D0205976

FRENCH ECCLESIASTICAL SOCIETY
UNDER THE ANCIEN RÉGIME

French Ecclesiastical Society under the Ancien Régime

A Study of Angers in the Eighteenth Century

by

JOHN McMANNERS

Emeritus Fellow of St. Edmund Hall, Oxford,
Professor of History in the University of Sydney,
(formerly Professor in the University of Tasmania)

MANCHESTER UNIVERSITY PRESS

© 1960
Published by the University of Manchester at
THE UNIVERSITY PRESS
316–324 Oxford Road, Manchester 13

First published 1960
Reprinted 1968

G.B. SBN 7190 0340 7

Printed in Great Britain by Lowe & Brydone (Printers) Ltd.,
London

To

A. M. M.

with gratitude

ACKNOWLEDGMENTS

THE writing of this book has been completed on one of those islands 'of the Southern Sea' which the Angevin abbé Mévolhan had hoped would one day be 'peopled with free men who will owe to the French in Europe their happiness and their liberty'. Only the first half of his dream came true. Seated on my verandah, looking through the pale leaves of the gum trees across a blue and sunlit bay, I am very conscious of the vast distance (in every sense of the word) which separates me from Angers of the eighteenth century. I hope that a proportion of the shortcomings of this volume will be excused by a consideration of geographical factors. On the other hand, I am glad to admit that my exile from Europe has provided me with an excuse for leaning on my friends and for soliciting their help more shamelessly than most authors dare to do. To their generous advice and criticism I owe more than can be expressed in any formal acknowledgment. Professor A. Goodwin of Manchester University has read the whole manuscript; Mr. R. Shackleton, Fellow of Brasenose College, has looked over the chapters on literary and intellectual life, and Dr. F. Sternfeld has reviewed the section on music; Mr. J. S. Bromley, Fellow of Keble College, my friend and collaborator in other matters concerning the eighteenth century, has read the early chapters of the manuscript and made brilliant and detailed criticisms; Dr. L. A. Triebel, Emeritus Professor of the University of Tasmania, has surveyed the final draft with his exact and scholarly eye. To Dr. R. Fargher, my former colleague at St. Edmund Hall, I owe a peculiar debt of gratitude; for some years, Angers was a daily topic of conversation between us, and now that we live at opposite ends of the world, he has spent many weeks of work on the typescript, amending errors, pointing out infelicities of style and guiding me on wider matters of treatment with an urbane and humorous insight.

My thanks are also due to a number of librarians and archivists in France—to Mlle Jeanne Varangot, *conservateur* of the Municipal Library at Angers and Mlle Jacqueline Maurice, to M. J. Levron, archivist of Maine-et-Loire and his successor M. d'Herbécourt, as well as to their assistants Mlle Héno and M. Bernier, to Mlle Chartier of the *bureau du Secrétariat général* of the Mairie of Angers, to the abbé Noye, archivist of Saint-Sulpice, to Mlle Langlois of the Archives nationales.

During the various visits to France which this work has entailed, I met with many incidental kindnesses; I remember how, at the instance of Mr. Gill, Fellow of Magdalen College, M. Prinet and

M. Rancœur of the Bibliothèque nationale made enquiries on my behalf from Canon Catta and Major Pinguet; how the Librarian of Carpentras, instead of sending a formal reply to my letter, sent a complete copy of the document which interested me; how one of the assistants at the Municipal Library of Angers, whose name, alas, I have forgotten, forwent the holiday of 14 July out of a friendly interest in my investigations. To these, and to many others, I would like to express my gratitude.

I am indebted to the editorial staff of the Manchester University Press for expert guidance at every stage of the printing and production of this volume, to Professor Scott, of the Geography Department here in Hobart, for assistance with the map, and to my wife, who has borne the drudgery of tidying up after the party, so to speak, by assuming the burden of compiling the index. Publication has been aided by a subsidy from the Publications Fund of the University of Tasmania. Angers is far away from this 'island of the Southern Sea', but distance makes no difference to the habitual generosity of the University in these matters.

JOHN MCMANNERS

Hobart,
  Tasmania

CONTENTS

MAP

(end of book)

Sketch-map showing the religious establishments at Angers, based on the 'Plan Historique
de la Ville d'Angers' of Moithey *ingenieur-
geographe du Roi*, Paris, 1776 (*by courtesy of the
British Museum*)

ABBREVIATIONS

A number of obvious abbreviations have been used. The chief are: *'Biens nat.'* = *Biens nationaux*; *'Bull.'* = *Bulletin*; *'Dept.'* = *Département*; *'hist.'* = *historique*; *'reg.'* = *registre*; *'Rev.'* = *Revue*. The titles of the two journals most often cited are abbreviated as follows:

Anjou hist. = *Anjou historique*
Mems. Soc. Agric. = *Société d'agriculture, sciences et arts d'Angers, Mémoires*
(for changes in title, see Bibliography)

The names of libraries and archival depositories are abbreviated as follows:

A.M.L. = Archives départementales, Maine-et-Loire.
A. Nat. = Archives nationales, Paris.
B. Angers = Bibliothèque municipale, Angers.
B.M. = British Museum.

From time to time the number of monks or nuns in a particular religious house, or of vicaires in a parish, or canons in a chapter, has been given. Where there is no indication to the contrary, these statistics refer to the position as it was in January 1789.

CHAPTER I

ANGERS AT THE END OF THE OLD RÉGIME

'THERE are few Cities in the French Dominions that afford the Curious a larger Field of Enquiry than Angers.' So wrote the much-travelled John Breval in 1738.[1] Arthur Young, who supped there and passed hastily on without comment, would hardly have agreed with the enthusiastic verdict of his compatriot, for this attractive clerical town was a backwater in the stream of economic progress, where the very secretary of the Bureau of Agriculture had no idea of the location of the domains of the improving marquis de Tourbilly.[2] But for those English travellers whose outlook was less severely utilitarian, Angers remained a favourite resort throughout the century. Dashing young gentlemen with a military career in mind came over to spend a year or two at the Academy of Equitation, to learn the arts of horsemanship under the eye of M. de Pignerolle, walk the streets resplendent in scarlet uniforms with gold buttons and blue facings, and dine splendidly but insubstantially at the duc de Brissac's.[3] The future victor of Waterloo was one of them, and long afterwards he would recount his reminiscences of youthful days in Anjou, where he had met the abbé Sieyès, and thought he had met Chateaubriand, and where the duc de Brissac's table, 'strong at the centre, but the flanks weak', bravely deployed its limited resources on a wide battle front.[4] Here was society enough, but provincial seclusion too, so that an Englishman disappointed in love might retire here to 'digest' his ill fortune.[5] Milord Southwell, a nobleman of the Roman persuasion, who had married into the family of Walsh, comte de Serrant, had made Angers his permanent abode, and in the eighties we find him resident in the parish of Saint-Julien, practising his religion in a private oratory in his house, and educating his daughter in the convent of the Visitation.[6] But the English visitor who was likely to appreciate most of all the Angers of the last years of the old régime was, as Breval suggests, the 'curious', the antiquarian minded. Such a traveller would find himself in a town haunted by memories of the Middle Ages, memories which belong to English as well as to French history. Our own Henry II, son of Geoffrey Plantagenet, count of Anjou, had given the silver gilt enchasement of the True Cross of the church of Saint-Laud; the stone tomb of an English seneschal of Anjou at the entrance to the Hôtel-Dieu inspired the sick with gratitude to their benefactor and sombre apprehensions of human transience; the city walls, of 'prodigious circumference', were reputed to have been built by King John; Margaret of Anjou, wife of Henry VI, rested in a tomb in the cathedral, and in a window of the chapel of St. Bonadventure at the Cordeliers, her effigy presided over the arms of England and Anjou quartered.[7] In Angers, the present generation lived in the shadow of the past. In this low-lying city astride the river Maine, the black and shapeless castle on the rock, the towers of the cathedral and the spires of churches dominate the huddled dark slate roofs that crowd within the massive useless walls and towers. Here, said Wraxall, you may savour 'the grandeur of decay and ruin'.[8]

The traveller who went to Angers after exhausting fashionable diversions in Paris, entered another world, provincial France, clerical France, where the pulse of life was slow, where old loyalties and traditions lingered longest, where news of the manœuvres of politics, the scandals of the court and the novelties of the *philosophes* filtered in unsensationally, smooth ripples on the edge of the pool of national events. The capital was far distant. A lumbering six-horse carriage which left for Paris twice a week arrived there seven days later, and even the speedier stage-coach of 1789 took three days on the journey.[9] Paying a debt at Paris was a difficult transaction for ordinary folk; the most convenient way was to hand the money over to the Seminary, and get the superior to arrange for his parent house of Saint-Sulpice to pay out the equivalent.[10] Until July 1773, Angers remained untroubled by the existence of a local newspaper, and when, from this date, the *Affiches d'Angers*[11] appeared, it made no contribution to political discussion, but week by week purveyed desiccated and formal news of municipal and ecclesiastical cere-monies, with respectful gossip about folk who mattered. Even so, in 1781, a new editor hastened to assure his respectable clientele that no article would ever appear which might shock even the most austere of readers. 'If in the past occasionally something of the sort has slipped past the attention of the editors, M. Mame gives his assurance that there will be no more of these inadvertencies. He will make it a genuine duty to respect religion, morals and the laws.' Only with the meeting of the Notables six years later was the *Affiches* tempted into politics—it printed the minutes of the sessions, without comment. This was, indeed, the appropriate journal of a self-contained and stable world, content with its one dull newspaper, and its two coffee houses.[12]

If in Angers we are far removed from the political and intellectual ferment of the capital, we are further still from the mania for financial and commercial speculation which struck Paris in the later years of the old régime. Angers could boast no banker, no millionaire among its citizens, though perhaps a prosperous parvenu, M. de Giseux, might qualify for the title of a financier in view of the fact that he obtained a duke as husband for his only daughter. Those who made money in business were very willing to retire with a modest competence, it being a generally received opinion that a man who could not manage on 3,000*l.* a year would never make ends meet, even with an income of 100,000. The chief investment of the prosperous classes of society was in landed property in the surrounding countryside, to which they were accustomed to withdraw in a series of family migrations once the fair of Corpus Christi-tide was over. Food was cheap, servants' wages were low, and the standard of living expected of successful men was not ostentatious. Few families kept a carriage, only the bishop and the marquis de la Lorie boasted a train of lackeys. Doctors and lawyers took their meals in the kitchen, and even the nobility, whose pride prevented them from appearing in the streets except with sword at side and gold lace on hat, were well known to give only modest dowries to their daughters.[13] Social inducements to commercial enterprise were lacking. Significantly, a far-reaching scheme for the establishment of sugar refineries using water transport to draw to Angers a share in the profits of the Antilles, had come, not from business men realizing its possibilities, but from the Jesuits. As might be expected, a suggestion coming from such a source met with scant favour from the jealous municipality.[14] Slate-quarrying, rope-making from the hemp of the Loire valley, the manufacture of woollen stockings and calico handkerchiefs, the printing of playing cards and the production of a certain amount of sail-cloth for the royal navy were the town's chief industries, together with some minor activities deriving from the fact that the city was an ecclesiastical centre, and exported a surplus of wax candles, church ornaments and the white Franciscan type of girdles called 'cordelières'.[15] Here the conservatism of small merchants for long prevailed over the more adventurous designs of bigger commercial men; it was not until 1768, for example, after three unsuccessful attempts earlier in the century, that a *Bourse de Commerce*, an institution which Nantes had enjoyed for 125 years, was securely established.[16] Government officials looked with despair upon this continued economic stagnation and lack of enterprise of the inhabitants. 'The present generation vegetates,' said a report of 1783, inelegantly, but emphatically, 'just as that which preceded it vegetated, and as the succeeding one will vegetate.'[17]

Manufacturing and commerce were not, then, the main support of the 34,000 inhabitants who lived within the sound of the cathedral bells of Angers.[18] Like Bayeux, Tréguier, Fréjus and many another provincial town, theirs was a metropolis of the Church and the law, where revenues drawn to the centre from the estates of ecclesiastical institutions and by the fees of lawyers took the place of commercial spending, and circulated to maintain a population of tradesmen and artisans. Angers was far from being a genuine administrative centre; it boasted neither Parlement nor intendant, fifty pensioners in garrison at the castle were the only justification for its claim to be the headquarters of a military governor, and the capital of the apanage of the comte de Provence gained nothing but sycophantic ceremonies and disputes over forgotten feudal dues from this connexion with royalty. Nevertheless, the owl of Minerva flies abroad when the shades of night have fallen, and Angers, deprived of a role in the administrative sphere, had become a centre of legal learning. No less than fifty-three full-scale courts or tribunals dispensed justice in the city,[19] settling the appeals which wound their way upwards from inferior sessions of royal or seigneurial justice, or providing, on the ascent to the *Cour des aides*, the *Cour des monnaies* or Parlement a half-way house where the weary litigant must pay his toll. It was a labyrinthine confusion of courts, and yet, even when this is taken into account, there were still too many lawyers, for the Crown, which sold most judicial offices, had no interest in restraining their numbers. Thus thirty-nine magistrates at the *Présidial* and thirteen at the *Prévôté* were engaged in administering justice in an area which comprised only two hundred and fifty parishes. The result of this royal policy of inflation was a rapid decline in the value of judicial office from the beginning of the century and keen competition between the various courts for the spoils of litigants. When a property-owner died in Angers, at least two, and probably three jurisdictions affixed their seals, and it was said that, before embarking on litigation, a preliminary law suit was necessary to find which court had competence.[20] Hence, too, a town full of legal officials and hangers-on, bailiffs and summoners, lawyers and notaries, and the distinguished magistrates and barristers whom Besnard remembered so well, with their long powdered hair or full-bottomed wigs, fumbling in ample robes for their door keys as they returned gravely home from the law courts. True, the *perruquier* who maintained sausage-shaped rows of curls in their portentous wigs had paid more to the Crown for the right to exercise his trade than they had for theirs, but they were none the less proud for all that.[21]

Without the great ecclesiastical institutions of the town, and all the legal business which flowed in from the affairs of their scattered estates, their feudal assizes and constant litigation, the lawyers of Angers could never have prospered. Medieval Anjou with its counts and feudatories had gone like a dream, but their pious foundations remained, ruling the air by the music of their bells and the eminence of their spires, ruling the ground by their leases, rents and feudal incidents. Packed close around the cathedral of Saint-Maurice were five other collegiate churches, Saint-Pierre, Saint-Maurille and Saint-Martin, all with their full quota of canons, while Saint-Julien and Saint-Maimbeuf were buildings which had outlived their chapters. Outside the walls was the chapter of Saint-Laud, and on the far side of the river was a minor collegiate foundation in the church of La Trinité, making a total of half a dozen extant chapters in the town altogether. There were five abbeys, four of Benedictines and one of canons-regular, and a Benedictine house for women, the abbey of Ronceray, which was the greatest corporation in the town after the cathedral. Seven houses of mendicant orders, the priests of the Oratory, the Lazarists and the Frères des Écoles Chrétiennes complete the total of communities of men, while of women, including the sisterhoods working in the three hospitals, there were fourteen communities in addition to Ronceray. One-third of the chapters, a quarter of the abbeys, and one in fourteen of the other monastic houses of the diocese were concentrated in its principal city. However, the proportion was very different in the case of curés, for out of more than 600 parishes in the diocese, only seventeen were in the town of Angers itself—though seventeen to serve a population of 34,000 would seem, had the division of population been equal, an adequate total. In addition to parish churches, there were fourteen chapels of ease scattered about the town; two were used as 'district churches', while most of the others were slipping into disuse and decay. It was hard to go any distance in town without stumbling across a cemetery—'our town seemed to excel all others in this type of reminder (of man's latter end)', said a curé of the diocese, with macabre relish.[22]

The old city (*cité*), where religious foundations clustered thickest, was also the centre of the diocesan administration. Here, next to the cathedral, stood the bishop's palace; nearby was the *officialité* or clerical court, conjoined with the court of the archdeacon, for the cathedral of Angers had a jurisdiction independent of the bishop. Here too was the Seminary, which provided priests for all the surrounding areas. Across the road from the façade of Saint-Maurice was the office of the administrators of clerical taxation, briskly attended from 8 a.m. to noon and from 2 p.m. to 5 (Sundays, Thursdays and major feasts excepted). 'Benefice holders are requested not to make payments to the doorkeeper, under penalty of having to pay twice over.' [23] At least once a year every parish priest presented himself here, duly noted this sombre warning, and departed poorer than he came. Much of our history arises from the emotions aroused by these melancholy transactions over the counter of the *Bureau des décimes*.

B

There was an enormous clerical population. In the monasteries there were in 1789 about 60 monks and 40 friars, and over 300 nuns. The crop of canons was prodigious, 72 all told, and more if we include the directors of the Seminary, who inherited the rights and revenues of the defunct chapters of Saint-Julien and Saint-Maimbeuf. Each parish had its curé, and there were 22 vicaires, the total of parochial clergy being only half that of the number of canons. This disproportion is even greater when we consider the clerical underworld that revolved around each collegiate church, *maires chapelains* and chaplains, deacons, sacrists and succentors. There was a whole hierarchy of them at the cathedral, and even the unimportant chapter of La Trinité had six of these officials, all priests. Similar employments, on quite generous terms, were offered to seculars by the great abbeys.[24] Country parish priests who reached retiring age came to Angers to spend their declining years, and took minor posts as chaplains to communities of women—such was the previous background of the confessors of the Pénitentes, the Visitandines, the Carmelites, and the houses of Le Bon Pasteur and La Croix. Monks who were freed from their conventual obligations found such employment a useful supplement to their pensions; one of the confessors of the Ursulines was a religious whose priory had been suppressed, and a monk of Cîteaux is found directing the nuns of Sainte-Catherine in 1790.[25] Seven priests were employed by the Hôpital Général, and as many by the Hôtel-Dieu.[26] Omitting tonsured clerks and students at the Seminary, it is true to say that one person in every sixty resident in the town was either in major orders or a member of a religious community. This is true of the town statistically and takes no account of the proverbial ubiquity of the clergy, which made their presence even more evident psychologically. In the *cité*, around the cathedral and the abbey of Saint-Aubin, every other person one met was likely to be an ecclesiastic of sorts. An idler who sat for half an hour on one of the stones which kept the traffic away from the paved centre of the cathedral square might pass the whole clerical world in review. The bishop himself might sweep up to the palace, fresh from his country house at Andard, or a prosperous young monk from Saint-Aubin ride past on one of the abbey horses loaned for his vacation, or with a flash of white sleeve in a black robe a nun of Ronceray would go by, aloof in her carriage, as befitted a member of that exclusive foundation. Then, more continually, one would see the alternating patterns of black and brown and white as the humbler religious orders went about their errands, and the daily activities of the great church of Saint-Maurice—a crocodile of choir boys being escorted thither in white cassocks and little violet skull-caps, a canon hastening to office, distinguished, if it be a feast day, by a red or violet cassock. Or, by contrast, there would be a threadbare canon of Saint-Martin, pathetically displaying the red silk girdle which his chapter claimed as its distinguishing monopoly, a doctor of theology resplendent in blue silk sash and ermine stole over a black gown, stalking across to the cloisters to vote at the Faculty, a curé in sober garb, perhaps the abbé Robin of Saint-Pierre, with snuff stains on his cassock and the unbuttoned disarray which was his own private badge of the independence of the parish priest, and inevitably there would be a procession, with cross and reliquary, banners and candles, moving, according to the calendar, on a yearly route as predictable as the orbit of the planets.[27]

Angers was a clerical city. Crowded within its walls was a mass of institutions characteristic of the rich and varied life of the Church of France. All facets of that Church's greatness and many aspects of its decadence were mirrored there. In Angers, its life is seen focussed into a concentration of clear-cut images, with every feature rendered more salient. There is an inbreeding which heightens the peculiar characteristics which ecclesiastical orders and corporations had acquired through the centuries, there is a narrowing down of their relations with secular society into basic permanent factors within the cadre of a tightly knit provincial life. Everyone knew everyone else, and everyone knew his own traditional rights, and those of other people. The whole process of development was going on as surely and as steadily as the building of a coral reef. It is not possible to claim that this town is a typical unit for study: French society in the eighteenth century was too diverse for that. Provinces were under various forms of government and customary law, weights and measures varied throughout the kingdom; society was honeycombed into groups and cells by dividing lines of privilege and tradition, as well as by economic cleavages; urban and rural existences were often as far apart as if the customs barriers at the gates of towns really marked international boundaries. The typical does not exist in eighteenth-century France. What can be said, however, is, that the life of Angers, confined and introverted, was a unity; men were bound together in a natural community, and in studying the Church within this community one at least avoids the injustice of considering bishops without dioceses, curés without parishes, monasteries without traditions. To describe the Church of France by the typical is to commit the error of the royal bureaucracy and, indeed, of the revolutionary assemblies, and see the whole confused genius of the land solely from the vantage point of Paris, that home of statistics and gossip—joint fruits of the centralization of both administration and fashion. Judged by either, the eighteenth-century Church fares ill. To obtain a more genuine impression, one needs to do what the kings of France had ceased doing, that is, to tour the provinces, indeed, to do more than that, and, at the risk of narrowness and partiality, to take up residence in some provincial *milieu*, and study its indigenous life. It was a life that was both nourished by the past, and its prisoner too. Ecclesiastical Angers lived by the privileges, property and traditions that so grievously bound it, like a tree casting out new green shoots in the harsh sunshine of a new century, yet with roots going deep into a medieval subsoil—while as yet no one had heard the approaching sound of a woodman's axe. Here, one studies, not the typical, but the highly concentrated, the commonplace, stepped up to the *reductio ad absurdum* of a whole social complex.

This pattern of events in eighteenth-century Angers is woven around the normal and slowly developing factors of ecclesiastical existence, and is not greatly affected by the movements of thought and pressures of opinion which would bulk large in a general history of the religious life of France in this period. In Languedoc and, in a cautious underground way, in Normandy, Protestantism remained a force. Thus the story of a futile continuance of persecution, the hollow hardening of clerical hearts, the revulsion of lay opinion, and the development of ideas among the Protestant *bourgeoisie* would be an essential consideration in the religious annals of towns like Montauban, Toulouse and Nîmes. But whatever force Protestantism had had in Angers was shattered by the revocation of the Edict of Nantes. The populace, which for long had shown its bitter hostility by dumping its garbage at the gates of the Protestant cemetery, took this official opportunity to turn out in force, and a crowd of 5,000 or so stood around in pouring rain singing the *Te Deum* while workmen and schoolboys pulled down the church at Sorges, three miles or so from the city.[28] The municipality, after awarding the furniture from Sorges to the hospital of St. John the Evangelist, put up the money for a prize essay competition, the subject to be 'the extirpation of heresy'.[29] This extirpation was soon completed. When, in 1707, bishop Poncet de la Rivière, a hammer of all dissent, attended in person at the funeral of Michel Renault, silk merchant, who had turned to the Roman faith after a life-time in the Reformed religion,[30] the work was almost done. 'Some debris of Calvinism' remained in the town, and the bishop's archdeacon and eventual successor, Vaugirault, is said to have cleared it away.[31] After this, we hear little more of Protestantism in Angers. When the danger was over, and no news of local heretics beyond the occasional abjuration of a watchmaker from Switzerland or La Rochelle[32] circulated, tolerance came easily. The Academy which had accepted 'the extirpation of heresy' as its essay topic, forty years later was requesting permission from the Crown to admit a Jacobite and Protestant Englishman to its own sacred circle, and in 1787 made a minor poet of Cambrai a corresponding member for verses demonstrating that Fénelon had been an apostle of toleration.[33] The hospital which boasted the plunder of Sorges in its chapel was re-emphasizing proudly that sick and poor of all confessions were welcome within its gates.[34] To the local clergy, Protestantism in Anjou became a subject for historical research rather than polemical debate. And as for the heretical cause in less favoured areas of France, let it be strictly but not harshly dealt with; let the Protestants enjoy the quasi-toleration given by the edict of 1787, and aspire to nothing more.[35]

Jansenism, once the period of brute enforcement of subscription and adherence to orthodoxy is over, is a more difficult phenomenon to analyse, lurking as it does in nuances of doctrine, and whetting the edge of clerical grievances rather than appearing in its own name. In Angers, once the diocese of Henry Arnauld, brother of the great Arnauld of Port Royal,[36] there had been no significant resistance to the Bull Unigenitus. Opposition came only from institutions which drew their inspiration and confidence from their extradiocesan affiliations—the Oratory and the three chief Benedictine houses, especially Saint-Aubin. 'I search in vain, my dear Sir, for this general opposition of which you inform me,' wrote the bishop to a Jansenist doctor of the Sorbonne in 1718. 'Surrounded as I am by twenty chapters, a populous University, seventy religious communities—in a word, by nearly 400,000 souls whom it has pleased God to lay to my charge, your party has been able to steal from me no more than two parish priests and a handful of Oratorians and Benedictine monks who, so far as I am concerned, are only, so to speak, members of my diocese by accident.' [37] This was true enough, and before the middle of the century, even the resistance of the Oratorians and the Benedictines of Saint-Maur had been broken.[38] Bishop Poncet de la Rivière was an ardent supporter of the Bull, and not only reduced his own diocese to subjection, but also did his best to bring moral pressure to bear on more tolerant members of the episcopate.[39] From his printing press emerged a stream of orthodox apologetic, including some 'consoling reflections', which were calculated to be anything but consoling for the good monks of Saint-Aubin, whom he pilloried ruthlessly.[40] Behind him was his cathedral chapter, which broke off its long-standing confraternity with the canons of Le Mans who had refused to accept Unigenitus;[41] behind him too was his Seminary[42] and the fanatically rigorist Faculty of Theology, exulting in papal congratulations upon its unanimity.[43] Bishop Vaugirault[44] continued this repression, and under their rule, Angers became a fortress of orthodoxy. The Oratorians and Benedictines were reduced to impotence and silence. Among the laity an undercurrent of dissidence persisted in certain families, but among the secular clergy true Jansenism was practically annihilated. Only three curés in the whole diocese (and none of these was from the town of Angers itself) had opposed their bishop in 1716[45] and twenty-one years later it was said that the only Jansenists among the secular clergy of the town were the dean and one of the canons of the chapter of Saint-Laud.[46] Such disputes as those that rent Tours, the metropolitan town of the ecclesiastical province, and Nantes, did not arise to scandalize faithful Angevins. Here was a refuge for the orthodox and a place of correction for heretics. A curé of Nantes fleeing from the wrath of Parlement after refusing sacraments to a Jansenist found secure retreat in the hospitable Seminary;[47] the nuns of Notre-Dame du Bon Conseil of Saumur, convicted of doubtful leanings, were transferred to the Angevin house of La Fidelité.

The main theme of the ecclesiastical history of Anjou in the later years of the old régime is the struggle of curés against the domination of monks and canons. This struggle had its ideological background, its conception of the nature of the ministry, its scriptural proofs, its appeal to history, its doctrinal arguments. But none of this was Jansenist. What in fact had happened, in France generally,[48] was that Jansenism proper, a doctrine of grace, a way of life, a resistance to certain papal pronouncements, had got into strange company. By now it was marching at the head of a motley army of camp followers. There was a practical alliance with the Gallican lawyers and, for a time, an involuntary one with the strange upsurge of 'convulsionism' from the underworld of popular imagination. Above all—and this was the driving force in the whole complex of ideas—there was an alliance with a movement among the lower clergy, which was economic in its basic origins and synodal in its fundamental tenets. The theology of the movement was not Jansenist, but 'Richériste', that is, it affirmed the right of the community of pastors to rule the church. The so-called 'Jansenism' of the eighteenth century gained its force in politics from Gallican affiliations, its significance among the clergy from Richerist affiliations. In Angers, as almost everywhere in France, we find Gallicanism deeply rooted, not only in the Faculty of Law,[49] which would be its natural seed-plot, but also in the Faculty of Theology. Bernier's thesis of 1786 showed a hatred of Jansenism—but at the same time it asserted the inferiority of Popes to Councils, and insisted on the autonomy of the lay State.[50] Just as these routine expressions of Gallican sentiment are found without any taint of unorthodoxy, so too Richerism flourished as a conviction and a rallying cry in its own right, strictly within the pale of orthodoxy as dogmatically defined. Richerism here was a weapon against authority; not because authority was on the side of a theological witch-hunt, but because authority refused to recognize the rightful status of the parish priest. It is true that the revolt of the curés of Anjou was long in coming, and that, when it did come, it owed more to news of the success of the lower clergy of other dioceses and to local incidents than to theoretical convictions or to logical schemes of reform. Even so, to the extent that the revolt had a basis of theory, that theory was Richerist, and inasmuch as it was directed towards a specific programme, it was directed towards the amelioration of the economic and honorific status of the parochial ministry.

To an unusual degree, the ecclesiastical life of Angers was free from extraneous and disturbing influences, so that the interplay of rivalries on questions of dignity, status, organization and property can be studied in isolation, as it were, under laboratory conditions. Nor, in the last few years of the old régime, was there serious episcopal intervention to disturb the steady development of these themes. From 1758 to 1782, after a century of rule by strict and worthy bishops, Jacques de Grasse ruled his see of Angers in the tradition of the more notorious prelates of the old régime, and though his occasional crafty interventions in diocesan politics had their significance, for most of his time he was an absentee in Paris.[51] Mgr Couet du Vivier de Lorry who succeeded him was a man of ability who had many accidental virtues, but sloth and good nature combined to persuade him against embarking upon any definite policy. Thus the ship ran into dangerous waters with a fair-weather pilot at the helm, and this ineffectiveness on the bridge of the vessel makes the set of the current more obvious in Angers than it would be in an episcopal town which was dominated by an outstanding personality.

'A simple town very rarely has a history.' The remark is attributed to Voltaire, who cared only for Paris, and in a bleak *mot*, this cosmopolitan exile made it clear that Angers was a strong candidate for his category of provincial nullity.[52] In Angers at the end of the old régime, one can study, not great events, but great survivals, history of a special kind, the history of things which had endured. It is a story, not of the sea with its waves and storms, but of a reed-grown river winding majestically through a monotonous plain. Even so, the scenery was changing and, perhaps, the current was imperceptibly quickening. There were tensions and oppositions in society; the stream was beginning to divide and subdivide to form the delta which marks the river's end. If men had cared to listen, they might have heard ahead of them the long slow murmur of the inconstant and ruthless sea.

CHAPTER II

THE LITURGICAL YEAR

EVERYWHERE in Angers one could hear the music of bells, a continual reverberation in the still air above narrow streets and black slate roofs, carrying messages of exhortation, invitation and warning. To a cynical observer, perhaps, they might have spoken above all of riches and poverty. There was thrift and penury in the dull metallic beat of humble bells in parish churches and in oratories of minor communities and in the austere monotony of the single bell of the Capuchins faintly sounding from distant Reculée; anticipations of revenue could be detected in the modest twin peal of Lesvière and a sufficient competence in the three and four bells of the Cordeliers and the Augustins or in the nine small bells of the Jacobins; broad acres and affluence spoke mellowly in the great harmonies sweeping down from Saint-Aubin's massive tower, suitably re-echoed from across the river at Saint-Nicholas, where dom Thibault had cast four magnificent bells a century ago, and all equally were drowned and dominated by the tremendous carillon of Saint-Maurice, nine bells in three towers, swung by a team of 17 ringers.[1] Yet these inequalities had come to be accepted as inevitable by the generality of folk, to whom the bells of Angers constantly reaffirmed the fixed hierarchical pattern of ecclesiastical society and gave a melodious background to daily life, a speaking calendar of the changing seasons of a picturesque liturgical year. Half an hour before the offices of each Sunday and Saint's day, and one hour before the cathedral sermon, the bells gave their warning; reminders of fast days were given by the 'silver' bell, the *Haranier*, from a little lead-covered steeple on the transept of Saint-Maurice; varying peals marked the graded hierarchy of feast days, and on solemn occasions, like the institution of a new bishop, the great bell of the cathedral, *Guillaume*, swung by five ringers, gave the signal for the outburst of all other bells of the city.[2] Daily routine and the passage of the night hours were musically indicated, workmen relied on the cathedral chimes to waken them at the beginning of the day,[3] and the four notes of the carillon of the clock struck hour and half-hour with a reminder of religion by playing the air of the hymn of Our Lady, 'inviolata, integra et casta'.[4] During the night, monasteries rang for their offices at varying hours, so that an old inhabitant could tell the time from his bed without a watch.[5] A nice calculation of peals allowed the faithful to synchronize their prayers with each liturgical occasion. One could say an *Ave*

Maria for the soul of a nun at regular intervals in the series of funeral tolls, and a *miserere* at each quarter of the hour; one could join in spirit in the first mass of the mendicants by saying a *pater* when the third bell took over from the second after the angelus was rung.[6] Not everyone could enjoy this perpetual music. Until the canons of Saint-Maurille allowed the parish to move its bell to their cloister, it was maintained that houses facing on to the square before the church were 'almost uninhabitable'. And nocturnal chimes were unpopular with some—'des tapages et les carillons qui se passent dans la ville, d'abord que la nuit vient', said an angry inhabitant suffering from insomnia.[7]

As the hours of the day and the seasons of the year were thus perpetually distinguished, a continuous succession of liturgical observances unrolled, in a pattern in which all the many churches of the town played parts which long-established tradition assigned to them. There were the usual parish, monastic and collegiate offices, in which the cathedral led the way in dignity and magnificence. Here, every day, five ecclesiastics in copes,[8] preceded by four vergers, processed for all services except matins, and three deacons, three sub-deacons and two canons, with candles, cross and incense, accompanied the celebrant to say mass.[9] Every week there was exposition of relics, on Mondays at Saint-Julien (when pregnant women came to wear the girdle of Saint-Lezin and pray for a safe delivery),[10] and on Fridays at Saint-Martin, and on the first Friday of each month at Saint-Laud. Each Sunday there was exposition of the Sacrament, sermon, procession and *salut* in two or three churches of the religious orders, according to a rotation established among the Jacobins, Cordeliers, Recollets, Carmelites, Minims, Augustins, and the abbey of Toussaint.[11] The staff of the Seminary contributed to public worship on Sundays by a sermon in their chapel after cathedral vespers were over, and by directing a meditation in the church of Sainte-Croix.[12] There was an afternoon sermon at the cathedral on Sundays and feast days. On the first Sunday of the month the canon lecturer preached at nine in the morning, after which a general procession left Saint-Maurice, and proceeded, according to a fixed yearly rota, to one of the other collegiate churches of the town for mass, the mendicant orders leading, the various chapters following, with the canons of Saint-Maurice bringing up the rear, all preceded by their crosses.[13]

The greatest festivals of the Church—and at Angers these included Epiphany and Ascension as well as Easter, Pentecost, and Christmas —were celebrated with overwhelming splendour, and with a wealth of quaint traditional observances.[14] A serious liturgiologist left to guide-books the dispensation of wine on the second Sunday after Epiphany from one of the original jars of Cana of Galilee,[15] but the fascinating Holy Week and Easter ceremonies drew his special attention. From Maundy Thursday, the ritual of the cathedral of Saint-Maurice re-enacted in a very literal form the events of the Last Supper, Passion and Resurrection. On Thursday, the bishop and the dean washed the feet of twelve children from the hospital, with the public executioner acting as their towel-bearer, the Johannine version of Christ's discourse to the disciples was read, wine was served by the choir-boys in the episcopal palace, and a Latin discourse on the institution of the Eucharist was given. On Good Friday, when the dean chanted the gospel, a canon sang the Dominical words, and the choir interpolated the voices of the Jews. At matins on Easter day, two chaplains, wearing copes, took the part of the angels, and concealed themselves behind long white curtains hanging from a canopy, which represented the sepulchre. Two other clerics in dalmatics and amices, wearing gloves and red hats, represented the mourning women, and presented themselves at the tomb, where the gospel dialogue with the angels was spoken. Finally, they emerged from behind the curtains, each bearing a silver-mounted ostrich egg, singing 'Alleluia, Resurrexit Dominus . . .', the choir responding 'Deo gratias, Alleluia' before the organ swept into the *Te Deum*.[16]

Above all else, the cycle of the Church's year at Angers was marked by processions.[17] There were general processions on Saint-Mark's day, Palm Sunday, Ascension day, and, pre-eminently, on the feast of Corpus Christi, the day of the famous *Sacre d'Angers*, reputed to be one of the most magnificent processions in Europe. Then there were particular processions of individual churches, like those which filled the whole octave of Corpus Christi-tide once the renowned *Sacre* was over, or that of the chapter and parish of Saint-Pierre which proceeded to the Carmes to sing mass there on Easter Monday. Lent began with a Shrove Tuesday parade of the canons of Saint-Julien, followed by an expedition of the canons of Saint-Maurice to the Jacobins on Ash Wednesday (one of their 19 annual progresses), then, on every succeeding Wednesday and Friday, other chapters went forth on penitential tours. Each of these processions had its special object of veneration or interest: for veneration there were relics, for interest there would be the Shrove Tuesday ox of Saint-Julien, driven through the streets in pagan fashion be-laurelled and with gilded horns, or the dragon with lolling mouth and flapping wings carried from Saint-Serge to Ronceray on Saint-Mark's day, and reputed efficacious to deliver the city from visitations of flies or serpents.[18]

In addition to this permanent liturgical calendar, the month of May was likely to be marked by special prayers and services for rain, and July and August for fine weather. Then, the appropriate collects were said at mass or the Holy Sacrament exposed, or at the cathedral, where every opportunity for special music was taken, there would be a sung high mass with an anthem, and a penitential psalm at *salut*.[19] Extremely unpropitious weather would call for a full-scale procession: such as was ordered by the diocése in May 1785, leaving the cathedral at nine in the morning bearing the relic of Saint-Loup from the church of Saint-Martin, then proceeding to Saint-Serge for mass, with singing of psalms and graduals on the outward journey, and litanies of the saints in plainsong on the return.[20]

A relic carried in state in its bejewelled shrine was an indispensable adjunct of these observances. On the feasts of Corpus Christi, the Ascension, Saint-Mark, Palm Sunday and Rogation-tide, the canons of the cathedral followed their bones of Saint-Sérené, carried for them by chaplains and dependent curés, while from the other side of town the monks of Saint-Serge came to meet them, bearing a reliquary containing remains of Godebert, bishop of Angers.[21] The True Cross of Saint-Laud was taken in state to Saint-Aubin on Passion Sunday, to the Recollets on Ascension day, and to the chapel of the nuns of Sainte-Cathérine on the day of the Exaltation (weather permitting), and was exposed for adoration on the first Friday of every month, at Good Friday and Easter, and on other occasions at the request of the administrators of the hospital on behalf of their inmates.[22] To the head of Saint-Loup, in the possession of the collegial of Saint-Martin, a particular meteorological significance was assigned. When a novena of prayers for propitious weather was called for, it would be exposed each morning of the nine days from matins to the end of high mass and carried in state after compline, and in the full-scale concluding procession.[23]

Possession of important relics was regarded as a sure sign of a church's greatness. Saint-Julien boasted a complete arm of its patron, and that was why its old dedication to Saint-John Baptist (represented only by a finger) had been popularly abandoned. It was the True Cross, intertwined with fleur-de-lis, which formed the coat-of-arms of the chapter of Saint-Laud, whose canons appealed to the fact that they were 'depositories of a considerable portion of the most authentic fragment of the True Cross' as a culminating argument for the preservation of their independence.[24] These possessions were jealously preserved and inventoried and housed with a magnificence appropriate to their intrinsic status and to the wealth of their custodians.[25] In the crypt of Ronceray, behind a stout iron grille, an angel upheld a tiny model church all encrusted with gold, enamel, rubies, sapphires and pearls; within was a cross adorned with pearls and diamonds, containing a fragment of Our Lady's clothing. On great feasts the cathedral displayed its principal relics enshrined in silver statues; there was an arm of Saint-Maurice enclosed within a representation of that saint in armour with shield and sword; there was a figure of Our Lady looking down at two silver angels presenting a lock of her own hair; there was Saint-Martin kneeling, holding a crystal phial containing blood of Saint-Maurice and his fellow-martyrs. In short, as a sceptical English Protestant visiting the cathedral had remarked, there was an '. . . abundance of reliques, the tooth of one Saint, the bone of another, etc., whose names I have quite forgotten as well as he had, of some of them, that shewed them us, though they were his old acquaintance'.[26] As opportunity presented itself, a church would add to its stock of relics by purchase or negotiation. When Saint-Décent's tomb was found at Rome the canons of Saint-Maurice made haste to acquire some portion of his remains for display in a glass panel in the front of their high altar;[27] on the other hand, from their relics they were able to make a gift of a fragment of a bone of Saint-Sérené to the church of Notre-Dame at Sablé where the saint had exercised his ministry—this was duly taken over in 1783, together with a certificate of provenance, and thanks returned by the bishop of Le Mans.[28] In 1775 the chapter of Saint-Martin obtained relics for its altar of Saint-Sébastien, and documents vouching their authenticity were locked away in the capitular strong-box;[29] this notable acquisition, however, was completely over-shadowed by a simultaneous coup of the canons of Saint-Maurille, who on 10 September solemnly installed within their church the relics of four martyrs, newly brought from Rome by canon Péan's nephew.[30] Parish churches might negotiate for a portion of a relic which particularly concerned them, as the church of Saint-Samson did in 1766 to obtain mementoes of its patron from Saint-Magloire at Paris,[31] but normally, they could not hope to keep pace with the eclecticism of chapters. Their main source of new acquisitions was the infrequent pilgrimages of parish priests to Rome, where pious souvenirs with impressive pedigrees were in generous supply. The famous True Cross of Saint-Laud set the standard for their purchases. Similar fragments were brought back by Bailly, curé of Plessis Grammoire near Angers in 1782, and by Bassereau of Lesvière five years later—

. . . which (relic) he has deposited in the sacristy to be exposed for public veneration, and to stand there as a monument of the tender love that the said curé has always had for his dear parish.[32]

The greatest ceremony of the liturgical year at Angers was the annual procession of Corpus Christi, the *Sacre d'Angers*. Everywhere in Catholic Europe such processions were held, but local patriots and an impartial connoisseur of liturgical curiosities agreed in describing that of Angers as having special features which made it unique in

Christendom.[33] Its distinctive peculiarity was a parade of twelve 'torches', which might be prosaically described as a portable wax-work display, or, more suitably, in the words of an English visitor, '12 Pageants of History in large Wax Work, but too Romantick for so August a Solemnity'.[34] Each 'torche' was composed of at least fifteen life-size wax figures arranged to form a biblical tableau, and housed in a square tower adorned with columns, garlands and ornamental cornices, the whole structure being carried on a hurdle by a dozen to sixteen porters.[35] Normally only two or three of the scenes depicted were derived from New Testament incidents—the Temptation in the wilderness, 'Render unto Caesar', 'Suffer the little children' or the Resurrection of Tabitha;—the rest would be drawn from the more lurid and dramatic pages of the Old Testament—David or Judas Maccabeus triumphing over their foes, Solomon in his glory, Joseph turning the tables on his brethren, with Daniel slaying a dragon as a constantly recurring popular favourite.[36] In theory, each tableau was provided by one of the guilds of tradesmen, but in practice, since 1743, the expense was shared by all the corporations, and the municipality allotted the contracts for their manufacture.[37] On the eve of the feast, these twelve 'torches' were borne to the cathedral, where they were inspected by the canon treasurer, who had power to fine the makers for poor workmanship or for lack of originality in repeating any of last year's subjects; then they were arranged down the nave on either side, with their candles burning for vespers that evening and for matins and lauds on the following day.[38] As soon as the mass of Corpus Christi was over, and terce begun, the tableaux moved off at the head of the great procession. The *crieur des patenôtres*[39] followed with his bell, then came the guildsmen marching two by two, preceded by whatever music they had seen fit to hire for the day. Each member carried a candle on a pole, and their leaders bore emblems representing the patron saint of the guild: Saint-Crispin for the shoemakers, Saint-Honoré for the bakers, Saint-Joseph for the carpenters; or indicative of their trade, a steeple, a fishing net, a turning windmill.[40] Next came the *juges consuls* preceded by their violins, oboes and drums (and if half a century's litigation had been successful, the notaries would have preceded them also),[41] then the triumphant notaries and *avocats*, then the magistrates of the *Présidial* and the municipal officers (eluding the question of procedure by walking side by side), after these the clergy—monks with their crosses, canons-regular, seculars; and finally, the bishop and the dean of the cathedral, bearing the Holy Sacrament in a golden monstrance. The canopy under which they walked was carried by the four oldest canons, the twelve choir-boys escorted them, crowned with flowers and singing hymns to the accompaniment of oboes and violins. As a rearguard came the *maréchaussée* in bright red tunics, amid a din of drums and trumpets.[42]

The procession crossed the river, and at the abbey of Ronceray the 'torches' halted and their candles were lit while the Holy Sacrament passed through and on to the Tertre Saint-Laurent.[43] Here was a chapel, surmounted by a dome on four arcades, which itself formed a little auxiliary chapel dedicated to Our Lady. The bishop mounted the stairway, and placed the Sacrament in the central arcade, from whence, to the south, one could see the whole city spread out below. There was a halt here for two hours, a motet was sung, and a sermon preached from the open-air pulpit in the cemetery adjacent to the chapel. According to strict liturgical theory, the people remained here, worshipping like the Israelites at the foot of Sinai;[44] in practice, there was a general adjournment for lunch, led by the municipal officers, who entertained the *subdélégué* and the officers of the *maréchaussée* together with their official party.[45] So the sermon was rather wasted. 'C'est bien prêcher dans le désert,' said a visitor to Angers in 1782, 'car les curieux vont dîner.' [46] After the sermon—and lunch—the procession reformed, and returned to the cathedral.

Such was the ritual of the famous *Sacre d'Angers*, a ceremony in which sacred and secular were inextricably blended. It was a spectacle, for which the prosperous hired strategic windows in town,[47] a carnival, giving opportunities for libertinage to less respectable inhabitants of the city,[48] and a parade, in which the inevitable disputes for precedence found their focus. All aspects of civic life were represented, and every organization played its appropriate part. The streets were hung with tapestry and roofed over with canvas as protection against rain and sun, artisans were obliged to be at the cathedral by 6 a.m. on pain of fine, guildsmen and officials marched in procession in strict hierarchical order. A general levy on all trades and corporations provided the 'torches', while other communities made contributions in accordance with their status or their geographical position: the cathedral paid handsomely for the band of the local cavalry regiment, and the parish of Saint-Maurille subscribed for the carpeting of the street altar near the pillory.[49] In spite of the great expense involved, the procession was thoroughly popular. In the *cahiers* of 1789 only watermen and wood merchants opposed compulsory attendance, while the movement for reform of the procession in 1790 did not aim at the abolition of the 'torches', but merely wished to lay the charge equally on all inhabitants.[50] When Angers substituted other festivals of a revolutionary nature, of Victory, or of the Supreme Being, their ceremonies were significantly modelled on the popular old ritual of the *Sacre*.[51]

It was not with laymen that ideas of making changes in these observances of the feast of Corpus Christi originated, but with clerics who wished to rescue and re-emphasize the religious significance of the day. Some changes were within the power of the ecclesiastical authorities, such as a regulation of the cathedral chapter in 1787 that the doors of its church should be locked at 8 p.m. on the eve of the feast to keep out idle sightseers who got a preview of the 'torches' by judicious tips to workmen and sacristy officials.[52] More radical reforms were impossible. All the organizations of the town had united to defeat bishop Vaugirault's proposal of 1741 that the order of procession should be changed to prevent the Sacrament from being kept waiting in the streets by the vagaries of preceding files. As the municipal officers pointed out, it was a civic procession, and though they were not so anxious to maintain their point in the eighties when payment for the storage of the 'torches' was in question, their description of the ceremony is a fair one—'this procession is not a purely ecclesiastical ceremony, but a mixed one, or, rather, it is the procession of all the inhabitants'.[53]

One is tempted to ask: to what extent were all the inhabitants celebrating the gift of sacramental grace, and to what extent were they merely indulging in a taste for civic pageantry and fairground frolics? That question, however, can never be satisfactorily answered in a society where spiritual and temporal were so closely bound together, and where the general imagination had no conception of the possibility of their separation. All legislation assumed that church-man and citizen were synonymous; the regulations of Parlement for the diocese, for example, not only state the obligation of furnishing *pain bénit* on Sundays at the behest of churchwardens, but also insist that the offering be made in person, or by a wife or a daughter, and never by a servant or inferior.[54] It was practically impossible, in the middle of the century at least, for a member of the upper classes to die unreconciled, for rumours of such a scandal would bring the bishop or his vicars-general in person to an impenitent death bed. Sacraments, said a sardonic Jansenist, are refused to those who want them and pressed on those who don't.[55] It is difficult to find criteria to assess the religious life of the common people, who followed the cycle of the Church's calendar in their daily life as automatically as they rose in the morning at the sound of the cathedral bell or inter-changed winter and summer clothing at All Saints and Easter.[56] An ideal test would be that of Easter Communions,[57] but in such a clerical town even this was likely to be a commonly accepted obliga-tion—and, for Angers, statistics are not available in any case. We hear of profane revellers who frequented dance saloons and billiard rooms on Sundays and Saints' days,[58] and there was a stirring of a sceptical spirit among the educated bourgeoisie, but making due allowance for these strata of the population, it seems true to say that most people's minds were deeply impregnated with the clerical atmosphere of Angers.

Prosperous citizens still made provision in their wills for mendicant friars and orphans from the Hôpital Général to attend their obsequies, for money to be distributed to the poor and for low masses to be said for their souls,[59] though these pious bequests seem to have been on the decline. Certainly, vocations to the religious life were rare among men nowadays, although one could still meet a dom Chevalier, 'jovial and worldly wise: he had been a pharmacien at Angers and married, then, having become a widower, he ranged himself under the banner of St. Benedict'.[60] Ordinary church-going habits, however, seem to have suffered but little change since the beginning of the century. 'Nowhere have I seen churches so well attended—so full,' wrote a visitor in the sixties.[61] On great occasions vast throngs poured into churches. Five thousand women carrying lighted candles packed Saint-Maurice for the mission of 1751—'the cathedral was never better illuminated'—and a procession of men a fortnight later was even more numerous.[62] Three years after this the nuns of the Visitation counted 4,000 communicants at masses for the beatification of their patroness, and when in 1772 Sainte-Chantal was finally canonized, their church and courtyard were full of people from four in the morning to evening benediction.[63] When in 1751 and 1776 a jubilee year brought round its offer of indulgences—'Seek ye the Lord while it is *so easy* to find Him', bishop Vaugirault announced on the first of these occasions, misquoting Isaiah to the scandal of Jansenists who deplored these facilities[64]—great crowds hastened to perform the requisite stations. Remarkable preaching by canon Raimbault of Chartres in the Lent of 1780 so packed the cathedral that the very chapter was ousted from its stalls.[65] Parish churches too were crowded for services of local significance—when a new bell was blessed, or an old couple celebrated their golden wedding by a mass of 'renewal', or when the parish midwife held a candle by the font before receiving her authorization to practice, or when a sad cortège of families accompanied the curé each All Souls day when he processed to the cemetery to sprinkle holy water on the tombs of deceased parishioners. We would like to know more about routine attendances at masses—there were four every day in the church of La Trinité, all 'usually preceded or followed by the communion of the people'.[66] As the clergy do not make their traditional complaints about empty pews, perhaps we can safely assume that church attendances were satisfactory.

Behind the façade of ceremonial statistics there were signs that ecclesiastical discipline was waning. The fast of Lent was generally observed up to the Revolution, but a contemporary noticed a decline in strictness from 1770 onwards.[67] Even at the beginning of the century *monitoires*[68] issued by ecclesiastical authorities had become a subject of ridicule in worldly circles, and their credit was only temporarily enhanced by a resort to the sombre ritual of the neighbouring diocese of Tours, which was equivalent to a cancellation of baptism—a white robe trampled, a candle extinguished, office book thrown down and church bells jangled out of tune and harsh.[69] Such lurid anathemas soon came to be regarded as bad form, the official view being that a curé, in publishing an excommunication in connexion with a *monitoire*, ought to do no more than the minimum required by law.[70] Year after year[71] at the request of the municipality, ecclesiastical thunders were directed against rogues who obtained their firewood by sawing down trees and seats in public promenades, and year after year passed without the culprits being detected, so that bishops became more and more reluctant to sanction such futile proclamations. On the other hand, a pious lady whose corn was being stolen from her barns, a few persons of quality whose conduct at a ball had been satirized by an anonymous versifier, or the magistrates of Royal courts seeking the authors of clericalist pamphlets against the Parlement of Paris,[72] were not unwilling to invoke an ecclesiastical supplement to the police, however ineffective. Thus it was that lay society was at once facile in its resort to ecclesiastical censures and indifferent to those censures once they were proclaimed, while the clergy generally wished to impose severe restrictions upon an undignified and obsolete practice.[73] Certainly, in the last decades of the old régime few *monitoires* were published in Angers, though the very last one was not promulgated until February 1788, being a call for information against the 'quidams ou quidannes' who had fraudulently cornered all local supplies of tallow and candles.[74]

Yet, while discipline slackened, simple piety still retained its hold on the popular mind. For three centuries the lame had left their crutches and prisoners their chains to decorate the walls of the Chapel of Notre-Dame de Recouvrance at the Carmes, and a stone statue of Our Lady on its altar (a statue miraculously rescued from Calvinist outrage) still drew pilgrims, more particularly nursing mothers.[75] It was believed that miracles were worked at a crucifix set up after the great mission of 1751, and there were still many superstitious people who were convinced that ashes from a bonfire outside the church of Saint-Julien on the feast of the Nativity of Saint-John the Baptist had healing powers, and that women who inserted themselves into ecclesiastical processions among the priests would be cured of fever.[76]

Institutional rivalries and the momentum of tradition played a

c

dominating part in the allegiance of the clergy to their relics; among simple folk, however, the motive remained what it always had been, a superstitious veneration for objects calculated (as an old Angevin writer had said) to frustrate the 'ambushes and plots of men and the deceits and wiles of the Devil, and to aid in speedily appeasing the wrath of God inflamed against the inhabitants of cities'.[77] A scandalous incident which took place in the cathedral in 1757 attests this. When an inquisitive canon opened a medieval tomb, the news spread in a flash, and

. . . stirred up the notion that the sepulchre contained the body of a saint, the people rushed to obtain fragments. The aperture in the tomb was sufficiently large to make it possible to pull out some pieces of bone. Vestments which covered the skeleton were almost entirely torn away and the whole contents would have become a prey to this pious brigandage had not the canon returned, and, aided by one of the bell-ringers, put a stop to their activities.[78]

Superstition was not imposed by the clergy from above; it welled up from the people below. 'Who could have believed', said the writer of the *Encyclopédie* article on Magic, 'that in this very century where the human mind has made such great progress . . . there are still people who are not undeceived?' [79] But to be fair to the good folk of Angers, this criticism applies to every stratum of French society in the eighteenth century. Crude peasants still feared witches (one indeed was tortured to death on a farm of the monks of Saint-Nicolas of Angers as late as 1780);[80] high society in Paris resorted to astrology, alchemy, black magic; a few ponderous theologians still warned their confrères against the pitfalls of sorcery;[81] and, for that matter, Angevin doctors still prescribed remedies for their patients which could have come direct from the cauldron in Macbeth.[82] Credulity was not a monopoly of simple people or of provincials, still less of ecclesiastics. On the contrary, enlightened clerics, as well as *philosophes*, condemned superstitious practices and the atmosphere they engendered—'the mistaken zeal for religion which intrudes itself everywhere, and principally among the simple, the feeble-minded, common folk, women, the super-pious'.[83]

Missions and confraternities were, as ever, the chief devices of the clergy for maintaining a sense of religious discipline and controlling and refining manifestations of popular piety. Most great churches had special preachers for their Lent and Advent courses[84] and, if anti-clericals are to be believed, they were not always so movingly eloquent as canon Raimbault—'Follow one of these doctors and see how he imposes on the vulgar. He arrives at Angers, goes to the church which pays him the highest fee, and mounts the pulpit. A stupid crowd throng round to hear him with pious respect; they believe him without understanding a word, and amid their yawns, they admire him.' [85] Parish missions took place from time to time with preachers brought in from neighbouring dioceses.[86] Every ten years there was a full-scale united mission for the whole town, which was financed by a pious legacy which furnished 1,500*l*. for the honoraria of the visiting priests who conducted it. Then there were catechism courses for children, sermons twice a day at hours convenient for workers, services of preparation for communion, special arrangements for hearing confessions, and monster processions, with occasional innovations like antiphonal singing of canticles by men and women, or the posing of questions (collusively one fears) to a 'brains trust'.[87]

Whatever success missions had (and no one ever knows whether missions are successful), the religious confraternities of Angers seem to have declined steadily throughout the century. Bishop Vaugirault, in an attempt to quicken devotion among people of the artisan class, had set up a confraternity for men meeting in the church of Saint-Maimbeuf and another for women in the chapel of the Lazarists; at his death in 1758, they are said to have mustered a total membership of over a thousand.[88] But their effectiveness did not long outlive their founder. One of the reasons seems to have been the suspicious attitude of the parochial clergy, who feared associations directed by canons, which would 'accustom the faithful to voices other than those of their natural pastors, and imperceptibly wean them from their parish churches'.[89] Meanwhile, there remained older confraternities established in the parish and monastic churches, each with its own peculiar organization and affiliations. There were five confraternities in the parish of Saint-Michel du Tertre, though three of them were more important as financial items on the accounts of the vestry than as religious associations.[90] In the church of Saint-Pierre, the curé was patron of the 'pilgrims of Saint-James',[91] and the canons exercised a somewhat dictatorial sway over the confraternity of the Purification.[92] A band of faithful layfolk was leagued together to maintain perpetual adoration before the Holy Sacrament in the little church of Sainte-Croix,[93] another group supported the prayers of the Dominican order, and received handsomely engraved certificates of membership as a reward.[94] Also in the church of the Dominicans was the confraternity of the Transfiguration which was patronized by the guild of weavers and met for services twice a year on the second Sunday in Lent and the second Sunday in August. Yet the general picture is one of decline. We hear of the revolt of the sisters of the Third Order of Saint-Dominic in 1778 and of their final exclusion from the chapel of La Bonne-Nouvelle by the prior, and of riots in taverns in 1781 and 1784 by the weavers, which resulted in the winding up of their confraternity of the Transfiguration by the civil police.[95] An observer in 1773 declared that only one confraternity retained its vitality.[96] He was referring to the 'Noble confrairie des Bourgeois', which met for a service in Saint-Laud on the day of the translation of Saint-Nicholas, and had a low mass said every Saturday by the curé of Sainte-Croix.[97] This association was, however, a prosperous exception that proves the rule of decadence, for it was a well-endowed company, whose meetings were formalized gatherings of well-to-do citizens. Membership was restricted to those exercising 'honourable' professions, or belonging to the official organization of merchants of the town; the six chapels in the patronage of the brotherhood provided sinecures for its ecclesiastical members; and its annual service was a parade of professional men and bureaucrats, where *Présidial* and municipality processed to kiss the paten after the offertory, with due regard to the rulings of precedence.[98]

Ceremony is, in its essence, corporate, predictable, and impersonal. It is impossible to judge the spiritual state of individuals from a description of their outward conformity, and for most individuals other evidence is inevitably lacking. And what can be said of the ecclesiastics, principally canons of collegiate churches, who maintained this continuous ceremonial round? Perhaps their activities had degenerated into formalism (though why all development towards formalism should commonly be called degeneration needs some examination); but if so, it was a formalism jealously preserved and lovingly elaborated. Chapters clung to their precedents and their precedences, and vied with one another in the splendour and dignity of their services and processions. Nothing must be left to chance. Regulations of the chapter of Saint-Maurice prescribed manifold details of dress, summer and winter, feasts and fasts, indoors and outdoors; the degree of bad weather which would justify the substitution of surplices for copes was defined, and great was the scandal when a canon of Tours presented himself in inappropriate garb to preach the Lenten course of 1779.[99] Did almanacs foretell an eclipse? Why then, the cathedral procession would set forth that day armed with candles (as it happened, it was a meagre and futile eclipse, and the canons regretted that they had not taken more scientific advice before making fools of themselves 'in an enlightened century like ours'.[100] The vergers policed the place neuve when the chapter was on progress, for the hay cart which had blocked the route at this strategic point in 1762 was never forgotten.[101] In the last decade of the old régime, capitular registers are full of details concerning ceremonial observances. The canons of Saint-Martin record how they welcomed their new bishop 'in long cloaks, preceded by their verger' and how their dean made a speech of welcome in French.[102] Those of Saint-Laud record how they formed two ranks with those of Saint-Martin to make a profound obeisance to the bishop, before returning chanting litanies at the end of the celebrations for the birth of the Dauphin; in 1787, the canons of Saint-Pierre summarize their new regulations for singing the epistle, gospel, responses and graduals in their church; the chapter of Saint-Martin notes the routes taken and the psalms sung in procession on great occasions, and in March 1789 was busy re-adjusting the itineraries.[103] These forgotten canons loved such formal and dignified details—it was their world—and when on a 1st of May the canons of the cathedral decided that their Rogation procession would take a new route to avoid the fair in the rue des Poêliers and the place du Pilory whenever Rogation day fell on a 1st of May again,[104] they were looking well ahead, pathetically confident in the permanence of their place in society. 'Cela arrivera en 1815', is their marginal note. This was in 1780. Five years later, the future duke of Wellington began his military training at the riding school of Angers.

CHAPTER III

PROVINCIAL CULTURE

I. CHURCH MUSIC AND ARCHITECTURE

FOUR years after the battle of Waterloo the prefect of the department of Maine-et-Loire received stern and unequivocal orders to restore the old musical traditions of the town of Angers.[1] But the arts, alas, do not spring to life fully armed at rumours of an administrative intervention and one had only to look at the *Conservatoire*, the *Opéra*, or the *Théâtre du Vaudeville* to realize how many musicians of Restoration France had received their education as choir-boys and church organists under the vanished old régime.[2] Before 1789 there were more than 450 choir schools teaching about 5,000 boys[3] to read Latin, sing and play instruments: from this reservoir of talent came choir-men and instrumentalists in various churches, an aristocracy of organists and *maîtres de musique* in cathedrals and royal chapels, and many of the singers and musicians who were drawn into the magic circle of Parisian entertainment and played at the *Opéra*, *Comédie Française*, the *Concert Spirituel*, and private performances given by courtiers and Farmers General.[4] Composition as well as execution was taught in these old choir-schools of France, and the standard way to become a composer,[5] whether of masses, sonatas or of comic operas, was to move steadily up the ladder leading from choir-boy to player of bassoon, violin or *serpent* in a church, and then on to organist or *maître de musique*. Lalande had been a chorister of Saint-Germain l'Auxerrois, Gilles a choir-master at Aix, Agde and Toulouse, Grétry, the son of a church violinist, became a choir-boy at Liège and was sent to Rome to study at the canons' expense, Rameau had been a church organist who, it is said, escaped from the barren mountains of Clermont to write operas in Paris by haunting his local bishop and canons with such barbarous music that they rescinded his contract.[6]

With music at the service of liturgical worship and the rich endowments of the Gallican Church at the service of music, an interlocking of sacred and secular took place which was very typical of France under the old régime. Cathedral chapters intrigued and outbid one another to entice able musicians into their service and scoured the countryside, sometimes well out of their diocese, for choir-boys.[7] *Maîtres de musique* moved rapidly from post to post as financial inducements and temperamental notions impelled them. Composers slid easily from sacred to secular, and secular motifs slipped easily into religious compositions. There were novelties like musical *saluts* and performances of *tenebrae* by professionals and women at Paris as early as the end of the seventeenth century, which made La Bruyère wonder if dancing would not soon be added to complete the resemblance to opera.[8] From then onwards the royal chapel at Versailles and various fashionable churches in the capital became centres of superb music, theatrically produced.[9] In 1725 the *Concert Spirituel* was founded, which throughout the century was to provide entertainment in Holy Week and on other days when theatres were shut,[10] while rich private individuals put on religious music for their friends' relaxation—memoir writers speak of carols at the duchesse du Maine's, of Rameau's improvisations on the organ of the chapel of M. de la Popelinière, of Pompadour producing and singing in a *miserere* in her drawing-room.[11] After the death of Couperin 'the great', organists tended to cultivate a worldly virtuosity, contrasting their tones and combining stops and manuals to titillate the senses of their audience and exhibit their own prowess.[12] In this respect the fame of Daquin and Balbastre at the end of the old régime might almost be termed notoriety.[13] Papal rescripts discouraging 'elaborate repetitions' and 'confusion of voices'[14] did not run in France. During the elevation at mass, said Mercier, they play ariettas and sarabands, and at *Te Deum* and vespers, hunting sons, minuets, sentimental airs and rigadoons.[15] There is whimsical exaggeration here, of course, and a hint of that instinctive connexion between Puritanism and journalism which is so interesting a psychological phenomenon. And, in any case, Mercier is speaking of Paris, that capital where all the peculiar tendencies working in French society contrived to reach their logical and scandalous extremes. In the provinces ecclesiastical leadership in musical life was more decorous. Sacred music did not become, as it were, 'secularized', but remained bound up with genuine liturgical observances. That was why the prefect of Maine-et-Loire had an impossible task when he sought to restore the old musical traditions of Angers. When the ceremonial pattern of the city's liturgical year had been shattered its chief established musical occasions had vanished, and when comfortable and abusive old institutions had been abolished, vocalists and instrumentalists had been deprived of their most consistent patrons. There had been a false new dawn of cultural enterprise with the symphony concerts of Theophilanthropy:[16] apart from this, the musical traditions which the authorities were lamenting had been obliterated in revolutionary turmoils, and the breach with the past can be dated precisely as September 1790, when the old cathedral chapter was ordered to wind up its affairs.

Before the Revolution, great music in Angers was almost a

cathedral monopoly. An annual exception to this rule arose towards the end of the old régime when the mayor and aldermen began to arrange charity concerts: these nevertheless were still dependent upon the presence of the choir of Saint-Maurice, which was loaned only on condition that ladies must not take part and that the words sung must be in Latin.[17] When the Ursulines celebrated their founder's day, or the royal chapters of Saint-Laud and Saint-Martin honoured the birthday of their patron the King's brother, or when the city fathers gave thanks for Louis XV's escape from Damien's dagger, the *maître de musique* of Saint-Maurice was called in to write an appropriate mass or motet; the choir also might be loaned out—on strict conditions—for the mayor's annual concert, or to grace services at Ronceray when new nuns were professed.[18] Amateurs and 'jeunes gens de condition' would bring their violins to supplement the cathedral instrumentalists and form a full orchestra—as they did when Gilles' requiem was sung for the soul of Louis XV, or when Voillemont, *maître de musique*, celebrated his first mass to an accompaniment of his own composition.

It was commonly said that, of all French cathedrals, that of Angers had the finest music.[19] Besnard, playing his violin and taking a hand at cards with his landlady's daughters while making up his mind about ordination, describes it as the town's greatest attraction during the pleasant idle years he spent there.[20] And comparisons could be levelled further afield than France, for nothing could be more horrifying to one brought up to the standards of this diocese than the cacophonous din at Saint-Peter's at Rome.[21] Proud of their church's great reputation, the canons of Saint-Maurice did everything on a grand scale. At high festivals, especially at Easter and on the eve of the patronal festival, the organ was supplemented by an orchestra of skilled performers hired for the occasion; a particular instrumentalist might be brought to Angers from Saumur, or even from as far afield as Poitiers.[22] For all ordinary purposes, however, the cathedral was musically self-sufficient. Its minor clergy were appointed under an obligation to carry on with musical studies; an automatic deduction of salary would be made to cover the cost of instruction in plain-song, or a bonus would be offered as soon as a reasonable standard of proficiency had been attained.[23] The qualifications for a post of *maire-chapelain* were: to be a priest under twenty-five years of age, 'who has a good volume of voice, and who knows plain-song, at least passably', and this office was awarded after a competitive test of vocal abilities.[24]

Every effort was made to obtain an able *maître de musique*, and, what was not so easy in those days of keen rivalries, to keep him. Down to 1775, the canons of Saint-Maurice had ill luck. Urbain

Grondeau, a promising young musician who produced a mass of his own composition for the patronal festival of 1758, died two years later.[25] After him came Louis Bachelier, a former choir-boy who had been ordained to the priesthood. But as he grew famous—he was even called to Versailles to play some of his severely formal compositions in the presence of royalty—his relations with his employers deteriorated, and in 1768, in spite of all the chapter's pleas, he chose a more strictly ecclesiastical vocation, and moved off to a canon's stall at Saint-Pierre.[26] No doubt the music of that church benefited greatly. Meanwhile, the cathedral was in difficulties; Bellanger stayed for two years, Nicolas Rozé lasted for five, and then succumbed to the lure of an appointment at Paris.[27] Then at last, the tribulations of the chapter were over. Voillemont, whom in their turn the canons enticed away from the church of Troyes, remained with them until the Revolution. Immediately after his arrival, the new *maître de musique* produced a setting for high mass at the Ursuline's founder's day, 'charming, well constructed, light and yet expressive',[28] and from then onwards his compositions were a feature of the musical life of Angers. Amateur musicians of the town, grateful for his patronage, came to play his music when he celebrated his first mass after his ordination in 1785, and his new *salut* in the following year was greeted by the local newspaper as giving him 'a place among the most distinguished composers of church music'.[29] Determined to retain his services, the cathedral treated him generously,[30] but in 1788, the inevitable crisis occurred, for Voillemont, anxious to assure his future, applied for the succession of Notre-Dame at Paris, and defeated 47 rivals in the examination. Possibly, his threat of accepting the new appointment was merely a gesture of independence. He had grown accustomed to living in that pleasant house[31] in the rue de la psalette in the shadow of the cathedral, with its classroom where generations of choir-boys had conned their grammar, and its convenient gallery and stair leading directly to the cloisters; provincial life was genial, and provincial adulation of his talents easily won and genuine. Certainly, his affections remained in Angers, and a guarantee of a retiring pension of 800*l.* at the age of fifty, given hastily by an anxious chapter, was enough to retain the celebrated *maître de musique* at Saint-Maurice.[32]

The choir-men under his direction were also full-time professionals, sometimes recruited from ex-choir-boys or other local talent, but more often brought in from far afield, a bass from Nantes, a tenor from Paris or Orleans.[33] They were handsomely paid; a suitable starting salary was 42*l.* a month, rising to a full 900*l.* a year, which was a permanent income, continued both in sickness and old age.[34] Senior musicians could expect to be allotted a convenient residence near their work, for the tangle of narrow streets around the church was all in the domain of the chapter;[35] then, too, there was hope of generous treatment from the canons in other respects, expectations which were put into lyrical form by a poetaster of the choir struck down by influenza.[36] On the other hand, the canons retained the right to fine their *psalteurs* for unsatisfactory conduct, a salutary provision, for the tribulations of those who employ temperamental professional musicians inevitably beset the chapter. Sometimes the trouble was unconventional dress, or absence from mattins, sometimes rudeness to a canon, or infiltration towards the vestry before service was finished; sometimes, individuals went on strike, and refused to sing as a demonstration of their grievance.[37] One Rosé, imported from Paris in 1769, was, four years later, making the 'new and chimerical' claim that he was not obliged to join in the psalmody,[38] the distinction between choirs and places where they sing, being, apparently, a very real one to him. At other times the canons complained of inattention and gossip during services. In 1772, measures were taken to deal with scandal caused by 'des conversations inutiles, souvent prolongées, même à haute voix, et par leurs rires immodérés', a description of chaos in the choir stalls which struck the chapter as so apposite that it used identical wording to justify further disciplinary measures three years later.[39]

All concerned in organizing church music, from that day to this, would agree that, while complacent and conceited senior musicians are most insufferable, a greater measure of original sin seems to manifest itself in choir-boys. However that may have been, in respectable households mothers looked longingly towards the spires of Saint-Maurice as their small boys were approaching the age of seven, for it was no minor honour to see one's son tonsured by episcopal hands, and thenceforward walking the streets in a white cassock (like the Pope himself), violet cap and red or violet cape.[40] These ten choristers who lived as boarders with their music master and Latin master in the *psalette* or choir school[41] were a formidable item on the chapter's expense account. There were surgeon's and apothecary's fees, the wages of their schoolmaster, payments for special music lessons for those 'who are found to show signs of proficiency on instruments', there was the outlay on robes, shoes and stockings, to which, from 1780 onwards, was added the item of linen and laundry, which parents were finding difficulties in providing.[42] On reaching leaving age, the senior boy received 160*l.*, partly as a reward for past services, partly to provide, as it were, his 'demobilization' clothing.[43] The canons showed themselves generous to their youthful charges. In the melancholy outbreak of ringworm in the winter of 1773 a handsome little payment was voted to three of the mothers for medical attention to their sons at home,[44] and when a boy turned out to have no musical ability and had to be dismissed, the chapter would send him off with quite a reasonable gratification.[45] If the failures were helped, naturally the successful were not forgotten; civil employment came easily to a youth who had the chapter's 'attestation of life and morals', good musical ability might lead to a further post at the cathedral, and outstanding intelligence might bring financial aid for a course at the Seminary.[46]

After exercising such care the chapter expected strict discipline and written permission was required before a boy was allowed out in town 'even to sing in churches',[47] a nicely worded prohibition which suggests precautions against unauthorized borrowing of choristers for special services by parish priests or canons of other churches.

Perpetually confronted with the example of Saint-Maurice, these poorer chapters struggled as best they could to maintain their musical standards in face of rapidly rising costs. As competition between churches intensified, organists demanded higher salaries. The cathedral paid 800*l.*—but this was for the great Bainville who had been a prodigy on the instrument when still a choir-boy at Chartres and had published a volume of original pieces.[48] Lesser chapters, however, had to offer at least half as much, or perquisites in lieu, like a rent-free house. It was no longer possible for a chapter with a full rota of services to pay a mere 250*l.* a year; for that sum a good performer would condescend to do no more than exercise a general supervision and send his pupils along to deputize at his instrument, possibly 'pupils who do not know how to play and who trouble the decency of the offices'.[49] Choir-boys were an even greater problem. The cost of their robes, education and food—the sacrist of Saint-Laud was neither the first nor the last to discover that it is a fallacy to assume that children eat less than adults[50]—made their maintenance a heavy expense. As for choir-men, at the best of times minor chapters were able to afford only four voices and to offer wages which were a third or a half of those given at the cathedral.[51] Effects of such penury were very evident at the church of Saint-Martin, where the canons were served by part-time musicians, like a shoemaker who agreed to accept 20*l.* a month for attending the offices and studying chanting and *serpent* playing; there were only two choir-boys (indeed for eleven years before 1780 there had been none at all) and as a measure of economy, full choral services were limited to Sundays and solemn feast days.[52] This poverty revealed another side of the character of choir-boys, whose lot at Saint-Martin's was not sufficiently enviable to allow the chapter to impose such draconian discipline as prevailed at the cathedral. A crisis came every Saturday night after compline when two boys sang litanies of Our Lady in the Chapel of Notre-Dame des Anges; or rather, sometimes they sang them and when they did it was 'to the scandal of the faithful', who heard 'deux enfants chanter avec précipitation, sans attention, sans décence'.[53] By May 1789 the canons had given up all hope of reforming this ceremony, and sought powers to have it sung by the whole choir at rarer intervals. But let us leave our choir-boys of Angers as they ought to have been, and maybe sometimes were; at Christmas singing one of those touching old local carols describing how each Angevin guild and community presents its homage to the infant Jesus, or in dalmatics and carrying candles, proceeding to the palace to welcome the bishop, or singing their cantata outside his window when they went to present their bouquet on May morning, or, perhaps, in some general procession obeying all the rubrics of the diocese,

habitu Chori induti, non turmatim aut promiscue, sed bini, composito et gravi passu, aliquanto intervallo . . . non vagis oculis circumspectantes, sed in librum Processionalem intenti.[54]

In matters of architectural taste and furnishings, the lead given by the cathedral to other churches of the town is almost as obvious as in the case of music. The writer of a guide-book in 1778 declared that the various churches of Angers had been handsomely decorated in the last thirty years,[55] which was true enough, though we are not compelled to agree that all changes had been for the better. Innovations began at Saint-Maurice, and were copied by the other canons as soon as they could raise the necessary money. It was in 1699 that the cathedral moved forward and isolated its high altar *à la romaine*, that is like the high altar of Saint-Peter's at Rome, which Angevin pilgrims throughout the eighteenth century agreed in regarding as a superb model for all other churches.[56] The chapter of Saint-Pierre followed suit seven years later after raising 6,000*l.* by a lottery; the canons of Saint-Maurille, jealous at being outpaced, changed their altar between 1714 and 1716, even at the expense of demolishing their chapel of Notre-Dame des Serpents with its tradition of miracles; Saint-Laud moved its altar six years later still.[57] Last of all among rich institutions came the abbey of Saint-Nicolas, which retained its old arrangements until 1732 when the monks made atonement for their tardiness by erecting in front of their choir a vast baldachin upheld by four life-size marble angels.[58] Parish churches too made what haste they could to follow the fashion set by the cathedral,[59] though it would take a whole generation before thrifty parishioners could be won over to changes which involved untoward expense. Thus it was in the second and third decade of the century that the cathedral remade its altars in marble, while parishes came into line only gradually, chiefly in the seventies and eighties.[60]

A description of the architectural exploits of ecclesiastics in this period tends at first sight to appear little more than a catalogue of annihilation. 'Revolutionary vandalism', it has been said, 'was responsible for a much smaller total of destruction and spoliation than the intransigent classicism of Jesuits and canons of the seventeenth and eighteenth centuries.' [61] Angers furnishes a sufficiency of startling examples. We read how the directors of the Hôtel-Dieu demolished their sixteenth-century altar carvings and threw the debris into their cellars, how the Jacobins sold the old tomb of bishop Loiseau, their founder, with its statue of gilded copper, how the Benedictines of Saint-Nicolas and the Cordeliers rebuilt or restored their cloisters, erasing portraits and dislodging statuary, how the Jacobins auctioned an old embroidered frontal to pay for marble to remake their high altar, how the Capuchins knocked down the hermit's chapel, which had been the first site of their house, 'to continue the terrace'.[62] It must be remembered, however, that old treasures were often replaced with new works of art which were regarded as better—like the lavish altar erected at the Hôtel-Dieu, or the new marble tomb of Michel Loiseau (even though the Angevin antiquary Pocquet de Livonnière thought it 'most inappropriate'). One must remember too that a great deal of very ordinary but expensive cleaning, furnishing and reconstruction went on—the lowering of the floor level of the parish church of Saint-Nicolas or the raising of that of Saint-Evroul, red and yellow mosaic paving of the floor of the Jacobins, a rose window to light the choir at Toussaint, an enlarged doorway for the south transept of Ronceray and repairs to pavements and the stonework of the façade, and, elsewhere, new side-chapels and new sacristies—which must have added greatly to the dignity and decency of churches.[63] There was more destruction—and more improvements—at the cathedral than elsewhere, and here, a consistent pattern and policy can be detected which gives a meaning to what might otherwise appear as a series of scandalous architectural incidents, and which, if it cannot win our approval, might at least arouse sympathetic understanding.

The canons of Saint-Maurice, in the full tradition of eighteenth-century ideas of decoration, for long had sought to make their church appear light and spacious, a building of sweeping perspective in which polished marble and richly carved woodwork would show to the best, if somewhat theatrical, advantage. Early in the century the floor was repaved, the six altars of the nave were remade in marble, and the high altar, brought forward in Roman fashion, was finally, in

1757, crowned with the great baldachin, where, borne aloft on six red marble columns, a flurry of cherubim supported a gilded orb and crown.[64] By now, a vast forest of organ pipes dominated the west end of the cathedral, and Suruge had completed carving four giant Atlases which upheld the gallery, and baskets of fruit and flowers and piles of musical instruments which surmounted its three towers.[65] The spacious interior necessary to set off this new work was achieved by making havoc of the legacy of the Middle Ages. The old screen, with its fifteenth-century silvered cross, and the odd pinnacled turret erected by Duke René to house the 'urn of Cana', were ruthlessly demolished.[66] No attempt was made to preserve antiquity; inscriptions on the floor vanished at the repaving, other vestiges of the past were effaced during excavations for the canons' new funeral crypt, the central pillar of the main door with its two fifteenth-century statues was demolished to facilitate the entry of the 'torches' of the *Sacre*, and eight of the twelve apostles above the door were removed for good measure.[67]

Worse devastations were to come. A painstaking ecclesiastic of Châteaugontier, who wrote a guide-book to Angers in 1778, had suggested further improvements at the cathedral—an obelisk on the square outside in the manner of Saint-Peter's at Rome, and, for the interior, a camouflaging of the joints of the stonework, on the principle that beauty of construction consists in putting together an edifice so that the stones comprising it appear a complete unity.[68] What he recommended was, in fact, plaster and whitewash. At Saint-Martin and the abbey of Saint-Aubin this reform had already been carried out, and the cathedral chapter now called in the Italian Baroni, who had done work of the kind at Chartres, and was willing to do his worst at Angers for 2,400*l.*[69] Remorselessly, Baroni pursued his fashionable trade; all the interior, the sacristy and the chapter-house were whitewashed. Medieval wall paintings were obliterated.[70] Already, the oldest tomb in the church, dating from the twelfth century, in which bishop Ulgar lay in state in the remains of his violet and red silk chasuble, had been stripped of its enamel; now the picks of workmen shattered its projecting carvings, and the plastering process engulfed it.[71] Then came the disposal of the tapestries. There was a rich endowment of medieval pieces among the cathedral treasures—an immense late fourteenth-century Apocalypse of seventy scenes, where the fiery sword sprang from the mouth of the Son of Man, where the seven candlesticks burned and the seven-headed beast rose from the sea,[72] a magnificent series given by Charles VII which rehearsed Christian history from the fall of the angels to the triumph of the Church militant, and a mid-fifteenth-century composition to the greater glory of the chapter, all emblazoned with its arms.[73] Canons of the eighteenth century were never quite at ease with these relics of medieval taste displayed around them on great feast-days. In 1768 they complained that tapestries were prejudicial to the acoustics,[74] and now, having decided on whitewash, light and simplicity, it was clearly time to get rid of them. All, with the exception of those needed for the Maundy Thursday altar, were put up for sale, only the vast Apocalypse surviving in storage to protect the orange trees of Saint-Serge from frost during revolutionary years.[75]

When new woodwork and panelling were erected in the choir, the canons were driven further in their career of archaeological crime. Scant respect had been shown already to the memory of Duke René, who slumbered in the choir, and in 1779 the chapter sought Royal permission to have the exterior masonry of his tomb removed. This granted, the effigies of the good duke and his lady, recumbent on black marble, were taken off to less distinguished quarters (obtained by evicting a bishop) and the arcade of the original tomb vanished behind the new woodwork.[76]

By now, the designs of the eighteenth-century canons were very largely completed. At great cost to themselves—though they recouped some of the expenditure by the sale of medieval silverwork, even including part of the reliquary of Saint-Maurille[77]—they had transformed their church in accordance with their own ideas of beauty and dignity. They were doing at Angers precisely what their contemporaries at other French cathedrals were doing. Almost everywhere we hear tales of the demolition of a Gothic past: stucco and gilt covering crude powerful frescoes, altars transferred and reredos pulled down, stained glass replaced by plain, old tombs and carving and pillars destroyed—Auxerre lost its gigantic statue of Saint Christopher, Autun its red and black marble tomb of Lazarus, Chartres its rood-screen, pounded into gravel to level the floor . . .[78]

It is not necessary to believe that these innovating canons scorned the Middle Ages as centuries of superstition and ignorance. They were simply being up to date and taking the best architectural advice available to them; they were following the rules laid down at the end of the seventeenth century by François Blondel, that builders and decorators should serve nature and reason, not private fantasies, that they should look to classical antiquity or to the masters of the Italian Renaissance for inspiration, that they should refuse to allow incompatible or distracting details, striving always to achieve harmonious proportions and 'un bel ensemble'.[79] Even so, Blondel had been prepared to give qualified praise to Gothic, for it was immense and permanent, well fitted to achieve its object of inspiring veneration in simple people[80]—and this admission became standard doctrine in the eighteenth century. Soufflot in 1741 drew attention to the superb play of light and shade and the soaring height and dramatic effect of medieval churches.[81] More than this, he also praised the technical skill and daring which had achieved these effects, using as his illustration the church of the abbey of Toussaint at Angers, where two slim columns less than a foot in diameter upheld the thrusting weight of the stone roof. After Soufflot, praise of this remarkable Angevin church became a commonplace among connoisseurs,[82] though as Thorode complained, ordinary people who saw it every day thought nothing of it. 'Reason', 'nature' and classical antiquity did not necessarily condemn the general lines and imaginative sweep of Gothic architecture; indeed, the cathedral of Orleans was being steadily rebuilt throughout the seventeenth and eighteenth centuries in imitation of the old medieval church which the Huguenots had destroyed.[83] It was medieval ornament and embellishments, incongruous details, clutters of tombs and un-fashionable statuary, rood-screens and other obstacles which broke lines of perspective—in the Angevin Rangeard's words, 'this Gothic over-elaboration, this profusion of ornaments, this almost invariably formless mass of pompous or paltry decoration with which our churches . . . were overloaded' [84]—which classical architects despised. 'For my part,' wrote a Jesuit expert in a handbook on architecture published in 1755,

I am convinced that up to the present we have not found a judicious style for this sort of buildings. Our Gothic churches are still the most satis-factory ones that we possess. Behind all this mass of grotesque orna-ments which detracts so greatly from their beauty, you gain a sure though indefinable impression of grandeur and majesty.[85]

Developing his theme in a later work this same author (who by now had been made an associate of the Academy of Angers[86]) recommended a Grecian style for the externals of a religious building and Gothic for interiors, though with marble pavements, and shorn of 'foolish' decorations characteristic of late medieval art, and of rood-screens, 'those horrible barricades', and of 'gilded tombs of frail and sinful mortals'.[87] He might have been describing the improving programme of our canons of Angers. Even after the Revolution had released their pens from all inhibitions Angevin commentators were still faithfully reflecting the sort of opinions which Père Laugier was setting forth in the mid-century. In 1797 one of them remarks upon the 'skilful architects' of those 'very ages which we call centuries of ignorance' and regrets the 'grotesque' devices with which their work is overlaid; another condemns the 'bizarre, monstrous and extrava-gant' ornaments in the church of Saint-Aubin and its 'hideous, deformed or terrifying' statues, yet goes on to praise the vast size of the building, its rows of pillars and the general effects of light and perspective.[88]

It was these good qualities in their architectural heritage which the canons of Angers believed they were enhancing and drawing out. Perhaps they went about their tasks too daringly, though as Laugier remarked, 'there can be no progress in the Arts if we always limit ourselves to imitation of things that have been done already'.[89] Only in an ironical and paradoxical sense was their work a prelude to revolutionary vandalism. They were simply men of their time, conscious of all its resources, sure of its continual progress, confident in their own judgment. A later generation of archaeologists of the school of Viollet-le-Duc was to be horrified, but the canons were only doing what their ancestors had always done themselves, proudly rebuilding the church they loved as seemed best in their own eyes, undeterred by reverence for the past.[90]

2. LITERARY AND INTELLECTUAL LIFE

Medieval canons would have understood and sympathized with their eighteenth-century successors, who were welcoming new art and new music, but were using both as adjuncts of liturgical worship in its traditional form. A relationship between historical and literary studies on one hand, and religious thought and apologetic on the other, was equally traditional, and was equally maintained in Angers. Here the clergy ruled the intellectual life of the town in a fashion which would have seemed incredible to a visitor fresh from the *salons* of Paris. As we shall see when we consider the religious orders and communities, the education of youth was under clerical control, but that was general throughout the realm and would have caused no surprise. It was ecclesiastical domination in the adult intellectual circles of the University and Academy which was significant, particularly as it was a domination which had been perpetuated by merit rather than by tradition. In fact, the University of Angers was proud of its freedom from the control of churchmen. Long ago, the canon of the cathedral who held the title of *maître-école*, had lost all real power to the Rector, being now a mere chancellor, whose functions were limited to signing *lettres de grade* and receiving a small sealing fee.[91] The Faculty of Law rejoiced in its precedence, unique among the universities of the kingdom, over the Faculty of Theology.[92] Even so, of all influences in university life, the ecclesiastical was predominant. While the medieval colleges affiliated to the University now existed only in name, the abbeys of Saint-Aubin, Saint-Serge and Saint-Nicolas and Toussaint, and the houses of the

D

Carmelites, Augustins, Dominicans and Cordeliers held an equivalent status, and their students could take degrees. At the beginning of the century, in spite of strong opposition, the Seminary had been granted a similar academic recognition for its two-year course in philosophy.[93] Whatever repute the University enjoyed in the country at large was derived from its Faculty of Theology, the most celebrated in France after the Sorbonne. A patriotic intellectual of Anjou might not be inclined to admit this qualification, for when curé Robin visited Paris in 1750, he considered that the doctors there were debating 'a very ordinary difficulty'.[94] Young men of the revolutionary bourgeoisie might laugh at two professors lecturing in the dilapidated cloisters of the cathedral,[95] but at least the degrees their faculty conferred were genuine, not snobbishly confined to students of distinguished families, and awarded after purely nominal interrogation.[96] People had grown accustomed to lawyers produced under this system, but it was proverbial in western France that if you felt ill you sent for a physician who had qualified at Paris or Montpellier, not at Nantes or Angers.[97] Theologians, on the other hand, achieved their degrees with difficulty. Even the brilliant young Bernier had a rough passage when upholding his theses, and the ecclesiastic who negotiated the Concordat might have done so with inadequate academic qualifications had his examiners been less forbearing.[98] Happy indeed the candidate who manœuvred through a barrage of questions from the doctors of theology to join them genially afterwards in the bonbons and wine of their well-earned collation—a great contrast to the Faculty of Law, where degrees were up for sale at 12 francs a question.[99]

In the more superficial life of the Academy, the clergy played an outstanding role to which social distinction and wide interests, as well as learning, entitled them. Angers boasted its own *Académie des Sciences, Belles-Lettres et Arts*, affording seats for forty immortals of local fame, who competed for the discriminating applause of the respectable *Affiches* and the more down-to-earth approbation of M. Mérau, their tavern-haunting *concierge*, 'Monsieur, je suis content de vous'.[100] Their themes were eminently respectable, omitting no opportunity for praises of the monarchy[101] or of themselves (for had not the emulation of academic societies excited men's minds and rescued Europe from the dark ages?)[102] and including none to offend ecclesiastical susceptibilities. 'C'est une bonne fille,' said Voltaire darkly, 'qui n'a jamais fait parler d'elle.'[103] When the bishop of Soissons, a prolific writer of pastoral letters, passed through town, what could be more fitting than a proposal to receive him among these conventional celebrities, and what could be more typical of Angevin orthodoxy than an angry clerical opposition, given that

Mgr Fitz-James was Jansenistically inclined? 'A great man,' said one of the vicars-general, 'I'll grant you that he's nearly six feet high.' [104] Throughout its history indeed, the Academy of Angers had a strong clerical element among its members. In the eighties, at public sessions of the Academy, one might have heard the bishop himself (who, incidentally, provided a gold medal biennially as an essay prize) on pulpit eloquence, canon Waillant of the cathedral on the dangers of public speaking, or on the utility of mathematics, canon Trouillard of Saint-Martin on systems of education, or be-wailing the neglect of letters, canon Burgevin of Saint-Pierre con-futing Montesquieu on patriotism, canon Barat in praise of Louis XVI.[105] And above all, in prose and verse, in season and out of season, came that long-standing member and consistent contributor, the abbé Rangeard, on diverse topics, a farewell to poetry in 1779, and an Ode to Virtue in the following year, prognostics and presenti-ments, rescues from drowning, France rules the waves, women's fashions, current politics, fables, metrical translations and para-phrases of psalms.[106]

When other societies, which would appear less suited for clerical membership, sprang up in the second half of the century, each could show its crop of public-spirited and literary-minded churchmen. One of the four founding members of the Royal Society of Agriculture in 1761 was the ubiquitous Rangeard, and when the membership totalled twenty, five of these were ecclesiastics.[107] For long the correspondence of this society with the central government was in the hands of Cotelle, dean of Saint-Martin. Methods of slate quarrying, titles to coal-mining rights, the distribution of clover seed, the chemical analysis of the poisonous official salt, the defence of his fellow-citizens against the 'crying injustices' of the tax-farmers—nothing came amiss to this practical dean. True, he hoped to obtain an additional benefice by the powerful contacts he was gaining in Paris, but he promised that if extra revenues came his way, he would lay them out on prizes to encourage scientific agriculture.[108] A benefice in plurality, prizes—'They have no notion of private people going out of their way for the public good,' said Arthur Young, harshly, after being courteously entertained by a later secretary of the Angevin society.[109] But this practical Suffolk squire was thinking exclusively in terms of efficient farming: a Swiss nobleman who had heard of the foundation of the Agricultural Society of Angers in 1761 showed greater insight by regarding it as a device for political self-expression, a sort of club of provincial reformers which could claim the privilege of giving advice to a despotic king.[110] There was, too, as the century progressed, a growing literary and amateur enthusiasm for country pursuits, which led in its next stage to the foundation of a Botanical Association in town, which enlisted all the youthful zeal of La Revellière-Lépeaux, the future Director, and in the eighties the *Botanophiles* struck somewhat feeble roots, with the aid of the prior of Lesvière, schoolmasters of the Oratory, and more distant patronage from the bishop.[111]

Freemasonry, of course, came to Angers. Its original advent had been rather sinister, if the *procureur du Roi*'s tales of wenching, brawling 'et même de l'irréligion' are to be credited.[112] Certainly, in 1754, the chapter of Saint-Maurice refused to allow masonic meetings in houses of which it held the ground lease,

believing that this sort of assemblies, composed of men only, were a mere pretext to facilitate loose talk on matters touching religion or the state, and even perhaps, the satisfaction of unnatural passions.[113]

But by the seventies no trace was left of this disreputable ancestry —or perhaps we should say, panic had died down in official circles. By then, masonry was an affair of two agreeable middle-class clubs, whose activities were exemplary.[114] They gave alms, commissioned masses for deceased brothers, and even their masonic 'Marseillaise' with its ferocious chorus[115] taught nothing more extreme than the duty of loving one's enemies, which is, of course, a subversive doctrine, though it was not meant in that sense by its clerical composer. Ecclesiastics of moderately progressive ideas joined quite freely. Canon Waillant of the cathedral was a founding member of the lodge *Père de Famille*; in 1774, the lodge *du Tendre Accueil* had three canons of the cathedral, one of Saint-Martin, one of Saint-Pierre, and two Augustins among its brethren, and clerical membership, especially of Oratorians, remained strong in the lodges in the following years. Whatever the fashionable intellectual activity in Angers, churchmen could be relied on to play a leading part, and local gossip and papal fulminations did not suffice to make an exception of freemasonry. The rule held good when in the early days of 1789, informal meetings were held at the shop of the printer Mame to hear and discuss the latest political news; it is significant that the *habitués* who were present when the packet from Paris arrived on 17 July included three canons, one curé, and the commendatory abbot of Toussaint, and it was they who first heard the dread news of the fall of the Bastille.[116]

Clerical Angers was free from the inhibitions that fear engenders. It was very difficult to convince oneself, in the bosom of this stable and conservative provincial society, that the irreligious writings of the age presented a serious danger, or that progressive and reforming thought might be turned effectively against the Church. Not that the writings of *philosophes* were unknown here—far from it. Young men of the middle class—and, if alarmists were to be believed, women too—read the new writers. In the early seventies an angry academician of Angers, denouncing the books of the 'criminal league' in Paris, more particularly those of d'Holbach, declared that 'scarcely have they been published in the capital than they spread like a torrent in the provinces'.[117] René-Jean Pantin, son of a local doctor who married in 1774 and settled down in a house in the rue Valdemaine leased from the priests of the mission, was a collector of anti-clerical manuscripts; he doubted the Old Testament miracles and prophecies, believed that Christianity was a product of pagan and Jewish mystery cults and that Christ was, as Celsus said, the son of a Roman soldier.[118] Unbelief of a less militant kind could even insinuate itself within the walls of the Little Seminary, where Mercier du Rocher, originally sent from La Rochelle to prepare for the priesthood, made his last confession in August 1771.

I was beginning to conceive of God as an uncreated being, supremely good and merciful, and of the whole drove of religions in the world as just so many political institutions. I thought that it would be enough if I followed the maxim, *Alteri ne feceris quod tibi fieri non vis.*[119]

Vague deistic ideas, the spectacle of monastic wealth and a visit to town of a troupe of actors, which made him yearn to be a dramatic author, turned him decisively from ordination and from Christian practice. Volney, who visited Angers for a while, had Hebrew grammars in his lodgings for no good purpose; La Revellière-Lépeaux was cherishing deistic ideas and a hatred of all aristocrats, including sacerdotal ones. Gabriel-Eléanor Merlet, an academician and an ally of La Revellière in botanical pursuits, was another cultivated young man of like progressive views whose correspondence with his friends Huard and Préseau reveals still more of the anti-clerical temper growing fashionable in his generation and social class. From Rome he writes satirically of that priest-ridden city where in cynical self-defence he moved around in ecclesiastical costume as if he were still a loyal pupil of the Angevin Oratory—

How you'd laugh if you saw me, hair cut short, clothed in black, with a silk mantle and clerical neck bands—in short with all the trappings of an *abbé. Si Romae fueris, Romano vivito more.*

This dress, it is true, did not handicap him in seducing a girl he met paying her devotions on the steps of the Scala Sancta. Later on in London he had an opportunity to contrast Protestant and Catholic Europe: here, he said, he had been delighted 'to have seen neither monks nor misery', not to mention having enjoyed excellent food.[120] Merlet was a cynic, even about the *philosophes*: some of his contemporaries were more uncritical in their admiration. Another Angevin worthy who went up to Paris in 1778 wrote back naïvely to his friends of Voltaire's appearance in the capital as the advent of a Messiah—'The cloud is rent asunder, the sacrifice is being offered and humanity is regenerated'.[121]

Such views, however, were aired in private correspondence and conversations. In public one had to be cautious, so that when the chemist Joachim Proust produced a masque in praise of Voltaire and Rousseau in 1788 it occasioned great scandal to many of his fellow-citizens.[122] The reception given to this dull and harmless masquerade was a measure of the conservatism and submission to authority which was characteristic of formal society in Anjou. The local printer confined himself to reprints of classics, harmless verse, treatises on agriculture and books of devotion; booksellers' advertisements chiefly concerned volumes like *La Journée du Chrétien*, *Le petit Paroissien*, *Vie intérieure*, breviaries, catechisms, meditations, 'Hours' as appropriate to the usages of various dioceses, or as used by the King, Queen, Dauphin or princes.[123] Within living memory, only one speech at the Academy had ventured to criticize the government and that was given by the theologian Cotelle de la Blandinière, concerning a religious issue—and it had been hastily disavowed by a panic-stricken municipality.[124] It was priests of the Oratory and the Seminary, and the curé of Saint-Julien who in 1786 suggested a minor break with old traditions in the interests of hygiene, and it was lawyers of the *Présidial* who insisted that stinking corpses of criminals continue to be publicly exposed near the city.[125] Innovation was not popular in Angers, so why should churchmen fear for their doctrines? The Academy was respectable, the Faculty of Theology was reputed infallible, the monumental *Conférences d'Angers* had settled all problems of Christian belief for generations to come. There were arguments in the Seminary to vindicate Genesis against Buffon,[126] and the learned priest of the parish of Saint-Pierre was prepared to prove Moses right from the annals of other ancient peoples—or even if he was wrong, 'it remains incontestable that the moral teaching is sound, and, by consequence, divine'.[127] Theology, at least, was safe from the corrosive acids which the *philosophes* were distilling in their godless laboratories in distant Paris. Envious eyes were being cast on Church property, and the absurd maldistribution of ecclesiastical wealth was a subject of comment, but there was no ideological inspiration, only a practical one, behind this movement of opinion. Plans for a system of national education[128] were winning favour in the University, especially in the Faculty of Law, and among the priests of the Oratory, but in strict logic, there was no reason why their adoption should undermine ecclesiastical control. The harsh white light of philosophic doctrines filtered into Angers confused and mellowed and refracted by the heavy still atmosphere of provincial society.

Indignation without alarm was the reaction of the clergy, and indeed of local dignitaries generally, when they aired their views at the opening of law or university terms, or at sessions of the Academy. When the discourse fell to the abbé Barat, canon of Saint-Martin, one could rely upon hearing outright denunciation of 'the unbelievers' of our age, 'whose ideas spell disaster to society and political government'.[129] Patriotism, said canon Burgevin at his reception into the Academy in 1782, must ultimately lose its force without the power of religion and morals to inspire it.[130] This could be proved from Roman history, argued another orator, for the great days of the Republic were those when the state paid due attention to religious ceremonies.[131] A lawyer like François Prévost, a Gallican, a supporter of state education, a sympathizer with Calas, a 'destroyer of idols', did not think otherwise; 'O unhappy century, where irreligion, ignorance, pride and corruption produce a world of *prétendus philosophes*'; for his part, he will have none of their doctrines, but will leave mankind in its 'good and sweet illusions', in the ignorance and innocence which are the only goods the gods approve.[132] He agreed with the clergy at least in regarding religion as a social necessity. These provincial *esprits forts* prided themselves, in fact, on their rectitude in withholding their daring and brilliant thoughts so as not to upset the moral foundations of simpler humanity. 'He was too honest, too wise, too well-bred to set up grim memorials of his independence or his scepticism upon the ruins of the faith of our fathers' [133]—that was the sort of praise which a worldly academician of Angers would covet. Even a cynic like Merlet, travelling through all the popish décor of Avignon, would write back to his Angevin friends disclaiming the title of *philosophe* and resignedly offering to suppress his genius and become 'a victim to prejudices'. With Fontenelle he was willing to say, 'if I held all truth enclosed within one hand I would take care not to open it'.[134]

As oblique and patronizing reflections of this kind show, those who defended religion on mere grounds of social utility were in danger of finding themselves saddled with unsatisfactory allies. Other apologists chose their ground with more subtlety and instead of denunciation or prophecy of social ruin praised the legitimate achievements of the age of Reason up to a point where religion began to be in danger. Canon Guillot was enthusiastic about Fontenelle's proof of life on other planets and admired Newton's 'angelic' genius, but he denounced 'system makers' who thought they knew everything—and those included Leibniz and Malebranche alongside Gassendi and Spinoza.[135] 'Liberty of thought', said Rangeard

which, contained within due bounds, has been able to extend the area of our knowledge, has degenerated into unbridled audacity, scorning reticence and breaking every restraint.

Even so, he spoke of a coming reform in France which had been prepared by 'the revolution which has taken place in our manner of thinking', by 'that judicious reason which insists upon evaluating everything by the test of public utility'.[136] Earlier in the century it had been possible to justify belief by denouncing reason, whose 'sad illumination merely serves to enlighten us about our own unhappiness', and by incessant self-contradiction, 'leaves us for ever curious, but always ignorant'.[137] Now, however, it became more fashionable to approve of reason, provided it were rightly directed, a useful sheep dog, obedient to the whistle of the ecclesiastical shepherd. Virtue and science, said canon Cosnier in 1776, can aid each other, thus religion has nothing to fear from the activities of the new philosophy.[138] This school of thought would allow some value to the works of 'the new philosophers', but would attempt to redefine the word '*philosophe*', and rescue it for application to Christian thinkers. 'The philosophic mind', it was said in the Academy in 1781, 'which respects the sacred barriers laid down by the wisdom of the Supreme Legislator, is not excluded from the sanctuary.' [139] Thus we would have a 'Christian philosopher', who would see nature as a continuous miracle, and reason as the handmaid of faith, but 'sacred reason', not the dissolvent reason of the profane.[140] This was the title Rangeard claimed for himself—'Philosophe chrétien, et chrétien soumis'.[141] A true philosopher, in short, would take his doctorate at Angers, and produce his daring speculations in papers to the local Academy.

In Angers, the thrusts of anti-clericalism were as effective as swordplay against a feather-bed. Here, as canon Cosnier had said, religion had nothing to fear from the new philosophy, and thus it was safe for the Benedictines of Saint-Aubin to install plaster busts of Voltaire and Rousseau in their monastery,[142] and for the clergy to praise the literary merits of a dangerous author in spite of his opinions. Witness their attitude to Voltaire. Curé Robin claimed to have confuted him—but in the self-same paragraph went on to praise his intelligence and style.[143] Even Cotelle de la Blandinière, a pillar of orthodox theology and writer of the diocesan handbooks, had been anxious to submit his maiden speech to the Academy for the approbation of its great anti-clerical patron.[144] Rangeard went further still, and allowed his liberalism to carry him on to ground

which some regarded as unholy. 'That is Voltaire's field,' a friend
wrote to him in 1766,

not a subject for a reasonable man, and above all, for an ecclesiastic . . .
This piece of writing seems to me to re-echo the declamations of Voltaire
against the spirit of the Church.[145]

Perhaps there is a reference here to Rangeard's critical opinions on
miracles subsequent to those of the earliest Christian centuries.
Though he was fascinated by the Middle Ages and admired the
Crusades he looked back sadly to times of 'feudal anarchy' when
religion became corroded with superstitions, when

false traditions and relations of legendary marvels filled practically all
the chronicles and the Church had to lament the relaxation of its
discipline amidst this multitude of imaginary events which, to some
degree, were made into a substitute for the penitential discipline which
up to that time she had so successfully imposed.[146]

Let those who would, believe that Saint-Maur came back from his grave
to beat Rainfray count of Anjou into insensibility, or that Foulques
Nerra was directed to a site for his monastery of Saint-Nicolas by
three doves with branches in their mouths—Rangeard would not.[147]
Thorode, lay secretary of the cathedral chapter, included these tales
in his 'Notice de la ville d'Angers' without comment, but he was
ironical about accepted chronology for the Flood and used a miracle
at Saint-Aubin's tomb as a mere indication of ancient burial
customs.[148] Even M. Emery of the Seminary, who spoke so sternly
against habitual scepticism concerning 'particular revelations', was
prepared to admit that a man could be too credulous, and (while not
disbelieving them himself) he omitted all visions from his volume
on *L'Esprit de Sainte Thérèse*—except that of hell 'which contains
very instructive moral lessons'.[149] There was no sign here of that
defiant assertion of marginal beliefs which has sometimes been the
fumbling response of churchmen to attacks on their doctrines. On
the contrary, there was among the clergy of Angers a modest independence of thought and a serenity in face of criticism which was
born of a confident feeling of immunity. To them the writings of
philosophes were but a distant sound of battle. They gave point to
the protest of the editor of the local newspaper that he will give
no offence to religion, and provide the canon-treasurer of the
cathedral with an argument for his inspection of the 'torches' of the
Sacre 'lest an opportunity be given to the detractors of our sacred
books and our dogmas' [150]—but they were not regarded as an
imminent danger.
     Official theology in Anjou proceeded on its stately way throughout

the eighteenth century, unmoved by preoccupations of apologetics, reiterating beliefs without rearguing them. Volume after volume of the *Conférences du diocèse d'Angers* appeared,[151] successively edited by Babin, Vaultier and de la Chalinière, canons of the cathedral, and finally by Cotelle de la Blandinière, sometime curé of Soulaines, each leaden tome dictatorially orthodox. Perhaps it was because this mountain of orthodox assertions barred all paths of theological speculation that the ablest minds among the clergy of Angers turned to a study of local history, reflecting like that famous antiquary, the abbé Du Bos, that 'I'll at least have one consolation: seeing that my subject does not involve theology or medicine, my mistakes won't create either heretics or assassins'.[152] On the other hand, it might have been argued that a sympathetic study of the past greatness of the Church of France would be its best defence in the present. If theologians could make no reply to 'reason' beyond renewed assertions, antiquaries might at least build up a cumulative refutation of those *grands seigneurs* of letters who were writing 'philosophical' history, scorning the 'centuries of ignorance' and the erudite slaves who cared for their barbarous monuments.[153] Then there were other and obscurer motives to incline ecclesiastics to study the past. Society was riddled with privilege, privilege depended on precedent, and precedent was deduced from history. That was why nobles and magistrates of Parlements, anxious to appropriate political power to their class, were turning to antiquarian arguments,[154] and similarly, churchmen defending their immunities against secular encroachments, higher clergy proving their rights against lower or lower against higher, were inevitably drawn into historical discussions. But apart from all other considerations the subject itself had its own intrinsic relevance and fascination. There were the conundrums posed by the Academy—why was the present diocese smaller than the actual province? why was the archbishop of Tours recognized as metropolitan and the archbishop of Lyon as primate?[155] There were the lives of five Angevin saints[156] to investigate—Maurille, Aubin, Lezin, Maimbeuf and Godebert—whose names still resounded in church dedications and whose relics lay in jewelled shrines on many an altar; and by contrast there were the medieval counts of Anjou, whose pious bouts amid careers of violence had given ecclesiastical institutions their great possessions—men like Foulques Nerra, founder of Saint-Nicolas and rebuilder of Ronceray, ruling like a brutal Caesar in Anjou, whipped naked on a hurdle through the streets of Jerusalem. Then there were lesser feudal families whose tombs lay heavy on the paving stones of churches and whose endowments were still remembered—the lords of Craon who slept at the Cordeliers, the Beauvau in the Augustins.[157] Here too was a diocese which had produced two popes and twenty cardinals and whose cathedral chapter had given twelve bishops to Angers and twenty-three to other sees. This at least was the computation given in a manuscript register proudly left by its finder at the palace for bishop de Lorry's inspection—'Forgive me, sir, if my writing is so bad as I am using an old pen of your porter's. I hope that you will be good enough to accord me an audience at your return' [158]—a pathetic little note which contains all we know of some forgotten antiquary of Angers.

All around, a wealth of material encouraged antiquarian attention. During the second half of the century, in the rich archives of chapters and monasteries, classification and cataloguing went on apace, in the care of expert feudists, Desportes at Saint-Maurille, Barthélemy at Saint-Aubin, Cloquet at Toussaint, Thorode at Saint-Maurice.[159] Here, at the cathedral, there was a veritable treasure house of medieval parchments: had not the great Mabillon, in passing through Angers, turned aside and respectfully kissed the cartulary containing charters of the Carolingian kings?[160] A general inventory of their titles drawn up by the canons in 1734 had filled an enormous register of over 1,500 pages, and it took Thorode nine years—from November 1761 to June 1770—to complete a final classification. Binding for 383 volumes cost nearly 1,400*l.*, the organization of a muniment room cost rather more than this, Thorode himself was paid 10,000*l.*, then there were other payments to Cloquet for additional assistance.[161] Thorode's next major task was the reorganization of the central diocesan archives, which up to 1778 had been stacked ingloriously in a loft above the hall of the bishop's palace. Now, however, the Assembly of the clergy of Anjou ordered their removal to the building which housed the receiver of clerical taxation, where the cold of winter would not prevent research, and the work of classification could conveniently proceed.[162] There was no unemployment among the feudists of Angers.

This zeal of corporate bodies for the preservation of their muniments is, however, only one side of the story. Scandalous examples to the contrary make one suspect that their enthusiasm had motives other than the promotion of disinterested scholarship. Some of the written records of the Middle Ages did, in fact, suffer the same fate as its architectural monuments. In the last few months of its existence, the chapter of Saint-Laud blandly informed an investigator that their manuscript of the *Gesta Consulum Andegavensium* had been lost thirty years ago.[163] We hear of the canons of Saint-Martin selling old parchments to bookbinders, and of the cathedral chapter attempting to find a buyer at Paris for old books, 'of which many are partly worm-eaten, and the others in a very bad state'.[164] On

the walls of the convent of La Baumette was displayed an earthen-
ware dish in which Duke René had washed his hands after laying the
foundation stone, and his armorial bearings glittered in the chapel
windows;[165] nevertheless, in spite of these perpetual reminders, the
hard-up friars were, throughout the century, selling off the good
duke's library to foreign collectors. For a mere 30*l.* an English book-
seller picked up a Fust bible, printed on vellum, a gift of the royal
founder, embossed with his coat of arms and authenticated by his
autograph—'a notorious instance', said Breval severely, 'of this
Monkish Indifference to Antiquity'.[166] It seems that the interest of
ecclesiastical institutions in the preservation and codification of
their archives was legal, rather than historical. Owners of large
properties and feudal dues, corporate bodies to whom prestige and
precedence were the very breath of existence, chapters and
monasteries needed to have their records exhaustively indexed for
use in law-suits. That clearly was the reason why the abbot and
monks of Saint-Aubin handed over the three keys of their charter-
house to Barthélemy in 1771;[167] confusion in the classification by
fiefs and priories would be damaging to both pride and pocket in
the long run. One sees a like motive in the smooth approaches made
by the great abbess of Ronceray to Rangeard in 1782 when her law-
suit against the priests of La Trinité was raging. We have to seek
out old titles, she said, to prove the antiquity of our foundation,
and 'as I know, *Monsieur*, that you have done much work on the
antiquities of Anjou, you might be able to unearth something that
would interest us'.[168] The cartulary Mabillon had kissed was decisive evidence against the claim of the comte de Provence to feudal
homage from the cathedral;[169] territorial surveys were a title for the
collection of *lods et ventes* on houses in town; and genealogical data
enabled lawyers to claim *deshérence* when property on fiefs passed
out of the direct line of the original holders. Anyone interested in
buying or selling property in Anjou did well to consult Thorode,
feudist and secretary of the chapter of Saint-Maurice: 'Pray hand
my letter over to master Thorode,' wrote one canon to another concerning the sale of some woods, 'and ask him to write to me on
Saturday if he has found anything relevant among the old titles.' [170]
It was the practical value of diocesan documents that moved the
deputies of the clergy of Anjou to call for a reclassification in 1778.
As the Crown proposed to deprive its faithful clergy of their right
to appoint Apostolic notaries in the diocese, a reimbursement of
monies originally paid for that privilege was due, that is, it was due
if receipts could be found; they were in the archives in a single file
somewhere, but where? It was to provide against such another
crisis that Thorode was called in to reorganize, and when at last

victory was won in this melancholy affair of the notaries, he was commissioned to supervise the publication of a new edition of a legal handbook which summarized all royal declarations concerning the privileges of the diocese. Two hundred ordinary copies, and twenty bound in majestic calf, were to remain as a monument of rights so dearly purchased.[171]

If great corporations regarded rich archives chiefly as a basis of power, nevertheless their very presence produced a race of antiquaries in Anjou. From early in the seventeenth century a tradition of local historical studies had been developing and had caught the imagination of lawyers and of churchmen. This was an age when the law really was complicated, when lawyers groaned and grew rich amid conflicts of Roman, feudal, monarchical, ecclesiastical and provincial precedents and customs, and when family pride and the exemptions of nobles made genealogical trees yield profitable harvests. Acquaintance with dusty archives might bring good fees from clients, and since the sale and multiplication of judicial offices was creating a class of leisured magistrates, what began as a professional interest sometimes developed into a consuming passion for curious knowledge or literary fame. Pierre Touraille, Bruneau de Tartifume, Claude Ménard, Germain Arthaud and Nicolas Pétrineau[172] published little, but their example and their manuscript collections survived to encourage and direct their successors. Other exploratory work in the seventeenth century had been done by ecclesiastics. Jean Hiret, a doctor of the Faculty, published a volume on the antiquities of Anjou in 1605, the first to be drawn from original sources, though, as Rangeard said, it was 'full of fables and anachronisms'. Claude Ménard became ordained late in life and enjoyed some unusual controveries. In one he outraged the canons of the cathedral by arguing that their church was junior to that of Saint-Pierre, in another he cast a spell of gloom over taverns and seminaries in Spain by demonstrating that Saint-James of Compostella had really been buried in the vaults of Saint-Maurille at Angers. A curé of Fontevrand wrote a history of his parish, Bonichon of the Oratory investigated the history of ceremonies, canon Arthaud (brother of the lawyer) contributed to the *Gallia Christiana*, canon Demesnil printed a collection of the cathedral statutes, canon Eveillon defended local saints against Jean de Launoi's scepticism,[172a] Barthélemy Roger, an ex-monk of Saint-Nicolas, settled down near Lesvière where he spent forty years compiling a history of Anjou which he did not live to publish. Meanwhile learning revived in the Benedictine houses: dom Laurent Le Peletier published two collections of charters of Saint-Nicolas, and dom Robert Hardy, prior of Saint-Aubin, deposited a manuscript history of that house, 'written from its original title deed', in its library, before leaving for higher promotion.[173]

All this led to Ménage, an author of European fame, in whom the legal and ecclesiastical traditions of Angevin erudition coalesced and bore fruit. His mother was of a magisterial family, his father was an *avocat du Roi* who was ordained after his wife's death and became dean of Saint-Pierre. Ménage himself was vain and amorous, though this did not deter him from accepting the sub-diaconate to inherit his father's benefices. Thereafter he spent his time on literary production, wherein articles on his own distinguised ancestors figured more frequently than was strictly necessary. His *Histoire de Sablé*, published in 1683, was really, as he said himself, 'a short history of Anjou and Maine' based upon research 'in a thousand places'. 'I am author of many books,' he added boastfully, 'but I am the creator of this. I made it from nothing.' [174] Ménage was accepted at his own high valuation. Angevin scholars reverently passed down from hand to hand unpublished materials which his graceless son had auctioned; and his remarkable pantechnicon of erudition became a model for aspiring historians of Anjou.

During the first half of the eighteenth century this antiquarian tradition continued. René Lehoreau, a canon of Chemillé, worked from the age of eleven to the day of his death compiling a description of the ceremonies and liturgical observances of the cathedral of Angers; canon Legouvello wrote a life of René, Duke of Anjou and King of Sicily;[175] Joseph Grandet, curé of Sainte-Croix and director of the Seminary, kept up a widespread literary correspondence, wrote minor ecclesiastical biographies, descriptions of miracles, attacks on Jansenism and a longer dissertation, *Notre-Dame Angevine*, a history of all religious institutions in the province which were under the invocation of Our Lady. Seventeenth-century researchers had left manuscript collections behind them and most of these now fell into the hands of Claude Pocquet de Livonnière, a *conseiller* of the *Présidial*, professor of law at the University and a founding member of the Academy. His son Claude-Gabriel, who inherited his father's professorship and interests, became the next Angevin scholar after Ménage to achieve extra-provincial fame, contributing as he did to all the great collections of the century—the Bollandist anthologies, the *Gallia Christiana*, dom Rivet's *Histoire littéraire*, Montfaucon's *Monuments*, Moréri's dictionary and dom Carpentier's continuation of Du Cange. After his death in 1762 ecclesiastics regained their domination over antiquarian studies from the lawyers. Ancestor hunting was still a dominant passion in society, so feudists and notaries continued to turn over private archives and parish registers for genealogical data, and professors of law still ground out treatises on feudal and customary codes and areas of jurisdiction,[176] but their work was episodic and had a narrowly professional aim. A lawyer, perhaps, needed ecclesiastical connections or interest to transform his investigational instincts into genuine antiquarianism. It is significant that in the last years of the old régime Thorode was the only lawyer whose researches took a directly historical direction. It was his work in the archives of Saint-Maurice from 1761, as secretary to the chapter, which turned his mind towards a comprehensive factual history of the monuments and institutions of his native city:[177] otherwise he might have remained a dour and cynical notary collecting materials on local families and (as the story went) threatening to use it as blackmail when anyone offended him.

Since Ménage's *Histoire de Sablé* the dream of a definitive history of Anjou flitted through the brain of every zealous local antiquary. Canon Brossier of Saint-Maurice made this his declared ambition, conferred with feudists and worked steadily through the archives of chapters, priories, monasteries and nunneries. As secretary of the cathedral chapter he had unique opportunities. 'Scarcely had I been received into the office,' he wrote, 'than my single desire was to learn to read the old writings.' This art he learnt very quickly, for within four years he had compiled five volumes of a work he entitled 'L'Ami du Secrétaire'—a friend to historians too, for it preserves much information from capitular registers which are now lost. It was a labour of love for this good canon to collect and tabulate historical details concerning the great foundation with which he so completely identified himself. By no means the least conspicuous entry in his catalogue is an account of a riot caused by one Hubert, a tonsured clerk of La Rochelle: 'Box on the ears given within the precincts of the church to me Brossier the Secretary, during the funeral service of M. Vaultier, the first canon to be buried in the new crypt.' [178] Out of gratitude to an enthusiastic chronicler we are bound to take notice of his bid for secular immortality. But his projected history of Anjou was never published and the story of Hubert's crime was never woven into the pattern of provincial development.

Gifts of style and imagination which would have breathed life into the dry bones of Brossier's indices were, by the universal consent of Angevins, possessed by his predecessor as secretary to the cathedral chapter, the abbé Rangeard. An uncle of his had been a friend of Grandet and had written a history of the University of Angers, while Rangeard himself had begun his ecclesiastical career as a tutor in the household of Pocquet de Livonnière and had inherited valuable documents from that family's collections, notably Roger's history and the second unpublished part of Ménage's *Histoire de Sablé*. In 1752, when he was still not thirty years of age, he was already reading sentimental odes to the Angevin Academy and secretly preparing to continue and emulate Ménage. But by now there were rivals in the field, professional historians whose resources in manpower and money could defeat all amateurs.[179] From the beginning of the eighteenth century the Benedictines of Saint-Maur had turned from patristic and monastic studies generally to concentrate upon work 'for the illustration and glory of Gallican history'.[180] Saint-Germain-des-Prés became a central institute under dom Luc d'Achery, Mabillon and Montfaucon, and teams of researchers toured France. An invitation from the Estates of Brittany to write the history of that province led to five monks being drafted to investigate cartularies in the peripheral areas of Anjou, Touraine and Poitou, and in 1698 dom Mabillon himself passed through Angers on a tour of inspection.[181] By 1711 a vast plan of French historical studies had been devised and in 1737 the Diet of the Congregation received with satisfaction volumes so far published on Brittany and Languedoc, and decided to press on to new triumphs in Normandy, Touraine, Maine and Anjou.[182] Fragments of Angevin chronicles had already been published by dom Luc d'Achery and dom Martène, while Montfaucon had a list of Saint-Aubin's manuscripts ready for inclusion in his *Bibliotheca bibliothecarum*.[183] Angers itself did not become a centre of studies,[184] but dom Rivet at Saint-Vincent du Mans nearby kept in touch with Pocquet de Livonnière to appropriate Angevin transcripts for his vast *Histoire littéraire de la France*.[185] 'The very idea of this work', it was said, 'makes slothful humanity tremble', and when Rivet gave way to Poncet, Colomb, and Clément, and the tenth enormous volume appeared, a young provincial abbé with historical ambitions might well begin to feel despondent.

Like industrious moles the Benedictines of Saint-Maur burrowed their way through the province, ransacking its archives. But who could tell? The Diet of that learned congregation might be generous and allow an interloper access to their transcripts. Dom Colomb of Le Mans, in thanking Rangeard for some researches carried out on his behalf, held out this glittering possibility and gave genial hints on the amount of work of which the human frame was capable, on methods of concealing from the public the extent of one's literary ambitions, how to skim authorities without actually reading them and how to choose a title that might mean anything.[186] This was in 1751. In the following year, when dom Taillandier visited Angers in search of material concerning Breton history and the genealogies of the Rohan family, it was 'M. l'abbé Rangeard' who gave him access to the cathedral charter-house and helped him in his researches 'with all possible politeness'.[187] Then in 1752 came a polished and complimentary letter from dom Géron of Saint-Benoît-sur-Loire conveying a formal invitation to collaborate in furnishing materials for the *Gallia Christiana*, which could be deposited with dom Monclair of Saint-Serge for forwarding 'and which we would acknowledge fully on publication'.[188] This sort of recognition was appropriate and flattering in the case of a general annalistic compilation, but it was a very different question two years later when dom Housseau, now in charge of all work on the history of Touraine and Anjou, offered Rangeard, in return for handing over his own materials, nothing more than an honourable mention in his preface. With dom Arnauld and dom Jarneau touring Anjou making transcripts and with Colomb and his team at Saint-Vincent du Mans to aid him, Housseau knew that he was in a strong position. Bland and somewhat sinister replies awaited all Rangeard's suggestions of a genuine partnership—references to shortages of books in the provinces, dark hints of pitfalls yawning ahead of those who were unable to work for long in Parisian archives, offhand mentions of conferences of experts, and of the Congregation's willingness to put twenty years of work and 10,000*l*. of money behind its production. Only the Benedictine machine could write the definitive history of Anjou: whatever rivals published could be no more than 'curious anecdotes'.[189] Rangeard, who had just been driven from his post at Saint-Maurice after a dispute with his chapter and now lived in poverty in the vicarage of Saint-Aignan, gloomily recognized defeat. 'Everything is lacking in this province to whoever wishes to write its history', he confessed, convinced against his will.

From then on, he turned his attention to belles-lettres, to poetry grave and gay, translations of psalms and readings to the Academy which made him unofficial laureate of the province. Under his tutelage, Mlle Charlotte-Marie-Ann Charbonnier de la Guesnerie, disappointed in love, found consolation in novel writing, and on his visits to Paris, our literary *abbé* smuggled up to the printers her manuscript of the *Memoires de Miledy B . . .* and *Les Ressources de la Vertu*.[190] Priestly patronage for these novels was really no scandal, for 'though she depicted love, it was virtuous love, always delicate and well regulated in its passion, providing an occasional embellishment to the dream that is life'.[191] Bishop de Grasse too found a use for the talents of his old friend whom he promoted to be rector of Andard:

My dear *archiprêtre*, do take in hand the task of writing something for me for the parish priests' retreat. Choose some subject concerning the sacerdotal life, and let it take rather more than half an hour to read, Best wishes. . .[192]

All the while, in the midst of many preoccupations, and fame

E

achieved in other disciplines, Rangeard remained faithful to his original Muse; in spite of everything, he gave some help to the dog-in-the-manger Benedictines and to Duboys, a professor of law who was researching fitfully on local history, kept up an erudite correspondence with canon Belin of Le Mans, and his extracts from Angevin archives were continually at the disposal of those who cared for such things.[193] Dom Housseau, eternally garnering, amassed a cartload of notes and never published a line.[194] Rangeard, though a definitive history of Anjou never issued from his pen, contrived to write extensively and always maintained that

> France will never be able to pride herself . . . on a general history worthy of a learned and artistic nation if the writer fit to undertake the task is not able to draw upon the information and guidance of individual histories of each of our provinces.[195]

Other clerics of Angers embarked on more modest historical ventures. Some read essays of an antiquarian vein to the Academy. Tonnelet, prior of Toussaint, corresponded with the librarian of Sainte-Geneviève on the early history of printing and made a search for early printed books in Anjou.[196] Canon Guillot produced a study of the early origins of the Bretons and a dissertation on the princes who had reigned in medieval Anjou,[197] while a humble curé in the seventies was painfully compiling his 'Anecdotes Angevines', a farrago of genealogical and topographical minutiae, gloomily spiced with an occasional sombre prodigy, a man alive on the wheel for 24 hours, or a duke of Anjou with two noses.[198] These were very minor figures, however, lacking the facile style and the ability to coin a phrase in tune with the epoch which made Rangeard the outstanding local publicist. But this fixed star of the Academy had one serious rival, a lurid and unpredictable comet, in the form of Robin, the fantastic curé of Saint-Pierre, an absurd and charming figure, whose crabbed learning and riotous individuality are as evident in his writings as in his life.

Let Rangeard and academicians struggle for immortality, curé Robin was confident that he had attained it—

> Mes écrits aux savants en diront d'avantage,
> Et mon nom avec eux passera d'âge en âge.[199]

To make assurance doubly sure, he inserted full records of his notable activities in his parish registers and immured copies of his books in the masonry of his church and other buildings. Inevitably, the will-o'-the-wisp of a history of Anjou flitted through his brain,[200] but research in archives was not for him. Haphazardly and as inspiration took him, he pieced together his curious learning, as he himself disarmingly confesses,

> I throw my reflections on to paper just as they come to me, without straining after ideas, or putting myself to any great effort; one idea gives rise to another, one piece of research leads to another, and, without my knowing it, a book is born.[201]

Archaeology was his *forte*. With studied originality he seems to have chosen that branch of scholarship which was most neglected by his contemporaries. Gossips of Angers could show you remains of the old inner walls of their town—hedging in one side of the Lazarists' garden, propping up the stables of the inn of Saint-Julien and of the Boule d'Or, with goodly gate pillars still standing erect in the shop fronts of M. Parage and the grocer Follenfant; if pressed, they might even point to a few hollows and stone blocks marking the site of a Roman amphitheatre in the garden of the nuns of La Fidelité. Connoisseurs could tell of stone coffins, bronze medals and bones which were unearthed when the monks of Saint-Aubin built two new shops and when various chapters dug funeral vaults or prised up paving stones.[202] But interest in these remains was confined to a narrow circle—to 'des gens prévenus et amateurs de l'antiquité'.[203] Certainly the municipal authorities, who had been glad enough to publish a collection of documents reciting their own privileges,[204] turned a deaf ear to Robin's plan for preserving information about the old amphitheatre. 'You have to have an important air and powerful friends before they'll listen to you,' said curé Robin.[205] Nevertheless, the world was kept well informed of his own discoveries and theories. His little country house at Empiré formed a base for his investigation of the so-called 'Caesar's camp' near that village, and he traced the line of the old Roman road from Nantes to Angers.[206] Yet Robin was not a strictly disinterested archaeologist, for he always hoped that among the broken monuments evidence might turn up to vindicate Claude Ménard's old hypotheses concerning the antiquity of his parish of Saint-Pierre. His opportunity came in 1757 when he was building a new sacristy and old tombs were unearthed which enabled him to prove—to his own satisfaction at least—that his church had been founded in the first century of the Christian era. Consequently, all other churches of Angers were 'emanated from and separated branches of the church of Saint-Pierre',[207] a suspicious conclusion which gave him immense personal gratification. Indeed, this labyrinthine antiquarianism turned out to be an interest cultivated with a particular end in view, namely to prove to the world his right to the title of 'premier curé cardinal de la ville d'Angers'. But it is hard to tell whether he published to defend his rights and avenge his quarrels, or invented rights and picked quarrels to afford excuses for his urge to publish. According to his own, not unduly modest declaration, writing books was his obvious duty:

> . . . . one of the ancients said that a big book is a big sin . . . however, happy are they, says Pliny, to whom the gods have given the gift of doing things worthy of being written down, or of writing down things worthy of being read, and most happy of all, indeed, are those whom they have favoured with both these advantages.[208]

To moral rigorists, who disapproved of clerical activities in spheres of non-theological, quasi-profane learning, Robin addresses a further word of self-justification:

> Now if someone says to me, as was said indeed with reference to my first book,—this is excellent and well said, but you, as a priest, could very well apply yourself to other things; I would reply to this, that it was nearly always the bishops and pastors of the peoples, ... the priests of the various nations, who transmitted to us the history of the most celebrated epochs and the most interesting events; and as for the time I spend, my writings are to me what social engagements are to others,—they are my tric-trac, my games of draughts, my hands at cards.[209]

This reply of Robin is less bombastic and more satisfying, and serves to put himself, Rangeard, Brossier and the rest of us, provincials as we are, on to the outer fringes of a great tradition.

CHAPTER IV

CANONS AND CHAPTERS

THE cathedral church of Saint-Maurice claimed Charlemagne as its founder, in an age before fiefs were invented and two centuries before the counts of Anjou had graduated from 'simple officers of the crown' to feudatories of the *comté*.[1] Forty proud and pious generations had laboured to build up its territories and form its traditions. Within the walls of Angers the cathedral chapter was the wealthiest proprietor and the greatest corporation. In the 'old city' (*cité*) its full feudal superiority was attested by the payment of *cens*, a small imprescriptible due which indicated feudal dependence.[2] Here, tradesmen still asked permission to put up signs on the street[3] and the property of individuals dying without heirs was confiscated;[4] here too, by converse obligations, the canons paid for public utilities like the installation of new street lighting, or for the maintenance of children abandoned in the area of the fief.[5] When aldermen were elected, two deputies of the chapter were invited to the municipal assembly and were given places of honour,[6] while at any official service in another church of the town, the officers of justice, who normally would be entitled to stalls on the right of the choir, had to yield precedence and take the left when the cathedral chapter attended.[7] The bishop himself had no domination in his own episcopal church. From a canon to a sub-cantor, all clerics of the cathedral were exempt from the jurisdiction of the see of Angers, rights of visitation being vested in the metropolitan, the archbishop of Tours.[8] In the parishes of Saint-Maurice and Saint-Evroul in the *cité* and in four capitular fiefs in the countryside the chapter itself exercised full episcopal authority, these parishes being subject to its *loi diocésaine*. Thus the canons of Saint-Maurice were entitled to convoke their six curés to a private synod on the Friday after Pentecost, the day after the allotted time for a diocesan synod;[9] they gave letters demissory to ordinands, approved confessors, permitted the publication of indulgences and jubilees and laid down the stations to be performed, made visitations of churches and reviewed audits of parish accounts, authorized schoolmasters, sent round instructive booklets on artificial respiration, gave marriage dispensations in cases of spiritual affinity and in some cases of consanguinity, granted dispensation from banns or 'fixation of domicile'.[10] Year after year they sent round to their curés a solemn declaration 'permitting the use of eggs in the coming Lent, from Ash

Wednesday inclusive up to Palm Sunday exclusive, and the use of meat on Sundays, Mondays, Tuesdays and Thursdays of each week, from the first Sunday inclusive, up to the Thursday of Passion week, also inclusive, to be by them published at the sermon time of their parish masses, and to be put into execution'.[11] In diocesan affairs generally, the cathedral claimed to be associated with the bishop on terms of high dignity. Any legal document which the officers of that church might require had to be furnished free of sealing fees by the diocesan registry.[12] On great national occasions, when royal injunctions prescribed festivities or mourning, the bishop was not entitled to issue instructions to his diocese on his own authority. The canons of Saint-Maurice insisted that all royal letters be passed on to them and that any directions concerning ceremonial which were subsequently circulated should contain a statement showing that they were drawn up 'in accord' with the chapter. The vicars-general, having inadvertently omitted this formula in their orders for the tolling of bells when Louis XV died, were compelled to apologize, and bishop de Grasse faced strong protests, tantamount, he complained, to 'threats', when he withheld the royal letters announcing the birth of a daughter to Louis XVI and victories in the war against England.[13]

This proud cathedral chapter did not enjoy the scandalous affluence which characterized some ecclesiastical establishments of the old régime; nevertheless, its canons were very comfortably off. A canonry was worth rather more than 3,000l. in the first instance,[14] which would be augmented, as time went on, by provision to various chapels of the foundation, or to similar benefices without cure of souls in the gift of other patrons. Thus Brossier, after being a canon for ten years, possessed six such additional benefices,[15] and Nioche de la Brosse, after sixteen years, held four.[16] Canon Boulnoy, who had been prevented by gout and other infirmities from rendering a complete return of his benefices earlier, in June 1790 informed the Ecclesiastical Committee of the Constituent Assembly that he held, in addition to his canonry, five chapels in the diocese of Angers, three having been bestowed on him by lay patrons. In addition, he held five priories of the Benedictines of Saint-Maur, scattered in the dioceses of Poitiers, La Rochelle, Nantes and Chartres, one being worth 1,000l. a year, one 800, another 400, and another, thanks to the beauty of its situation, was farmed to a rich individual for a substantial rent in kind. This considerable accumulation of benefices was not, however, all profit; indeed, the abbé Boulnoy argued that he had consumed his patrimony of 30,000l. in repairs, re-building and lawsuits. One chapel brought in 100l. income and had cost him 3,600l. in repairs; the priory farmed for 1,000l. had swallowed up more than a year's income in repairs and had been saddled with a pension and a lawsuit costing 8,000*l*.—'jamais liste de bénéfices plus imposante n'a moins fait le bien être de quelqu'un'.[17] Pluralities, indeed, were speculative investments, rather than assured increments to income. However, ignoring all additional benefices other than those in the direct gift of the chapter itself, it is clear that canons of Saint-Maurice were enjoying considerable incomes. This is so on their own showing, for while they no doubt erred on the side of caution, it is significant that in the abortive negotiations of 1784 for the union of two other chapters of the town to the cathedral, their terms envisaged arrangements which would ensure new revenue in the proportion of over 5,700*l*. for each new prebend created.[18] As canon Brossier's personal accounts reveal, it was possible, in the early sixties, to live in Angers at a basic expense—on wine, bread, meat, coal, lodging and the wages of a servant—of 515*l*. a year.[19] Prices had risen since then, but even so, when all necessities were paid for, the surplus remaining was enough to enable a canon to furnish agreeably one of those dignified capitular houses on the cathedral square, the place du château or the rue des Jacobins,[20] to entertain and move in society, and, perhaps, maintain a small estate in the country as a retreat in the summer.

Canonries of Saint-Maurice[21] were distributed with the injustice which was common form in the disposal of all well-endowed benefices in France. It is true that, of the canons of 1789, one was the son of a tanner, and another had risen to the priesthood after a five years' apprenticeship as schoolmaster to the choir-boys,[22] but these were exceptions and the chapter was very largely a preserve for younger sons of distinguished families, who could hope to crown an ecclesiastical career with dignity and modest affluence before reaching the age of thirty. Dutertre des Roches, son of a royal officer at Saumur, became a canon at the age of nineteen,[23] Charles de Creny, descended from a noble family of Normandy of six centuries' standing, was appointed at the age of twenty-three, when still only a sub-deacon, and four years later became archdeacon of Outre-Maine as well. These were unusually youthful appointments, but even those who decently took a theological doctorate before promotion to a stall had not long to wait: Poulaine de la Forestrie, whose family accepted municipal office in Angers only on condition that its claims to *ancienne noblesse* were not thereby impugned,[24] was a canon at twenty-eight; Louet, son of a *conseiller* of the *Présidial* at Angers, whose line went back to a fifteenth-century treasurer of the Dukes of Anjou, joined the chapter, which a hundred and fifty years ago had had a Louet for its dean,[25] at the age of twenty-seven; while Lenoir de la Cochetière, of a noble family of Lude, took his doctorate a year younger than Louet and was a canon at twenty-five. At the same age, Waillant received both his doctorate and his canonical stall, a rapid promotion which was no doubt connected with the fact that canon Wiot was his uncle. The dean himself, César-Scipion de Villeneuve, had not come to the cathedral until the age of thirty-four, but this comparative hold-up in his career was due to the fact that he had at first been a Jesuit, and the delay was compensated by his appointment as dean only two months after taking up his canonry. A profitable alternation between Church and Army was the standard method of providing for younger sons of the nobility, and a stall at Saint-Maurice took its place in the economy of various families. Dean de Villeneuve was a second son, with an elder brother who inherited the manor of Tourettes-lès-Vence, and a younger brother who became a dashing major of cavalry.[26] Another second son was Charles de Creny, whose three brothers were all Army officers.[27] Dary d'Ernemont, who, but for an accident to his family archives, could have proved descent from a companion of William the Conqueror, was a third son; his elder brother had inherited Ernemont, another brother was a canon of Saint-Waas at Arras, and the other three took up military careers.[28] One of the canons of Angers was himself an ex-soldier, for Le Perrochel, son of a general, had originally followed his elder brothers into the Army, where he had been an officer in the dragoons of *Monsieur*, before turning to the Church and becoming abbot of Toussaint and a canon of Saint-Maurice.[29] Every noble family had its network of ecclesiastical connexions. Tugal-François Hullin de la Maillardière had had a second cousin a canon of the cathedral before him, his sister was a nun at Beaufort, more distant relatives had taken the veil at Le Calvaire and the Ursulines of Angers, and a half-cousin was a canon of Saint-Martin.[30] A brother of Lucien-François de la Corbière had been chaplain to the princess Adélaïde and another relative dean of the cathedral of Verdun, which no doubt accounted for his elevation to a prebend at Verdun at the age of twenty-three, before returning to Angers, the place of his university studies, as a canon eleven years later.[31] But while appointments at Saint-Maurice were regarded as rightful perquisites by noble families of Anjou in particular, and, in a widening circle, by those of Normandy, Brittany and the Vendée, they were not rich enough to attract solicitations by the greatest courtiers, and at the beginning of 1789 only two stalls were affording supplements to the salaries of clerics at Versailles.

One of these had fallen to Fayon, a priest in the royal chapel, who was appointed a canon in 1784. The other was held by one Chaussard, who in twenty-six years of office had never graced a service in his cathedral. He was in minor orders only, and was, perhaps, adequately punished by his task of tutor to the most riotous and refractory pupils in France, the pages of the *grande écurie du Roi*.[32] A third canonry fell into the hands of an absentee sinecurist in January 1789, being appropriated by Dumouchel, rector of the University of Paris, to the despair of the senior graduate of the diocese, who at seventy-five years of age had still not given up hopes of ultimate recognition,[33] and the anger of Dumouchel's enemies in the capital, who regarded the affair as a shameless piece of jobbery.[34] With these exceptions, the chapter consisted of canons subject to normal obligations, and residence was enforced strictly, without favour to the great. Le Perrochel, holding his prebend in virtue of his position as abbot of Toussaint, indulged in his hobby of foreign travel, and, being absent from chapters-general at St. John Baptist-tide, was deprived of the fruits of his benefice.[35] Supplies were cut off during Waillant's illegal and suspicious absence in Paris[36] and the dean was instructed at one time to summon Poulain de la Guerche back to town.[37] Le Noir de la Cochetière lost his turn for a canonical residence which fell vacant during his absence in Rome, even though his journey was authorized, his application for the house received, and his delay in returning fully explained by 'a feverish cold on the chest', attested by a medical certificate endorsed by cardinal Bernis in person.[38]

Residence was enforced, and discipline was strict in minor matters too. Registers of attendance at services were kept, the bald needed capitular permission to wear wigs, as the gouty did to remain seated, during the offices.[39] Standards of morality, in the narrower sense of that word, were high. In the last years of the old chapter, there was but one serious offender, canon Waillant, who, ten years after his appointment, decamped to Paris and refused to come back. His eventual return revealed his reason for staying in the capital and gave his colleagues cause to regret their complaints of his absence. His uncle Wiot and the grave Louet were sent to urge him to send away the woman he had installed in his house. They persuaded him to send her to a nunnery in town, but this proved to be only a staging point on the way to Waillant's country retreat; finally, however, after asking for three days to think over his position, he sent the lady back to Paris, and the chapter decided to pursue the offender no further.[40] In the light of this major scandal, it is not surprising to find Waillant failing to fulfil his preaching duties, so that the chapter now had cause to complain of unauthorized preachers turning up on the first Sunday of the month to fill his place in the pulpit, and of one Sunday without any sermon at all.[41] But Waillant's adventures are a startling exception, and his colleagues' groping efforts to deal with the crisis reveal their confusion and consternation in face of untoward circumstances.

Free from the grosser vices, canons of Saint-Maurice seem also to have been—through lack of opportunity—but little tempted by promptings of ambition. Dean d'Autichamp moved off to become bishop of Tulle in 1741, and eleven years later Joseph de Saint-André Marnay de Vercel, newly consecrated, toured Anjou 'to enjoy the sweet satisfaction of showing himself in cross and mitre in this Diocese where he had formerly been Grand Vicar and canon'.[42] But these were unusual cases, the result of unusual influence. Fate perhaps left a loophole for Le Noir de la Cochetière, who happened to be in Rome in 1786-7 at a time when the Clergy of France were anxious to settle an affair of dispensations with the Papal Curia. For a time, the pilgrim became a diplomat, and cherished hopes of 'a flattering recompense'. But outmanœuvred by cardinal Bernis, the French ambassador, who wished to smother the matter, he received nothing more than a bishopric *in partibus*, a Roman reward which the Crown refused to recognize, and was reproached by bishop de Lorry for 'foolishly missing the only chance that I might hope for, to come, in my state of life, to the office which marks the term of ambition'.[43] Such opportunities were rare. A canon of Angers at the end of the old régime seemed certain to remain where he was for life. His office was not a spring-board for promotion: it was a dignified *cul-de-sac* in the ecclesiastical hierarchy. Idleness was, no doubt, the greatest temptation. Even so, many canons were more active than their critics supposed. Six were vicars-general of the bishop,[44] seven were doctors of theology (including Dutertre des Roches, who redeemed his youthful appointment somewhat by taking his doctorate seven years later), their ermine stoles bearing witness that the theological tradition of the cathedral created by Babin and de la Chalinière in the first half of the century was not defunct. Much time was lavished on the management of property, care of the fabric and supervision of fine music and magnificent ceremonial. After all, the life of a canon was what the individual chose to make it. Some drifted along in their agreeable sinecures; Le Perrochel took possession of his prebend[45] and departed for England, Germany and the bracing north; some found scope for literary or social activities at the Academy or in freemasonry;[46] Brossier plunged into the archives. Canon Louet was a scholar, an administrator and a divine.[47] Four years after his induction he became one of the two professors at the Faculty of Theology of the University, after holding this post for six years he became *maître-école*, an office corresponding to that of Chancellor of the University, in 1782, a senior canon of thirty years' standing, he was appointed Vicar-General, and as *official* was in charge of the legal and disciplinary business of the diocese. He was much in demand as a preacher. The municipality sought him for public occasions (unavailingly when the virtues of Louis XV were to be extolled), the comtess de Brionne presented him with a handsome snuff-box as a token of gratitude for his funeral oration on her husband, and Fleury's *Histoire Ecclésiastique* on his shelves and presentation silver at his table bore witness to the admiration of his colleagues for his Lent and Advent courses at the cathedral. Leisure which Louet devoted to administration and preaching was very differently but no less worthily employed by canon Cassin,[48] whose death in 1783 was shortly followed by the opening of an instance of canonization. Urbain-Élie Cassin, son of a wealthy merchant of Angers, had obtained his stall at Saint-Maurice at the age of twenty-five, and lived a comfortable worldly life, until a chance remark of his friend Tourny, *intendant* of Bordeaux, made in casual conversation at a country house party, led to a fit of remorse and a startling conversion. Conscience-stricken by his facile promotion, he resigned his canonry and, when the bishop immediately re-appointed him, gave away his furniture, sent his tapestries to the hospital, and thenceforward lived a ruthlessly ascetic life, wearing a hair shirt, abjuring meat and fish in his diet, refusing fires even in the depths of winter. Instead of taking the fashionable summer vacation in the country, he remained at the cathedral until All Souls day every year and then went off on foot to his rural property for a fifteen days' retreat. Since ecstatic seizures obliged him to renounce preaching, his entire work in his later years was that of a director of souls, being confessor to the Carmelites, the hospital of the Incurables, and the nuns of Ronceray. On the 3rd of September 1783, knowing all the while that his last illness was upon him, canon Cassin was at the cathedral at 4.30 in the morning, half an hour before mattins, said his mass, heard confessions, attended chapter, took several interviews afterwards, returned to his house, where he received the mother superior of the Incurables, said his own vespers alone as he did not feel well enough to sit in choir, then set off for the abbey of Ronceray to hear confessions, down the short steep hill to the bridge where the dark river flowed between the crowded quays in the shadow of the cathedral towers, and there, on the bridge, he collapsed and died. Which is very far from the traditional picture one forms of a day in the life of a canon of the old régime.

Around the great church of Saint-Maurice the other collegiate churches revolved, like minor planets round a sun. They were never allowed to forget their inferior status. Attendance at the cathedral was obligatory for them on certain occasions. When a canon of the latter foundation died, all other chapters of the town had to present themselves to sing a *subvenite* over the coffin,[49] and for the obsequies of bishops, invitations were issued to the minor chapters as commands, not honourably conveyed by fellow-canons, but aloofly, through a verger.[50] An annual service for the repose of the soul of Charles Miron, a former bishop of Angers, was another of these events of ceremonial obligation, irrespective of any traditional observances which might happen to coincide with it. In August 1774, the canons of Saint-Laud absented themselves to perform their own procession of the True Cross, but the jealous chapter of Saint-Maurice refused to allow them to shelter behind the sanctity of their notable relic. This monthly celebration of Saint-Laud, the cathedral held, was merely 'a new foundation, much posterior' to the yearly one of Miron.[51]

There were six collegiate churches below the cathedral, all taking their places in a nicely graded hierarchy of precedence. Lowest of all came the phantom chapters of Saint-Julien and Saint-Maimbeuf, which were united to the Seminary, whose superior and staff, however, still clung to the decanal and canonical rights that went with the defunct churches.[52] At the opposite end of the scale and highest in order of dignity after the cathedral, came the two royal chapters of Saint-Laud and Saint-Martin, which, at some time since the fifteenth century, had contrived to steal ahead of the other chapters and usurp an unwarranted priority.[53] These two royal chapters had bound themselves together in an indissoluble alliance or 'confraternity'. Representatives of one church were always present at the patronal festival of the other, funeral tolls from the bells of both churches announced the demise of any of their canons, the chapter of Saint-Laud was always invited to and always attended Saint-Martin's procession of the relics of Saint-Loup, while at all general ecclesiastical ceremonies the canons walked together and adopted a uniform ceremonial.[54] Every year, on 17 November, the two collegials combined to celebrate the birthday of *Monsieur*, the king's brother, their joint patron; mass was sung on odd years at Saint-Martin and even at Saint-Laud, with the dean of the visiting church officiating and the visiting canons accommodated in the highest stalls on the right of the choir.[55] It was a notably weatherproof alliance, secure amid the storms of a furiously litigious age. In November 1781 and in April 1782, the canons of Saint-Martin did battle royal against the canons-regular of the abbey of Toussaint concerning precedence in singing a *subvenite* over defunct canons of the cathedral,[56] but when, in the following October, a point of procedural dignity was raised against them by their brethren of Saint-Laud, they displayed a very different temper, admitting 'that they had not paid attention to the customary formalities, and that they besought the canons of Saint-Laud not to draw any inference from this lapse from the ordinary usages'.[57] The two remaining chapters, Saint-Pierre and Saint-Maurille, were also allied by treaties, said masses for each others' dead and attended funerals;[58] but their relations were far from being as harmonious as those of the royal chapters. Canon Jubeau of Saint-Maurille (locally famous for having spent a few weeks in the Bastille as a guest of the Crown), spoke his mind at a general procession on the first Sunday of November 1773, and, as a result of his 'indecent and injurious remarks', the canons of Saint-Pierre insisted that the bishop cancel their alliances.[59] This was done, though three years later, the jubilee of the Holy Year, appropriately enough, found these two chapters reconciled. Once again, their confraternity was observed,[60] and indeed, it now flowered into a joint project for regaining their precedence and ensuring their prosperity by a permanent union of their canonries with the chapter of the cathedral. But the hump of accumulated riches could not easily pass through the needle's eye of such a compromise. A detailed investigation of the finances of the two inferior chapters failed to satisfy the wary canons of Saint-Maurice, who made progress impossible by insisting that only six new titles of prebends or canonries could be allowed under the proposed merger.[61]

Indeed, all these other collegiate churches of Angers were much poorer than the cathedral. Early in the century, the chapters of Saint-Julien and Saint-Maimbeuf, united to the Seminary, were reckoned to yield to that institution 7,000l. and 6,000l. respectively.[62] Estimates of total income show Saint-Martin with 22,479l.,[63] Saint-Pierre with 23,040l., Saint-Maurille with 19,478l.,[64] while Saint-Laud was rather richer than any single one of them. This revenue, in the case of Saint-Maurille and Saint-Martin, was, to an important extent, drawn from property and feudal dues in the town itself. Earlier in the century, the provident canons of Saint-Maurille had deconsecrated part of their cemetery and cleared a square in front of their church, work which was done at their own expense, though the city contributed towards the cost of paving. As a result, their successors in the seventies had been able to construct a few fine new houses facing on to this square, in an eligible position which would draw good rents.[65] By 1784 the chapter owned twenty houses in town, which brought in an income of over 6,600l. In addition to this, the fief in Angers was reckoned to bring in 1,500l.[66] *Deshérence*, that is, the right of a *seigneur* to escheat the property of individuals dying without direct heirs, brought in a naturally fluctuating, highly unpopular, and sometimes bitterly contested revenue. This came, of course, in occasional windfalls—sometimes very large sums, like the 3,250l. which fell due in April 1789 as a half share of the selling price of a house whose previous owner's paternal line was extinct.[67] *Lods et ventes*, a sort of purchase tax on the acquisition of houses within the area of a feudal jurisdiction, normally levied at a rate of about one-fifteenth of the price, yielded a more constant income, bringing in from time to time sums of 200 or 300, sometimes as much as 600*l*.[68] However, the leases of Saint-Maurille's country property were worth over 4,700*l*.,[69] so this chapter was less dependent on its feudal incidents in Angers than was the royal chapter of Saint-Martin. Here, there was the continual lottery of escheats,[70] and the steadier *lods et ventes*, which in a good year come near to the 3,000*l*. mark. 748*l*. fell due when the marquis de Contades sold his house in 1784, and over 1,000*l*. were later paid by M. Arbin de Narbonne on acquiring three houses at the corner of the rue Chaudron.[71] It was all very well for the chapter of Saint-Maurille to be generous and allow a rebate of 25 per cent on its *ventes*:[72] the canons of Saint-Martin were much more dependent on revenue from this source. In 1783 they resorted to the opposite procedure, and limited their customary remissions,[73] justifying this severity by the argument that 'the charges they are at in respect of their fiefs are many in number, and are continually augmenting'.

This was true enough, because incomes so constituted were subject to considerable charges. Firstly, there were fixed permanent outgoings; the obligations of acquitting masses and foundation services (680*l*. in the case of Saint-Pierre, 861*l*. in that of Saint-Maurille), taxation paid to the Clergy of France (2,200*l*. and 2,000*l*. for these two chapters respectively), pensions, and payments to curés of dependent parishes. It was calculated in 1784 that with these deductions made, the disposable income of the chapter of Saint-Pierre was little more than 15,000*l*., and that of Saint-Maurille a little less than 13,000*l*.[74] Then there was the upkeep of property. In 1763, the houses owned by the canons of Saint-Martin were reported to be in a parlous condition,[75] and in 1784, those owned by Saint-Maurille were far behindhand in their repairs.[76] Income from feudal incidents was a lottery, which brought corresponding obligations to counterbalance profits. A *seigneur* enjoying escheat had to rear all foundling children abandoned in his fief, putting them out to nurse, or paying for them at the *Enfants trouvés* at Paris, or finding adoptive parents, who would require something like 100*l*. for their pains.[77] This burden could be a heavy one—from March 1786 to March 1787, no less than twenty children, of whom ten ultimately survived, fell to the charge of the chapter of Saint-Martin.[78] Also, in a town fief, the costs of administering justice, particularly criminal justice, might be heavy. When these commitments had been met, minor officials, ecclesiastical and lay, had to be paid, involving a yearly wages bill of something over 4,000*l*.[79] It is clear then that income remaining for distribution among the deans and canons (ten canons in the chapters of Saint-Laud and Saint-Martin, nine at Saint-Pierre, eight at Saint-Maurille) could not have been very large. A canon of Saint-Laud, who received 1,400*l.* a year,[80] must have been considerably better off than his brethren in other collegiates. Cotelle, dean of Saint-Martin, after continual appeals for supplementary income from benefices in royal patronage, forwarded through his diocesan bishop, the maréchal de Brissac, the Imperial ambassador and others, renewed his plea in 1768, stating that his income as dean was barely 900*l.*, together with a house which brought on him a heavy burden of repairs.[81]

There were of course various supplements to canonical incomes. A canon, like a curé, had his surplice fees and was paid for saying foundation masses.[82] Small benefices without cure of souls—priories, prebends and chapels—might be held by cumulation. Dean Cotelle admits to holding such an additional benefice worth 150*l.*, and states that one of his canons holds the priory of Lude and that two others have pensions of 800*l.* from such sources. As the years went by, good luck and appropriate contacts created a gravitational vortex around a canonical stall which drew minor satellites into the main orbit. One canon of Saint-Pierre obtained a family chapel in 1775, another benefice eight years later, then five years later added the chapel of Saint-John Baptist at Jallais, just before its revenues were diverted to a charitable institution.[83] With reasonable good fortune, the average canon could hope to build up an income of 2,000*l.* to 3,000*l.* a year.[84] Then there was always the value of a canonical house to be considered. This was a perquisite of varying value. The deanery of Saint-Laud was a handsome building, well fitted to receive company and set in the midst of extensive gardens; that of Saint-Pierre, opposite the church in a crowded corner of the city, was a less-well-appointed house, with no land attached to it save a courtyard shared with the house next door. A modest little dwelling in the rue Saint-Aubin or the rue Cordelle was all that Saint-Pierre or Saint-Martin could offer to canons Prevost or Mongodin, while the two Gautreau brothers, canons of Saint-Martin and Saint-Laud, enjoyed spacious houses and gardens.[85] Within the same chapter, canonical houses varied in value; if Mongodin was austerely lodged, his *confrère* Tremblay could be reasonably content with a residence which he leased out for 500*l.* a year.[86] The terms on which a house was held might be more or less favourable; up to 1788, when the chapter finally brought parity into its arrangements, four of Saint-Laud's houses were held on condition of the tenant being responsible for all repairs, while the other houses had their dilapidations compounded for at a nominal figure of 6*l.* a year.[87] Extensive repairs and improvements might be the subject of a special agreement, like the curious concordat of canon Corbin with his colleagues in May 1789, by which he undertook to spend 6,000*l*. on the house *du petit cloître* which had fallen to him in the last 'option', on condition that his sister should retain this house free of rent if she survived him.[88] Canonical residences were not attached to particular prebends; this was a traditional ruling in the town of Angers, which survived the challenge of a formal lawsuit against the chapter of Saint-Martin in 1765.[89] Thus each chapter had its housing queue, and canons moved up to improved quarters as they attained seniority, a general post of lodgings taking place whenever a house fell vacant.

Following the principles upon which benefices were awarded under the old régime, the fact that canonries in these four collegiate churches were inferior in revenue and prestige to those of the cathedral meant inevitably that their holders belonged to comparatively lower reaches of society. Some of the canons, it is true, belonged to families of the old nobility or of the *noblesse de robe*, who might well have aspired to a stall at Saint-Maurice. From this social stratum came the deans of these chapters, and some of the canons of Saint-Laud and Saint-Martin, where royal nomination prevailed with all its accompanying influences. At Saint-Martin,[90] there was dean Frémond de la Mervellière, and canon Sauvage, third son of a prosperous family of San Domingo which traced its origin to the cadet branch of a feudal line of Burgundy.[91] Of local families, there was a Boylesve, who could boast an ancestor who had crusaded with Saint-Louis and another buried in state in the Cordeliers beside the casket which contained the heart of good King René;[92] there was, too, the son of a *correcteur de la chambre des comptes de Bretagne* resident in Angers, Mathurin Gautreau de la Grois,[93] who owed his appointment to influence with the former bishop of Limoges, who supervised the distribution of benefices in the patronage of the comte de Provence. Mathurin's younger brother, Armand Gautreau de Villeneuve, had been made a canon at Saint-Laud through the same influence; his dean du Chilleau,[94] who at the age of twenty-seven had been a canon of Saint-Martin, had been promoted only two years later to the deanery of the sister church, as befitted one born at the château de la Tour-Savary. There was an Angevin dean at Saint-Pierre, Daburon de Mantelon, son of a magistrate at the *Présidial*, who followed the normal course of an elder son who sought ordination, and made over his inheritance of lands and feudal dues to his younger brother in return for a yearly pension of 1,200*l*.[95] But, generally speaking, most of the canons—in the case of the two chapters in episcopal collation, practically all of them—were from a middle-class *milieu*, sons of notaries, *avocats*, officials, merchants and tradesmen. Not that this could justify their appointment in the eyes of ecclesiastical reformers who were urging that canonries be used to solace parish priests 'grown grey in the ministry'; for most members of these chapters had been in possession of their stalls before their early thirties were passed. Applying the test of age to the canons of Saint-Maurille[96] in 1789, we find that only two are vindicated on this score, and if we allow indulgence to Touchet on grounds of learning, we are left with five canons whose average on appointment was thirty years five months. One of them, Couraudin, son of an *avocat au Parlement* resident in the fashionable parish of Saint-Michel du Tertre of Angers, had been only twenty-six years of age at his installation. The *bourgeoisie*, like the aristocracy, had its sinecures.

Perhaps sinecure is too hard a word. France was full of magistrates of fossilized courts, auditors of non-existent monies, directors of obsolete organizations, who had bought or inherited their establishments. Canons held abusive offices of the same accepted sort. They enjoyed a modest but secure income for life, an assured place in society, with the right to perform some distinguished functions. State and Church alike were honeycombed with innumerable narrow oligarchical corporations, whose privileges were consecrated and cherished abuses and to which entrance was gained by influence or favour. Naturally, and without a twinge of conscience, a canon moved into his chapter as a master moved into his guild or a magistrate into his court, and was there absorbed into a narrow world of dignity and precedence, corporate pride and ceremonial observance. The continued existence of four collegiate churches with their horde of dependent canons in a city which already had a cathedral chapter, was clearly an abusive survival, so too was the principle upon which canonries were bestowed. Yet, within each of these chapters individually, the rules were strictly kept. With one exception—a mere tonsured clerk still studying in a seminary in Paris, who had been imposed on the payroll of Saint-Pierre in 1781[97]—all canons were resident. As Corbin of Saint-Martin discovered, even a very brief unauthorized absence involved loss of retribution.[98] There were tariffs of fines for absence from services, which at Saint-Maurille were worked out to cover every contingency. There the customary heavier fine for mattins was combined with a fifty per cent increase for solemn feasts, with a further surcharge on officers with incomes over 300*l.*, while absence was defined to begin at the *gloria* of the *venite* at mattins, at the last *kyrie* of high mass, and at the *gloria* of the first psalm of vespers.[99] At Saint-Laud, sluggards were coerced to mattins by a usage which forbade absentees from early service to join in the later offices.[100] Capitular deliberations are full of censures on minor officials, adjustments to minutiae of ritual and schemes for

F

beautifying and adorning the church. Whether the work done was spiritually or socially useful or not, there was a good deal of it to do. Administering scattered properties, tangled leases and absurd feudal dues was no easy task in this fantastically litigious age; one of the canons of Saint-Maurille was procurator for legal affairs, another supervised the care of foundlings left on the fief of the chapter, another looked after repairs and sacristry expenditure, a fourth had the onerous task of directing the collection of income.[101] Eight years in this latter office proved too much for poor Denis Péan, who, in 1777, admitted to his colleagues that 'by inadvertence, and in all good faith, many errors had crept into [his accounts]'. Pathetically, to end all contestations, and 'as a last mark of my zeal and attachment for the aforesaid chapter', he offered his vestments and church furniture as a gift, all except a chasuble of silver thread that the late bishop had given him, and four chasubles that the expelled Jesuits of La Flèche had left in his keeping. Mercifully, the canons accepted this offer, 'as a sort of indemnity' from 'our very dear, greatly beloved, highly respected colleague of so many years, whose memory will always be precious to us'.[102]

Even so, a canon's life was a leisurely one, and idleness, like adversity, is a test of character. Du Chilleau, when he moved from his stall at Saint-Martin to the deanery of Saint-Laud, was a sleek young man, who took tobacco, knew how to order an expensive dish of fish in Advent and was prepared to lose up to 9*l.* a time in his daily hand at cards.[103] Canon Sauvage of Saint-Martin was gay and hospitable; Chivaille of Saint-Pierre, who was appointed at the age of twenty-four, had a reputation for sociability;[104] his senior colleague Mongodin sought his niche in literature, and pursued the great with insipid odes and his foes with pedestrian epigrams.[105] The abbé Aubery of the chapter of Saint-Martin was a vicar-general of the diocese and a ruthless man of business, spending much time in Paris tracking down creditors of the bishop.[106] His dean, Frémond de la Mervellière, had once been a vicar-general himself, but had resigned that dignified office to become chaplain to the Incurables. New promotion had come his way, but he still remained a friend of the unfortunate, and being the only priest in town who knew the newly invented deaf and dumb language, he acted as confessor to the children in Mlle Blouin's charitable establishment.[107] Cotelle, his predecessor at Saint-Martin, who died in 1777, had lived more fashionably, and had been a leading spirit at the Academy and the Society of Agriculture, the dean before him had been an incorrigible absentee who was ultimately deposed by his despairing chapter.[108] It is impossible to generalize about deans and canons: they made of their office what they would. Gautreau de la Grois rose to be *promoteur* at the *officialité* in charge of

clerical discipline in the diocese,[109] and his brother Armand followed
their uncle, the saintly canon Cassin, as director of the Carmelites at
the request of the nuns. To these two the sheltered existence of a
canon was an opportunity to cultivate the spiritual life. 'Most men',
writes Gautreau de la Grois to his brother, 'live only by trouble and
agitation. They cannot believe that retreat and solitude are the true
place of sojourn for the yearning soul, and that it is only when all
creatures are silent and in the flight from all unnecessary business
that a man can draw near to his God and hear his voice more
clearly.' [110]

Each chapter had its clerical underworld of subordinate choir
officials, some in major orders, others merely tonsured clerks. The
succentors, *corbelliers* and chaplains of the cathedral, with salaries of
over 700*l.* a year, and even the *épistolier*, with his 540*l.*, were superior
officials,[111] financially as well off as some parish priests. Needless to
say, each of them clung to such peculiar precedences or traditional
distinctions as had accumulated around his office. If *corbelliers* were
first in rank, chaplains could claim a longer ancestry, and if chaplains
were above succentors the latter had priority in processions; a first
deacon whose post went back to time immemorial was superior to a
second deacon whose ancestry could only be traced to the early
sixteenth century. Even the *épistoliers* had their precedences, for the
senior of them rejoiced in the title of 'Grand sous-diacre' which
ensured that he was never confused with his junior colleague who
humbly acted as doorkeeper at chapter meetings, calling out canons
required on business with a 'Dominus X—desideratur'. All of these
cathedral officers would claim to be rather better than their opposite
numbers in other collegiate churches; certainly the latter had to be
content with much smaller emoluments. A sacrist[112] might receive
as much as 800*l.* a year, but the two chaplains of each chapter[113]
came into the category of ecclesiastical hacks, earning 300 to 400*l.*,
which surplice fees and windfalls might bring up to 600*l.*, while the
succentor[114] would be a tonsured clerk earning considerably smaller
emoluments. All liturgical administration, from the ringing of bells to
the maintenance of choir-boys, was normally the responsibility of the
sacrist. When the offices were said or sung, the chaplains were in
their places on opposite sides of the choir stalls, except on great feast
days, when, resplendent in copes, they flanked the precentor; they
blessed holy water on Sundays and Saints' days, kept relics, and,
where there was no evangelist, read the gospel at mass. Their duties
were purely ceremonial, they had no status in the chapter or voice
in its affairs, and they remain anonymous to us except when some
revolt or impertinence brings their names into the capitular registers.

'I am very surprised that it should be you who asks me these questions, you *M. le Doyen'*, said succentor Mérand when interviewed by the chapter of Saint-Martin concerning his 'superstitious and scandalous practices' in church.[115] But this was a rare outburst. Generally, canons dispensed their patronage, amended salaries, transferred duties, administered collective and individual rebukes, fined the slothful and distributed the proceeds to the most assiduous without overt complaint from their humble subordinates.[116]

When we have reviewed the cathedral and the other four collegiate churches, we still have not reached the sum total of canons of Angers. Four still remain, but so downtrodden and browbeaten are they that they hardly qualify for the proud title—they are mere shades of true canons.[117] Across the river, in a populous and poverty-stricken quarter known as La Doutre, was the parish church of La Trinité, built alongside the church of the wealthy abbey of Ronceray, to which it was joined in a dependence that was much more than architectural. Here, the abbess and nuns exercised all rights of 'dames de fief, châtelaines, patronnes, fondatrices et de curé primitif'. Originally, the abbess had appointed four canons, who acted as joint curés of the parish. Since 1701, however, a separate curé had been installed, who had his own vicaires to aid him. The four canons now remained as canons merely, free from parochial responsibility, and the three former 'perpetual' vicaires became their chaplains.[118] It was a typical reform of the old régime. A new agent was created to do all the work, and vested interests remained. The canons of La Trinité were left adrift, and their chief task henceforward was to repel boarders from all sides of the vessel. Like all canons, they had to face challenges from the curé of their dependent parish, but in addition to this, they had difficulties with their chaplains, who had inherited from their previous parochial status rights beyond those of their fellows in the other collegiate churches.[119] The canons did not appoint, and were unable to dismiss them; they were appointed by the bishop on the presentation of the abbess of Ronceray, and were able to dispose of their benefices by permutation or resignation. In the thirties and forties, canon Darlon had fought continuously to reduce the chaplains to a subordinate place, insisting that the offices they celebrated be announced by the ringing of an inferior bell, and at second vespers one St. Andrew's eve had taken a prominent personal part in a tug-of-war with the bell ropes.[120]

During these melancholy disputes, the abbess of Ronceray had given aloof encouragement to her canons. Yet while their underlings rebelled, the canons knew that they were in greater danger from lightning which might strike from above. Successive abbesses showed a clear determination to keep the canons in a position of inferiority. In 1741, the old ceremony of taking an oath of fidelity to the abbess, which had been in abeyance for nearly a century, was revived and was enforced by the bishop on the recalcitrant clergy of La Trinité.[121] Then there was a spiteful episode concerning canon Boufteau's windows,[122] which reveals the domineering tendencies of the abbey, and forms a minor comic prelude to a great lawsuit in 1781. It was then that canons Duval and Leroy, worthy successors of Darlan of battle of the belfries fame, went before the court of the *Sénéchaussée* of Angers to demand that they and their colleagues be confirmed in their exclusive right to administer the sacraments within the precincts of Ronceray. In April, a nun who was ill had asked to make her Easter communion, and the abbess, instead of sending for the canon of the week, had sent for the sacristan. Duval could produce a letter from the nun in question which proved that this attempt to oust the canons from their rights was a deliberate one. Hard words were said on both sides. Duval was reported to have declared that the abbess ruled her nuns 'with an iron sceptre', the abbess alleged that it was not possible to call on Duval for duty as he was never present at mattins, but 'gives himself over peacefully to the sweet balms of sleep while his colleagues are singing the praises of the Lord'.[123] In reality, the abbey had no case, for its own lawyers had, in the past, used as their chief argument against the pretensions of the chaplains the fact that the canons had an exclusive right to officiate in Ronceray.[124] Thus, in the end, Duval and Leroy won their case, though the Parlement of Paris, on appeal, allowed the nuns freedom to choose their own confessors.[125] Unedifying as this dispute may seem, one must remember that the canons were fighting, not only for their rights, but for very existence. On the one hand, there was a danger that they would lose all independence and become mere chaplains to the nuns. That in fact was how the abbess disdainfully described them—'Two chaplains of the royal abbey of Ronceray have conceived the ambitious project of shaking off the yoke of obedience, and setting themselves up on equal terms with the lady abbess.'[126] 'Their chaplains!', the canons reject the title with panic-stricken eloquence.[127] On the other hand, the canons realized that a successful attempt to whittle down their remaining functions might mean their complete ruin. The various chapters of Angers were difficult to justify by any sort of logic, ecclesiastical or profane, and the canons of La Trinité had the least justification of all for their existence, either by current activities or by historical traditions. Between abbey and parish, they held hollow and unnecessary offices. A reforming utilitarian wind was beginning to blow in France, and those who held sinecures did well to cover their nakedness, and clutch to themselves the few rags of duties which still remained to them.

CHAPTER V

MONASTERIES AND RELIGIOUS COMMUNITIES

A FEW minutes' walk through narrow streets to the south of the cathedral brought a visitor to Angers to one of the finest relics of the Middle Ages that the town boasted. One went past the miserable half-subterranean church of Sainte-Croix, down the rue Courte and under an arcade and covered gallery which joined the big and little seminaries, to come out at the massive twelfth-century tower of the abbey church of Saint-Aubin. Beyond it lay the monastery proper, a range of fine late-seventeenth-century buildings, with a pleasant garden behind its handsome façade.[1] 'Saint-Aubin the rich',[2] this abbey was called, to distinguish it from the other Benedictine houses in town; not that the others were poor, but because Saint-Aubin was exceptionally wealthy. Estates and fiefs brought in over 50,000*l.* a year.[3] Clerical taxation, as was only just, drew off nearly 7,000*l.* of this revenue, and a certain fixed tariff of alms had to be met: 1,810*l.* to the Hôpital Général, 400*l.* to prisoners in the town jail, small sums to the mendicant orders and the poor of the countryside. Then there were repairs to property. But all these outgoings taken together did not, for the year 1786, come to more than 11,000*l.* There was thus a handsome surplus, of which the lion's share went to the abbot, who could be sure of receiving not far short of 20,000*l.* a year.[4] There was, of course, no resident abbot, for notable sinecures like this were inevitably disposed of at Versailles. After keeping the wolf from the door of a bishop of Rennes and a bishop of Angers, these rich revenues went, in 1781, to the bishop of Séez, who from thenceforward, in view of the poverty of his endowments, schemed steadily to make this union of the abbatial income of Saint-Aubin to his see a permanency. The not inconsiderable revenues which remained to the monastery and the extensive buildings were enjoyed by fifteen Benedictine monks of the order of Saint-Maur. Dom Mansel their prior and young dom Soulet were doctors of theology, and a few students were accepted by the monks to share their lodgings and their table for the duration of the university course;[5] nevertheless, Saint-Aubin was not a house of learning. It seems that the policy of the congregation of Saint-Maur was to use this particular house as a centre for younger monks; certainly, on the eve of the final suppression, the average age of the fifteen professed was thirty-six and nine of them were under thirty-two years of age.[6] Whether they were usefully employed or not, it seems clear that their daily liturgical routine was carried out with decent formality. Low mass at 6 a.m., high mass at 10, vespers at two o'clock, compline at 5 p.m. and mattins at midnight were regularly attended, and gave the lie to a mean anti-clerical proverb which was current in Angers, 'That goes without saying, like the mattins of the monks.' On the other hand, life was undoubtedly comfortable. Monks no longer wore their habit as a badge of separation from the world: their tonsure was nominal, their frocks were cut to resemble the cassocks of secular priests and beneath appeared elegant shoes and black silk stockings. Pleasant social occasions relieved the tedium of Benedictine life—a hand at cards, a musical concert on Sunday evenings after vespers.[6a] Meat was banished from the common table, but the best sea and river fish, ducks, teal, hares, and woodcocks were lavishly supplied, and the 'infirmary table', where the prior himself habitually dined, was free from restrictions. Each monk received 120l. a year as pocket-money, and was allowed to take a month's holiday, on condition of attending offices at a house of the order if one were conveniently near.[7] The abbey provided a horse, or, for older monks, a two-horse cabriolet with grooms, so that once every year the comfortable boredom of existence was broken by a pleasant excursion, with relaxation in the company of relatives at Tours, Brest, Rennes, or even as far afield as Cambrai.

Saint-Aubin is an illustration on a grand scale of the general state of the other Benedictine houses of the town. None was so rich of course. Lesvière, on the riverside near the castle walls, had, indeed, an accumulated debt of 32,000l. in 1790; even so, it owned 3 fiefs, a farm in the parish of Saint-Samson, various houses and gardens and the tithes of six parishes. Its revenues had been steadily rising since the beginning of the century—so that they now produced nearly 10,000l. yearly for its absentee prior alone.[8] This was, however, a full two-thirds of the revenue of the house and its loss was the root cause of insolvency. The handful of monks (four in all)[8a] remaining in residence seem to have made small effort to redeem their situation. Bills went unpaid, in 1790 the tobacconist and confectioner awaited their money, over 1,000l. was owed to the baker, over 2,000 to the draper and a full 6,000 to the butcher, while the cook's wages were two to three years in arrears.[9] Repairs were neglected, the buildings became more and more dilapidated and the rock on which the house stood was slowly crumbling away. The almonry, on the very edge, bore up bravely until the spring of 1791, and then, as if in sympathy with the evicted monks, subsided in ruinous confusion into the castle moat.[10]

Not far from decaying Lesvière, but on the other side of the river,

stood the abbey of Saint-Nicolas. The main road from Angers to
Rennes and Nantes left the city walls and ran westwards through a
straggling and poverty-stricken suburb—a single shop, two miserable wine bars, three small workshops, and a few houses belonging
to day-labourers and washerwomen.[11] Dominating this pathetic
scene was the Benedictine house, situated on a broad terrace facing
southwards. On one side was an old ruined tower and the great barn
of the monastery, on the other, rocks and clumps of trees provided
a picturesque background to the building and served the monks as
rabbit warren. The conventual house itself was newly constructed,
with a vaulted refectory, two handsome reception rooms and a
library; there was, too, an old wing containing nine rooms, and a
separate house for the abbot.[12] Needless to say, this house was never
occupied nowadays by its rightful owner. Saint-Nicolas had as its
abbot the abbé de Mostuejouls, principal chaplain to *Madame*, and
former tutor to the royal children, a typical ecclesiastical courtier,
who drew more than 50,000*l.* a year from his two abbeys, a priory
and his canonry at Lyons.[13] He belonged to a noble house which
provided for itself handsomely from church revenues; his elder
brother, the marquis, inherited the family property, the abbé himself was the second son, the third son was a canon of the exclusively
noble chapter of Saint-Julien de Brioude, and a daughter was a
noble canoness of Remiremont.[14] The disposable income of Saint-
Nicolas was at least 25,000*l.* a year—probably much more.[15] Abbot
de Mostuejouls pocketed almost two-thirds of it, and remained in
permanent residence at Versailles.

On the opposite side of the city to Saint-Nicolas was the abbey of
Saint-Serge. It was, perhaps, more agreeably and more strategically
situated than any other religious establishment of Angers, lying as it
did just outside the city walls, surrounded by its own rich gardens,
its impressive stone façade half-concealed by trees which lined its
great courtyard and provided shady promenades for leisure hours.[16]
Saint-Serge vied with Saint-Aubin for pride of place in Angers. Its
privileges and honorific distinctions were many: it was 'Saint-Serge
the noble', as distinct from 'Saint-Aubin the rich'.[17] Every year, on
the 1st of May, the municipality went in procession to the chapel of
Saint-Brieuc in the abbey church, and here the mayor kissed the
ring of the saint and swore to preserve the privileges of his foundation, a not inappropriate ceremony, for the monastery owned the
very ground on which the town-hall was built.[18] From its fiefs and
from rents paid by contractors who leased its slate quarries, Saint-
Serge drew a considerable income, 12,000*l.* to 14,000*l.* for its monks,
and 6,000*l.* to 7,000*l.* for its abbot.[19] Once again, the abbatial dignity
was held *in commendam*, in this case, from 1784, by the bishop of

Angers himself. This general application of the revenues of Benedictine houses as supplements to income for clerics of high station or
courtiers was, of course, an abuse, although, if it was 'the leprosy of
the monastic order', it was an affliction which was a symptom of
decline rather than a cause of it. But before being too censorious,
one ought to look at the tribulations of a commendatory abbot as
exemplified at Saint-Serge.

Monseigneur Couet Vivier de Lorry, bishop of Angers, took possession of his abbey on 17 April 1784 with all customary ceremonies;
he entered the church by its main portal, took holy water, prayed
before and then kissed the high altar, touched the gospel book, sat
in his abbatial stall, rang the bell, sang a *Te Deum*, processed to the
abbot's lodgings, where his bulls of provision were read aloud.[20]
But after this he did not merely retire and draw 7,000*l*. a year.
Having just terminated a lawsuit over the abbey of Saint-Martin of
Troyes, which had been his former source of supplementary revenue,[21]
he now embarked on a long course of litigation to extract money for
the repairs of Saint-Serge from the heirs of his predecessor. Experts
estimated what was due while the family of the former abbot, de
Hérouville, ignored these proceedings. By 1786, the *Sénéchaussée* of
Angers had decided in the bishop's favour,[22] by 1788, the *Châtelet* at
Paris had done the same.[23] This disposed of claims from the em-
battled creditors of de Hérouville, leagued together in Paris under a
former farmer of the abbey lands, who had hoped to win priority
for his mortgage of 19,000*l*. over the 12,000*l*. bill for repairs.[24] Meanwhile, the brothers of the dead abbot had concealed such assets as
had fallen to them[25] and the bishop had to maintain one of his
vicars-general continually in the capital prosecuting an investigation of their shifts and schemes. Taking into account repairs, litigation and fluctuations of income, even sinecures in eighteenth-
century France were something of a gamble. An abbot had to hope
that he would live long enough to recover his outlay. It was an
investment he undertook rather than a pension which he appropriated.

If commendatory abbots were filching monastic revenues, there is
one thing at least which can be said in their defence: that is, that
the monks usually retained more than enough for their needs. There
was only a handful of inmates in each of the four Benedictine houses
at Angers. When the Commission of 1768 had investigated the state
of the monasteries of France, Saint-Serge, with a mere thirteen
residents, had been recommended for suppression;[26] nevertheless, it
still survived. At the time of that inquisition Lesvière had been only
seven strong, and these had declined to four by 1790. Saint-Nicolas,
which earlier in the century had cut its woods to finance a notable

building programme, had failed to justify this optimism of its monks, who were reduced to nine by the end of the old régime.[27] Even the great Saint-Aubin had only fifteen permanent residents. The population of these houses had declined dangerously near to, or even below the absolute minimum required by royal edicts.[28]

This decline in recruitment was, in part a reflection of a new secular spirit in society, in part a natural result of the alarm and uncertainty caused by the inquisitions and suppressions carried out by the Royal Commission of 1768 and its raising of the age for taking vows,[29] and to some extent it was an epiphenomenon of the monastic decadence which had been that commission's justification. In the course of the seventeenth century the Benedictine houses of Angers had been rescued from disorder and scandal by joining, or being constrained to join, the reforming congregation of Saint-Maur. According to the historian of the congregation, the Angevin houses became centres of 'learning and piety', 'examples' and 'ornaments' to the city.[30] Since then the reform itself had declined. Chapters-general became scenes of tumult and faction. Disputes between abbots and priors added to the anarchy. The persecution of Jansenism discouraged zeal in favour of a hollow and insincere orthodoxy, dividing houses between 'Jansenists who make a show of their regularity to accredit their party and Constitutionals who affect submission to the Bull (Unigenitus) as an excuse for neglecting their observances'.[31] Learning flourished, though, like orthodoxy, it too could serve as a cover for worldliness. There were skilled schoolmasters in the congregation, directing *collèges* whose instruction was as good as any in Europe. There were great scholars, addicted sometimes to wine, tobacco or intrigue, but working twelve hours a day to complete their quota of folios before fate pushed them down into that 'damned worm hole through which you have to go to Paradise'.[32] But for every scholar or schoolmaster there were one or two others who drifted comfortably through their curriculum,[33] and after two years of classical studies, two of philosophy and four of theology remained content to be modestly learned and moderately indolent. The reform of Saint-Maur had restored monastic finances, and a steady decline in vocations, together with a steady rise in the value of rents, made Benedictine communities very prosperous. The late-seventeenth and eighteenth centuries showed the agreeable architectural results of this solvency.[34] Amid trim formal gardens new convents arose. Balanced neoclassical façades in harmonious local stone (there was none of the baroque and rococo exhibitionism of South German and Italian abbeys) were pierced by great windows which admitted light and air to sweeping staircases and vast corridors leading to panelled parlours and reception rooms. This was how

Saint-Aubin and Saint-Serge had been rebuilt, with Saint-Nicolas following suit in the seventeen-thirties.[35] 'The congregation of Saint-Maur', said an Angevin observer of those building programmes darkly, 'is jettisoning every monachal appearance; I am surprised they are retaining cloisters seeing they don't fit in with lordly country-houses.'[36] A secure existence in agreeable surroundings became one of the motives inclining men to take monastic vows. 'If I am on the road to heaven,' wrote one of them, 'I find the carriage very comfortable.'[37] Not that the monasteries filled up with the dregs of society, as their critics sometimes chose to suppose. When we can break through the anonymity of the cloister and catch glimpses of our Maurists of Angers—dom Boislinard a polished ex-infantry officer,[38] dom Braux, gentle, mild, professing theology and botany with equal zeal, Mansel and Soulet, doctors of theology, Locatelli and Marchant, future librarians and teachers—we have to set the worthiness of individuals against the decadence of the original ideals which they were supposed to be serving. A fair verdict is that of a novelist writing in 1787, who speaks of 'agreeable retreats where Christian philosophers and good company know how to combine duty and pleasure',[39] and the title of his novel might be applied with sad irony to this transmutation of fervour and self-abnegation into decent learning and comfort—*Ainsi finissent les grandes passions*. Thus it was that three large and one small Benedictine houses in Angers, possessing a total income of over 200,000*l.*, had come, without great scandal, to be serving very little social or religious purpose. They provided four lofty ecclesiastics with supplementary pensions and afforded shelter to fewer than fifty monks.

The abbey of Toussaint, whose church lay just outside the north wall of Saint-Aubin's gardens, may be placed in the same category as these four Benedictine monasteries. Like them it presents a spectacle of a shrunken kernel within a large and solid shell. It was a house of Augustinian canons of the Order of Sainte-Geneviève,[40] which had had eleven inmates at the time of the Commission of 1768, but whose numbers had declined to six by 1777.[41] Then in the eighties came a revival, when five young men were professed as canons, so that at the final suppression the house had eight members in major orders and three others.[42] These canons-regular were men of importance, with their white cassocks and well-creased cambric surplices, their elegant manners and their honorary title of 'M. le prieur'.[43] Although they looked with envy upon the extensive gardens of their Benedictine neighbours,[44] for a prior and five priests their own buildings, lavishly restored in the seventeenth century, remained absurdly large. A great courtyard led to a spacious vestibule opening into a vaulted dining-hall; there was a salon with a panelled chimney-piece, a parlour for everyday use and, exclusive of the infirmary, twenty-two other rooms, eight with fireplaces.[45] From country estates and leases of twenty-one houses in town the abbey drew an income of 17,000*l.*; there were, in addition, certain grain rents, and, although the gardens did not produce enough fruit and vegetables for all their meals, a vineyard in the parish of Saint-Barthélemy provided all the wine the canons required.[46] Even so, Toussaint was always in financial difficulties. When clerical taxation and a small annual subsidy to the headquarters of the congregation had been found, sacristy expenses met,[47] and repairs paid for, only 12,000*l.* remained. Of this, the abbot took a share, and the canons-regular, for their part, lived extremely well.[48] They lived, apparently, beyond their means, for in 1772, the capitular registers record negotiations for a loan, 'the position of the house being delicate, and its embarrassment extreme'.[49] From then onwards there was an attempt to rationalize expenditure. Contracts at a fixed yearly sum were made for window cleaning, repair of kitchen utensils and the adjustment of the clock; the locksmith and mason were to offset their bills against the rent of the houses they occupied, and connexions with the established wood merchant were severed to enable the monastery to buy in the cheapest market.[50] Negligent administration on the part of the commendatory abbot did not help the canons-regular in their struggle towards solvency. As usual, this office served to pension an absentee nobleman. Le Perrochel, a younger son of a younger son, had served as a lieutenant in a regiment of dragoons, then turned to the Church in search of an assured position in life which the camp did not afford. His family had nothing to leave him beyond a coat-of-arms, but two gold crescents and a star on azure were enough to entitle him to a monastic sinecure.[51] He took possession in 1783, and from the abbatial establishment of Toussaint and the prebend at the cathedral which went with it, he drew sufficient revenues to be able to shake the dust of Anjou off his feet, departing on a grand tour of the Protestant North.

In addition to Benedictines and canons-regular there were seven[52] houses of mendicants in Angers, containing a total of about forty friars of different observances. There were in 1789 four Dominicans, four Augustins and nine Carmelites, the rest belonging to the various offshoots of the Franciscan movement—Recollets, Capuchins, Minims and Cordeliers.[53] Vocations to the mendicant orders had been declining steadily. A desire for a career of ecclesiastical learning no longer drew recruits to them. There had been a time when the religious had as many doctors regent in the Faculty of Theology of Angers as the secular clergy, and as late as 1715 doctor Cheverue of the Cordeliers had won a lawsuit justifying their claim to equal representation on committees to examine theses.[54] But since then the secular doctors had come to predominate and a prejudice had arisen against the doctors of theology in mendicant houses, who, it was said, used their privileges to escape the obligations of their rule. 'There are more coffee pots and tea-sets, snuff boxes and knick-knacks on their tables than books of theology', Pocquet de Livonnière remarked, 'preaching is their resort against the vow of obedience, the doctoral cap against that of poverty'.[55] Mattins at midnight and other offices till three in the morning, silence after eight o'clock at night and two meals a day—the official programme of the Recollets[56]—provided a forbidding prospect for the unlearned who were not entitled to mitigations. Begging tours, gardening, washing up and penance, 'abstinence and ignorance' as applied at the Capuchins had no attractions for the youth of the eighteenth century, who even in the seminaries mocked at the friar's white hood, 'a mushroom on a dunghill'.[57] Recruitment was drying up. The story of this decline may be read in the register of the noviciate at the Cordeliers. In the decade following 1747, thirteen young men of good families in Angers entered to essay their vocation; in the fifteen years following 1757 only one came forward and he departed after four months.[58] In 1783 the fine new convent of the Dominicans housed five friars—in 1789 they were reduced to four.[59] Everywhere the picture was the same. Most of the mendicant houses in the town had had twice as many professed at the time of the Monastic Commission of 1768 as they had in 1789.

By definition, all were poor. Earlier in the century, an ecclesiastical writer referred to the White Friars, the Carmelites, as 'rich',[60] but this was an inference, no doubt, from their fine library of over 7,000 volumes and the gossip of the poor parish of La Trinité in which their house was established. In fact, they owned twenty-seven houses in Angers, bringing in a yearly rent of 4,600*l.*, and enjoyed various fixed alms and minor rents which did no more than bring their total income up to 5,000*l.*,[61] which was more than adequate for mendicants, or indeed for any kind of monks, but not riches by normal eighteenth-century standards. The Cordeliers were more prosperous, having an income twice as large as that of the Carmelites.[62] There were silver dishes on their dinner table, 160 sheets in their linen store and 24 pipes of wine in their cellars. Individual friars were given a dress allowance and were allowed private possessions—one even employed his own servant.[63] But such affluence was exceptional. By steady investment throughout the century the Dominicans had built up a revenue of about 5,000*l.* a year.[64] It might have been a good deal more than this had bene-factors in the past given real property instead of contracts conferring money rents. 'Our forbears thought of nothing but contracts', said Père Faitot bitterly as he devised ways and means of restoring the conventual buildings; for contracts, he said, were often dishonoured, subject to lawsuits and always at the mercy of inflation.[65] However, his friars lived comfortably enough. If their table was modestly served—for a capon, partridge, rabbits or dish of pigs' feet was a delicacy, worthy of entry on the registers as 'extraordinary expenditure' [66]—each member of the community could possess his own furniture and keep for his own use money earned on preaching expeditions.[67] Below the Dominicans in the scale of poverty came the Augustin friars. Eight small holdings, seven houses, a stable, a patch of vines and a few fractional rents brought them in rather more than 4,000l. a year; their buildings were in an advanced stage of neglect and the total value of their furniture was less than 500l.[68] Lower still came the Recollets, proverbially penurious, who had survived only by selling off some of the fine medieval volumes in their library[69] and allowing their property to fall into fantastic disrepair.[70] Minims and Capuchins had never built up any sort of financial independence and were still under the necessity of going round daily, soliciting alms. The Capuchins' only property was a house to lodge their laundry-woman and a plot of land whose revenue served to maintain their church ornaments. 'Two dozen shirts for the sick' were the only items of wearing apparel in their linen cupboard. Each cell was furnished with nothing more than 'a very poor bed, a table, chairs and a few pious books'.[71] If then they were to entertain the General of their order or put candles in their windows at seasons of national rejoicing, the municipality had to finance them, and ferrymen who plied on the river were obliged to give them free passage when they came into town on their begging tours.[72]

While they were comparatively or absolutely poor in actual income, the mendicants were rich in other respects. They had attractive churches, extensive buildings and strategic development sites. 500l. would have bought the entire furniture of the Augustins' personal quarters, but one walked on rich Turkey carpet in their sanctuary where Biardeau's huge *Adoration of the Magi* adorned the high altar. No parish church in town could vie with the thirteenth-century church of Saint-Sebastian where the Cordeliers worshipped, with its coats of arms, mediaeval tombs and memories of Jean de Laval and good duke René, its forty oil-paintings lining panelled walls and its high altar spanned by a great baldachin borne aloft on columns of black marble.[73] Early in the seventeenth century the Minims had begun with a tiny chapel. Now, thanks to wealthy patronage which curés could only envy, it had become a spacious church—'et sic de Minimis Majora', said a spectator of this expansion, maliciously.[74] Few parochial sacristies were so well furnished as those of Recollets, Carmes or Augustins, abundantly supplied with altar linen, copes, chasubles, silver candelabra and chalices.[75] Citizens who strolled down the rue du Pilory peered through iron railings into the twin quadrangles of the Cordeliers, an oasis of quiet shaded by old elms: or, passing down the rue de l'Hôpital, they could glimpse this cool interior through the stone gateway surmounted by the arms of France and Lorraine and flanked by statues of Our Lady and Saint Bernardin.[76] It was only twenty years since the Dominicans had built a new convent, judging that their old one was too 'sad and sombre', with an 'air of poverty' about it which would discourage novices and visitors.[77] Now their old five-roomed house was deserted and four surviving Jacobins had their new building three storeys high, eight windows wide, cloisters, library, refectory, parlour, reception-rooms and ten cells to themselves.[78] Four or five friars in the black habit of the Minims kept their perpetual Lent in the echoing vastness of a building which might more suitably have been a barracks. The house of the Capuchins out at Reculée was one of the finest in the kingdom. It was said, early in the century, that a hundred monks could easily have lived there.[79] That was an exaggeration, but there were at least 44 separate cells as well as many public rooms, and the friary was well situated in a salubrious position outside the city in the midst of broad alleyways planted with hornbeams and magnificent gardens running down to the riverside.[80] The Recollets' main house in the parish of Saint-Laud had been completed in the course of the seventeenth century, but they still retained their convent of la Baumette, perched on a steep rock over the river Maine in a spot so beautiful, it was said, that it ravished the eyes of all beholders and cured the sick in soul.[81] Newly repaired in the middle of the eighteenth century,[82] it was a whole empty labyrinth, complete with servants' quarters, staff dining-hall, cellars and stables. Here the four surviving friars received company in one of their seventeen public rooms, dined at the end of one of the five oak tables in the silent refectory and took their leisure by the fountain in the courtyard, or wandered among the walnut trees, drooping willows and formal lawns of half a dozen different gardens.[83]

The reactions of the laity to the spectacle of mis-applied wealth presented by the declining Benedictines and canons-regular were, no doubt, the natural reactions to such phenomena in any age: regrets by the pious, and envy among the profane. With the abbey of Saint-Serge particularly in view, the *cahier* of the parish of Saint-Samson[84] urged that each monk be given a pension of 500 or 600*l*., and that the surplus of monastic revenue be confiscated before it flowed away down the well-worn channel to Paris. 'We hope that these gentlemen will pardon us these observations, since they are never done preaching to us that the superfluity of the rich is the daily bread of the poor, and they ought to show us an example.' But the mendicant orders, which were immune from such direct criticism, were nevertheless included with the richer monasteries in a ruthless syllogism which needed no anti-clerical sentiments to increase its force. Parochial reformers were bound to consider that a better use might be made of their churches, and above all, an improving municipality, motivated equally by philanthropy and considerations of local trade, would certainly cast envious eyes on empty buildings and strategic acres. The demand for barracks, hospitals, orphanages and offices for bureaucrats was becoming stronger every day, and sixty monks and forty friars occupied thirteen institutional buildings, some of an immense size. There was an almost inevitable final term to this syllogism.

The time was approaching when religious institutions would be judged by strict and unimaginative standards of social usefulness. But even on these grounds, no possible objections could be made to the other three male religious communities settled in Angers, new foundations, contrived for specific useful purposes. In 1674, the Lazarist fathers had arrived[85] to occupy a little house presented to them by a pious lady. Their order, founded by Saint-Vincent de Paul, had already swept out far afield, to Tunis, Algiers, Madagascar and Poland; it was an unadventurous inner ripple of the movement which lapped into the quiet Angevin countryside. Gradually they collected alms enough to add a simple chapel to their building, to purchase three parcels of land at Andard,[86] and even, ultimately, to invest about 20,000*l.* with the Clergy of France. Otherwise they neither grew rich nor extended. Retreats for laymen and courses of instruction for ecclesiastics met within the garden walls of their house in the rue Valdemaine, and from time to time curés of sleepy country market towns called in the 'Petits Pères' to take parochial missions. Pious ladies (and even, it appears, bishop de Grasse) gave them capital sums to support such campaigns, which were held at ten-year intervals, generally in specified parishes.[87] One or two little funds were also made over to them 'to contribute to the conversion of scandalous libertine women or girls of town or country who are in danger of losing their virginity or to assist peasant families to separate children of both sexes who sleep together, to provide books of piety for family use, to wind up or forestall a lawsuit'.[88] No one envied the Lazarists and the superior and his three priests[89] were too little entangled in the web of recorded mundane things to become better known in history.

The other two communities, the Congregation of the Oratory and the Frères des Écoles Chrétiennes, both almost exclusively occupied in educational work, were less retiring, and both have left a significant impress on the history of Anjou in the eighteenth century.

On Sundays the Oratorians preached to the sick of the Hôtel-Dieu and visited the prisoners in the town jail,[90] otherwise their days were spent in teaching at the Collège d'Anjou, where sons of the nobility and the prosperous middle-class were educated. Here, the chevalier de Caqueray gained some smattering of learning before departing gleefully for the more congenial life of the camp,[91] and Marin Boylèsve de la Maurouzière walked off with the leading academic prizes and the acting honours of *Landor, ou la Force de la Nature*, as befitted a son of the syndic of the nobility of Anjou. Meanwhile, Choudieu, a future *Conventionnel*, was justifying the rising middle class by creeping steadily up to the prize 'for diligence',[92] and La Revellière-Lépeaux and his friend Leclerc, lost in the 'mass of ridiculous subtleties and barbarous formulae' of logic, were taking refuge in the reflection that Boylèsve de la Maurouzière's success was not unconnected with the excellent coffee and Jansenist conversation with which his distinguished father entertained their Oratorian schoolmasters. Gendry, a baker's son, was cleverer than all of them, but his brilliance had no embarrassing consequences, as his parents could not afford to buy him decent clothes to attend prize-giving day.[93] Most of the students were from noble or prosperous families and most of them were 'day-boys'. It was a continual lament of the municipal authorities that the Collège took so few boarders; people who counted always retired from Angers to the country in the hottest months of the year, and as the school could not accommodate their sons, they were obliged to leave them, for the completion of the academic term, in lodgings 'little suited to their birth and fortune'.[94]

The Congregation of the Oratory was ideally fitted to produce masters for such 'public schools' of the old régime. It was not a monastic community, for no permanent vows were exacted; as Bossuet said, there were 'no rules but the canons of the Church, no other superior than the bishop, no bonds other than charity, no vows other than those of baptism and ordination'. Even the latter commitment was not obligatory, and laymen who took an oath of temporary obedience were able to join the community and teach in its schools. A meagre yearly allowance of 120*l.*—it was even less at the Collège d'Anjou—was not likely to attract men who had not a vocation, at least to the teaching profession, and the liberal nature of the internal constitution of the order encouraged inclinations towards progressive ideas in education. La Revellière-Lépeaux said

G

hard things of the formal logic that was taught, yet he admitted that the philosophical teaching of the Oratorians of Angers was the best that could be done with an impossible subject;[96] they had, after all, turned to Cartesianism at a time when scholasticism was officially enforced, and later they had welcomed the physics of Newton into their syllabus.[97] Latin themes and, of course, a general religious bias in education were taken for granted, but they were not allowed to warp a developing and widening curriculum. The teaching of French was held in honour, and Viger, another future member of the National Convention, testified in 1787 to the vitality of the history course, which brought to life great geniuses of the past rather than wallowing in 'a sterile nomenclature'.[98] At the Collège d'Anjou traditional educational formulae were being enlarged to admit the wider interests of the urbane and liberal Oratorian masters. There was the genial Héron, who taught his pupils the humanities in the widest sense of that word; Bénaben, an elegant man of the world; Mévolhan, who, under a discreet anonymity, sketched the influence of women in politics; Leballeur, who had squared the circle and challenged sceptics to a public demonstration, and Olliver, who turned from erudite disquisitions on history and Hebrew usage to write a best-seller on the classification of wines.[99] Politics were not excluded from their many interests or their liberal outlook, and only an opportunity was needed to demonstrate that 'a congregation for long accustomed to regarding liberty as the essence of man' would gladly march with its fellow-citizens on dangerous paths of freedom.[100]

It was a doctrinaire and intellectual liberalism which was to dispose the Oratorians to accept the ideals of the Revolution; the Frères des Écoles Chrétiennes were to accept these ideals with the equanimity of professional schoolmasters, whose sphere of duty remained the same so long as there were children to educate and a roof to cover them. Jean-Baptiste de la Salle, the founder of their Institute, died in 1719, having created an educational organization which, during the next sixty years, built up a teaching force of 800 brothers living and working in more than 140 houses and teaching more than 30,000 pupils.[101] There was no attempt to compete directly with the old *collèges* of France with their classical education and distinguished clientele; on the contrary, the Frères forswore Latin and taught practical subjects—writing, mathematics, navigation, surveying, book-keeping and manual arts—to the children of poor and lower middle-class families. It was a principle of the Institute that education should be gratuitous, though in the eighties its Superior General had to use his utmost authority to maintain this tradition against the intrigues of municipal officers who begrudged having to find the meagre remuneration of the Frères from city funds.[102] Two particular types of exception were, however, allowed to this rule, and a limited number of houses (Angers was one of them) grew prosperous from these opportunities of compromise. Boarders could be taken and quite high fees accepted on their behalf;[103] so too a few houses were allowed, or rather in this case obliged, to accept boarders of a very different kind, lunatics, vicious youths locked up at the request of their families, mad clergymen or other individuals who were removed from ordinary society by the authority of a royal *lettre de cachet*.[104]

The Frères had arrived in Angers in 1741[105] at the invitation of bishop Vaugirault, to teach in the parish school of La Trinité. Very soon they had acquired a building in the parish of Lesvière and here they struggled on miserably for the next forty years. The site on the stale muddy riverside was unhealthy. Respectable society was indifferent to their zeal to educate poor children, while the municipal authorities bluntly declared that they 'came to Angers without the agreement of the mayor and aldermen. Their establishment is prejudicial to the good of the city.' [106] From 1745 the government sent ne'er-do-wells and misfits to be confined at Lesvière. If the fulfilment of this social obligation ensured backing from the intendant at Tours against a snobbish municipality, only a cynic would maintain that acting as warders in a lunatic asylum was a suitable spare-time occupation for schoolmasters. There were dangerous incidents—we hear of 'writings, arms, ropes and files' being lowered to prisoners from the steep rocky scarp which dominated the buildings and of riots which ensued, 'when several brothers were victims . . . and perished from the ill-treatment which they suffered'.[107] But by 1782 persistence and patience were rewarded and the Frères moved triumphantly to a site amid fields and orchards to the south of the city. Their new house, brought from the bishop at a bargain price,[108] was the Rossignolerie, a decorative three-storeyed building contrived around three sides of a formal courtyard and set in extensive gardens adorned with rustic pavilions and alley-ways of laurels and hornbeams. What was lacking in this paradise the Frères devised for themselves. Brother Martin used the mechanical skill he had acquired in his native Franche-Comté to contrive a well-nigh infallible clock for the central façade, while brother François, an ex-architect, built a new chapel in the style of Louis XVI, which dean de Villeneuve of the cathedral duly consecrated.[109]

As early as 1751 Angers had been one of nine centres selected by the Institute as a suitable site for a boarding school. Now, in the idyllic surroundings of the Rossignolerie, this establishment grew and flourished. A wing of the house, with sixty or so unfortunate inmates,[110] still fulfilled sombre functions as a state prison and asylum, but the main buildings now housed more than 40 teaching brothers and their 180 pupils. These boys, whose ages ranged from seven to fifteen years, came from comparatively prosperous families of the minor bourgeoisie, for artisans and peasants could hardly have afforded to provide twelve changes of linen and maintenance fees of 400*l.* a year. These favoured pupils lived under a strict but enlightened discipline. Corporal punishment[111] and ironical rebukes were forbidden; when the dunce's stool or impositions failed to obtain obedience an offender was simply sent home. Each boy had a room of his own and was responsible for making his own bed, cleaning his shoes, and opening his bedroom window when he arose at 5.30 each morning. There were three periods of recreation each day and communal walks on Tuesdays and Thursdays, otherwise all waking hours exclusive of meal times were filled with classroom studies or pious observances. Though the Frères included Voltaire in their prose anthologies they made no concessions to dangerous intellectual tendencies. The least taint of Jansenism sufficed to exclude a volume from their library, they went out of their way to give special honour to the feasts of the *Sacré Cœur*, the Assumption and the Immaculate Conception, and in spite of their curriculum of commercial subjects, their catechism was uncompromising about the wickedness of loans at interest. Prayers, meditation, mass, the litanies of the Child Jesus and the rosary before breakfast, self-examination, a *De profundis* and the Angelus before dinner and litanies of the Passion and St. Joseph afterwards, catechism at 6 o'clock and prayer and meditation in the classroom at the day's end—such was the pattern of daily life at the Rossignolerie. Then, after eight years, an adolescent would leave for his father's shop or office in Angers or Saumur to 'undertake commerce in the name of God and under the protection of the glorious Virgin Mary'.[112]

It is interesting to compare the attitude of the official clique which governed Angers towards the Congregation of the Oratory and towards the Frères des Écoles Chrétiennes. In effect, the municipality was an old boys' association of the Collège d'Anjou. It paid for the completion of the buildings, hired an adjoining house for use as an infirmary and subscribed towards the salaries of the masters.[113] When the government banned the reception of boarders (a mean incident in the campaign against the Jansenist leanings of the Oratorians) the city fathers made continual lamentations; when news of the suppression of the Jesuit *collège* at La Flèche began to circulate, the first thought of the town council was to ask for an appropriation of revenue to benefit the Collège d'Anjou.[114] On the other hand, the Frères, who arrived to educate the lower orders, were regarded as a scourge. According to the municipal officers, they sabotaged a whole network of excellent parish schools, deprived pedagogically-minded ecclesiastics of well-deserved supplements to their incomes, drove out no less than twenty established schoolmasters who made stout contributions to local rateable values, and drew together undisciplined hordes of 'children of the dregs of the populace', who held up traffic, frightened horses and threw stones 'always and indiscriminately'. The Frères were doing all this, it was said, as part of a deep-laid plot 'to aggrandize themselves at the expense of the citizens'.[115] And then, in the eighties, came a remarkable conversion. By now the Frères des Écoles Chrétiennes have become 'very advantageous' to the town and are asked to furnish additional teachers for drawing and mathematics. Meanwhile, declining numbers at the Collège d'Anjou are darkly ascribed to the laziness of the masters.[116] This change of heart requires explanation. It began, perhaps, as a grudging acceptance of a *fait accompli*. In spite of opposition at law raised, for divergent reasons, by the Oratorians and by the curé of Lesvière,[117] and in spite of a long and sinister delay by the Parlement of Paris to register appropriate letters patent,[118] the acquisition and occupation of the Rossignolerie had been completed. The bishop, the intendant and loftier and more mysterious powers at Versailles had remained unwaveringly friendly towards the Frères, while brother Agathon, who had ruled the little community at Lesvière from 1771, six years later was elected Superior General of the whole Institute, becoming a man of wide and unpredictable influence.[119] Then, as overt opposition died away, approval began to manifest itself. Once they had moved from the riverside slums and were virtually confining themselves (with the exception of continuing extra-mural teaching commitments in the parishes of Lesvière and La Trinité) to educating fee-paying pupils, the Frères became respectable. Their pedagogy began to look much less like a subversive experiment. And whatever else they were doing, they were certainly succeeding. The municipality, more concerned with economics than education, was prepared to praise any institution which would make the town a centre of trade and consumption.

This then was the state of the male orders and religious communities of Angers. In five great monastic establishments, Benedictines and canons-regular lived on in decorum and outward decency: if they bore no wheat in the ear, neither did they produce tares for burning. These houses, like great declining trees, remained upright, drawing from their roots lush sap which still proliferated in fleshy leaves and richly corrugated bark, in everything, indeed, except fruit. Then there were seven establishments of mendicants, no longer poor, yet still not rich, respectable and institutionalized, not open to condemnation for what they were, but for what they might have been and were not. Then came a sharp boundary-line between old foundations and new, which coincided with the intellectual horizon where medieval twilight faded into the sharp clear air of the utilitarian eighteenth century. The Oratory sprang from the genius of the seventeenth century, the Frères des Écoles Chrétiennes had arisen in the new age itself, and whatever they achieved stood as a criticism of an unreformed past.

In contrast to the communities of men, among the communities of women in Angers there was only one surviving medieval corporation; but that indeed was the greatest monastery of all, which rolled into one that spirit of aristocratic monopoly which was embodied in the institution of commendatory abbot, the riches which were characteristic of Saint-Aubin, and the honour and dignity associated with Saint-Serge. In fact, in the whole of Anjou only the cathedral chapter of Saint-Maurice took pride of place before the Benedictine nuns of the abbey of Ronceray. Among narrow squalid streets on the north side of the city their church was the one great architectural landmark, just as their close was the one centre for high society on that side of the river. The cure of La Trinité which served this populous and poverty-stricken area and thirteen other cures of the diocese were in the nomination of the abbess.[120] On this abbey, eight priorities depended, which were given to individual nuns, who paid lodging expenses to their monastery, and retained what remained to them as private income.[121] The Angevin countryside was studded with enclaves of Ronceray's feudal jurisdiction: peasants in distant hamlets came before its lawyers' assizes to plead their suits of debt or inheritance, bakers and butchers sold bread and meat at prices fixed by the abbess, and innkeepers did not dare to sell liquor during the hours of high mass or vespers for fear of her wrath.[122] Five manors, a dozen barns and wine-presses, half a dozen mills and forty-six farms in the countryside, and six houses in town formed the domain of Ronceray, yielding a yearly income of 27,000l. to the abbey and other considerable revenues to the abbess herself. Rumour exaggerated the value of those great possessions—an angry canon of La Trinité declared in print that they were worth 80,000l. 'if the property was administered with strict honesty'.[123]

The purpose of this wealthy foundation was summed up with laconic directness by its abbess in a report to the Ecclesiastical Committee of the Constituent Assembly—'Object: for the poor noble ladies of Anjou and Maine'.[124] Poor is to be understood comparatively, nobility was essential. 'The advantages which the nobility draws from this house can be paralled with those which the establishment at the *École Militaire* procures for its (sons).' [125] Like the chapters of canonesses of Lorraine, Flanders, Alsace and Hainaut, the abbey of Ronceray was part of a system of luxurious outdoor relief which the church had been obliged to provide for surplus daughters of the nobility of France. Generally speaking, such institutions of the old régime maintained only lax discipline—for as the nobles of Grenoble insisted, when faced with rumours of reform in the chapter of Montfleury, their daughters 'would never think of entering if it was as forbidding as the bishop . . . prescribes . . . which would cause a notable prejudice to all the noble families of the province'.[126] This being so, it is not surprising that at Ronceray nuns wore no veil, were free to go out in their carriages unescorted and could receive visitors in the abbey parlours without chaperons.[127] However, it was a genuine monastic life which they led, and no scandal-monger ever dared to allege impropriety. A long noviciate awaited a new entrant, possibly even as much as twenty years, according to the abbess's discretion. Then came a full and formal ceremony of consecration, resembling the old rites for ordaining deaconesses. The bishop in person welcomed the novice in her white dress and garland of flowers, and gave the gold ring and black peplum of the order.[128] After this, life was a steady round of canonical offices, mattins and mass in the morning, nones and vespers and spiritual reading in the afternoon, compline before retirement at eight o'clock at night, nocturn and lauds at midnight and three in the morning.[129] In Angers, as elsewhere, abusive privileges of particular classes were imposed upon the Church and religious institutions became formalized—but here, decorously so, and without scandal. The high office of abbess of Ronceray was held from 1763 by a daughter of one of the great families of France which inevitably monopolized such offices, Léontine d'Esparbez de Lussan Bouchard d'Aubeterre. Her father, the marquis, died in 1740 when she was twenty-two years of age, but her brother, as he rose to distinction, to marshal of France and minister plenipotentiary to Vienna, had influence enough to see to her establishment.[130] It was in the cloisters of Ronceray that local life in Angers came nearest to the charmed circle of Versailles. During her first seven years of rule, the new abbess could boast of her brother as royal ambassador at Rome, enforcing the policy of France against the Jesuits with bluff soldierly directness:[131] later he added to his fame by sternly and successfully presiding over the turbulent Estates of Brittany,[132] and after his death, his wife, *la maréchale*,[133] came to stay with her sister-in-law, bringing memories of courtly high society into the dull cyclical gossip of provincial existence. When the elections to the Estates-General began, the abbey of Ronceray remained in full possession of all its great privileges. A cautious suggestion of reform had been mooted, but it did not extend beyond a proposal to consolidate the revenue of chapels served in the dependent church of La Trinité; the number of nuns was declining, but not seriously so, for there were still twenty-three professed.[134] The abbess had just reached her seventy-first year and her eye-sight was failing, but she remained as active as ever, shrewd and direct in all business affairs, autocratic and exact in the government of her house, a formidable and aristocratic old lady presiding over the greatest convent of Anjou.

Like Saint-Aubin and Saint-Serge, Ronceray was one of those great hulks, laden with treasure, which the receding tide of the Middle Ages had left stranded on the shores of the modern world. Envious coastal dwellers gained no pickings, for official salvage laws allotted rich derelicts to the aristocracy: of the twenty-three nuns of Ronceray in 1789, only one, Ursule-Louise-Madeleine Charbonnier de la Guesnerie, came from a family resident in the town of Angers. Local families, even distinguished ones, did not normally enjoy sufficient influence to open the gates of this great and wealthy abbey, and their daughters who felt drawn to a religious life found their way more often to the convent of the Visitation. Here, in 1790, there were two de Monteclers, whose father was director of the official tobacco monopoly and *seigneur* of the manor of Montbenault, a de Raspieller, whose father was *écuyer* to the marquis D'Autichamp, a Poulain de la Forestrie, a de Penneveau, a Milscent, while the aristocracy of commerce was represented by a Gouppil, daughter of a *juge consul*.[135] When little Sophie de Milscent began her schooldays at the Visitation in 1781, she was welcomed by two of her maternal aunts, both nuns, and she always remembered how one of them waylaid the visiting bishop to make a proud recital of their complete family genealogy. A lawyer in government employ who was a man of importance but whose family tree was something of a sapling compared with that of the Milscents, would more naturally send his daughter to the Ursulines, while fathers of prosperous bourgeois status without any gilding probably had to turn elsewhere. The Benedictine house of La Fidelité was attractive; in 1789 seven of its twelve places were filled by Angevin ladies coming principally from the more prosperous parishes of the town.[138] Next in priority would probably come the Calvariennes and the Carmelites. These two institutions normally, though not invariably, required payment of a dowry or guarantee of a subsistence allowance when a nun was professed.[139] The Neveu household and their friends furnished 7,000*l.* altogether to Le Calvaire in the seventies and eighties on behalf of three daughters who took the veil, while at the Carmelites, merchants of Angers in the silk, wax and ironmongery trades, who paid dowries ranging from 800*l.* to 2,500*l.*, were escaping with sums smaller than were customarily given. One-third of the 140 nuns who inhabited these four leading convents were drawn from the town of Angers itself, where the families who were most likely to be able to afford appropriate endowments might be expected to live. Dowries were also exacted in other houses. Even in the Bon Pasteur 1,000*l.* had to be invested to establish each nun,[140] and though the humble sisters of the Saint-Charles were not required to bring large sums with them, those who came from rich parents might give more—as much as 1,600*l.*[141] However, convents would generally be prepared to stretch a financial point where good birth was concerned, for it was admitted that one of their functions was 'to provide decent and honourable retreats for that numerous portion of the nation which is too well-bred to degrade itself by doing the humble tasks to which lack of income seems to condemn it'.[142] In any case there were fifteen communities of women altogether and one imagines that their diversity of system would open a way to the religious life for girls of both town and country of whatever social antecedents.

This network of spiritual and social organizations, which included within its cadres three hundred nuns, had been almost entirely the achievement of a brief period of recent history. Ronceray lived on its medieval memories and endowments, but none of the other convents traced its foundation back beyond the year 1600. The great outburst of piety which regenerated the Church of France in the first half of the seventeenth century was their source and origin. Within a period of less than sixty years, Angers had seen the arrival of the Ursulines, Visitandines, Calvariennes, Carmelites, Penitents, the nuns of La Fidelité and of Sainte-Catherine, the sisterhood which served the Hôpital Général, the sisters of Saint-Vincent de Paul at the Hôtel-Dieu, and, towards the end of the seventeenth century, the establishment of the houses of La Croix, La Providence, and Le Bon Pasteur. It was very difficult afterwards to found any new community in Angers. Spiritual saturation point had been reached, not to mention territorial overcrowding. As enthusiasm died down and as the development of the town generally moved forward, it began to be apparent that the new institutions had inserted themselves into the most valuable strategic interstices between the properties of the older corporations. The municipality fought successfully in 1687 to prevent the Ursulines from buying the college of the Oratory,[143] and unsuccessfully later to prevent the foundation of the houses of the Bon Pasteur and the Petite Pension.[143a] The house of the Visitandines, situated in 'an extremely vast field or park, more extensive than that of any other monastery in or near Angers',[144] aroused particular envy. In 1759, the town built a pyramid before the gates of this convent, with inscriptions noting the dimensions of the roads round about;[145] it was a practical step to prevent encroachment but it was also a gesture of suspicion, and might well be taken to have a wider symbolical significance. The seventeenth century had peppered the map of Angers with a pattern of new ecclesiastical properties, and it is in defensive warfare against their extension that we see a first hardening of the attitude of the municipality towards the possessions of churchmen in the town.

Once established, a community could never be evicted. The way in which these houses of women consolidated their possessions and rounded off their territory in spite of adverse circumstances was a standing proof of the unfailing tenacity of religious institutions. For if the nuns of Ronceray resembled the rich and comfortable Benedictine monks, the nuns of other organizations of Angers resembled rather the mendicant orders, rich in possession of strategic buildings, but, for the most part, desperately poor in every other respect. A diocesan return of 1731[146] noted the houses of La Fidelité, Sainte-Catherine, Le Calvaire, the Carmelites, the Penitents, La Croix and La Providence as the poorest convents of the diocese. Their painfully amassed savings had been wiped out by the great crash of Law's Scheme under the Regency,[147] which singled out for ruin those new foundations whose investments were not secure in real property. The story of the Carmelites' 45,000*l.* in useless paper[148] may be read in the history of their church, whose foundations were laid in 1715 on the proceeds of a lottery, and which was still not finished by the middle of the century.[149] Gradually, however, these thrifty little communities of women fought their way back to solvency. In 1730, Le Calvaire probably had little more than a revenue of 1,620*l.* derived from the farms of its lands,[150] and the Carmelites had been running at a loss on a total income of just under 3,000*l.*;[151] rough estimates of monastic finances made in the sixties show the one house enjoying 5,000*l.* a year, and the other 10,000*l.*[152] Certainly, more reliable later figures show that by 1772, the Carmelites had investments of 39,000*l.* with the municipality of Paris and the Estates of Brittany,[153] and eighteen years later they had five houses leased out in Angers, rents from various small farms and other incomes which in the upshot totalled just short of 10,000*l.* a year.[154] At the same time it was noted that the nuns of Le Calvaire now had just over 6,000*l.* coming in.[155] The house of Sainte-Catherine was rather richer, but was still ten years behind in its payments to some of its tradesmen.[156] La Croix however never quite recovered and remained miserably poor;[157] nor did the Penitents succeed in building up a large basic income, for, 'obliged to receive girls in need of correction, the house has always been over-full'.[158] The return of 1731 had not included the Visitation as a poor community, nor was it; even so, the nuns had obtained their property only by incurring debts which were a perpetual burden[159] and which prevented them from completing their church or their buildings. In 1776, their bursar was using her connexions at Court in an attempt to persuade the Bureau of religious communities to advance money to pay off outstanding loans, and trembled lest her importunity brought about the suppression of her convent on grounds of insolvency—'I'd be in despair to have drawn such a storm on a house which is as dear to me as my own life'.[160] More recent foundations like Le Bon Pasteur[161] and La Petite Pension[162] were much poorer than any of the establishments of the early seventeenth century; indeed, the municipality's argument against their foundation had been that they would compete with official hospitals for alms. Only the Ursulines could be described as wealthy. From the very first, they had put their money into real property, cloth mills, paper mills and farms, and, more especially, into a considerable estate at Genetay. Thus, in 1789, they could pay two chaplains, two confessors and eight servants, meet bills of 5,000l. for repairs and administrative expenses on their lands, and still be able to give 2,650l. in charity.[163]

Poverty, as well as riches, can play havoc with ideals. Under the pressure of penury, some convents became to all appearances little better than rest homes for retired ladies of middle-class families, who would withdraw to the cloisters, paying board and lodging for an apartment in which they could end their days. This had been the fate of the house of La Croix, originally founded to educate girls converted from Protestantism, which was now described as 'rather a *pension bourgeoise* than a monastery'.[164] The nuns of La Fidelité eked out their profits from the sale of *guingnolet*, a cherry brandy for which their cellars were famed,[164a] by taking boarders from time to time.[165] At La Croix there were 20 boarders each paying 250l. a year pension and an additional room rent.[166] It was natural enough that fallen girls sent to the Penitents privately and not through the usual channels of justice, should be charged for at 120l. a head, but it was less obviously right that seven permanent residents paying 440l. a year each should have settled there.[167] The Petite Pension had its boarders, and even Le Bon Pasteur, which was a refuge for fallen women, had its quota of two dozen respectable guests who paid 'more or less according to their ability'.[168] At the house of Sainte-Catherine, boarders occupied the four handsome apartments looking out on to the courtyard—which was undeniably just in the case of the two of them, as the ladies in occupation had built the rooms at their own expense.[169]

Yet these financial shifts are not necessarily proof of spiritual penury. What happened to a nun at her profession when she crept under the mortuary sheet in her new-won veil and crown, re-enacting in symbolic terms her death to the world?[170] What thoughts were in her mind through the long day's round of religious observances, from dressing at first light thinking of Christ on the cross to retiring at night reflecting on the folly of attachment to earthly vanities?[171] Did the spiritual reading from the lectern and the pious images on the walls always maintain the attention of an Ursuline as she dined at one of the seven refectory tables amid the noise of children—or did the piece of family table silver which she had brought from home sometimes rouse memories of what was lost or might have been?[172] The cell of a nun of Le Calvaire, with a mattress, a *prie-dieu* and a chair for its sole furniture must often have seemed forlorn;[173] the 500 books of devotion in the Carmelites' library and, worse still, the 100 in a parlour cupboard at La Croix must often have proved boring.[174] Meditation, teaching, and for relaxation, sewing the violet damask and silver chasuble, clipping useless sheets to pieces to repair others only slightly less decrepit, offering a glass of home-made liqueur to the preacher of a retreat or a doctor who gave a free consultation, polishing the brass chandeliers in chapel or refectory[175]— these were the external circumstances of a series of mysterious little closed worlds. And the realities behind them? The objects of their foundation the Carmelites described as purely spiritual, prayer for the Church, the King and the kingdom, and 'penitence . . . to appease the wrath of God against the sins of the world'; while the Calvariennes placed first among theirs 'devotion to the mother of God sharing the sorrows of Jesus Christ on Calvary'.[176] These are words which, in 1790, they themselves chose to describe their aims, at a time when there was every temptation to emphasize more utilitarian ends. There is no evidence to show that they did not sincerely follow them, and in the nature of the case, there is no reason to expect any evidence that they did, for spiritual things are not the monopoly of those who preserve their private prayers in notebooks, but slip easily on through the mesh of statistical history like water through the fingers of a clumsy hand.

Education, however, was an activity in which it was possible to combine loyalty to the objects of founders with modest profits and a genuine contribution to the social utility which the age was demanding. 'Every reasonably sized place inhabited by rich bourgeois needs a retreat where they can leave their children to be brought up in the practices of piety', wrote a bishop of Angers towards the middle of the eighteenth century, in defence of his communities of women.[177] 'What use are so many convents?' 'What use are they, ungrateful men?' replied an orator at the Academy—'to rear for you good mothers of families, chaste and loyal spouses, vigilant housewives, women who are virtuous citizens. Can the sweet voice of Nature be heard amid the tumult and worldliness at your own homes? Will your children find the true notions of virtue and learn to love them under the tutelage of venal souls, of hired school-mistresses?' [177a] Three institutions in Angers filled this educational role, nicely graded according to social classes. Girls of aristocratic families were educated at the Visitation; daughters of prosperous middle-class families went to the Ursulines, which, as pupils of the first school condescendingly admitted, 'was exactly the same as the Visitation, only less well run'.[178] Then, in the rue Saint-Jacques, there was La Providence,[179] originally founded as a home for un-employed servant girls and orphans, but now giving board and lodging to sixteen paying guests, and providing thirty backward children with a pale imitation of the education offered by the two more exclusive academies. It is true that vestiges of a more demo-cratic purpose survived in the obligation of the Ursulines to teach, free of charge, ordinary children to read and write, which duty they continued to perform, taking a daily class of sixty children, if we believe their account, or of twenty, if we accept the word of their enemies.[180] Whatever the truth of the matter, this activity was a sideline; as educational establishments the Ursulines and the Visita-tion were chiefly concerned with their upper-class pupils, particularly the twenty to thirty[181] boarders which each house accepted. In theory, the aims of a convent school were strictly religious. The girls were to be taught 'to preserve their baptismal innocence, to love our Lord and do all things for love of Him, . . . to become true and perfect Christians, and examples of piety to their families'. To this end, they were to learn to scorn 'the maxims of the world and the vanity of their sex', to abjure curls, powder, daring fashions, cards, and the reading of novels and comedies.[182] In practice, the education they received was much more worldly and more liberal. They learnt to dance, to move in polite society, to act and to sing. An annual play brought round pleasant lighthearted social occasions, with canon Louet, superior of the Visitation, in the chair, a song sung in his honour, written by the versatile curé of Lesvière, and dashing acting in masculine parts by the gay young niece of the bishop's vicar-general de Sapineau.[183] Or, at the Ursulines, there would be pastorals, and burlesques on the tenants of the convent, written by one of the nuns, with lines reflecting that sentimental egalitarianism and praise of the gallant American revolutionaries which were too fashionable to be omitted.[184] As for religion, there was catechism twice a day, taught from the same dog-eared note-books that had

been in use in 1700, a round of services, visits of the confessor, a
bow to the crucifix every time one passed it.[185] The Christian life
here, said an angry Jansenist, 'is reduced to a few external practices
which they ally with the maxims of the world'.[186]

Sixty (or twenty) free places, with free bread for lunch, at the
Ursulines, was not the only educational provision made for girls of
the working class by the religious houses. Classes for poor girls were
held by the sisters who worked at the Hôtel-Dieu and the Hôpital
Général, while at La Petite Pension, schoolmistresses were trained
and sent out into the countryside to dispense medicines and the
alphabet.[187] These communities, however, were primarily devoted
to care of the sick, and it is here that the women religious of Angers
did their noblest work. There were three major public institutions
fulfilling this role in the town: the traditional Hôtel-Dieu where
disease was treated, the Hôpital Général set up early in the seventeenth century to care for the infirm and destitute, and the eighteenth-century foundation of the Incurables (set up by the generosity
of a wealthy widow resident at Ronceray) which was a refuge for
the bedridden and impotent. In these three hospitals was crammed
a whole unchronicled history of human misery. The 120 places in
the Hôtel-Dieu were always filled, and a constant clamour arose for
more, so that to lie one in a bed was a peculiar privilege which the
municipal authorities awarded to workers in certain favoured
trades.[188] In the Hôpital Général, there were nearly 600 poor in
1780,[189] and ten years later there were more than 200 beds at the
Incurables, with 60 epileptics of both sexes in two separate rooms.[189a]
Yet these major works of social welfare were desperately poorly
endowed. Only the Hôtel-Dieu had inherited any of the wealth of
the Middle Ages. From its country estates, feudal dues and grain
rents, it drew a basic revenue of 58,000*l.*; thirty-six miserable houses
in the town produced a small addition of 4,000*l.*[190] From the municipality came a grant of a tax on theatrical productions and on the
sale of meat in Lent, but this income made very little difference. In
1782, 82,000*l.* came in and commitments totalled 149,000*l.*, of which
68,000*l.* were ordinary running expenses and 81,000*l.* were interest
on debts in the form of *rentes viagères.*[191] Taking into account its
vast and inescapable responsibilities, the Hôtel-Dieu, in comparison
with Ronceray and Saint-Aubin, had been unlucky in the lottery of
piety. Throughout the century it was cutting its woods, reducing
salaries, taking fewer inmates and excluding local applicants in
favour of wounded soldiers who brought with them a government
gratuity,[192] so that in December 1783, curés were warned that they
must enquire if there was an empty bed before sending in their sick
parishioners for treatment.[193] Law's scheme, with its ruinous infla-

tion, had shattered the finances of the Hôpital Général, which drew only 15,000l. a year from real property. Now it struggled to make ends meet with odd and fragmentary supplements; foundation alms of corn paid by the great abbeys, an *octroi* on wines entering the city, profits from the sale of wool and cotton spun by the inmates and stockings that they knitted, dues derived from a monopoly of funeral undertaking, and tips given to the orphan children who marched in procession at dignified obsequies and paraded the town with placards advertising furniture sales.[194] The Incurables, with less than 8,000l. a year of permanent income from property, was in an even more precarious situation.[194a] It was impossible not to envy the broad acres and feudal dues which the great abbeys had inherited.

The temporalities of these struggling hospitals were under lay control. Even the Hôtel-Dieu, which had been a priory of the rule of Saint-Augustine up to the end of the sixteenth century, had been brought under administrators appointed by the municipality, an early example of ecclesiastical revenues confiscated to preserve them against churchmen 'who entered into the heritage of the poor like ravening wolves'.[195] Lay control seemed more than ever necessary in view of the inefficiency which not uncommonly accompanied genuine piety. No one denied that these nursing sisterhoods rendered devoted service to the sick, but their management of business affairs was another matter. At the Incurables, where the board of 'trustees' [196] had neglected its duty of supervision, the mother-superior was found in 1789 to have kept no inventory of title-deeds, no accounts, no records of the certificates of doctors and curés which gained admission; there were few free places available, and the dispensary was in the hands of an unqualified boarder.[197] It could be taken, by those who had not yet had experience of secular inefficiency in such institutions, as an object-lesson of the need for a further rationalization and laicization of charity. Charitable obligations were slipping out of the ecclesiastical sphere, and would continue to do so, but endowments which had originally been bound up with charitable purposes were not accompanying them. Compulsory alms[198] furnished by the great monasteries did not arouse gratitude, but merely whetted the appetite for more. If, as a current phrase had it, 'the revenues of the Church are the patrimony of the poor', a clear conclusion followed; future charitable foundations—an *Enfants trouvés* for example—must be endowed from the start with a share of the surplus wealth of the Church.

Intervention by laymen in temporal administration did not alter the fact that hospitals were still ecclesiastical institutions. Certificates from parish priests were required as admission tickets, and a daily routine of religious observances was prescribed for the sick or destitute who entered the wards. For example, at the Hôtel-Dieu[199] masses were said at 6 a.m. for the staff, at 9 for the night sisters, and later for the sick in every part of the hospital, so that a minimum of four priests was required for this duty alone; at the Incurables, there were prayers at 7 a.m. ending with a '*stabat*', then mass, then a spiritual reading during dinner, recitation of the Rosary before the afternoon work began, and a *de profundis* for the souls of bene-factors when it was over.[200] All the hospitals were served by religious sisterhoods which were independent of the administrators in spiritual matters. There were 35 Filles de la Charité de Saint-Vincent de Paul at the Hôtel-Dieu,[201] 23 Sœurs de Sainte-Marie at the Hôpital Général,[202] and a Mother-Superior with four chief assistants, and, no doubt, other auxiliaries, at the Incurables.[202a] They lived under a freer and more spontaneous discipline than formal orders of nuns. The Sœurs de Sainte-Marie made a promise of obedience, chastity and poverty, which did not become an actual oath until the eighties.[203] A *gouvernante* at the Incurables took no vows, but under-took to spend half an hour in prayer each morning, wear brown or black habits, and to go into retreat for eight days each year.[203a] Members of the sisterhood of Saint-Vincent de Paul, though con-trolled in matters of recruitment and postings from their head-quarters in Paris,[204] were equally free from permanent obligations; 'they take no vows,' said Rangeard, 'and they are none the less devoted to the most edifying practice of piety and generous charity.'[205] The role of these hospital sisters in the underworld of the dispossessed was like that of the Oratory in the intellectual world, giving an example of communities bound together only by the services they rendered and their love for a common task. Free from temptations of institutionalism and preoccupations with cor-porate possessions, which bulk so large in the affairs of the other religious organizations, and serving people whose lives are chronicled only by brute statistics, they have little formal history.

Three minor ecclesiastical institutions supplemented the work of the hospitals proper. At La Petite Pension in the parish of Saint-Maurille, the sisters of Saint-Charles were dispensing remedies to the sick as well as training schoolmistresses and laying up a fund of good will which served them well in the chaos of revolutionary years.[206] Prostitutes were normally arrested and confined in the Hôpital Général, but fallen women and girls who were not beyond reclamation, especially those whose families were willing to pay for their lodgings, could go to the Penitents,[207] and here, eternally learning the trade of tailoring, or following practices of piety in the incongruous shadow of the feudal battlements of the old fortress of

Saint-Nicolas, they would find a refuge, often for life, from the censures of the world. Or they could go to the Bon Pasteur,[208] where life was much the same. Righteous laymen thought such people were too well provided for under the easy discipline of nuns and at the expense of rich ladies of the town whose alms would otherwise have gone to the hospitals; they considered that all fallen women could be crowded into the large seventeenth-century mansion which Le Bon Pasteur had appropriated and the Penitents suppressed altogether.[209] No doubt that handsome carved head amid a confusion of arabesques, monkeys and fantastic birds on the chimney-piece of the Penitents would have looked down with more composure on a bureaucrat in his office or a substantial citizen in his *salon* than on a troop of erring girls.

There was a richness and a diversity—as well as decadence—in the monastic and quasi-monastic communities of Angers which defy full analysis. The vagaries of medieval generosity and of the inspirations of seventeenth- and eighteenth-century founders, the deadening burden of penury and the even more ruinous drag of riches, love of old traditions and the imaginative independence of new ideas, had given each community a peculiar bent of its own, a special atmosphere which became more tense—or more drowsy—in an introverted life of corporate loyalties. Monks here do not appear to have fled the country with monastic funds or women; there is no evidence in convents of nuns of those forced vocations, abductions and perversions so cherished by scandal-mongering diarists and erotically sentimental novelists of the eighteenth century.[210] The nearest wine-drinking contest we have found was at an abbey at Saint-Florent-le-Vieil,[211] and the Cordelier imprisoned at Angers for breaking open offertory boxes with chisels and skeleton keys had plied his trades at Rennes and not locally.[212] Sloth, narrow-mindedness,[213] institutionalism, pettiness, and not startling vices, were the temptations which beset the religious of Angers. But fundamentally, their tragedy was, that at a time when lay society was becoming more and more doubtful of the value of the celibate and contemplative life, they remained caught in a network of tradition and of property owning which perpetuated inequality and ineffectiveness. Orders of women can at least be paid the compliment of a description according to their scale of social usefulness; orders of men fit better into a simple quartermaster's table of numbers on one hand and revenues and buildings on the other, with no reasonable proportion between the two sides. Altogether, one thing is clear. Those who had arrived earliest had retired to the shade, and later arrivals (though not all of them) were bearing the heat and burden of the day, without any hope of receiving the traditional equal penny. Five Benedictine

H

houses (that is, including Ronceray) whose wealth was being siphoned off by the privileged classes, enjoyed a total revenue greater than that of all other nuns and monks and friars and parochial clergy of the town together. These monasteries provided a culminating example of the indefensibility of the distribution of Church property within the Church itself. Revenues so manifestly misappropriated were a dangerous sight in an age when a steady growth of opinion in favour of the laicization of charity was inevitably raising questions concerning the re-allocation of endowments which had been quasi-charitable in original intention.[214] The municipality of Angers was in search of *Lebensraum,* and projects of social welfare were an unexceptional text on which to base its side of the argument.

CHAPTER VI

THE CHURCH AND SECULAR SOCIETY

I. CHURCHMEN AS EMPLOYERS AND CONSUMERS

THE life of most individuals in the past cannot be recreated. They survive, if at all, only by name, in account books or wages bills, or in the abstract, in generalizations about their social class. We have seen that it is difficult to analyse the spiritual role of the Church in the life of ordinary people in Angers; it is only possible to evoke something of the atmosphere of an ecclesiastical town, give some account of routine religious practices, and some rough statistics of outward conformity. We get nearer to ordinary people and their day-to-day life when we consider their economic relationships with churchmen, for records of monetary transactions can easily be kept and, such is the bias of human nature, they generally are. Angers was dominated by a vast complex of ecclesiastical institutions, which were a centre of consumption and a focus of employment; it is to this aspect of the relations of the Church with secular society that we now turn. The picture that can be given is an impressionistic, not a statistical one. It is not possible to trace right through all consequences of employment and expenditure, to see money passing down from artists and lawyers to their craftsmen and clerks, down to artisans and primary producers; but some idea can be given of the uppermost structure of this pyramid and of the relationships which existed between ecclesiastical institutions and their direct employees.

The many churches of the town, with their rich liturgical life and their keen rivalries, provided continual patronage to a whole colony of artists.[1] Early in the century, Angers was already established as a provincial metropolis of ecclesiastical art and design. Resident there were the architects Baudrillier, who built the new monastery of Saint-Nicolas and the great staircase of Saint-Serge, and Jouin, who reconstructed the choirs of the cathedral and of Saint-Laud, Barauderie, who designed the high altar of Saint-Samson, and the Saint Simon brothers who piled doves and cherubim, vases, flames and garlands on the altar of the Hôtel-Dieu in a frenzy of gilding. Sculptors and woodcarvers set up their workshops in the dark narrow streets of the parish of La Trinité, made their names by producing a masterpiece or two in city churches, and then, as news of

103

the new fashion spread about the diocese, further commissions came in from country districts. Artists from other parts of France and from foreign lands were drawn to this centre of opportunity. Pierre-Etienne Suruge, brother of a famous engraver, came across from Paris, and graduated from work on three minor altars of the church of Sainte-Croix to the monumental task of carving the casing of the cathedral organ. Crescini, an Italian plaster moulder, was working at Saint-Maurice in the sixties, while his compatriot Baroni painted the chapel of the Seminary in 1770. From Würzburg came a German sculptor, Leysner, who adorned the tomb of bishop Vaugirault and designed the woodwork of the cathedral choir. Meanwhile, the tradition of indigenous artists flourished. Ten years before the Revolution, François Bordillon was running a school of architecture and sculpture at his house in the place Cupif; Pierre-Louis David, father of a more famous son, was carving credence tables and church furniture, and Jacques Gaultier of the place du Pilori was in high favour at the cathedral, where he executed new woodwork from Leysner's models, until the sad affair of certain allegorical figures in terra-cotta brought him into temporary disrepute.

Then the churches provided continual employment for skilled craftsmen of various kinds. There were the professional bell-founders of Angers, the families of Trony and Daviau, and Jean Tichant the recluse, living pathetically alone in the rue Châteaugontier;[2] there were organ-builders like Jean Luck, who rented a house from the chapter of Saint-Maurille in the rue de la Roë.[3] We find Chartier, a bookbinder, repairing battered registers of the Faculty of Theology; Landeau, a marble polisher recutting the cathedral credence tables, and in the same year, Deville a jeweller who furnishes four footstools in morocco for the bishop's throne.[4] Denis Lachese, a silversmith, in the course of three years did seventeen items of repair to the ornaments of Saint-Aubin: to chalices, holy-water sprinklers and stoups, censers and their chains, incense boxes, book clasps, the furnishing of new silver nails for a crucifix and a new screw for the precentor's staff, and the replacement of a fragment chipped from a gilded pax.[5] Less romantic articles of church furniture were also required. Thus it was that Eperon, who did routine carpentry repairs to the properties of Saint-Aubin, was called in to devise a five-foot oak box as a spittoon for the vestry, and a mysterious detachable contrivance to raise the seat of dom Lorraine in the choir stalls to a more dignified height.[6] With Eperon, whose yearly bill to the monks came to 600l. or so, we come to the many small craftsmen and artisans of the building trade who were continually employed by ecclesiastical institutions, for repairs and reconstruction were always necessary— to churches, conventual buildings, canonical residences and presbyteries, to extensive housing property within the town and on scattered estates in the countryside. The mason, carpenter, locksmith, plumber, tiler and glazier who figure by name on the registers of the abbey of Toussaint,[7] were representative of trades whose main commissions came from ecclesiastical customers.

Around each monastery there was a hinterland of small tradesmen, who had grown accustomed to supplying consumer goods in a steady stream and to receiving the dilatory payment of the monks. The canons-regular of Toussaint,[8] for example, found their baker, cabinet maker, *perruquier*, carpet seller, mason and locksmith in the street which bore the name of their foundation. Running westwards from their house was the rue Saint-Laud, where their hatter and linen-draper had shops and the furrier who lined their amices against the winter's rigours, while on the other side of the abbey was the rue Sainte-Croix, where they patronized a grocer, a glazier and a chandler; and who should be their apothecary but M. Gouppil, permanent churchwarden of the parish of Saint-Evroul and resident at the very gates of the abbey—it was unthinkable to go past his door to the other side of town where M. Olliver dispensed rhubarb and senna to the Augustins.[9] Then there was always the great item of laundry. Altar linen, albs and surplices, table-cloths and napkins (for the clergy had considerable responsibilities of entertainmant and no wives to supervise their households); everything conspired to ensure constant profits to the laundresses of Angers. Perhaps the bishop[10] was being overcharged when he paid 3*l.* to have his best alb laundered (though its lace-work was delicate), but even an institution which was trying to economize and employed its own washerwoman had to provide a house and 700*l.* or so a year for the service.[11]

Though there was many a thrifty shift or delayed payment,[12] the continual expenditure of the ecclesiastical corporations of Angers on the maintenance of extensive properties and vast buildings, their public obligations in the way of liturgical observances and hospitality, and their steady routine patronage of shopkeepers and artisans, made their activities the central feature of the unprogressive economic life of their city.

Indirectly, the town's economy was parasitic on the Church; a whole legion of people of varying social grades was also directly employed by ecclesiastical institutions. Lawyers supplemented their fees of office by managing the affairs of monasteries and chapters as a side-line. Each fief had its *sénéchal* and a big corporation needed a receiver to collect its diverse and episodic revenues, together with an *avocat*, as a day-to-day legal adviser. The assizes of fiefs had to be held by qualified practitioners, registers had to be maintained, and sales and leases of property recorded and investigated so that feudal incidents could be duly claimed.[13] The diocese employed accountants, registrars, and other lay officials of various kinds, ranging from Apostolic Notaries who took office for the exemptions it carried rather than the fees it produced, to the receivership of clerical taxation, which was worth more than 2,000*l.* a year. Diocesan office might be profitably combined with a clerkship to one of the great corporations; Feuillatreau of the diocesan registry was also secretary to the cathedral chapter, in virtue of which employment he enjoyed a commodious house[14] in the steep narrow street running down from the cathedral to the riverside. Thus, he contrived to achieve a comfortable status in life, at the expense, it is true, of 'wearing out his eyesight', but then, who would not do as much to 'keep the wife he loves so dearly and three small children still in their cradles'?[15]

Musicians of reasonable ability and singers in good voice were certain of employment in Angers. Chapters and abbeys competed for organists, and each chapter had its choir-men, paid from 300*l.* to 400*l.* a year for their services,[16] while terms of appointment at Saint-Maurice were handsome and professional. Next in the lay hierarchy of the liturgy came a goodly company of vergers and sacristans. In monastic and capitular churches the sacrist's office was one of dignity, held by a priest or a tonsured clerk, who would have a lay subordinate under him, someone like the short-sighted individual who groped his way around routine duties at Saint-Maurille for his yearly 180*l.*,[17] or like M. Body, a master tailor who served in his spare time as lay sacristan at Toussaint.[18] No ceremony was complete without its verger. Every year, the *noble confrairie des bourgeois* of the town hired one of the professionals to wear its green velvet gown and lead its procession with due decorum.[19] There were many to choose from, for the cathedral had four (suitably distinguished from all others by red velvet tunics beneath their decent gowns), other chapters two,[20] while even the smallest parish could not be without that dignified decrepit figure who conducted the curé from his house to the church, escorted preachers to the pulpit, and during lulls in his ceremonial duties exercised the traditional function of whipping dogs out of church.[21] In the parishes, the office of verger and of sacristan were combined, though even so, only very small salaries were offered. At Saint-Maurice (the parish church, not the cathedral), which boasted a prosperous congregation, 82*l.* a year was available, while poor Lesvière could rise no higher than 20*l.*[22] Saint-Aignan offered 30*l.*, but its sacristan had to launder the linen and furnish altar breads, incense, brooms and brushes.[23] There was no salary at all at the chapel of La Madeleine (which was the outlying 'district church' of the parish of Saint-Julien) but only perquisites from the occasional offices, the use of a plot of land at a peppercorn rent, and 'voluntary liberalities', like the eggs at Easter.[24] Small rewards indeed for a general factotum whose activities were continually under review by zealous curés and cheeseparing churchwardens. Even so, a gown and staff and a small but regular supplement to income were not to be despised, and the post of parish sacristan was much sought after.

In a parish, the omnicompetent sacristan rang the bell, but monasteries and chapters, with their proud peals and more frequent offices, provided further part-time employment for the able-bodied poor of Angers. Voluntary bell-ringers were frowned upon nowadays by ecclesiastical disciplinarians, who forbade gifts of wine, and positively locked up the belfries at Hallowe'en.[25] That being so, small fees had now to be paid, something in the nature of thirty to forty *livres* a year, with, perhaps, a measure of corn as a supplement.[26] Then, in addition to its bell-ringers, a monastery or a chapter would need to hire other assistants for its manifold ceremonies: hire, for in these days of ecclesiastical wealth, no one performed a liturgical function without being paid for it. Toussaint had not money to spare; even so, its canons-regular found salaries for an organist, an organ-blower and a server at mass, not to mention importing a small boy to act as 'acolyte extraordinary' on Sundays and feast days. Apparently, the original reward for this latter service was dinner at the abbey, but by 1779 the canons had grown tired of eating their soup under the goggling scrutiny of 'le petit Esnault'—'agreed with his mother that he will no longer eat at the abbey, and that instead of a dinner when he attends church, he will be given a 6*l*. gratification'.[27] A modest yearly sum, but it sufficed to place young master Esnault among the hierarchy of juvenile employees of ecclesiastical Angers, far below the aristocracy of choirboys, but well above the proletariat of urchins which earned its yearly tips by opening and closing the doors of the library and lecture rooms of the Faculty of Theology.[28]

Finally there was all that army of household servants that history takes for granted and who intrude themselves upon our notice only when the Revolution ousted them and drove some of them to complain—grooms and footmen at the palace, cooks, laundresses, charwomen, gardeners and porters at the monasteries,[29] the housekeepers of canons and curés and the boys who did odd jobs at vicarages. Great monastic houses, whatever their shortcomings in other respects, were kindly employers, paying modest salaries but either retaining or otherwise providing for their servants in old age and infirmity. Thus Pierre Moreau, after thirty-seven years' service at Saint-Aubin, was given a pension of 50*l*. in 1767, with an assurance of a further 25*l.* so long as he chose to continue performing some nominal duties—which in fact he was still doing twenty-three years later.[30] In 1789, Jean Rogue the verger at Saint-Nicholas was over seventy years of age and had been in office for thirty-four years— his food, lodging, two pair of shoes and 60*l.* p.a. provided him with that 'modest but sufficient subsistence' which his poverty-stricken grown-up children could not afford him.[31] The verger of Saint-Serge, though a younger man, had put in fifty years' service, while the cook there, Pierre Pigeon, who was going blind, pathetically relied upon his Benedictine masters to look after him in his retirement.[32] At the same time, Jean Girard had been gardener at Ronceray for thirty-five years, a woman domestic servant had been there for seventeen years, another employed in the infirmary for twenty-seven, a sempstress for over thirty, while Marie Tramblay had been brought up in the abbey precincts where she had been born, sixty-seven years ago.[33] So it was that Marie Tramblay found her refuge— just as Nicholas Sevière, an illegitimate child, had been taken in by the Benedictines of Lesvière, and found his niche in life as their domestic.[34] It was not only professed religious who found sanctuary in the monasteries.

Urbanity, it is true, did not come so easily when worldly prosperity was in decline; certainly, under the warping pinch of retrenchment, the canons-regular of Toussaint seem to have grown to expect too much from too few for too little. Their porter[35] not only kept the keys, he also rang the bells, swept the courtyard and tailored the monastic habits, all for 120*l.* a year, though it is true that he was free to ply his needle on his own behalf in any spare time that remained to him. Six assistant cooks followed one another in as many years, until at last one was found willing to cook, hew wood, draw water, act as groom, errand boy, supplementary organ-blower and bell-ringer. And the vital problem of a cook proper was never satisfactorily solved. Charles Philemon was an excellent performer, who impressed the visitor of the abbey so much that he ordered an increase in his salary. What inflation of pride or deflation of pastry followed, we do not know, but in the next year, 1772, the canons-regular were looking for a successor. Nine years saw a procession of seven delinquent cooks. Perhaps their terms of appointment give a clue to explain this culinary *malaise* at Toussaint, for a cook there was employed 'on the express condition that he will not take the fat, but will melt it down and strain it for frying or for soups; he will receive 150*l.* wages, without wine, and a New Year's gift of 6*l.*, with permission to sell skins and feathers to his own profit, but nothing more. If his conduct is satisfactory, if he does work about the house, runs errands in town when required, goes to the vineyard to supervise and examine the work there (when services of this sort are compatible with his duties in the kitchen), he will receive 200*l.* a year instead of 150*l.*, and that even in his first year, the whole agreement being based upon the supposition that he knows the art of cookery and pastry making.' At last, in 1781, a man of mature years and a stranger to the province accepted this thankless office, and stayed for six years, when in April 1789, the cycle of inconstant cooks began again.[36] By then, it was very soon to be a question of getting rid of the canons rather than of their cooks.

Painters, architects, carvers, decorators, craftsmen, jewellers, bellfounders, and their assistants; lawyers, notaries, feudists, estate agents, clerks, registrars and receivers; musicians, choir-men and choir-boys, bell-ringers, vergers, sacristans, grave-diggers, sweepers (we must apologize to sacristans for not distinguishing them from this latter class, even in the poorest of parishes);[37] housekeepers, cooks, servants, gardeners and grooms; tailors and robe makers, apothecaries, chandlers and all the members of guilds of provision sellers—a whole economic nexus of trades and professions depended on revenues drawn from the countryside by the great ecclesiastical corporations of Angers. The enumeration may seem fastidious, but it is a catalogue that can bring us very near to the real life of Angers under the old régime and enables us to recreate the atmosphere of a society which the Revolution destroyed more decisively than we sometimes imagine.

When, eventually, Church property had been sold, curé Bernier of Saint-Laud, returning to Angers with a brief foray of Vendean armies, delivered a tremendous sermon in his old parish church regretting the passing of old-fashioned charity. The clergy, he said, 'received with one hand to give with the other. They were the beneficent syphon which drew up the water, distributed it and fertilized the land. . . . The clergy were almsgiving itself. Their property belonged to the people.' [38] An accountant would have to describe all this as wild exaggeration. Alms of great corporations to parishes where they drew tithe, weekly and seasonal distributions of loaves, herrings, broad-beans and the like by great abbeys, cauldrons of soup sent round to prisoners in the town jail, and other routine charities do not form an impressive percentage of ecclesiastical wealth.[39] On the other hand, in crises of public misery churchmen made great contributions and individual ecclesiastics were often remarkably generous. More than this, almsgiving apart, in another and less direct sense, when we study ecclesiastical property-owners, we can see Bernier's 'beneficent syphon' working. They transferred capital, inefficiently enough, into artistic, cultural and educational development, and into maintaining status, rather than into economic progress. Lawyers and artists at the top of the scale, tradesmen in the centre, and many very ordinary folk at the bottom of the scale drew a living from the Church, which was a steady patriarchal employer and customer, encouraging respectability rather than initiative or advertisement. The kind of employment ecclesiastical institutions had to offer was suitable, not only for the able or the able-bodied, but often for the weak and the misfits of society, and it was, too, in many cases part-time employment which served to preserve the indigent from the utmost consequences of their state. The poor were cushioned against the rigours of outright economic competition, not so much by alms, as by employment, and were, for good and for ill, held back from rapid absorption into the developing cadres of capitalist production. Those who benefited most from the Church were, however, by definition, those whose voices counted least. The history of the relations of ecclesiastical life with the rank and file of secular society is the story of censured cooks and commended choir-boys which we have told, a series of relations which have no thread to link them together into formal history.

The dull and unenterprising administration of their property by ecclesiastical corporations and their dealings with their many grades of servants and officials form one aspect of the relations of the Church with secular society in this period, but it does not provide us with an eventful or developing theme, or indicate the desires and passions which were to mould future events. It is only when we consider the municipality of Angers, a bourgeois oligarchy, full of improving zeal, oddly but genuinely representative of its own social class, envious of the properties, exemptions and distinctions of ecclesiastics, that the pattern of tensions in provincial society begins to foreshadow social metamorphosis and revolutionary events. Here there is a developing attitude, a steady formulation of policy, and it is to this that we must turn.

2. AN ENVIOUS MUNICIPALITY AND THE FIRST ORDER IN THE STATE

In eighteenth-century France temporal and spiritual were closely knit together. When a King was crowned or a criminal executed their ceremonies combined to manifest in outward symbols an inter-dependence on which the social order was founded. 'Rome was never more flourishing', said a speaker at the Angevin Academy, 'than when its citizens, loyal to their religion, made it a duty to show respect to the gods and to begin their military and civil exercises with religious ceremonies.' [40] In Angers as elsewhere, on all occasions of municipal or national celebrations, ecclesiastical pageantry, copes and crosses, sermons and sonorous *Te Deums* were interwoven with profane flags and fireworks, bonfires and volleys of musketry. When a peace treaty was signed, or a royal child born, the bishop was invited to assist the mayor in lighting a bonfire on the fairground, while all civic officials attended a general procession and a *Te Deum*. Outside Saint-Maurice the town militia paraded, to honour the temporal power by a salvo of musketry when the mayor entered the cathedral, and the spiritual by a salvo at the elevation of the mass.[41] Every year, the city magistrates were in attendance when the royal chapters of Saint-Laud and Saint-Martin observed the birthday of *Monsieur*, brother of Louis XVI and count apanagist of Anjou; they took their place in the *Sacre* and in the cathedral's procession of Saint-Sebastian, and on Palm Sunday they walked behind the bishop when he went to hear a sermon at Saint-Michel du Tertre.[42] A Mass of the Holy Spirit was celebrated at the church of the Cordeliers when new aldermen were installed,[43] the merchants of the *Bourse de Commerce* paid their hebdominal corporate devotions,[44] and a religious service marked the opening of the law terms—'the path which brings you back to the temple of justice,' said a magistrate sententiously, 'leads through the sanctuary of the divinity.' [45]

Lawyers and aldermen did not, however, forget their due rights of precedence when passing through the sanctuary. Invitations from the spiritual authority must come in due form; the municipality was bitterly affronted by being invited through the mayor, instead of corporately, to a *Te Deum* for the peace of 1783, and threatened to retaliate in kind by issuing future invitations to the cathedral chapter through the dean instead of to the assembled canons.[46] And at official services, those who came to praise God or honour the King were determined to do so from pews appropriate to their rank and station. Ecclesiastical and lay corporations alike kept careful records of precedents. There was a strict rule at Saint-Maurice, for example, that officers of the *Présidial* and *Sénéchaussée* were confined to benches in the choir, except at the five episcopal feasts of the year, when they had a special allowance of three stalls, but then only if the bishop himself was actually present to celebrate.[47] Unforeseen circumstances nevertheless sometimes did arise and cause a scandalous dispute, like that between the municipal officers and the canons of Saint-Martin at a service of thanksgiving for the preservation of Louis XV from Damiens' dagger stroke.[48] In a provincial town, churches were the chief public places where men could make display of their rank;[49] thus it was that this specialized form of rivalry had arisen, for which a Jesuit wit of Angers coined an appropriate name —*Scamnomanie*, 'pew-mania'.[50]

Behind these disputes for barren honours, deeper interests and emotions were concealed. On the one side there was jealousy, on the other distrust. The clergy formed the most powerful corporation in the city. Not only did they own vast possessions and enjoy signal exemptions, but also, at a time when every other order of society was divided and atomized, they alone formed a strong and united group, which never failed to bring its full influence to bear in defence of its privileges. While a map of ecclesiastical Angers reveals a loose federation of institutions, at once united and divided by alliances and feuds and all the whimsical stratifications which history had imposed, even so, the Church which faced secular society in the town was a unity. There was no divided weakness in its negotiations with the intendant at Tours, or his *subdélégué*, with agents of the Farmers-General, or with the municipal officers. It was a local branch of the most powerful and self-conscious organization in France, the first order in the state, which held its own assemblies, voted, assessed and collected its own taxation, and appealed directly to Versailles on all matters affecting dignities and privileges. The business affairs of a diocese were concentrated in the hands of its *syndic*, and he was in constant touch with headquarters in Paris. Here, two 'Agents-General' of the clergy of France, polished young aristocrats awaiting their episcopal purple, administered the Church in intervals between Assemblies; behind them was a permanent bureau with its neat files of precedents, and a council of expert lawyers which met for consultations every week. From thence, dioceses drew their legal advice, and to the centre of this web went their complaints, to set in motion all the stratagems of politics. On routine matters, a syndic would be in touch with the lawyer who was permanent head of the bureau, a Beauvais or a Duchesne; and if he was wise, it would be an affable correspondence. We find many a brace of red-legged partridges of Anjou accompanying the mail up to Paris from our diocese, and some cunningly drafted legal memoirs coming in return—unknown to the agents of the clery, 'for you'll understand that a general of any army is jealous to keep the battle honours for himself'.[51] In important matters, a deferential address,[52] embellished with good wishes for the season of the year, or for a suitable see, would be sent to one of the agents-general directly: in a crisis, the bishop himself would write, or call when he was in the capital. A distinguished personage like the abbess of Ronceray would also feel entitled to call in person, and would come across from her Parisian lodging at Port Royal to discuss the business of her abbey.[53] From the office of the agents-general came a continual stream of advice, and sometimes, an intervention would be made with the government in favour of the diocese. A letter might be sent to the intendant to save some pious institution from financial exactions, or to establish the privilege of officials employed by the clergy, a complaint might go to the duc de Choiseul at the War Office to rescue a gardener from the draw for the militia, or a signature be obtained from Turgot himself to defend a curé against victimization by the tax-farmers.[54] If by any chance the council of lawyers at Paris made a wrong decision, they were quick to amend their mistake, and if it so happened that a case was won which they had expected to be lost, they immediately requested copies of all documents, so that the benefits of the triumph could be spread to all dioceses.[55] Thus it was impossible for the privileges of churchmen of Angers to be gnawed away, either by agents of the government or by the municipality. Behind the clergy of town and diocese stood the most efficient bureaucracy in France.

This central administrative organization of the Church had as its chief function the defence of clerical immunities from ordinary taxation, and it was this privilege in particular which the municipality of Angers looked upon with a jealous eye. As the ecclesiastical order voted its own finance directly to the Crown, any municipal levy destined to buy off a national tax could not apply to churchmen.[56] For example, a duty on wines which was imposed in the seventeenth century to provide a composition in lieu of the *taille* was paid by laymen alone.[57] Similarly, ecclesiastics were exempt from the due of *franc-fief* paid by commoners who acquired noble property. Difficulties over this privilege were raised by financial officials at Tours, but they were overcome by the aid of the legal staff of the agents-general, so that the clergy of Angers never had cause to regret their refusal to join with the town in buying off this burden.[58] Naturally enough, the municipality was not willing to concede more than the letter of the law allowed. A royal edict of 1758 concerning dues levied at town gates defined clerical exemptions as applying to 'food-stuffs that they bring in from the produce of their benefices, and for their own consumption only'. A great deal depended on that 'and'. The syndic of the clergy of Anjou persuaded the authorities to give 'benefices' its wide and, indeed, obvious meaning, but he could not convince them that 'and' did any more than combine two limiting factors, each being an indispensable condition for enjoyment of the privilege. Thus, he said, 'the exemption for the diocese is reduced to nothing, or practically nothing, for the ecclesiastics of towns'.[59]

The central government was no less interested in reducing clerical exemptions to a minimum. For three centuries, the abbey of Saint-Aubin had enjoyed a generous measure of tax-free salt—they 'lived on fish', its monks disingenuously explained, as well as sharing their salt with their abbot, a dependent priory at Châteaugontier, the farmers on their estates and the curé of their parish. All these arguments were of no avail when the brusque abbé Terray became

Controller General. He roundly accused our Benedictines of dishonest trafficking and reduced their exemption by 75 per cent. 'All representations on your part to obtain a greater quantity of salt will be absolutely useless . . . furthermore, it is only right that every order of citizens should contribute to a burden which has become necessary to provide for the needs of the state.' [60] With such sentiments, the local authorities were in full agreement, and they co-operated with conspiratorial glee in any official designs against the clergy. Discussions in January 1772 between canon Mezeray, syndic of the clergy of Anjou, the mayor of Angers and a local agent of the Farmers-General[61] illustrate this triangular relationship of clergy, town, and central government in matters of taxation. Two officers of the local militia called on the canon asking him to sign in a register a declaration of the numbers of persons in his household. As this census was manifestly concerned with tax assessment, the syndic refused. On the following day, he sought out the mayor to demand an explanation. According to the mayor, the Farmers-General were complaining that the town was furnishing them with inexact statistics, so that the muncipality was now covering itself by making each householder responsible for his own statement; canon Mezeray replied that ecclesiastics could be under no obligation to sign declarations concerning taxes which did not apply to them. That afternoon, the syndic proceeded to the office of the *directeur des gabelles* and flourished at him the 'contract' of 1765 which officially reconfirmed the privileges of the clergy of France. Finally, both officials agreed to write to their higher commands in Paris to invoke verdicts from the experts. Clearly, as this incident shows, the municipality was not concerned to go out of its way to be accommodating; where a purely local imposition was concerned, it might even resort to a certain amount of sharp practice to extract a contribution from an ecclesiastical institution. When the streets were paved, the monks of Saint-Nicolas, who lived well outside the walls, were called upon to subscribe, and when new street lighting was installed, an equally unjustifiable requisition was made upon the canons of Saint-Laud, which the intendant quashed out-of-hand on appeal.[62]

The clergy defended the outworks of their privileges with as much vigour as they applied to maintaining their central fortress. This was an age when liberties depended on precedents, and when it was hard to guess what subtle form the next exaction would take. It was impossible to relax, so that every minor issue must be fought, as no one could tell whether or not a major battle would soon depend upon its outcome. Canon Louet, of the cathedral, wrote in 1787[63] concerning an Apostolic Notary who had been subjected to the *corvée*, that, even though this system of forced labour had now been abolished, a protest must still be made. 'It is in any case a blow at our privileges, which might have repercussions if *corvées* are at any time re-established, which might well be the case.' Such lay officials of the church, Apostolic Notaries, lawyers, registrars, receivers of clerical taxation and the like were supposed to share clerical immunities, thus not only had their rights to be maintained as a sort of outer line of defence, but also, more practically, able men would be willing to accept such offices with their meagre perquisites only so long as the accompanying privileges subsisted.[64] At the end of the old régime, from various places in the diocese came news of Apostolic Notaries haunted by their fellow-citizens to bear their share in the burden of billeting troops, in *corvées* or in paying a *vingtième*.[65] In Angers itself, however, the clerical grip had been strong enough to force an advantageous settlement of such questions before the turn of the half century. In 1743 the municipality unearthed a half-forgotten royal declaration of 1715 which was used as a pretext for subverting the privileges of these lay officials in ecclesiastical employment, sub-jecting them to augmentations of capitation, and to billeting, and rejecting the claims of their servants to immunity from militia service. Faced by threats of an appeal to the Royal Council, the town gave way and in 1746 agreed that three Apostolic Notaries and five other officials of the clergy in Angers would be left undisturbed in their rights.[66] This concordat lasted, precluding further disputes except with regard to the drawing of lots for the militia. In 1766, great difficulties were raised over the exemption of a gardener of one Le Roux, *avocat du clergé*, and even the servant who looked after canon Mezeray's country-house was in some danger.[67] But the agree-ment of 1746 proved conclusive, and it was not until 1774 that the municipality found an opportunity for revenge. News of a ruthless royal ordinance against those who fraudulently took the tonsure to escape conscription arrived, and the local officials decided to insist upon a strict and retroactive application of the law to students in the Seminary.[68] It was odd that a lawyer's gardener should escape and seminarists be threatened; it is an illustration of the military fallacy of a too rigid line of defence.

But the main factor in the relations between the Church and bourgeois society in Angers was property rather than privilege. Churchmen and citizens were in constant touch along a whole frontier of debts, leases, rents and feudal incidents. Bishop de Lorry was, no doubt, an aloof and distant figure to Massoneau in his bakery and that good lady Renée Coudray in her butcher's shop, yet both knew him well enough as the creditor who had prior claim on the inheritance of bishop de Grasse. The story of the 'petit livre parti-cular que la dem[lle] Coudray tenait exprès pour M. De Grasse', with its outstanding debt of 1,891*l*. 10*s*. 9*d*. is a sad one, yet a prelate who was left with 100,000*l*. worth of repairs on his hands and only half that amount available from the sale of the furniture of his predecessor could not afford to be sentimental.[69] This legal priority given to repairs on the property of ecclesiastical benefices brought about hard cases, but it was not unreasonable. Trouble arose more often from the demands of chapters and monasteries in their capacity as overlords of fiefs. By now, feudal rights had more financial than administrative significance, but even so, an attempt to revive latent powers might lead to an extravagant incident. In 1762, the cathedral chapter decided to take its position as 'baron du grand fief' in the old city seriously, and appointed two canons as its commissioners of police. Two years later, ordinances were printed ordering householders to have the streets swept and a beadle went round with sommations to ensure performance. Great was the rage of magistrates of the *Présidial* at this incursion of ecclesiastics into temporal affairs: 'one of them, M. de Livonnière, a *conseiller* resident in the *cité* in the house called Saint-Laud, tore down with his own hands the ordinance which was affixed to the pillar near the corner of the diocesan registry of finance'.[70] Generally, however, litigation and ill-feeling on matters feudal arose from the network of financial incidents in which property owners of the town were entangled.[71] Of these, *deshérence* or escheat was the most contentious. It went far beyond the common-sense right of a property owner to sell off the possessions of a lessee who died without any claimant to his succession appearing;[72] it was not a logical and practical right, but a feudal exaction, extending over the whole fief, and capable of subtle legal interpretations of the various customary laws of inheritance. Professional feudists, with the archives of chapters and monasteries to aid them, were a potential menace to the expectations of heirs. At one and the same time in the seventies the canons of Saint-Martin and Saint-Maurille and the monks of Saint-Nicolas were engaged in lawsuits over inheritances they hoped to confiscate. The opposition lawyers affected to believe that a feudal onslaught on the citizens was beginning. 'Your courts will resound with disputes of this kind, which are always burdensome to citizens of limited means, though the chapters of Angers, opulent feudal lords, count outlay on a lawsuit a mere nothing if it can bring them some pickings from their fiefs. The glamour of these proceedings will attract the attention of our lay holders of feudal rights. That is what makes this whole business dangerous.'[73]

Lawsuits between private citizens and landowning corporations are phenomena too inevitable to be employed in isolation as evidence of general opinion. The municipality of Angers, however, was less concerned with the dues and rights derived by ecclesiastics from their possessions, than with the vast extent of those possessions themselves and the barrier which they imposed across all avenues of civic development. Privileges, immunities and obsolete feudal perquisites form a less significant theme in the relations of the Church with local society than the sheer fact of property holding in itself. The chief common interest of the Angevin bourgeoisie in the eighteenth century, an interest which became more consciously defined in their minds with each year that passed, was to change the medieval ground plan of their city to a form better suited to both their patriotism and their purses. Progress demanded changes, and changes could only be made at the expense of ecclesiastical property owners.

3. THE ISSUE OF CHURCH PROPERTY

Throughout the eighteenth century the municipal oligarchy of Angers had been anxious to adorn and modernize the city, and in the seventies and eighties this improving zeal redoubled. Houses were numbered, special plates were put on the doors of firemen,[74] street lighting was installed, rescue stations set up by the riverside, the old iron chains across the streets were removed, fountains were restored, a square named after *Monsieur*, the King's brother, and a new promenade were cleared. Economic motives were not absent from the minds of town-planning enthusiasts, for eight new free fairs were established, the canal of the port Ayrault was dredged and new quays and loading areas planned. A mayor or alderman could have no greater ambition than to be embalmed for the memory of posterity either in a street name, or presiding in marble effigy over the regimented shrubs of some formal garden.

The vast property of the Church—men spoke of it generally as comprising 'three-quarters of the town'[75]—was inevitably involved in all schemes of improvement. Twenty years after the failure of its project to make a public square on the site of the deserted church of Saint-Maimbeuf,[76] the town council turned its attention to the congested place Saint-Maurille, which was enlarged in 1783 by the purchase of land from the canons of Saint-Maurille and Saint-Pierre.[77] However, it proved much easier to buy a cemetery from canons than a dilapidated house from a religious order, as the comedy of the quai de la poissonerie was to demonstrate. In 1786, the town was offering 1,200*l.* to the Augustins for a house they owned on the quayside; a year later, the friars are being summoned to demolish the ruinous building within twenty-four hours (an order issued by authorization of Parlement itself); in 1788, the good monks are still holding out.[78] Other religious orders in Angers were more enlightened but equally tenacious. In 1782, the Benedictines of Saint-Serge

I

closed a path through their meadow which was the only means of communication for carriages or horses between the suburban hamlet of Saint-Serge and the town, 'seeing that various individuals have tried to make this concession into a definite right of way'.[79] It so happened, however, that floods made this path impassable during several months of the year, so that when M. de la Besnardière, who was setting up a factory in the quarter of Saint-Serge, offered to make a new road, the municipality negotiated an agreement with the monks, who received an appropriate compensation.[80] In town the Cordeliers were also astride an equally strategic route, and they exacted a tribute from the city as price for their complacency in allowing a passage from the pillory to the place Falloux. The municipality offered 600l. in 1784, but the friars stood out for a much more expensive compensation which was ultimately granted— 'a handsome and solid grille of iron-work', ten feet high, with points 6 to 8 inches long, to be erected in front of the porch of their church.[81] The property of Saint-Serge was again under discussion in the summer of 1788, when M. de la Revellière-Lépeaux informed the municipality that this monastery was willing to surrender some land to form a botanical garden, 'being anxious to favour such a useful establishment'.[82] It was true that the only land available on the fashionable side of town belonged to Saint-Serge, but the 'anxiety' of the Benedictines to be helpful owed something to the enthusiasm of amateur botanists. Certainly, investigation showed that an 'exorbitant' rent was being demanded,[83] and our disillusioned *Botanophiles* invoked the standing committee of the Provincial Assembly of Anjou to put pressure on the monks through its influential aristocratic members.[84] These negotiations with Saint-Serge had been paralleled by the negotiations of the Society of Agriculture with Saint-Aubin twenty years earlier.[85] Those who had urgent reason to seek land within or near the city walls of Angers were at the mercy of ecclesiastical proprietors.

One may detect a continuous hardening of the attitude of the municipality towards this question of ecclesiastical property throughout the century. In 1715, it hoped to do no more than prevent any new religious houses establishing themselves in the city and 'cool the embarrassing and unnecessary zeal' of prospective founders,[86] but by the last decade or so of the old régime, schemes of downright expropriation became a commonplace of local politics. To understand the mental climate in which these ideas grew, one should remember that Church property in France was regarded as, in a certain sense, public property. It was held in *usufruct*, the clergy were its administrators, and the King, or the nation, or 'the national will' (according as to whether it is Louis XIV speaking early in the century or Cerfvol or Talleyrand towards its end), could intervene to ensure that it was used to best advantage.[87] By this title, the state could deprive the clergy of their common-law liberty of acquiring landed property; hence, there was a steady tightening-up of the laws of mortmain, which in 1749 were brought to their highest point of stringency. 'According to the ideas expressed in this Edict', wrote the then bishop of Angers,[88]

it seems that churchmen are foreigners, and not the children and relatives of the King's subjects, and as if their income is not spent in the kingdom or used to help the other subjects of the King and the poor; and all of us who are subject to mortmain are depicted as men who have no other aim than getting hold of the property of the laity.

Without formal authorization by letters-patent, the clergy could make no new acquisitions; meanwhile a *droit d'amortissement* was levied ruthlessly on any improvement or extension made to property they possessed already. Tax-collectors made the most fantastic claims. If a decayed priory were united to the Seminary, or a canonical house repaired, or a new lease made, or a building changed to a different use, or a composition accepted for the surrender of a feudal due, they were there immediately demanding their fine.[89] By systematic espionage on the part of its agents, the government was teaching the country at large to keep a watchful eye on the posses-sions of the Church.

From 1774, this lesson was continued by *Monsieur*, the comte de Provence, who held the duchy of Anjou as part of his apanage. In February of that year, all old ecclesiastical corporations of the province were bombarded with circulars demanding 'foy et hom-mages, aveux et dénombrements'.[90] This grotesque revival of claims to feudal homage was a financial device which the Crown had already attempted to use against the clergy of France, but the lawyers of *Monsieur*, unlike the lawyers of the Crown, were not will-ing to allow delays for discussion. There was a great ransacking of archives among the clergy of Angers. The monks of Saint-Serge and the canons of Saint-Martin laboured to collect evidence to confute the allegation that their predecessors had rendered such homage earlier in the century,[91] while the cathedral chapter proved from its charters that it had held its lands a century before fiefs were in-vented.[92] From the agents-general at Paris came exhortations to stand firm, lest a precedent detrimental to the whole Church of France be created.[93] The benefice holders of Anjou did stand firm, though their gloom deepened, as in the following year feudal seizures began, and a first wave of bailiffs come in to confiscate the revenues of Saint-Serge and Lesvière.[94] In the end, clerical obstinacy and procrastination weathered the storm, and defeatists like canon Roustille of Saint-Maurice were proved mistaken. Nevertheless, the legal rights or wrongs of the affair had not been decided, while later events in the apanage of the duc d'Orléans showed that claims to homage might be revived.[95] It seemed as if the privileged classes at the end of the old régime were determined to draw attention to the absurdity of their pretensions and to the extent of their possessions.

From 1777 onwards, the landed property held by religious corporations in Angers was brought to the notice of every inhabitant by an acrimonious debate which sprang from a royal declaration of March of that year.[96] By this new regulation, municipalities were ordered to transfer their cemeteries out of town to new locations in the countryside, which parishes would have to acquire at their own charges. This reform was long overdue: everywhere in France one heard lugubrious stories of 'cadaverous odours' and 'mephitic vapours' hanging over pestilential graveyards and dank funeral vaults.[97] Each parish in Angers had its own cemetery near its church: now, the municipality and the bishop, in obedience to orders from an enlightened government, sought to interdict their use and prevent further burials within the town.

For as long as they were able, parsimonious parish councils, more conscious of considerations of hard cash than of hygiene, resisted, and a discussion of parochial population and boundaries, and a review of all available land near the town ensued—which was, in fact, a review of the property of ecclesiastical institutions. In any case, men regarded it as only fitting that compulsory purchase for such a purpose should be exercised at the expense of churchmen; the aldermen of Tours, consulted by their opposite numbers in Angers, recommended this as a matter of policy. We have looked out suitable sites, they said, 'and have had the honour to indicate them to our prelate; these sites are lands which belong to ecclesiastical corporations'.[98] In 1784, a solution to the problem was found for two groups of parishes. La Trinité and Saint-Jacques shared a new site with the Hôtel-Dieu, purchased from the lands of a chapel known as *Guinefolle*, while the parishes of Saint-Maurice, Sainte-Croix, Saint-Aignan, Saint-Evroul and Lesvière were allowed to use the cemetery of Saint-Laud.[99] This left seven parishes within the town walls still in search of a suitable plot of land. A commission of the municipality and of the *Présidial* had suggested territory occupied by the Minims,[100] and in the following year the parish of Saint-Denis was prepared to survey in the exact location—'the land of the second garden of the Friars Minor of this town, that is to say, the area which is at the far end of that garden, now planted with vegetables'.[101] But when this new cemetery was put into use in 1784, it proved to have solid rock near the surface, and no drainage. As curé Robin of Saint-Pierre protested, it was theologically undesirable to commit bodies, not to the earth, but to water, 'which is not their element'.[102] Surveyors and churchwardens renewed their searches, and sites belonging to the chapter of Saint-Martin, the monastery of Saint-Serge and the house of the Visitation were investigated.[103] Saint-Michel du Tertre now contracted out of this coalition of parishes, buying its own plot of land from Saint-Serge, which was duly consecrated by the curé on 15 December 1785.[104] It was not until three years later that the other parishes found a suitable place for their cemetery near la Croix-Montaille, which was consecrated by Huchelou des Roches, curé of Saint-Julien, on 10 August 1788. But the great dispute was still not over. The path to the new cemetery was unsatisfactory and circuitous, leading to a demand for higher wages by grave-diggers and constituting a danger to life and limb for mourning parties; consequently, the combined curés made an appeal at law against their bishop's interdiction of their old burial grounds. And the solution proposed to this new difficulty again involved the property of an ecclesiastical institution—a new road was required through the park of the Visitation.[105] The parish priests concerned petitioned the municipality for ruthless action to obtain a right of way. 'In view in these circumstances, *Messieurs*, could you ask these ladies to agree voluntarily to this project, and if they refuse, which we think is unlikely, could you use compulsory means of action, seeing that this is a question involving the public interest?' [106]

Attention had thus been focussed on the details of ecclesiastical property owning. Peripheral areas of these vast possessions had, indeed, already become a no-man's-land, in which churchmen were unable to put their rights of ownership to effective use. There was a lesson visible in the abandoned chapels of the town.[107] Two were used by parishes as 'district churches', but a dozen others were falling into ruin or were being applied to secular uses. Lepers had once worshipped in the chapel of Saint-Lazare, but there were no lepers now; the Recollets had not been allowed to annex the Commandery of Saint-Laud for their offices, so that this old home of the Knights Templar was abandoned and its dependent chapel of Saint-Blaise was a ruin;[108] the doors of the little church of Saint-Fiacre were never opened now; the chapel of the Saint-Esprit was a private house and garden; the fashion of attending services at Saint-Eutrope had waned, and since the day of Saint-Laurent had been removed from the calendar of holiday feasts few pilgrims came to the shrine that bore his name.[109] Then, there was the church of Saint-Maimbeuf, once the seat of a chapter, but now empty and useless. Even so, when the municipal officers sought a building where the *torches* of the

Sacre could be stored, none of these was made available. The Seminary refused to allow Saint-Maimbeuf to be used, and the monks of Lesvière were persuaded to hand over the keys of the chapel of Saint-Eutrope only on condition of receiving a rent of 50*l.* a year.[110]

This leasing out of property which could no longer be maintained in its ecclesiastical usage was typical of monasteries. A certain widow Goujou rented a house and orchard in the domain of the Cordeliers, old Miss Coineau had a lease for her lifetime of a tiny cottage which was inextricably entangled with the main building of the Jacobins, and poor widow Brault lived in a coach-house in the stable yard of Toussaint.[111] At the Jacobins, too, M. Falloux du Coudray, an official of the *Chambre des Comptes* of Nantes, leased the *maison Saint-Dominique* directly adjoining the friars' church, while M. Prezeau de la Haie lived in a building which had once served the Dominicans as an infirmary.[112] Rich laymen lived in the old abbatial mansion and the new one at Saint-Aubin, and poor laymen paid small rents for a room in the tower, a lodge at the entrance, and a flat over the main gateway,[113] not to mention Pierre Tourneur, who stored his wood in a little cellar under the great tower.[114] Half-empty convents hired out their state rooms for public purposes. *La Nation d'Anjou*, one of the six 'nations' of the University, met in the Cordeliers, the Faculty of Medicine and the notaries of the town held their assemblies in the Jacobins, so too, from October 1787, did the standing committee of the Provincial Assembly of Anjou.[115] The apothecaries held their guild sessions in the Recollets, the dyers in the parlour of the Augustins, and the fishermen of the hamlet of Reculé in the Capuchins.[116] Business agents of absentee abbots inserted notices in the local paper advertising abbatial houses to let. Mr. Swinfort, an Englishman, occupied the prior's residence at Lesvière in 1777, after him came a cavalry captain, and in 1782 the tenancy was on the market again; the residence of the abbot of Saint-Nicolas, with apartments improved by milord Southwell during his stay in Angers, was being offered in 1782 and 1785.[117] The church was shrinking back inside its territory, leaving a fringe of secular leaseholders on its boundaries.

And this was at a time when, in other respects, churchmen were busily engaged in winding up the legacy of the Middle Ages. In the cathedral, axes and hammers broke up the carved work thereof, and in 1782, old woodwork of the choir, more than a hundred stalls, an episcopal throne, a sacristy door and 'the stand of the reliquary of Saint-Maurille, enriched with gilded ornaments', were up for auction.[118] Clearly, there was nothing sacred about the past, or about the traditional uses of ecclesiastical property. An irreverent carpenter who stored his planks in the cemetery of Saint-Maurice[119] was but imitating his betters. Benefices and revenues were also being re-allotted. Chantry chapels were ruthlessly suppressed to bring about a logical consolidation of revenues. A whole batch of forty-five of these foundations was absorbed by the chapter of Saint-Maurice in 1769,[120] and five years later it was agreed that masses in the chapel of Saint-Denis des Bretonniers should be reduced from sixty-five a year to twenty-four.[121] In other chapters, and in parishes, foundation masses and traditional observances were discontinued when their revenues had become insufficient to acquit the charges.[122] They were forgetting that the best method of teaching men to violate the private rights of the living is to take no account of the wishes of the dead.[123]

When some useful ecclesiastical foundation was projected it was common practice for bishops or ministers of the Crown to look around for decayed old institutions which could be united with the new to supplement its revenues. That was how the almonry of Saint-Jacques-de-la-Forêt and the Collège de la Fourmagerie had been absorbed by the Hôpital Général of Angers in the seventeenth century,[124] and the chapters of Saint-Julien and Saint-Maimbeuf by the Seminary. Such unions were enforced quite often and spoken of continually. As recently as 1746 the Jesuits of La Flèche had been given the Angevin abbey of Asnières-Bellay to add to their other abbeys and priories;[125] when in their turn the Jesuits were suppressed the municipality of Angers first thought was to attract endowments from La Flèche to its own Collège d'Anjou.[126] New expectations were aroused by proposals of suppressions put forward by the Monastic Commission of 1768: the Assembly General of the Clergy of Anjou for example, which thirty years ago had obtained the priories of Cunault and Broc for the 'Seminary of Saint-Charles', now asked for the priory of La Haie aux Bonshommes, a dependency of the doomed order of Grammont.[127] The Commission had also scheduled Saint-Serge for liquidation. It had survived, though from the beginning of his rule bishop de Lorry had manœuvred to make the union of his abbey with his episcopal see a permanency.[128] 'Unions' then were a commonplace in ecclesiastical reforms or intrigues; nor did laymen fail to notice any tamperings with traditional revenues.

More especially were they watchful when such suggestions were made by the wealthier ecclesiastical institutions of the town. Rumours of a project to unite the chapters of Saint-Maurille and Saint-Pierre to that of the cathedral in April 1784, and a direct proposition by the abbess of Ronceray rather less than a year later for a union of various benefices to her abbey, led to immediate reactions on the part of the municipality.[129] In the latter business the town council had a sound case on purely religious grounds against the abbess: quite rightly, it insisted that there was a primary need for an increase in the income of the curé of La Trinité and the creation of a new parish in the faubourg Saint-Lazare. Essentially, however, lay opposition to such attempts to consolidate ecclesiastical incomes had more interested motives, which had been clearly formulated in 1702 when the town protested against the union of the chapters of Saint-Maimbeuf and Saint-Julien to the Seminary—'the town has a notable interest to conserve the titles of benefices, which ought to be possessed by local men, rather than by strangers'.[130] But disputes raised by these issues were very minor affairs compared to the storm which arose when news was received that the bishop of Séez, titular abbot of Saint-Aubin, intended to have that dignity permanently united to his see. The municipality trembled at the thought of these rich revenues leaving the province for ever,[131] and, as year after year, this alien bishop's sinister design moved forward, town and clergy in Angers formed a firm alliance to oppose it.[132] If the bishop of Séez could propose to appropriate the revenues of an abbey, why should not the town of Angers do the same, forestall him in fact, and use the income for its charitable projects? In 1784, the city magistrates were hoping, that if their attempt to rescue Saint-Aubin failed, at least they might be allowed 12,000l. from its revenues towards the establishment of an Enfants trouvés.[133] Afterwards, they reduced their anticipations by half, but hope never quite died away, and the same theme generally recurs whenever they were driven to speculate upon the bishop's machinations.[134]

For long, indeed, the municipality had cherished this hope of setting up a foundling hospital in Angers. If there is any truth in the statistics cited by town officials, the situation was appalling, and the need desperate. They spoke of 500 children abandoned in a single year, of one wretched infant that was devoured by scavenging dogs, of waggon-loads of babies carted off to Paris by contractors whose profits on deaths were greater than those on survivals.[135] Other provincial towns had established orphanages long ago;[136] Angers was well behind-hand in philanthropic initiative. Such a worthy venture was one in which the aid of ecclesiastics was naturally expected, and given. Bishop de Lorry, whose interest was solicited as soon as he arrived, contrived to make his usual judicious interventions,[137] the Benedictines of Saint-Serge had already made a generous offer of financial aid,[138] and in 1787, an ecclesiastic who insisted on remaining anonymous gave 22,000l.[139] But chapters and monasteries which drew feudal increments from their fiefs in Angers and the surrounding countryside were involved in the project in a more mundane and obligatory fashion. Abandoned children were the responsibility of the feudal overlord, who appropriated inheritances when heirs failed and was therefore not unjustly constrained to set the expenses of births against the profits of deaths. The establishment of an Enfants trouvés would gratuitously lighten the burden on feudal superiors unless some scale of contribution was laid down and enforced against them. A draft project of 1769 suggested a total levy of 2,000*l*. a year on fiefs in the town itself,[140] and from what we know of the finances of the three institutions chiefly concerned (the chapters of Saint-Maurice, Saint-Pierre and Saint-Maurille), it appears to have been a fair estimate. The municipality continually reverted to this business of a contribution without being able to come to a definite settlement.[141] It is true that the bishop promised to unite benefices to the new foundation in proportion to the value of its services to ecclesiastical fiefs, but it proved impossible to extract reliable statistics of the numbers of children abandoned in the various quarters of the city. Indeed, in 1786, an angry official accused churchmen of deliberately refusing to keep records so that their responsibilities could not be brought home to them.[142] Perhaps it was expecting too much to ask for such figures without giving any guarantee of how they would be used. Even if fiefs paid their share, there would still be a large initial outlay for which the municipality would be responsible, and its zeal in the cause of orphan children did not extend to an enthusiasm for paying out monies on their behalf. There was a general hope in Angers that some ecclesiastical revenues would be confiscated, and an Enfants trouvés set up at no expense to the citizens whatever.

Long ago, a scheme for taking the priory of Lesvière had been mooted, and in 1769 this was still regarded as the obvious location.[143] Let the revenues of a neighbouring monastic house and of the *Confrèrie des bourgeois* be added to those of Lesvière, and 12,000*l*. a year would be available as a basic income for the proposed foundation. Five years later, the municipal officers were still hoping to annex the revenues of the *Confrèrie des bourgeois*[144] and set up their orphanage out in the countryside, this time, in the buildings of the decayed priory of La Haie aux Bonshommes. Its titular prior had agreed to the suppression of his benefice, provided he was allowed to retain a life interest in the revenues, though it was supposed that he would surrender this too in the end. Here, once again, hopes were raised that the new institution would be founded, 'without its costing a penny, either to the State, or to the subjects of the King'.[145] These projects failed. 'Zealous citizens', said a propagandist, 'had cast their eyes upon various monastic establishments, but the opposition of these corporations and the influence they still enjoy have always been insuperable obstacles.' For his part, this 'friend of humanity' had an alternative suggestion: let the nuns of La Providence, now running 'a badly organized boarding house', be constrained to return to their original duties of caring for orphan children.[146] This idea of annexing monastic revenues was subsequently kept alive by the haunting question of the designs of the bishop of Séez on the abbey of Saint-Aubin. In the summer of 1787, negotiations for royal letters patent giving permission to found the orphanage were approaching a conclusion. The diocesan bishop, who was visiting Paris, played his part, after suitable prompting from an agent of the municipality in the capital—'the bishop of Angers desires this establishment as much as we do, he has promised to speak to M. le baron de Breteuil about it, and I won't leave him until he has carried out his promise'.[147] When letters patent were duly forwarded, the town provided a house in the place Monsieur as an initial site, and a committee of management was formed which included the bishop, the dean of Saint-Martin, and a canon of the cathedral.[148] By towns-people in general, this good news was greeted with a clamour for the appropriation of ecclesiastical benefices. Both the general assembly and the town council made this recommendation, the latter adding a pointed comment concerning the clergy of Anjou—'it is difficult to find a province where benefices are in a greater number, and where the clergy are more opulent'.[149]

The zeal which had established an Enfants trouvés was not entirely humanitarian. There was a general impression in Angers that trade and commerce were declining, reflected in an essay title set for competition by the Academy in 1787, 'Quels sont les moyens d'encourager le commerce à Angers?' [150] The prize was won by Viger, *procureur du roi* and a future revolutionary administrator, who took this opportunity to indulge in strictures against the dead hand of ecclesiastical property owners, and ask that young men of the middle classes be given a more progressive education in tune with the epoch. But the main argument of Viger, and of rival essayists, was one of which the municipality had long been aware: that is, that local sales of foodstuffs and merchandise should be increased by developing the town as an institutional centre. A foundling hospital was one step in this direction, so too would be an increase in the numbers attending educational establishments. In 1745, the town petitioned Louis XV to allow the Oratorians to take boarders, point-ing out that the Collège d'Anjou, which had once had over a thousand pupils, now had only five hundred. 'The town of Angers, which owes its prosperity to letters rather than commerce, feels the disadvantages of this reduction in numbers of students by the decline of the demand for consumer goods.' [151] But the Oratory was not co-operative, and although by 1768 boarders were again being taken, never more than twenty-six were resident at any one time. This being so, there were two possible solutions. The obvious one was to enable the Collège d'Anjou to expand by increasing its financial resources, a plan which was put forward by both town and University on the occasion of the suppression of the Jesuits. New income would be derived, of course, from ecclesiastical benefices—'No diminution to the receipts of the Royal exchequer, no increased charges on the people.' [152] When this application failed, the alternative proposal was to endeavour to persuade the abbey of Saint-Aubin to found a school and take in boarders. 'I think that the rich Benedictine order, possessing four houses at Angers in the most strategic sites, would have as much to gain as we have by giving up one of their houses and taking over a boarding school or collège,' so wrote one of the municipal officers early in 1765.[153] This project of the sixties foundered, and was revived in 1788. It had many advantages. Saint-Aubin was situated within the walls in an accessible position, yet had enough land around it to allow for expansion, the abbatial house could be used to lodge students, and the Benedictines of Saint-Maur, 'supreme masters in the art of training good citizens', could draft in expert teachers to begin the work.[154] All the while, of course, these good citizens in embryo would be spending their pocket-money in Angers, and in any case, the scheme was the town's third line of defence against the designs of the bishop of Séez on the revenues of Saint-Aubin.

If Minerva failed to draw in an influx of sojourners with money to spend, the municipality was willing to turn to Mars as second preference, and develop Angers into a flourishing garrison town. It was strictly a question of economics; there was no real enthusiasm for the presence of soldiery. Indeed, in 1774, the town had appealed to its Count apanagist against the despatch of a new detachment of musketeers, and the local military commander, worn out by civilian complaints, reciprocated by declaring that he would prefer not to have to send his men to this 'receptacle of the most despicable *canaille*'.[155] What the city fathers wanted was a garrison in barracks, not one quartered on the population depriving families of their houses and scattered riotously about the town far from the eyes of its officers. So the town council argued in 1780, and proposed an obvious solution. Let the four or five surviving Minims and the four or five Augustins retire into a section of their large enclosures and considerable buildings, taking for themselves only what would suffice for an honest family of the same size, and let the soldiers occupy the rest. 'The greater good is that which turns to the profit of society in general. No corporation or community can be allowed to go on living in a property which is useless to it, and which is rendered profitless to the State by the mere fact of their retaining it.' [156]

After eight years of chequered negotiations,[157] the plea of the town for the despatch of a cavalry regiment was granted, and then a decision about barracks had to be taken. The town council unanimously favoured the appropriation of the monastery of Saint-Serge, arguing that the Benedictines would still retain three houses in Angers, and 'when it is a question of the general interest, an opulent congregation ought to be disposed to make sacrifices'.[158] Failing this, a composite confiscation, at the expense of the Recollets, the nuns of Sainte-Catherine, and the riding school might provide a new barracks. The Minims with an adjoining meadow belonging to the Oratorians was another possibility, but the town would prefer to reserve this as a future residential area; and finally, of course, there was always Lesvière.[159] By February 1789, the Council of War in Paris decided on the house of the Minims, and by the end of July, the resistance of the monks had been overcome[160] and an appropriate figure for their pensions established. Then came all the problems of winding up a religious establishment; what arrangements were to be made for saying foundation masses, how were family tablets from the walls of the church to be disposed of, were the Minims allowed to sell their marble altar?[161] The whole of France was shortly to be confronted with similar problems, for seven months later, the Constituent Assembly made the first of its decisions concerning the sale of monastic property. Angers had already had its dress-rehearsal.

CHAPTER VII

CURÉS AND PARISHES

I. THE PAROCHIAL STRUCTURE

THE river running from NNE to SSW divided Angers, geographically and socially, into two unequal parts. On the right bank was a poor and crowded quarter called *La Doutre*, on the left bank was the city proper, with its castle, cathedral, town hall, fashionable residential areas and its multitude of churches. Directly to the east of the castle, within the shadow of the towers of the cathedral and Saint-Aubin and within sound of the bell of the Seminary chapel, no fewer than ten parish churches were found. Each of the collegiate foundations of Saint-Pierre, Saint-Maurille, Saint-Martin and Saint-Julien, and the cathedral itself, had its parish, served by its own curé and functioning, for all practical purposes, independently of the chapter whose name it bore. The parishioners of Saint-Maurice passed through a door in the nave of the cathedral to reach their church, those of Saint-Pierre worshipped in a side-chapel of the collegial, those of Saint-Martin, Saint-Maurille and Saint-Julien had their own altar in the nave of their capitular church,[1] for if canons had withdrawn from pastoral ministrations, they still retained their architectural and honorific domination. Of these parishes, the three largest were Saint-Pierre (which, with the country district of Empiré reckoned in, totalled 4,000 souls[2]), Saint-Maurice (which was estimated to have 3,000 communicants[3]), and Saint-Maurille. This latter church, situated centrally in town and on the fringe of the ecclesiastical establishments around the cathedral, could draw on a residential area lying to the east towards the Collège d'Anjou and the hôtel de ville, and was thus considered 'the first in Angers, both by its situation and by its nobility and honourable inhabitants'.[4] Saint-Martin and Saint-Julien were smaller parishes, probably not exceeding 2,000 inhabitants in number; indeed, Saint-Julien was saved from complete insignificance only by the fact that its boundaries extended beyond the city walls into the surrounding countryside. Although this country population had its own separate 'district church' in the chapel of La Madeleine, Saint-Julien still remained the parochial centre, and when possible, churchwardens were elected alternately from town and country.[5] There was only one other parish in this area —that of Saint-Michel de la Palud—which could compare even with Saint-Julien in numbers of inhabitants, and this again was due to the fact that this cure was in the south-east corner of the city walls, and thus had a hinterland in the countryside, served by a vicaire stationed at the dependent chapel of Saint-Sébastien.[6] Sainte-Croix also boasted a vicaire, not on grounds of population, however, but because of duties connected with the perpetual adoration of the Holy Sacrament established there. This pious work was, indeed, the only visible justification for the continued existence of this tiny parish, for its church was under the very walls of the cathedral choir, the building was ruinous and, thanks to the fact that its floor was eight feet below ground level, perpetually damp.[7] The three remaining parishes around the cathedral were microscopic in size. Poverty and lassitude after long rivalries had brought about the fusion of Saint-Denis and Saint-Maimbeuf in 1721, but the parish of Saint-Denis which arose from this union could still afford its priest no more than two baptisms and five burials in the course of a year. Under the castle walls, only a hundred yards apart, lay the churches of Saint-Aignan and Saint-Evroul; the latter, with its 300 communicants,[8] absorbed most available population, though Saint-Aignan was strengthened by its status as a chapel for the castle and its military pensioners.

If one started from Saint-Maurille on the edge of this concentration of churches, and walked north-east through prosperous streets where most of the principal inhabitants resided, within fifteen minutes one arrived at the town hall, and adjoining it was the one other parish church within the city walls on the left bank. This church of Saint-Michel du Tertre, which depended on the abbey of Saint-Serge, had risen to a position of first importance by reason of its proximity to the centre of municipal life. The official pew of the mayors of Angers dominated its nave and its aisles were lined with tombs and funeral chapels of great families of the Angevin magistracy.[9] Within this parish lived an oddly assorted population. Its curé had under his pastoral oversight the grave *conseilleurs au Présidial*, *avocats*, notaries, and teachers at the Faculty of Law, who lived around the place du Pilory and the porte Saint-Michel, the prisoners in the town jail, the erring souls who frequented tennis courts, billiard saloons and gaming-houses which abounded in this area, the ordinary folk of the faubourg Saint-Michel and mine hosts at *Le Pélican*, *Le Cheval Blanc*, and other inns which lined the main road leading towards Paris.[10]

Thus, on the left bank, there were eleven parishes: on the other side of the river, a single parish, that of La Trinité,[11] served the entire town within the walls and also ran far out into the countryside, its total population being about eleven thousand. A few noble families resided here, the de Gibot, the de Crissé and the d'Andigné, and here too was the rich abbey of Ronceray. Otherwise, this was a poor quarter, half the inhabitants being artisans who had drifted into town in search of work throughout the eighteenth century. Thus, in one single parish, the greatest pastoral obligations and opportunities of the town were concentrated. But for all his great responsibilities, the curé of La Trinité was in a dependent situation. Other priests had livings which depended on chapters or on monasteries; he had to face pretensions of both, for he shared his church with canons, and both canons and curé were subject to Ronceray.

The parochial map of Angers may now be completed by surveying in five peripheral cures, each lying just outside the city walls. Leaving La Trinité and going westwards on to a main road which ultimately followed the river down to Nantes, after twenty minutes' walk one came to Saint-Jacques and Saint-Nicolas. The former depended on the abbey of Ronceray,[12] the latter on the abbey of Saint-Nicolas, an unfortunate circumstance, for from a pastoral point of view, this separation of the district into two parishes was illogical. United, they might have formed a unit rather smaller in population than Saint-Maurille, rather larger than Saint-Julien. Indeed, Saint-Nicolas, the smaller parish, had in some ways already become dependent on Saint-Jacques. Its church, which was in a chapel of the monks, had no font, and its vicarage was inconveniently situated, so that the curé was accustomed to rely on his neighbour's font and tabernacle and communicate his parishioners at Easter in the church of Saint-Jacques.[13] From this latter building, an open sweep of meadows belonging to the abbey of Saint-Nicolas skirted the city walls and ran down to the river. All the far bank, dominated by the gaunt bastions of the castle, was in the parish of Lesvière. There was nothing notable here, save M. de Pignerolle's riding-school[14] and the monastery whose church the parish shared. There were very few inhabitants and very undistinguished at that, 'boatmen and ferrymen and other poor folk'.[15] The *Académie d'Equitation* was on the eastward fringe of this cure, just where the neighbouring parish of Saint-Laud began, and in 1761, when its buildings were extended, there had been a serious lawsuit between the two curés, jealous of their boundaries.[16] Though Saint-Laud contained only 130 households, it was more populous than Lesvière and had more prosperous inhabitants, including half a dozen noblemen and the canons of the chapter, whose chapel of Saint-Joseph formed the parish church.[17] Then, on the far side of the city, comes the last of these peripheral parishes, that of Saint-Samson,[18] a small but prettily situated cure depending on the abbey of Saint-Serge. Its role on the north-east of the town resembled that of Saint-Laud to the south-west, and it served the scattered habitations which had sprung up outside the porte Cupif and along the edge of the lush river meadows where the abbey's cattle grazed.

One might conclude that the town of Angers fell into four natural areas. There was the historic centre around the cathedral, in a triangle marked out by the castle, Saint-Maurille and Saint-Aubin; there was a modern residential and official centre to the east; there was a poor quarter on the far side of the river; and finally, there was a belt of small suburbs and dependent countryside around the circuit of the walls. By standards of the day, such as the clergy of Anjou accepted in their deliberations in 1766,[19] the optimum size for a compact town parish was 3,000 souls. Using this criterion, we see how ill-adapted the old parochial organization was to eighteenth-century circumstances. The residential and official centre was adequately served by the distinguished parishes of Saint-Maurille and Saint-Michel du Tertre. On the north-west, the peripheral belt was incomplete, leaving the already over-worked parish of La Trinité with much extra-mural responsibility; on the south-east, the countryside was rather inefficiently divided between some of the urban parishes; while to the west, Saint-Nicolas and Saint-Jacques might with advantage have been fused, so too might Lesvière and Saint-Laud. Four parishes in the decayed medieval town were mere fossils, serving only a handful of inhabitants, and four others were rescued from insignificance by a rather illogical extension into rural areas: eight parishes serving a total population no larger than that which fell to the single parish of La Trinité on the unfashionable side of the river.

It is true that such a parochial survey of Angers needs to be completed by a consideration of other factors. A map of monastic establishments, for example, should be super-imposed on it when one is considering opportunities for attending divine worship, and among the many decayed chapels scattered about the town, there were two or three which retained some local importance. Also, vicaires were allotted to each curé in a way which did something to atone for manifest inequalities of population. In 1790, Saint-Nicolas, Saint-Evroul, Saint-Denis and Saint-Aignan were served by their curés alone, the other parishes had one vicaire, except Saint-Pierre, Saint-Maurille, Saint-Maurice and Saint-Michel le Palud, which had two, Saint-Michel du Tertre which had four, and La Trinité which had five.[20] Thus, when one says that this latter parish was responsible for 11,000 souls, one must remember its five vicaires, the presence of seven religious communities in its midst, and its 'district church' at the chapel of Saint-Lazare, where masses were said and catechisms taken.[21]

Even so, when all allowances were made, the case for reform of the parochial system of Angers was overwhelming. It was advocated, pungently and pugnaciously, by the abbé Robin, the eccentric curé of Saint-Pierre, in a brochure, *L'Ami des Peuples*, in 1760. Though his subject matter would have corresponded better with a title 'l'ennemi des chanoines', he did advocate, incidentally, a scheme of parochial redistribution which was independent of his ruthless views on the future of collegiate churches. His proposals involved uniting Saint-Nicolas with Saint-Jacques, Saint-Evroul and Saint-Aignan with Saint-Maurice, Sainte-Croix with Saint-Michel de la Palud, Saint-Julien and Saint-Denis with Saint-Martin, and the division of La Trinité into three new units, to make a final total of eight parishes within the walls and five in the suburbs.[22] This plan deals with all obvious inequalities and absurdities. There were, of course, many possible variants and parochial patriotism or prejudice was likely to influence a would-be reformer in his choice—very naturally, curé Robin did not propose to alter the status of his own church of Saint-Pierre. Thirty years later, when a revision of parish boundaries had become a matter of practical politics, an anonymous theorist[23] with different sympathies proposed to dismember Saint-Pierre and elevate Saint-Julien to the status of a town parish worthy to compare with Saint-Michel du Tertre and Saint-Maurille. On the other hand, he was not prepared to be so radical on the far side of the river, where he proposed to leave La Trinité intact, but to form a new parish to take in a population of 4,000 or so outside the walls. At the same time, the young and ambitious curé of Saint-Laud produced a project for preserving his own parish and adding to it the villages of La Cornouaille and Empiré, which, he argued, naturally gravitate towards it.[24] The usual annexionist arguments of manifest destiny were well known to these humble empire builders.

No progress in this question of parochial boundaries was, in fact, made between Robin's proposal of 1760 and the Civil Constitution of the clergy. In 1766, government investigations into the inadequate salaries of parish priests brought the Diocesan Bureau to consider the possibility of uniting small and poor livings,[25] and two years later, an edict which enjoined the union of cures with a revenue of under 500*l.* led to a draft proposal for the absorption of Saint-Evroul into either Sainte-Croix or Saint-Maurice. There was an outcry of dismay and anger from the inhabitants of the threatened parish.[26] They said hard things about the distribution of the revenues of the Church of France in general, and their successful resistance illustrates the fact that parochial reform by itself could never have been carried through without a parallel reformation of the abuses and sinecures which were even more damaging to efficiency than parochial maladjustments. Ideas of reorganization were again in the air in 1784. A project to unite various collegiate churches of Angers was being canvassed[27] and these discussions probably did something to awake the consciences of those in authority to the more pressing problem of the

K

huge parish of La Trinité. On 9 July, Canon Gautreau de la Grois, *promoteur* of the diocese, presented a report to his bishop summarizing the situation.[28] A curé with modest revenues, with only three official vicaires and a fourth whom he paid at his own expense, was responsible for ten to twelve thousand inhabitants—'it is not possible for such a small number of ministers to be in personal relationships with all the parishioners and give them the spiritual aid which they continually need'. He did not propose startling changes: the canons of La Trinité were to be replaced by chaplains, and the money saved would go to increase the stipend of the curé, pay his supernumary vicaire, and provide a fifth assistant priest. Although this scheme foundered on the opposition of the canons and the abbess of Ronceray, the inquiry *de commodo et incommodo* which it entailed gave the parishioners a chance to add their request that a new parish be formed to serve the area outside the city walls. Their case was strongly supported by the municipality, whose representatives waited upon the bishop and the abbess to ask for this new parish for the faubourg Saint-Lazare.[29] Nothing was done, except that in future La Trinité had five vicaires, and an echo of Gautreau de la Grois' disappointment may be heard in the *cahier* of the chapter of Saint-Laud, which demands the suppression of useless parishes.[30]

In 1789, the Church of France was full of inequalities and illogicalities, which extended to its basic parochial structure. Traditions and loyalties of priests and people and vested interests of ecclesiastical corporations stood in the way of a new delimitation of boundaries, yet, if a great national crisis were to enforce these changes, it would be impossible to deny that they were 'for the good of the people, for simplicity, and economy'.[31]

2. PARISH PRIESTS

With one exception, all the parochial clergy of Angers in 1789 were local men.[32] Suchet, curé of Saint-Michel de la Palud, and Follenfant of Saint-Maurice, were both from families resident in town and each had his own nephew for vicaire. For more than twenty years the tiny parish of Saint-Evroul had been run by the Gouppil family, one brother being curé and another sole churchwarden in permanent and unchallenged possession of that office. Indeed, eleven of the clergy (five curés and six vicaires) came from Angers itself, four came from Château-Gontier, two each from Saint-Florent-le-Vieil, Chemillé, Chalonnes-sur-Loire and Champigné. A circle with a radius of forty miles, drawn with the town as its centre, would include the places of origin of all except one of the seventeen curés and twenty-two vicaires. By contrast with his autochthonous colleagues, Ferré of

Saint-Samson, born on the distant Mediterranean coast and a licentiate of the Faculty of Law of Paris,[33] was a cosmopolitan adventurer.

Huchelou des Roches, who was inducted to Saint-Julien in 1768 at the age of twenty-nine, came from a family of some local distinction: his father was a *conseilleur de la Prevôté*, and his mother was a Benoist, a name well known in the annals of the Angevin magistracy.[34] The social origin of the others varied, but none rose higher than what may conveniently be termed 'lower middle-class'. Curé Gouppil's brother, our permanent churchwarden at Saint-Evroul, was an apothecary, and a house near to his shop was owned by another Gouppil, curé of Alençon, and occupied by a Miss Gouppil— all presumably being brothers and sisters;[35] Boumard of Sainte-Croix came from a family of agricultural middlemen which earned its competence by farming the scattered property of ecclesiastical landlords;[36] the father of Robin of Saint-Pierre was an iron, coal and corn merchant at Saint-Florent-le-Vieil, who had exhorted his son to weigh well the profits available in their business before he sought ordination—'Tu pourras amasser du bien dans mon commerce.'[37] One vicaire at La Trinité, Tardif, was the son of a merchant at Château-Gontier and had a brother practising as *avocat* in Angers.[38] Another vicaire of this parish, René-Jules Houdet, was a son of a surgeon of Chalonnes-sur-Loire who had died leaving his widow with four children to educate. She had discharged her task well: one son was a priest, another a surgeon at Saint-Florent-le-Vieil, another a merchant at Nantes, and a daughter was married to a notary at Durtal.[39] Others of the parochial clergy came from lower social strata than this minor professional and commercial bourgeoisie. A hard-pressed saddle-maker of Beaupreau with twenty-one children on his hands had brought up three sons for the ministry of the Church; one was parish priest of Saint-Florent-le-Vieil,[40] another, our abbé Gruget, had become an assistant priest at La Trinité in 1775, and nine years later was promoted to the cure.[41] Bernier, a brilliant young intellectual who served at Saint-Michel de la Palud from 1787 and became curé of Saint-Laud three years later, was accustomed, in his episcopal period, to hint at a descent from the famous traveller of his name; but in fact, his father was a weaver of Daon-sur-Mayenne who eked out his income with his perquisites as sacristan and his wife's earnings as village schoolmistress.[42] Suchet, curé of Saint-Michel de la Palud, had a sister who married a Viger and was collector of ticket-money for official lotteries in Angers. A daughter of hers entered the Carmelite house in town, and a son, Augustin-Jean, studied at the Seminary (and, if the story be true, lost his pocket-money there in pursuing an infallible system which he had deduced from his mother's records), and finally became vicaire to his uncle.[43]

Whatever their origin, all the parochial clergy of Angers seem to have been men of a respectable education. One of the curés was a doctor of medicine, two were doctors of theology, while the others, if the general custom of France was observed, ought to have had university degrees of some kind to qualify for holding benefices in a walled city.[44] Two vicaires, Tardif of La Trinité and Forest of Saint-Michel du Tertre, were the envy of their contemporaries, for the blue silk and ermine of their theological doctorates marked them out for early promotion in a diocese which had a special reputation for encouraging learning. Students at the little Seminary competed eagerly to be included in the select apostolic twelve (*soutenants*, they were called) who were chosen to argue a thesis at Easter or at the beginning of August, for 'In the diocese of Angers a *soutenant* of the Seminary was a man of importance; if he became an ecclesiastic, the best places were reserved for him, sometimes he chose those he preferred, and in any case he was made a curé or a canon many years before his contemporaries'.[45] Parish priests of the diocese had not necessarily attended at the little Seminary, for this was, as it were, a school attached to the Seminary proper, which gave a general education towards the degree of master of arts in the University to both ordinands and others. But all, wherever they had previously been educated, came to the Grand Séminaire to make their final preparation for ordination. For some, this meant an attendance of three years, keeping terms for seven and a half months in each year, and attending daily lectures at the Faculty of Theology in the cloisters of Saint-Maurice. Others, 'fiacres' as they were nicknamed by their more fortunate contemporaries, were too poor to aspire to academic heights. Their course lasted for fourteen months only, and while they shared common-rooms and refectory with University men, they had a separate curriculum for recreation and study.[46]

At five in the morning a seminarist's day began, when a priest of the staff came round the dormitories, waking his students with a 'Benedicemus Domino'.[47] From then to nine o'clock at night, life followed a strict routine.[48] Meditation and religious observances rather than study were its keynote. It was not the library, where 9,000 volumes[49] slept secure on ordered shelves, but the chapel, which was the centre of life and discipline. This restriction of emphasis was to some extent an accommodation to the intellectual quality and background of most candidates for the priesthood, and to some extent it was a faithful reflection of the original aims of founders of French seminaries in general and of this one in particular. M. Olier was described by Sainte-Beuve as having 'more charity and zeal than breadth and stability of intellect, was full of ceremonies and imagery, a mystic, even a visionary',[50] and the imprint of his powerful will still lay upon the institution which he had founded. One must remember, too, that in the mid-seventeenth century there had been appalling disorders among the ordinary clergy of France.[51] M. Olier in setting up his community of Saint-Sulpice and bishop Pelletier who had called the Sulpiciens to Angers in 1695, were naturally preoccupied with problems of clerical recruitment, morals and discipline. 'The first and last end of this institute', began the *Pietas Seminarii* of Saint-Sulpice, 'is to live supremely for God, in Christ Jesus our Lord, so that the interior dispositions of His Son penetrate the very depths of our hearts.'[52] 'I live, yet no longer I, but Christ liveth in me', said Saint-Paul, and the professed aim of the Sulpiciens was to build up their pupils to this ideal—by meditation, discipline, and, more particularly, by devotion to the sacrament of the altar and to Our Lady—*Jesu Vivens in Maria*. But concentration upon an ultimate ideal can have unexpected results when translated into institutional terms. In Paris under Cardinal Fleury's unlucky patronage the mother-house became a haunt of graceless young aristocrats, while in the provinces there was a greater propriety, but a narrow and clericalist education was given. From the first the sacramental and marial devotion of Saint-Sulpice and its infallibilist theology had been anti-Jansenist in flavour,[53] and the use bishops made of their seminaries as engines against Jansenism led to a concentration upon orthodoxy which discouraged independent thought. Certainly this was the view of the *Nouvelles ecclésiastiques*, whose commentators throughout the eighteenth century referred to the Sulpiciens of Angers as purveyors of superficial instruction and leaders of a Molinist conspiracy.[54] In Angers, too, a fortuitous circumstance served to intensify this tendency to concentrate upon spiritual and liturgical, as distinct from intellectual instruction. The directors were responsible, not only for services in their own chapel, but also for obits and anniversaries of the chapters of Saint-Julien and Saint-Maimbeuf which were united to their house, and for the role in general religious processions of the town which had been played by the old canons. On most of these occasions their pupils were also obliged to attend, so that in Lent when there were two general processions each week, normal lectures and study were practically at a standstill.[55] There were those who considered that in a critical and utilitarian century the education given to parochial clergy should be more liberal and intellectual. Under bishop Vaugirault, an Angevin commentator was bitter in criticism of his local seminary, whose rules, he said, revealed every sign of 'the most ridiculous and tedious bigotry' and produced priests 'infected with an attitude of mind diametrically opposed to that of the age in which they live; the Seminary is nothing more than a noviciate for monks, or rather a penal establishment for galley slaves'.[56]

Granting that an ordinary course at the Seminary had its intellectual limitations, what of its moral and spiritual value? This is very hard to assess, partly for intrinsic reasons concerning the nature of the evidence required and partly because the Sulpicien type of discipline and training depended very much on the personal qualities of individual directors and, more especially, of the superior of a house. M. Emery, who took over in 1775, was a rigorous unsparing man who would tolerate no slackness—not even from his bishop, whom he turned out of bed to take an ordination service. For seven years he ruled in Angers before being called to Paris to direct the whole community, and during and after his time everything indicates an outward strictness and regularity of life.[57] Before this opinions could differ concerning the spirit in which the Sulpiciens ran their institution. Besnard talks of their favourites, and of the hypocritical piety of these 'mignons' or 'mystiqueurs', and hints at homosexuality.[58] Another student, who was there some time before Besnard, writes to his father of 'the kindly faces of my teachers, the tone of piety which reigns in the house, the grave studies we do here', of his fellow-students 'pious as angels'—'I swim in an ocean of grace, grace surrounds me and penetrates my being, as the waters surround and penetrate the fishes in the sea'.[59] They were very different characters, of course. Charles d'Aviau du Bois de Sanzeny preferred his little cell to all the 'gilded plasterwork of the world', while Besnard intrigued steadily until he was given one of the twelve rooms with a fire.[60] Perhaps students at the Seminary got out of it what they put into it.

Once his training was completed, a newly-ordained priest was likely to serve for ten years or so as a vicaire before obtaining a parish of his own.[61] As he became ripe for a benefice, he must attract the notice of a patron. It is true that a 'resignation in favour' might come his way, and if a graduate, he knew that no non-graduate could compete with him in the months of January, April, July and October.[62] But apart from these circumstances, he must look towards the city of Angers, for here was the well-spring and fountain-head of promotion for the whole diocese. A quarter of all livings, one hundred and two in fact, were in the bishop's gift.[63] Taken together, the cathedral and the abbey of Saint-Serge controlled as many; the absentee abbot, with forty local nominations on his hands, would appoint some prominent Angevin ecclesiastic to supervise his interests, while vacant benefices depending on Saint-Maurice were allotted by the 'canon of the week'. Fifty-nine livings depended on the abbeys of Saint-Nicolas and Saint-Aubin, the canons-regular of Toussaint and the abbess of Ronceray, while the chapters of Saint-Laud, Saint-Pierre, Saint-Martin and Saint-Maurille appointed to twenty-one others. Altogether, the bishop and these great ecclesiastical corporations of his episcopal town controlled nearly three-quarters of parochial patronage within the diocese. In the city itself, we find a reflection in miniature of the diocesan situation.[64] The bishop presented to Saint-Julien and Saint-Denis, the canon of the week at the cathedral to Saint-Maurice and Saint-Evroul, and the holder of the particular prebend of St. John the Baptist also had the gift of Sainte-Croix. Saint-Samson and Saint-Michel du Tertre depended on the abbot of Saint-Serge, Saint-Michel de la Palud on the abbot of Saint-Aubin, Lesvière on the abbot of La Trinité of Vendôme. With the assent of her two chief officers, the abbess of Ronceray disposed of La Trinité and Saint-Jacques, while the monastery of Saint-Nicolas and the four collegiate churches of the town appointed in the parishes which bore the names of their foundations. Ecclesiastical promotions ought, no doubt, to be decided only 'within the precincts of the sanctuary',[65] but in these circumstances, solicitations by, or on behalf of, junior clergy were invitable. 'The curé of Saint-Laud', says a letter writer in September 1783, 'is at his last extremity. After mattins at four o'clock, he received extreme unction . . . the precentor is canon of the week. Already he has been approached for the cure.'[66]

Promotion then did not conform to the psalmist's rigid schedule, but might come from any point of the compass where a great ecclesiastical corporation was to be found. Appointments, too, were a lottery within a lottery, for livings throughout the diocese varied greatly in importance and income. Parish priests were becoming increasingly conscious of their identity as a class, yet not all were members of a clerical proletariat: some belonged, so to speak, to the bourgeoisie of the church. Benefices like Soulaines, which rewarded Cotelle de la Blandinière, the theologian, or Andard, which was an episcopal recompense to Rangeard for a loyalty which had cost him his canon's stall at the cathedral,[67] were much superior to the majority of cures. There were many livings of intermediate importance, and at the bottom of the scale came the *vicaires amovibles* of forty subordinate parishes of Anjou, who did a curé's work without having his title or independence or income. 'Don't you think . . .', wrote one of these wretched priests in 1789, 'that all curés ought to be equal, both in title and revenue? . . . For is it not true that, when benefices are distributed, favour plays a greater part than merit?'[68] In respect of inequalities, as in respect of patronage, the city of Angers is again a microcosm of the diocese at large. None of its curés enjoyed the income of a Soulaines or Andard, a few were more modestly prosperous, most were in indifferent circumstances, and one or two were almost as poor as this priest of Saint-Pierre du Lac whose complaint has just been quoted. The distinguished parish of Saint-Michel du Tertre was worth over 1,000l. a year, Saint-Pierre yielded nearly 900, then came Saint-Maurille, though, oddly enough, when the *congrue* was raised to 700l. in 1786, the incumbents of the parishes of Saint-Nicolas and Saint-Samson, and possibly of Lesvière also, received a larger basic income. Saint-Maurice and Saint-Julien came next, while Saint-Jacques, Sainte-Croix, Saint-Denis, Saint-Michel de la Palud and Saint-Martin were worth about 400l. The tiny cures of Saint-Aignan and Saint-Evroul were absolutely poverty-stricken. 'Cent sols de perte et bien servie' ran a local proverb with reference to this latter parish, and even when an extra 200l. was obtained from the cathedral in 1774, the curé still had less than a living wage.[69] La Trinité is a special case.[70] Its curé could make no financial claim on Ronceray, either for himself or his vicaires, though the abbess was accustomed to bestow on him a chapel in the church of Sainte-Croix at Rochefort which was in her gift. His revenue was derived from two pieces of land and eight houses belonging to the living, which in a good year might bring in 3,000l. Out of this, the property was maintained, and the vicaires paid, so that ultimately a curé of La Trinité was no better off than most of his brethren.

These bald official figures of benefice income do not, however, tell the whole story. Our curé of La Trinité was not the only holder of a chapel without cure of souls. When the Civil Constitution of the Clergy came into force, parish priests were entitled to claim half the value of any additional benefices which they had enjoyed under the old régime, and it is then that we learn new details concerning such chapels and priories which had not been fully revealed during previous controversies concerning inadequate incomes.[71] Suchet of Saint-Michel de la Palud had nearly 1,000l. from these sources, Ferré of Saint-Samson and Robin of Saint-Pierre had more, Doguereau of Saint-Aignan, who received practically nothing as a parish priest, had 1,500l. clear of all deductions from the income of eight chapels, while Boumard of Sainte-Croix had accumulated three chapels whose value was about half that of his actual living.[72] However, this whole business was haphazard. Luck and good connexions brought prosperity to some, but curé Noel of Saint-Jacques had only one additional benefice, worth less than 100l. a year. Well-known vicaires in town-like Taillebuis and Viger had already begun their accumulation of supplementary benefices,[73] while an assistant priest in the countryside might struggle on for forty years before a reasonable opportunity came his way.[74] Then there were other and more rational supplements to incomes. A curé who was a regent doctor of the Faculty of Theology and who was assiduous in attendance when theses were examined, could expect to earn 40 to 50*l*. a year in academic fees.[75] Surplice fees were a considerable item in more populous parishes. Foundation masses brought their remuneration, which at Saint-Maurice was as much as 300*l*. a year.[76] Gifts in kind quite often came the way of a parish priest, from the silk stockings and plate left at the confessional for curé Robin (and appropriated by one of his vicaires), to a buss of white wine which the churchwardens of Saint-Maurice were accustomed to hand over each November.[77] Some allowance must also be made for the value of the vicarage, and in some cases, of its garden. All these additions and adjustments, however, serve merely to show how it was possible for parish priests to maintain any sort of dignified standard of living at all. One hundred *livres* was the annual wage of an agricultural labourer in the north; three hundred *livres* was an amount that a country surgeon might charge a wounded soldier for a year's board and medical attention; 500*l*. was what was needed in Angers in the early sixties to pay for food, lodgings and the wages of a single servant; 1,200*l*. was the annual expenditure of a canon of Saint-Omer, who lived quite well, and kept a lackey and a maid.[78] These figures of the cost of living in provincial France may serve as a scale of comparison by which to estimate the prosperity of our curés of Angers, ranging from comfort to a bare subsistence. Some of them may have inherited a little money of their own from their families—one imagines that it was the fortune of the wholesale merchant of St. Florent-le-Vieil rather than 2,000*l*. of income from various ecclesiastical sources which paid for Robin's country-house at Empiré and his fantastic litigation. But none was rich, and some were poor. If it be true that a certain parish priest of Anjou had a hundred shirts in his linen cupboard and a dozen beds in his guest rooms,[79] he must have been a wealthy man in his own right, or have held one of those few fortunate country livings with fat tithes coming in. Standards were very different in the town of Angers.

Vicarages were built on a scale which made some concessions to the dignity of their occupants, but was more consonant, on the whole, with their modest incomes. A kitchen where a single servant lived and cooked, a sitting-room where parish meetings were held and where the curé studied and entertained, and a single bedroom upstairs, was a minimum accommodation, such as was afforded at Saint-Denis before reconstruction took place.[80] Most vicarages were rather more spacious. At La Trinité and Saint-Pierre, which were exceptional, there was room for the parish priest and his staff to live in common; elsewhere there would be a parlour, a dining-room, and from two to five other rooms with fireplaces. In town, there would be a little courtyard behind the house with a well in the middle, a flower-bed, latrines and an outbuilding or two, with perhaps a little door leading into the sacristy of the parish church;[81] in parishes bordering on the countryside, there would be room for a walled garden or a vineyard.[82] Concerning the domestic arrangements of curés, it is not often that we can pry into these humble details, except by using rights of entry peculiar to auctioneers and undertakers. If we follow in the wake of a posse of bailiffs and enter the vicarage of Sainte-Croix in 1789,[83] we find a kitchen with two fire-dogs, a fire-guard, a little square table, a shovel, pincers, a triangle, a spit and a frying-pan; in the sitting-room there are two arm-chairs and fifteen ordinary ones, two tables one with turned legs and a drawer, a mirror in a gilt frame, a chest of three drawers with brass knobs, and three umbrellas ready to hand, for it was the dangerous month of April when this inventory was taken; then in the bedroom, there is the obvious furniture, together with six arm-chairs covered in voluted silk.

These possessions of the abbé Boumard were the accumulation of a residence of over twenty years, for once appointed to a living in Angers, even a very poor and obscure one, a curé rarely changed. An important parish in Saumur, which had a population of 11,000 and was served by five vicaires,[84] tempted Martin du Chesnay away from Saint-Laud after a stay of only three years, and Bassereau, a doctor of theology and an influential man, was not long content with Lesvière.[85] Changes like these, however, were exceptional. In 1789, Follenfant had been at Saint-Maurice for twelve years, Huchelou des Roches at Saint-Julien for twenty-one, Gouppil at Saint-Evroul for longer still, Robin at Saint-Pierre for thirty-seven years, and Roussel at Saint-Maurille for as long as most people could remember. Probably none of our parish priests of Angers at the end of the old régime, with the exception of the brilliant young Bernier at Saint-Laud, had any hopes or expectations of further promotion.

These long years of ministry within a single parish have a history, which, for most curés, inevitably remains unchronicled; yet it is one which can easily be evoked in imagination, for a priest's duties within a community have changed but little in the course of time. As between larger and smaller parishes, there was great variation in the incidence of daily and occasional offices. At Saint-Aignan and Saint-Denis there were not likely to be more than three baptisms a year, at Saint-Pierre, Saint-Maurice and Saint-Maurille, there might be a hundred, at La Trinité more than three hundred.[86] Every day in this huge parish there were four low masses between 5.30 and 11 a.m. and a high mass at nine o'clock.[87] At the other extreme, at

Saint-Evroul there was generally nothing more than a low mass, even on Sundays and Saints' days, though on these occasions there would be a spiritual reading or a homily on the gospel for the day. This system was preferred by the parishioners, who declared that, after all, 'sung masses and vespers are not obligatory'.[88] In parishes of intermediate size, an incumbent might arrange matters to suit his own ideas. Curé Robin had fixed times for mass on Sundays and feast days, and a rule that one of his priests must always be on duty, either in the vicarage, or at an address in town where he could be sent for at short notice.[89] Otherwise, his clergy said their masses and daily offices at times which suited themselves. Robin himself was always at the altar at midday, but only attended the mattins of the canons when his health allowed. Often, he said his morning offices alone, preferably before daybreak, for 'the silence and calm of the night are full of charm for him, the *Venite exultemus* and all the fine canticles of the Psalmist fill his soul with joy'.[90]

At great festivals Angers was ablaze with devotional pageantry. Parishes then did their best to vie with chapters in every punctilio of ritual. The cathedral itself could not have elaborated upon the standing orders for the Corpus Christi-tide procession of the parish of Saint-Julien, 5,000 words in length, which lay down robing stations for 6 priests, 4 masters of ceremonies, 12 thurifers and 46 other acolytes, crossbearers and the like. From the length of albs to the disposal of the key of the chapel of Saint-Lezin all preliminaries are minutely regulated, until at last we heave a sigh of relief when the First Master of Ceremonies sets off the procession with a code of smoke signals from his thurible.[91] But though parishes did what they could with limited resources, it was monks and canons who monopolized the greatest splendour, and though each curé had his due place in general processions, all too often it was in a humiliating subordination to a chapter or monastery.[92] This being so, the proudest occasions for a curé and the most striking ones for his flock were those when services were held to commemorate unusual events of purely parochial significance. Golden weddings, when a mass was celebrated and husband and wife, as it was said, 'renewed their marriage' in the presence of children and grandchildren, were popular festivals which called for the attendance of all local inhabitants. A new bell would be consecrated with an elaborate ritual,[93] which so closely resembled baptism that liturgical handbooks were at pains to point out that bell-metal was not capable of receiving justifying grace. Great personages, such as the abbess of Ronceray or the chevalier de Gibot, would be present as 'godparents', giving their names to the bell and a donation to the parish, and some distinguished diocesan official like canon Louet would be called in to preside, arrayed in a white cope; there would be exorcisms with salt and water, washings and anointings while psalms and the antiphon *vox Domini super aequas* were sung and the tenth chapter of St. Luke read, for the bells call the Marthas of this world from their manifold pursuits to quietness and reflexion. Like the bells, a parish midwife had also to be blessed by the Church before entering upon her work. There were several admissions made to this office in 1778, following the termination of a course on midwifery given by Mme Le Boursier du Coudray, an expert from Paris who was touring the provinces under government patronage. The ceremony took place at the main mass of Sunday morning. A certificate from the intendant, and a testimonial from the curé vouching for the candidate's good character and knowledge of the baptismal formula (for use in emergency) were read out, and the new midwife was taken to the font, where she held a lighted taper, and took the oath of her profession with her right hand on the Bible.[94] Crowds flocked to these services, so that at least one curé congratulated himself on his foresight in transferring this admission ritual to the end of mass, so that the 'tumult' did not 'detract from the sacrifice'.[95]

Parish priests, having larger audiences on these occasions than they normally had for their homilies at Sunday mass, naturally seized their opportunities. When Etienne Janeau, a master wood-carver of eighty years of age, celebrated his golden wedding, curé Robin, 'always attentive to inspire in his parishioners all those sentiments of holy and peaceful living which will lead them to happiness, both in this world and the next, took this occasion to give a discourse on the union, peace and fidelity which ought to reign in the family and make it both happy and fruitful'.[96] No doubt, in blessing the union of this aged patriarch of the parish of Saint-Pierre, Robin was on his most correct behaviour, but pleasant stories also circulated concerning his genial informality in the pulpit. After a bad harvest, he is reported to have ended a gloomy call to penitence with 'luckily the vineyards have done well, we will make up for it in wine', and there was a notorious interruption of his discourse on another occasion while he gave instructions about a leg of mutton for his supper that evening.[97] Some of his colleagues favoured a more sombre vein. 'In dolore paries filios. . . . Thus spake the Lord to the first and most unhappy of all mothers, and thus He spake to all her guilty posterity', began one of our curés of Angers, welcoming a new midwife with a display of Augustinian theology and harrowing his audience by describing the fate of unbaptized children, 'for ever banished from the presence of their God, or baptized under doubtful forms which are inadequate to set at rest our fears for their eternal destinies'.[98]

These are extraordinary sermons. A good idea of the continuous routine teaching given week by week in parish churches is afforded by voluminous notes and common-place books left by curé Boumard of Sainte-Croix, mostly in his own hand, though some are summaries of courses of instruction inherited from his predecessors. There is an alphabetical reference dictionary of moral and religious topics, running from 'Adoration' to 'Stage plays';[99] there is a catechism course for children to teach them that 'they have a God to serve, a soul to save and a Paradise to win'. There are sermon notes on the gospel for the day throughout the year, and on set themes—the Ten Commandments, the Lord's Prayer, and the Sacraments. Then there are outlines of more formal doctrinal teaching—the Creation, 'the different hierarchies of angels', the making of man, the Fall, the promised Messiah, the Immaculate Conception of Our Lady, the life of Christ, 'Dialogues on the Passion', the Last Judgment. Here, due and literal attention is given to the terrible 'signs which precede the Judgment', but Doctor Boumard does not allow himself to degenerate into an apocalyptic commentator. 'We are made for Eternity, . . . we approach our Eternity', but it is a judgment to which all hearts are open, a judgment which is occurring now—'it is not necessary to wait for the other world to see a lecherous man in Hell, he is in it in this world'.[100] Homely homilies on church discipline bulk largely in this collection. Curé Boumard tells his flock why they must fast in Lent, and why they must stay to hear the whole mass on Sundays and feast days; he explains the importance of regular confession (for the rule of once a year is a mere minimum for the hard-hearted), and the benefits to be derived from 'the very useful practice' of praying before the Holy Sacrament, which is perpetually exposed in the church of Sainte-Croix. In the year 829, lightning had struck down peasants who tilled their fields on a Sunday; that was a long time ago, but we too would do well to abstain from Sunday labour to obtain God's blessing on our weekday work. The 'precepts of the Church' are fully expounded, and no false modesty inhibited our preacher from including number four, concerning 'the honour due to priests'—a salutary commandment which parish priests generally were attempting to bring home to monks and canons, as well as to laymen. No concessions were made to the eighteenth century. There is no retreat from dogma in favour of morality in a vacuum; there are none of those sermons beloved of *philosophes* which could be preached indifferently at Paris, London or Constantinople.[101] Riches are a menace to the soul, comedies are 'schools of demons'.[102] Let there be no praise of natural religion; there is nothing to be said for Mahomedans, Calvinists or Jews, and as for 'virtuous pagans', they are only virtuous through secret pride and self-esteem. Yet Jubilee year with its tide of facile indulgences was, apparently, something of an embarrassment to our clergy of Angers. For this occasion, Boumard had his lively and extremely unaccommodating 'dialogues' to refute critics—'I see very clearly that you have only an imperfect idea of the Church's treasury of merits, which the Council of Trent calls *heavenly treasures*'.[103] Wits and intellectuals might be undermining religion, but no word of compromise was ever uttered from the pulpit of Sainte-Croix. 'Never doubt any article of our faith, for to be wavering on a truth of the faith is to be a heretic.'

Nor were any concessions made to childish fears at catechisms. Why are the wicked inconsolable in Hell?—'For three reasons. The first is that it pleases God to make them suffer; the second is that the demons study to invent new punishments to torment them; the third is that the gnawing of their own conscience gives them no repose. The saints are pleased to watch them suffer.'[104] However, this grim example is not typical. Training in prayer and the sacramental life predominated in diocesan syllabuses. In their first class children under the age of six learnt the Pater, Ave and Credo, in French and Latin. The second class (6 to 11 years) was more highly organized, with boys and girls sitting apart and competing for posts of honour—'intendants' of the class, 'seniors' and 'first in the pew'.[105] Here the whole of the Church's liturgical year was studied in detail and full training in methods of prayer was given.[106] Perhaps these classes were taken by a vicaire, more often though, by a catechist, with two assistants to keep order and record the names.[107] It seems that the curé's role was limited by custom to general supervision.

Study and the preparation of sermons normally occupied a curé's weekday mornings, with pastoral visiting in afternoons. But these morning sessions were continually interrupted by visits of 'poor folk asking him for bread or confiding their little troubles (which are nevertheless big troubles to them)'.[108] A certificate signed by a parish priest was required before a loan from the Mont-de-Piété could be solicited, or free medicine obtained from the dispensary in the rue de la Chartre Saint-Maurille, or meat bought from butchers at a reduced price in Lent, and it was under their auspices that poor folk obtained gratuitous treatment from the doctors-regent of the Faculty of Medicine.[109] It was generally believed, in high society at Versailles as well as among simple provincial folk, that the only cure for the bite of a mad dog was a course of sea-bathing, and the clergy were expected to make out a sort of passport for victims, to ensure them a free passage and help on their way to the coast.[110] Poor parishioners applied for all kinds of help as of right. Collegiate churches were free to give alms as they were inclined,[111] but a curé was regarded by public opinion as under a complete obligation to find resources for charitable distribution, whether from pious foundations[112] or collections, or, in the last resort, from his own stipend. A diocesan official stated in 1784 that it was difficult to find priests willing to accept the living of La Trinité— 'they prefer the humblest title to that of a benefice, which, though more honourable, would put them in the position of hearing every day the groans and lamentations of the poor, without having power to aid them'.[113] Clavreuil, who resigned in that year, had in fifteen years spent 15,000l., partly his own patrimony, partly debts which he had been obliged to incur. The winter of 1788-9 was a grim time, and the abbé Robin tells us that his tribulations were increased by the smallness of the charitable contributions be received; for while the rich gave alms, they did not give them through the curés, to whom the poor continued to make their applications, so that he himself paid out 300l. of his own money.[114] When the parish priests of Angers leagued together in August 1789 to insist that places in the Hôpital Général be allotted free of charge,[115] they were fulfilling collectively that role of guardians of the interests of the poor which public opinion had for long assigned to them in their individual parishes.

A curé's responsibilities towards the indigent extended also to seeing that their children received some sort of education. Families of the lower middle-class and above enjoyed adequate educational facilities in a graded hierarchy of institutions. For girls, there were convent schools, for boys, the Collège d'Anjou and the humbler boarding-school of the Frères des Écoles Chrétiennes. There were, too, independent schoolmasters, often ecclesiastics—like the abbé Faucheaux, a chaplain of the collegial of Saint-Martin—who took pupils at their homes under licence from the University.[116] But for children of ordinary folk, who could not afford to pay more than a trifling fee, opportunities were very limited. A girl might be one of those who was allowed to attend free classes of the Ursulines or of the sisters at the Hôtel-Dieu, a boy might be lucky enough, if he had a good voice, to receive his education as a choir-boy. Failing this, there was no resort but the parish school. Government edicts assumed that such an institution would be everywhere maintained,[117] but in practice, the efficiency and, indeed, the very existence of parish schools owed much less to official directives and the collective activity of local inhabitants than to the accidental incidence of pious benefactions. In this respect, by comparison with nearby country districts, Angers was well provided for, and during the eighteenth century, these endowments were steadily renewed. We hear of legacies to a girls' school in the parish of Saint-Samson, and a boys' school in that of Saint-Julien, of gifts by the cathedral to its parish of Saint-Maurice and by the Seminary to Saint-Pierre, of a house bought and leased to provide a salary for a schoolmaster at Saint-Martin.[118] Some parishes owed their schools to the generosity of a former curé, men like René Gasnier, who provided his people at Saint-Jacques with a building and enough money to maintain it, pay a teacher and provide prizes for the children.[119] Thus it was, too, that Saint-Nicolas enjoyed the services of an ecclesiastic and a sister from the Hôpital Général by virtue of a legacy from a parish priest earlier in the century, and Saint-Michel de la Palud had a school-house in the *cul-de-sac* at the end of the rue Courte, given to his people by curé Behier.[120] The parish of Saint-Maurille could boast a charity school for girls run by the little community of Saint-Charles, which had been founded early in the century by a pious lady with the object of training schoolmistresses who could be sent out to dispense medicines and the alphabet in the surrounding countryside.[121] It was gifts such as these, rather than votes of money by thrifty parish assemblies, which gave education to the poor. The wealthy inhabitants of Saint-Michel du Tertre, for example, voted a trifle of 16*l*. a year towards their two schools, which were otherwise maintained by old foundations, whose income was carefully noted in a dossier kept separate from ordinary vestry accounts.[122] It can be shown that at least ten parishes of Angers had a school in the eighteenth century, and the claim of the municipal authorities in 1763 that this was true of almost all of them seems very credible.[123]

Here, amid the babel of classroom, the word of the parish priest was law. He drew up a list of children whose parents' circumstances entitled them to free education,[124] and he appointed the master or mistress. In country districts, a village schoolmaster was likely to be sacristan, grave-digger and clerk as well,[125] but in Angers, where there were so many ecclesiastics and ecclesiastical institutions, this not entirely congruous plurality was unnecessary. The Frères des Écoles Chrétiennes sent teachers across the river every day to the tumble-down *maison du Saint-Esprit* which served as school-house to the parish of La Trinité.[126] Elsewhere, sisters or ecclesiastics from the hospitals fulfilled these functions, or unbeneficed priests would be employed, 'finding there a part of the livelihood which fortune had refused them'.[127] The bias of the curriculum may be gauged from conditions laid down in the seventeenth century in the parish of Saint-Jacques, and from the terms of appointment of a schoolmaster for the canton of La Madeleine in the parish of Saint-Julien in 1754.[128] In the latter case, lessons were to be given from 8 to 10 in mornings, and from 2 to 4 in afternoons, and reading, writing, the Catechism and all the duties of religion were to be taught. René Gasnier was more specific still concerning details of religious obligations. Latin and plain chant were included in his curriculum, rosaries and images in his list of prizes, while the most important features in the training of girls were to be 'prayer, and learning the art of laundering all types of church linen'. It was a haphazard, inefficient and clericalist education which was given in these parish schools of the old régime, but this at least can be said in its favour—for most children, it was gratuitous. In 1816, there were no free schools left in Angers.[129]

Along with these functions of a pastor of souls, relieving officer and educationalist, went those of a public official. High mass on Sundays was still the chief occasion for making official secular announcements, though a growing sense of liturgical decency now prevented their inclusion with ecclesiastical notices at sermon time, and courts of law were no longer able to require proclamation of their sentences in church, the Parlement of Paris having by a decision of 1727[130] relieved the curés of Angers of this incongruous obligation. Public order was still, however, under religious sanctions, though by the middle of the century the *monitoire* was becoming obsolete.[131] Since excommunication had become unfashionable, a curé's direct responsibility to the state was largely reduced to the less lurid task of maintaining parish records. From the sixteenth century, his registers were official secular documents as well as ecclesiastical, and they furnished legal evidence of births, marriages and deaths. Two independent entries were made; one remained with the parish, the other was deposited at a state registry.[132] It was proverbial that, in this age of exact and exacting notaries, these records of curés were, by contrast, ill-kept and slipshod. 'Why are the children of this world wiser than the children of light?' asked a lawyer.[133] A reason is not far to seek. Registers, costing anything from 3*l*. to 15*l*. a year, were bought by the parish, which even had to pay 5 sous a time to a local *procureur fiscal* who paged them;[134] and the curé himself received no fee for his services.[135] Harassed with continual spiritual duties, he felt no particular moral obligation to be efficient as an unpaid agent of the government. It was one thing to keep a parochial record, and quite another to render accurate duplicates to the civil authority, or to make fool-proof arrangements for lawyers to consult his registers in the course of their lucrative business. In 1770, Robin of Saint-Pierre was in difficulties with the courts over his negligent custody of his parish records. An entry of 1495 had been partly erased, under suspicious circumstances of which he could give only a very halting explanation.[136] An unnamed clerk of Murault, a notary of Angers (this clerk could be recognized by the fact that his fingers of one hand were twisted) had called to look over the registers, and as Robin had had pressing duties in church, he had left his visitor with his sacristan,

L

the sacristan's son and a boy who did odd jobs at the vicarage. The latter had deserted to go on a shopping errand, and the sacristan and his son went off to see some wretched man being pilloried, being encouraged in this dereliction of duty by the notary's clerk, who said he 'wouldn't eat their books'. Nor had he, but when someone else called to make an extract of the same information, it was discovered that three words had been erased, though it was true that they remained faintly visible, and a former vicaire of the parish could give evidence that they formed part of the original entry.

Curé Robin, in fact, kept his parish registers to serve historians of the future rather than lawyers in the present. Other parish priests inserted notes on important ceremonies in their churches, or recorded increases in their stipends.[137] Robin went further, and kept a chronicle of curious events of general importance. His record of births, marriages and deaths is enlivened by descriptive passages— we hear of the mild winter of 1758-9, 'like a continual spring', and of the fantastically hot summer that followed, of the extraordinary duration of the winter of 1766, when 'on Ash Wednesday, 12 February, we were still going to see the skaters on the meadow of Saint-Serge', and of the tremendous winter of 1788-9, when the ice on the river bore horses and carts, followed by two great thaws which flooded whole streets, so that the curé of Saint-Pierre had to use a bridge of planks to regain his house after celebrating a midnight mass on Christmas eve.[138] Above all, there is his account of how news of the fall of the Bastille reached Angers, how he was coffee-housing with a select little group of canons awaiting the arrival of despatches from Paris, how as soon as the first word was read the room filled with people, how there was a rush to the town hall to demand the formation of a militia, while the duc de Brissac, 'all trembling and pale as a corpse', dared not go out of his lodgings even to inspect his troops.[139] These were stirring events, more worthy of a chronicler than the dry facts which lawyers demanded to prove wills or dispute inheritances.

The curés were full of pride in the dignity of their office: but in Angers, at least, it was a pride in their spiritual responsibilities rather than in the secular and social functions which they so often performed. *Le bon curé* of eighteenth-century literature, charitable to the poor, an aid and accomplice of true love, and an 'officer of morality' in his parish, too often fell rather short of being a priest in strict theological beliefs.[140] But here, our parish clergy made no attempt to separate their role as philanthropists from the commission they had received at ordination, on the contrary, the latter was primary. God relies on men, said Boumard, for the regulation of the internal order of states, 'on the saints for the establishment of religious orders, on the angels when He wished to give His laws, but He chose to institute the priesthood Himself, to demonstrate its greatness, and to show how much respect is due to those He has chosen from mankind to serve Him in so perfect an estate'.[141] But this manifestation of pride, is pride in an office; the man himself, Boumard insists, must be humble, and his function of leadership is to be exercised by example rather than command.

It is by prayer that curés can finally achieve the good results which God withholds from their works. When their efforts bear little fruit, that is always a serious warning to them to return to God, and their success is always a reason to render thanks to Him. A curé who has been led by God to the sacred life returns into the world only with the aim of sanctifying it by his teaching and example. The first characteristic which should be noticeable in a parish priest is moral purity: his life ought to stand as a censure of all average standards.[142]

3. PARISH ASSEMBLIES

Within his parish, a curé had independent authority in matters concerning the organization of divine service and administration of sacraments, but he was excluded from control of matters involving church property and revenues, which were considered by lawyers as 'purely lay and temporal'. These were dealt with by a general assembly of inhabitants, and by churchwardens (*marguilliers*) who were elected there. Thus it was a parish, and not its priest, which was responsible for providing confessionals and other furniture, liturgical books, wine, wax, and oil, for doing laundry and repairs, for cleaning the church and appointing a sacristan and choir-boys, for keeping accounts, collecting pew-rents and accepting legacies.[143] Where spiritual and temporal overlapped, there were various regulations and customs which covered debatable ground. A foundation mass was accepted by the parish, though its incumbent would have to give his consent. Churchwardens, with the agreement of their curé, were entitled to spend up to 10*l.*, but a greater expenditure required an authorization from the assembly. Commonly, all title-deeds to property, loose cash in hand and church plate were kept in the sacristy in a coffer with two or three locks, the priest having one key, the warden in office another, and a third, if there was a third, would be held by a royal or seigneurial official, or, as at Saint-Michel du Tertre at Angers, by a delegate named by the parishioners.[144]

In strict theory, a general assembly ought to have been open to all inhabitants. Although this democratic system survived in some rural districts, by the eighteenth century, in most parishes, especially urban ones, it had declined into oligarchy.[145] In the eighties, law books were assuming that this would inevitably be so, and that a summons to an assembly would be confined to nobles, officers of courts of justice, *avocats*, ex-churchwardens, and 'notables'—that is, inhabitants paying from 12 to 15*l.* in *taille* or *capitation*.[146] By an ordinance of 1786, the Parlement of Paris laid down this sort of membership for all parish assemblies in Anjou. Routine affairs were to be run by a *Bureau ordinaire*, meeting on the first or second Sunday of each month, and consisting of the curé, churchwardens in office, and from four to six ex-wardens, while at least twice every year, a general assembly was to meet, composed of this *Bureau*, all other ex-wardens, nobles, magistrates and *avocats*, together with twelve principal inhabitants, taken from among those who pay at least 12*l.* in *taille* or 6*l.* in *capitation*.[147] This regulation was not imposing any startling change, in fact, it was doing little more than confirming and codifying a state of affairs already in existence. One factor which had contributed to bring about this narrowing down of general assemblies was the pressure of dignified residents who did not care for the rough and tumble of democratic procedure. In the seventeenth century, the staid official parish of Saint-Michel du Tertre had been much troubled by a caucus of the faubourg Saint-Michel tumultuously pressing its candidates for sacristan and assistant clergy, and a 'sage regulation' of the Parlement of Paris had been obtained to limit attendance to the curé, wardens and ex-wardens, officers of the *Présidial* and other royal jurisdictions, the senior notary of the parish, and twelve notables chosen by these.[148] Here, in fact, is a standard formula for the future. In other parishes it had probably been less a matter of pressure from above than reluctance from below, coupled with considerations of administrative convenience, which led to such a change. On 13 April 1766, the parishioners of Saint-Julien agreed (having obtained authorization from the Parlement of Paris) to model their constitution upon that of Saint-Michel du Tertre—and already there were only twenty people present to vote.[149] Three years later, the assembly of Saint-Evroul fought, and fought successfully, to prevent the suppression of the parish—out of 300 communicants, twenty-nine were present at this crucial meeting.[150] When we find a large concourse of 47 people gathered in the vicarage of Saint-Denis, we can be sure that householders' pockets were gravely threatened, as they were indeed on this occasion by curé Courtillé's designs for an expensive new wash-house and boiler. Thus, it is not surprising that parish affairs fell into the hands of notables, for after all they were those substantial citizens who were eligible to be constrained to serve in the time-consuming task of *marguillier*. The parish of La Trinité, for example, could hardly complain, if, enforcing service in this office on pain of a fine of 100*l.*, it found its general assembly had become an oligarchy.[151] Those who paid the piper called the tune. In most parishes, only the second half of the traditional formula 'la plus grande et saine partye des dits paroissiens' was now relevant. The grave magistrates, *avocats* and notaries who predominated in the assembly of Saint-Maurice took five years to find a new *cliché* which would satisfy their legalistic consciences. In 1765, they were 'the parishioners and inhabitants', three years later 'the parishioners and notable inhabitants' followed by 'the parishioners and inhabitants' with 'notable' inserted as an afterthought. By the end of 1769 they were 'the notable parishioners and inhabitants'. At last, in January 1770, they described themselves as 'the notable parishioners', and at this they stayed.[152]

These parish assemblies were in mesh with the administrative machinery of state and municipality. All meetings, even for purely internal affairs, required an authorization in the form of a civil ordinance of convocation. For most routine purposes, this warrant was given, on payment of a small sealing fee, by the lieutenant of police of the *Sénéchaussée* of Angers.[153] If it was a question of repairs, reconstruction, or levying a rate, instructions came from the final authority in these matters, that is, the *intendant* or his *subdélégué*. The municipality also summoned parish assemblies to review the names of candidates for municipal office, or to elect deputies to attend at the town hall when new officers were installed. Sometimes, there would be a request for an opinion on a proposed course of policy; should the city invite the Benedictines of Saint-Aubin to found a boarding-school, should street lamps be introduced, should a barracks, or a foundling hospital or a *bureau de charité* be set up in town? Parochial replies were usually conservative: by all means let us have a *collège* at Saint-Aubin, provided that no prejudice is caused to the already existing Oratorian establishment, by all means ask for barracks, but not at the expense of our present riding-school.[154] And above all, these parish assemblies were parsimonious. They were determined not to say anything which could ever be construed into an argument for extracting money from their pockets. There are two ways of viewing the proverbial nexus between consent and taxation, and when a request for advice came from the municipal oligarchy, taxpayers could be forgiven for adopting a suspicious attitude. Let the central government preach hygiene and progress at other people's expense, it was not for a parish to admit that its old cemetery 'could prejudice the salubrity of the air'.[155] Economic arguments proved that a barracks would bring trade, but the parishioners of Saint-Julien were still not reconciled to contributing to the initial outlay; there are too many taxes, they said, 'vu la difficulté des tems qui ne peut estre plus grande'.[156] Later, they were enthusiastically in favour of a foundling hospital, and painted a vivid picture of the tragic fate of abandoned children, 'who might become useful to the state, to industry and to agriculture'. But there was a rider added to their agreement—'on condition that the upkeep and feeding of the foundlings who are left at the said hospital shall in no case fall chargeable to the inhabitants of this town but, on the contrary, shall remain chargeable to the *seigneurs* of fiefs'.[157] There was little enthusiasm for street lamps. They will be, said the inhabitants of Saint-Denis, 'much more expensive than they had at first thought, for which reason they are of the opinion that the said establishment should not take place'.[158] Saint-Evroul, thoroughly reactionary, deplored the whole march of progress, manifested in 'les innovations journalières que l'on fait dans la ville'.[159]

Parish councillors were instinctively parsimonious, as befitted men whose principal duty was to preserve their church in decent solvency, gathering its revenues, and laying them out on routine maintenance with occasional major repairs or improvements. Detailed control was delegated by an assembly to its elected churchwardens, and most ordinary business was transacted at monthly meetings of the *Bureau ordinaire*, composed of wardens and ex-wardens. Normally, there would be two *marguilliers*, though the large parish of La Trinité had three, and a small and poor parish like Lesvière had only one. Their term of office varied from one year to three years, and a newly-elected warden usually began by taking over responsibility for the accounts, being known as *marguillier comptable* or *procureur de fabrique en exercice*. As nobles were exempt from serving, a parish chose its most prosperous commoners; Saint-Julien or Saint-Denis might boast a notary or an *avocat au parlement*, Saint-Michel de la Palud might have a gunsmith, La Trinité a merchant tanner or wax-maker, poverty-stricken Lesvière could rise no higher than a carpenter or a cooper.[160] A small parish, whose supply of eligible men was limited, was lucky if it found a Monrif de Montergon, who was willing (on conditions) to accept a further term of office at Saint-Denis,[161] or an *avocat* like Blanchard, who fortified Saint-Aignan with his legal expertise for over twenty years.[162] At Saint-Evroul, all problems were solved by the excellent Gouppil, master apothecary and brother of the curé, who took up his burdensome office in 1762, and was still presenting accounts in 1790.[163]

It is by reading between the lines of churchwardens' financial statements, and by eavesdropping when financial ways and means are discussed in general assemblies, that we can evoke something of the peculiar flavour of parish life under the old régime. Pew-rents, a standard source of revenue in all churches, probably serve to bring us closest of all to local gossip and to local worthies.[164] At the cathedral, the right of hiring out chairs was farmed to a contractor, so that it

was something of a curiosity when the municipal authorities made
arrangements for free seats for all at a service for the repose of the
soul of Louis XV.[165] A parish church might, in its minor way, follow
this example and make a contract with its sacristan,[166] but more
usually, a parish council preferred to keep the allocation of pews in its
own hands. There was an official charge of 30s. a year for a place at
Saint-Denis, 15s. (with an initial entrance fee of 3l.) at Saint-Evroul,
and 1l. at Saint-Maurille.[167] Thus, a vestry would obtain a small but
fairly constant yearly income—47l. only for a tiny parish like Saint-
Evroul, rising to about 100l. in more extensive parishes like Saint-
Maurice, Saint-Michel de la Palud, and in the wealthy 'official' parish
of Saint-Michel du Tertre as much as 300l. for chairs and 486l. for
pews in a single year.[168] Thorny problems of family traditions and
precedence were involved whenever places were allotted. When the
parish assembly of Saint-Denis decided to raise its rents from 20s. to
30s., senior inhabitants were to be given first choice in the redistribution, which was to take place at Easter, before wealthier parishioners
moved out to their country-houses for the summer.[169] It was not
always easy to ensure that the great paid for their privileges. This
increase of pew-rents at Saint-Denis was followed by an enquiry into
titles of possession. Canon Guerche, precentor of the cathedral, and
Mme de Langotière were found to be occupying free places without
adequate evidence to support their exemption, and the curé was
deputed to dun them for their 30s. The marquis de Contades,
another offender, was approached, and made an obliging reply;
which was noted, respectfully, but very firmly, by the parish
assembly.

> Concerning what has been represented to M. le marquis de Contades,
> that up to the present the rent of the pew that he occupies has only been
> paid on the tariff of three places, while it actually contains four, and that
> nothing has been paid for two chairs that the aforesaid marquise his
> wife occupies at the back of the church, near to and adjoining the con-
> fessional of M. le curé (of which one is for sitting, the other for kneeling),
> the aforesaid nobleman, the marquis de Contades, to prove his desire to
> contribute to the well-being of the aforesaid vestry, has offered, and has
> undertaken to pay, every year, starting on the first of this month, 6l.
> rent for his aforesaid pew, and 30 *sols* for the aforesaid two chairs.[170]

It would be hard to make a mistake after that! But alas for all these
calculations, three years later, in 1785, the bishop transferred the
parish services to Saint-Maimbeuf, and the assembly of Saint-Denis
had to reallocate all its seating. However, there were compensations,
as the choir stalls of the former canons of Saint-Maimbeuf were here
available for male members of the congregation. Twenty *sols* were
to be charged for its lower seats, and forty *sols* were not regarded as

too high a levy on those who aspired to sit in the lofty splendours of this canonical Olympus.[171]

In addition to rents for pews and chairs, a parish also drew other revenues from church services—from collections, offerings from pious confraternities, the sale of candle ends, and fees for hiring the pall at funerals. The new pall of the parish of Saint-Julien, bought in 1787, could be taken to a house of mourning by the sacristan at a charge of 6l., which was doubled if this involved going outside the parish boundaries.[172] Even Saint-Michel du Tertre was not so expensive— 1l. 10s. for the use of the ordinary funeral furnishings, and 3l. for 'le drap mortuaire de luxe'.[173] Generally, a parish would also possess some property, a small plot of land leased out for anything from 8l. to 102l. a year,[174] and one or two houses. Saint-Michel de la Palud owned a considerable house in the rue Saint-Aubin, and four others in the rue basse de Saint-Martin, while even poor Lesvière enjoyed a house rent of 60l. a year.[175] Then there were the main parish invest- ments, put into 'gilt-edged'. The parish of Saint-Laud drew 106l. interest each year from three small investments with the Clergy of France, Saint-Evroul steadily increased its holdings in the funds of the Clergy from 1,800l. in 1776 to about 3,000l. fourteen years later, the assembly of Saint-Pierre had 7,400l. salted away yielding an in- come of just over 400l., while comparatively small sums might be deposited at interest with some local monastery.[176] Churchwardens had a complicated task gathering in such fragmentary revenues. At Saint-Maurice,[177] there were pew-rents, church collections, donations by the confraternity of Saint-Sebastien, various endowments created at the end of the seventeenth and beginning of the eighteenth century by the hatmakers, wax merchants and shoemakers, 304l. interest from investments with the Clergy of France, a house in the montée Saint-Maurice leased for 30l. a year, and another leased for 12l., 56l. from the Benedictines of Montreuil Bellay, and three permanent annual gifts in kind—two candles at Christmas, one at Easter, and a buss of white wine on November 3. Occasionally, a churchwarden proved unequal to these complications of parochial finances and was unable to render a satisfactory account of his stewardship. Delay in presenting accounts was fairly common, though actual defaultation was rare. Even so, some parish assemblies found themselves saddled with deficits which retiring wardens were unwilling to meet. The parish of Saint-Denis decided in 1771 to take action against M. le Page, who still owed 556l. from his term of office seven years ago;[178] and in 1772, one Le Roy gave his note of hand (invalid as it turned out) for 384l. to balance a financial statement which he had presented to the parish of Saint-Evroul ten years previously.[179] Parochial days of reckoning, like Judgment Day, if long delayed, were nevertheless inevitable. Even in troubled revolutionary times, the demands of ex-churchwardens, 'ancestral voices prophesying war', were heard, smugly insisting on the verification of their successors' accounts.[180]

However, when all is considered, it is remarkable how providently even very poor communities contrived to manage their affairs. The miserable little church of Saint-Aignan,[181] with few parishioners and fewer endowments, in strict logic might well have been expected to decline into a mere garrison chapel of the castle. But not so. Its little congregation was faithful, its meagre finances were well managed, and slowly and painfully, money was set aside for maintaining and adorning the church. In the mid-century, there was a yearly income of 30*l.* from pew-rents, rather less in burial fees, a little from collections, and 25*l.* from investments. This investment income declined to 10*l.*, but the pew-rents were developed, until in 1780 they yielded over 70*l.* annually. A special collection for repairs to the fabric in 1758 brought in 340*l.*, the curé, a former curé and the cathedral chapter made handsome contributions, and when in 1785 a pious lady added 2,500*l.*, the parish was more than solvent. All the while, routine maintenance was carefully attended to; new slates were put on the roof, church ornaments were repaired, lead was substituted for wooden guttering, worn-out linen was patched or replaced. We hear too of expensive new acquisitions, of a gradual and a missal bound in morocco, of two palls, one black and one white, of a chasuble and paten costing 330*l.* In 1758, well over 1,000*l.* was expended on decorating the walls, erecting three new altars, gilding the tabernacle, constructing a new pulpit, and furnishing images of Our Lady and Saint-Aignan. This work of adornment was completed by further improvements in 1781 and 1788. Saint-Aignan may have been, so to speak, a toy parish, where everything was in miniature, but it was a perfect replica of a real one. All things were done efficiently and in due order. Churchwardens, although not obliged to do so, took out expensive letters of nomination on appointment, gave receipts on properly printed notepaper, and kept meticulous accounts. Without considering the ample supplementary benefices which he contrived to amass, one can guess that the abbé Doguereau found many compensations in being *prieur-curé* of a humble but well-organized parish like Saint-Aignan.

Normally, a parish assembly met in the vicarage, with its priest present, sometimes writing up the minutes, and generally signing first at the end of proceedings.[182] La Trinité was something of an exception, for here meetings were held in the old sacristy, and the community of priests of that church was entitled to send a deputy to preside over deliberations. Even so, this theoretical right had fallen into disuse, and from the mid-century, the curé was accustomed to assume precedence of place and signature.[183] Where co-operation is a matter of routine and disagreement a subject for debate, minute books are not likely to give a fair history of relationships between the clergy and their parish councils, though in unusual circumstances, these unsentimental records may afford us a glimpse of mutual friendships which do not normally find a chronicler. The abbé Rangeard of Academy fame, living comfortably in the country on the rich tithes of Andard, sent a gift of 300*l.* to his old parish of Saint-Aignan; his successor added 500*l.* of his own money to pay off standing parochial debts, as well as giving a pulpit cloth, 'a pall embroidered with gold', and 'a new multi-coloured chasuble with gold flowers'.[184] From the other side, we occasionally find the people expressing generous sentiments towards their clergy. When a vicaire of Saint-Julien asked for a wall to protect his garden from passers-by who stole his fruit, the assembly decided that at least it would allow him a hedge and a little extra land—'It is very natural for us to do everything possible for *Monsieur le vicaire*, he merits it in every respect.' [185] Enthusiastic eulogies of curé Gouppil were elicited from his parish council when news was received of a project to terminate the independent existence of the church of Saint-Evroul. 'They loudly proclaim that there are few parishes where instruction is provided with such assiduity, and where spiritual and temporal succour is given with more devotion, zeal and humanity.' [186]

In thus applauding their pastor's zeal (and, it must be said, all too complacently approving his willingness to accept a less than living wage), the parish councillors of Saint-Evroul were not being entirely disinterested. If they were incorporated with Sainte-Croix, there would be a definite danger to their pockets. 'This church is much decayed, and will be in danger of collapse in the not very distant future; proprietors of houses in the parish of Saint-Evroul have an interest in remaining responsible for the repairs of the church of Saint-Evroul, whose building is solid.' [187] This is typical. Here, local patriotism and affection for a parish priest are allied with dictates of thrift: on other occasions, these considerations might clash, and whatever happened, the evil day when a rate had to be levied must be postponed. Churchwardens reckoned very strictly with their curé. In 1774, the abbé Lepron proved with some difficulty to his parish council of Saint-Maurice that he was being underpaid for his foundation masses to the tune of 23*l.* a year,[188] and in 1781 curé Courtillé of Saint-Denis demonstrated, by an investigation of accounts since 1762, that the vestry owed him 374*l.* 15*s.* 5*d.* However, this latter affair ended magnanimously. Courtillé, taking into consideration his parishioners' outlay on rebuilding his vicarage, waived his claim, while the assembly in return awarded him all profits accruing from the disposal of candle ends after funerals and other services.[189] In the case of curé Blouin, who ordered repairs to vestments and altar furnishings without permission from his churchwardens, the technical fault lay clearly on the other side, and it was not surprising that his parishioners of Saint-Julien refused to pay a bill of 204*l.* He knew perfectly well that the church's revenues were very modest, 'therefore', they argued, 'his intention has been to have the said ornaments repaired at his own expense, and indeed, we are more than persuaded that his design was to make a present to the aforesaid vestry'.[190] A year later, Blouin's successor, Huchelou des Roches, went about this business more diplomatically. The eight chasubles, of satin, of black velvet, of green and ruby damask, faced with imitation gold and silver braid, must have been very fine once—but they were now worn out. He suggested that he buy two chasubles and a stole at his own expense, and that the vestry could repay him as its revenues became available.[191] This was agreed, but in the following year, Huchelou des Roches met with a rebuff when he advanced a project which was suspected to conceal more serious financial obligations. The chapter of Saint-Julien was now defunct, and the Seminary which had inherited its church, merely kept up some formal semblance of services there. Why then should the parishioners continue to huddle together in the nave, and their curé continue to celebrate at an inferior altar? Very reasonably, Huchelou des Roches had asked the bishop to allow him to use the whole building, and had shown his foresight by insisting that his parish should not thereby become responsible for any further repairs. On this score, however, his parish councillors were not willing to run any risks, judging, probably rightly, that sooner or later, possession would turn nine-tenths of the law against them. They admitted that, in particular, it was their ambition to have a sacristy of their own, but on one condition, 'that the said parishioners be not contributable towards it'.[192] A similar situation arose at Saint-Maurice when curé Lepron put forward a request for a contribution towards the salary of his vicaires. He could point out that, since the cathedral had absorbed the foundations which had once been available to pay assistant priests, curés had had to find aid at their own expense, that he himself had no private income, and that surplice fees had been steadily declining. This plea was coldly received by his parishioners—'the facts that the curé adduces have nothing to do with them and do not concern them in the least; that this being so, he is the only one in a position to try to get justice (from the cathedral), and at his own costs, risks and perils'.[193]

On the other hand, there was some expenditure which a parish priest could legally insist upon as being the sole concern and unavoidable responsibility of his people, and all major repairs to the vicarage came into this category. It was a heavy burden, which proved quite beyond the resources of a poor parish like La Trinité, where a rambling and ruinous presbytery was maintained only by the generosity of individuals and the sale of wood from the property of the cure.[194] Elsewhere, the inhabitants managed to fulfil their obligations, not without disputes, for the state of the law rendered disagreement inevitable.[195] An incumbent was obliged to do running repairs; if he failed in his duty, and major repairs were finally necessary, who was responsible then? So argued the parishioners of Saint-Pierre against their redoubtable curé Robin, who raised an expensive alarm when the roof beams broke over his bed; it was, they held, his neglect of running repairs for thirty years which had thus endangered his sleep and safety.[196] Then who was to pay for extensions and improvements? Sooner or later, a vicarage would have to be brought into line with improved housing standards, and a curé's ideas of minimum requirements was likely to be higher than those of his parishioners. Robin, whose two vicaires lived with him, appealed right up to the *Conseil du Roi* to ensure that his house was rebuilt on a more generous scale, and even when this dispute was settled, he was found to be adding an unauthorized window in one of his gable ends.[197] Each parish had its own peculiar problems. At Saint-Denis and Saint-Laud there were two vicarages, inherited from previous unions of benefices, and when it was a question of expenditure, a legal quibble could be raised as to which of the two ought to be the official residence; the curé of Saint-Laud, for example, preferred a convenient house in the cloisters, but his people would rather have him established in 'Monplaisir', further away, but in better repair.[198]

Here is a typical and unusually well-documented instance of a parish assembly dealing with a problem of vicarage reconstruction, in a general atmosphere of gloomy goodwill towards its parish priest. On 18 April 1775, by authority of an order of convocation signed by M. Ayrault, lieutenant-general of police, and after due warning by circulars and announcements at sermon time at mass, the representatives of the parish of Saint-Denis foregathered in their curé's house, on the very scene, as it were, of the crime. It was a comparatively full meeting, with a total attendance of nineteen. Ecclesiastical corporations whose property lay in the parish were entitled to be represented, so the Seminary had sent the abbé Ferrand, famous for his enormous nose, an infinite capacity for snuff, and unfailing business acumen.[199] A small committee of three (one being the abbé Ferrand) was set up, which was authorized to appoint two expert surveyors, and make a 'provisional' decision as to whether the vicarage 'could be safely lived in without being entirely rebuilt'. Their report was to be discussed at a later meeting. Everyone signed the minutes, our curé cautiously adding a rider to his signature, 'present without prejudice to my rights'.[200] After this, there was a delay, until curé Courtillé shook off the tax farmers, who, with 'insatiable avidity' were proposing to levy a fine on this projected improvement to ecclesiastical property;[201] meanwhile, the dilapidated house was rented out on a lease terminable at one month's notice.[202] Finally, it was decided to begin rebuilding in the spring of 1777. On 27 April of that year, in a meeting authorized by an ordinance of the *subdélégué* of the intendant of Tours, three commissioners were appointed to be present at the auctioning of the contract, which was actually taken up for a sum of 5,900*l*.[203] However, curé Courtillé soon pointed out that the plan agreed upon omitted an addition which was very dear to his heart, 'a wash-house, and a little attic study in the roof above it, with a fire-place in each'. This turned out to be an expensive supplement. The contractor (a master carpenter of the parish of Saint-Michel du Tertre) and his cautionary backer were adamant, in spite of repeated appeals, on an extra payment of 1,685*l*. 12*s*. On 12 June, the curé put his case to a huge meeting, with forty-seven present in place of the normal eight or nine.[204] This additional building, he explained, would be a wash-house, with a large copper or boiler; above it, in the roof, would be a small room provided with a solid stone fire-place, while below the whole structure would be a cellar. Documents relating to the temporal of the cure would conveniently be kept in this little upper room, the copper would be used every Saturday to heat up soup which the parish provided as alms to prisoners in the town jail, and the cellar would house the fuel needed for this purpose. 'It was neither possible nor fitting', he said, 'that a curé of a town, who was being allowed nothing more in the way of ground floor accommodation than a little sitting-room fourteen feet long (both for taking his meals and for fulfilling the obvious social obligations of a man in his position) and a little kitchen of the same size (where his meals would be prepared and where his servant-girl would have to live), should also be compelled to give up this latter room every Saturday of the year for the cooking for the prisoners; furthermore, he would find himself reduced to the parlous necessity of putting all firewood, both for his own use, and that of the prisoners, all higgledy-piggledy alongside his stocks of wine in one and the self-same cellar which was under the said kitchen and no more than fifteen feet in dimensions, which would infallibly cause the deterioration of this latter article of consumption.' This cry *de profundis* carried the day. All agreed to contribute. In February of the next year, payment was becoming due, and the intendant authorized the levy of a rate on all property owners within the parish. Rather half-heartedly, under a tentative formula, curé Courtillé drew attention to a transaction of

1750 which was alleged to make the Seminary responsible for half the bill; 'it would', he said, 'be interesting' to know if this was the case. The abbé Ferrand left no doubt about the matter. This claim, he declared, was 'irregular and unfounded', and he offered payment in strict proportion to the value of the Seminary's possessions within the boundaries of Saint-Denis.[205] No one could refute him, and in its meeting of April 1778, the parish assembly proceeded to make an assessment. As town dwellers were free from *taille*, and ecclesiastics enjoyed exemption from *capitation*, the incidence of the rate was independently calculated, one fifth on the value of house rents, and four-fifths on the value of property in general. There was an original contract for 5,900*l.* to be honoured, then an additional 1,685*l.*, together with the curé's expenses for lodgings during the time of rebuilding, and fees due to royal officials and surveyors. Thus, a tiny parish, which might expect two baptisms and five burials in a year, was saddled with a tax of 8,500*l.*[206] And the Seminary, which had inherited the rights of the old chapters of Saint-Julien and Saint-Maimbeuf, had not been made liable for half the cost. However, the suggestion that it might have been was typical, and it is the relations of parishes with dominant monasteries and collegiate churches which forms a central theme of the ecclesiastical history of the town of Angers in the last decades of the old régime.

CHAPTER VIII

CANONS AND CURÉS

I. PATTERNS OF RIVALRY

GENERALLY speaking, parish priests of eighteenth-century France fell into two distinct categories. There were beneficed curés, named by a bishop or lay patron and holding their tithes in their own hands; some of these were very comfortably off, and even those who were not, were at least independent. On the other hand, there was a whole class of curés who were nominated by abbeys, chapters, congregations of canons-regular or the Order of Malta. These corporations and communities retained the title of *curé primitif*— to use English terminology for this phenomenon, they were 'rectors' in their parishes, while the actual parish priests were their 'vicars'.[1] Royal declarations had given security of tenure to a curé in this position, but the galling honorific superiority of his *curé primitif* remained, most usually demonstrated by the right of celebrating divine service in his parish church on the four solemn feasts of each year and the day of the patronal festival. A monastery or chapter would also, like as not, have impropriated the tithe and revenues of the living, paying its priest a mere 'portionem congruentem', which, though congruous with law, certainly bore small relation to the cost of living. Hence, such curés were described as 'curés à portion congrue', though it is important to notice that the *congrue* did not automatically accompany dependence on a *curé primitif*. The latter's rights might be honorific only, though, as such, a blow to the pride of both priest and parish, or, they might extend to possession of revenues which ought more properly to have constituted an endowment for the living, and thus be doubly hated.

At the beginning of 1768, that is, before the royal edict of May of that year, we find all seventeen parishes of our town of Angers dependent on monasteries or chapters. The tiny parish of Saint-Aignan, which had the status of *prieuré-cure*, is an exception, but only technically so, for the canons-regular always turned it over to a secular priest on account of its miserable income.[2] Six parishes had a monastery as *curé primitif*: Saint-Michel du Tertre and Saint-Samson depended on the abbey of Saint-Serge, Saint-Michel de la Palud on Saint-Aubin, Saint-Jacques and La Trinité on Ronceray, and Saint-Nicholas on the Benedictine house of that name. Three parishes, Sainte-Croix, Saint-Maurice and Saint-Evroul, came under the cathedral, while Saint-Pierre, Saint-Maurille, Saint-Laud and

Saint-Martin were dependent on the other four collegiate churches whose names they bore. When the moribund chapters of Saint-Julien and Saint-Maimbeuf had been suppressed at the end of the seventeenth and the beginning of the eighteenth centuries, their privileges, including the status of *curé primitif* in their respective parishes, had fallen to the Seminary, though actual appointment to these benefices was from henceforward vested in the bishop.

Financial provisions were heterogeneous. Saint-Nicolas and Saint-Samson were, quite simply, on the *congrue*, which had been fixed, by a royal declaration in 1686, at 300*l*. for a curé and 150*l*. for a vicaire. One says 'quite simply', but no arrangement in eighteenth-century France was ever very simple. While the abbeys of Saint-Nicolas and Saint-Serge were responsible for finding most of the money, small contributions towards each *congrue* were made by other ecclesiastical institutions; the abbot of Saint-Aubin gave 15*l*. towards that of Saint-Nicolas,[3] and the canons of Saint-Maurille, the Seminary (on behalf of the defunct chapter of Saint-Julien), and the treasurer of the cathedral were obliged to assist in paying the parish priest of Saint-Samson.[4] In addition to this complication of composite payments, the curé of Saint-Nicolas was entitled to free salt from his abbey, and both he and his colleague on the other side of town enjoyed *novales*, that is, tithe on any new crops cultivated within their boundaries. The other four parishes dependent on monastic houses had their own revenues. Such miserable tithes as there were in the parish of Saint-Jacques were collected by its curé,[5] and the priest of La Trinité drew his income from the property of his benefice, thus neither received a subvention from the abbess of Ronceray. Saint-Michel de la Palud and Saint-Michel du Tertre were also, in the main, financially independent of the abbeys of Saint-Aubin and Saint-Serge.[6] When parishes had been split off from their chapters, varying agreements on finance had originally been made. Thus the canons of Saint-Laud had left their curé in full possession of his temporal, reserving only a share in parochial oblations to themselves.[7] On the other hand, the chapter of Saint-Pierre had undertaken to pay a *congrue* of 300*l*., without prejudice to surplice fees, which were very large; this it had exchanged, early in the century, for the usufruct of a farm and tithes from certain lands, and when this income proved inadequate, it had been compelled to make an additional money payment.[8]

As prices steadily rose, some revision of the edict of 1686 became an obvious necessity, and in the seventeen-sixties, the *curés congruistes* of France began to league together to press their demands.[9] Finally, in May 1768, a new edict raised the *congrue* to 500*l*. A parish priest could opt for this payment if he wished, though to obtain it, he would have to surrender, not only any rents and normal tithes which his benefice might still hold, but also any *novales*, or new tithes, which he might be enjoying. In spite of these qualifications, this was joyful news in the vicarages of Saint-Nicolas and Saint-Samson. In the former parish, the *novales* consisted of a mere composition of 50*s*. from the Hôpital Général for new cultivation in a single paddock;[10] a greater income was drawn from tithe on the fields of Saint-Samson, but it was uncertain and variable. Thus an exchange for an extra 200*l*. in perpetuity was a welcome one. More especially, our curé of Saint-Nicolas was jubilant. Earlier in the century, his parish registers had taken envious note of the abbey's ostentatious building programme: now they record this triumph of the *congrue*, with a special note for posterity telling how monkish machinations to withdraw the yearly gift of salt were also defeated.[11] His neighbour of Saint-Jacques, seeing this new opulence of some of his colleagues, decided to follow their example and abandon the land and tithes of his benefice to Ronceray, in exchange for this newly augmented *congrue*. By 19 December 1770, he had plucked up courage to make his request to the abbess. That great lady, however, was a shrewd woman of business, not anxious to give away any of her revenues as a Christmas present. She therefore abandoned her rights as *curé primitif*, retaining only her patronage and her curé's obligations in the church of Ronceray. These legal formalities went through, as her lawyers said, 'without discussion of the question as to whether it is a fact that the revenue of the cure of Saint-Jacques, in fixed income, surplice fees and foundation masses, is not adequate to provide the curé with a reasonable amount to live on'.[12] In resorting to this mean shift and abandoning privileges which were transforming themselves into obligations, the abbess was but imitating the action of the cathedral with respect to its parish of Saint-Evroul, whose curé had applied for the augmented *congrue* two years earlier.[13] When the chapter of Saint-Maurice had heard of the edict of May 1768, it had hastened to consult its lawyers, and to put up various subtle objections to the agents-general of the Clergy of France.[14] On the whole, these evasive suggestions had been rejected, but a legal right to abandon the title of *curé primitif* (while retaining all rights derived from other sources) had been established, and this was enough to outmanœuvre the parish priest of Saint-Evroul. The canons probably quietened their consciences by arguing that article 16 of the edict of 1768, which ordered the union of small and poor benefices, was a more reasonable remedy for penury than sacrifices on their part. Whether this is so or not, a diocesan project to unite Saint-Evroul to Sainte-Croix, Saint-Maurice, or Saint-Aignan was brought forward in the following April.[15] The parishioners of

M

Saint-Evroul gave this design a bitter reception. Angers, they pointed out, needed more parish priests, not fewer.

There are in this diocese an infinite number of benefices without cure of souls, many chapters and monasteries, and the unions of these would be more than sufficient to augment the temporal of the cures of this town, which are already too few in number. His highness has just united forty-five chapels to his chapter of the cathedral of Angers, a proof of the multiplicity of benefices without cure of souls, and they (the parishioners) hope that his love for the Church and for his co-operators of the second order of clergy will produce a proportionate beneficence to satisfy the intentions of his Majesty indicated in the edict cited.[16]

It is true that, in their zeal to preserve their parish, they went on to use arguments which contradicted their pastor's claim for a higher income. He was, they said, satisfied with what he got, and managed to save enough to give handsomely to the poor—'Bel exemple à suivre'. Even so, these modest requirements which they ascribed to their parish priest only served to sharpen their criticism of rich benefice holders. The living of Saint-Evroul, they darkly admit, would never satisfy 'a priest who might be drawn to the ministry by ambition rather than by the holiness of that state of life'.[17] Saint-Evroul remained an independent parish, but its curé failed to obtain the *congrue*. He did, however, get something from this crisis of the early months of 1769. In alliance with his colleague of Saint-Maurice, he had formed an opposition at law to the union of forty-five chapels to the cathedral which had so angered the parish, and in February 1769, the chapter of Saint-Maurice agreed to buy off this opposition by promising 200*l.* a year to each of these parish priests once the proposed union of benefices had been accomplished.[18]

While the edict of 1768 had evoked speculation on the maldistri-bution of ecclesiastical revenues, it had benefited only three of our seventeen curés of Angers. History repeated itself when the *congrue* was raised to 700*l.* in 1786. Once again, a welcome augmentation was presented to Saint-Nicolas and Saint-Samson, while the parish priest of Saint-Michel de la Palud, who now decided that it was worth his while to apply for this revised income scale, found that his abbey of Saint-Aubin preferred to renounce its rights as *curé primitif* to escape its obligations.[19] In Angers, the steady success of the de-pendent parochial clergy of France in their demands for increased salaries was exasperatingly irrelevant. Three peripheral parishes of minor importance were rising in income at the expense of three monastic houses, while all other livings, holding their own property or tangled up in complicated arrangements with their chapters, were stationary. Every increase in the *congrue*, in fact, made it more unlikely that this increased *congrue* would ever be granted, and merely served to underline the rising cost of living as well as illustrating the need for parochial reorganization and for the redistribution of monastic and capitular wealth. And then, concerning honorific precedences and monopolies—what claim had they to respect if a monastery or chapter was willing, in the last resort, to abandon some of them rather than pay two or three hundred *livres* a year to a struggling priest?

Indeed, it was these distinctions of dignity, rather than financial disputes, which aroused the parochial clergy of Angers to ire against dominant ecclesiastical corporations. This was a fantastically litigious age, when courts resounded continually with expostulations of claimants to precedence and empty formal honours. Eighteenth-century France was too civilized: the term of an introverted existence had been reached. Society had settled into an infinitely complex hierarchy of caste and privilege, whilst passions and aspirations of a new age, so long as they continued to grow within traditional cadres, found expression in the law courts. Legal subtleties manifested society's attempts to sublimate revolutionary tendencies into the labyrinthine complexities of accepted forms. It was in this context of chicanery, and under a disguise of argument from precedent, that a battle against privilege was being waged within the clerical order, which itself was divided by a steadily developing rivalry of nobility and *Tiers Etat*. We have seen that this rift between aristocrat and commoner within the Church does not strictly coincide with a frontier drawn between monks and canons on one hand and curés on the other, but that, in so far as monasteries and chapters afforded well-paid sinecures, they had become aristocratic preserves. Here, no doubt, is an important factor in the growing class-consciousness of our parish clergy of Angers, and yet it would seem that their stirrings of common interest and resentment were really more of an ecclesiastical phenomenon than a social and economic one. It was less a question of hatred of privilege on logical and egalitarian grounds, than of a pride in their own office, and a desire to rescue its rightful dignity from eclipse or belittlement. Curés did not wish to be able to rise out of their station so much as to receive proper recognition in the place to which they had been called. They were men accustomed to command in their parishes, they performed innumerable social functions, and every day of their lives made them conscious of the importance of matters ceremonial. Naturally, they resented a system whose absurdities served no purpose beyond that of guaranteeing an artificial superiority to corporations whose privileges now greatly exceeded their social and religious usefulness. 'The title of *curé primitif*', said the canons of La Trinité in 1781, unconscious of the beam in their own eye, 'is foreign to pastoral direction, and to the care of souls. It is a vain and meaningless rank in the Church.' [20] How vain and meaningless it was, a survey of the complicated pattern of capitular and monastic domination over parishes will serve to show.

The most remarkable example of this domination is seen in two parishes of the old city, where the cathedral enjoyed unprecedented powers, extending far beyond any normal rights of patron and *curé primitif*. It is true that Saint-Maurice and Saint-Evroul had their own churches, and that the chapter had not absorbed such meagre possessions as formed the endowments of these livings.[21] Yet in all other respects, the church of Angers was supreme, being patron, rector, feudal overlord and diocesan superior all rolled into one. The curé of Saint-Maurice was held in complete tutelage; he was, said the canons (replying to a circular of the chapter of Perpignan, which was experiencing some difficulties with its dependent parish), merely a chaplain.[23] He was obliged to take an oath of obedience, and could be fined for negligence, he was forbidden to have his cross or banner carried aloft before him, he had to ask permission before he could expose the Holy Sacrament or stage new ceremonies or processions— indeed, the cathedral registers contain twenty pages of orders and prohibitions issued at one time or another by the chapter to its curé of Saint-Maurice.[24]

This peculiar enclave of interlocking jurisdictions was a remarkable anomaly. In all other parishes of Angers, the powers of monasteries and chapters were simply those of *curé primitif* overlaid and embellished by local variations and idiosyncrasies. Generally, a parish priest, whether he were the pastor of poor Lesvière or of the rich official parish of Saint-Michel du Tertre, was excluded from his own altar at the High Mass of Christmas, Easter, Pentecost, All Saints and the patronal festival.[25] Saint-Laud was an exception. Here, a succession of watchful incumbents had contrived to restrict their canons to minor usurpations—blessing the fonts on Easter Saturday and the eve of Whit-Sunday: which, said an ecclesiastical annalist earlier in the century, proved the value of constant vigilance, 'for against a chapter one cannot be too careful...O happy, happy curé!' [26] When an abbess of Ronceray was installed, ceremonies in the church of La Trinité were calculated to leave no possible doubt as to her supremacy.[27] She sat with her nuns in the principal stalls of the choir, her parochial clergy presented incense and holy water and brought the gospel book for her to kiss, and finally, she moved off in procession back to Ronceray under a canopy held by the four senior churchwardens. Excluded by her sex from exercising sacerdotal functions, the abbess nevertheless demonstrated her domination when the sacrament was administered, for a parish priest had to receive the key of his tabernacle from her hand.[28] A double servitude weighed upon this curé who ruled the largest parish in Angers. The canons of his church took their toll where the abbess left off. They celebrated mass on great festivals, they blessed ashes and palms and fonts according to season, they gave absolution on Maundy Thursday, they claimed a right to bury nuns and canons and other persons of distinction, they had first voice in the nomination of a precentor and choir-men and even of preachers.[29] In parishes dependent on monasteries, a curé who suffered some usurpation of honourable functions in his own church might find himself obliged, by an unequal exchange of courtesies, to render humble services in the church of his *curé primitif*. The incumbent of Saint-Jacques had to say an early mass once a month in the choir of Ronceray, his colleague of Saint-Michel de la Palud was obliged to attend high mass on feast days at Saint-Aubin.[30] When the Benedictines of Saint-Serge processed in town, the prior was escorted by the curés of Saint-Michel du Tertre and Saint-Samson, and preceded by the crosses and banners of these two dependent churches. At all major processions of the cathedral, the parish priests of Saint-Aignan, Saint-Evroul and Sainte-Croix had to take their turn in carrying a reliquary which held the bones of Saint-Séréné. Every parish had its tariff of such ceremonial obligations, thoroughly codified by the decisions of law courts.

As the liturgical year rolled on, its lofty festivals revived memories of rivalries, precedences, feuds and litigation. In some churches, too, every daily service was held in the shadow of tutelage. At Saint-Maurille, Saint-Pierre, Saint-Laud, Saint-Martin and La Trinité, high altar and choir were a canonical fortress, while curés said their masses in bleak naves or in humble side-chapels. The parishioners of Saint-Nicolas crowded into the chapel of Saint-André of their abbey church, and had to decamp to Saint-Jacques for their Easter communion, those of Lesvière used the monastic nave until its tottering roof became too dangerous, and then were allowed, under due restrictions, to borrow the high altar of the monks.[31] In the church of the extinct chapter of Saint-Julien, monopoly achieved its crowning absurdity. Dust gathered on derelict choir stalls, while the parish worshipped in the nave; once or twice a year, the Seminary staff came down in hoods and surplices and copes of violet velvet to say a minimum of offices and preserve their prescriptive rights.[32] Bells reverberated eternally to the glory of chapters and monasteries, rather than calling the faithful to their parochial duties. At Saint-Pierre and Saint-Maurille, the parish bell was banished to an obscure gable-end belfry, while the cathedral would not grant even this minor privilege to Saint-Maurice, lest a plebeian tintinnabulation detract from the ordered beauty of the mightiest peals of Angers.[33] Parishes which had obtained a right to share the main bell-tower had still not achieved equality of status, for a sacristan would have instructions to distinguish between capitular and parish offices by his method of ringing.[34] However, while the faithful laity envied the bells, choirs, high altars and sacristies of monks and canons, as things were, they certainly did not wish to take them over. Financial apprehensions overwhelmed their pride and their interest in the splendour of liturgical worship. Saint-Samson and La Trinité, parishes with their own churches, never ceased to bewail the ill-fortune which had left their monastic patrons free from responsibility for repairs to their bell-towers,[35] and where buildings were shared with chapters and monasteries the chief concern of ratepayers was to avoid any action which might furnish an excuse for a transfer of financial burdens. Those who used a church were, in the end, likely to have to pay for its upkeep. 'Subtle and crafty politicians', the directors of the Seminary had watched all the century for the inhabitants of Saint-Julien to make a false step. Every crack in the paving stones or wormhole in the beams was a warning to thrifty churchwardens of the parishes of Angers.

Desultory warfare between parish priest and *curé primitif* took place along a well-surveyed battle-front, which traditional rulings and old litigation had very largely stabilized. At one point, at least, all strategic features were held by the curé. It was his exclusive prerogative, within his parish boundaries, to administer sacraments and bury the dead. Lawyers cited Angers as a town which provided the clearest case law to justify this contention, and a secret consultation of the legal experts of the Clergy of France in 1759 admitted that these precedents were conclusive.[36] In 1737, the crucial victory had been won. It was then that the united curés of Angers, backed by their bishop, had obtained a decision of the Parlement of Paris against the royal chapters of Saint-Martin and Saint-Laud. By this ruling, parish priests were confirmed in their rights of administering the sacraments to all parishioners, and of saying the last suffrages over all who died within their boundaries, even if the dead man were a canon, or a chaplain or a benefice-holder of a chapter.[37] This case would not be valid, perhaps, against the powerful cathedral,[38] but it seems clear enough as regards all other chapters. Law-suits still continued, however—curé Robin was sued by the canons of Saint-Pierre, the canons of La Trinité began an action against the abbess of Ronceray—for every general rule in the eighteenth century was subject to qualifications of privilege or tradition. A dispute of 1774 between the Seminary and curé Huchelou des Roches of Saint-Julien illustrates one of these manifold contingencies which baffled human foresight. Huchelou des Roches claimed his simple legal right—to bury a parishioner, the deceased abbé Blouin. However, until 1768, Blouin had been curé of the parish himself, and the Seminary, as heir to the privileges of the chapter of Saint-Julien, was entitled to preside at the interment of its own parish priest. Furthermore, Blouin had been an honorary canon of Saint-Julien, and in his will had asked to be buried by representatives of that chapter. There was, inevitably, a scene. Just as Huchelou des Roches was singing a *subvenite* over his predecessor, the clergy of the Seminary arrived, and drowned his chant with their own; he replied by taking the names of witnesses of the scandal with a view to prosecution. By way of corporate protest, all other parish priests of the town refused to be present at the actual burial. From the first, it had been a shabby comedy. This is how the registers of the Seminary recorded the receipt of news that the abbé Blouin had died—'The differences which have arisen during many years between chapters and curés made us in no hurry to ring the big bell, as the custom is.' [39]

Another class of disputes, less macabre, but no less unedifying, concerned the joint use of churches by chapters and parishes, and here, the law was more likely to favour the former. We have seen how the Seminary lay in wait for an opportunity to unload its repairing obligations upon the parish of Saint-Julien, insisting meanwhile upon all obsolete rights in a strategy of patient provocation. A curé was not allowed to 'take possession' of font and sacristy—he merely had permission to use them. [40] Similarly, while he could borrow the plate and chalices of Saint-Julien for his celebrations, it was always made clear that this loan was of favour and not of obligation. Indeed, on one occasion, a sacrist of the Seminary established his point by depriving curé Blouin of communion plate altogether, an incident which caused a dispute of twenty-four years' duration, ending only in 1783, when the parish was granted a sacristy of its own and at last admitted that the altar silver was loaned out of 'pure goodwill'. [41] A chapter might also be under an obligation to make loans of a very different sort, and send some of its chaplains or inferior clergy to assist at a parish mass as deacons, sub-deacons or precentors. Each Sunday, for example, the Seminary had to send six ecclesiastics to high mass at Saint-Denis, [42] and, up to 1723, the cathedral had been under a similar obligation towards its parish of Saint-Maurice. In that year, however, various stray benefices were suppressed and their income annexed to general capitular revenues, a reform which had logic on its side, but which ignored the interests of curés of Saint-Maurice, and deprived them of their accustomed assistance. As late as 1768, memories of this injustice were still green in the mind of the abbé Lepron.[43] The chapters of Saint-Laud, Saint-Martin and Saint-Maurille still continued to send minor ecclesiastics to grace parochial masses, and up to 1763 all went smoothly. Indeed, the chapter of Saint-Maurille had just congratulated itself upon 'the concord and good relations which have always reigned between the canons and their parishioners',[44] when a difficulty about precedence, hitherto unsuspected, was suddenly discovered. Chaplains of chapters claimed priority over vicaires of parishes. Although both the diocesan bishop and the lawyers of the Clergy of France decided in favour of the parochial clergy,[45] our canons still took up the cause of their subordinates; the three chapters leagued themselves together by 'concordats' and 'procurations' to fight a law-suit to a final conclusion,[46] and representatives were sent off to initiate litigation before the Parlement of Paris. This apparently trivial dispute had wide repercussions: so much so, that two chapters, Saint-Laud and Saint-Martin, were very glad to fade out of a debate which was receiving dangerous publicity. There were those in high places who sought occasion to confiscate the revenues of useless benefices, and at Court they were suggesting that these two royal chapters, incurably quarrelsome and litigious, should be 'reformed' and united into a single and more economical institution. As soon as this rumour became current, we find the chapter of Saint-Laud very anxious to prove that it had always aided its curé in his functions, and had striven 'to forestall any possible complaint by showing politeness and avoiding everything which might have the appearance of resentment'.[47] But the chapter of Saint-Maurille, which ran no such risks, made no attempt to be genial. Curé Roussel lost his income from capitular distributions, anniversaries and foundations, and as late as 1768 he was still complaining that the ecclesiastics of the chapter were absent from his parish mass, with the connivance of their canons.[48]

While this dispute was laying up a fund of ill-will between parish and chapter at Saint-Maurille, other minor vexations were accumulating. The canons built a new rood-screen which deprived the parish of pew space worth 18l. a year. They refused to pass on any of the fee paid by M. de Tremblay for a plot of land in their main cemetery, and when the 'little' cemetery was levelled and cleared and handed over as a public square, none of the indemnity paid by the city found its way into the churchwarden's accounts. There was some controversy, too, concerning a right to appoint two choir-boys, and to renumerate them by selling off candle ends remaining after high masses and funerals. Royal officials, lawyers and notaries predominated in this parish assembly and they were wordly-wise, legalistic and uncompromising. 'There is no further hope of agreement,' they minuted in August 1765, 'nothing remains but a resort to the courts.' [49] A conference with canons Péan and Guillot failed to clear the air—'It is henceforward impossible to rely on any of the promises of the gentlemen of the chapter, they break them all.' [50] Already, thanks to the feud of vicaires and chaplains, curé Roussel was an angry man, and he now volunteered to prosecute a parochial law-suit in person, at his own costs and charges. His parishioners accepted this offer, and promised to recompense him with the yearly interest on any sum of damages to which the chapter might be condemned.

Sixteen years later this furious litigant was senior parish priest of Angers and a pillar of sobriety, even somewhat suspect by his more advanced colleagues as a weak collaborator in canonical dominion. Law-suits were expensive, lay support was fickle and, after all, Christian charity counted for something. Age and the passage of time soothed and mellowed the discontented. And so it would have gone on, had not the curés become more conscious of their identity and interests as a class and developed a common set of arguments to defend their rights. Once this was the case, natural leaders could arise and clerical revolt could be organized.

2. CURÉS, BISHOPS AND RICHERISM

Behind this chronicle of random feuds, financial and liturgical, can be detected a growing self-consciousness and developing tradition of common action among the curés of Angers. We have seen how they leagued together over burial rights in the thirties and how the priests of Saint-Laud, Saint-Martin and Saint-Maurille united to defend their vicaires in 1763. In both cases the diocesan bishop had favoured their claims. Between these two crises, however, a further development had taken place, for our Angevin curés, under the episcopate of Mgr de Vaugirault, had also begun to league together against their diocesan bishop himself. What was more significant still was that Mgr de Grasse, who succeeded to the see of Angers in 1758, showed himself fully conscious of his curés' growing power and deliberately directed his policy towards winning their support. The contrast between these two prelates and their rule in Anjou was both absolute and paradoxical. The first, austere, pious, hovering dutifully over every detail of diocesan life, was fanatically orthodox and a foe to all Jansenists. The second was idle, worldly and lived by pre-ference in Paris, yet, being a notorious hammer of Jesuits, he was praised by Jansenists as 'a prelate zealous for the purity of morals and for the preservation of our precious (Gallican) maxims'.[51]

Virtue and zeal made Jean de Vaugirault dictatorial: sloth and worldliness inclined Jacques de Grasse to make crafty, friendly advances to his lower clergy. Thus one prelate stirred up a united opposition and his successor called for united support, both in their own way assisting the curés of Angers to move into a closer alliance for the furtherance of their common interests.

When Jean de Vaugirault[52] ascended the episcopal throne of Angers in 1730, his clergy might well have reflected upon the good fortune which had preserved their diocese from becoming yet another apanage for young aristocrats of the Court. Their new bishop came from a comparatively obscure noble family of Anjou and was already fifty years of age when Fleury raised him to the episcopate on grounds of sheer merit. Older parish priests could remember him as a student at their local *collège*, as a young doctor of theology at the University, as a canon of Saint-Maurice and as vicar-general busy with the manifold details of pastoral administration. Apart from one brief visit to Paris, he spent his twenty-eight years as bishop entirely in his diocese, reprinting its liturgical books, beautifying its cathedral, organizing confraternities and good works, supervising clerical morals and, above all else, scouring away every taint of heresy. When a Jansenist fell mortally ill at Angers, Mgr de Vaugirault came in person to the death-bed.[53] If his exhortations proved fruitless, an episcopal order would limit funeral ceremonies to a few hasty strokes on the bell and a few formal prayers.[54] By the mid-century his zeal had breached and overthrown the last Jansenist strongholds in Anjou. As early as 1733 (on the very eve of the feast of St. Thomas, their theological patron) the Dominicans had admitted defeat.[55] In 1747 an escort of fusiliers removed the last Jansenist nuns from La Fidelité at Saumur and brought them to orthodox custody in Angers;[56] in September 1749 the superior of the Angevin Oratory and three of his priests signed their capitulation and were granted powers to preach and hear confessions once again.[57] The Seminary, the Faculty of Theology and the pressure of official patronage had done their work on the secular clergy and they in turn had moulded popular opinion. Jansenists, said a woman at the funeral of M. de Grimaudet du Landru, are 'Huguenots', and the coffin bearers put the corpse in its grave face-downwards, regretting only that they were not allowed to throw it in the river.[58] Even the *Nouvelles ecclésiastiques*, never prone to minimize the numbers of the remaining elect, had to admit that Jansenism was a lost cause in Anjou—a 'Sulpicien bishop', an agent of Jesuit and Molinist policy, had prevailed.[59]

Yet it was at this very moment when orthodoxy was triumphant, that a minor incident in bishop Vaugirault's repression of Jansenism aroused hostility among the curés of his episcopal town.

Mme Desplaces, a prominent resident in the parish of Saint-Michel du Tertre, died, an impenitent Jansenist, on 16 May 1752. The bishop sent for her curé, no doubt intending to prescribe abbreviated funeral rites. Curé Deniau, however, failed to report and buried Mme Desplaces with full ceremonies. He was punished by being deprived of power to hear confessions or preach outside his own parish, and his misfortune evoked expressions of sympathy and solidarity from all except one of the other parish priests of Angers.[60] This particular incident was trivial enough, but it was an unusual one in such an orthodox diocese and it formed a prelude to a series of law-suits which troubled the remaining years of bishop Vaugirault. Twelve curés of his episcopal town rejoiced in a curious title, that of *curé cardinal*, and by virtue of this otherwise obsolescent distinction they were entitled to be present in chasubles at the cathedral on solemn days when their bishop officiated pontifically. This privilege was not disputed, though a claim to wear hats along with the chasubles was;[61] a crisis arose when an episcopal order treated attendance as an obligation rather than a privilege and relegated the 'cardinals' to a position of subordination as compared with the archdeacons and canons of the cathedral. Our curés reacted strongly against this combination of episcopal presumption and canonical encroachment. An *appel d'abus* was laid before Parlement: the bishop had the affair 'evoked' to the jurisdiction of the Royal Council. Normally, once an evocation had by-passed the hurly-burly of ordinary anti-clerical justice, a persecuted prelate could regard his case as won; but the cardinal-curés interposed innumerable legal obstacles and rejoinders, to such effect that by March, 1757, they had won their case.[62] The Jansenist press rejoiced in this unexpected check to 'episcopal despotism', an 'evil which ordinances of the Council and *lettres de cachet* have continually aggravated since the entry on scene of the Bull Unigenitus'.[63]

Now, so far as Unigenitus was concerned, there is nothing to suggest that the curés of Anjou deplored it—the contrary appears to be the case. Nevertheless one must take notice of the fact that their opposition to Bishop Vaugirault coincided with that onslaught of parliamentary Gallicanism against the hierarchy which filled the mid-century with tumult. While the curé of Saint-Michel du Tertre was conducting Mme Desplaces' funeral, the Parlement of Paris was pursuing ecclesiastics who obeyed their archbishop's command to refuse the last sacraments to dying Jansenists. Parlement was ordering all universities to teach the Gallican Articles of 1682 (a command which the monks of Saint-Aubin gleefully noted in their capitular registers)[64] and maintaining its own right to act as a court of appeal in ecclesiastical matters[65] at the very time when the *curés cardinaux* made an *appel comme d'abus* against their bishop. In 1753 and 1756 the *Sénéchaussée* of Angers suppressed pamphlets—one inspired by Mgr de Vaugirault himself—which denounced the claims of lay magistrates to intervene in spiritual affairs,[66] while the Law Faculty censured one of its professors (a younger brother of an archdeacon of Angers) for dictating notes to his pupils which magnified episcopal pre-eminence and defamed the Gallican liberties.[67] Yet while these circumstances no doubt afforded encouragement to the curés in their law-suits, their motives at this time probably had as little direct connexion with the arid anti-clerical Gallicanism of lawyers as they had with the Augustinian doctrines which Unigenitus condemned. To them 'episcopal despotism' was the live issue and it is in this respect only that we are justified in attempting to link their quarrels with a wider movement of opinion which was spreading among the lower clergy of France.

In 1695, in return for a vote of benevolences, the prelates had obtained a royal edict giving them power to license confessors and preachers and to condemn their subordinates to a period of three months' incarceration in a Seminary without trial.[68] If more arbitrary intervention was needed, they could always apply to the Crown to imprison or exile trouble-makers by *lettres de cachet* and could protect themselves from the secular courts by having their law-suits evoked before the Royal Council. Not every bishop who accepted Unigenitus thought it politic to be logically ruthless and pursue all Jansenists,[69] but those who did so employed arbitrary devices to the full and had thus provoked a reaction, not so much against orthodoxy as against the kind of authority they were using to enforce it. So it was that from a submerged and declining Jansenism arose a new theological contention with very direct practical implications. It was a question now of the nature of authority in the Church. Was it true, as the prelates argued, that the second order of clergy had only a derivative divine commission and no more than a consultative voice in doctrine and morals? Or was it true, as Edmond Richer had argued at the beginning of the seventeenth century, that the Church ought to be ruled by the whole company of its pastors? From Père Vivien de la Borde's *Témoinage de la Vérité* in 1714 Richerist ideas were spreading. Official theology in the diocese of Angers made no concessions to such novelties. Volume IV of the *Conférences* which appeared in 1709 was devoted to the subject of ordination and was explicit on 'the jurisdiction which belongs in origin and by divine right to Bishops, as holding the first rank in the Hierarchical Order, and as successors of the Apostles, from whom all other inferior Ministers ought to hold, and to receive their power'.[70] Even so, in 1717, bishop Poncet de la Rivière thought fit to issue an 'instructive advice' to his curés, warning them against propagandists who offered them a right to take part in Councils of the Church—angry replies, at least one coming from his own diocese, showed that he had not convinced everyone.[71] Theologians and canonists, more especially the 'three Nicolas' ", Le Gros, Petitpied and Travers, published learned volumes in defence of Richerist hypotheses and thirty curés of Paris appealed to the King to protect the rights of their order. 'In the government of the Church,' they said, 'all things should be regulated in common.' [72] This was in September 1727, a date which marks a beginning of practical Richerist agitation among the parochial clergy. The financial grievances of curés, their hostility to capitular and monastic domination, their desire for guarantees against arbitrary power, their resentment against the aristocratic monopoly of more lucrative benefices were to be brought to a focus around a specific complex of historical and doctrinal argument concerning authority in the Church.

Some time was to elapse before these ideas could take firm root in a ruthlessly weeded garden of orthodoxy like the diocese of Angers. Antiquarian studies first of all suggested a possible route to subvert the monumental theological assertions of the *Conférences*; that was why dom Ros of Saint-Nicolas in 1746 gloated over discoveries in the archives of his house which showed that in the twelfth century priests used the same formula of absolution and the same prayers to bless chasubles and patens as their episcopal superiors.[73] It was possible also to evade questions concerning the jurisdiction of bishops and to do research into the rightful status of chapters, a line of attack which curé Robin of Saint-Pierre was to follow with noisy effectiveness.[74] But the decisive implantation of Richerist ideas came about in a more practical fashion through contact with ecclesiastical lawyers in the great dispute over the status of the *curés cardinaux* in the fifties. In handling this case, the legal experts who appeared for the parish clergy argued, not from pettifogging precedents, but from wide general principles. The twelve curés, they held, had a right to appear in the cathedral as co-celebrants with their bishop and as his natural advisers and assistants.[75] Their supporting arguments proceeded on Richerist lines. A superficial observer, we are told, might imagine when he sees the ample revenues, broad fiefs, palaces, retinues and honorific titles of bishops that there is 'an infinite distance' between them and their collaborators of the second order. 'Religion and justice', however, do not judge by such external circumstances, which have only arisen because the revenues of dioceses have been unfairly distributed on non-Apostolic principles.[76] Bishops in fact are 'simple depositories, accountable for their actions'.[77] Parish priests have their own direct Dominical institution to validate their ministry, being descendants of the 72 disciples sent out by Christ. Together with their bishop they form 'the Pastorate of the diocese', its 'Presbyterium', 'Senate' or 'Council'.[78] If cathedral chapters have usurped the role of an episcopal council, they should be deprived of it or, better still, their stalls should be taken over by senior curés, men well qualified by experience to give advice to their 'first pastor' and entitled by virtue of age to a quieter life.[79] Canons are officials 'of purely human institution', so too are archdeacons, who ought to be mere gatherers of information entitled to no superior rewards beyond their travelling expenses.[80] This in outline was the argument of the lawyers, and while not all curés would necessarily have agreed with the full rigour of these extreme claims or felt as ardent a passion of revolt as Jansenist journalists in Paris ascribed to them, it is clear that this prolonged litigation must have provided them with the basic principles of a Richerist education.

At this point, however, the grouping of opposing forces in the diocese of Angers shifted. Within a year of his defeat, Mgr de Vaugirault was dead and the alliance between bishop and canons, for the moment at least, came to an end.

Jacques de Grasse, who in 1758 succeeded bishop de Vaugirault without replacing him,[81] was a dissipated nobleman who lived as much as he could in Paris, where he ran through the income of his bishopric and two rich abbeys, as well as accumulating enormous debts. Here was a scandalous prelate indeed, but one who had a mind of his own and shrewd notions about the balance of power in his diocese. Whatever theological opinions he may have had were vividly anti-Molinist; on the other hand, his way of life was far from Jansenist austerity and it was obvious by now that there was no hope of a revival of Jansenist opinion in Anjou. Among a few families in town and among some of the older Benedictine monks and canons-regular gibes were still levelled at Unigenitus, but only two Jansenists remained at the Collège d'Anjou and a prior ruled at Saint-Aubin who was reputed to be 'more Molinist, if that was possible, than the Jesuits themselves'.[82] 'A Mussulman', said doctor Jubeau of the Theological Faculty, 'would enter Paradise before a Jansenist,' [83] and if theses[84] examined there are any guide, the precedence of Angevins over polygamous followers of the Prophet remained fully assured. A new volume of the diocesan theological handbooks was ruthlessly orthodox on grace so that in Jansenist circles its compiler was set down as 'an impudent falsifier, a dishonest summarizer, an outright Pelagian'.[85] Possibly Mgr de Grasse had never read it: however that may be, he gave his *imprimatur*.[86] It seems that he really cared for none of these things. What passed with him for theological convictions were really political opinions and he stands out as an episcopal example of that 'entirely political Jansenism, which allows many to be of the party without being of the dogma, or, indeed, of religion at all'.[87] At the core of this 'party' were the magistrates of Parlements and Richerist canonists, its principles were the Gallican liberties and its immediate object was the ruin of the Jesuits. It was this destruction of the Jesuit order which Mgr de Grasse, in defiance of the Pope[88] and a majority of his episcopal colleagues, was determined to pursue.

A bishop, more particularly an idle one, must have allies. In towns where the Jesuits had established themselves they had inevitably raised up enemies, but they had not gained a foothold in Angers and lay society's disapproval of their intrigues was lukewarm and vicarious.[89] The directors of the Seminary felt no loyalty towards their new bishop and Mgr de Grasse reciprocated by making no secret of his desire to discourage the Sulpiciens from staying in Angers.[90] Supporters of the Vaugirault régime were thunder-struck to find that their new master was a tough and unspiritual Gallican. Canons Louet and Houdebine and their dean, a select little group at the cathedral which had presided over the former bishop's policy of super-orthodoxy,[91] now made the chapter of Saint-Maurice a centre of opposition. Ill-will on both sides soon built up a feud. The bishop failed to include the traditional references to his canons in ordinances, or, even when he did, he would not call them 'confrères', and he ignored their rules concerning ceremonial dress within the precincts of Saint-Maurice. For their part the canons refused to adjust the gutters of the church which continued to cascade water on to the leaking palace roof. In reprisal the bishop's vials poured out more effective plagues than water, for he arranged for an increase of clerical taxation to fall upon his cathedral.[92] One can understand then that Mgr de Grasse was not unwilling to call in the second order of clergy to redress the balance of his diocese. By 1760 he could be in no possible doubt concerning the feelings of his parish priests towards the dominant monks and canons, for in that year he received an open letter from Robin of Saint-Pierre, which exalted the cause of curés with a wealth of antiquarian learning and whimsical invective.[93] When, therefore, in this same year the curés of Angers appealed to their bishop to put into effect an instruction of the Parlement of Paris suppressing confraternities which were not authorized by letters patent duly registered,[94] he seized his opportunity with alacrity. As soon as he could contrive to get back from Paris, he called a meeting of parish priests to concert measures. An episcopal ordinance in September sealed the compact between this cynical bishop and his curés: the former got support for a Parliamentary ordinance directed against Jesuit and Sulpicien organizations, while the latter were rid of competition which drew parishioners away from parish masses and sermons.[95]

Royal edicts of August 1764, and May 1765, establishing a new form of municipal election in France,[96] provided Mgr de Grasse with a new opportunity for improving his alliances. Fourteen notables were to be nominated by a plurality of votes in a general assembly of representatives of ecclesiastical institutions, law courts and other communities and corporations; this assembly of representatives and the notables they finally selected were to include one representative of the town's principal chapter and one 'for the ecclesiastical order'. According to the abbé Mezeray, canon of Saint-Maurice and *syndic* of the clergy of Anjou, this 'ecclesiastical order' consisted of the Diocesan Bureau[97] and representatives of the cathedral, the abbeys of Ronceray and Toussaint, the three Benedictine houses and the two royal chapters—'these constitute, and have constituted from time immemorial, the order of the clergy of the town of Angers'. True, this meant that only two curés would be present, but all others were assumed to be virtually represented by the great ecclesiastical corporations which dominated their parishes, and as for vicaires, they were 'birds of passage', unworthy of consideration.[98] For his part, bishop de Grasse, with democratic and revengeful insight, decided that it was these great corporations themselves which would be virtually represented by a canon of the cathedral; that being so, he proposed to assume that the 'ecclesiastical order' meant parish priests and their assistant clergy. Canon Mezeray called the traditional oligarchy to assemble on Wednesday, 26 June. Meanwhile the bishop issued a summons to curés and vicaires, ordering them to attend at his palace on Tuesday morning. This news did not reach the cathedral chapter until Sunday night, by which time the bishop had made himself inaccessible in his country-house, with no intention of returning to Angers until Monday evening. Representatives of all chapters and of Ronceray hastily met and drew up a protest which notaries delivered, but it was too late to circumvent the episcopal manœuvre.[99] And the curés played their part by refusing to be intimidated. In a municipal assembly held on 3rd July, the mild Chotard of the parish of Saint-Martin replied briskly to objections raised by canon Louet, and Boumard of Sainte-Croix was elected as notable for 'the ecclesiastical order'.[100]

Curé Boumard was well suited to represent the growing independent temper of the second order of clergy. Rigidly orthodox, a doctor of theology who had gained some notoriety as an opponent of Jansenist doctrines,[101] he was nevertheless a champion of the rights of curés, an angular and unyielding man with no respect for canons and no fear of law courts. Two years later he embarked upon a career of liturgical sabotage which carried the guerilla warfare of canons and curés to new and scandalous extremes. Like his colleagues of Saint-Evroul and Saint-Aignan, the curé of Sainte-Croix was obliged, by legal decisions of a century's standing, to carry the bones of Saint-Séréné in major processions of the cathedral. More and more, these three parish priests had grown recalcitrant. They cast doubts upon the necessity of wearing an alb and stole for the ceremony, they argued that a commitment which kept them away from their duties on St. Mark's day, Palm Sunday and Rogation days might imperil the salvation of sick folk in their parishes.[102] On 26 May 1767, the canons of Saint-Maurice set out on their Rogation day itinerary to the monastery of Saint-Aubin. Just opposite the church of Saint-Denis, their great procession came to a disorganized halt. No tributary ecclesiastic had presented himself to take over the reliquary of Saint-Séréné. The dean despatched a verger to investigate, who reported that the abbé Boumard had gone off to the country, and that his vicaire had no instructions to replace him.[103] Legal sommations followed this incident, and Boumard was brought to book, but he remained an irrepressible opponent of liturgical monopolies. In 1773 he was opposing (unsuccessfully) the chapter of Saint-Martin's claim to descend processionally upon his church and sing suffrages before its altar of Saint-Nicolas, parish services notwithstanding.[104] And eight years later, it was hardly an accident that the cathedral's Assumption Day procession was ingloriously delayed, while the humble parishioners of Sainte-Croix, with uplifted cross and uninterrupted chant, swept across the path of the peregrinating canons.[105] Once a furious litigant, curé Roussel finished up as a pillar of sobriety. But age did not mellow the abbé Boumard. His election as a municipal notable in 1765 had been significant, for an election weighted in favour of the parochial clergy, with a curé returned as deputy, was a novelty in Anjou. When the experiment was renewed, twenty-four years later, in a strictly clerical context, though on a larger scale and in national circumstances, Boumard was again a prominent candidate.

3. THE ADVENTURES OF CURÉ ROBIN

Naïve tourists might believe that the crypt of Saint-Pierre contained the tomb of Saint-René—local people knew better. Our countrywoman, Mrs. Craddock, who visited Angers in the early eighties in search of cultural curiosities, insisted on investigating this mystery and found a venerable vault full of bottles, for as her guide laughingly explained, the curé stored his choicest wines in the coolest place of his parish.[106] Here is an incident which may serve to re-introduce us to the abbé Robin, doctor of theology of the University of Angers and curé of Saint-Pierre for the last thirty years, a singular

N

priest whose activities amused and scandalized his contemporaries and have been a delight to subsequent generations of local antiquaries. Long after his death, his remarkable figure was well remembered in Angers. Hat on the side of his head, cassock unbuttoned, nose, upper-lip and front of his garments powdered with tobacco, hands thrust into his sash, he would wander the streets with a pre-occupied air, or stand ruminating on his doorstep, occasionally making a gesture or addressing a few humorous words to working-girls or artisans as they passed, and laughing heartily if they scored off him in return.[107]

He is quick-tempered, lively, impatient, impressionable, susceptible; he hates vice and the vicious as he hates awkwardness and clumsy people; without melancholy, without boredom, without bitterness; born with a gay, light-hearted and satirical temperament, though pensive at times; little seriousness, gravity or mystery in his make-up—the sort of man you like at first, then you despise him, and in the upshot, if you are a knave, you positively hate him.[108]

Add to the details here enumerated the fact that this amiable character-sketch was written by Robin himself, and nothing is lacking to enable us to picture the man.

If in considering the rivalries of canons and curés and in describing the formation of an alliance between Mgr de Grasse and his parochial clergy, we made few references to this particular priest and his parish it was not because the church of Saint-Pierre was an oasis of quietness or because its curé's character was unobtrusive. On the contrary. Ten years before Roussel was aroused to fury by the dispute between vicaires and chaplains, Robin had embarked upon a long struggle with his canons, and he it was who in 1760 greeted bishop de Grasse with a petition for reforms which would have completely reversed the respective positions of chapters and their dependent parish priests. It was a sad day indeed for the somnolent canons of Saint-Pierre when Robin permuted a canonry at the neighbouring church of Saint-Maurille to take over their parish, for this learned, litigious and long-lived curé did battle against them for nigh on forty years, for as long, in fact, as either chapter or parish survived.

There was a fund of resourcefulness, truculence and independence in Robin's character which made him a most redoubtable opponent. He was of solid bourgeois origin, and as proud of it as another man might be of four quarters of nobility. A little country-house which he built at Empiré, on the outskirts of his parish, was adorned with busts of himself and of the wholesale corn, iron and coal merchant of Saint Florent-le-Vieil who was his father, while his boastful autobiography in Latin verse does not allow us to forget that he had sacrificed a profitable inheritance in the family business by seeking ordination.[109] Perhaps our good abbé insists too much on these worldly advantages nobly forgone, yet we may readily forgive him, for, while at different levels of the hierarchy, to the son of a noble or a peasant an ecclesiastical career was an avenue of advancement, for children of the prosperous lower bourgeoisie it was likely to entail genuine sacrifice. Minor promotion pleased those who escaped from poverty, major promotion went to those with influence: those who were neither poor nor influential could more easily be disappointed. Robin's vocation certainly involved him in a long period of apprenticeship as a vicaire in various parishes before he obtained the modest living of Chênehutte,[110] and he was thirty-seven years of age when he finally rose from the morass of minor country clergy to a stall at Saint-Maurille at Angers. Being no careerist, he does not complain of this comparatively slow promotion, but there is nevertheless a bourgeois pride and self-conscious rectitude about him which forms the basis of his vivid and combative personality.

His egocentricities were reinforced by another and very different passion, which added a delightful touch of extravagance and whimsicality to his character. An oddly erudite student of the past, he was caught up in fantasies born of his own learning, and was deliberately acting a part on the stage of history. He believed that his writings were destined to immortality, and to make assurance doubly sure, he immured copies of his books in walls and public monuments for the benefit of future archaeologists.[111] 'They call me impossible,' he confided to one of his vicaires, 'but they will come in pilgrimage to my tomb'—and that tomb, complete with a Latin epitaph, was already prepared for veneration in the chapel of his little house at Empiré.[112] The canons of Saint-Pierre were faced by an opponent who could not easily be brought to reason by practical or cautionary considerations, for while they fought for their profits and their privileges, he had posterity in mind as well. In 1752, six months after acquiring a stall at Saint-Maurille, Robin exchanged to return to parochial work. It seems that the role he had set himself to play and which filled his imagination was essentially that of a curé, and for no worse reason than a genuine love of the manifold duties of parochial responsibility, which brought him into daily touch with common people, who saw little of his pride and inflexibility, and loved him for his unconventional sermons, his care for children and his genial accessibility. In everything, our curé was a partisan—witness his opinions, pungently expressed, on a trip to Paris and Rome in 1750. After being present at a disputation of the Sorbonne, he observes that this was an 'ordinary' difficulty compared with subjects normally set at his own university; when he first sees Genoa, he reflects that the tiles on the roofs are of poorer quality than those in Angers; his considered opinion of Rome is that only 'a French pope with 50,000 men of his own nation' could possibly 'introduce good manners and honest morals' there. And above all, he is a partisan when he considers the dignity of his own office of parish priest. To a footman, who tried to exclude him from watching the King at table, he replied, 'I am one of the King's men, I am a curé of his dominions, and I desire the honour of seeing him dine'; that being so, he stayed to examine the gold plate and sample the dessert. After seeing the Pope at his devotions, complete with guards and jewelled snuff-box, he declares openly and dangerously, that he'd rather be curé at Chênehutte than Pope at Rome.[113] If the humble priest of Chênehutte admitted no superior, clearly the curé of Saint-Pierre would not yield an inch of ground when his just rights were in question. If this was the green tree, what would he be in the dry?

Saint-Pierre was an important parish, containing 4,000 souls, and its income, though modest, was far from exiguous. Against these attractions, however, must be set the disadvantage of a relationship of dependence and subordination towards the chapter, which was *curé primitif* and owner of the church itself. Parochial offices were said in a side chapel, humbly announced by the canons' bell, and the curé had no status in chapter, though he was entitled to a seat in choir immediately after the canons and controlled burials on the left-hand side of the nave. A *congrue* was supplied in augmentation of surplice fees, partly in lands, partly in tithe and partly in cash—a confused and disputable system of payment.[114] Hence there was an accumulation of quarrels. Curé Milscent had been a sick man, anxious to retire from this scene of confusion; Robin seems to have assumed that no battle was complete without his intervention and was very willing to inherit these quarrels and improve upon them, so that his appointment in 1752[115] marks the start of a period of thirty-eight years of guerilla warfare between curé and canons.

Robin was no diplomat, and his ill-timed obtrusiveness provoked the jealous canons to score a preliminary victory. Since it had been customary for curés of Saint-Pierre to be made honorary canons, as an ex-canon of Saint-Maurille, Robin naturally expected that no difficulties would arise in his case. However, when the chapter, lacking a quorum, imposed a delay, he foolishly observed that 'one monk missing is no obstacle to the election of an abbot', a jest which cost him dear, for the chapter, recognizing its sinister implications, black-balled him and appointed his vicaire to the vacant stall, thus providing their head verger with an insoluble problem, and curé Robin with a permanent grievance.[116] A macabre wrangle over funeral ceremonies followed. Normally, parishioners were buried by their curé, though, at Saint-Pierre, persons of distinction whose relatives were willing to pay inflated fees could be buried by the chapter, on condition that the parish priest received half the candle wax as his perquisite. Such distinguished obsequies were generally followed by litigation, and after various disputes, Robin decided to strike a dramatic blow. It was Wednesday in Holy Week. The capitular schedule of services for that day included a funeral, that of Mme Taupin, aunt of one of the canons. The parochial clergy of Saint-Pierre made a sudden raid, kidnapped the coffin and bore it off to their church, where the usual suffrages were said before the corpse was returned to canonical custody. As a result, the tribunal of the *Sénéchaussée* did brisk business. It gave judgment by default against the curé, who, oddly enough, failed to appeal, though had he known it, the expert lawyers of the Clergy of France considered that his case was unexceptionable.[117]

Peace descended on the troubled church of Saint-Pierre when the abbé Saillant became dean, for he sought no more for his chapter than a right to bury its own members and was willing to leave all parishioners to the curé. These were indeed halcyon days. 'Si dilexerimus invicem Deus in nobis manet et charitas in nobis perfecta est'—so apposite seemed this versicle, and so sentimental was canon Boislève, that he applauded in choir and cried, 'That's worth a sermon!' But the sermon, like most sermons, was not lasting in its effects. When a new dean was installed, this era of mutual tolerance came to an end. The parish had already been given permission to build a little house for its sacristan in an angle of the walls of the capitular church; now new and difficult conditions were imposed, including payment of a feudal rent and a bann on digging latrines. Robin ignored these terms and completed his building, adding an inscription in Latin verse celebrating his successful defiance. The canons went to law, alleging that his workmen had destroyed some of their gutters and that the chimney of the new house smoked into their church.[118] More profits of wholesale trade at Saint Florent-le-Vieil were pocketed by lawyers of the *Sénéchaussée*. According to Robin, the canons were determined to ruin him— 'Nous lui ferons vendre jusqu'à sa marmite'—and he maintained that only news from Paris of the Parlement's inclinations in favour of curés brought them finally to a more Christian frame of mind.[119] But, in truth, it seems as though Robin himself found the struggle overwhelming, for in June, 1774, before he was reduced to the sale of his cooking pot, he sent a signed statement to the dean, offering to submit to arbitration on this matter of the sacristan's house and all other outstanding questions.[120]

Having fought the chapter to obtain a house for his sacristan, an ominous cracking of roof beams in his own bedroom ceiling now warned curé Robin that he must do battle for his own. As was not unusual when a vicarage needed expensive repairs, there were disputes and litigation, and while the affair dragged on, Robin lived inglorious in lodgings, his furniture covered by nothing better than a partition of planks, and guarded only by a huge homeless dog which took up residence among the ruins. 'The curé', people said, 'ought to present a claim to the chapter for a pension for this faithful animal.' [121] The victim of these tribulations ascribes all delay to the ill-will of the chapter: what he fails to record for posterity is the fact that opposition to rebuilding his house came chiefly from his parishioners, though they were undoubtedly inflamed and abetted by the canons. When a parish meeting was called, the curé failed to appear. His flock insinuated that his absence was due to a guilty conscience, for, they alleged, he had neglected running repairs for thirty years, and had received a contribution from his predecessor for other repairs which he had never executed.[122] In June 1780, the intendant at Tours approved a plan of reconstruction. Robin declared that there would not be room enough in this new vicarage for himself and his two vicaires, and appealed to the Royal Council, which ordered a new survey.[123] At last, rebuilding started. Even so, the curé still made trouble concerning his lodging allowance,[124] and the canons still haunted him to ensure that no untoward additions were made to plans so far approved.[125] Canons and parishioners in league against a parish priest—here was an unnatural alliance, cemented by parsimony and not by sympathy. But in 1783 financial considerations brought pastor and flock together again. When the town proposed to make the old graveyard of Saint-Pierre into a market-place, the chapter was prepared to sell. Robin did some research and discovered a legal judgment of sixty years ago which implied that his parish was co-proprietor of the land in question. All was now set for another battle of litigation, but the cautious parish assembly, once it had extracted a promise that the canons would pay for a new cemetery, was not disposed to arm for combat. The curé, finding himself leading a crusade with an army of camp followers, rated his people for 'alienating the temporal of the parish' without consulting him.[126]

While the fortunes of the main battle thus ebbed and flowed, the flanks of the field were occupied with numerous indeterminate skirmishes. There were questions concerning payment of a *congrue* to vicaires, and of repairs to a farm called 'la Petite-Lande' which was allotted to the curé as part of his income; there was a dispute concerning control of the confraternity of the Purification, another over the right of parochial clergy to use the sacristy door of the canons, another involving a ciborium used for Easter communion, which was kept in the tabernacle of the collegiate church, in spite of its engraved legend 'Je suis de la paroisse'.[127] And all the while, between law-suits, feuds were kept warm by a mutual exchange of courtesies. Bull-necked canon Mongodin, a laborious inventor of lightweight epigrams, drably satirized Robin's publications, while the latter dryly exhorted those who were unable to find seats in his church not to stand at the back, but to move on to the service of the canons, 'where there's lots of room'.[128] So many were the questions at issue that, in the end, their very multiplicity facilitated the conclusion of a peace, in which claim was cancelled against claim, without investigation of the validity of any. In 1787 a concordat was made, which the bishop himself ratified.[129] All law-suits pending before Parlement, *Présidial* and *Sénéchaussée* were withdrawn, Robin gave up his *congrue*, renounced his claim to bury members of the chapter, withdrew all pretensions to a right of way through the sacristy and to a share in ownership of the cemeteries and ciborium of Saint-Pierre; for their part, the canons surrendered their title of *curé primitif*, admitted the curé as first in rank among their honorary canons, paid a compensation of 172*l.* in respect of the ciborium, and handed over a piece of land near Empiré in compensation for the *congrue*.

Towards the beginning and towards the end of his fantastic career of litigation, our curé of Saint-Pierre issued manifestos, in which his strange erudition and fertile pen were active in marshalling theoretical arguments in favour of his fellow parish priests. In 1760 he published a pamphlet calling on the bishop to initiate a scheme of parochial reorganization[130] and, in 1785, in a volume of 200 pages, he described at length his own struggle with the canons of Saint-Pierre.[131] There was a time, he argued, when curial functions were inseparable from canonical ones; his own church, for example, had been in origin a college, in which the curé was equal to the dean and enjoyed independent revenues.[132] Such churches were plebeian in origin, they were founded for their parishioners, yet now they have fallen, buildings, bells, organs and revenues, into the hands of chapters or monasteries, who do no parish work, and whose youthful members, scarce out of their catechism or their seminary, take rank above venerable pastors who care for the flock.[133] When he himself came to Saint-Pierre, not a single canon preached or heard confessions, except the dean, who was spiritual director to two pious old ladies.[134] And yet, we find curés in such churches celebrating a low mass as in the time of the persecutions, in concealment and in secret, under rood-screens or in little side-chapels, at hours inconvenient for the public, without decency, with a sermon hurried and truncated so as not to incommode a few canons or monks who are going to say an office for themselves alone.[135] In fact, only one or two chapters are now necessary in Angers. The others could be suppressed and their prebends given to curés; not that canons in strictly limited numbers are not useful, of course—'nothing so sanctifying as psalm singing'.[136]

This champion of the cause of parish priests was not a leader of a movement. His campaign against canons was carried on without assistance from his colleagues; indeed, they objected to his pretensions as much as any one. On the strength of his journey to Rome, Robin arrogated to himself a title of 'Patron of Pilgrims', which presumption caused an initial breach with the other curés of Angers.[137] Then, in 1764, was published his *Camp de César*, a labyrinthine dissertation, incomprehensible to most people, but all too clear on one point, that is, that the parish of Saint-Pierre was utterly senior to all other parishes of the town.[138] Twelve curés were entitled to call themselves 'cardinal', but Robin, not content with a title he shared with others, insisted on being 'premier curé-cardinal', and so proclaimed himself. At monthly meetings of the Faculty of Theology, the curé of Saint-Pierre was a continual source of confusion and embarrassment. 'Rendez-moi mon argent, et je ne serai plus docteur', he would cry when aroused, and there must have been many who would have wished to take him at his word. It was at such a stormy session that he insulted the mild Chotard, curé of Saint-Martin, by accusing him of obscurantist notions on the furniture of Hell, so that henceforward Chotard conducted his necessary negotiations with the parish of Saint-Pierre through one of its vicaires.[139] Even priests of his own church found Robin a difficult man, one who was to be treated with deference and reserve, and local gossip had it that a pious gift of silk stockings and silver plate very nearly involved the abbé Pauvert in one of those citations before the courts which his curé showered so prodigally on his foes.[140] Thus it was that the protagonist of the parochial clergy's cause in Angers remained an isolated figure, distrusted by his colleagues and waging a lonely feud against canonical domination. As he himself wryly observed, he was 'like a dog at the head of a procession',[141] causing merriment, but arousing little sympathy. However, eccentric though he was, the long tragi-comedy of his litigation was beginning to win him favourable recognition by 1785, when the *Affiches* welcomed his *Exposé* with remarkable geniality.

It is written concisely, in a gay light-hearted style, with an occasional touch of mockery when the subject is appropriate. The character and outlook of the author is revealed in all its *naïveté*, for he discusses his own shortcomings and recounts the story of his humiliations with the sort of moderation and charity one would expect in the confessional. The respective rights of chapters and of curés on the *congrue* are discussed and analysed, and researches are made into their origins. Curés on the *congrue* and priests in charge of dependent parishes will find here strong arguments for the improvement of their lot, suitable to be brought to the notice of the Commissioners of the Clergy.[142]

But in less than three years' time, curés were to have an opportunity to bring their grievances before a much wider audience, and a more efficient and ruthless propagandist than Robin was ready to take over the leadership of the parochial clergy of Anjou.

CHAPTER IX

THE ATTACK ON THE DIOCESAN OLIGARCHY

At this point, our chronicle of controversy between curés and canons in a sleepy provincial town merges into the general history of the diocese, and from henceforward plays its minor part in a build-up of forces which was to shape French history. A dispute over clerical taxation arose, which welded together heterogeneous discontents and formed a rallying point for the parochial clergy of Anjou, who now moved into an alliance against canonical domination, and found a natural leader for their cause.

In France, absolutism had failed to subvert the independence of the clerical order, which still voted its own taxation in quinquennial General Assemblies. A General Assembly was composed of two bishops and two deputies of the lower clergy from each ecclesiastical province, and these in their turn had been elected at provincial meetings to which each diocese sent its bishop and one other clerical representative. Once taxation was voted at Paris, local assessment was calculated by diocesan committees, variously called *bureaux diocésains*, *bureaux des décimes*, and *chambres ecclésiastiques*, which had power to settle disputes involving sums of under 20 or 30*l*., and to seize the revenues of defaulting benefices.[1] But these liberties of the Church of France were oligarchically administered within. A mere curé never found his way up to the General Assembly at Paris[2] and, what concerns us more particularly here, most of the Diocesan Bureaux had become closed preserves of the privileged, oddly 'elected', or co-opted or nominated to their office.[3]

Such was the case in our diocese of Angers. Here, there was a central bureau, which was an inner council of a body rejoicing in the democratic title of 'General Assembly' of the diocese. Again, however, 'general' was to be understood relatively. Of 25 members, only two were curés. Otherwise, the Assembly was a club of monks and canons of the town of Angers: the abbeys of Saint-Aubin, Saint-Serge, Saint-Nicolas and Toussaint each sent a deputy, as did the abbess of Ronceray, all collegiate churches of the town were represented, including even the humble canons of La Trinité, while the cathedral took pride of place with four of its canons present.[4] In theory, this Assembly ought to have met four times a year,[5] in practice it met only once or twice, and oligarchy as it was, it was still a mere façade, with real power resting in the hands of its inner ring.

Thus, the whole business of assessment of taxation and verification of accounts was left to the Diocesan Bureau, which met every Thursday in the court room of the bishop's ecclesiastical lawyers, and more formally, each quarter, in the *bureau des décimes* itself. The two curés of the Assembly were always members of the Bureau, together with two canons of Saint-Maurice, one deputy for all the Benedictine communities, one for the canons-regular, one for the royal chapters and one for the other collegiate churches.[6] Membership was for life, or until retirement, and vacancies were filled by co-option, a procedure so undemocratic that even the cathedral chapter, a principal beneficiary of the system, deplored its inability to indicate which of its own canons should be nominated to serve.[7] Disputes among the other monopolists were eliminated by a fixed rotation of office among the various chapters and monasteries; thus the post of deputy for royal chapters fell alternately to canons of Saint-Martin and Saint-Laud, and the place allotted to Benedictines was passed on from Saint-Aubin to Saint-Serge, and from Saint-Serge to Saint-Nicolas. There was an election formula which included a proviso that the clergy were not bound to choose from any one chapter or monastic house within the various groups; nevertheless, when a vacancy occurred, the diocesan *syndic* always reminded the Bureau of the traditional succession, and appropriate election always ensued.[8] When curés were appointed, there was not even this abusive safeguard of a customary rotation, and the canon-ridden Bureau naturally did not choose to take to its bosom the parochial firebrands. For nearly thirty years before the Revolution, Chotard of Saint-Martin, a self-effacing priest who disapproved so strongly of curé Robin's adventures, was a member, and when Roussel of Saint-Maurille was appointed in 1782, he had had seventeen years in which to live down his feud with his canons, and was now grown staid and very senior. Nominated, not elected, and in receipt of a welcome salary of 200*l.* which could easily be interpreted as a badge of dependence,[9] these two curés could hardly claim to represent their colleagues. Even if they could, that would have made no difference, as they were inevitably doomed to be outvoted in all affairs coming before the Bureau and could never hope to be appointed to the all-important office of *syndic*, or even that of secretary. When in 1786 canon Nioche de la Brosse of the cathedral became *syndic*, and canon Corbin of Saint-Martin became secretary, the former was succeeding to an office whose three previous holders had all been canons of his own chapter, while the latter was succeeding dean Voison of Saint-Pierre who had been secretary for no less than twenty-three years.[10]

Diocesan finance was thus controlled by a 'committee of canons'.[11] Most taxation levied from benefice holders went to meet the demands of the General Assembly of the Clergy of France, though any surplus which remained for purely diocesan objects was allocated by the Bureau. It was distributed to thoroughly respectable causes; even so, the financial dealings of an oligarchy are not likely to remain immune from accusations of patronage or arbitrary favour. Pensions to retired priests[12] were an obvious necessity, but were monks and canons best fitted to choose the most deserving recipients? Why, from 1763 to 1767, was 600l. a year paid over to the house of the Visitation at Angers,[13] which, as everyone knew, was primarily a boarding-school for daughters of distinguished families? The Seminary had its own endowments, and in any case was peculiarly a responsibility of the bishop; why then was it such a constant drain on diocesan resources? In the heyday of its insolvency, from 1756 to 1765, it received over 10,000l. towards running expenses, and nearly 3,000l. for its buildings.[14] Nineteen years later, when times were harder, the Bureau hardened its heart and claimed six years' arrears of taxation, a fine angry gesture which led nowhere. Shortly afterwards, the Seminary was authorized to set down its deficit against the board of poor students, so that nothing was paid.[15] Then there were the honoraria paid to members of the Bureau, its *syndic* and its secretary, modest sums, not large enough to cause scandal but sufficient to arouse adverse comment, particularly in so far as the two curés were concerned.[16] The lay office of Receiver of clerical taxation, which was handed down from relative to relative in the Lointier family,[17] was no sinecure, yet parish priests of the diocese might be forgiven if they considered it well rewarded, carrying as it did a salary of 2,000l. a year, with various extra gratifications from time to time.[18] In dealing with its officials and clerks, the Bureau continually showed itself aware of the problem of rising prices,[19] and it might have been as well if it could have shown an equal concern with the lot of hard-hit curés on the *congrue*.

In addition to clerks and a few financial officers, the Bureau also appointed the eighteen Apostolic Notaries of the diocese. There was nothing very distinguished about these minor officials—they dealt with routine legal business of churchmen, resignations, permutations, taking possession, notification of degrees to patrons, and were also entitled to deal with testamentary affairs generally, like ordinary notaries.[20] Their perquisites were modest, so that the real motive for competing for such offices was to obtain exemption from *corvées* and billeting. Nor had the clergy much to gain from their exercise of the right to appoint; the diocese could regulate fees for ecclesiastical documents—that was all. Nevertheless, at the end of the seventeenth century, the clergy of Anjou had paid good money to the Crown to bring Apostolic Notaries under their patronage.[21] It was satisfying and appropriate that the diocese, or rather its Bureau, should exercise this privilege, though it would not have been easy to demonstrate what tangible benefit most clergy gained from it. It was, no doubt, worth having, but events were now to force the question, was it worth paying to have?

Early in 1778 a royal ordinance announced that, from 18 June following, the secular notaries of Anjou would take over the functions of their rivals of the Apostolic variety. These latter, it was said, were too few in number to provide adequate service for their clientele, and too ignorant of Latin to construe the wording of Bulls.[22] It so happened that these remarkable revelations of inefficiency coincided with a payment of 6,000*l.* to the coffers of the Crown by the ordinary notaries of the diocese. The actual royal ordinance bore the date 10 November 1776—the clergy had not been served notice of it until fifteen months later, a fact which made the whole affair even more shabby and sinister.[23] On 22 April, an Assembly of the Clergy of Anjou decided to send the bishop and canon Louet of Saint-Maurice to Paris to countermine this notarial conspiracy.[24] It was a treacherous business to negotiate, as an unwary offer of money might conjure up further 'buyers' of offices and touch off a chain-reaction of blackmail.[25] However, by 5 July the bishop reported that all was well, and that the diocese would retain its patronage, provided it reimbursed to the notaries their 6,000*l.*[26] It shortly became apparent that this optimistic episcopal bulletin was quite unreliable and that nothing had been surely established so far beyond the principle that the Crown had to be bribed by somebody. On 19 September the Assembly of the clergy of Anjou reaffirmed its bellicose intentions, though with a note of thrifty hesitancy. Enquiries were to be made as to what expenditure was likely to be involved, and Mgr de Grasse, who had received a handsome allowance for his first trip to Paris, now encouraged his wavering clergy by promising not to ask any subsidy for a further expedition.[27] This offer was gratefully accepted. Two days later, however, the Bureau, ignoring its parent Assembly, ordered the Receiver of clerical taxation to pay 6,000*l.* to the bishop in respect of his imminent departure for the capital. This action, sycophantic and spendthrift, raised a storm of opposition. Mgr de Grasse lived in Paris most of his time anyway, leaving his episcopal functions in Angers to a suffragan:[28] his expenses account was little better than a subsidy to scandal. On 23 September there was an angry scene in the cathedral chapter-house, when canon Mezeray the *syndic* and his fellow-deputy to the Bureau refused to explain their conduct to their assembled colleagues and stalked out of the meeting. On the following day, the dean and canon Cassin waited on the bishop and formally asked him to state what sums of money he had received, to which the bishop simply replied that he had been given as much as was officially laid down by the Clergy of France for the expenses of deputies of the first order, and that it appeared 'natural' to him that his diocese should pay for his journey, 'notwithstanding the ruling of the General Assembly of the Clergy of Anjou'.[29] In Paris, the bishop found time from other distractions to give his backers value for money, and in October he again obtained a ruling of the Council against the notaries.[30] Still the battle was not over. *Monsieur*, the King's brother, who held Anjou as his *apanage*, was too deeply involved in the whole fraudulent business for any action to be taken without his agreement, and the new ordinance lay unsigned upon the Chancellor's desk.[31] Then came an awkward compromise offer cunningly put forward by business agents of the *apanage*: the clergy were to be allowed to nominate Apostolic Notaries and have 'some sort of proprietorship' in these offices, but their choice was to be limited to Royal Notaries, who would receive their provisions from *Monsieur*.[32] Victory on these terms was worthless, and on 8 April 1779 the bishop gave a new account of the machinations of the notaries which brought him a vote of a further 2,400*l.* for Parisian excursions.[33] This time, he brought everything to a conclusion. 6,000*l.* were duly repaid to the notaries, a further 600*l.* went to the ecclesiastical lawyers in the capital for their good offices, the bishop's residences there ceased to be subsidized, and the Bureau resumed its right to appoint Apostolic Notaries. This privilege had been retained, as an angry curé later pointed out, by levying a surcharge of no less than 40,000*l.* on benefice holders of the diocese.[34]

No doubt such mismanagement was much discussed in country parsonages when tax demand forms came round. The cost of living was rising and financial burdens were increasing. Revised assessments by the Clergy of France, which came into force in 1766, had increased the global sum due from the diocese of Angers by more than 20,000*l.* a year. The diocesan oligarchy protested, alleging victimization—'we have been chosen out of all the dioceses of France'—and painting a gloomy picture of the meagre possessions of benefice holders under the auctioneer's hammer. Replies from Paris were ruthless. Let verified accounts be furnished, and let a positive demonstration be given that anyone was being forced above the level of taxation laid down for his category.[35] These new scales of taxation were weighted in favour of parochial clergy and graded according to means; by referring to them, the agents-general were politely hinting their suspicion that, if rich benefice holders of Anjou paid their full minimum, there would be no need to send auctioneers into humble vicarages. This suspicion seems to have been justified, for the

Bureau was incapable of making the demonstration required. Nevertheless, its *syndic* went up to Paris in 1770 to lobby for support at the Assembly General of the Clergy of France. He returned 'very sadly', and was sadder still afterwards when his story of concessions wrung from the archbishop of Narbonne was denied by the agents-general in language just within the bounds of civility.[36] Five years later deferential but despairing appeals were still being forwarded from Angers to officials in the capital.[37] Meanwhile, the curés of Anjou had been driven to reflect on their exclusion from the management of their own affairs and to question whether increasing financial burdens were being fairly distributed. Signs of a new and challenging temper became evident in the early seventies, when fifteen parish priests leagued together to defend themselves from the financial exactions of the archdeacons. Neither natural law nor ecclesiastical polity could justify an archdeacon in levying a permanent tax over and above his visitation fee on parish priests within his jurisdiction: the courts, however, were only concerned with legal prescription. The archdeacons won easily. With the cathedral archives and legal advice from the office of the agents-general at their disposal, they brought before the Parlement of Paris 150 sentences and 8 decisions of its own, 400 titles, and complete receipt books from 1586 onwards.[38] Their victory was an object-lesson. Individual abuses in eighteenth-century France were so securely entrenched at law that the only way to break through hierarchical domination was to appeal to natural right on a more general issue. News now coming in from other dioceses showed that for the curés of France the composition of Diocesan Bureaux was such an issue, and the most strategic point for attack.

Here an abuse was crumbling, and precedent could not hope to outface justice much longer. This admission had been specifically made by the General Assembly of the Clergy of France in 1768 when dealing with a serious agitation in the diocese of Troyes—it was far from fitting, it was said, 'that the councillors of the Bureau, who are supposed to represent the different ecclesiastical corporations, should be nominated by the bishop alone'. Among the lower clergy there had been a steadily growing pressure to link taxation and representation.[39] For thirty years the curés of Tarbes, Dax, Toulon, Coutances, Chartres and Gap had been insisting that they had a right to choose their own representatives to their Diocesan Bureaux. This claim, and a demand for an increased *congrue*, formed the programme of the 'insurrection of the curés' which began in January 1780, when agents of the lower clergy of Vienne and Grenoble caballed in Paris with Gallican and Jansenist lawyers. A royal declaration of March 1782 forbidding parish priests to league together came too late to prevent a general movement throughout the kingdom. When, at the end of that year, Loménie de Brienne, archbishop of Toulouse, was found making plausible promises to a synod of his clergy, it was obvious that the agitation was powerful and popular. The surest weathercock of ecclesiastical politics was turning.

A great deal would now depend upon the attitude of particular diocesan bishops, and in this same year, 1782, a crucial change took place in the government of the diocese of Angers. Jacques de Grasse's twenty-four years of absentee misrule ended. 'He died on Wednesday,' Rangeard was informed by a letter from Paris dated 29 July, 'but his death was concealed until Thursday. The saddest thing about it is, he died without sacraments.' [40] Duchesne the postillion trotted out from Angers with half a dozen horses[41] to escort the bishop back from the capital for a more permanent stay in his episcopal city. 'To put everything in order,' wrote a pious army officer stationed in the town, 'we need a bishop who loves and understands the duties of his office, kind and genuine, but very strict— who lives in Angers.' [42] Michel-François Couet du Vivier de Lorry, who succeeded, had some of these qualities, or at least an outward appearance of them. Debts drove him in the end to fulfil the residence qualification, and eighteen years spent in minor bishoprics had developed in him a sort of shrewd evasiveness. At the age of thirty-four he had become bishop of Vence, five years later he had been translated to Tarbes, thirteen years later he was promoted to Angers —a rise to great office which he owed to an ancestor who had held legal office under Catherine de' Medici, thus establishing his family among the *noblesse de robe* of Lorraine.[43] This facile progress through the ecclesiastical *cursus honoris* was normal, for the episcopate at the end of the old régime was an exclusive aristocratic preserve. These consecrated noblemen brought to their task both the vices and the virtues of their race; a few were immoral, many were luxurious and non-resident, a few were deeply pious, most were decent and dignified and a number of them showed remarkable administrative ability.[44] The new bishop of Angers seems to have struck a mean between vice and virtue, being at once able and slothful, worldly and decorous, a smooth uncontroversial figure, who, had zeal and energy been intermixed with his talents, would have fully deserved his mitre. If we reject the testimony of the bilious Choudieu,[45] a rabid anticlerical ever since (if we believe the story) bishop de Grasse had confirmed him with a box on the ears, we may describe Mgr Couet du Vivier de Lorry as a man of excellent morality in the narrow sense of the word, the sort of churchman who contrived to live luxuriously without breaking any of the rules.[46] As a prelate, he inspired few, but offended none if he could help it. 'A social figure, but not much capacity for business';[47] that was true, but too harsh a verdict never-theless, for attention was now given to those outward things, like a new edition of the liturgical books,[48] which indicate to the uninitiated that a diocese is flourishing. Whether explaining why he is delayed in Paris away from his new flock,[49] or exhorting to unity and con-cord in revolutionary times, he was a master of judicious pro-nouncements and flattering words. While not a great orator, he was a polished and attractive public speaker, capable of delivering a 'dis-course which appeared quite spontaneous considering the ease with which it was spoken, but which you'd have sworn had been prepared beforehand, given its apposite terminology, appreciative references, and its well-turned and engaging phraseology in general'.[50] His official correspondence strikes a personal note—a slight family connexion, a happy memory shared: 'I have a niece who last year married M. le comte de Montaubon'—'do you remember an abbé Lorry, grand-vicar at Orleans?' [51] In a retreat for priests he could pay a touching compliment to a saintly canon; writing to the intendant he could feelingly depict the miseries of the province; quick-witted and sensitive, he could rescue a schoolgirl from the embarrassment of having to make a formal speech.[52] If the bishop lost his temper occasionally it was only because he had an idle man's hatred of being disturbed. He liked things to be done but not to do them. And be-neath all this, as later events were to show, he was a man who cherished neither rancour nor ambition; in his slothful aristocratic fashion, a good man. Nevertheless the first five years of Mgr de Lorry's episcopate were to be a story of missed opportunities. A Jean de Vaugirault might have exercised an influence by his manifest zeal and sincerity; Jacques de Grasse might have done so by shrewd diplomacy. In the troubles which were to bedevil his diocese, how-ever, bishop de Lorry neither led nor mediated, was neither loved nor hated, but drifted along as a lukewarm partisan of great ecclesi-astical corporations against the second order of clergy.[52a]

In Anjou grievances were accumulating and, as we have seen, the parish priests of the central city of the diocese had begun to unite to forward their claims. As yet, however, there was no clear programme of action and the inert mass of rural clergy had still to be heated and fused into a common purpose. Thus a revolt of curés was long in developing. When it came, it owed much to the leadership of one man, who had followed attentively the course of events in other and more vociferous dioceses. The abbé Chatizel, doctor of theology of the university of Angers, held the living of Soulaines, an important parish nine miles from town. Son of a Royal Notary himself, he had looked with particular disapproval on the affair of the Apostolic Notaries, and as principal of the collège of Laval he had waged a feud

o

with his local canons[53] which was to form a preliminary exercise for his forthcoming battle with the chapters of Angers. His mind was harsh and clear, free from those antiquarian whimsicalities and personal prejudices which disqualified curé Robin from leadership among his contemporaries. About episcopal despotism, too, Chatizel had made up his mind, witness a resounding treatise on marriage dispensations which he published in 1782. Here he proposed to reserve to the Pope the right of dispensation in important cases, and to leave all routine cases to parish priests, who alone knew their people's motives and who would not attempt to extort money from their flocks. Bishops he would exclude altogether from this sphere of authority. This book affords an early illustration of the tendency of the lower clergy to turn towards Rome as a counterbalance to episcopal domination. Also, by his ultramontanism, Chatizel was able to give his treatise an air of super-orthodoxy, and, incidentally, to have it published at Avignon. There was more than a flavour of Jansenist austerity about the character and writings of the learned curé of Soulaines, but his basic theological arguments go no further than Richerism, that is, it was the rights and status of parish priests that he defended and not wider hypotheses in doctrinal fields. From the New Testament, Chatizel demonstrated, by using standard Richerist texts,[54] that the priesthood has a divine origin and status independent of the episcopate. St. Paul told an assembly of presbyters at Ephesus that the Holy Spirit had given them power to rule the Church, and it is manifestly impossible to translate presbyter here as 'bishop'. They were priests, the only bishop present being St. Paul himself. Apollos was a presbyter, yet St. Paul describes his ministry as co-equal with his own—'I planted, Apollos watered.' It is the same at Lystra, Iconium and Antioch; priests, not bishops, are put in charge of churches. In fact (and this is the key Richerist text, the Dominical authority), parish priests are descendants of the 72 disciples who were independently commissioned by our Lord. It is true that these 72 were not present at the Last Supper, nor did they receive the promise 'as the Father hath sent me, even so send I you'. But St. Matthias was not there on the first occasion and St. Thomas was absent on the second. In any case, bishops of today were present on neither; they, like priests, receive their powers by transmission. If presence at the Last Supper were a crucial test of sacerdotal ancestry, that would imply that a priest does not consecrate at the Eucharist as validly as a bishop, which is absurd. Possibly Christ gave more formal ordination to the 72 after His resurrection: however that may be, He did commission them and they have His authority, which is vested, in the first place, not in one class of men, but in the whole Church.[55] Thus, while a bishop lays hands on the head of a priest in ordaining him, he is merely acting 'as the channel of divine grace', he is not its orginator. He gives the sign, but not the thing signified. Actual authority comes from Christ. So episcopal authority and priestly authority come from one source, and a curé is head of his parish in the same way and by the same title as a bishop is head of his diocese.[56] A parish priest is not the recognized minister of ordination, but with this exception he ought to exercise 'episcopal' powers. He ought to be able to confirm in an emergency (as in the Greek Church),[57] to give marriage dispensations to his parishioners, to exercise jurisdiction under sanction of spiritual penalties, to be a councillor of his bishop in all important affairs.[58] The survival of a title of *curé cardinal* in Angers was a testimony to the great role parish priests had once played, when, like cardinals at Rome, they were minor bishops in their own right. As for other ecclesiastical ranks and orders—monks, canons and priests without cure of soul or titles—they were nothing in the Church.[59] Chatizel's subject was marriage dispensations: his object was to sketch his ideal of an ecclesiastical hierarchy of parish priests led, but not ruled, by a virtuous and democratic episcopate.

All this was very far from the doctrine taught in volume after volume of the *Conférences d'Angers*, which, in 1780, brought to Cotelle de la Blandinière, their composer, a pension of 1,000*l.* a year from the episcopally dominated Assembly of the Clergy of France.[60] Chatizel had been cautious and avoided overt reference to the sacred *Conférences*. Nevertheless the direction of his argument was clear enough, and three years later he received devastating support from Paris, where the greatest canonist of the century joined in the onslaught against the official theology of the diocese of Angers. Maultrot was old and blind now, but many a thick volume in defence of the rights of curés was still to issue from his pen. While the incumbent of Soulaines had used marriage dispensations as a text for his reflexions, Maultrot chose the discipline of the confessional for his, and in 1785 published two treatises[61] denying the rights of bishops (and, indeed, of popes) to withhold absolution of particular crimes from the ordinary powers of parish priests. Cotelle de la Blandinière in his *Conférences* for the diocese of Angers, had not only argued that bishops ought to retain graver sins for their own more expert assessment, he had gone further and justified the reservation of trivial offences if diocesan discipline were in any way involved. These contentions gave Maultrot opportunities for satirical remarks about bishops in general and their despotic tendencies in particular. Essentially, however, Maultrot's argument, like Chatizel's, consisted of the central Richerist hypothesis that priests received a direct commission from Christ and were not beholden to bishops for jurisdiction over their parishioners. Although he had been promoted out of his original diocese and was now archdeacon and canon of Blois, the abbé de la Blandinière continued to defend the theological handbooks he had written at Angers, and produced a supplementary *Conférence* on the hierarchy, in which he showed that bishops alone are judges of the faith, that the power to preach and hear confessions in derived from them and that they and not their curés must choose parochial vicaires.[62] In reply Maultrot produced his most comprehensive work, the *Défense du Second Ordre contre les Conférences ecclésiastiques d'Angers*.[63] This was a laborious distillation of every Richerist argument, a dry legalistic presentation of a clerical Utopia in which every parish priest would be independent in his own parish, choosing his own assistant clergy, preaching and hearing confessions by his own inherent authority and travelling in to his episcopal town once or twice a year to cast his vote in the synod which governed his diocese. Scarcely was the ink dry on the third of Maultrot's volumes than the abbé de la Blandinière, who at 78 years of age was still willing to add a final volume to 'the already too voluminous *Conférences d'Angers*', launched his reply. With calculated magnanimity he lavished praise on diocesan synods and described with a wealth of learning the old synodical traditions of the diocese of Angers, which Henri Arnauld had revived and which had continued until Mgr de Grasse's sad episcopate.[64] However, he goes on, these synods were held by bishops simply to obtain advice or to promulgate statutes with a maximum of publicity.[65] Priests, successors to the apostle's priesthood but not to their apostolic jurisdiction, could discuss laws, yet only their bishop, in synod or out of synod, could make them.[66] Though Maultrot made his inevitable counter-reply,[67] by the end of 1787 both controversialists had exhausted their arguments and more than elaborated them.

Thus from 1782 to 1789 a debate was in progress which would inevitably come to the ears of our Angevin curés, shaking their faith in those awe-inspiring volumes of *Conférences* which loaded their sparsely populated book-shelves, and spreading Richerist ideas more widely among them. During this same period the abbé Chatizel was to bring the financial and constitutional grievances of the curés of Anjou to a focus, and we can imagine their progressively taking comfort, as the agitation developed, in a vague reflexion that their mundane claims were, after all, not without a respectable backing in theology and canon law.

These financial and constitutional grievances suddenly came to the fore in 1784, when, unfortunately for their own peace of mind in the coming years, the members of the Diocesan Bureau over-assessed the formidable curé of Soulaines for clerical taxation.

In the past he had paid 319*l.* a year: he was now asked to pay 527*l.*[68] It was true that, for a parish priest, Chatizel enjoyed a handsome income. According to the Bureau's reckoning, he had 4,000*l.* a year, and even in 1789 its *syndic* still maintained that the cure of Soulaines was farmed for 5,000*l.*[69] But it would seem that these figures took no account of heavy permanent outgoings—the salary of two vicaires, repairs to property, and, above all, outlay on barrels and labour for collecting a tithe on wine. If these had been subtracted, it is probable that very little more than 2,000*l.* of disposable income would have remained.[70] With a sure propagandist instinct, however, Chatizel did not drag into open discussion these domestic details of his disputable affluence. He attacked on grounds of general principle. In 1785 he published a pamphlet in the form of a letter to the bishop, in which he censured the Bureau for 'the obscurity of its administration, the unrepresentative character of its recruitment, and the inequality of its assessments'.[71] Thirty canons of the cathedral, he pointed out, have two deputies, twenty canons of other collegiate churches have one, while hundreds of parish priests only have two, who are in any case nominated by the Bureau itself.[72] Theologically speaking, this is indefensible, for pastors should be next in importance to bishops, instead of being 'victims of a multitude of man-made institutions', that is, of chapters and their canons. There is no sanction in the law of the Church for such an oligarchy; indeed, the Council of Trent prescribed triennial diocesan synods. Human reasoning is here in agreement with divine, for by 'common law' and by 'the very nature of things', curés have an imprescriptible right to elect their own representatives.[73] In other parts of France, he points out, these arguments prevail. Just representation has been given to the lower clergy in half a dozen dioceses, Avranches and Nantes in particular, and in the latter, the *syndic* himself is now a parish priest.[74] Then, as to details of assessment to taxation. Chatizel observes that the new scales of taxation published in 1765 adopted the principle that curés ought to pay less than other clerics in proportion to their revenue, which was only just, in view of their greater usefulness to the Church. But consider how this new assessment is being applied in Anjou. A certain parish priest with 4,000*l.* a year pays one-seventh of his income in taxation; the cathedral, which must have at least 100,000*l.* coming in, pays a total of 3,000*l.*; the bishop, who farms his temporal for 60,000*l.* and has 12,000*l.* in registry fees, pays a derisory sum—'Your Highness knows . . . if that is one-seventh of your income, or if indeed it is the seventh part of the tax that it ought to bear.'[75]

Early in March 1786 the General Assembly of the Clergy of Anjou was hard at work repairing the breaches made by Chatizel's cannonade.

Some reply to his accusations had to be devised: the *syndic* produced a memorandum and it was decided that a thousand copies should be forthwith printed and distributed. It was a laboured and unconvincing document. From it parish clergy would learn that bishop de Grasse had farmed his temporalities and those of Saint-Aubin for a mere 50,000*l.*,[76] that poor canon Roustille of the cathedral had only received 3,000*l.* a year from the priory of Champigné and that he had now resigned it to his brother in consideration of a pension,[77] that the cathedral had heavy annual charges in respect of its swarm of minor officials and paid extra taxes on chapels united to the foundation.[78] *Congruistes* were assured that the Diocesan Bureau had generously refrained from exacting the full amounts to which they were liable, and tithe-owning curés were reminded that their revenues had been increased by extension to new crops and by the rising price of foodstuffs.[79] It was agreed that taxation might have been fairer, had it not been for the false declarations which benefice holders habitually rendered—it was suggested that the curé of S—— himself was enjoying 1,200*l.* more income than he admitted.[80] Nowhere, however, was it precisely stated what income the bishop or a canon of the cathedral was enjoying, while inequalities of clerical remuneration were blandly accepted as inevitable. Similarly, the composition of the Bureau was treated as sacrosanct on no other ground but that of hoary prescription.[81] Curés were bluntly described as, in origin, 'mere delegates' of canons and regulars, who had handed over their parishes to be free to devote themselves to the celebration of divine office, study and contemplation.[82] These 'delegates', now grown so numerous, and as a consequence forbidden by the government to league together into a corporation, should content themselves with virtual representation on the Diocesan Bureau by their betters.[83] It is true that the General Assembly of the Clergy of France has laid down a model procedure for the election of representatives in synods, but this is only good enough for benighted dioceses which have no old custom of their own to guide them.[84] If the art of controversy necessitates beginning with concessions to one's opponent's views, nothing could have been more inept than this long and sonorous compilation.

While this memorandum was circulating, a hasty move towards nominal reform was pressed forward. A draft of a new constitution for the Diocesan Bureau was produced and canon Aubery of Saint-Martin was sent post-haste to Paris to arrange for royal assent and promulgation.[85] These new regulations were put through with unparalleled expedition, being registered by the *Conseil d'État* on 13 April.[86] A preamble plausibly described the new system as an adaptation of that laid down as a pattern by the Clergy of France in

1770. It was then—after a scandalous election dispute in the diocese of Troyes and an enquiry by the Crown into the working of Diocesan Bureaux generally—that the Clergy of France had produced a declaration, for the information of the government, defining the method in which these bodies ought to function. According to these proposals there ought to be one member for a cathedral chapter, three more representing other canons, simple benefice holders and monks respectively, and two members for the parochial clergy.[87] Some dioceses had already adopted, or been compelled to adopt, this reform, which was now, apparently, to be extended to Anjou after a delay of sixteen years, which shows how sluggish the Angevin curés had been in pressing their just claims. But in fact even this modest reform was not being honestly applied and the reference in the preamble to the regulations of 1770 was very largely camouflage. On 22 March, the bishop informed the agents-general of the clergy that he had intended to ask for the regulation of 1770, 'but after careful consideration I thought it my duty to respect and maintain the old constitutional system of the clergy of Angers, a system which is peculiar to it, and which is dear to all the orders who compose it'.[88] How dear the system was to the order of curés events were to show. All that actually happened in 1786 was that the so-called General Assembly of the Clergy of Anjou was restored to 'the form and rights it has enjoyed since time immemorial',[89] that is, it was from henceforward to elect the members of the Diocesan Bureau, name Apostolic Notaries, and settle important questions of taxation. Though the Bureau could no longer recruit its membership by co-option, representatives of chapters, monasteries and curés remained there in the same proportions as before, and, in practice, the customary rotation of places between the various chapters and monasteries was maintained.[90] An alteration in the composition of the General Assembly was made as a concession to the curés, but it could have no significant effect on voting strength, as only two more parish priests were added to its membership. The oligarchy had been freed from the domination of its inner ring, that was all.

While this constitutional window-dressing was in progress, the curés of the town of Angers began to organize. Boumard of Sainte-Croix, whose grievances we have already noted, Martin du Chesnay of Saint-Laud, Ferré of Saint-Samson and Follenfant of Saint-Maurice (three future supporters of the Civil Constitution of the Clergy) joined in a formal petition against the machinations of the diocesan oligarchy.[91] They raised the central question of just representation for their order and pressed home more ruthlessly Chatizel's allegations of unfair taxation, drawing attention to the failure of the Bureau to fulfil its legal obligation to publish complete assessment lists for comparative purposes. This growing tendency towards common action among the parish clergy was given scope and encouragement by one significant provision in the otherwise illusory reform which the diocesan oligarchy had sponsored. The two additional representatives of curés for the Assembly General were to be elected by their fellows.[92] Voting began forthwith. On 18 May the clergy of rural deaneries elected their representatives, who met on 30 May in the presence of canon Louet, one of the bishop's vicars-general, to proceed to a final nomination of their two deputies. In the first stage of these elections, the country clergy had done more than meet, vote, enjoy the good cheer provided by their rural dean or *archiprêtre*[93] and return quietly to their parishes; they had also taken steps to safeguard their interests and show their resentment. Their representatives to the final electoral assembly were sent up furnished with procurations stating that the new regulations were being executed 'provisionally' and with reservation of a right to make representations to the Crown against their inadequacy, which reservation was inserted in the minutes of the meeting of 30 May and in the minutes of the General Assembly of the Clergy of Anjou when the two new deputies were admitted.[94] A movement of re-sistance had crystallized, and its natural leaders had appeared. One of the delegates at the electoral meeting of 30 May was Rangeard,[95] curé of Andard, laureate and historian of the province, who was now willing to abandon the pose of Olympian serenity which had befitted an academician and use his indefatigable pen to serve the curés' cause, and one of the two deputies finally chosen to attend the Assembly General was Chatizel. The events of 1786 had provided the lower clergy of the diocese of Angers with their dress-rehearsal for 1789.

As it was, however, this extra representation gained by the curés merely served to emphasize their continued impotence in the affairs of the Clergy of Anjou. Along with Chatizel, Courtillé, curé of Saint-Denis, had been named as deputy. Resident in town, with a very small population to care for, he could give his full interest to diocesan business. He was well qualified to appreciate his colleagues' grievances, for his living was ill-endowed, and in his church the Seminary exercised rights of *curé primitif* inherited from the old chapter of Saint-Maimbeuf. As negotiations for rebuilding his vicar-age reveal, he was a man of practical business capacity, and his declamations against the 'insult', 'rapine', and 'woeful oppression' of the Farmers-General some years previously give an impression of a man who would not meekly tolerate abusive privilege or jacks-in-office.[96] For two or three weeks before their first attendance at the Assembly General Chatizel and Courtillé lobbied for support for an attack on canonical domination—formed 'cabals', as the *syndic* put it.[97] Together, at the meeting of 13 June, they protested against the office of *syndic* falling once more to a canon of the cathedral,[98] and the representatives of one chapter and of one religious community were brave enough to break away from the oligarchy and join them.[99] But these were all the votes they obtained.[100] The presiding vicar-general rejected their plea for vote by secret ballot, and as a result the two down-trodden nominated curés had not sufficient courage to declare for their own cause. Canons Nioche de la Brosse and Corbin became *syndic* and secretary respectively by nineteen votes to four.[101] Needless to say, when the time came round for the Assembly to appoint two of its curés to sit on the Bureau, it was nominated, not elected, deputies who were promoted. The parochial clergy of the diocese had received a right to elect, but their representatives remained as powerless as before.

Originally, bishop de Lorry had smoothly assured the agents-general that this new constitution would restore his diocese to its traditional tranquillity.[102] He still maintained that there was but a handful of malcontents, but by the beginning of July he was already appealing to Paris for aid in restoring 'the peace and harmony of my sanctuary'.[103] Certain curés—the 'seditious' party, the newly elected *syndic* always calls them—were attempting to stir up a general agitation against the Diocesan Bureau, and Boumard of Sainte-Croix is now referred to as their leader.[104] What we know of the abbé Boumard, whether haunting the offices of the Farmers-General in Paris to complain of the exactions of their agents,[105] or taking to the ecclesiastical *maquis* on the fine afternoon when he sabotaged the cathedral Rogation procession, suggests an extremely obstinate man. Like Chatizel, he knew his Church history well from a Richerist point of view, and looked back with envy to an age when 'the bishops did nothing important without the consent of their priests, deacons and people'.[106] He had joined with his friend Courtillé to denounce the fraudulent reform of the Assembly General of the Clergy of Anjou,[107] and now that hopes of constitutional concessions had proved illusory, he proposed to drag the Bureau and its doings into sinister publicity in the law-courts. It had all begun over a matter of 16*l.* 5*s.*[108] Precisely two years ago, the diocesan Receiver had summoned Boumard to pay this amount of tax on his chapel of St. Francis in the church of Melay, being a sum left outstanding by the previous titular, who had died bankrupt. Taxation, it was argued, was levied on benefices, not on persons, so the actual holder must pay whatever was due and recoup himself by legal action against his predecessor's heirs. Boumard had held out for nearly a year, then finally presented himself at the diocesan office, accompanied by a lawyer's clerk as a professional witness of proceedings. Here he had solemnly counted out on the table the exact sum owing for taxation since he had actually taken over his benefice. When this was refused, on the ground that old debts must be settled before current payments could be received, the angry curé of Sainte-Croix paid over his 16*l*. 5*s*. under protest, reserving a right to ask the Diocesan Bureau questions about the unpaid taxation of the former bishop. Since then, Boumard had become thoroughly embittered and was no longer prepared to pay any taxation whatsoever, even under protest. To all sommations from Receiver and *syndic* for impositions due from his cure and his chapels, he now replied that he would welcome a law-suit, and that he was anxious to bring to light the dealings of the Bureau with bishop de Grasse.[109] Behind this minor dispute, indeed, lay a major scandal, 'disagreeable for the Bureau and devastating for the memory of M. de Grasse'.[110] During the first fourteen years of his deplorable episcopate, the late bishop had defaulted on his tax returns for a total sum of 16,000*l*., and when brought to bay, had coolly offered to pay exactly in future if his past debt was remitted. The Bureau made no actual reply to this offer, but accepted it in practice. Verbal orders were given to the Receiver to allow the bishop his receipts when he made current payments. From then onwards, Mgr de Grasse had paid his taxation, but clearly restitution formed no part of his theory of penitence, and importunate deputations and the opprobrium of appearing as a debtor in every yearly balance-sheet failed to shame him into surrendering 16,000*l*. When he died, the Bureau had taken no action against his heirs, 'no doubt out of respect for the dignity of the episcopal office', no doubt also out of regard for the fact that nothing but debts remained from the episcopal succession. Nor had the Bureau, naturally enough, made any attempt to recover its money from the new bishop. As to who was now responsible for this debt, it was impossible to say. The old Receiver was dead, but in any case, it was not for him to distrain upon a benefice holder, and he had brought the matter to notice on his accounts every year. Of the Bureau of 1772, only one member survived, curé Chotard, who, being a sensible man, exercised the privilege of age and 'remembered nothing about it',[111] while present members of that body could argue that the dead bishop had quittances for the last three years of his life, which precluded them from an action against his succession. But whoever was responsible, this whole affair was, as the lawyers of the Clergy of France observed, 'a sad commentary on the dishonesty of a bishop and the weakness and inexactitude of the Diocesan Bureau'.[112] While curé Boumard was being dunned for a sum of 16*l*. owed by his minor benefice, the greatest benefice in the diocese still owed 16,000*l*., and this bad debt had been incurred with the positive connivance of the ruling oligarchy.

Canon Nioche de la Brosse, the *syndic*, would have preferred stern measures against Boumard, lest any sign of weakening should encourage the 'seditious party'.[113] His bishop, however, wished to prevent 'the ashes of M. de Grasse from being disturbed and humiliation brought upon his memory',[114] while from Paris came positive legal advice to 'let the facts alleged against the late bishop of Angers remain buried in the most profound oblivion'.[115] It was too late. The curé of Sainte-Croix had quite decided on his law-suit,[116] and had accumulated other grievances concerning the affairs of the Bureau which he intended to air in the courts. Meanwhile he refused to pay any sort of clerical taxation on his cure or other benefices. Nor had he, when in April 1789 bailiffs arrived to seize his furniture.[117] It may seem ludicrous to mention this minor tragedy amidst the events of one of the most significant years in history; but the victory of the *Tiers État* was gained as a result of a split in the clerical order, and the revolt of the curés was the outcome of a whole intricate pattern of events, trivial and pathetic, like the over-assessment of abbé Chatizel, or curé Boumard's 16*l.* 5*s.*

CHAPTER X

CLERGY, NOBLES AND THIRD
ESTATE (1787–1789)

In 1787 political life suddenly revived in Anjou. There was electrifying news from Paris. Here, the Parlement, in alliance with all other sovereign courts of the realm and backed by the populace of the capital, had refused to register Loménie de Brienne's edicts imposing a stamp-duty and a land-tax, and demanded the calling of the Estates-General. By November, Louis XVI had promised to summon this great assembly of the nation before 1792, and it was already clear that the date of its meeting would have to be advanced. Angers was not the seat of a parlement, but magistrates of the *Présidial*, from their minor vantage point in the judicial hierarchy, exhorted the King on behalf of his Parlement of Paris, 'hoping that His Majesty would wish to defer to the requests and representations of all his courts'.[1] Meanwhile, a newly-invented Provincial Assembly of Anjou had met, and its existence, if not its activities, brought political speculation to a focus. From October 6 to 27 its grave deputies conferred at the town hall of Angers, heard masses at the Cordeliers and the cathedral said by dean de Villeneuve, their senior ecclesiastical member, and set up a permanent commission which remained in session in town to collect information and advocate reforms.[2] France seemed well on the way to receiving a constitution, the intendant at Tours would no longer dominate local life, and, it was said, the 'great tree of despotism, mighty and oppressive, without being startlingly uprooted, would nevertheless finally wither away'.[3] An era of liberty was approaching, and the inevitable question as to who should rule in the name of liberty now arose.

This withering away of the tree of despotism which the duc de Choiseul-Praslin hoped for was to redound 'to the great advantage of the trees of the countryside'—in fact, to the nobility of Anjou, who would 'enrich themselves by despoiling the intendant'. So wrote the duke to Walsh, comte de Serrant, in a correspondence concerned with rigging nominations and co-options to make up the membership of the Provincial Assembly. Walsh,[4] of an Irish family but lately come to Anjou from Brittany, with connexions at Versailles and great possessions in the province, had established himself as the oracle of its nobility, and was already meditating a 'system' which would devolve effectual political power into the hands of his own class. Boulainvilliers' dreams of a revival of feudal constitutionalism and Montesquieu's designs for an aristocratic barrier against despotism lived again in this man's ambitions. His disciple, Boylèsve de la Maurouzière, put their aspirations into terms of political theory when he said that the hierarchy of three estates is a fundamental law of the monarchy like the established succession to the throne: without it, central power would triumph easily over a confusion of classes, 'a flock of sheep for the shearing'.[5] Constitutionalism of some kind was now inevitable, and to this aristocratic cabal the inauguration of the Provincial Assembly of Anjou marked a beginning of opportunity for the Angevin nobility. Boldness and circumspection were needed: courage to sail forward into uncharted waters, caution in trimming one's sails to every new wind; but given these qualities, provincial, and possibly national, leadership could fall to their class.

The Provincial Assembly and its permanent commission began well, enlisting local loyalties by protesting against the loss of a few parishes to the neighbouring province of Maine,[6] taking a lead in reforming projects by demanding fair and equal taxation and attacking the *gabelle*, and flattering the town of Angers by renewing its pleas for a foundling hospital and barracks.[7] And then, inspired by news from Dauphiné and anxious to shake off its dependence on Tours, the permanent commission, on the last day of October 1788, petitioned the Crown to restore the old Provincial Estates of Anjou.[8] This was a popular demand to make, but the motives for making it almost immediately became popularly suspect. Provincial self-government was one thing, an exhumation of archaic liberties was another, for in the old Estates of Anjou the commons had been kept in tutelage, all three orders enjoying equal representation. This *démarche* of the permanent commission coincided with events in Paris which served to underline its disingenuous motives: the Notables, recalled by Necker, refused to accept a doubling of the commons and vote by head in the approaching Estates-General.[9] There was a piquant flavour of ambition in the constitutional recipes of the aristocratic cuisine.

At this point, a revolt of the bourgeoisie began. After all, the permanent commission of the Provincial Assembly was a residual executive of a nominated oligarchy; as the municipality of Angers put it, the zeal of its members could be applauded, but their status could not be recognized—they were 'administrators set up without our consent'.[10] Representatives of the commons who sat there were not those that the commons would have chosen for themselves, and the two representatives of the clergy, d'Alichoux of the cathedral and canon Burgevin, an ornament of the Academy, stood for the higher ecclesiastics who ruled the diocese, and not for its parish priests.[11] By proposing to retain political arrangements of the fifteenth century in the reconstituted Estates, the permanent commission was calculating on perpetuating a domination of great ecclesiastical corporations over lower clergy on one hand, and of nobles over commonalty on the other. It was from lawyers of the Angevin bar that protests against this design originated.[12] The municipality of Angers took courage from their initiative. A general town assembly was called, and a schedule of questions to which deputies were to bring their answers was circulated. More especially, they were to say whether the Third Estate, 'which bears the greater part of the burden of taxes and public charges, ought to have as many deputies and votes as the clergy and nobles in combination'.[13] On 9 December, mayor and aldermen, the *syndic* of the clergy and deputies of the cathedral, *Présidial*, university, royal jurisdictions, *avocats*, *juges consuls*, notaries, *procureurs*, merchants and parishes of Angers met in general conference. Canons Louet and Guillon of Saint-Maurice argued that the municipality had proposed questions which were beyond the competence of a gathering which did not contain formally commissioned representatives of the first two orders in the state, that it was premature to make pronouncements on the form of Provincial Estates before the Crown had sanctioned their re-establishment, and that the approaching meeting of the Estates-General would provide a more suitable opportunity for such representations.[14] Only the parish of Saint-Denis showed any sympathy for these tactics of conservatism.[15] Fortified by this virtual unanimity, the municipality petitioned the Crown to restore the Estates of Anjou in a new form, that is, with double representation of the commons and vote by head, and these propositions were circulated to other chief towns of the province for their adhesion.[16] Throughout this month of December, the central government was bombarded with petitions from every part of France asking for double representation of the Third Estate in the approaching Estates-General, petitions which the Angevin comte de la Galissonière darkly hinted were formulated at the minister's desk before returning to him stamped with a seal of popular approval.[17] However that may have been, on 27 December Necker yielded to this outcry. Henceforward, in both local and national affairs, the commons would be able to negotiate with the other two orders on at least equal terms.

Now the nobility was on the defensive, anxious to prevent an augmented Third Estate from dominating the approaching Estates-General. In Anjou, they were talking of their willingness to relinquish financial privileges, but with a few eccentric exceptions, like the left-wing comte de Dieusie, they were insisting that they would not relinquish their corporate identity as an order in the state.[18] Their *cahier*, when it was finally drawn up, was explicit on this point: their representatives were instructed to oppose vote by head, and to refuse any propositions to unite their order either to the clergy as a whole or to higher ecclesiastics only. For Walsh, comte de Serrant, however, the fight was still for domination rather than for survival. From November 1788 Angers was inundated with brochures of his party, which appealed to voters of the commonalty over the heads of their middle-class leaders. Let the people distrust the newly-ennobled, whose 'so-called rights' are but 'the Dead Sea fruits of the extravagance of kings';[19] so, too, let them distrust vote-catching lawyers with political ambitions—as the verger of Saint-Michel du Tertre observed, 'the protection you are pretending to extend to the Third Estate is, in fact, a cajolerie, which you are using to win its confidence and to get yourself elected as its representative'.[20] This blatantly opportunist propaganda was suspect from the very first. 'Where are the titles of this new apostolate that M. le Comte de Serrant comes to exercise in our midst? Where are the proofs of his mission. . . . *Numquid Saul inter Prophetas?*' [21] Other replies of genuine prophets to Saul were less genial. Volney, who was principally engaged in fomenting troubles in Brittany, kept his left hand disengaged, so to speak, to lash the nobles of Anjou—'know this, that all men, whatever their class or condition . . . are equal'. Reply and counter-reply (not to mention forged ironical approval) were poured out in response to the comte de Serrant's pamphlets, and when Volney wearied, La Revellière-Lépeaux came in to relieve him. 'Do not choose either nobles or priests, however good their personal character', he wrote. That was already a foregone conclusion. Meanwhile, as a sinister background to this paper war, came echoes of street-fighting from Rennes, where law students were crossing swords with Breton gentry. Early in February 1789[22] law and medical students of the University of Angers were girding themselves up to march to the aid of their contemporaries at Rennes and causing no small sensation in their own town by so doing. The struggle was bloodless in Angers (though on 10 March the marquis d'Autichamp feared that 'the Nobility will be obliged to look to its arms');[23] nevertheless, in this tense and feverish atmosphere it was impossible to obtain any hearing for the 'system' of Walsh. In February and March, the bourgeoisie of Angers managed the preliminary elections for the Estates-General[24] without intervention by the aristocracy from above, or protest from the working-class below. The town itself was organized by two successful lawyers, the Delaunay brothers, now on the threshold of their career as revolutionary deputies and administrators. The countryside, swayed by model *cahiers* distributed by La Revellière-Lépeaux and his friends, elected inhabitants of Angers who held rural property, or local notaries, surgeons and lawyers. In the united assembly of the *Sénéchaussée* of Angers, these 800 voters, suitably organized in bureaux, were shepherded by the urban middle-class, and Volney and La Revellière-Lépeaux were members of the committee appointed to draw up a *cahier*. Representatives of five *sénéchaussées* were to attend a final electoral meeting on 16 March, but as those of Angers outnumbered all the rest by two to one, there could be no doubt of the final issue. Leaders of the Angevin bourgeoisie like Volney and La Revellière-Lépeaux would go to Versailles, and the *cahier* they presented would be a summary of their aspirations.

In this sharp and decisive struggle, the clergy had remained neutral. More sincerely than the nobility, they were liberal in outlook and anxious for reform. Rangeard, watching political events from his rectory at Andard, had constituted himself laureate of a new era, welcoming the meeting of the Provincial Assembly, the victory of the Parlement of Paris and the calling of the Estates-General with metrical prophecies of a new golden age. Soon, constrictive exemptions would be removed, and the erstwhile destructive torrent of taxation, spreading more evenly over all the land, would become a fertilizing stream, commerce and agriculture would flourish, and Louis, 'wisest of princes' (this laudatory epithet was for public consumption—in a private letter to Héron of the Collège d'Anjou, the poet expresses himself rather differently), who had already 'submitted himself to the empire of the laws', would rule as a constitutional king.[25] The *cahier* of the clergy of Anjou[26] reveals that, as yet, Rangeard was only slightly ahead of his brethren's opinions. Here, they ask for control of taxation by the nation, a sweeping reform of financial abuses, annual Estates-General, provincial estates, guarantees of individual liberty, better conditions for soldiers, and the preservation of common lands for the peasantry. For their part, provided that the nation will take over all debts of the Clergy of France, they wish to relinquish their own exemptions from taxation. These are aspirations, not only of the lower clergy,[27] but of the clergy of Anjou as a whole. Similar propositions are found in individual preliminary *cahiers* drawn up by the chapters of Saint-Martin and Saint-Laud,[28] while the canons of Saint-Maurice, protesting later on against the proceedings by which clerical deputies to the Estates General have been elected, are at pains to make it quite clear that they have no wish to go back on these liberal demands; 'they consent, nay, they enthusiastically propose that they should bear the burden of public charges equally with the other two orders'.[29] Everywhere in France, churchmen were adopting a similar attitude. They belonged to an order which had enjoyed a privileged constitutional position; they were now willing to allow the whole nation to take over their heritage.

Choudieu, a bilious anti-clerical then resident in Angers, looking back on these days, grudgingly admitted that 'the clergy, which by its exaggerated pretensions and encroachments upon the civil power has always taught peoples that kings are not inviolate, itself asked for the convocation of the Estates-General and the reform of the old order'.[30]

But clerical support for a liberal régime in politics did not imply any desire to weaken the links that bound Church and state together, or any willingness to surrender control of machinery which gave the Church its power to sway the minds of men. The public exercise of religion, said our Clergy of Anjou, should be allowed to the Roman church alone. The state should suppress all anti-religious propaganda, enforce observance of Sundays and holy days and maintain moral standards by forbidding lotteries and speculation, while education was to be brought more tightly under ecclesiastical control.[31] A curé of the diocese who yielded place to none as a reformer and an opponent of aristocracy was equally uncompromising in defence of his Church. He would transfer papal dispensing powers to an apostolic vicar in France and subject bishops to yearly synods, but he defended popes from charges of extortion and the episcopate from the insinuations of libellists, and drew up schemes to increase the dignity of parish priests and to impose strict moral discipline in every parish.[32] Behind the liberalism of nobles and bourgeois lurked strategems of ambitious individuals anxious to play a part on the stage of politics now that absolutism was breaking: behind the liberalism of the clergy there was a less personal, less selfish but more permanent desire for influence, not so much in politics, as in the national life as a whole, not on behalf of individuals, but on behalf of an eternal corporation. Nobility and bourgeoisie hoped to rule in their generation: the clergy intended to mould society in centuries to come. Thus, in this triangular battle for domination, the conflict of the second and third orders for control of the state was both logically prior to and historically more urgent than any clash of interests in which the first order was directly involved.

There may be argument as to whether the *cahiers* of associations and corporations within the town of Angers are fully representative of popular opinion, but at least they represent the opinions of the dominant bourgeoisie. From them one may illustrate various grounds of conflict which might arise between churchmen and commons. Ecclesiastical property is under continuous and envious review[33] and the maldistribution of revenues within the Church itself is a subject for bitter utilitarian comment. Naturally, a good deal is said of exemptions from taxation, billeting and guard duties.[34] General reforms within the Church of France are recommended, possibly

P

through the agency of a national council summoned by the Crown.[35] Bishops and abbots are to fulfil their duties of residence, 'which would have more charms for them', says the Law Faculty tartly, 'if their revenues were more modest'.[36] Ecclesiastics are not to grow rich by accumulation of benefices.[37] The balance of power and the incidence of promotion are to be tilted in favour of the parochial clergy.[38] A number of *cahiers* would wish to see the French Church freed from dependence on Rome, mostly in minor matters like annates and dispensations,[39] though two refer to more radical possibilities—setting up a Patriarch in France, or even ending the Concordat altogether.[40] But for the most part there is little that is remarkable in these requests, and nothing which must inevitably cause an unbridgeable gulf between clergy and bourgeoisie. If the Third Estate was casting envious eyes upon church property, so too was the nobility. Attacks upon abuses and maldistribution of income had wide support within the Church itself. Hatred of clerical exemptions was counterbalanced by the clergy's spontaneous offer to relinquish them. Acid references to Rome probably had no deeper motives than parsimony, second-hand Gallican prejudices and a hatred of the law's delays—even the pharmacologists, ancestors of M. Homais and plotting to establish a Patriarch in Paris, hoped to arrange everything by friendly agreement with the Vatican.[41] The church-state connexion and clerical control of education are assumed to be established features of national life. True, lawyers, merchants and municipal officers would have been glad to see commercial lending at interest made legal[42] and some *cahiers* complain of the testamentary laws which made repairs to the property of benefices a privileged debt.[43] But these were not great matters. Only the Law Faculty, with a proposal to deprive the clergy of its status as a separate order in the state,[44] was advocating anything seriously detrimental to the power and prestige of the Gallican Church. Envy of wealth and privilege is inevitable and must be assessed comparatively. The inhabitants of Angers, who had much more reason to envy the first order of society, show in their *cahiers* much more bitterness towards the second.[45] Nobles, rather than churchmen, were the enemies of the Angevin bourgeoisie.

Just as the faction of the comte de Serrant was appealing to the people to abandon its middle-class leaders, so too the bourgeoisie was appealing to parish priests over the head of the diocesan oligarchy. Canons, said Volney (he was referring more particularly to the chapter of Rennes), are like rats and mice who, when the mistress of the house is ill, profit by disorder and gnaw hams and cheeses. 'My friend, in this business you have no ecclesiastics in your favour except the curés and their vicaires, that is to say the only clergy in

France who are really useful.' [46] The *cahiers* of Angers, with their bias in favour of parish priests, reflect these opinions in more judicious and practical terms.[47] But spokesmen of the Third Estate also appealed to the clergy as a whole, using arguments of both morality and expediency. At the end of February 1789, La Revellière-Lépeaux declared that ecclesiastics who were unable to see their duty to join the people's cause ought at least to remain neutral and, 'Bible in hand', stand between the opposed factions. Their policy, if they were true to their principles, could not be framed on self-interest, for they were obliged to consider the interests of religion in itself, and that alone. 'Misled by mistaken ideas, you have grown accustomed to see the glory and grandeur of the Eternal as coincident with that of his ministers. . . . Do you wish to make us think that, after you have preached self-abnegation, you are merely seeking to deceive us, and to monopolize to our hurt all the sweets of social existence?' [48] There was some force in this argument. Churchmen had not only to follow their convictions: they had a duty to appear disinterested. Thus the first order was obliged to leave the battle for supremacy to the two lay orders. Both its internal divisions and its principles forbade effective intervention.

Canon Mongodin of Saint-Pierre, it is true, did not think so, and on New Year's day 1789 he gave the commons of Anjou the benefit of his opinions. His pamphlet[49] was as hearty and truculent as his personal appearance. 'Bon jour, bon an, messieurs du Tiers, un mot s'il vous plaît.' Away with all this nonsense about natural equality, contract and reciprocal rights! Government is a result of the Fall of man, 'force made the first sovereign', and men go on obeying to obtain protection. That is why the Bible tells us to render to Caesar the things that are Caesar's. A hierarchy is essential in a state, and the nobility are not your enemies. Do you wish to unleash a *jacquerie* in the countryside, while cobblers are presiding over cardinals in your central assembly? 'Vote by head and not by order simply means without a head and in most frightful disorder.' So do not listen to lawyers who preach to you like Savonarola while their only aim is to get themselves elected and to govern. 'O worthy people, always too credulous, will you never cease being the dupe of windbags and charlatans?' In reply to this blend of theology, Hobbes and snobbery, Volney evoked Christian principles as expounded by an inevitably virtuous curé of his own invention.[50] Brought to a melancholy conviction of sin by our canon's declamations, Volney presents himself at his parish confessional and there recites his manifold evil ambitions, which, oddly enough, are all reckoned to him for righteousness. Reducing the Crown to an executive role and ensuring popular liberty, these are duties which religion itself enjoins, and as for deploring the luxury of the higher clergy, 'pass on, that isn't sin, councils of the church have said twenty times more than that'. One sin alone this virtuous curé imputes to our tribune of the people—he had read Mongodin's pamphlet.

However, this 'mongodinade' which Volney satirized was an eccentric outburst of an odd blunt individual, whose foible was to claim acquaintance with all the best people. No such diatribes came from the dignified and diplomatic higher clergy of the diocese. Perhaps, like Cotelle de la Blandinière, the aged and absentee but still accredited theologian of the diocese of Angers, they were groping for a decent attitude towards the approaching revolution; believing in the King's divine right to rule yet admitting that religion, public opinion, and, so far as taxation was involved, the Estates-General could limit him; hostile to the pretensions of nobles and parlements, yet very concerned to ensure the sanctity of that fundamental law 'as old as the monarchy', which separated the nation into three distinct orders.[51] But whatever their political opinions may have been, in any case they bore no love for Walsh, comte de Serrant; indeed, for two years past they had been co-operating with the municipality of Angers and the province generally to oppose his feudal claims. As long ago as 1769 this grasping nobleman had been enclosing waste-lands and ending customary grazing rights;[52] in 1784 he proceeded to claim all roadside trees within the area where he exercised anachronistic powers and non-existent duties as *seigneur haut justicier*. By August 1786 he had won his case before the Parlement of Paris,[53] and a sound of saws in the country-lanes of Anjou proclaimed that the count had turned timber merchant. Other *seigneurs hauts justiciers*, notably the marquis d'Autichamp, had followed this mean example.[54] Mindful of *Monsieur's* claims to feudal homage, the cathedral chapter was suspicious of all feudal revivals, and decided to collaborate with various orders and corporations in both town and countryside to organize resistance.[55] On 17 January 1787 the Assembly General of the Clergy of Anjou agreed to join the municipality of Angers and other interested parties in a concerted opposition for which the clergy would subscribe one-tenth of the expenses; as this matter was one which concerned higher ecclesiastics rather than lower, it was agreed that curés should pay only one-sixth of taxation levied for this purpose.[56] By now, this wretched dispute was, as an officer in garrison at Angers wrote, 'a major affair which interests the whole of Anjou'.[57] Nioche de la Brosse, canon of Saint-Maurice and *syndic* of the clergy, was the leading spirit in the attack upon feudal reaction. Together with Gastineau of the Law Faculty he went up to Paris to interview the minister, who cautiously referred him back to the Provincial Assembly.[58] The permanent commission, faced with a very awkward decision, decided to be neutral, though the comte de Dieusie implored Walsh to withdraw his claims and spare their consciences.[59] De la Brosse made a similar appeal, couched in bland and sardonic terms which constitute a masterpiece of polite ruthlessness. 'I write,' he said, 'not with the preachings of a St. Bernard or a Peter the Hermit, but simply as a man who believes in your intelligence and in the goodness of your heart.' There is an appeal to fashionable sensibility, a diplomatic suggestion that the lawyers have mishandled the affair, a direct but unexceptionable hint at the count's foreign origins, and, behind all this, an uncompromising insistence that his whole claim is baseless and unjust, an attempt to reap what has not been sown. In Anjou, Touraine, Maine and the neighbouring provinces, de la Brosse declares, 'you are spoken of quite openly as the enemy of the common weal'—'pourriez-vous vous consoler de ne paraître désormais aux yeux de vos concitoyens (j'ose trancher le mot) qu'un usurpateur avide?'[60] Walsh did not yield. Clergy and town therefore pressed on their case before the permanent commission of the Provincial Assembly, canon Louet of the cathedral and M. de Lesrat of the municipality handing in a formal complaint which compelled that vacillating body to make further appeals to *seigneurs hauts justiciers* to renounce their pretensions. This was in December 1788, and in January canon Louet was still haunting the commission and goading its members into reluctant activity.[61]

This affair of the trees, dragged out as it was from 1786 to March 1789, provided a standing refutation of the comte de Serrant's propaganda, and a proof that he was not fit to lead his own class, let alone the province. More important still, it had set up a barrier between him and the higher clergy of the diocese, and indicated common ground on which first and third orders could co-operate. Having done his best to make the privileges of greater local aristocrats thoroughly obnoxious, Walsh nevertheless, with remarkable effrontery and naïve malice, exhorted commoners to join him in attacking the privileges, and more particularly the property, of the Church. Victor Bodi, an *avocat* of Angers who was the count's legal agent and journalist, in November 1788 was proclaiming the necessity of such an alliance. He denied that the clergy had any right to claim an independent place in the social structure, for they form a corporation which 'is outside ordinary society, since it does not accept the fundamental laws of all societies, those of property, marriage and defence of the state'. It has renounced the ordinary obligations of men, and must be 'reminded continually' that certain temporal consequences follow: its property is merely held in *usufruct*, and really 'belongs to the nation, which alone has the right to dispose of it'. Despotic in its own instincts, yet submissive to despotism by policy, the first order represents a danger to constitutionalism against which Third Estate and nobility must ally.[62] Apart from the suggestion of an alliance to plunder Church property, which showed an opportunist instinct for the obvious, Walsh's dreams were chimerical. Even so, the idea that the two lay orders were natural allies persisted in face of facts, and was again alluded to by the comte de la Galissonière in his discourse at the opening of the final electoral assemblies of Anjou on 16 March.[63]

It was then that 427 gentry of Anjou met under de la Galissonière's presidency in the chapter-house of Saint-Aubin to elect their deputies to the Estates-General and to agree upon their *cahier*.[64] The commons (now at last in the final stage of their indirect elections, and the clergy, were also separately assembled. Now was the time to strike bargains and form alliances. It was the clergy who seized this opportunity. On the morning of 18 March they sent a deputation to the commons to announce their willingness to surrender immunities from taxation, and during that afternoon they received a deputation in return[65] which praised 'this spirit of patriotism and equity which is always characteristic of the ministers of a God of peace'. The nobles, taken by surprise, were angry with the first order for not giving warning of this *démarche*,[66] which made their own renunciation two days later something of an anti-climax. As for the withdrawal of *seigneurs hauts justiciers* in the matter of roadside trees on 21 March,[67] that was useless as propaganda, being two years overdue already. While the clergy made haste to conciliate the commons on a fundamental issue, the nobles spent their time annoying the clergy on matters indifferent. There are hints of anti-clericalism in their *cahier*, not mean plebeian details of course, but grand sweeping references to ecclesiastical discipline, a national plan of education and the status of Protestants—subjects suitable to embarrass churchmen.[68] Such ingenuity as was not applied to preparing a *cahier* was expended in engineering a dignified revenge upon the chapter of Saint-Maurice. In the mid-fifteenth century, an ephemeral order of chivalry, the *Ordre du Croissant*, had hung its escutcheons in the cathedral, where they had remained until the whitewashing of 1783, when the canons seized the opportunity to relegate them to decent obscurity in the chapel of Sainte-Anne.[69] An order of chivalry which had scarcely outlived good Duke René, its founder, was not likely to arouse genuine emotions in the breasts of Angevin nobles, and it is hard to believe that any of them wished to revive its excellent rules—to be present at mass every day, to say the hours of Our Lady on penalty of not sitting down at table, to visit the sick and take care of widows and orphans.[70] However, here was a pretext to score off the clergy.

A formal protest was organized. On 20 March a deputation of six noblemen waited upon the cathedral chapter and entered ceremoniously by the great doors, specially opened for the occasion—or rather, four of them did, two being wary committee-men who had urgent business which took them away without further waste of time. The comte de Cossé and dean de Villeneuve read solemn discourses to each other, then the canons escorted the deputation back as far as the entrance to their cloister.[71] Three days later, six canons proceeded to the assembly of nobles, where Louet made a speech, conceding the particular point at issue, but making no relaxation of principles—'a Christian church displays the heraldic symbols of religion, not those of the nobility'.[72]

This complaint against the cathedral had been unearthed by the marquis de Beauvau, who now conjured up his medieval ancestors to confound the clergy once more.[73] In the fifteenth century, Bertrand de Beauvau had showered gifts upon the monastery of the Augustins of Angers, on condition that its endowments should revert to his descendants if this particular congregation ceased to occupy the house. According to the strict letter of the law, there were now too few friars resident here for 'conventuality', so the marquis proposed to transfer his rights over the property to a new object, that is, to found a chapter of noble canonesses 'solely reserved for daughters of Angevin houses'. No doubt His Majesty would wish to add other ecclesiastical income to so worthy an establishment. The open-handed marquis was duly applauded, and a place in this hypothetical new foundation was voted to ladies of his family in perpetuity. This is how the nobles of Anjou spent their time at the crisis of their fortunes. Very soon, all chapters of noble canonesses of France would be dispersed, and uncanonical hands would deal with coats of arms that spoilt the austere splendour of whitewashed churches.

CHAPTER XI

THE REVOLT OF THE CURÉS AND THE ELECTIONS TO THE ESTATES-GENERAL (MARCH 1789)

'AH! above all else let a sympathetic regard be paid to the curés, those worthy pastors, who relieve the poor and console the broken-hearted, let their lot be ameliorated; nor should their zealous collaborators the vicaires be forgotten, let them be given a living wage and freed from the degrading necessity of collecting from door to door.'[1] This eloquent plea of the *Présidial* was echoed generally by other corporations and communities of Angers when in February and early March of 1789 they were compiling their *cahiers*. La Revellière-Lépeaux had been circulating specimen *cahiers* which advocated increased incomes, and he proposed to reserve canonries at the cathedral for priests grown old in the parochial ministry.[2] These suggestions were taken up in greater detail. The Apostolic Notaries put forward the realistic figure of a *congrue* of 1,200*l.*, with half this amount as the salary of an assistant priest, but others proposed as much as 1,000*l.* for a vicaire, and this higher figure was accepted in the final conflated *cahier* of the Third Estate of the town.[3] No difficulties were foreseen in obtaining revenue for these new salaries. The property of abbeys and chapters could be sold, and what remained after clearing off national debts could be applied to relieving the poverty of the lower clergy.[4] Meanwhile, Volney[5] was declaring that parish priests were the only useful members of their order in France, and a pamphleteer of more narrowly local celebrity was exhorting his fellow-citizens to reorganize charity in the town in collaboration with the curés, to the exclusion of 'any ecclesiastic who does not bear the title of pastor'.[6] At least one chapter, that of Saint-Laud, reflected this general movement of opinion in its *cahier*. Benefices without cure of souls, said these canons, should be united to parish endowments, so that *congrues* might be increased and vicaires relieved from their begging tours.[7] However, it was rather late in the day for chapters to transform themselves into champions of curés. It was the Third Estate which had taken over that role and was already looking forward to reaping its reward in the form of deputies of the lower clergy acting as its allies in the approaching Estates-General. Let us, said one pamphleteer, 'unite our forces to counterbalance the power which the Nobility and higher Clergy have massed so effectively against our common interests. . . . Ah! our very dear Pastors, will you be so weak as to pay regard to rank and birth? . . . Can your votes be won or wrung from you by the imposing glance of your presiding (bishop) or by his brand-new air of affability?' [8] The writer went on to promise the usual generous salaries from the incomes of abbeys and chapters —'rejoice, the days of justice have come'. Clearly reforms were at hand and parish priests could rely on widespread support in pressing their grievances. 'It is high time', said the Faculty of Law, 'that the respectable class of pastors should be avenged for the long indifference, nay almost, scorn, with which it has been treated, to the prejudice of the maintenance of public morality.' [9]

This is what Chatizel had been saying for some years past. At the end of 1788 he published a manifesto[10] summarizing the grievances of curés, oppressed and degraded for a century and a half by a 'conspiracy' of canons and regulars. Chapters and monasteries hold property which was given originally to support pastoral functions, and from these acquisitions they now pay *congrues* unrelated to rising costs of living. They, too, own the finest churches and have a monopoly of music and ceremony, so that the splendour of their deserted services 'makes one doubt if the religion of the parishes is the same as that of the chapters'. We have no diocesan synod, our so-called 'General Assembly' is a confederacy of canons, the newly established provincial administration gives no place to the second order of clergy. But Chatizel was not merely asking for justice on these standard points of controversy. His specific object now was to demand a reversal of the balance of power in the approaching elections to the Estates-General. What the dominant diocesan oligarchy would have wished in this respect we may deduce from individual *cahiers* of the chapters of Saint-Martin and Saint-Laud[11] and from suggestions put forward by the permanent commission of the Provincial Assembly of Anjou.[12] The two *cahiers* recommend a system of election which would award places in five equal blocks— bishops, canons, monks, holders of benefices without cure of souls, and curés; while the permanent commission blandly declared that 'there could be no difficulty with regard to the clergy', whose 'usual and periodic assemblies' could easily form the cadre for new elections. It was hard to tell which system would have given fewer seats to curés. Chatizel was protesting in advance against any such arrangements. 'The curés', he said, 'are to the Church of France what the Third Estate is to the nation',[13] that is, if we add a gloss from Volney or Sieyès—everything. In the Estates-General they must be represented in proportion to their numbers, their value to the community, and their service to the Crown. Royal authority had everything to gain, Chatizel speciously argued, by weighting voting power in favour of a body of men who were in constant touch with the people, aiding the poor, censuring the spirit of revolt, teaching obedience, and conveying the sovereign's will 'to the ears of the great and to the hovels of the poor'.[14] On 23 December, Chatizel and his colleague Courtillé, curé of Saint-Denis, sent copies of this manifesto to Necker and to the King himself. 'One of the principal aims of our ministry', they told Louis XVI, 'is to maintain among your people respect and submission towards your sovereign authority.'[15] A month later the government's decision was announced. Curés could attend electoral assemblies in person, canons and monks would only be allowed to send representatives, one for every ten canons, and one for each monastic establishment. 'By a stroke of the pen, Necker had set up a clerical democracy alongside the lay democracy.'[16] Parish priests of the diocese of Angers (with assorted reinforcements from such fragments of the dioceses of Poitiers, La Rochelle and Nantes as lay within the same electoral area) would have decisive power to nominate the ecclesiastical deputies for Anjou—that is, provided they could be organized and united in their choice.

In the rectories of Andard and Soulaines, incisive pens were at work to remind curés of their discontents and to ensure that they did not falter in their hour of opportunity. Rangeard presented a theological and historical case, Chatizel concentrated on practical exposure of administrative scandals within the Diocesan Bureau. 'Post hoc . . . designavit Dominus et alios septuaginta duos: et misit illos binos ante faciem suam'—this commissioning of 72 disciples, said Rangeard, using the key text of Richerist exigesis, is the parish priest's charter, his warrant that his mission is as well authenticated as that of a bishop.[17] But what are monks and canons? They enjoy man-made offices in a Church which originally knew no other distinctions than those which ordination conferred. Yet, in the confusion of the dark ages (and who could deny that Rangeard, despite all obstacles put in his way by the rich and leisured Benedictines, was Anjou's greatest expert on this period of history?), they contrived to appropriate cures and annex property and tithes, leaving the true pastors to languish like exiled Jews beside the waters of Babylon.[18] These depredations have continued, and even in the last fifty years the six or seven richest churches of the diocese have appropriated to themselves more ecclesiastical income than all the five hundred parishes together.[19] The arguments of the archpriest of Andard were not all theoretical, however: he had particular grievances in mind, and against canons of the cathedral he was specifically and especially bitter. Rangeard, now a champion of curés, had once been a canon of Saint-Maurice himself, until he had been compelled to resign his stall after an unedifying dispute with his colleagues.[20] That had been many years ago, but perhaps memories of those days still rankled, and he notes sardonically that sons of aristocratic families might find their way into parishes rather than cathedral chapters if only the revenue of the Church of France were justly re-allotted.[21] To enforce his point he devised a debate between a canon and a curé with an impartial philosopher as umpire: a humble parish priest confronts a mincing canon of less than half his age, while the grave philosopher totals up their respective incomes—700l. as against 4,600l. on which full taxation is not paid.[22]

For details concerning such injustices of clerical taxation an enquiring voter could turn to Chatizel, who, since his election to the General Assembly of the Clergy of Anjou, was in an excellent position to enlighten his colleagues about the machinations of the diocesan oligarchy. The so-called 'reform' of 1786, he reminds his readers, was contrived without our consent, and has still left the General Assembly a 'private committee of the canons'. As a result, says Chatizel, we have been unable to do anything save unearth abuses, but these, as he ruthlessly lists them, form an impressive total. Taxation had been increased, while at the very same time there had been a fantastic and unexplained surplus of over 130,000l. in hand. 16,000l. were still owing from the previous bishop: a debt of 5,000l. had been remitted to the Seminary; the affair of the Apostolic Notaries wasted 40,000l.; in fact, when various gratifications and other useless expenditures are taken into account, there had been a surcharge of 200,000l. on the diocese.[23] Finally, and most obnoxiously, the higher clergy had under-assessed themselves for taxation. Four abbeys and eight chapters in Angers had escaped to the tune of 30,000l. a year: that is, over the last twenty years, the parochial clergy had paid out half a million on their behalf.[24]

So much for old grievances. The electoral assemblies of the three orders were to meet in Angers on 16 March, and Chatizel's party published a complete specimen *cahier* as a guide to voters. In general national concerns their attitude is liberal—and clerical. Privilege is to end, individual liberty is to be guaranteed, feudal rights are to be swept away for ever; but the 'Catholic, apostolic and roman religion' is to remain established and 'dominant', and 'seductive and dogmatizing impiety' is to be repressed.[25] Apart from these provisions the whole pamphlet is a sweeping statement of the lower clergy's demands. A picture is painted of a reformed church of France, wherein a curé would enjoy over 2,000l. a year of independent revenue from tithes in his own hands, and could hope to end his days as a canon of a cathedral.[26] Parishes in the town of Angers, where tithe was negligible, would have their incomes increased by a generous union of other benefices to their temporalities, annual synods would meet to discuss all diocesan affairs and to elect at least half of the bishop's vicars-general, while in ecclesiastical courts curés would act as assessors for all cases. Vicaires, no longer humiliated by an annual examination, would enjoy 1,000*l.* a year with a guarantee, after fifteen years of service, of absolute priority for the next vacant living.[27] Here was a programme for a clerical Utopia, a shrewdly calculated golden age. Then, as to its achievement, a brief administrative note at the end of the brochure gives instructions on this vital point. 'We remind *MM. les curés* that M. Leroux, restaurant keeper of the Place Neuve in the parish of Sainte-Croix, will be open from Sunday, 15 March, and throughout the assembly'—so too will his brother in the rue Baudrière—'and for the private business of *MM. les curés*, they can meet in the main hall of the Palais des Marchands, on the aforesaid day, 15 March, at five in the evening, on Monday morning at seven and so on for the rest of the time.' [28] Here, in these simple but effective arrangements, was the result of caballing, circulation of anonymous writings and requests for signatures which the *syndic* of the diocese had complained of two months previously,[29] and of messages smuggled out of Angers to Soulaines by a baker who sold his bread every Wednesday and Saturday on the square outside the cathedral.[30] But there is no reason to disbelieve Chatizel when he protests, in a private letter, that he did not wish to be represented 'as the chief of a sort of federation'.[31] He, Courtillé, Boumard and their friends, had simply hired a hall. The curés would come together before the electoral assembly and their grievances would do the rest.

Early in January the bishop and *syndic* had been hoping to persuade the government to intervene and suppress Chatizel's 'seditious' writings and the 'dangerous ferment' they were causing in Anjou. At the same time, they were declaring, somewhat paradoxically, that the vast majority of clergy were not affected by this propaganda—it was a question of 'a faction of five or six curés', 'thirty or so' admitted the bishop, whose sense of proportion never entirely deserted him.[32] However, since then the royal power itself had favoured the parochial ministry. Representations by pious and influential ladies failed to conciliate our angular controversialist at Soulaines,[33] so that nothing now remained but to organize to fight the elections in March. The chapter of Saint-Maurice kept in close touch with other chapters of Angers and with the Benedictine monasteries, and on 5 March circulated its *cahier* to these corporations.[34] To canon Nioche de la Brosse fell the thankless task of defending the past activities of the Diocesan Bureau. His pamphlet in reply to Chatizel was well timed, being distributed shortly before the electors met. Thus the *syndic* had the last word—but how ineffectively! It was too late in the day to talk of Chatizel's 5,200*l.* a year,[35] for everyone knew by now what expenses and outgoings had to be deducted to arrive at a statement of net income, and in any case, a vital question still remained unanswered—what were the revenues of a canon of the cathedral? An ecclesiastic who himself came from Saint-Jean d'Angely could hardly hope to arouse antagonism against a curé who had come from Maine 'to inform the clergy of Anjou about their true interests'.[36] Anyone could make an error in assessing taxation;[37] true, but errors on a large scale over an extended period in favour of one class of taxpayers were not easily shrugged off as accidents. Appeals for unity in troubled times[38] were one thing, but lessons of the past were another, and the question at issue was, who could be trusted to represent the clergy in the central councils of the nation?

United, the parochial clergy could dominate the approaching elections. However, the will of seven or eight hundred curés, scattered over the countryside in villages, hamlets and market towns, and owing allegiance to various dioceses,[39] remained an unknown quantity. De la Brosse was neither dishonest nor entirely deluded when, on 9 January, he claimed that three-quarters of them had not even heard of Chatizel's agitation.[40] It was impossible to guess how many rural incumbents would trouble to make an uncomfortable journey to Angers, especially those who had no vicaire and who thus would be obliged to find a *locum tenens* for the period of their absence.[41] Under these circumstances every assured vote might count, and the chapters of Angers examined the regulations carefully to see what evasions or interpretations might suit their interests. Strictly speaking, each group of ten canons was entitled to send only one representative. Almost invariably, however, canons held other benefices, abbeys, priories or chapels, and on 22 February de la Brosse applied formally to the government asking if they were free to vote in respect of such titles held in plurality.[42] This request was granted, and the leaders of the lower clergy were too late in hearing of it to take effective counter-measures. Boumard of Sainte-Croix obtained the signatures of four other curés of Angers and of Rangeard to a protest which was hastily forwarded to Paris on 10 March, but a ruling had already been given.[43] Canons who held benefices which entitled them to vote in their own right duly stood aside and left the choice of capitular delegates to their colleagues.[44] Provision was thus made for a strong attendance of canons and Benedictine monks at the electoral assembly of the clergy, and those attending also furnished themselves with the procurations of absentees like the commendatory abbot of Saint-Aubin or of communities of women like the Carmelites, Visitandines, Ronceray, Le Calvaire and La Fidelité. As a result, on 16 March, the cathedral had fifteen of its canons present, holding among them a total of thirty-three votes, the chapter of Saint-Maurille disposed of five votes, that of Saint-Laud five, that of Saint-Pierre four.[45] Even so, monks and canons were hopelessly outnumbered. Out of a total vote of 831, four hundred and fifty-five were curés, without counting unbeneficed ecclesiastics and others who might be expected to support their cause. If the parochial clergy clung together, victory would be theirs.

Assemblies of all three orders began on Monday, 16 March, but the real elections for the clerical order had already taken place on the Sunday night. The country curés had flocked to the Palais des Marchands at five o'clock as instructed, and there everything had been concerted. Two possible clashes of interest might have arisen to divide them: the canons-regular of the Congregation of France (the so-called *prieurs-curés*) who held over 100 votes, or the priests of dioceses other than Angers, who commanded about 80 votes, might have diverged from the line of the main body. But once it was settled that a post of deputy or of *suppléant* should go to each of these groups, the rest was straightforward. Names were agreed upon and the conspiracy organized. To make assurance doubly sure, the very 'tellers' for the forthcoming elections were nominated, and lists of approved candidates and the order of voting for them were distributed.[46]

From the first, the parochial clergy took the offensive. Official proceedings opened on the Monday with a united assembly of all three orders, whose unreal and platitudinous harmony was rudely disturbed by two curés who insisted on registering a protest against the extension of the regulations which had allowed so many canons to be present. There was a design, they affirmed, 'to annihilate the class of curés'. The comte de la Galissonière, gravely presiding, declared that this matter was one for the order of clergy to discuss by itself when it verified electors' powers under its bishop as chairman. To this, one of the objectors replied 'in terms that a man in his position should never allow himself to use'; alleging 'cabal and intrigue' on the part of canons and casting doubts upon the bishop's impartiality.[47] According to de la Galissonière's smug account of the crisis, these troublemakers were 'confounded by the calm, reasonableness and honesty that I showed in my replies', and many of their colleagues disavowed their turbulent insistence, though 'generally speaking, most of the clergy of the second rank are gravely lacking in elementary decorum'.[48] This disregard of decorum persisted when the clergy met separately on 18 March. Various speakers insisted that the original objection must be debated, and, an inevitable deadlock being reached, the comte de la Galissonière was called upon to give his decision. It was in favour of canons and regulars,[49] but so far as effective voting strength was concerned, that made no difference. The system of the curés was already in operation. Canons and monks were given reasonable representation on a deputation to the nobility and on committees to check procurations and to draft a *cahier*,[50] but the important post of secretary of the assembly went to a parish priest, amid tumultuous acclamation from one side and strong protests from the other.[51]

For the next two days, the bishop was absent. Having a keen sense of realities and a hatred of disturbance, the 'clamour' and 'motions' of the 18th had induced a tactical indisposition.[52] Business proceeded in his absence under the presidency of d'Alichoux, grand archdeacon and canon of the cathedral. Canons Barat and Burgevin and the prior of Toussaint achieved barren honours by leading another deputation to the nobility, while the three tellers appointed for the forthcoming elections were all parish priests.[53] Mgr de Lorry rejoined his sorrowing clergy in time to see their *cahier* through its last stages.[54] In this document, the lower clergy's demands were embodied in inoffensive and general terms: diocesan synods were to be held annually, higher ecclesiastical offices were to be made open to all priests 'without distinction of birth', plurality and non-residence were to be suppressed, the endowments of livings were to be increased, and 'an exact and precise regulation' was to settle disputes between parishes and chapters which shared the same church.[55] This *cahier* was approved on the morning of the 23rd. That afternoon, the bishop's indisposition beset him once more and elections began in his absence. Chatizel was voted as first deputy to Versailles by a sound majority, though if it be true that there were 300 votes cast for the bishop, it would seem that if Mgr de Lorry had bestirred himself more, he might have influenced the obsequious and the wavering and made the contest a real one.[56] Rangeard was next elected, by an overwhelming majority which showed that his great reputation in the province could draw him support from all quarters. There was a holiday for the feast of the Annunciation, then Rabin curé of Notre-Dame of Cholet and Martinet, *prieur-curé* of Daon, were elected, with Jacquemart, curé of Brissarthe, and Boumard of Sainte-Croix as *suppléants*.[57] Victory did not disarm the controversialists. At this very moment Chatizel and Boumard were concocting open letters to canon de la Brosse, which were rushed through press to be available before the clergy returned home. Boumard was particularly rude to the *syndic*, challenging him to exchange signed lists of benefices and income so that all the world could judge which of them was paying his fair share of taxation—'I complained of your partiality, was I wrong?'[58]

Voting finished on the morning of the 27th, and the bishop, who bore no malice, returned that afternoon to preside over administrative arrangements resulting from his own defeat.[59] Even so, his troubles were not over. Immediately after this session of 27 March was concluded, the cathedral chapter met and decided to challenge the validity of the whole proceedings, and in alliance with the other chapters and monasteries a protest was drafted and formally signed before a notary of Angers three days later.[60] On general theoretical grounds, this protest argued that it was unjust for all clerical deputies to be drawn from the single class of curés; on legal grounds, the canons adduced old laws of the kingdom forbidding clerical combinations; finally, and under the circumstances, this was their most telling argument, they pointed out that the procedure of discussion and election had been irregular, witness the fact that no proper minutes were in existence.[61] This was true enough, to the great embarrassment of the bishop, who was responsible for forwarding a duly authenticated record of proceedings to Paris. M. Coulonnier, the aged and half-blind curé of May who had been swept into the office of secretary by the enthusiasm of his colleagues, had scribbled away in utter confusion, and, immediately deputies were named, had hurried off to his parish, leaving behind him an unsigned, and, indeed, indecipherable document.[62] On 2 April the clergy met again to attempt to elicit some sort of minutes from the memories and general will of the survivors. This session of recollection was interrupted by a procession of canons and Benedictines, accompanied by two notaries who made lengthy speeches of objection to the proposed compilation. In the ensuing hubbub, the bishop, after helpless calls for order, departed in despair, and the meeting broke up in confusion.[63] However, minutes still had to be produced, so Mgr de Lorry appealed to the comte de la Galissonière to convoke the clergy again for 6 April. The cathedral chapter decided to abstain from further attendance,[64] so that the order of clergy at last wound up its affairs in peace. Two days later, the deputies of all three orders took their oath in the cathedral. Rangeard came forward to compliment his bishop and d'Alichoux on their sage exercise of the presidential office.[65] The intendant at Tours reported these remarkable changes of fortune with dispassionate wonder—'the clergy of Anjou, a province which has . . . a famous university, innumerable ecclesiastical dignitaries, great religious houses and monastic orders of the utmost distinction, finds itself represented by town and country curés'.[66] 'The clergy behaved scandalously,' de la Galissonière informed Barentin, 'and this order by itself has given me more trouble than the other two together.'[67] Canon de la Brosse appealed to the agents-general of the clergy for justice, only to receive a peevish reply from their once all-powerful organization. 'No doubt you are aware that your chapters and your regulars are not the only ones who consider they have grounds for protest at this juncture. The abuses you complain of have been of universal occurrence.' [68] In fact, out of 296 deputies of the clerical order for the whole of France, 208 were curés.

CHAPTER XII

THE CLERGY AND THE DOMINANT BOURGEOISIE (MARCH 1789– SEPTEMBER 1790)

ONCE these elections were concluded and the deputies had departed, all eyes in Angers and in Anjou were turned towards Versailles and Paris. Provincial history and national history now meet and interweave. On 4 May, amid all the religious and secular pageantry with which men of the old régime honoured God and their King, the Estates-General was opened. Its deputies processed from Notre-Dame to the church of Saint-Louis for mass, a *Te Deum* and a sermon, bishops in glittering vestments walking apart from their clergy, contrastingly austere and humble in ordinary cassocks and acutely conscious of the slight upon their status. This division, said Rangeard, was 'doubtless necessary to the dignity of prelates, so that distant spectators would not confuse them with the lower clergy'.[1] But outward pomp bore no relation to political statistics: while there were only 42 bishops there were more than 200 parish priests. Chatizel curé of Soulaines, Rangeard archpriest of Andard, Martinet *prieur-curé* of Daon, Rabin curé of Notre-Dame of Cholet—they and their fellows could, if they wished, dictate the policy of the First Estate, and with it, the destiny of France. The Third Estate with its double representation was demanding verification of powers in common and was already speaking as if it was the nation. That was why Volney of Anjou insisted on publicity of debates, for, like the philosopher of old, he would have his house made of glass, open to popular scrutiny; that was why Milscent of Anjou attacked great nobles and higher ecclesiastics who separated King from people.[2] For six weeks the orders disputed, nobles opposing union, clergy divided and wavering. From the Third Estate came appeals, public and private, to parish priests, urging them to throw in their lot with their natural allies and their own social class. From Rangeard's account of proceedings in the clerical chamber there is no doubt that he was one of a pressure group of 60 to 80 clergy of the second order which at the end of May was holding evening meetings to concert details of a proposal to join the Third Estate,[3] while Rabin was one of the speakers put forward by this group on 28 May in a debate calculated to force a final decision.[4] Louis XVI then commanded conferences of the three estates to seek a conciliation, but by 6 June all hope of compromise had faded. 11 June was the feast of Corpus Christi (the day of the *Sacre* at Angers): Chatizel was one of twelve clerical deputies who were selected to attend the King at Notre-Dame when he went to do reverence to the Holy Sacrament.[5] It was a day when a priest must think seriously of his duties towards social concord—and on the morrow the Third Estate proposed to issue its final ultimatum to the clerical order. The commons of the deputation of Anjou sent Milscent, La Revellière-Lépeaux and Brevet de Beaujour to invite their own Angevin curés to join the national cause. Rangeard, Rabin and Chatizel 'gave reason to hope that they would perform this act of patriotism'.[6] Rabin came over first, the other two followed him, and all three were present in the church of Saint-Louis on 22 June when the archbishops of Vienne and Bordeaux brought 150 clerical deputies to join the Third Estate.[7] On the following day came the *séance royale*, when Louis XVI made a last fumbling bid to prevent the divided Estates from becoming a single Parlement of the nation and when Mirabeau replied with his defiant 'bayonet speech'. More clergy came over, and on 25 June nearly fifty nobles joined the commons. Curé Martinet remained deaf to liberal clamour, and was still on the side of reaction when, on 27 June, the King himself admitted defeat and commanded the orders to unite.[8] An English visitor who normally had more foresight now packed his bags and left the capital to see more interesting events in the provinces—'the whole business is now over, and the revolution complete'. Eighteen days after his departure, Paris, stirred by Necker's dismissal and news of troop concentrations, rose and consummated the revolution, or, rather, brought it to an end of the beginning. The fall of the Bastille ensured Necker's recall, defeated King and Court, ended all threat of a military reaction, created a National Guard, swept the bourgeoisie into power in the provincial towns of France, and reduced the nobility 'to a level with the rest of the nation'.[9] Curé Martinet interpreted these signs of the times and on 18 July appealed to be allowed to attend meetings of his fellow Angevin deputies. His conversion was accepted and a magnanimous report was sent back to Angers explaining that 'he had only erred in his choice of means, but as soon as he realized that the union of all classes was necessary to achieve a new order of things, he came over to this way of thinking with all imaginable enthusiasm'.[10] Meanwhile, on 16 July Volney and La Revellière-Lépeaux had informed the Assembly that Angers was governed by a mayor and aldermen who were unrepresentative officials, possessing only a 'venal and arbitrary title'.[11] Even as they spoke, news of the fall of the Bastille was racing westwards. On the following day, the oligarchy which they had denounced was overthrown.

17 July was a Friday. In Angers that day, canon de la Brosse and one of his colleagues at the cathedral, canon Chivaille of Saint-Pierre the bishop's secretary, Perrochel ex-soldier and abbot of Toussaint, and the ubiquitous curé Robin were coffee-housing in Mame's bookshop, awaiting the day's despatch from Paris, that sure catalyst of political discussion. But as soon as the courier arrived, there was a surge into the room, the secret was out, and a panic-stricken crowd rushed off to the town hall.[12] Immediately, a militia was organized. Lawyers, magistrates, professors and substantial citizens generally armed themselves and patrolled the streets. Enthusiastic youths marched off to the *châteaux* of the comte de Serrant and the duc de Brissac, and finding it difficult to decide what to do when they got there, appropriated a few superannuated artillery pieces and hauled them back to defend the city. Within two days, the Angevin National Guard was over a thousand strong.[13] Angers had been saved from nameless horrors. The marquis de Lostanges, an officer of its military garrison, believed that prompt action by the bourgeoisie had prevented a rising of the lower orders, more especially of workers in the neighbouring slate quarries, who would have pillaged indiscriminately under cover of red, white and blue cockades.[14] Abbé Houdet, vicaire at La Trinité, an enthusiast for liberty, knew better. Angers, like Paris, had sprung to arms to defend itself against despotism. In the capital, thousands of German soldiers in civilian dress had been lurking, awaiting a signal from the 'diabolic committee' of the Queen to massacre the inhabitants. Only the alertness of the duc de Liancourt and the King's good heart had saved the people. But 'the dreadful project of the court is unmasked, the mystery of iniquity is revealed and confounded . . . now we have everything to hope from the Estates-General'.[15]

Further news from Paris was reassuring. On 29 July the clerical deputies of Anjou wrote to their constituents, informing them that perfect peace and security were now restored, that the union of the orders on 27 June had ended divisions, and that Necker had returned and visited the Assembly 'to mix his tears with our applause'.[16] In Angers itself, the bourgeoisie, through the National Guard, remained in control, a 'permanent committee of the Angevin militia', which was set up on 2 August, taking over all effective power from the discredited municipality.[17] Universal fraternity now reigned. A reconciliation was effected within the clergy. The Diocesan Bureau had refused to pay expenses to its four curés at Versailles, alleging that they were not fairly representative of all classes of taxpayers and instancing the renunciation of clerical privileges, which absolved dioceses from fulfilling obligations which should now fall upon the nation. On 28 July, however, it was decided that, 'although all these reasons are still valid, the new order of things, the long-drawn-out meeting of the Estates-General, and above all the wise and genuinely patriotic conduct of the deputies ought to make us overlook the form of their election'.[18] For the moment, there were few external signs of hostility among the three orders. The nobles were not content and looked askance at the rule of a permanent committee 'more despotic than Louis XIV would have been',[19] but they declared their allegiance to the National Assembly, and their wives joined ladies of the middle class in embroidering a banner for their new defenders.[20] Relations between the clergy and the dominant bourgeoisie were more obviously and more genuinely friendly. Priors of various religious houses, de la Brosse, *syndic* of the diocese, and other ecclesiastics, including even our fire-eating authoritarian canon Mongodin, had declared their adherence to the National Guard, and Perrochel, abbot of Toussaint, thanks to his previous military experience and to his present reforming enthusiasm, was one of the sixteen members of its permanent committee.[21] This body of new unofficial administrators was welcomed by the Oratorians at their prize-giving day as if it had been in name, as well as in fact, the municipality.[22] Bishop de Lorry, a master of well-timed platitudes, judiciously celebrated 'the august assembly of the nation' in a pastoral letter, and praised the generous sacrifice of privileges made by its deputies in August.[23] When the province defied the Constituent Assembly's decision to prolong the *gabelle* for a year, ecclesiastics demonstrated their solidarity with lay society. It was Duboys, a country curé, who appeared before the permanent committee on 17 September with a letter from his parish which became the manifesto of revolt.[24] Representatives of chapters, Benedictines and parish priests were present at a town meeting on 1st October, and abbot Perrochel was chosen as one of the deputies of Angers to attend a provincial meeting five days later—a meeting which formulated a final protest which was taken up to Paris by de Houlières, head of the permanent committee, and the elder Delaunay.[25] It is true that there was momentary dissatisfaction with the attitude of clerical deputies to the National Assembly. One or two of them had apparently returned to Anjou, and as a result they were regarded as 'deserters',[26] absent from their posts at a time when the province needed every voice and every vote. However, local pressure soon drove them back to the capital, and by 4 November de Houlières and Delaunay were praising their loyalty.[27]

This halcyon year of social concord was a hard year materially. A bitter winter had ruined most nut-trees and blasted half of the vines;[28] common folk had nothing better than cider to drink, and the permanent committee of the militia of Angers had to import rice to supplement declining stocks of grain within the city. As always in hard times, ecclesiastics led the way in generosity. An official *caisse de subsistance* raised rather more than 20,000*l.*, of which churchmen contributed almost half. The bishop, who was pouring out alms on his country estates,[29] gave 1,900*l.* to the town, the cathedral gave 1,200*l.* with a further 221*l.* from three canons individually, other chapters gave 900*l.*, the Benedictine houses 2,400*l.*, the unendowed Frères des Écoles Chrétiennes 1,500*l.*[30] No doubt most of these corporations could well afford it, but their figures contrast favourably with the community of notaries 150*l.* and 600*l.* from the Royal-Picardy regiment. The surplus in the coffers of the clergy of Anjou which Chatizel had complained of was put to good use, 40,000*l.* being lent to the town to purchase grain. As it was not possible to call an assembly to vote this loan, curé Roussel of Saint-Maurille and Gaudin of Saint-Nicolas discussed it with their colleagues in town and wrote round to curés of the countryside to obtain their agreement.[31] In November, the cathedral chapter made haste to obey instructions and send in all plate not needed to celebrate divine service—'to aid the State in its necessity'.[32] The state had just taken steps to aid itself by putting all ecclesiastical property 'at the disposal of the nation'.

Meanwhile, reformers in Angers wished to give a formal constitution to charitable organizations as well as to the nation. Elsewhere in France, and more particularly at Le Mans, *bureaux de charité* had been set up to centralize good works and knit together the patch-work pattern of ecclesiastical benevolence. It fell to the bishop to give a lead, and a town assembly which was convoked at his suggestion appointed a committee of eight, including the curés of La Trinité and Saint-Michel du Tertre, to investigate how the system worked at Le Mans. Their report suggested a council of 33 ecclesiastics and 44 laymen, with an inner directing body consisting of one deputy from the cathedral, one from other chapters, two monks, three curés, eight nobles and fourteen commoners, presided over by the bishop.[33] It was a step towards laicizing charity, but a very moderate one, which gave full recognition to ecclesiastical interests. More radical suggestions were abroad, which would have excluded monks and canons, but even so, the bishop was still to preside, and curés were to supervise the distribution of alms.[34] While these administrative principles of almsgiving were being discussed, the parish priests of Angers demanded an urgent and specific reform. Their complaint before a municipal assembly[35] compelled an investigation of administrative efficiency at the hospital of the Incurables, where poor patients were no longer received free of charge. A strong committee dealt with this scandal, and its work was, perhaps, the only activity in which canon de la Brosse, leader of the higher clergy, and Delaunay, presiding genius of the urban bourgeoisie, ever co-operated.[36]

The new order in France and the grip of the middle-classes on local administration were consolidated in the first half of 1790. On 13 January, royal letters patent authorizing a creation of new municipalities in accordance with the law of December 1789 were received at Angers. De Houlières, head of the militia's permanent committee, was elected mayor, the younger Delaunay became *procureur* of the Commune, merchants, lawyers, *avocats*, doctors and notaries were instituted as municipal officers and notables. The clergy had no power in this renovated administration. Curés no longer took their places as of right in parish assemblies and out of thirty notables there was only one ecclesiastic, Bougier, curé of Saint-Michel du Tertre.[37] In May, electors of the second degree met in the abbey of Saint-Aubin to make a final choice of administrators for the new department of Maine-et-Loire. The militia received its official title of National Guard by decree of the National Assembly, and re-dedicated its banners on 1 July. All this while, as if to counter-balance an over-logical and unsentimental reorganization of the country, a federative movement was gaining impetus, with Anjou and Brittany giving a lead to the rest of France. Angevin youths, who a year ago had sworn to march to Rennes, now resorted to Pontivy to renew their pact of association with their Breton contemporaries under more peaceful circumstances.[38] On 1 February, their fathers foregathered at Pontivy also, where Delaunay the elder proclaimed an end of provincial distinctions before going on to Paris leading a deputation to teach the Jacobins that a 'general federation is the sole method of consolidating the Revolution'.[39] His wishes were fulfilled by the great festival of 14 July. Each parish sent a representative, and enthusiastic citizens of Angers hired carriages at their own expense to go up to the capital[40] to see Delaunay receive a flag from the hands of the King. When, on the evening of 29 July,[41] the returning representatives were feted, and the streets of Angers resounded with dancing, banqueting, toasts and cannon shots, it must have seemed that the Revolution was indeed assured.

Individual ecclesiastics were outright enthusiasts for the new order. Abbot Perrochel now found his own country sufficiently interesting to give up continental wanderings; he advised his militia friends on military discipline, and he it was who was chosen by the deputies of Anjou to present the town with an official copy of a map of the new department of Maine-et-Loire.[42] Vicaire Houdet was delighted when he saw municipal officers and departmental administrators being elected: 'the new order of things which is being organized is going to bring into evidence the quantity and quality of each individual citizen's abilities'—perhaps even his own. Above all, he approved of the federative movement, which would teach a lesson to 'introverted patriots, for whom the fatherland extends no further than their own backyard'—'you double and triple your own being by allying with you fellow-citizens'.[43] Schoolmasters of the Oratory were in the vanguard of constitutional enthusiasm. Père Roy, their superior, presented his colleagues and a deputation of their pupils to the electors of the Department on 13 May, and claimed that his order, with its voluntary discipline, had been a precursor of ideals of freedom. 'For two centuries . . . we have been children of the new constitution.' [44]

Others were more reserved in their attitude, but the clergy as a whole, throughout this first half of 1790, showed a formal approval and lent a modest co-operation to the advent of liberty. On 21 February, after taking the civic oath, the new municipality, accompanied by its militia, proceeded to the cathedral, where the bishop celebrated a mass of the Holy Spirit and a *Te Deum* was sung.[45] Five days later, canon Burgevin of Saint-Pierre and the comte d'Autichamp appeared to congratulate these new officers on behalf of the permanent committee of the Provincial Assembly of Anjou,[46] which, in defiance of all laws of political therapeutics, still lingered on. Canon Burgevin's role in this ghostly embassy from the past symbolized the attitude of the higher clergy of Angers. They proposed to co-operate with the régime in power. 'Moses was the legislator of the Hebrews, Aaron was their pontiff: they were brothers, their union will serve us as an example', said the bishop, when, accompanied by the dean of the cathedral, he visited the electors of the Department to renew his oath to 'the Nation, the Law and the King'.[47] The militia paraded at Saint-Maurice on 14 June to have its standards blessed, and again on 1 July to have them re-dedicated; the bishop officiated on the first occasion and gave a sermon marked by 'the purest patriotism and the greatest solicitude for his flock', while dean de Villeneuve deputized at the second service and made a gracious reply to a speech by that most fervent of local anticlericals, Choudieu.[48] Church and state remained in close alliance. Those who ruled in the name of the Nation and the Law, as well as of the King, inherited ecclesiastical ceremonies which had consecrated those who had administered in the name of the King alone. More than that, the Angevin clergy's patriotism was celebrated all over France, thanks to Mgr de Lorry's skill at striking off a phrase in tune with the epoch. His pastoral letter of 30 May welcoming the new departmental administration was read at the tribune of the National Assembly by La Revellière-Lépeaux, and was officially printed and distributed.[49] 'Teach your children to lisp the words *God, brother* and *country*. Teach them to pronounce the oath to be faithful to the Nation, to the Law, to the King, an oath which has become the rallying cry of every French citizen.' To his clergy, the bishop insisted that there was no conflict between the Church and the new order.

Successors of the apostles and disciples of Christ, let us show forth in our conduct the simplicity of their lives, the saintliness of their characters, the kindliness of their devotion and the constancy of their charity. These religious and good-hearted people of ours are not divorced from us. They will always come back to us, to seek in the bosom of the Church the only true consolations.

'We are waiting to see M. de Lorry applying these weighty and worthy lessons to himself as well as to his co-operators', said a cynical commentator who, however, went on to praise the bishop's frank acceptance of the political situation.[50] Indeed, when this pastoral letter was written, Church property was 'at the disposal of the nation', the municipality of Angers had offered to buy ten millions worth, and its commissioners had inventoried monastic houses. In Paris, the Civil Constitution of the Clergy, which was finally adopted on 12 July, was already half voted. Which suggests to us that whatever churchmen thought of the sale of ecclesiastical property, of the attack on monasticism, or of the reorganization of their functions, we must look elsewhere for the essential cause of their approaching clash with the Revolution.

The new patriotism, to be sure, regarded religion as an adjunct, even though a necessary one, of its ceremonies. When deputies of the Federation were welcomed back from Paris, Angers erected its own altar on a 'Champ de Mars' and deserted the cathedral. Canon Louet led an embassy from the chapter of Saint-Maurice to protest against this innovation. Their days were numbered, but so long as they remained in office, the canons had no intention of countenancing a *Te Deum* on a 'Champ de Mars—alias the fair ground', and indeed, the three who were present mingled with the crowd as mere private individuals, inglorious in everyday cloaks and cassocks.[51] Such ecclesiastical welcome as the deputies of the Federation received was led by 'Mr le Grand Curé de Saint-Maurice', supported by a host of parochial clergy.[52] At first, bishop de Lorry also raised difficulties about open-air religion, but he soon yielded, and presided over a *Te Deum*. 'My children, let us love God and let us all be brethren,' was his brief but expressive sermon, which was cheered to the echo.[53] However, though the canons of Saint-Maurice refused to follow their bishop into a liturgical compromise, we should not interpret their abstention as a calculated manifestation of hostility to the Federation in general principle. Up to now they had been taking great care not to do anything which might be interpreted as reactionary. It is true that at the end of May, Etienne Bardou,[54] a discontented Gascon tenor of their choir, had accused his employers of anti-democratic prejudices, but his fellow-choirmen hotly disowned his libellous invention. 'Far from our chapter having been against us when we showed ourselves full of zeal for the reform of abuses,' they said, 'on the contrary, it ruled that we should be marked as present at divine office every time we were absent on business to do with the new Constitution.'[55] It would seem that this dispute of July concerning prayers on a fairground, was, for our canons, not an affair of politics, but simply a question of precedence and decency. Intransigence over ceremonial formalities was, after all, an occupational disease of canons of the old régime.

A 'Champ de Mars' in place of a cathedral—at least some of those who planned this new departure meant it to have symbolic significance. On his return from the Federation at Paris Delaunay made no secret of his belief that religious ceremonies should play an inferior role to national ones. Renewed every twenty-five years, the federative pact ought to replace the 'ridiculous usages' and 'Gothic formulae' of the coronation, and the clergy be deprived for ever of 'the right they have usurped of receiving the oaths of him whom the nation crowns'.[56] Anti-clericalism was a rising force, and it took the form, not of excluding the Church, but of subordinating it. That this subordination could be genuinely accepted by churchmen, more particularly by higher ecclesiastics, was something that anti-clericals found difficult to believe. There was a growing distrust of the clergy, and sinister literature was beginning to circulate. Marie-Joseph Chénier's *Charles IX*, fresh from triumphs on the Parisian stage, was much talked of, and in February 1790 copies were on sale at Pavie's the printer in the rue Saint-Laud. Those who rejoiced to reflect upon a cardinal blessing daggers on St. Bartholomew's eve no doubt subscribed also to the new *Observateur Provincial*, a dull left-wing broadsheet, which made occasional gibes at clerical wealth and influence, and which in the summer of 1790 was campaigning for legalized divorce to complete the liberties of patriots.[57] This propaganda was having its effect. Although he was a recognized enthusiast for the Revolution, the abbé Houdet decided to stay away from the primary elections for the departmental administration—'I didn't go to those of our district. Our habit is an obstacle in the eyes of some people; I thought it prudent to abstain from appearing.'[58]

Even so, when in the middle of 1790, one of the *Amis de la Constitution* of Angers published a list of classes who were supposed to be plotting against the Constitution, he said nothing of clerics, neither good nor ill.[59] Presumably they were still regarded as neutral and pliable. It was not until the beginning of September, when Angers had its first real taste of rioting, that accusations of counter-revolutionary activity were levelled against churchmen. These riots were the work of the 'Fourth Estate', of that class which André Chénier had just disdainfully described as one which 'understands nothing, takes interest in nothing and which knows only how to sell itself to those willing to buy it'.[60] On 4 September a shortage of grain led to tumults, and on the next day, the *perreyeurs*, barbarous workers in the slate quarries, invaded town and were repulsed only after sixty or so of their number had been slain. On the evening of the 7th, two captured rebels were hanged on the 'Champ de Mars.' With a few conspicuous exceptions,[61] members of the National Guard had not won much distinction for valour in this fighting—unlike curé Robin, who at Empiré quelled a riot of women armed with cudgels by the sheer majesty of his disapproval.[62] Worse than that, the bourgeoisie had fired on the people. This especially needed explanation. An obvious one was given. It had been an 'aristocratic rising', 'une dernière convulsion aristocratique', a plot on the part of dissatisfied nobles who had stirred up the proletariat.[63] This was not impossible, but self-exculpatory rumour went further and accused the clergy. They had ordered church bells to sound a tocsin; dean de Villeneuve's savings had paid the rioters.[64] Here was an absurd story, but the curé of La Trinité was terrified when he heard it was in circulation, and a vicaire of Saint-Michel du Tertre who absolved one of the executed rebels took care to obtain a statement that no one had incited them.[65] Department and municipality remained in a state of panic. An imbecile girl with sulphur in her pocket was arrested. A man in a blue coat with incendiary bombs in his was sought everywhere. The Minister of War was asked to provide ferocious armaments.[66] This was in early October, and two months later, as everyone knew, the sale of ecclesiastical property was to begin. That was why it was so easy to suspect the clergy of disloyalty to the new order. The Angevin bourgeoisie judged everyone by its own standards.

CHAPTER XIII

THE END OF CHURCH PROPERTY
(1789–DECEMBER 1790)

'I SINNED through ambition', Volney confessed, early in 1789. He was not referring to his yearning for political prominence, an ambition which ultimately enabled this tribune of the people to find repose as a count of the Empire: he was accusing himself of no greater crime than an altruistic zeal for the development of his own city of Angers. 'I wanted to see . . . this town of Angers become a superb city, with numerous factories, brisk manufactures, to see an Exchange, a public library, a fine building for the Provincial Estates, a fine courthouse, a fine theatre, a vast botanical garden, a high school for all the sciences . . .'[1] Here was an appeal to a basic passion of lay society. New squares, roads, quays and footpaths, gardens, a foundling hosptial, a boarding-school, a barracks—these had been subjects of the ambitions of the old municipality. A new era could realize them. Church property would provide sites, indeed, might bear the whole cost of new establishments. Royal policy, mean shifts of a count apanagist, ecclesiastical leasehold, law-suits over feudal incidents, cemetery discussions, the designs of the bishop of Séez, the Academy essay topic two years ago—everything had conspired to bring ecclesiastical possessions to envious notice. By mid-February, the decision of the Council of War confiscating the house of the Minims for a barracks was known.[2] A first step had been taken.

As we have seen, the comte de Serrant was suggesting an alliance of the two lay orders to plunder the Church, proclaiming the nation's right to re-enter upon its heritage; rather later, the marquis de Beauvau was even proposing to reclaim his heritage as a private individual. Needless to say, the clerical order was anxious to deny that its property was held on different terms to that of laymen.[3] The chapters of Saint-Martin and Saint-Laud went further and asked for the withdrawal of the *droit d'amortissement*, declaring that 'citizens who are already deprived of their common-law liberty of making new acquisitions ought at least to be free to make good use of what they possess already'.[4] Yet all the while, propaganda by curés against rich ecclesiastical corporations was providing arguments for envious laymen, who were willing to translate suggestions of redistribution of income into extremely secular terms. Rangeard revealed the medieval usurpations of monks and canons, who had successfully imposed upon a superstitious age by threats of excommunication and interdict.[5] Chatizel pointed a contrast between the dedicated life and the possession of broad acres.

To strangers [he wrote] the town of Angers presents an astonishing spectacle. Four palaces worthy of the pomp of kings serve as refuges from the world for the disciples of the famous hermit of mount Caffin and his sister St. Scholastica. Five huge abbeys, a royal priory and eight chapters occupy half of the vast area within its walls. Their immense possessions cover practically the whole province of Anjou. A well-informed observer has said that you can scarcely travel a league without setting foot on their domains. Rivals of the sovereign power itself, they all enjoy dues, jurisdictions, fiefs, vassals, coats of arms and guards, cures where they don't reside and tithes which they do not earn.[6]

That this wealth should be used to ameliorate the lot of curés and vicaires—Chatizel's point—was taken up by the commons of Anjou in their *cahier*, but with a difference. Property belonging to abbeys, chapters (except cathedrals) and benefices without cure of souls (except those in lay patronage) was to be sold, and if the parochial clergy were to receive a living wage from the proceeds, this was incidental to the main object, that is, paying off the national debt.[7] To do so, said the Law Faculty, would simply be an 'act of justice and of reason'. The Faculty of Medicine considered that this end would be served by confiscating the temporal of bishoprics and abbeys for twenty years, 'as old domains of the nation now reclaimed to restore its finances'.[8] From the assembly of non-incorporated inhabitants came a more radical suggestion—to abolish tithe also and leave payment of clerical salaries to the Provincial Estates.[9] Less sophisticated folk argued from municipal, rather than national, needs. Pension friars, and use their convents for 'advantageous public establishments', annex a Benedictine monastery as a site for a foundling hospital, suppress several of the collegiate churches and convents 'whose gardens and buildings occupy an immense area in town', or, more sweepingly, 'suppress the host of chapters, convents and priories whose vast houses and enclosures crowd the whole city to no useful purpose'.[10] Commendatory abbots spending their money outside the province were unfavourably noticed by the button-makers and the parish of Saint-Samson.[11] More deeply versed in economics, the drapers had clearly read the Academy prize essay of 1787—'the infinite number of benefices without cure of souls, canonries, prebends, etc., which abound in the town of Angers, offer to its youth hopes of an easy and comfortable existence, and distract them from useful work in favour of vain studies, and, to the detriment of the state and of morals, multiply the number of the idle and the unmarried'.[12] The inhabitants of Angers, as their *cahiers* reveal them, were not anti-clerical. Few were as crudely philistine as the drapers with their disapproval of scholarship, few were as parsimonious as the wigmakers who would cut bishops down to 12,000*l.* a year, and probably few were as severely calculating as the cutlers and cabinet-makers, who estimated that nobles and clergy between them owned two-thirds of France.[13] Nevertheless, there was clearly substantial agreement among the laity on one point: measures must be taken to deal with the vast extent of ecclesiastical property in Angers.

All over France, *cahiers* were showing similar preoccupations.[14] Once the Estates-General met, a confiscation of church property, at least in part, was inevitable. Churchmen assumed that theirs was an exclusive national Church entitled to a monopoly of education and civic recognition. This assumption now turned against them, for it might imply, as Talleyrand argued, that *ecclesia* and assembled people were identical—and now the people really was assembled and its demands were heard. In France the state had always exercised a right of uniting or suppressing benefices and religious communites, and could forbid ecclesiastical corporations either to acquire or to alienate property. The comte de Serrant, whose ideas were otherwise so chimerical, had used language both of popular sentiment and of legal exactitude[15] when he declared that the clergy merely held its lands in *usufruct*. This thesis was upheld in the National Assembly as early as August 1789 by some of those who successfully opposed an offer of compensation for the loss of tithes, abandoned in altruistic delirium on the night of 4 August. Tithe went, and Rangeard shed no tears over his sheaves and wine barrels at Andard. 'The clergy', he reflected, 'is infinitely richer in lands than has been admitted. It will be easy to make generous provision for parish priests.' [16] Easy perhaps, but would it be done?—already some curés were losing their revolutionary enthusiasm.[17] At the end of September, a decree invited the clergy to hand in church silver, a measure which, under the old monarchy, had proclaimed a last degree of national emergency.[18] Faced by utter bankruptcy, the assembled nation would have courage to pursue this precedent further. Even before the union of the orders, a deputy of the commons had darkly hinted that an auction of property whose revenues merely supported a luxurious higher clergy would be a more logical measure than a voluntary melting down of sacred vases.[19] On the evening of 28 September, Volney pressed the Assembly to adopt the propositions of the *cahier* of his Angevin constituents. Certain monks had offered to surrender their property, and there was some dispute as to how heartily they ought to be thanked—in fact, was it really theirs to surrender in the first place? Volney asked that the 'veil of mystery' be forthwith lifted from this question and a definite decision made concerning the ultimate ownership of ecclesiastical temporalities.[20] Within a few days, Volney's proposal was taken up in fuller detail by a more authoritative voice, so that our deputy from Anjou was left to play a minor, though still uncompromising role.[21] On 10 October, four days after Louis XVI had been compelled by the Parisian mob to take up residence in his capital, a direct scheme for 'an operation on ecclesiastical property' was put forward by an opportunist who had well read the signs of the times—Talleyrand, bishop of Autun. A vast loan secured on church lands, or a re-allocation of surplus income might have met the financial crisis, but the Constituent Assembly was not prepared to adopt half-measures which would imply that the clergy still remained a separate order.[22] By a decree of 2 November, the state undertook to care for the poor and pay the clergy, leaving ecclesiastical property 'at the disposal of the nation'. Here, thought curés, was a poor reward for loyalty to the popular cause—no more, perhaps, than Martinet had expected, but this time Chatizel was with him in opposition to the majority of the Assembly.[23] Disillusionment had begun. In December, an actual sale of 400 millions worth of *biens nationaux* was decided. There is no doubt that a primary object was to take money where it could most easily be found: even so, an idea was soon abroad that the *assignat* would 'cement' the new constitution, giving all citizens an equal interest in defending it.[24]

From the municipality of Paris came an initiative which made this vast transaction both possible and certain of success. It was proposed that municipalities of the kingdom should act as intermediaries in the alienation; once it had agreed to this on 17 March, the Assembly could go forward to decisive action without fear of a fiasco. At Angers, this news produced an immediate reaction, for the new town government had inherited all the improving zeal and territorial ambitions of the old oligarchy. At the end of March, the municipal council decided to follow the Parisian example, though petitioning the Assembly to allow twenty years' grace for completion of payments. Of 400 millions worth of property up for sale, Angers would take over 10 millions worth, which 'we will use . . . to establish divers institutions of public utility for the town and for the department which had been solicited in vain from the old established order'.[25] Circulars were despatched to other principal municipalities exhorting them to do their share,[26] and on 6 May it was announced that prospective buyers should hand in their names at the town hall.[27] Volney, no doubt with justice, claimed some credit among his colleagues in the National Assembly[28] for this zeal of his constituents, and Delaunay the elder, leading a deputation of his Breton-Angevin federation, made haste to boast of his city's patriotism before the Jacobins at Paris. 'We should count ourselves happy, *messieurs*,' he declared, 'if by great sacrifices, we are able to save the state, and with it the liberty which your courage and genius have won for us.' [29]

For the next seven months the District authorities of Angers collected rents from ecclesiastical properties,[30] and as they had had sufficient foresight to appoint Feuillatreau[31] of the cathedral and diocesan registry as their clerk, things went smoothly. Even so, there was some evidence of that popular dishonesty and bureaucratic muddle which might be expected to accompany a great spoliation. Thieves looted the sacristy of Saint-Pierre and carted off organ-pipes from the Augustins' chapel, trees were sawn down on the estates of Saint-Aubin, and cattle grazed there freely until soldiers of the Royal Picardy regiment marched out from Angers to impound them.[32] Department and District fell out, each claiming a right to publish lists of property for sale;[33] the municipality rendered its returns to the National Assembly in an incorrect form;[34] the Department was dilatory in its decision concerning which monastic houses were to be conserved, and this angered some potential buyers, more particularly two citizens who wished to set up a spinning factory.[35] Meanwhile, the more prosperous inhabitants of Angers had time to reflect on their opportunities for investment in real property: as Delaunay had said, they would spare no sacrifice to save the state.

The nation was to pay its clergy, but not all who had waxed fat on income from possessions which were now being confiscated would be allowed to come under that rubric. When the Estates-General met, one thing was even more certain than an 'operation on ecclesiastical property', that was a suppression, wholesale or selective, of monastic houses. Louis XV's government had ended the Jesuits and instituted inquisitions and confiscations in monasteries generally, a practical illustration and precedent for the demands of the *cahiers* and for the Constituents' theory that 'all corporations being created by society, society can destroy them if they are useless or harmful'. At the end of October 1789, the taking of vows was provisionally suspended, and shortly afterwards the doors of monasteries were opened to those inmates who preferred their freedom. After bitter discussions,[36] a final decree was passed on 13 February 1790. Educational and charitable establishments were to remain 'for the present', but all others would be dispersed. Monks who chose to leave would be pensioned, those who chose to stay would be grouped together in certain houses which would be specified later.[37]

In Angers, at the end of April, commissioners from the municipality (or, in the case of the Visitation and Saint-Serge, outside the city boundary, from the new municipalities of Saint-Laud and Saint-

Samson) presented themselves at monastic houses to make inventories and receive declarations from their inmates. Practically without exception, communities of women were agreed on wishing to stay, to 'live and die in their house'.[38] Everywhere in France, nuns were showing a similar fidelity to their vocation—in great contrast to monks. There was, it is true, a very great difference in the fashion in which male and female religious were treated. The former were to be grouped on principles of rough justice into selected houses, the latter were to be allowed to stay in their own house and in their own order.[39] It was harder, too, for women to leave the shelter of their convent and start life again. Families which had subscribed to endow their establishment in the cloisters would not necessarily welcome the return of maiden aunts and elder sisters. Nor were the National Assembly's intentions concerning communities of women very clear. Most had some sort of claim to be doing educational or charitable work, and in March each house had sent to the Ecclesiastical Committee of the Assembly a statement of its aims and social functions.[40] Sixty gratuitous educational places, 'with free bread for lunch', had figured prominently on the Ursulines' return, while the nuns of La Fidelité had positively distorted truth in referring to their large number of boarders. So, for some at least, there was still hope of preserving independence and possessions. Yet, when all is said, the fidelity of women was both remarkable and genuine. Even girls who were unprofessed regarded leaving their convents as a tragedy. Thérèse Sophie d'Arandel, twelfth child of a noble family of the diocese of Rouen, begged to be allowed to stay at Ronceray—'Her situation was such that she could anticipate nothing but unhappiness in the future if she did not continue to be aided by the charity of Mme l'abbesse.' [41] Tearful scenes took place at the Ursulines and the Visitandines when monastic vows were suspended and novices had to be sent home. Mlle du Tertre wept when her father arrived to take her away, and at the Ursulines, when Mlle de Brassé left, no one could pluck up resolution to remove her veil or unbar the door. 'I armed myself with faith and courage and did both', said Jeanne-Jacquine Moutardeau, severely practical.[42]

Very different reactions were seen in communities of men when the civic authorities made their visitations. Saint-Aubin, as we shall see, was a special case; the monks of Saint-Nicolas reserved their opinion; five monks of Saint-Serge ultimately asked for freedom;[43] the four inmates of Lesvière were fairly firm in April, but by 27 July dom Julliot offered to obey the National Assembly as he had always obeyed his superiors and asked for a pension, 'seeing that with such small numbers community life is impossible'.[44] The canons-regular of Toussaint[45] seem to have been particularly lukewarm in their vocation.

R

Prior Tonnelet had five with him in wishing to maintain their vows, though one insisted that he move to a house nearer to his own family, taking his furniture with him, while the remaining four made an essential point of their right to remain in their own congregation. Five others, whose ages ranged from 30 to 23, chose freedom. One of these said that he would rather stay but that 'imperious circumstances' drove him out; two others said that they had joined to be 'useful to the public' but that as they could no longer fulfil this aim within a monastery they would go, another bluntly declared that he had become a canon-regular 'in the hope of enjoying the prerogatives which are attached to that state, and being uncertain whether or not the said prerogatives will be taken from him, his intention is to take advantage of the offer of a pension'.

Of the mendicant orders only the Carmelites were unanimous in wishing to remain under their vows—even so, on 23 August, when another visitation was made by the District authorities, two chose independence.[46] Three out of nine Capuchins wanted to be out, and of the majority, only one, a poor crack-brained friar confined in the house by royal order to keep him out of mischief, was unequivocally desirous to stay.[47] The Augustins reserved their opinion. Two out of the four Recollets of La Baumette and four out of seven Dominicans (led by their superior) chose the liberty that the decrees afforded.[48] Of the Cordeliers,[49] three were willing to stay in any house of their order, three, including Loyau, the superior, were willing to stay, but only in their house at Angers, and only one, Favereau (and he was partly paralysed and died soon), was willing to stay unconditionally. The other five chose freedom, together with a lay brother who added 'as soon as possible' to his request. These decisions were still not final. Notwithstanding his declaration Loyau moved out to lodgings in town and it was rumoured that Favereau had changed his mind before his death on 18 June. The District authorities chose to believe this and sent down to the monastery to take over his personal effects on behalf of his relatives; the friars, who had proposed to divide them among themselves, 'gave vent to the most scandalous invectives and curses', so that Viger and Delaunay sent for troops of the Royal Picardy regiment to keep order while they put locks on the cell door and a seal 'of red wax representing in the manner of antiquity the head of Socrates'.[50] According to a malicious statement of Viger to the Department on 22 July, the desire of Cordeliers in particular and of monks in general to flee their cloister was now almost universal— 'I have the honour to observe to you that since the time of the first declarations made by the monks most of those who stated their intention of remaining in their house have changed their mind and are asking for the pension and liberty to quit'.[51]

This conduct of monks and friars was unheroic, but not unnatural in the circumstances. Monastic life in France seemed doomed to extinction and one might guess that a bleak future in declining institutions was all that could be expected by those who attempted to maintain their vocation. Fourteen years later Marchant, who had been a sub-deacon at Saint-Aubin, declared that he had anticipated how events would turn out and 'being still young . . . I believed it prudent not to take any further engagements within a corporation whose members, it was easy to foresee, would be a target for all the disorders of the Revolution'.[52] And for those who looked ahead more complacently, secularization was to be sweetened by not ungenerous pensions—700 to 1,000l. for a friar and 900 to 1,200l. for monks;[53] it was tempting to close with the offer while it was still open. Furthermore, monks and friars had grown accustomed to their own little community, its gossip and its devotions and the pleasant buildings and gardens which were its home. That was why the faithful section of the canons-regular of Toussaint appealed to be allowed to stay in their abbey, shorn of their property and living only on their pensions. When this request met with no favour, within three days three of the petitioners applied to benefit by the decrees and to be given a first quarter of their pension for use as private individuals.[54] Three Cordeliers wished to remain friars—but only if they could stay within their monastery at Angers. So, too, did all nine Carmelites, and one of them 'reserved the right to leave when it might seem good to him' and another expressly said that he would only stay 'so long as the house remained composed of persons who suited him'.[55] Similarly in August the two faithful Recollets qualified their constancy by the proviso that they must be allowed to remain at La Baumette.[56] Prior Chabanel and his three Benedictines were willing to stay on at Lesvière, or in some other monastery chosen by the departmental authorities, so long as they found this new place of residence convenient, otherwise they proposed to take advantage of the release which the law afforded them. At the end of July we find them still attempting to avoid making individual declarations of willingness to leave their community, yet at the same time applying for pensions with a view to betaking themselves to Saint-Serge—a naïve attempt to get the best of both worlds which the Department quickly vetoed.[57]

These were parochial loyalties which had grown and flourished in days of mellow decadence, taking the place of a wider monastic patriotism. And not only were these agreeable religious clubs to be dispersed, there was also no guarantee that individual orders would be able to maintain any sort of separate identity. Monastic vows, as taken originally, had implied a commitment to a certain order, and to a certain way of life. Now all was confusion. Monks and friars would be huddled together arbitrarily in a new house and no one could foresee what conditions of existence or possibilities of useful activity would prevail under the new régime. That was why the Augustins unanimously declared that they 'wished to remain in their community of Angers until the houses are specified, the allowances fixed, the manner of life set forth, reserving their right to give definite explanations of their intentions after these points have been settled'.[58] The Benedictines of Saint-Nicolas, replying to the municipal officers on 26 April, insisted that a decision was impossible until alternatives were clearly defined. 'We cannot state our way of thinking until the houses set aside for us are named, the pensions assured, the rule of life laid down, and until we are told whom we will have to live with and who our superior will be.' [59] As these questions remained un-answered, it was not surprising that, when commissioners of the District arrived at Saint-Nicolas in August, two monks had already departed. When in September the archives were carted away and the town decided to ask for the buildings to house a school of artillery, three more monks chose to leave. They were young men, who could easily start life anew. The prior and three older monks lingered on for a further eight months until the day for the sale of their furniture drew near and all hope was ended.

Municipal and District authorities carried out visitations and enquiries with reasonable courtesy. Of their final inventories taken in August, vicaire Houdet observed that there was here 'a new matter of declamation for the discontented', though he himself could vouch at second-hand for the moderation of proceedings at the Capuchins and at third-hand for those at Ronceray.[60] But there was no doubt that the lay administrators were determined to proceed with ruthless legality. The appeal of the canons-regular to be allowed to remain at Toussaint was rejected by the Department, as were other appeals from smaller institutions,[61] so too was a claim of the Ursulines to be recognized as an educational establishment exempt from confiscation. The latter might have escaped, had it not been for a devastating analysis of their position given by Delaunay on 30 August. According to him, this community taught only twenty pupils (omitting boarders, who paid handsomely): on its own showing it enjoyed a large income, 'and we know that religious houses never give a complete statement of their revenues'.[62] Maliciously said, but the law being what it was, it was not unjustly done.

This, however, could hardly be said of the eviction of the monks of Saint-Aubin by the municipality, hurriedly pushed forward under circumstances of doubtful legality.[63] True, there was an urgent need for accommodation. On 17 April, commissioners appointed by the

Crown to concert measures for the formation of the new Department of Maine-et-Loire appealed to the town to provide a building in which electors from primary assemblies could meet to choose their new administrators, and, once this new departmental administration was constituted, a permanent site would be needed for its head-quarters. Angers would no longer be inferior to Tours: old dreams of making the town an administrative centre were approaching their realization. The new municipality seized its opportunity. On 18 April, that is, before official inventories of monasteries had taken place and before the monks had been asked to state their intentions, six commissioners served a notice to quit on the prior of Saint-Aubin. Two days later, a time limit of eight days began to operate, within which period the Benedictines were required to withdraw to another house of their order.[64] It seems that the municipal council was relying on a decree of the National Assembly of 5 February, which proposed to confiscate monastic houses in towns where several foundations of the same congregation were in existence. However, if this was their argument, there was no gainsaying a point made by prior dom Mansel, that the decree could be validly enforced only by the new departmental administration, which was not yet in being.[65] Three monks of Saint-Aubin supported their prior's intransigence and were not willing to go further than an offer of their church and build-ings, provided they could remain in their cells. Four declared that they would prefer to withdraw to lodgings of their own rather than begin again in other houses. The six youngest monks asked outright for their liberty, dom Charles Lorraine, their spokesman, pointing out, not unreasonably, that a removal to other monasteries merely to await removals elsewhere would be frustrating, and that life in their cells, once church and main buildings were lost, would be sheer 'agony and paralysis'. Therefore, he said, give us the first quarter of our pension and let us go out into society to defend the new Constitu-tion. 'Even if you had not the right to expel us,' he added, 'it would have been a pleasure for us to co-operate with the great work of regeneration which is going forward, by making voluntary and individual withdrawals.' This conventional statement of progressive enthusiasm may or may not mean anything—René Marchant of the Lorraine brothers' party (for there were two brothers of that name at Saint-Aubin) feared most of all the danger of becoming 'a target' for revolutionary disorders, while dom Boniface was to throw him-self into those disorders and win sinister notoriety as a terrorist.

Eviction proceeded. A dozen monks left of their own free-will. Five were turned out and went to Saint-Serge, where the mayor sent them six out of forty-five barrels of wine found in the cellars of Saint-Aubin—a matter of angry complaint for those who had departed willingly and who yet had been denied these facilities for drinking to the new Constitution.[66] The bishop arranged for relics and sacred ornaments to be removed, one of the richest collections of old charters in France went to the archives (and, thanks to Toussaint Grille, was mercifully preserved);[67] innkeepers did their utmost to thwart enterprising competitors who sought licences to set up coffee-houses in the cloisters; and finally, on 10 May the electors arrived. On 28 June the Department administrators moved in,[68] appropriating the refectory of the monks for a council-chamber, their parlour for a reception-room and installing a secretariat in the sacristy; twelve offices were established on the ground floor, and there was room above for copyists and flats for officials. One might reflect that it was unfortunate for France that at this formative period in her history bureaucracy was so easily able to allot itself impressive premises.

Once all this was done, the town council excused its illegalities by declaring that it had acted, not under the new decrees, but under a law of the old régime which ordered the closing of all religious houses having less than a minimum conventual population. This number was nine, and Saint-Aubin had had sixteen monks. It was argued, however, that eleven of these had chosen to depart, so that, after the event at least, not enough remained to form a quorum—such was the explanation made by the mayor to the Ecclesiastical Committee of the Assembly at Paris,[69] and disseminated locally in the *Affiches* on 11 May. But in this same article, the real argument for confiscation was given, one towards which lay society in Angers had been working its way for some years, 'le salut de la ville devait être la suprême loi'.[70] Meanwhile, the envious District administrators remained homeless: from Saint-Aubin they migrated to the castle, from the castle to a house formerly occupied by milord Southwell, 'awaiting the evacuation of a religious house suitable for the installation of their important administration'.[71]

The sale of *biens nationaux* began in Angers on 9 December, the earliest possible date after full authorization had been obtained from Paris. A mass of eligible urban property was thrust on to the market; indeed, during the past few months, experts had surveyed and priced more than 400 houses in town.[72] Near great foundations, monasteries and chapters, whole streets were for sale. Widows and spinsters in modest houses in the rue des Carmes[73] gossiped apprehensively awaiting new landlords; shopkeepers in the rue Toussaint and the rue Saint-Aubin[74] counted their savings to see if they could afford to buy out their leases. In every corner or alleyway, something was for sale, sometimes, perhaps, to the surprise of all but very old inhabitants and the actual tenant—a house in the rue des Tonnelliers belonging to the chapel of Saint-Anne, another in the rue Saint-Nicolas belonging to the chapel of Malmorte.[75] Sixty-one houses previously owned by chapters and fifty-three previously owned by monasteries were included in the first series of auctions,[76] and others were to follow. For immediate sale, too, were lands and vineyards of Saint-Nicolas—a better long-term investment, perhaps, than housing property on crowded sites. All around the city walls small patches of rural land were to be sold, suitable to afford country-retreats for prosperous citizens and provide their tables with wine and fresh vegetables, or to form grazing grounds for butchers and drovers, or yield profits to agricultural speculators. So many ecclesiastical corporations had held land around Angers that lots were already subdivided and parcelled out for auction in detail: there was something for every taste and every pocket, and an unrivalled opportunity for those who already possessed rural acres to round off their heritages. In the parish of Saint-Samson, property once owned by the bishop, Saint-Serge, two chapters, a cure, the Seminary and six chapels, was for sale, which, in addition to the buildings and gardens of Saint-Serge and the bishop's country estate made up twenty-five lots— three large farms and eight small ones, three vineyards and eleven paddocks or enclosures.[77] On the other side of town, in the parish of Saint-Laud,[78] there were ninety-one items of rural property, 300,000*l.* worth, which had once belonged to thirty-three different ecclesiastical landlords. *La clauserie de la diablerie, le clos de mon conseil, le lieu du chesne vert, le lieu de la Grenouille, l'enclose nommé le petit veau*—there was a breath of hay harvest and orchards in their very names—awaited new owners. Who would not wish, had he six or seven thousand *livres* to spare, to purchase such a retreat within an hour's journey of his court-room or counting-house, there to read Jean-Jacques under an oak tree or supervise his tenant's labours?

Bidding was enthusiastic. 'There is keen rivalry to obtain possession of properties fertilized by apostolic benedictions', said the local anti-clerical journal sardonically.[79] Possessions of churchmen in Angers were strategically situated. Estimated prices had been calculated on former leases, which had usually been on a milder and more traditional basis than secular ones, and terms of payment were easy, even to those who did not foresee a coming inflation: 20 per cent down for urban property, further payments to be completed in 12 years.[80] Thus it is not surprising that bidding outran estimates. Eighteen houses, supposed to be worth 74,084*l.*, went for 130,325*l.* on the first day.[81] Eleven houses of the chapter of Saint-Maurille brought 40,225*l.* instead of 32,125*l.*, and the nine houses of the chapter of Saint-Pierre sold for 42,100*l.* instead of 24,645*l.*[82] By the end of April 1791, lands and buildings which had been expected to yield a little short of six millions had been auctioned for eight and a half.[83]

The municipality also bought on its own account. For years blue prints of town-planning schemes had accumulated. Now at last all obstacles had vanished. While the District was still seeking a location, the departmental administrators were installed in Saint-Aubin and were shortly to consider taking over the Jacobins also; soldiers were billeted in the Minims and from the president of the Military Committee of the National Assembly came assurances that 'Angers has always appeared to me to be a town which possesses every facility requisite for the various types of military academy which we have considered forming'.[84] This was good news, for the town council hoped to persuade the government to set up a military school and, better still, an artillery training unit. This, it was argued, could be sited in the abbey of Saint-Nicolas, have a firing range over the monks' pond and use the river for heavy transport and for power to turn its powder mill.[85] At the same time the castle was to be bought as a jail, the long-awaited foundling hospital was to be set up, preferably in Lesvière,[86] and the National Assembly was to be petitioned to set up a mint in Angers which could make a cheap start on local materials by coining the bells of chapters and monasteries.[87] Not only was ecclesiastical property now on the market, but there was also the approaching parochial reorganization dictated by the Civil Constitution of the Clergy, which would render many old churches of the city centre redundant. Roads could be cut through the cemeteries of Saint-Maurille and Sainte-Croix and through the Cordeliers' garden; Saint-Michel de La Palud and its graveyard need no longer constrict the rue Saint-Aubin; Saint-Maurille, Saint-Pierre and Saint-Maimbeuf could be demolished, leaving space for a public square and a market; lands of the monastery of Saint-Serge and the little church and cemetery of Saint-Samson could be united to form a magnificent botanical garden.[88] The town could now set itself free from the patterns imposed upon it by medieval piety, and urban geography would no longer reveal a map of clerical domination.

There was very little overt opposition to the sale of Church property in France. Many believed, as the administrators of the Department of Maine-et-Loire declared, that it was 'the only way to save the Empire and assure the success of its regeneration'[89] and those who did not see this necessity, from Marie-Antoinette downwards, were generally willing to take this opportunity for investment, so that even some of the clergy were prepared to buy.[90] 'Now the religious orders are suppressed, *Grand Dieu*, when will this legislature make an end?' wrote the marquis de Lostanges from Angers on 17 February 1790; yet three days later he was hoping to obtain from the municipality the use of the abbatial house of Saint-Aubin, formerly occupied by milord Southwell—'c'est une belle occasion'.[91] His attitude proved to be a fair anticipation of the opportunist temper of lay society ten months later when church property generally was up for auction. Even so, there were some misgivings in Angers and some regrets. Economic arguments for making the town a centre of consumption had been used continually: some people now began to wonder if perhaps, after all, monasteries had not been performing fairly adequately this function of sucking in wealth from the countryside to line the pockets of tradesmen and craftsmen. Being a supporter of the Church, Gastineau of the Law Faculty took a malicious delight in elaborating this after-thought, pointing out that a sovereign court or similar judicial institution was an absolute necessity to atone for loss of revenue caused by the departure of the monks.[92] The municipality took up this argument from the first and bewailed 'the losses which (the town) must bear by the suppression of its religious houses, which are very numerous and which spend all their revenue here'. In August the 'loss caused by the reduction in the amount of goods which were formerly consumed' was again being considered, this time as the basis of an appeal to the government to establish a military academy in Angers.[93] The minor municipality of Saint-Samson, equally aware of the force of this reasoning, inventoried the goods of Saint-Serge with a rider that 'the community of Saint-Samson has the greatest possible interest in the conservation of this religious house, the only one which exists on its territory'.[94] Trades-people who had worked for ecclesiastical establishments wondered whether the nation would settle old debts and foresaw a decline of orders in the future;[95] citizens who had rented houses or leased plots of land on favourable terms feared the advent of new owners.[96] Paper money, whatever its real backing, made simple thrifty men remember what their fathers had told them of Law's Scheme and its iniquities under the Regency, so that not everyone hailed the advent of *assignats*. Fifty small tradesmen of Angers set their hands to a petition against them, so that La Revellière-Lépeaux had to explain to the National Assembly the insignificance of this ignorant minority before he could continue to bask in the reflected glow of Angevin patriotism.[97] Pious folk found 'matter for declamation' when monastic furniture was inventoried.[98] Three municipal officers, all lawyers, resigned from their posts as a protest against the unjust seizure of the abbey of Saint-Aubin, and one of them, the *avocat* Benoît, afforded a refuge in his home to some of the monks.[99] Yet another lawyer, Henri Bodard, *procureur du Roi* at the *Présidial*, at the end of May and later in September, publicly denounced the sale of ecclesiastical property, and circulated pamphlets

arguing that the Church held its possessions by a title quite as valid
as that of a parish or a municipality.[100]

These protests came from laymen. One or two country curés
re-echoed them, talked of 'spoliation' and 'shipwreck', and scared
peasant farmers by issuing 'threats of excommunication from their
pulpits'.[101] But, whatever their private opinions might have been,
the clergy in Angers itself made no overt gesture of opposition, a
reticence which was typical of ecclesiastical France in general. To
sabotage sales and ruin the *assignat* would have unleashed every
latent anti-clerical passion.[102] 'After all, is it the sanctuary that you
are defending, or is it the money-changers at the gates of the
temple?'[103]—patriots were prodigal with such accusations. When
our curé of Saint-Julien, acting upon sound advice from Paris,
refused to publish in his pulpit departmental notices concerning the
sale of ecclesiastical properties, local anti-clericals raised a dis-
proportionate outcry, alleging that clerics were 'regretting their
riches', making 'secret efforts' against the Constitution, showing a
'factious spirit'.[104] The ugly rising of the *perreyeurs* in September[105]
had at once scared and shamed the bourgeoisie, so that they were
willing to see reactionary stratagems everywhere. In face of such a
suspicious temper, why jeopardize religion's cause by fighting against
the inevitable?—far better be co-operative, and follow the example
of two complacent canons of Saint-Laud, who offered to look after
certain artichokes on lands of their former prebends, and were
praised for services 'advantageous to the nation'.[106] After all, state
pensions were to be paid, and parish priests at least could rejoice to
see an end of inequalities and injustices in clerical revenues. But one
need not be so cynical as to seek only for politic reasons for their
attitude. 'We will always be rich enough to live and never poor
enough to starve', bishop de Lorry told his priests in May 1790, 'let
us live as they did in the days of the early Church.'[107] Within his
limitations, he was sincere when he said it. The root cause of diver-
gence between Church and Revolution is not to be found in this
confiscation of ecclesiastical property: for that we must turn to the
Civil Constitution of the Clergy.

CHAPTER XIV

THE CIVIL CONSTITUTION OF THE CLERGY (JULY 1790–MARCH 1791)

'A GRAVE error, which was the origin of many deplorable consequences'—'Perhaps the greatest political blunder of the Assembly'. Subsequent historians, clerical and anti-clerical alike, have agreed in endorsing these verdicts of Alexandre de Lameth and of Talleyrand on the Civil Constitution of the Clergy.[1] The magic unity of '89 was shattered, religion and patriotism became opposed causes, Church and Revolution diverged decisively, and a schism was created in the soul of France which remains to this day. The Constituent Assembly blundered into a tragic conflict, tragic because (though it is easy to say this in the comfortable retrospect of history) such an urgent and irreconcilable clash was unnecessary. On one hand, the men of the Assembly had no wish to separate Church and state. They were not swayed by masonic plotters or by a Jansenist cabal, and if their minds had been moulded by the *philosophes*, their enemy was not the Church, but despotism: they did not aim to free men from prejudices in the manner of Voltaire, but to win political freedom after the manner of Rousseau. A leaven of anti-clericalism was ever working in their midst, but outwardly they were conformist, and inwardly they were bourgeois, moral and conservative. They wished to preserve their national Church, suitably reformed, as a bulwark of a new state, just as it had been a bulwark of the old monarchy, and when they declared that they proposed to 'found institutions on the sacred basis of religion' they were sincere.[2] On the other hand, many churchmen were willing to go half way to meet them—not only 'patriotic curés', but also leaders of the aristocratic episcopate. Some bishops, it is true, hastened to emigrate and shake the dust of constitutional France from off their feet. It is true also that the two bishops on the Ecclesiastical Committee of the Assembly withdrew from its discussions at the beginning of February 1790, that twelve of their colleagues solicited a legal opinion against the proposed decrees, and that by the end of August pastoral letters were fulminating threats of resistance.[3] Yet the fact remains that there was a solid body of moderate episcopal opinion, led by the politic Boisgelin, archbishop of Aix, which hoped all the while to find some provisional solution, to 'baptize' the Civil Constitution, to persuade the Pope to patronize some 'interim expedient'.[4] Not all bishops had the trick of sounding a fashionably patriotic note as had our bishop of Angers, but most of those whose sees would be preserved were willing to take their place in the new era and co-operate with the inevitable. An *Exposition des Principes* of 30 October, to which one hundred and nineteen bishops adhered,[5] was unyielding on principle, that is, ecclesiastical authority must sanction the Civil Constitution, but it was moderate in tone and inspired throughout with a regretful yearning for an eleventh-hour compromise. That there was a real and grave clash of convictions is not to be denied—but neither party wished to have the dispute embodied in a ruthless and inescapable dilemma. An alliance between Church and state is one of those useful things in a nation's life which can only subsist if fundamental illogicalities in the entente are tacitly admitted and questions of ultimate authority are discreetly buried, preferably under a tangle of old traditions, failing that, under sonorous and plausible formulae. This is what ecclesiastical France hoped to bring about, and this is precisely what Assembly and Papacy failed to contrive.

Final disaster arose from the manner of enforcing the Civil Constitution rather than from its matter, though the matter was in some respects startling and disquieting. Yet, leaving aside for the moment propositions designed to seal the triumph of a bourgeois democratic erastianism under guise of a return to apostolic spon-taneity, we find that the decrees, tragically enough, were not ill-designed to bring about those reforms which the Church of France so desperately needed. Benefices without cure of souls were annihi-lated, chapters of cathedrals and other collegials were swept away, curés, guaranteed incomes on a scale ranging from 6,000*l.* to 1,200*l.*, were at last to receive economic justice, and new and logical parochial boundaries were to be drawn in both town and country. These changes were ruthless, particularly in regard to chapters, but ruthless changes were needed, as a survey of ecclesiastical institutions in Angers at the end of the old régime demonstrates. This programme contained the substance of what Chatizel, Boumard and Rangeard had fought to obtain. Louis XVI sanctioned the Civil Constitution on 22 July 1790, and the decrees were promulgated on 24 August: it was not until 27 November that the oath which forced a decision on the whole issue was imposed on the clergy, while the King's sanction to this oath was not wrung from him until 26 December. There was thus a period from the end of August in which the new church polity was law, while the question of its canonical 'baptism' was still under negotiation. The clergy had not yet come under the desperate obligation of declaring their allegiance and the business of elections to ecclesiastical office was only urgent in isolated local cases where vacancies occurred. During these interim months, the chief events in the clerical world at Angers were the suppression of chapters and the discussion of schemes for revising parish boundaries. Both went forward smoothly, which suggests that, in this town at least, the removal of abuses and inequalities by the Civil Constitution was not the cause of the ultimate revolt of churchmen against the National Assembly.

As a result of the decrees concerning ecclesiastical property, chapters had already wound up their material affairs and handed their property over to the civil authorities pending final auction. Individual canons had furnished statements of their old revenues, the last one to come in being that of canon Boulnoy of Saint-Maurice, who pleaded the tortures of gout as his excuse for failing to give consecutive thought to the value of his manifold benefices.[6] Appropriate pensions awaited canons, but the future outlook was bleak for their employees, and in May and June the musicians and registrar of Saint-Maurice appealed to the Ecclesiastical Committee of the Assembly to be compensated for their loss of expectations.[7] As the cathedral no longer drew rents from its central fortress of property in the *cité*, early in July its chapter requested the municipality to take over all street lighting there.[8] An enterprising citizen took advantage of this period of indeterminacy to remove silver chalices and ornaments from the sacristy of Saint-Pierre, whose canons hastened to call in the police lest they should be accused of complicity in a pious burglary.[9] Shorn of their property, the chapters lived on, offering 'their vows and prayers for the prosperity of the state',[10] maintaining their registers with scrupulous care and clinging to their honorific distinctions in the twilight of their days. Though on 24 August the Civil Constitution of the clergy was promulgated, the King's ministers still delayed as long as they dared in circulating the decrees to Districts, and Districts themselves varied greatly in the speed with which they acted, so that Notre-Dame at Paris was not suppressed until 22 November, and the chapters of Troyes and Bourges were still in existence at the beginning of 1791.[11] Nearer home, the District of Saumur proved dilatory in carrying out suppressions within its jurisdiction, and in mid-November had to be goaded into action by the Department.[12] There were no such delays at Angers. Agents of the District administration served notices to quit on Saturday, 18 September. That afternoon, a deputation of the bishop and the dean and canon Dutertre of Saint-Maurice waited on the departmental authorities to point out that the decrees had not yet been registered by the *Sénéchaussée* of the town, and asking for permission to continue to celebrate divine service until they were. This appeal was rejected. It was not even possible to say vespers that evening.[13] Throughout October and November, furniture was being inventoried and registers carted off to the departmental archives.[14] M. Follenfant, curé of Saint-Maurice, left his humble parish church and celebrated his parochial offices amid the splendours of the cathedral. There were sharp arguments at Saint-Martin and Saint-Maurille when the District administrators came to take over the sacristy furniture. Curés Chaloigne and Roussel and their churchwardens arrived to claim the sacred ornaments and revenues of the old capitular churches; the resentful canons tried to demonstrate that parishes would henceforward find liturgical expenses a burden, and they had claims to make concerning the vestments (or 150*l.* in lieu) which each of them had presented to the sacristy of their church on appointment.[15]

At Lyons, Saint-Omer, Arras and Rouen, voices were raised in protest against the disappearance of chapters, and at Tours[16] an official plea had been put forward to preserve the canonries of Saint-Martin which supplemented the patrimonies of poor families. But at Angers, the suppression of chapters passed almost unnoticed. Their existence had been too obviously abusive for their disappearance to leave lively regrets. But life in town no longer seemed the same when the music of so many bells was silenced. 'The workers of Angers are quite put out by the fact that the bell which formerly chimed the hours of the day is no longer heard,' wrote the District to the bishop on 29 October, 'we beg you to be good enough to give orders that it be rung every day at five in the morning.' [17]

Vacant monastic and collegiate churches now awaited embodiment in a final plan of parochial reorganization. Bernier, newly appointed to his cure of Saint-Laud, made the fine church of the old chapter, 'its solidity, its grandeur, its antiquity' and its store of precious relics, his chief arguments for a scheme which would enable him to annex Lesvière, fragments of Saint-Martin and Saint-Michel de la Palud and the whole countryside as far as Empiré.[18] At the same time, other ecclesiastical geographers were in the field with more impartial projects of redistribution which came nearer to the plan which was ultimately adopted.[19] Then there were other petitions representing minor local interests. Inhabitants of the faubourg Bressigny, the rue Châteaugontier and the place Monsieur wished to preserve at all costs their little district chapel of Saint-Sébastien; the parishioners of Saint-Samson, abetted by curé Ferré, wanted to worship in the church of Saint-Serge and not be treated as country dwellers, while villagers out at Empiré wanted to stay in the parish of Saint-Pierre or join that of Saint-Laud, so that they would retain their urban affiliations.[20] Meanwhile, at Saint-Laud and Saint-Martin, parishioners were looking covetously upon property and plate belonging to their chapters, and making ineffective pleas to be allowed to annex some of these endowments before the auction of church property began.[21] Whatever happened, it was obvious that the huge parish of La Trinité must be subdivided, and Houdet as one of its vicaires greeted this prospect with interested enthusiasm. 'It appears decided that they are going to make a new parish from ours at the Capuchins. If only I could be lucky enough to be given it!'[22] Thrifty laymen, however, looked with dismay on prospects of taking over more imposing buildings. Threatened with a move to Saint-Aubin, the parishioners of Saint-Martin produced every possible argument by way of objection: the church was situated in an inconvenient *cul-de-sac*, its bell-tower was separate from its nave, pillars and a walled-in choir obstructed the view, and (here was their essential reason) the crumbling walls and roof would necessitate repairs.[23]

It was impossible to please everyone, but the final plan, 'drawn up by the directory of the District of Angers in conjunction with the bishop and upon the advice of the municipal officers'[24] was eminently reasonable. Five handsome churches were taken over for parochial use—the cathedral, and those of the chapter of Saint-Laud, of the Cordeliers, and of the abbeys of Saint-Serge and Saint-Nicolas. On the left bank, five parishes would remain, Saint-Maurice and Saint-Pierre in the city centre, and Saint-Samson, Saint-Laud and La Madeleine (the former district church) on the perimeter; while on the right bank, La Trinité would dispose of surplus population to Saint-Nicolas and Saint-Jacques.[25] The brilliant young Bernier of Saint-Laud and the staid and simple Gruget of La Trinité were priests whose opposition to the Civil Constitution of the Clergy was to be uncompromising, so their verdict is not suspect when they praise this new delimitation of parishes. It was, said the first, 'for the good of the people, for simplicity and for economy'. 'One cannot but admit,' Gruget reflected afterwards, 'that this plan was quite well conceived. By it, the parishes would have been neither too large nor too small. Both priests and their flocks would have found it advantageous.'[26]

These new parochial boundaries were decreed by the Assembly on 25 January and received royal sanction on the 30th. By then, ecclesiastical society in Angers was in revolt and the religion of the Civil Constitution was reduced to official prayers offered by patriots, National Guards with bayonets and municipal officers in tricolour sashes. In so far as the National Assembly was imposing a rigorous measure of ecclesiastical reform, its work would have been accepted, but the decrees went far beyond a reform of abuses, and it is to these other aspects of the Civil Constitution which we must turn to explain the final tragedy.

The Constituents aimed to 'nationalize Catholicism, to put it at the service of the new order'.[27] It may have been reasonable to attempt this, but to attempt to do it quickly was a dangerous undertaking, involving all the recklessness, said Lameth, of 'combining an ecclesiastical reform with a political one'. For example, a sweeping revision of diocesan boundaries and of the whole plan of the hierarchy was proposed. It is true that this was needed. Vast sees like Rouen and Limoges stood in absurd disparity to clusters of minute dioceses in the south which were a legacy of electioneering tactics of the popes of Avignon; conflicting claims of Paris and Lyons, of metropolitans and primates, gave profits to lawyers rather than leadership to the Gallican Church. Here were grounds enough, not to mention economy in national housekeeping, to bring bishoprics into correspondence with Departments and confer titles of metropolitan upon ten archiepiscopal diocesans. However, while a revision of political areas could be performed by the sole will of the sovereign Assembly, and a reform of parochial boundaries could be carried out with the consent of local bishops, this readjustment of dioceses demanded higher ecclesiastical sanction. Some bishops would have to resign, others would have to take over their jurisdiction in certain areas, and however much Camus might argue that by consecration a bishop received power to exercise his functions anywhere, the formalities of canonical institution and the decisions of the Council of Trent strongly suggested the contrary.[28] Even bishop de Lorry, with his pose of dignified conformity to the new order, was unyielding here. His reorganized diocese, now coincident with the department of Maine-et-Loire, included strips of territory from the old dioceses of La Rochelle, Nantes and Poitiers; at least one bishop, the bishop of La Rochelle, was determined not to surrender his jurisdiction, and was sending defiant circulars to his old parishes.[29] A dispute between a country curé faithful to the observances of Poitiers and a local mayor zealous for the rites of Angers, brought matters to a crisis, and Mgr de Lorry was asked to exercise his extended jurisdiction. 'We congratulate ourselves on having you for our bishop', said the local authorities persuasively on 3 December, soliciting his intervention.[30] They received a reply which was 'vague and in no way satisfactory'. The other bishops, said Mgr de Lorry, 'no doubt still exercise their jurisdiction; I cannot and I am not entitled to take it away from them'.[31] This refusal was at once good form among colleagues and good law by law books.[32] Authority for a transfer of jurisdiction could be given by a national council, or by the Pope acting through delegates, or, as Boisgelin argued, by provincial councils dealing with their own areas. But whatever method was adopted, one thing was certain: approval must be given by ecclesiastical authority acting through canonical procedure.

While this identity of civil and religious areas would put dioceses into mesh with the new system of government, the intention was to go still further, and interlock the national Church with the state ideologically as well as administratively. Bishops would be nominated by electors of departments, and curés by electors of districts. Rights of appointment which had been enjoyed under the old régime by the Crown or by patrons would now be vested in the sovereign people. Though the Constituents were being logical, they were outpacing opinion in the country, for if ideas of lay election had been abroad in 1789 (they are found, for example, in one of the specimen *cahiers* which were in circulation at Angers)[33] they had not been taken up seriously in the *cahiers* generally.[34] On the other hand, in Anjou and in most of the rest of France, demands for changes coming from the lower clergy had been Richerist in flavour, not presbyterian: that is, they wished to see their Church ruled by synods of priests and not by gatherings of laymen. The identity of Church and nation which clerical *cahiers* insisted upon was an identity in which the clergy had a role of spiritual leadership aided by a censorship and by their control of education. It was not to be an identity in which the hierarchy of the pastorate was an emanation from the General Will. The Civil Constitution did limit the powers of bishops by allowing them to perform no act of jurisdiction without the assent of their vicars-episcopal, but the Assembly adjourned *sine die* discussion of the reform which the lower clergy most desired—the re-establishment of diocesan and metropolitan synods. Rousseau had defeated Richerism; the rights of the second order of clergy had been swallowed up in the rights of the nation at large. 'Liberty', said a Jansenist, was 'the Medusa's head which must petrify everything.' As a result, indifferent Laodiceans, cynical *philosophes*, and even Protestants, provided that they were prepared to attend the mass which preceded elections, could cast their votes for candidates for ecclesiastical office. In some parts of France, more particularly in Alsace, the right of Protestants to participate caused grave problems,[35] and even where this special difficulty was not present, the clergy were troubled when they saw that the people politically organized was being equated with the *ecclesia* of primitive Christianity. Jacquemart, curé of Brissarthe, who had replaced Chatizel as a deputy for Anjou in April,[36] spoke brilliantly in the Assembly on 8 June and 15 June against this delusive analogy. 'Let us put away chimerical dreams, let us cease building castles in the air. Times have changed. By all means let us look back with regretful admiration to the virtues of the apostolic age, but let us not flatter ourselves that we will see them revive again in our midst. When the name of Christian was synonymous

s

with that of saint, when the faithful, united by charity, formed one single family of brothers, when their ambitions rose no higher than the yearning for a martyr's crown—then you could have confided to the People the duty of choosing their Pastors.' As it was, dull-witted country farmers and mayors of villages, he said, would be dazzled by wealth, seduced by oratory, deceived by ambition, vicaires would court prosperous landowners as obsequiously as ministers in England court the local squire.[37] Here was plain speaking about democracy. Clearly the suppression of Jansenism among the Angevin clergy had not weakened their belief in the doctrine of original sin. Jacquemart's own suggestions concerning methods of making ecclesiastical appointments were strictly clerical: let bishops be elected by the priests of a diocese assembled in synod, either alone, or in the presence of the administrators of the Department, and as for cures, let them be conferred by a synod, by the bishop himself, or by competitive examination. As Robespierre pointed out, his argument would logically culminate in a re-establishment of the clergy as a separate corporation in the state.

A national Church, whose officers were chosen by the people, must be a church independent of foreign control. To this effect, article 20 of the Civil Constitution ruled that newly-appointed bishops would despatch a letter to the Pope indicative of unity of faith, but would receive canonical institution, not from Rome, but from their own metropolitan. Gallican governments of the old régime had been accustomed 'to kiss the Pope's feet while tying his hands'; the nation would carry on this policy but omit ceremonial camouflage. Article 20 was a unilateral breach of the Concordat of 1516, but so too had been the cancellation of annates in August 1789, which had been quietly accepted by the Vatican. This idea of institution by metropolitans was one which took its origin with a few ultra-Gallican canonists, yet it was an idea which, once stated, appealed to the pervasive Gallican spirit of France, and which in itself did not shock the clergy.[38] Rome might be expected therefore to yield once more under pressure.

The Papacy, however, was much more deeply concerned with the Civil Constitution in general than with this article in particular, for whatever the Assembly might claim to be doing, it was certainly legislating on matters concerning the spiritual sphere.[39] It is true that temporal matters were concerned equally vitally. Yet, even if it were argued that churchmen were under a constant obligation to adjust their organization to the demands of the state, it remained true that changes were being made which required the agreement of ecclesiastical authority. How was this agreement to be obtained? The Assembly wished to obtain it without having asked for it. Two propositions of Camus—that it would be an abuse of political power to change religion, and that the representatives of the people could change religion if they were so minded—must be held in tension. So the method adopted was to present the Church with an ultimatum, then to leave the King's ministers to negotiate its acceptance. 'Il faut consulter l'Église'—this was an insistent complaint of Boisgelin and the moderates, and the archbishop of Aix argued that there were only two methods of doing so: either by calling a national council, or by applying to the head of Christendom 'in accordance with the ancient forms of the Gallican Church'.[40] How far recourse to the first method would render the second unnecessary was a question that never required answering, for the Assembly was determined not to allow a national council to meet. To do so would be to admit that the clergy remained an order in the state, besides giving aristocratic bishops a chance for counter-revolutionary manœuvres. Since, therefore, the Constituents were treating ecclesiastical France as a collection of unconnected dioceses,[41] only one method of consulting the Church remained open.[42] The Pope must speak. Rome would be arbiter, and the French clergy would have to abide by a Roman decision. Political Gallicanism had thrown away its most useful ally, ecclesiastical Gallicanism.[43] If the French Church was to be independent of the Pope and fulfil the hope of Camus that it would support the nation even when that nation exceeded its legitimate powers, one thing was necessary—it must be allowed power of autonomous action. An ecclesiastical decision alone could prevent schism, yet the Church of France was not allowed to decide. Loyalty to the spiritual power was made entirely coincident with loyalty to Rome.

Governments of the old régime had dealt in very cavalier fashion with the Holy See: Joseph II had reformed his Church, Catherine II had re-organized Polish dioceses, Louis XV had suppressed monasteries, and the Papacy had been ignored. It was a point of honour with the Constituents to be as disobliging in the name of the nation as absolute monarchs had been in their own name.[44] From the writings of the *philosophes* a similar policy of cynical and enlightened erastianism could be deduced. 'When the sovereign believes a reform necessary,' said Treilhard, 'no one can oppose it.' Then came a hardening of anti-clerical opinions when the Assembly moved into Paris and came under the influence of bitter propagandists in the capital. There was a general conviction that bishops (whose conduct under the old régime had given some ground for such a suspicion) would yield in any case to save their revenues, it was unthinkable that the mass of curés would desert the Revolution, while it was assumed that churchmen in general would do anything rather than face the ultimate tragedy of schism.[45] As for the Pope, Avignon revolted on 10 June against his rule, and an appeal by its patriots for union with France gave the Assembly an unrivalled bargaining counter. Whether Pius VI was so base as to hope to barter his authorization of the Civil Constitution in exchange for his rebellious dominions is a question that does not concern us. What is certain is that the Assembly thought he was, and was therefore confident that blackmail would succeed. In this mood of false confidence, the Constituents made their cardinal error under an ever-mounting pressure of circumstances. The sale of *biens nationaux* was imminent, and a secure settlement of Church matters would give confidence to prospective buyers. Local difficulties arose throughout September and November after the Civil Constitution was promulgated. Bishops could refuse to give marriage dispensations or to collaborate in drawing up new parish boundaries, and the bishop of Rennes flatly denied canonical institution to the newly elected bishop of Quimper. So on 27 November the Assembly took decisive and fatal action. It was decreed that all clergy must take an oath to the constitution of the kingdom, which, of course, included the Civil Constitution of the Clergy. 'The law of 27 November', said Montlosier, 'cut all the bridges.'

On 26 December, after procrastinating as long as he dared, Louis XVI was driven to sanction this decree, and forthwith local authorities proceeded to require the oath from their clergy. In Angers, sommations reached the bishop, curés and vicaires, directors of the Seminary, professors of philosophy and theology and the Oratorians, at six o'clock on the evening of Saturday, 1 January. All parish priests also received a long proclamation, which embodied the terms of the decree and declared that ecclesiastics who would not comply with the Assembly's order were disturbers of public tranquillity: this document was to be read out to the faithful at high mass on the following morning.[46] It was too late in the day, especially on the eve of the Circumcision, a feast of obligation, for curés to concert their measures. Even so, none of them read the announcement. A week passed, and on the following Sunday the departmental administrators published the orders themselves, making them more comprehensive by adding a gloss denying papal rights in matters temporal.[47] This second attempt at publication was abetted by the two vicaires of Saint-Pierre, who, in defiance of curé Robin, now read the proclamation in their church.[48] Another week of caballing, speculation, propaganda and heart-searchings ensued. Then on 16 January the oaths were formally taken in various churches, the mayor and municipal officers touring town to supervise and record proceedings, supported by their full civic pomp of tricolour sashes and martial music. And the result? On 16 January[49] and on subsequent Sundays, two curés, three vicaires, the Oratorians and a handful of monks and minor chaplains became jurors.[50] Ecclesiastical Angers decisively rejected the Civil Constitution of the Clergy. In France generally, statistics show an almost equal balance of constitutionals and refractories, but here is a crisis where statistics have little meaning apart from their grouping and interpretation within local cadres. National history deals with great or influential men but with average motives, with the lowest common denominators of human passions: local history deals with ordinary men, but with their real passions, rough, untrimmed and angular, neither added together to form a sum nor divided again to form an average. We have seen the traditional institutions of Angers crumbling before the onrush of a new era. The Civil Constitution hastened this work of demolition, and marks the beginning of the end of a connexion between religion and social life which had given this town its peculiar atmosphere and character. A static world was brought to a conclusion too confused and unjust to be called a judgment, but one which forms a significant test, nevertheless, of men's motives and of the moral fibre of the order in which they had been living.

First, consider the motives of jurors. 'I swear to be a faithful pastor in the parish which is confided to my care, to be loyal to the Nation, the Law and the King, and to uphold to the best of my ability the Constitution decreed by the National Assembly and accepted by the King.' Here was a declaration whose terms were only superficially innocuous, for there was no doubt, as all contemporary polemicists were well aware, that the Civil Constitution of the clergy was included in 'the Constitution decreed by the National Assembly and accepted by the King'. However, it was still possible to argue that the main point of the oath was to give a general recognition to the new form of government.[51] If this was so, its rejection would imply disaffection to the Revolution, and local authorities were here presented with a powerful patriotic argument, which was deployed with all the pressure of fashionable jargon and ceremony. Ecclesiastics, and more especially curés, faced a barrage of propaganda and social blandishment. A letter from the mayor, written with his own hand, conveyed smooth congratulations or reassurances to every presbytery.[52] The patriot press gave exaggerated statistics of clergy in Paris and elsewhere who had taken the oath or were about to do so, rehearsed a few *clichés* from the Fathers and Church history to show that learning was not a reactionary monopoly, and accused non-jurors of playing the game of the counter-revolutionary nobility.[53] Bernier was warned that his brains would be blown out in the pulpit if he made impudent remarks about the

Constitution. Anti-clerical watch-dogs packed the pews to scare him. 'At least I have contrived to attract to my sermon today people who don't turn up very often', he observed.[54] Influential individuals made personal visits with flattering or threatening speeches.[55] Curé Robin suddenly found himself invited to dinner-parties,[56] and the pious and simple Gruget was besieged by Changé, his parishioner and president of the District Assembly.[57] Two deputies from the municipality came round in the week following 16 January to assure those who had not sworn that they still had another chance.[58] There was a widespread rumour bruited abroad by patriots that the bishop would lead in taking the oath. We have not forgotten his pastoral letter of May, 1790, said the *Journal du Département de Maine-et-Loire*, and we know his love of peace.[59] Others pointed to Mgr de Lorry's co-operation in redrawing parochial boundaries as a promising omen. The wife of a municipal officer rushed into the church of La Trinité and hustled a vicaire out of his confessional to confide in him the news that his bishop was going to yield.[60] Above all, there was the pressure of friends and relations. Janin, vicaire of Saint-Michel du Tertre, stood out against the solicitations of his brother, a priest at Mazé, who took the oath.[61] Curé Suchet of Saint-Michel de la Palud was immovable, but his nephew and vicaire, Viger, conformed to their family's policy. At La Trinité, Gruget out-argued his life-long friend, Bouchet, who had been sent to convert him, and Houdet, who for so long had yearned for a parish, manfully but reluctantly resisted appeals from his brothers, the merchant at Nantes and the surgeon at Saint-Florent-le-Vieil, who were achieving local celebrity as supporters of the new Constitution.

There were priests in France—and their numbers should not be underestimated—whose enthusiasm for the Revolution knew no bounds. In it they found a lay counterpart to their sacerdotal vocation and it was in their ranks that ideals of patriotism and national regeneration reached sincerest heights of fanaticism. They were prepared to put the Constitution on a plane with revelation, to equate it with the Bible, and declared that God's voice was heard more clearly in deliberations of the representatives of the nation than in fulminations of the ecclesiastical authorities. The latter were in any case proving singularly vague and ineffective in their guidance to struggling consciences—'eyes have they and see not, ears have they and hear not, neither speak they through their throat'—while the nation was speaking with ruthless clarity.[62] At Angers, the Federation of 1790 had moved such an enthusiast to notable utterance. J.-B. Coquille, an ex-Recollet, chaplain of the National Guard of Beaufort and a member of the society of the *Amis de la Constitution* of Angers, had printed and distributed a *Discours Patriotique* in which he praised the seizure of Church property and the ending of monastic vows (he later proclaimed his own matrimonial bliss as an object-lesson on this point) and urged his readers to take their Bibles in one hand and the Constitution in the other and observe their concordance.[63] Few local clergy were afflicted with Coquille's naïve exhibitionism, but some shared his genuine enthusiasm. Gaudin, curé of Saint-Nicolas, 'for long a defender of the work of our legislators', who embellished his taking of the oath with a patriotic discourse and an announcement of *biens nationaux* still for sale,[64] and Taillebuis and Fautras, vicaires of Saint-Pierre, 'for long panegyrists of the work of the Assembly',[65] may fairly be ascribed to the category of those who became jurors from emotion and conviction. So too may the Oratorians, for whom even the Constitution itself was not sufficiently democratic.[66] For them, the new Church settlement was a step towards the egalitarianism which was presupposed by Rousseau's doctrine of the General Will, an end of the rule of birth and fortune in the hierarchy, too long divorced from the people. Thus, there would be no return to days described by Bénaben of the Oratory in his first discourse to the club of the *Amis de la Constitution* of Angers, when 'religion, which ought to have served as a continual reminder to men of their natural equality, seemed, on the contrary, to be giving its sanction to principles which are destructive of all true society, in establishing an odious line of demarcation between individuals'.[67] Bénaben and his brilliant colleague Mévolhan fortified the case for the oath by a modicum of respectable clerical leadership of a more intelligent and edifying kind than was supplied by Coquille's effusions, and there were also a few other distinguished examples which drew some attention in the province. From Paris came news that Rangeard, oracle of the Academy and omnicompetent *littérateur*, had taken his oath before the National Assembly.[68] Martin du Chesnay, formerly curé of Saint-Laud and now in charge of a large parish at Saumur, wrote to his friends in Angers in favour of compliance,[69] and an aged Cistercian, Couthard, ex-abbot of Chaloche and one-time censor of the Assembly of the Clergy of France, 'sanctified by fifty years of study and meditation and a life passed in the practice of all the Christian virtues' took the oath in the church of Saint-Pierre on 23 January.[70]

Some jurors were swayed by conviction or convinced by argument, while others (though these two classes cannot be neatly separated) were influenced by material considerations, the logic of patriotism being supplemented by the 'logic of the cooking-pot'. Reasonable incomes and a chance of rising to the very summit of the hierarchy were to be the lot of clergy of the new Constitutional Church: refusal of the oath meant loss of office to those who held it and loss of opportunity to those who did not. Maupoint, curé of Cantenay, who was a frequent visitor to Angers, caused great scandal by cynically admitting his motives to one of the vicaires of La Trinité. A friend of canon Louet of Saint-Maurice and canon Tremblay of Saint-Martin, and by natural instinct 'an aristocrat', Maupoint had no reason to approve of the work of the National Assembly—'cependant il faut vivre', he said, and took the oath.[71] Yves Besnard, a former vicaire of curé Robin, who returned to Angers to take over Saint-Laud, was probably more interested in acquiring an important town parish than in niceties of theological scruple, though he had studied these deeply.[72] There was a pool of unemployed priests in Angers now, chaplains and minor officials of the former chapters and monks on subsistence pensions; while for them the oath was not an obligation, to take it opened the door into the parochial ministry with its assured income and status in society. One suspects that this was why Lego and Faucheux, chaplains of the chapters of La Trinité and Saint-Martin, and the brothers Mongazon, readers at the cathedral, are found in the ranks of jurors.[73] As for monks and friars, they were completely disorientated: their habit received no respect, their vows no recognition, their future, in or out of their order, was doubtful, and in most cases their original homes and their relatives were far away from Angers. They had lost heart, they were 'tired of their state', they 'wished to be out of their community',[74] and so, generally rather late in the day, some of them slipped into the Constitutional Church: dom Locatelli and dom Soulet of Saint-Aubin, Hallé, the lonely Recollet, P. Ecot, sub-prior of the Carmelites, P. Boutou, a Dominican, and PP. Perrot and Garnault, Capuchins, Marchand, Roger, Ragot, Bonneau and Delange of the Cordeliers, followed in the end, in December, by their prior, P. Loyau.[75]

Three of our seventeen curés of Angers took the oath. One was Gaudin of Saint-Nicolas, an enthusiast, the others were Ferré of Saint-Samson and Follenfant of Saint-Maurice, both, significantly, being priests who were to retain their parishes under the new organization, only with extended boundaries and increased incomes. No longer would they be humble satellites of great ecclesiastical corporations; on the contrary, their parish offices would now be said in the magnificent churches of the old chapter of Saint-Maurice and of the abbey of Saint-Serge. Long ago Ferré had left the Mediterranean coast to make Angers his home, and for thirty years he had been comfortably installed in his charming little vicarage among the trees and gardens just outside the city walls; at the age of sixty, Follenfant had been appointed to Saint-Maurice, and since then had lived for fourteen years in the shadow of the cathedral, fulfilling with exemplary care the duties of a pastorate in which he hoped to end his days. It was hard for them to leave their people, their work and the pleasant niche in life which they loved and the new dignity which had accrued to them, and go out into the wilderness. To the very last moment, both hesitated and wavered. Follenfant was torn between advice he received in letters from Du Chesnay and the continual warnings of his own nephew and vicaire, while in a last-minute consultation the bishop used a mirror as a parable and told him that his own venerable white hair should be argument enough.[76] Ferré agreed to swear, then listened to the exhortations of his fellow parish priests and withdrew his promise on the very eve of the fatal day.[77] On 16 January, Follenfant, bemused and bewildered, took the oath, then retracted sadly a few days later.[78] It was not until 13 February that Ferré became a juror, but he remained adamant once the die was cast, and for ever afterwards refused to make any gesture of regret.[79]

So much for adherents of the Constitutional Church in Angers. In other parts of France, pathetic attempts were made to avoid a clear-cut decision. In some districts the clergy devised a common restrictive formula to which they all adhered;[80] elsewhere, individuals masked their compliance by wrapping up the legal formula in a long evasive discourse,[81] while municipal officers occasionally broke the letter of the law and allowed qualifications to be 'inserted in' or 'annexed to' the minute of proceedings.[82] There was no such category of 'demi-jurors' in Angers: the municipal officers were too un-co-operative for that. While the Ecclesiastical Committee of the National Assembly, thunderstruck by the schism, invariably told local administrators to accept any kind of explanation along with the oath,[83] from the very first the municipality of Angers made it clear that no restrictions would be allowed.[84] In any case, the majority of clergy in town was too clear-sighted to be willing to adopt such expedients.

But before turning to great questions of principle which were at stake, we should consider one flaw in the material provisions of the Civil Constitution which dissatisfied our parochial clergy of Angers. They saw the vast traditional endowments of their Church under the auctioneer's hammer, and it was impossible to avoid asking oneself the question whether the nation, which was gaining so much, was acting justly? According to Jacquemart, who had replaced Chatizel in the Assembly, stipends allotted to priests in small country parishes were inadequate.[85] Grégoire, the future leader of the Constitutional Church, hotly disavowed this assertion, but protested nevertheless against a greater injustice done to clergy of the towns. Behind a long overdue revision of parochial boundaries, he declared, lurked a base design of economizing at the expense of present incumbents—'money is our God'. There was no provision for delay until the death of present titulars, but all whose parishes were not to be conserved would simply be turned out. Most of these evicted priests would be too old to start life again, and celibacy and an ecclesiastical career would by now have deprived them of the relatives and ties with civil society which could have afforded them comfort in retirement.[86] In Angers, out of seventeen parish priests, only three would remain in office without being subject to popular election[87]—Follenfant and Ferré were two of them—and there were only eight new cures, a fact of which the mayor was uncomfortably conscious, for in his personal letter of 1 January 1791 he congratulated those whose parishes were to be retained and tried to reassure the others concerning employments which were destined for them in the future.[88] But what employments could be destined for them, and what could compensate for loss of the pastoral office? Inevitably, there was going to be a race for parishes, with the District electors deciding between candidates.

Since such competition would be indecent, the natural inclination of clerical society to adopt a common policy was doubly reinforced. In towns generally (Orleans was a conspicuous exception) the oath was refused, and while one reason may be found in the superior education and theological enlightenment of the urban priesthood,[89] probably more weight should be put on its greater cohesion. An isolated country curé would come into town to consult his oracles— as Bardoul of Brain-sur-Authion came to Angers to consult curé Robin—but once he returned home, fell a prey to rumours and apprehension.[90] In the closely-knit ecclesiastical society of a small provincial town, however, it was possible to gossip together and exchange news continually, to satisfy oneself concerning the honesty of other people, to haunt waverers and give mutual moral support all round. In a matter like this it was more important to hang together than to be right in theory: there was a primary duty to be loyal to one's colleagues. Away in southern France, the abbé Veri, who had long ago ceased to exercise any sacerdotal functions, put this point of honour very clearly. It was impossible, he said, 'to desert one's order, one's brothers, one's companions at arms. Whoever betrays the duties of fraternity is the most infamous of men.'[91] After all, if the clergy of France remained reasonably united, they could not be defeated, and the Assembly would have to seek some compromise. On 28 January, vicaire Houdet of La Trinité was consoling himself for following his conscience and thus missing the new parish for which he had yearned. He believed that all over France the oath was being resisted, and that, as a result, the Assembly was already giving secret orders to local authorities not to elect new bishops—

'this uniformity of conduct in the whole body will probably bring about the salvation of all its members, and, one might add, the salvation of religion too'.[92]

Doubts and hesitations of individuals were thus suppressed, and a premium, as it were, was put on unanimity one way or another. Normally, the need for unity might be expected to be conducive to compromise; as it was, the circumstances in which the Civil Constitution was being put forward were exasperating and just as calculated to favour a unanimity in refusal. By imposing an oath, the National Assembly had cruelly narrowed decision into a dilemma which few clergy wished to face.[93] Whether the Church could or ought, or ultimately would accept the Civil Constitution, was no longer relevant. Representatives of the nation had legislated in matters ecclesiastical on their own authority and were now demanding adhesion to their decrees before the Church had spoken. It was as simple—and as difficult—as that. The clergy of Angers were being asked to accept a *fait accompli* and to give a forthright subscription to the will of the representatives of the nation.

Yet by now, with the exception of a few enthusiasts, they had learnt to be suspicious of the whole tendency of the National Assembly's policy, which was directed towards founding a state Church which bore only a delusory external resemblance to the ideals of the clerical order. Before returning to Soulaines Chatizel had demonstrated the gulf between these two conceptions by casting his vote against the granting of rights of citizenship to Jews.[94] In their *cahier*, the clergy of Anjou had asked for a restoration of synodical discipline: lay election to pastoral offices involved a very different view of the relation of the Church to civil society, for to fight for the independent status of curés *vis-à-vis* bishops was one thing, and to make both parties equally dependent on the common run of voting citizens was another. As the content of the decrees was suspect, so, too, the manner of their enforcement implied a concept of spiritual and temporal relationships in which the state, in the last resort, dictated. 'The curés', said Gruget, 'would not have refused their consent if canonical forms had been observed; but our legislators did not wish to do this. They wished to be the only ones capable of making all these changes.'[95] News from Paris indicated that churchmen who were deputies had already revolted against the will of the Assembly in which they sat, and that even after the attempted roll-call of 4 January and a full outcry of anti-clerical demonstrations, only one-third of them had adhered to the Civil Constitution. It was said that, in the capital, ne'er-do-wells were being hired to dress as priests and take the oath to bolster up the morale of patriots—honest Gruget had this story of a man who live at Montrevault, who had been told it by his wife, who had learnt it from a chimney-sweep.[96] In Angers itself, clergy and revolutionary bourgeoisie had drifted apart. Since the riots of September 1790 there was a hardening of anti-clerical feeling. A country vicaire of Anjou complained that 'priests are nothing more now than valets . . . we are not yet at the end of the drama: they want to marry us off and make us cuckolds'.[97] To confirm his fears, *L'Observateur Provincial*, which so smugly cited St. Paul and the Council of Chalcedon in favour of the Civil Constitution, at the end of December embarked upon a coarse and lurid campaign against clerical celibacy.[98] In this same month, the Department saw its first 'civic baptism' in the church of Saint-Pierre, when god-parents swore allegiance to Nation, Law and King, a liturgical innovation which received full discussion in the patriotic press, in spite of the bishop's pleas against publicity.[99] The gloss of respectability on revolutionary enthusiasm was wearing thin. The attitude of departmental and municipal officers concerning the oath did not help matters. Their portentous solicitation and pompous insistence was galling and degrading. As curé Robin pointed out, his conscience did not need enlightening by the brothers Delaunay 'to whom he had never been able to teach the catechism'.[100]

The honeymoon period was over, and the clergy, who in 1789 had saved the Revolution, would now decide their attitude by strict formulae of logic, and exacting theological logic at that. Angers, seat of a bishop, a flourishing Seminary where most local priests had been educated, and a Faculty of Theology which proudly boasted an unbroken record of inerrancy, was well provided with focal points of discussion and decision. Not a single doctor of the Faculty took the oath.[101] Most of them were in any case ex-canons, and members of old collegiate churches suppressed by the Civil Constitution were under no inclination to comply, even if the oath had been formally applicable to them, which it was not. Theological doctors in the parochial ministry, Robin of Saint-Pierre, Boumard of Sainte-Croix, Bernier of Saint-Laud, Frontault of Saint-Aubin des Ponts de Cé and Tardif, vicaire of La Trinité, were as unyielding. Martin du Chesnay wrote from Saumur to Boumard as he had written to Follenfant; his letter was coldly returned.[102] Bernier was not seduced by his personal ambitions and hopes for an extension of his newly-won parish. Curé Robin was unpredictable and reckless, and he yearned for a few peaceful years at the end of his days, to publish his remaining manuscripts[103] and to enjoy the house which he had reconstructed at the expense of so much litigation. Even so, he refused to subscribe —though he made no parade of martyrdom, and covered his confusion at finding himself submerged in an orthodox majority by the buffoonery of pretending that he would reconsider if his title of 'premier curé cardinal de la ville d'Angers' was recognized.[104] Before the turn of the year, M. Meilloc, superior of the Seminary, had been distributing his brochure *Préservatif contre le Schisme*, and he now carried all of his staff and most of his pupils with him in opposition to the Civil Constitution.[105] Letters went out to sleepy rural hamlets, bringing old students up to date on principles of casuistry and reminding them that 'we have a greater master to hear and to obey than the National Assembly'.[106] In the countryside, such communications were only an incidental factor in decisions—M. Elias, curé of Saint-Barthélemy and brother of one of the directors, took his oath in spite of all the best efforts of the Sulpiciens;[107] but in town, personal consultations and example exercised a more constant effect. To the very end, the Seminary was in the van of resistance, witness a subject for meditation laid down for students on the feast of St. Joseph, even as the cathedral bells thundered their schismatic welcome for the solemn entry of the new constitutional bishop— 'that wicked pastors are the most redoubtable scourge that God uses to afflict his people'.[108]

Long ago, in the controversy over Unigenitus, the Seminary and the Faculty of Theology had taken up an attitude to complicated problems of authority in the Church. Curé Boumard, saboteur of capitular processions and exponent of the rights of parish priests, might have sympathy with many clauses of the Civil Constitution, but doctor Boumard of the Faculty could not possibly approve it in entirety. Years ago he had aroused the ire of Jansenist controversialists in the capital by his adherence to the thesis that ultimate authority in the Church rests with the Pope and a majority of the episcopate, and that a bishop's silence in face of a papal directive implied consent.[109] Here were propositions which could form a basis for theological discussion in a crisis of obedience. 'The Church is the body of bishops with the sovereign pontiff at their head', wrote the abbé Supervielle, chaplain to the nuns of Le Calvaire, on 15 January, in an article which appeared in a royalist paper in Paris a few days later.[110] Cotelle de la Blandinière, the great theologian, whose monumental tomes were on the shelves of every presbytery in Anjou, had now left the diocese, but if anyone had written to him for advice, he would have received a similar answer.[111] There is no sign here of the idea of episcopal Gallicanism, that a national council might have been an alternative to a Roman pronouncement, and one might wonder whether our clergy of Anjou, independently of a chain of miscalculations which had thrown exclusive power of decision into papal hands, would have turned to the Pope rather than to the episcopate for their lead. It is difficult to be sure. They rarely looked southwards towards Avignon and Rome, and when they did, what picture formed in their minds—that given in curé Robin's Rabelaisian diary of his pilgrimage, or Jacquemart's most 'humanitarian and paternal' government in the world?[112] Whatever the answer, the question now at issue was a doctrinal one, not one of sympathies, and in doctrine authorities spoke with two voices. In 1782 Chatizel had been willing to magnify papal rights as part of his design to depress those of bishops, an early example of ultramontanism as an epiphenomenon of the lower clergy's restlessness under episcopal 'despotism'. And yet, in conformity with the Gallican Articles of 1682, Chatizel made it quite clear that popes were not infallible and that they could exercise no temporal power in France.[113] Christ gave authority to His Church in general, and gives it directly to bishops and to curés, even though their bulls and visas come from Rome.[114] It is just possible that provincial councils could give marriage dispensations instead of the Pope, and it is certainly true that bishops could be confirmed in their office by metropolitans.[115] The Holy See had power, but not exclusive power; indeed, as St. Hugh of Lincoln said (though his words are daring), the Holy See can be disobeyed, for it has power only for edification.[116] But when all this is said, Chatizel still regarded the 'Bishop of Rome' as 'the Head of the Church and the centre of unity'. At his episcopal town were the tombs of the apostles and there Paul's extraordinary commission had expired and was united to Peter's chair. Rome was 'that refuge where passions have no sway, to which error has no access. Throughout the centuries the voice of Peter is heard in that of his successors.'[117] The voice of Peter, free from errors and passion, always provided that he was speaking only for edification, with no interference in things temporal and subject to the authority of the Church in general—here was matter for endless dispute in vicarage parlours while the candle dripped its grease on to Cotelle de la Blandinière's handbooks and tattered old notes of Seminary courses.

As it happened, by its precipitation the National Assembly had made such discussions unnecessary. Rome, whatever its ultimate limit of authority might be, must speak and lead this time, for the Church of France had been left with no alternative 'centre of unity' or guidance, no other authoritative herald. At the end of October, 1790, the bishops, led by Boisgelin, had admitted as much. Only the Pope could save the country from schism. Four months before this statement was issued, the Pope had, in fact, condemned the Civil Constitution, only his condemnation had been kept secret, both by the executive government and by the Vatican. Thus, this crisis of January 1791 engulfed the Clergy of France at a time when the papal attitude was still not known. In Angers, however, there was a circumstantial rumour, amounting to a certainty, that

Rome had spoken, for a papal 'brief' dated 22 September 1790 was in circulation.[118] Mayor de Houlières and Delaunay, *procureur général syndic* of the Department, denounced it on 20 January[119] and sent a copy of this 'incendiary' document to the Ecclesiastical Committee of the National Assembly five days later.[120] It so happened that the local authorities were right when they declared this 'papal' rescript fraudulent, but there is little doubt that they would have used similar arguments against a genuine pronouncement. In any case, the damage was done, and when the authentic voice of Rome was heard, it spoke with the accents of the pious forger.

Seminary and Faculty of Theology were solid in opposition to the oath, and to their influence was added that of the communities of nuns, zealous for orthodoxy, determined to have no communication with schismatics, and ready to cry 'scandal, impiety and heresy' against all jurors.[121] If patriots were to find a respectable figure-head for their cause, their one hope was to win the pliant bishop, who had so far distinguished himself by facile adherence to all constitutional *clichés*. Although to the very last, rumours of his willingness to yield were in circulation, bishop de Lorry had never had any intention either of taking the oath himself or of urging anyone to decisive action for it or, indeed, against it. He was idle and comfort-loving, but there was nothing mercenary or mean in his character. His lot was cast with the vast majority of his episcopal colleagues.[122] It was impossible for him to be a Gobel, a Jarente or a Talleyrand, for that would be to make himself an object of angry recrimination by some and of too vociferous acclamation by others. Thanks to birth and favour he had proceeded with easy assurance into high office which he did not deserve. With the same aristocratic dignity, he left it when his hour struck.

On 6 February, the electors of the Department met at Saint-Maurice and chose Hugues Pelletier, a native of Angers and now *prieur-curé* of Beaufort, as their new bishop. M. de Lorry, lodging ingloriously in the Seminary, received his supplanter without reproaches,[123] and left town on 18 March, two days before the ceremonial installation. Early in May, the furniture of the episcopal palace was put up for auction. The municipality acquired a minimum from this sale to make the palace austerely habitable for its new bishop, while superfluities of the old régime, wardrobes and bureaux, beds of many sorts with canopies and decorations, fire-dogs and chimney-irons in resplendent gilt, and armchairs upholstered in damask and velvet were carted away by their purchasers.[124] Bishop Pelletier's arrangements were as make-shift as his furniture. No neighbouring bishop would consent to join in his consecration, so he had to travel up to Paris for the purpose.[125] When he took possession of his cathedral, only a dozen to fifteen priests were available to walk in procession, a figure which patriots multiplied by four or five to keep up revolutionary appearances.[126] The episcopal-vicars who were appointed were an undistinguished if not absurd collection: a former vicaire of Saint-Maurille brought back from the diocese of Blois, Voillemont, master of the choir school, and Guillier de la Touche, the mad curé of Epiré who lived on curdled milk and took his exercise on a treadmill.[127] Pelletier was a grave priest of unblemished reputation, but everyone conspired to blacken him, or at very least to find him ridiculous. Some declared that when he was elected he had read his speech of acceptance from a paper concealed in his hat;[128] Chatizel accused him of having painted extracts from Voltaire and Rousseau on his vicarage walls.[129] Anonymous letters were delivered at the palace, 'full of holy censures and menaces of the other world, and, what is worse, of this one too'.[130]

On 26 March the new curés who had been elected by the District Assembly a fortnight before[131] arrived to take possession of their churches, escorted by detachments of the National Guard, 'like Judas, accompanied by soldiers'. Ferré stayed at Saint-Samson of course, Gaudin took over Saint-Jacques, a country priest was installed at Saint-Pierre; 'il faut vivre' Maupoint got La Trinité, and Besnard, studious and unspiritual, came back to Angers as curé of Saint-Laud. Two local vicaires were also promoted, Taillebuis, formerly of Saint-Pierre, going to the living of Saint-Nicolas, and Viger, fortified by administrative connexions, obtained La Madeleine. At Saint-Laud, Bernier had inspired a whimsical welcome for his successor. Plate and vases were locked away, candles doctored so they would not light, the priestly vestments were cunningly sewn up, and the bell-ropes hitched aloft out of reach.[132] Otherwise, all was quiet at Angers, too quiet in fact, for the faithful were conspicuous by their absence from the masses of their new pastors.[133] Legacies of medieval piety and traditions of generations had been squandered, and the days of chapters and monasteries, bells, candles, processions, social conformity and ecclesiastical domination were over. The old régime in Angers had ended.

CHAPTER XV

EPILOGUE: THE FATE OF INDIVIDUALS

OUR study of ecclesiastical society in Angers at the end of the old régime is concluded, but social history is primarily a history of persons, and it would be austere and abrupt to insist on cutting their story short at the moment of the collapse of the old order. To describe their ultimate fate with strict justice is not easy, for the destruction of an established society is inevitably a tragic process; tragic events arouse sympathy and too much sympathy may be a foe to impartiality. The Revolution had its ideals and enthusiasms, its own inner logic and its peculiar meed of tragedy for its own sincerest adherents, but these, not being subjects of our study, cannot be considered in that detail of motive and human circumstance which alone leads to sympathetic understanding. We can review the revolutionary events externally only, as if they were unmotivated facts, like rain falling on the just and the unjust, or like shell-fire directed upon an objective by gunners who are thinking in terms of strategic contours and not of individuals. As war is cruel, so the Revolution was cruel, and here, we are concerned solely with tracing the history of a few of its victims who were cast adrift in a new world and trapped in a monstrous procession of events which they never understood and which they were powerless to influence.

Some of our clergy of Angers had been seminarists when M. Emery was superior and they remembered a famous remark of his which turned out to be a prophecy. He spoke in anger, suppressing a careless custom which had arisen of leaving the refectory at the end of the martyrology and at the beginning of the formula commending those who had suffered but had no memorial. 'You can never expect that your name will one day be admitted to the martyrology, but you can very reasonably hope that one day you will be included in the *alibi*.'[1]

The epilogue which follows is not meant to be fully-rounded history. It is an essay on some forgotten Angevin ecclesiastics of the *alibi aliorum*.

I. FROM CIVIL CONSTITUTION TO TERROR

The rest of this year 1791 accorded with its beginning. Curé Robin whimsically reflected that old prophecies were coming true—a great earthquake in 1755, an outpouring of God's wrath in 1790, with revolution, famine and war close at hand—a prelude to the stars going out in 1799 and the end of the world.[2] At the end of March canon Le Noir de la Cochetière sadly left Angers for Paris, and there, brooding amid the ruins of the Bastille, foresaw a future when liberty, that 'blessing from heaven', would become 'the scourge of the earth'.[3] As he had feared, the months that followed were filled with religious strife and growing bitterness. Stones were thrown at Besnard when he processed to the cemetery of Saint-Laud to bless the tombs on Palm Sunday. Bernier, his predecessor in the cure, who was held responsible for this riot, escaped from the vengeance of the National Guard by a matter of minutes, being present at vespers at Toussaint when a force of armed men surrounded the house of canon Gautreau where he had been lodging. Two women who had mocked at constitutional religious ceremonies were pilloried.[4] While parish churches were deserted, people flocked to hear the masses of religious communities. Early in April the administrators of Maine-et-Loire closed all monastic chapels and oratories and at the end of that month ordered the Carmelite friars, the Cordeliers and the Augustins to evacuate their houses and depart to Fontevraud.[5] The Frères des Écoles Chrétiennes feared that the oath might be next demanded of them and had also begun to murmur that, in view of the Rights of Man, they ought to be paid for their toil. Their discontent became known and in April it was rumoured that they, too, would be leaving. This was a very different question. The Departmental, District and Municipal authorities, panic-stricken at the prospect of losing an institution of practical utility, constrained them to stay.[6]

The new constitutional bishop bravely toiled on, administering a few shreds of his diocese. In May he announced that the Seminary would re-open and he optimistically asked the secular authorities to seek out thirty copies of the diocesan theological handbooks for the use of its students.[7] A stern pastoral letter forbade the faithful to make their Easter Communions outside their parish churches.[8] Only patriots heeded these exhortations. Such influence as the new bishop exercised was derived, not from his mitre or his palace, but from his membership of the Club. Here at the convent of the Jacobins, the *Club des Amis de la Constitution*, locally known as the *Club de l'Est*, gathered together the cream of the Angevin bourgeoisie, with Bénaben of the Oratory as their secretary and spokesman. As yet their temper was respectful towards monarchy, though subordinating it always to the General Will, and as far as the Church concerned them, they regarded it as a prop to the new Constitution and a guarantor of that equality which churchmen in the past had done their best to subvert.[9]

Sullen discontent seethed in the countryside. In the Districts of

Angers and Vihiers a considerable number of curés had remained in office, fortified as they were by the nearness of Angers and Saumur with their National Guards and revolutionary bourgeoisie, but in the Districts of Cholet and Saint-Florent out of 83 parish priests there were only six jurors.[10] Obstinately faithful to their old pastors, the peasants greeted intruders with silent contempt, or obloquy, or worse. The ousted clergy still remained in the midst of their congregations, presiding over services in barns and kitchens. Rabin of Notre-Dame de Cholet, the former left-wing clerical deputy, now a non-juror, said open-air masses before congregations of two or three thousand people.[11]

Schism had become a menace to the stability of the new political order, so that when Louis XVI attempted to escape from France at the end of June, various local authorities instinctively reacted by interning all non-juring priests within the areas of their jurisdiction. News of the flight to Varennes reached Maine-et-Loire on the morning of the feast of Corpus Christi, the day of the *Sacre*. After marching solemnly in that once-famous procession, the departmental administrators immediately instituted measures to suppress clerical pamphlets which were stirring up the countryside. On the following day they ordered all refractory priests to be brought to Angers and kept there under surveillance.[12] It was a beginning of penal measures against the clergy. The King's flight had conjured up spectres of civil and foreign war. Perrochel, ex-abbot of Toussaint, wrote from Paris denouncing 'cowardly tyrants' who 'abandon the fatherland which has laden them with benefits' and asking the Department to reserve him a place as a soldier in its volunteer battalions.[13] Men now talked of extreme solutions. J.-B. Cordier, a youth who had played Voltaire in Joachim Proust's masquerade three years ago, made a reckless republican speech in the *Club des Amis de la Constitution* of Angers, saying that the inviolability of the King was as absurd as the infallibility of the Pope.[14] Some of the priests under surveillance were actually imprisoned in the Little Seminary. Fear bred cruelty; the pillory was not good enough now for women who mocked at the Constitutional Church—they were whipped naked at cross-roads.[15]

Meanwhile the municipal authorities were fortifying the position of the national clergy in less ferocious ways: they ensured that the procession of the *Sacre* was held and voted wages to choir-men who were still performing their duties, in order to give divine service 'all the majesty that is due to it'.[16] Simultaneously, unwanted churches were being demolished. Saint-Maimbeuf, Sainte-Croix, Saint-Maurille and Saint-Pierre were now reduced to ruins and Saint-Martin, stripped of ecclesiastical furniture, was a store.[17] The abbey of Toussaint was soon to be purchased by the town as an auxiliary barracks for passing troops.[18] Saint-Nicolas was unvisited now except by pilferers who hauled away doors and window-frames, marble slabs, iron railings.[19] A new club, the *Club de l'Ouest*, a proletarian and lower-middle-class counterpart to the *Amis de la Constitution*, had been formed in May, and the church of Saint-Jacques was allotted to it as a meeting-place until it moved within the walls into more convenient quarters in the chapel of the convent of the Bon Pasteur.[20] Tenants of former ecclesiastical properties who had not troubled to register their leases under the old régime found themselves faced with eviction orders from new landlords.[21] Mévolhon of the Oratory was proposing to consolidate the Revolution by a comprehensive scheme of spelling reform[22] and other enthusiasts were busy with a new plan of street names which would eliminate religious prejudices—reference to the Constitution in place of the Cross, Social Virtues in place of All Saints, Washington instead of Saint-Aigan and J.-J. Rousseau in place of the Visitation of Our Lady. A wit contrived to have the rue du Ronceray changed into the impasse Amoureux, but there was grimmer and less conscious humour in the promotion of the rue Creuse to the rue de la Liberté.[23]

On 7 August the *Club de l'Est* decided to petition the National Assembly to expel all refractory priests, that 'malevolent horde'.[24] As it happened, such sentiments were temporarily inapposite. Louis XVI renewed his oath to the Constitution, thereby becoming officially reconciled to his suspicious subjects, elections for a new Assembly went forward and the Constituents marked the end of their labours by voting an amnesty. This was duly proclaimed in Angers on 16 September, when the president and *syndic* of the Department went in person to the Little Seminary to announce to the imprisoned clergy that they were once more at liberty.[25] Yet there was no relaxation of tension in the countryside. Even at Andard, which was not too far from town, Rangeard could hear the roll of insurrectionary drums and asked for some 'good citizens' to be sent out to show themselves armed within his parish boundaries.[26] Early in its career, on 21 October, the Legislative Assembly began to discuss the nation's religious crisis. Tardily but sincerely, the Constituents had turned towards liberalism, proclaiming an amnesty and separating the Civil Constitution of the Clergy from the Constitution proper. But members of this first Assembly had not been re-eligible for the second and thus another generation of revolutionary legislators had been called into being. Many deputies came up to Paris directly from departmental administrations with fresh memories of forays, insults and pious propaganda and with a crude prejudice in favour of ruthless solutions. Delaunay of Maine-et-Loire was one of them and his exaggerated accounts of assemblies, riots and sieges in the Angevin countryside had a significant effect in promoting stern penal legislation.[27] On 29 November the Legislative Assembly passed its coercion law by which all refractory ecclesiastics could be deprived of their pensions and expelled from communes where troubles had occurred. No loophole was devised for clergy who wished to be faithful to both Church and country: no distinction was made between conscientious obstinacy and counter-Revolutionary agitation.

Tension and suspicion increased everywhere as manœuvres of ambitious intriguers of both right and left and blind patriotic fanaticism drove the nation towards war. In Angers a first battalion of Volunteers to fight the foreign foe had been formed in September. In December the *Club de l'Est* proclaimed its enthusiasm to march against tyrants. 'Let the standard of war be unfurled, it is the will of the people', cried the *Journal de Maine-et-Loire*. At a joint session of the *Club de l'Est* and the *Club de l'Ouest* in March 1792, Bénaben dramatically indicated the flags of France, England, America and Poland, a potential federation of free peoples before which despots would tremble—he proposed to give the latter fair warning by sending them copies of the minutes of this meeting. Angevin patriots believed that France would be invincible, even though, as La Revellière-Lépeaux reminded them, 'proud nobles and knavish priests prolong our internal dissensions'.[28] On 1 February the Department took its precautions against clerical knavery, against 'the black aristocrats'. Once again, all non-juring priests were to be concentrated in Angers; they were not to be allowed to stray more than half a league from town and were to be obliged to answer a daily roll-call.[29] The abbé Roussel of Saint-Maurille, 'homeless, penniless and without resources', published a warning that these severities would defeat their own object. 'You know only too well, Sire,' he wrote, apostrophizing the King, 'of what men are capable when they believe that they are acting from purely patriotic motives. What then will they not do when they believe that they are but following their consciences and striving to preserve or regain their churches, altars and religion?' [30] The urban bourgeoisie was under no illusions about his meaning: the west country was on the verge of a new and terrible *jacquerie*.

By the beginning of June more than 400 priests[31] were concentrated under surveillance in Angers, reporting twice a day at the town hall amid jeers, but surrounded by their faithful peasants on market days. The great fair of Corpus Christi began on 7 June, bringing many more country-people into town, so that in the interests of public order roll-calls had to be transferred to the other side of town at Saint-Aubin. '*Enfermez-les*—lock them up . . . as much for their own safety as for ours', was the tenor of a petition signed by 200 prosperous citizens led by Bénaben. On the 17th the National Guard took matters into its own hands. Priests reporting at Saint-Aubin found themselves surrounded by armed men, arrested, and interned in the Seminaries. When the mayor asked who was in charge, the self-appointed jailers said that they all were, and when he tried to read them an extract from the official laws they put their hats on their bayonets and shouted 'Vive la Nation! Vive la Liberté!' [32] '*Salus populi suprema lex*', said the commander of the National Guard, taking his cue from his subordinates, and the departmental authorities acquiesced in this reading of the situation.[33]

A first general law of proscription against the clergy was voted by the Legislative Assembly on 26 May. Priests were treated as members of a fifth column in league with the Emperor and the émigrés; any one of them who was denounced by twenty 'active' citizens was immediately subject to deportation. Louis XVI refused to sanction this measure and so hastened his own inevitable ruin. On 20 June a Parisian mob invaded the Tuileries. On 10 August the Sections overthrew the throne. Refractories were now ordered to leave France, and a new oath, that of 'Liberty and Equality', was devised for all priests, whether office-holders or not. When news of the fall of the throne reached Angers, any non-jurors who were still at liberty (and who could still be found) were immediately interned.[34] The Seminary became a crowded prison-camp—there were no students here now, for bishop Pelletier's exiguous stream of ordinands had quite dried up.[35] In the old days its inmates had competed to be one of the apostolic twelve who had a room with a fire-place; there were no fires now, and priests were herded together on straw and fed on bread and water.[36]

The shadow of civil war crept nearer. On 26 August a detachment of National Guards marched out to defend the District of Châtillon against its local peasantry. Four days later news came of the fall of Longwy on the north-east frontier. The Angevin volunteers at Verdun would be next to face the terrible Prussian infantry, and behind them the road to Paris lay open. A band of 144 priests from Le Mans arrived in Angers on 1 September on their way to the coast. National Guards with bayonets kept back vindictive crowds as they were conducted to their staging-post at the castle.[37] Eleven days later at six in the morning a convoy of deportees left Angers for Nantes. There were 264 priests from the Seminary and those of Le Mans from the castle, some on foot, some riding in carriages. For escort they had 500 National Guards and police, with two artillery pieces.[38] On the 14th they arrived at Nantes, where they were well treated, though officious patriots protested against pedlars being allowed to sell them knives and amateur strategists advised against deportation to Spain lest the enemy should acquire clerical guides for a coastal invasion.[39] A week later embarkation proceeded on two ships, the *Didon* and the *Français*. A storm delayed sailing for a fortnight, but on 2 October, with a favourable north wind, the vessels left Nantes with their cruelly crowded cargoes,[40]—the curé of Saint-Michel du Tertre and three of his four vicaires, the curé of Saint-Denis, the vicaires of Sainte-Croix, Saint-Laud and Saint-Martin, dean de Villeneuve and canon Brossier of the cathedral, canon Touchet of Saint-Maurille, dean Frémond of Saint-Martin and dean de Mantelon of Saint-Pierre, Montalant and Breton of the Little Seminary, P. Donat of the Capuchins, dom Foulard and dom Julliot of Lesvière . . . these, and many others, saw the coast of France fade behind them and wondered what existence awaited them amid the monks and superstitions and sun-parched wastes of Spain.[41]

Aged and infirm priests were exempt from deportation and 125 of them remained in the Seminary at Angers. Young Gouppil, son of our churchwarden of Saint-Evroul and nephew of its curé (who was one of the prisoners) came over from his apothecary's shop with remedies for the sick who could pay—as for those who could not, he cannily insisted that the 'nation' must agree to meet his bills first.[42] Curé Robin was there and at some time during his captivity he wrote the last of his angry and eloquent letters, addressed to the municipality, District and Department. After all his work for historical learning and for his parish, he said, at the age of 79 he found himself penniless and in jail, and he asked for liberty in the name of justice, truth and humanity, 'three attributes of the Divinity, a guiding principle of our life, a source of all brotherhood in the world and of the beauteous order which here prevails, three virtues which pagan antiquity deified, so to speak, in the person of heroes and great leaders who were just, honest and magnanimous, three virtues which are worthy of your attention, gentlemen'.[43] Liberty was out of the question but on 10 October the authorities offered priests in the Seminary another opportunity to choose deportation. Only one elected to leave.[44] This was a disappointment to the National Guards who complained at having to be absent from their firesides to guard 'a considerable quantity of idiots, bigots and fanatics'. Besides, they added, they wanted to fight against foreign despots. This reluctance of the jailers to continue their work resulted in the prisoners being moved to pleasanter surroundings at the Rossignolerie, where the Frères des Écoles Chrétiennes still held their classes. Canon Tremblay of Saint-Martin died there soon, though not before he had arranged for his little fortune, put out at interest to a cloth merchant, to be preserved for his heirs.[45] He was lucky in the occasion of his death, for as it turned out, by a process of unnatural selection the deportation laws had spared the old and infirm for execution.

Meanwhile the nunneries of Angers were being closed by a simultaneous application of a law of 18 August 1792 (which suppressed all congregations) and of the decree enforcing the new oath of Liberty and Equality. The *Club de l'Est* hastened progress by a discussion of the futilities of convent education. Girls, they declared, had been made into coquettes lacking in practical accomplishments and clinging to distinctions of the old régime. 'Dolls might be suited to slaves but free men want women.' Communities of sisters who cared for the sick were spared but all other nuns were ordered by the municipality to leave their houses. Some returned to their families, others formed themselves into 'cells' and lived in rented rooms, working for their living and maintaining their common devotions.[46] New educational arrangements to make girls into revolutionary women had not yet been devised; the old curriculum, however, was still thought adequate for boys, always provided that metaphysics were omitted, 'being more fitting to mislead the mind than to enlighten it'. Early in November Bénaben and seven other ex-Oratorian teachers reopened the Collège d'Anjou, the municipality praising their zeal but failing to pay their salaries.[47] Twenty-seven Frères des Écoles Chrétiennes took the new oath of Liberty and Equality and, though their congregation was dissolved, they carried on their teaching functions as private individuals.

Sacks of provisions were now stacked high around the tombs of the Angevin magistracy in the church of Saint-Michel du Tertre, Saint-Martin remained a book-store, and workmen were demolishing medieval tombs and ornaments in the church of the Augustins to enable the *Club de l'Ouest* to meet there with republican dignity.[48] Saint-Michel de la Palud was transformed into a foundry: parishes were allowed to keep one bell apiece and the rest were carted there to be melted into cannon balls.[49] The monastery of Saint-Serge was a depôt for pictures and statuary, the priory of Lesvière housed the long-projected foundling hospital,[50] vagrants were camping in the Cordeliers and blackening the walls with their cooking fires.[51] Utility had reached its heyday. The municipality was hoping to make the house of the Visitation into yet another barracks, and sent a committee of inspection to the episcopal palace to survey its suitability for a combined criminal court and police station.[52]

In making this proposal, no one considered bishop Pelletier's feelings. He was a peace-loving man who pathetically sought to win sympathy from both sides. In spring, when the snuff-taking abbé Ferrand of the old Seminary had died, the constitutional bishop attended his funeral service;[53] in autumn when the club demanded emancipated women for wives, Pelletier, secure in his celibacy, joined Bénaben in signing the proceedings.[54] Yet the frosty contempt of supporters of orthodoxy was not thawed and, crueller still, patriots were beginning to exhibit an open indifference towards the Church which they nominally supported. St. Luke had been banished from the title-page of university theses in favour of a cap of liberty[55] and at least two couples had taken the new Constitution at its face value and united themselves in civil marriage before a Justice of the Peace without any religious rite.[56] When in October Angers mourned its hero Beaurepaire, commander of the first battalion of volunteers, there was no ecclesiastical ceremony. The bishop was not invited and Voillemont, his episcopal-vicar, dominated proceedings in his lay capacity of conductor of massed choirs.[57] Music, rather than the priesthood, had always been the vocation of this former choirmaster of Saint-Maurice, who now, at the beginning of his career as director of revolutionary festivities, was offering to teach the Marseillaise 'to all his comrades in general who have any sort of voice. He will regard it as a genuine pleasure', he announced, 'to teach them kindly and with all possible patience.' [58]

Had he obeyed the law, Bernier, the dispossessed curé of Saint-Laud, would have been an exile in Spain.[59] But on 14 September, the day his contemporaries arrived at Nantes for deportation, he had been hiding in a farmhouse in an 'almost inaccessible' corner of the countryside. News of the massacres in Paris had just arrived. He saw the emotion of the peasants around him—'a single spark falling on this centre of discontent', he wrote,[60] 'would, I believe, produce a vast conflagration. God grant that the Revolution does not go to this extremity.' But further news from the capital showed that the revolutionary events were moving on into still more desperate courses. On 21 January 1793 Louis XVI was executed. War with England and Holland followed swiftly. More recruits were needed for the frontiers and the Convention ordered a national levy of 300,000 men. It was a restoration of the dreaded conscription of the old régime with the same old privileges for the bourgeoisie in the form of exemption for officials. The horrors of the last autumn campaign had been widely related by deserters from the first battalion of volunteers of Maine-et-Loire who had crept back home in droves after their *débâcle* at Verdun.[61] An unpopular government which had deprived the peasants of their 'good priests' and their inoffensive King was proposing to march away their sons to distant battlefields. Here was that fatal spark which, as Bernier had feared, set the west country aflame.

Tumults began at Cholet on 2 March. On the 12th peasant bands sacked Saint-Florent. Country squires and ex-army officers joined the rebels and gave them organization and purpose. In the Mauges a 'Catholic and Royalist Army' was formed under La Rochejaquelain, Bonchamp, d'Elbée and Stofflet—and the fugitive abbé Bernier came into their camp and became a member of their council of government. By 9 June the Vendeans had seized Saumur. Angers was now in danger and its citizens were talking openly of surrender to the 'brigands' and showing hostility to republican troops.[62] The Departmental authorities and their armed forces withdrew. On 20 June the city was occupied by the royalists. There was no pillage, only office furniture of republican bureaucrats, the guillotine, the patriotic altar and tree of fraternity were destroyed.[63] Priests still in the Rossignolerie were released and enjoyed a few illusory days of freedom. Curé Gruget and two of his vicaires emerged from their hiding-places to hear confessions night and day in the church of La Trinité, whose steeple now flew the white flag of the Bourbons.[64] But Bernier did not attempt to take over his parish of Saint-Laud again;[65] the occupation, he knew, could be no more than an incident of civil war. And so it was. The Vendean army marched on towards Nantes and early in July the republican forces returned.

The restoration of the tricolour above the church of La Trinité marks the beginning of terrorist rule in Angers. A *comité de surveillance* met from henceforward at the *évêché* to direct arrests of suspects—one of its members was dom Boniface, a former monk of Saint-Aubin, another was Rosé, once a choir-man at Saint-Maurice.[66] At the Jacobins a military commission was established to dispense summary justice to traitors. Directing everything were *représentants en mission* of the Convention, for the Department and District authorities, discredited by 'Girondin' and 'federalist' leanings, were removed from office in September for 'lack of revolutionary energy'. The Seminary, the Ursulines and La Fidelité were again tenanted— by suspects under guard. By the end of November the cathedral itself was full of Vendean prisoners, men and women, herded there 'until their departure', as the president of the military commission euphemistically put it. Cruel fighting was raging in the countryside. Perrochel, ex-abbot of Toussaint and now a captain of dragoons in revolutionary service, was shot through the chest in a skirmish at Martigné-Brienne,[67] and in September a large Angevin detachment was cut down at Pont-Barré, so that, it was said, there was hardly a family in town which had not lost a father, son or husband.[68] Civil war, with its tragedy and bitterness, set its stamp on every heart and every activity.

All refractory priests who could be found were back under lock and key at the Rossignolerie. A play of local composition acted in Angers in November (and highly recommended by the revolutionary committee as containing none of the intrigues of Molière) described them as 'heartless and inhuman tigers'.[69] The sisters of Saint-Vincent de Paul were summoned to take the civic oath and abandon ecclesiastical costume. They refused, and were given notice to leave, which did not become immediately effective, as a municipal appeal for patriotic women to take their places met with no response.[70] Religious monuments were mutilated and profaned—at the Cordeliers workmen played ball with the casket containing the heart of good Duke René.[71] Educational activities were swallowed up by war. The Collège d'Anjou became a warehouse for flour and Bénaben and three other masters went off as civil commissioners to the armies. Their colleague Mévolhan, now by revolutionary deed-poll 'Civique Penn Mévolhan', unable to fight by reason of ill-health, offered to found a 'republican school' which would omit Latin from its curriculum.[72] Even the clergy of the Constitutional Church were in danger. Angers, like the rest of France, felt impulses which were turning the Revolution towards 'de-Christianization'—the cult of patriotism and exigencies of national unity, an upsurge of sentimentality in the face of tragedy, along with bitter hatred of all authors of divisions, a sudden fantastic play of obscure forces and fanatical individuals thrown up to the surface through cracks and landslides in the old social strata. A new calendar began in October, with Nature's cycle, pagan gods and botanical specimens in place of Christian martyrs; early in November the archbishop of Paris was forced to abdicate and the pageantry of Reason surged and flowed under the vaults of Notre-Dame. Though de-Christianization in Angers was not a popular movement, but rather an introduction from outside by *représentants en mission* and revolutionary committeemen, it was yet powerful and menacing enough to drive bishop Pelletier to abjure his orders. On 19 November he handed over his letters of ordination and made a sad declaration of his belief in 'natural religion' shorn of all 'diversities of practice' arising from human agencies.[73] Twelve other priests did likewise, including Besnard, the former vicaire of Saint-Pierre, who added to his abjuration an announcement of his approaching marriage to 'une républicaine'.[74] Rangeard was summoned and laid down his letters of priesthood, not as a 'sacrifice to Reason', however, but defiantly, refusing to disavow his convictions of a life-time 'fortified by study and reflexion'.[75] On 20 November Angers had its festival of Reason in the cathedral, from which all traces of Vendean prisoners and of 'vain baubles of superstition' had been effaced. A hymn was sung on this occasion written by Coquille, now 'Horatius Coclès Coquille' and husband of a wife, a departure which he justified in seven long verses proclaiming the victory of 'chaste affection' over 'false continence'.[76] On the 30th, medieval charters and registers of Saint-Maurice were ceremonially flung on to a bonfire as an encore.[77] Four days later sentries on the tower of the temple of Reason announced a new approach of Vendean armies.[78] This time the republicans had made their preparations and awaited assault behind newly fortified city walls. The Rossignolerie was outside their defensive perimeter, but the imprisoned priests were not liberated again, for they had been sent off down river on barges shortly before the royalists appeared. Vendean forces concentrated in Saint-Serge and from thence directed a murderous fire on the porte Cupif. Bénaben, who had just returned from the armies, saw the danger, and accused the general in charge of the defence of cowardice and inefficiency. Even so, the town was too strong to be taken and on 4th December, after a siege of a single day, the royalist army shambled away.

The next five months were unprecedented in the city's long history. The *représentants en mission*, with their revolutionary committee and military commission, wreaked a feverish and panic-stricken vengeance. An end was made of the bourgeois *Club de l'Est*, Mévolhan of the Oratory, its leader, fleeing from Anjou; the *Société de l'Ouest*, representing a lower social stratum on the other side of the river, now met in the church of La Trinité under the presidency of dom Boniface, and was the only organ of opinion.[79] Firing parties and the guillotine made a clean sweep of prisoners, stragglers and suspects.[80] When on 16 March the members of the first revolutionary committee were replaced, dom Boniface, their spokesman, summarized their achievements with terrible enthusiasm. 'We have defederalized, and what is more, defanaticized the Department of Maine-et-Loire. Today it pleases the national will . . . to dismiss us; good,—if they think they can find in this Department bigger revolutionaries than we are, long live liberty!—that's all we ask.' [81]

Striking down 'fanaticism' was a primary aim of this Angevin Terror, for ecclesiastics were rebels. Congratulations from Paris on the town's successful resistance ended with warnings—'surveillez les prêtres!' [82] A great festival of Victory on 30 December which swept round the city like the old procession of the *Sacre* (with a goddess of Liberty on a mountain top in place of the old Scriptural waxworks) taught the same lesson. Priests, recited the goddess, were a 'filthy horde', 'vile flatterers of crowned brigands'.[83] Those who could be found met with a swift fate. Doguereau, curé of Saint-Aignan, who had been too ill to be imprisoned, was now seized and guillotined amidst shouts of 'Vive la République'!; so, too, was Tessier, a vicaire of La Trinité, in an ecclesiastical *fournée* specially devised to form a funeral cortège for the Vendean 'Bishop of Agra'; so, too, was canon Barat, who was detected in town disguised as a miller and 'carrying on his person the instruments of fanaticism'; so, too, was the abbé Laigneau de Langellerie, chaplain of the Carmelites, who was arrested while taking the sacraments to a sick woman.[84] Fugitives with the royalist armies were rounded up in the countryside and brought back to Angers to die—Marguerite de Gressau, a nun of Ronceray, Rosalie du Verdier de la Sorinière of Le Calvaire, dom Chabanel the aged prior of Lesvière, who was found hiding in a trench roofed in with planks and who was guillotined along with the three women from a nearby farm who had concealed him.[85] The abbess of Ronceray, who had escaped to the château of her sister-in-law at Beaupréau, was arrested, brought back to face the tribunal and shot. 'She was eighty years of age, blind, good and charitable, but in those days they did not know the meaning of the word mercy.' [86] M. Meilloc, former superior of the Seminary, survived in hiding, so too did curé Gruget, who from a half-opened window near the scaffold extended hands to bless and absolve his friends as they went by to death. 'Citoyenne Manette', alias Denise-Marie Boussinot of the Petite Pension, who was too greatly loved by the poor to be condemned, risked her life to help such fugitives.[87] The sisters serving in hospitals were arrested in February and March, and other nuns who had remained in town after the evictions of 1792 were imprisoned shortly afterwards. Some took the civic oath. Those who did not were condemned to deportation, except two sisters of Saint-Vincent de Paul who were shot.[88] On 24 June 1794 a convoy of 96 nuns left for Lorient watched by silent crowds; on arrival at their port of departure they were incarcerated in the prison called 'La Grande Cayenne', where they remained until their eventual release nine months later.[89] Of the captives in the Rossignolerie, fifteen aged and infirm priests had been left behind during the evacuation of December; in March they, too, were sent down the river to Nantes to share the fate of their fellows.[90]

That fate had been mass execution by a new method, 'de-Christianization by immersion'. About seventy priests had been taken from the Rossignolerie before the Vendeans arrived, and put on barges to sail down the Maine and the Loire to Nantes. Among them[91] were four canons of Saint-Maurice and at least five of other chapters, curés Boumard, Roussel, Robin and Suchet, P. Anaclet who had ruled the convent of La Baumette, and other less-well-known ecclesiastics of Angers. Six were drowned en route, including, it is said, the famous curé Robin of Saint-Pierre.[92] If this was an accident it was, as Carrier declared, an accident 'that rejoices the heart of every citizen'.[93] As the other priests approached their destination women of Nantes crowded the pont de la poissonerie to rain down stones on their heads as the boats passed by.[94] Such were the passions of civil strife. The executions that followed aroused no concern, being regarded as 'a necessary episode of the Vendean war'.[95] Already on 19 November a batch of priests had perished in a *noyade* at Nantes. One of these victims had been a Benedictine of Saint-Aubin and another was Poulain de la Guerche of the Cathedral of Saint-Maurice, who had been arrested in the summer of 1792 while trying to find a ship for England.[96] The 58 ecclesiastics from Angers who arrived on 6 December were disposed of in the same fashion. Their pockets were rifled, they were bound together in pairs and packed in a boat in the estuary.[97] 'Last night they were one and all swallowed up by the river,' wrote representative Carrier, 'what a revolutionary torrent is the Loire!' [98] But it was Bénaben of the Angevin Oratory who hit upon the neatest turn of revolutionary phrase—'we call that sending them to the *Château d'Eau* . . . they can't complain that they are being left to die of thirst.' [99]

2. 1796

By the autumn of 1796 an uneasy weary peace reigned in Anjou. The Vendean armies, after a year of fitful truce, had marched again at the end of 1795, but Stofflet was captured and shot at Angers in February and Charette passed through the town on his way to execution a month later. Thereafter fighting declined into isolated forays and Bernier, the sole intelligence left behind incoherent insurrectionary forces, was seeking an opportunity to negotiate a final pacification. In Angers the bourgeoisie was in power again, for the revolutionary committee had been suppressed in December 1794 and by the following April the municipality no longer contained representatives of the lower classes. Dom Boniface and Gouppil enjoyed a new and momentary prominence when they founded a *babouvist* club at the end of 1795,[100] but their activities were banned by the police and these ex-terrorists sank back into impotence and contempt. Some leaders of the liberal and anti-clerical bourgeoisie of 1789 had perished, for the Terror in Anjou had claimed other victims besides Vendeans and priests. Five members of the old administration, including the *ci-devant* comte de Dieusie and La Revellière's elder brother, had been executed in Paris in April 1794. In that same month Joseph (the elder) Delaunay had been guillotined—not for Girondism, however, for he was a man of the left; not for Dantonism, though he died in the same *journée* as Danton and Desmoulins, but for corruption. His apartment in the boulevard Montmartre, where his mistress, the actress Descoings, had presided over a brilliant salon, had also been the centre of a tangled conspiracy of Jacobin profiteers who grew rich on the spoils of the Company of the Indies, and it was the unmasking of this political blackmail which had brought him to the scaffold.[101] But other middle-class leaders of the first revolutionary generation of Anjou survived to emerge from hiding after Thermidor.[102] Pierre-Marie (the younger) Delaunay, who had been a moderate in the Convention, was now a *grand seigneur* of the new administrative world, and from the end of 1794 to the summer of 1795 he had presided over the re-establishment of bourgeois domination in the Department of Maine-et-Loire.[103] La Revellière-Lépeaux and his friends Pilastre and Leclerc, were returned as deputies to the new Legislative in Vendémaire year IV (September–October 1795). La Revellière was now a Director, one of the rulers, and Leclerc was showing his nostalgia for the old cultural life of Angers by pressing the government to set up schools of vocal and instrumental music in all the old cathedral cities of France.[104]

If the Vendée was to subside and past hatreds find oblivion one thing was indispensable—religious peace. Since Robespierre's fall the pendulum had swung, first towards a tentative and insincere toleration, then back to persecution. In 1796 it appeared that the Directory was turning again towards liberalism and it was known that the Papacy, on conditions, would authorize Catholics to accept a *de facto* government. Anti-clericals were jaded and La Revellière had not yet begun his attempt to revive deism by enforcing his charming but faintly ridiculous Theophilanthropy. Priests could show themselves cautiously and in mufti, and though churches were closed to them, the faithful could pay their devotions elsewhere. In the summer of 1795 petitions had been organized in Angers asking that Saint-Serge and Saint-Maurice be restored to ecclesiastical use,[105] and Rangeard, never lacking in courage, announced on 15 Thermidor year IV (2 August 1796) that he proposed to say mass again in the cathedral.[106] Though the road to a final accommodation was at last open the journey was to be longer than men suspected: once more, after the military and dictatorial coup of Fructidor (4 September 1797) the government was to deviate towards repression, whose severities endured, at least in formal decrees, until Bonaparte's final intervention.[107] Even so, this autumn of 1796 was a period of *détente*. Masses were being said though church doors were closed and bells were silent; ecclesiastics had emerged from their hiding-places though few exiles had as yet returned. The threads of individual lives, like marine plants uprooted from the ocean-bed by deep-searching storms, came drifting to the surface in the calm and there began to weave themselves once more into a living growing pattern.

In those great storms some of our Angevin ecclesiastics had perished. A few others had died in their beds in the course of nature— old Follenfant of Saint-Maurice; the abbé Ferrand; Gaudin, curé of

Saint-Nicolas; Noel, curé of Saint-Jacques; Brûlé, vicaire of Saint-Julien.[108] Some had sought refuge with the Vendean armies, only to meet death from disease or republican bullets. Rabin of Notre-Dame de Cholet died miserably of dysentery in a farmhouse near Angers,[109] while Guérif, vicaire of Saint-Jacques, M. Elias of the Seminary[110] and dom Flosseau of Saint-Aubin[111] were consigned to unrecorded graves on rural battlefields. Others who cast in their lot with the Vendée came through. Bachelot, vicaire of Saint-Samson,[112] who had been too infirm to be deported, miraculously survived his roaming life with guerilla bands; so did Grasset, vicaire of La Trinité, and dom Jagault of Saint-Nicolas, who became a member of the governing council of the insurrection and vainly sought to bring to its armies a monastic and military idea of unity of command;[113] so too did curé Bernier, rendered sick in body, sharpened in intellect and embittered in soul by years of unremitting cruelty and fear.

Others had survived by flight beyond seas. In Spain the deportees were entering upon their fifth year of exile. Canons of the cathedral had naturally made for Compostella to enjoy the benefits of confraternity which linked their chapter with that of Saint-James; dean de Villeneuve went directly there, put up at the 'Grand Admiral' hotel and received a generous welcome—others followed him.[114] Some Angevin ecclesiastics—Breton and Montalant of the little Seminary and five other Sulpiciens, the curé of Saint-Martin and vicaire Forest of Saint-Michel du Tertre—were among the serried rows of refugees in the dining-hall of the hospitable bishop of Orense.[115] A lucky few became tutors in noble households,[116] an unlucky many lived meagrely on monastic rations,[117] others were boarded out with families and received a dole from pious offerings. 'I am in an excellent country,' wrote one village curé smugly soon after his arrival, 'with good folk who feed me very well. I have practically nothing to do and every day I get 15 sols from collections.'[118] But corroding idleness and continual poverty became unbearable to all but the most complacent, and, in spite of all difficulties, some more enterprising spirits migrated further afield. Canon Le Noir de la Cochetière went on to England,[119] Janin, vicaire of Saint-Michel du Tertre, to Louisiana,[120] while Montalant set off to be an evangelist in China.[121]

Clergy who had escaped deportation and had emigrated were now widely scattered. By devious routes, Chatizel,[122] canon de la Corbière of Saint-Maurice and Bancelin, vicaire of Saint-Michel du Tertre, had fled to England; dom le Coursonnais of Saint-Aubin to Jersey;[123] Huard, vicaire of Saint-Maurille, had gone to Italy where he published a comparative study of French and Italian pronunciation; Houdet of La Trinité, who had been so enthusiastic for liberty, had gone to San Domingo where he died soon, perhaps before he had learnt that the military commission of Angers had shot his mother and his three sisters.[124] Canon Louet had been imprisoned in the Seminary in June 1792 but had contrived to escape to Jersey, where, with typical thoroughness, old and broken as he was, he laboured assiduously at the mysteries of English grammar.[125] Even so, he always intended to go back to his native land and one of his last actions was to make a formal application for permission to return. By the waters of Babylon these exiles ever turned their thoughts towards Jerusalem, to 'the gentle slopes of the Loire' and to 'the meadows of Anjou'. When he saw Canterbury cathedral, 'so like Saint-Maurice of Angers, my own church', canon de la Corbière was overwhelmed by a flood of nostalgic memories, 'an indescribable emotion, sweet and yet so cruel'.[126]

There were other refractories who had outwitted the Terror yet spent most of their time within sight of the towers of Saint-Maurice. Gruget curé of La Trinité and one of his vicaires, and the young abbé Follenfant remained hidden in and about Angers throughout the Revolution, as did curé Chaloigne of Saint-Martin who escaped from the Seminary and thereafter contrived to hide not only himself, but also sacerdotal ornaments and altar linen of the abbey of Ronceray.[127] For six years Guillon vicaire of Saint-Maurille successfully escaped detection, until in the renewal of· persecution after Fructidor he was caught and sent to the crowded prisons of the Île de Ré.[128] M. Meilloc of the Seminary, exercising vicarial powers on behalf of bishop de Lorry, stayed on near Angers and then in the town itself, even when his protector, 'citoyenne Manette', had to flee.[129] As for Mgr de Lorry himself, typically, he had acted with a circumspect courage untarnished by foolhardiness. At first he had wandered unhappily in Normandy, then during the September massacres he had gone to ground in a quiet rural hamlet;[130] afterwards he had gone directly to Paris as 'citizen Couet', where, according to his own description of his conduct, he had paid his taxes, never spoken of public affairs except to obey, and asked for exemption from deportation on grounds of old age and infirmity.[131] In the summer of 1796 he returned to his old diocese for a season, but he would not take back his see[132] or give any opinion on religious affairs. 'I have never . . . directed anyone's conscience concerning the oaths,' he replied to one of his curés nearly two years later, 'I have never asked nor counselled, still less exacted retractions.' [133] He was one of the few bishops of the old régime who had not fled from France: that being so, he felt justified in playing for safety and being one of the few who kept his opinions to himself.

Seven years ago, in that almost forgotten battle of curés against

U

the hierarchy, Rangeard and his bishop had fought on opposite sides, but they had always respected one another in spite of their differences, and tragedy and disillusionment had drawn them together again. 'We differ, but thought is free,' wrote Mgr de Lorry to the curé of Andard a few weeks after the September massacres, 'and I would no more ask you to sacrifice your opinions than I would sacrifice to you my own—my principles, in which I wish to live and die; but there will always be a mutual sympathy in our hearts and you will always be dear to me, and I wish I were able to prove it to you.' [134] No doubt in the summer of 1796 he again demonstrated this friendship and visited that little house in the faubourg Bressigny, where Rangeard, now a humble employee in the local archives,[135] lived in decent obscurity, giving what leadership he could to members of the discredited and disestablished Constitutional Church. Three years ago Hugues Pelletier had died in a house in the rue des Jacobins in the shadow of the cathedral where he had been elected bishop, where he had celebrated pontifically and where he had abjured his vocation. Viger, for a while constitutional curé of La Madeleine, was dead; Taillebuis had renounced his ministry during the Terror; Ferré had given up his letters of priesthood but still lived in the vicarage of Saint-Samson and was known to be saying masses again;[136] Gaudin, constitutional curé of Saint-Jacques, was still living in his old house, but as early as February 1793 he had renounced all ecclesiastical functions and turned to secular teaching to earn a living; Voillemont was now married and an administrative official, busily engaged in his spare time in forming a symphony orchestra whose performances a year later were to make Saint-Maurice once more a home of good, though Theophilanthropic music.[137] Of jurors, only Rangeard and Ferré remained respected and only Rangeard remained significant. He had continued to pay visits to his old parish until, in May 1796, his two assistant priests were murdered by *chouans*; thereafter he stayed in Angers, making no secret of his loyalty to his ecclesiastical vocation and of his confidence that the Church of France, purged of its wealth and nominal adherents, would arise once more.[138] In spite of fate's harsh ironies he was still on the side of the Revolution: he hated proud Britain, tyrant of the seas,[139] he hated the Vendée and Bernier its evil genius, whom he believed capable of every immorality and treachery of republican legend.[140] But the ex-curé of Andard had only another year to live and when he died, leadership of the constitutional cause was left to the somewhat self-righteous obstinacy of Ferré.

The monasteries and religious communities of Angers had gone, their inmates were dispersed and, for the most part, forgotten. Of the abbey of Toussaint men remembered only its abbot, Perrochel, who had left a military career under the old régime to obtain a monastic sinecure, who had been obliged by his wound to leave the revolutionary armies, and was now a diplomat who served the Directory with aristocratic distinction in Sweden, Spain and the Helvetic Republic.[141] The Benedictines of Saint-Aubin were scattered afar. Prior Mansel had vanished; dom Marchant had gone with the Lorraine brothers to their home at Douai, from whence he moved to his own home at Cambrai to teach in the local *collège*, and now he was a clerk in the army of the Pyrenees and had just married a very young and unsatisfactory wife at Toulouse;[142] another monk was a refugee in Jersey; another was wandering around the Angevin countryside and was picked up by the police early in 1798 near Sablé; a former prior of the house was working as a library assistant in Paris; dom Flosseau had died with the Vendée.[143] Only two remained in Angers. One was Boniface the terrorist, the other was dom Locatelli, who had been a constitutional curé for a while and was now living in the rue des Poêliers and demonstrating 'good principles' to the authorities, which ultimately brought him to an official post as librarian.[144] Garnault (formerly, as a Capuchin, father Athanasius) now kept a school; Écot, an ex-Carmelite friar, was married and a clerk in a hospital; Loyau, the ex-Cordelier, nursed his gout in lodgings in the place du Pilori.[145] Since the Benedictine community of Saint-Nicolas had been dissolved,[146] dom Braux, simple and learned, had spent all his time cataloguing the books of religious establishments stacked in the nave of Saint-Martin, until in February 1796 he was appointed librarian of the École Centrale of Angers.[147]

This new school was opened on 21 March with Héron and Bénaben of the old Angevin Oratory among its professors. There was a *Fête de la Jeunesse* at the end of that month when Bénaben passed on to a new generation a political philosophy which he had deduced from his own chequered experience. Equality, he said, means equality before the law, no more—'beyond that point, young citizens, beyond that point, this precious equality, the very basis of free government, will not avail to remove differences between men which have been ordained by nature and by society'. His speeches in the two following years continue to afford glimpses of a revolutionary re-establishing his respectability. 'Rebellious priests' waving 'the torches of fanaticism' and sinister intrigues by an Orleanist faction, he declared, had set the Revolution on to evil courses which produced that 'horrible volcano' the Mountain, that 'execrable régime' of Terror and the 'ferocious cannibals' who were its instruments.[148] The guillotine and the 'Château d'Eau' were no longer fitting subjects for humour in Anjou.

3. 1802

On 6 June 1802 Charles Montault-Desisles, brother of the prefect of Maine-et-Loire and former constitutional bishop of Poitiers, was solemnly installed in his cathedral church of Saint-Maurice as first concordatory bishop of Angers. A sermon was preached by M. de Villeneuve, dean of the old chapter, newly returned from exile. 'Satisfaction glowed on every countenance', [149] reported Bernier, bishop of Orleans, and one-time curé of Saint-Laud, present as an agent of the government to see that everything went smoothly.

Since December 1799, when the municipality had declared that priests had no influence except on the consciences of old people,[150] the whole atmosphere of public opinion had changed. Middle-class citizens were demanding a religious education for their children and sending them to former nuns, ex-Frères des Écoles Chrétiennes and constitutional curés for instruction. A clerical boarding-school in the old vicarage of Saint-Maurice had more than 50 pupils and another in the devastated old abbey buildings of Saint-Nicolas under Godefroy and Villemot, formerly of the Rossignolerie, had three times as many.[151] From the spring of 1800, one by one, churches had been reopened.[152] Saint-Serge had been turned over to its parishioners for religious services in February and the last of the revolutionary *fêtes décadaires* was held in the cathedral in August.[153] The cross replaced the bonnet of liberty on spires and the *Te Deum* was sung for French victories.[154] Bernier, triumphant from his somewhat oblique pacification of the Vendée, had returned to his old parish in June, where he issued a printed pastoral letter resonant with an almost episcopal unction.[155] Then, in September, the curé of Saint-Laud had been called away by Bonaparte to negotiate the Concordat—a strange choice, perhaps, but where else in France could the First Consul have found such a man, a priest devoured by ambition who had taken no revolutionary oaths, a Vendean who was not a royalist, a theologian who was also an adventurer? In July 1801 the Concordat was signed. Bernier received his reward by promotion to the episcopate, though not, as he had hoped, to archbishop of Tours with residence in Angers. Mgr de Lorry was still alive and he had been offered the diocese of La Rochelle, which his rapidly failing health had obliged him to refuse.[156] Oddly enough, if we are to believe his own story, Besnard was invited to accept a see (although after all he was a doctor of theology, who, to say the least of it, had avoided compromising company), but he excused himself on the ground that he was unable to say mass, his health not permitting him to get out of bed without taking light refreshment.[157] Apparently Le Noir de la Cochetière was regarded as another possible episcopal candidate, and he certainly would not have refused a mitre for early-morning coffee's sake. Bernier, however, found him cold and proud towards ex-constitutional priests and reported him unsuitable[158]—thus for a second and last time this former canon of Saint-Maurice lost his opportunity of arriving at 'that office which in my station marks the term of ambition'.[159]

Others besides Le Noir marred the new religious settlement by recalling past feuds. Priests with uneasy consciences not unnaturally found M. Meilloc something of a dragon.[160] Families which had been prominent in buying Church property were coldly received when applying to their clergy for baptisms and weddings.[161] An ex-constitutional himself, bishop Montault found that some members of his old persuasion were less humble and pliable than he had been. A few men in town—Delaunay, now presiding judge of the Criminal court, La Revellière and one or two Theophilanthropic enthusiasts—still had 'some of the audacity of Robespierre's days' and they encouraged former jurors in their reluctance to sign any form of retraction.[162] Not until 13 August were these old constitutional clergy reconciled. Then an absurd comedy ensued at Saint-Serge. The aged abbé Ferré, who had been inditing pamphlets in justification of his past conduct,[163] now forced open the church doors and tried to reinstate himself as curé. Bishop Montault showed an equal lack of decorum and 'transforming himself into a police officer', rushed up to renew the locks and plaster then with his episcopal seal, encouraged, as he did so, by ironical applause from idle soldiers and market-women. One Garreau, a retired gendarme who had played the *serpent* at Ferré's masses for many a year, thereupon demonstrated his loyalty by prising off the episcopal padlocks and bearing home the litany desk as a pledge and trophy. Fortunately, however, bishop 'Monte à l'assaut' was fundamentally a reasonable man. He discontinued lawsuits he had initiated in his first flush of anger, and Ferré, who had only another year to live, was consoled with a canonry.[164]

Otherwise, ecclesiastical re-establishment proceeded smoothly. Six old curés of Angers had perished during the Terror, three had died natural deaths, one had demoted himself into the laity, one was a bishop. Excluding Ferré, five remained, and four of them eventually received parishes in town again. La Trinité of course went to Gruget. For nine years as vicaire and for seven years as curé he had ministered in those mean and crowded streets, then for a decade he had lived there obscurely, often in danger of his life. Now he was restored and for another 38 years he ruled his church, a stern and simple priest whose conduct was always supremely sincere and honourable even though his judgments on weaker contemporaries erred through lack of subtlety and sympathy. Bougé, formerly of

Saint-Michel du Tertre, died curé of Saint-Serge. Huchelou des Roches and Chaloigne were successive parish priests of Saint-Joseph, and the latter, in consideration of a small yearly income, left to his vestry the third best ornament of the old abbey church of Ronceray.[165] Bernier's visit of 1802 was his last appearance in Anjou. Before his departure he toured the countryside, proceeding in episcopal splendour through hamlets where he had wandered as a fugitive during the civil wars. In the parish church of Saint-Laud (which was now, since the old collegial had been destroyed, in the chapel of the Recollets) he celebrated a pontifical high mass, with generals and army officers, the prefect and civil officials crowding in alongside his old congregation. Women whose husbands had been killed by the Vendeans gathered outside to stone him. On the day of the Octave of Corpus Christi he walked in the parochial procession of the Holy Sacrament, guarded by a military escort.[166] Then he left for Orleans. Four years later he was dead.

The abbé Bastard, who had served under Bernier at Saint-Laud, inherited the parish and with some assistance from two of the ex-canons restored the old popular devotions to the relic of the True Cross there.[167] Of other former vicaires of Angers one had died with the Vendée, one had been guillotined, three had died naturally. Ten of the survivors, including Fautras and Taillebuis, ex-constitutionals, obtained country-parishes.[168] Four others took minor ecclesiastical office in Angers. Tardif, formerly of La Trinité, became a canon at the cathedral, as befitted a doctor of theology, though all the influence of the new bishop of Orleans could not prevail to have his old friend made a vicar-general.[169] Janin of Saint-Michel du Tertre was still in Louisiana, being the only living parish priest of the town who did not at once reappear in his diocese. The others, curés and vicaires, returned, seeking again the gentle slopes of the Loire and the meadows of Anjou and the sound of the cathedral bells.

> *Si oblitus fuero tui, Jerusalem,*
> *oblivioni detur dextera mea.*

They came back to the province where they had been born, catechized and ordained—it was their world. The essential religious history of Angers under the old régime had been their history, for canons, monks and even nuns had been, as it were, super-imposed upon the basic pattern of their routine ministry. The essential religious history of Angers in the future would be their history again, a continuous history, for the Revolution, which had altered parish boundaries, broken monuments and annihilated church property, had not diverted, broken or annihilated the vocation of these very ordinary men.

During the next few years we catch glimpses of others who were also drawn back to the town by the magnetism of memories and by their hopes for the future. There was ex-dean Villeneuve, one of the bishop's vicars-general; ex-dean Frémond of Saint-Martin, humble and active as ever, assisting M. Meilloc to resurrect the Seminary;[170] canon Touchet restored to a stall at Saint-Maurice, along with canon Jubeau formerly of Saint-Maurille; Leroy, once a canon of La Trinité, now a chaplain at the Hôtel-Dieu. There was Chatizel, who, after a few more years at Soulaines, came to spend his retirement in Angers; Montalant, of the old Little Seminary, who was first a country curé, then a canon, and finally a vicar-general, and his friend, Breton, curé of Saint-Maurice and much in demand as a preacher on solemn occasions.[171] Dom Piolane, ex-prior of Saint-Nicolas, died in Angers two days after Mgr Montault's installation as bishop.[172] P. Donat, who had ruled the Capuchin house at the end of the old régime, returned as chaplain to the Pénitentes—perhaps he was able to visit two of his former colleagues who died in the hospitals of the town in 1805 and 1807.[173] Sisters of Saint-Vincent de Paul—all of them members of the old Angevin establishment—were sent back to Angers from their Parisian mother house in 1806; the bishop and Delaunay gave them a warm official welcome.[174] Three charitable ladies still dispensed remedies to the sick at the Petite Pension.[175] Fifteen years later the surviving nuns of Le Calvaire returned to buy back their old convent buildings: they found old dom Blisson of Saint-Serge still in town and glad to become their chaplain.[176] Monks who had been bibliophiles in their cloister made their interest their career when the books were secularized. Dom Locatelli was assistant at the municipal library, conscientiously warding off masters of the École Centrale who claimed a right to take out volumes to read at home.[177] The chief librarian was dom Braux who died in March 1803, mercifully, perhaps, for a few months later his collections were broken up and evicted from the bishop's palace to make room for Mgr Montault.[178] In the secular academic world schoolmasters continued to be schoolmasters. Bénaben and Héron, ex-Oratorians, taught at the École Centrale, then at the Lycée. All that remained of the former's revolutionary past was a hangover of anti-clericalism—he wanted a system of national secular education, growing 'in the shadow of the august throne and all its influences'.[179] Voillemont, who had been an ecclesiastic so long as provincial music was a cathedral monopoly, fell into obscurity once his Theophilanthropic symphony concerts were ended, and his place as a leader of musical life was soon filled by two of his former choir-boys returning from the wars.[180]

From time to time news arrived of those ecclesiastics who had sought a niche outside Anjou. Of canons, Burgevin of Saint-Pierre lived with the Boylesve family at Paris where Le Noir now held a prebend, Duval of La Trinité was chaplain to the Gibot at their château de la Mauvoisinière, Brossier lived in retirement at Nantes, his historical ambitions abandoned since his vast collection of notes had been dispersed by parcel-wrapping grocers. Ex-dom Mercier of Lesvière settled down at Souvigny, and his former colleague Foulard was back at Nantes, his native city; René Marchant of Saint-Aubin was a librarian at Cambrai, separated from his frivolous wife and doing his best to bring up a young daughter; dom Jagault, as befitted a hero of the Vendean campaigns, sent a subscription to bishop Montault to encourage the building of a chapel at the 'Champ des Martyrs' where so many Angevin Catholic royalists had perished; Locatelli soon left his librarianship to become a curé at Saint-Dié and Chambord; two of the ex-Cordeliers and one Capuchin found minor ecclesiastical posts in the countryside of Anjou; another Cordelier succeeded Chatizel in the living of Soulaines; another, after holding a parish of his own, retired to Château-Gontier to end his days. Alhoy of the Oratory became principal of a collège in Paris and an expert on the education of the deaf and dumb. Five of the Sulpiciens of the old Seminary had emigrated to the New World, where two became bishops and a third vicar-general of Montreal. In 1815 vicaire Janin was heard of: he had grown rich in America, and three years later a prosperous abbé came back to Angers to die.[181] Besnard lived simply at Paris, writing a great antiquarian treatise which was never published. Secularized though he was, he could never forget his orders, regarding himself as 'an amphibious being in the world'. He did not read at night because he had been warned against this practice at the Seminary of Angers. The Bible given to him by the prior of Lesvière was lost, the snuff-box given by the prior of Saint-Nicolas was broken, but he still had a red leather wallet dom Mansel had presented to him when he had left curé Robin's tutelage and gone to a parish of his own in 1780.[182] In his declining years Besnard dwelt more and more upon Angers of the old régime and his dull and voluminous memoirs brighten into something approaching vivacity when he considers those happy pre-revolutionary years. When he died in 1842, two years after curé Gruget, Angers was changed out of all recognition.[183] Broad tree-lined boulevards swept through the city where the old ramparts had stood; the parish churches of Saint-Maurice and Sainte-Croix (demolished, with others, during the Revolution) and a jumble of surrounding houses had vanished, leaving the cathedral in dignified detachment; Saint-Aubin's tower still stood as a landmark but its church had been removed 'to open a passage to the Prefecture' which occupied the old abbey buildings;

the roof of Saint-Martin's church had caved in and the tower had lost its summit; the principal public square of the town with its memories of the guillotine occupied the site of the churches of the canons of Saint-Pierre and Saint-Maurille; Lesvière church and cloister existed no longer, not even as a saltpetre factory; the tower of Ronceray was gone and part of the west transept was in ruin; a few broken columns marked the site of the abbey church of Saint-Nicolas; Toussaint's proud vaults had collapsed and were overgrown with grass and bushes.

The mellow and unprogressive clerical world which the Revolution had overwhelmed was well-nigh forgotten. Like the city of Ys of Breton legend[184] seas had covered it, and there were few remaining who still heard in memory the slow sound of its bells rising upwards through sharp bright waves. But unlike the submerged city as Renan imagined it, Angers never was a dream, an Atlantis, a paradise founded on a superb error. It was real and tangible, patterned with passions and petty strife, injustices and anomalies, comedy and farce—all the dust and gilt with which the ambition, selfishness and wit of man contrives to overlay the solid things in which he sincerely believes. If there were magic peals and haunting choirs there were also battles over bell-ropes and tumults in vestries. But this angular prickly complex of mingled good and petty evil formed a natural community and a spiritual abiding place. It may have saved some souls: it certainly inspired many loyalties. With all its injustices and rivalries, it had the essential quality of homeliness—it drew its children back again when their years of exile were over. Anjou had always been like that—

Malheureux l'an, le mois, le jour, l'heure et le poinct,
. . . .
Quand pour venir icy j'abandonnay la France!
La France et mon Anjou.[185]

REFERENCES

CHAPTER I

[1] John Breval, *Remarks on Several Parts of Europe* (1738), II, p. 23.

[2] Arthur Young, *Travels in France and Italy*, 26–7 Sept. 1788.

[3] J. Mathorez, 'Notes sur les Étrangers en Anjou sous l'Ancien Régime', *Rev. Anjou*, LXX (1915), p. 166; O. Raguenet de Saint-Albin, 'Livres des Pensionnaires et des Externes à l'Académie d'Equitation d'Angers (1755–90)', *Rev. Anjou*, LXVIII (1914), pp. 165, 178, 342, 351; 'Bedingfeld Papers', ed. J. H. Pollen, *Catholic Record Soc. Misc.*, VI (1909), p. 205; MSS. *Duke of Rutland*, H.M.C., XIV (I), 1894, p. 365. For the uniform see Desjobert's notes on a journey in Anjou (1780) in *Andegaviana*, 1911, p. 118; for other details, P. Guedalla, *The Duke* (1931), pp. 24–5.

[4] Philip Henry, fifth Earl Stanhope, *Notes of Conversations with the Duke of Wellington* (1888), pp. 164–6.

[5] MSS. *Lady Waterford*, H.M.C., XI (VII), 1888, p. 78.

[6] Mme Letondal, *Mémoires*, *Anjou hist.*, V (1905), p. 7; 'La paroisse Saint-Julien d'Angers', *Anjou hist.*, XXXI (1931), p. 71. See also 'The Diary of the "Blue Nuns" or Order of the Immaculate Conception at Paris, 1685–1810, *Catholic Record Soc.* 1910, pp. 180-1, 414; and 'Records of the English Canonesses of the Holy Sepulchre of Liège, 1652–1793', *Catholic Record Soc. Misc.*, X (1915), p. 164.

[7] Péan de la Tuillerie, *Description de la Ville d'Angers et de tout ce qu'elle contient de plus remarquable* (1778), ed. C. Port, 1868, p. 225; C. Port, *Cartulaire de l'Hôpital Saint-Jean d'Angers* (1870), pp. 10, 59; N. Wraxall, *A Tour through the Western, Southern and Interior Provinces of France* (1777), II, p. 405; Breval, pp. 23, 25. According to the abbé Prévost, the portrait of Margaret of Anjou in the window of the Cordeliers made evident the beauty 'qui fit l'admiration de son siècle', *Histoire de Marguerite d'Anjou, Reine d'Angleterre*, 1741, IV, p. 198.

[8] Wraxall, II, p. 403. For the numerous old dwelling houses which survived in Angers, see Prosper Mérimée, *Notes d'un voyage dans l'Ouest de la France* (1836), p. 341. The castle had suffered serious demolitions from the end of the fifteenth century onwards (Rangeard, 'Etat . . . de l'Anjou avant la Révolution de 1789'. B. Angers MS. 1020 (894), f. 10). A Breton squire who had no interest in antiquities found Angers (riding-school and promenades apart) impossibly boring—'Nous quittons sans regret cette ville, dans l'espoir d'objets plus agréables et plus intéressants' ('Un voyage en Anjou (1782)', *Anjou hist.*, XLI, p. 29).

[9] F.-Y. Besnard, *Souvenirs d'un Nonagénaire*, ed. C. Port (1880), I, pp. 130–1; J. Denais, 'Le Portefeuille d'un Curieux', *Rev. Anjou.*, XIX (1889), pp. 177 ff.

[10] Correspondence of the curé of La Trinité with the agent of the Order of Saint-Lazare, 31 Dec. 1772 (A.M.L. G. 1792).

[11] *Affiches d'Angers, Capitale de l'Apanage de Monseigneur le Comte de Provence, et de la Province d'Anjou* (B. Angers H 5423). For what follows see B. Bois, *La Vie scolaire et les créations intellectuelles en Anjou 1789–99* (1929), pp. 84–6.

[12] Besnard, I, p. 134.

[13] For all the foregoing see Besnard, I, pp. 129–30, 127–8, 137, 143.

[14] C. Port, *Inventaire . . . des archives anciennes de la Mairie d'Angers* (1861), pp. 7, 147.

15 A. Le Moy, *Cahiers de Doléances des Corporations de la ville d'Angers pour les États Généraux de 1789.* (Documents Inédits Hist. Revn. Franç, 1915), p. ix; F. Dumas, *La Généralité de Tours au xviiie siècle. Administration de l'Intendant du Cluzel 1766–83* (1894), pp. 89, 161; V. Dauphin, 'Recherches pour servir à l'histoire de l'Industrie Textile en Anjou', *Rev. Anjou*, N.S., LXVI (1913), p. 19n. and 'La manufacture de toiles peintes et imprimées en Anjou', *Méms. Soc. Agric.*, XXVI (1923).

16 J. Levron, *La Bourse de Commerce d'Angers au 18ᵉ siècle* (1933), pp. 17, 23, 45–6.

17 'Mémoire sur la Généralité de Tours en 1783, par M. Harvon Receveur Général des Finances' (ed. Marchegay), *Archives d'Anjou*, II (1853), pp. 359–60.

18 C. Port, *Dictionnaire historique, géographique et biographique de Maine-et-Loire* (1878), I, p. 34; cf. 'Les Naissances et les Décès à Angers avant la Révolution', *Andegaviana*, I (1904), p. 94. An official figure for the population of the town in 1745—22,607 inhabitants, or 34,900 if one included the country areas directly dependent on the town—agrees with other estimates (Fr. de Dainville, 'Un dénombrement inédit au XVIIIᵉ siècle. L'enquête du Contrôleur Général Orry, 1745', *Population*, VII (1952), p. 66). In 1787 this figure was given as 28,188 (E. Levasseur, *La Population Française*, 2 vols. (1889), I, p. 227). By way of comparison one might add that Angers was one-sixtieth the size of Paris, one-third of the size of Marseilles and Bordeaux. On the other hand it was twice the size of Angoulême, Perpignan, Bayonne, La Rochelle, Châlons. Provincial towns like Rheims, Troyes, Montpellier, Dunkirk, Besançon and Bourges were roughly as populous as Angers (see Necker, '*A Treatise on the Administration of the Finances of France*' (Eng. trans., 1785), I, pp. 234–303).

19 A. Meynier, *Un Représentant de la Bourgeoisie Angevine à l'Assemblée Nationale Constituante et à Convention Nationale. La Revellière-Lépeaux, 1753–1798* (1905), pp. 77–9; F. Dumas, *op. cit.*, pp. 314–22.

20 Dumas, *op. cit.*, pp. 314–15.

21 Besnard, I, pp. 143–4, 126 (Port's note). A certain amount of statistical information about social classes can be gathered from the *Almanach de la Province d'Anjou* (1790), especially p. 68, and from V. Dauphin, *Angers il y a deux cents ans, 1730. Étude économique et sociale d'après le registre de la capitation* (1931). On the eve of the Revolution, there must have been about 80 magistrates of various courts, 40 to 60 avocats, 20 or so notaries, 26 procureurs, 4 Apostolic notaries, and about 74 minor legal officials—say, including the families they supported, 1,000 souls living directly by the law. It is also interesting to see that there were about 700 or more bourgeois living on income with no profession, at least 12 doctors, 20 surgeons and 10 apothecaries.

22 Rangeard (extracts in *Anjou hist.*, IX, pp. 466–8).

23 See the receipts in the archives of the Faculty of Theology (A.M.L. D 31).

24 E.g. Aubert at Ronceray and Marquat at Saint-Serge, both priests. 'Département de Maine et Loire. Traitement des officiers des chapitres d'Angers', with letter of Department, 5 Feb. 1791 (A. Nat. D XIX 80, file 612, no. 10).

25 F. Uzureau, *Un Martyr de la Foi en 1794. M. Laigneau de Langellerie, aumônier du Carmel d'Angers* (1913); E. Querau-Lamerie, *Le Clergé du Département de Maine-et-Loire pendant la Révolution* (1899), pp. 34–6; *Rondeau, Histoire du Monastère des Ursulines d'Angers 1618–1910* (1911), p. 219; 'Les Visitandines d'Angers pendant et après la Révolution', *Anjou hist.*, IX (1908–9), p. 49n.; P.V. Directory Dept., 10 Nov. 1790 (A.M.L. 1 L 68). The nuns would sometimes provide a house: for the Visitation, see P.V. Directory Dept., 18 Jan. 1791 (A.M.L. 1 L 69); for the Pénitentes, see estimation of *Biens Nationaux* (A.M.L. III Q 2, vol. IV, no. 13 in the 4th series of numberings). For the chaplain at the castle, see Municipal Reg. (Mairie), II, p. 36. The nuns of Sainte-Catherine paid their chaplain 200*l.* and board (A.M.L. 13 Q 8 'Etat'), the Carmelites 500*l.* and board (A.M.L. 14 Q 8), the Pénitentes 300*l.* and board (A.M.L. 13 Q 14). An ex-vicaire who served as a deacon at Ronceray was given lodging and 900*l.* (A.M.L. 16 Q 3), while an ex-curé had a pension from Ronceray of 400*l.* and one from the Pénitentes of 250*l.* (A.M.L. 16 Q 3).

[26] Queruau-Lamerie, *op. cit.*, p. 36. For a chaplain at the Incurables, 'M. Noel Pinot', *Anjou hist.*, III (1902–3), pp. 375–6.

[27] Details here which are not referred to later in the text are in Uzureau, 'Les Religieuses de l'Abbaye de Ronceray', *Mems. Soc. Agric.*, IX (1906), p. 252; De Moleon, *Voyages Liturgiques de France ou Recherches faites en diverses villes* (1757), p. 83. For dress of choir-boys; A.M.L. G 269, p. 53 (23 April 1768); for dress of canons of the cathedral, Lehoreau, 'Cérémonial de l'Église d'Angers' (early eighteenth century) in *Anjou hist.*, XV, p. 248; G. Letourneau, *Histoire du Séminaire d'Angers* (1895), p. 152, for robes of a Doctor of Theology.

[28] R. Reuss, 'Les Réformés d'Angers et la destruction du Temple de Sorges en 1685', *Soc. de l'histoire du Protestantisme Français, Bulletin*, LXIV (1915), p. 633. For the abjuration of Protestant ministers in the two preceding years, see Port, *Dict.*, II, pp. 262–3, and L. Demaison, *Cat. Gén. MSS. ... Reims (Coll. P. Tarbé)* (1909), p. 279. The son of one of them became dean of Saint-Laud (died 1762).

[29] 'Tables de la Loi', *Bull. Prot.*, 1932, p. 37; Godard-Faultrier, *L'Anjou et ses Monuments*, 3 vols. (1839–40), II, p. 483; *Andegaviana*, I (1900), p. 102.

[30] See *Anjou hist.*, XII, p. 582n. For two girls sent to nunneries and 'converted', see *La Semaine Religeuse d'Angers*, 4 Oct. 1908, pp. 1037–9.

[31] René-Jean Bailly's life of Vaugirault (*Anjou hist.*, VII, 1906–7), pp. 487–8. There were hardly any Protestants in the countryside around Angers; see J. Orcibal, 'État présent des recherches sur la répartition géographique des *Nouveaux Catholiques* à la fin du XVIIᵉ siècle', *Rev. de l'histoire de l'Eglise de France*, XXXIII (1947), p. 106.

[32] A.M.L. G 271, p. 548 (12 June 1774), p. 625 (18 Sept. 1774). For an abjuration in 1769, Guy de Chateaubriant, 'Glané dans les Archives d'Anjou', *Méms. Soc. Agric.*, XIX (1945), p. 138.

[33] Corr. Academy of Angers (B. Angers MS. 611 (568), nos. 34–37); cf. Port, *Dict.*, I, p. 729; Cherel, *Fénelon au 18ᵉ siècle* (1917), p. 437. The minor poet of Cambrai was François Marchant, elder brother of dom René Marchant, a monk of Saint-Aubin of Angers (M. Chartier, 'A travers les papiers Caprara. Bénédictin d'Angers et bibliothécaire de Cambrai. René Marchant', *Revue du Nord*, XXIV (1938), p. 192).

[34] Port, *Cartulaire de l'Hôpital Saint-Jean*, p. 18.

[35] Cahier of the Clergy of Anjou, 1789 (in Proust, *Archives de l'Ouest* (1868), IV, p. 31); cahier of the chapter of Saint-Laud, A.M.L. G 942, f. 125 (12 March 1789). Research, if it can be called by so exalted a name, is found in the abbé Gaudin's 'Anecdotes Angevines' (1774) (B. Angers MS. 1550 (6)). Rangeard's 'Mémoires pour servir à l'histoire du Calvinisme et de la Ligue en l'Anjou' (B. Angers MS. 1019) is much more serious—it was written during the revolutionary years.

[36] For the University of Angers' resistance to Arnauld's Jansenism, see C. Cochin, *Henry Arnauld, évêque d'Angers (1597–1692)* (1921), pp. 261–90.

[37] O. Marcault, *Le Diocèse de Tours*, 3 vols. (1918), II, pp. cxcv–ccii; cf. pp. 209–10. For Jansenist claims that they had supporters in the diocese who 'groan in secret', see Pletteau, 'Le Jansénisme dans l'Université d'Angers', *Répertoire archéologique de l'Anjou*, 1862, p. 381.

[38] Lens, *L'Université d'Angers*, I (*Faculté des Droits*) (1880), pp. 39, 67–8,

243; 'L'Oratoire et le Jansénisme en Anjou', *Andegaviana*, XXIV, pp. 396-7; Breval, *Travels*, II, p. 25.

[39] L. Bassette, *Jean de Caulet, Évêque et Prince de Grenoble, 1693-1771* (1946), p. 37. For bishop Poncet's nephew, a notorious foe of Jansenism and of the Parlement of Paris, see G. Livet, *L'Intendance d'Alsace sous Louis XIV (1648-1715)* (1956), p. 942.

[40] Extract in Raison, 'Le Mouvement Janséniste au diocèse de Rennes', *Annales de Bretagne*, XLVIII (1941), p. 28n. The bishop's Charge of 1716 is in A.M.L. G 4; his printing of the *Indiction du Concile Provincial d'Embrun* (1727) in A.M.L. G 5; his 'Ordonnance' of 1704 in Bodl. G. Pamph. 2240, no. 4. For other pamphlets of the bishop, see J. F. Thomas, *La Querelle de l'Unigenitus* (1950), pp. 125, 138.

[41] The confraternity was not re-established until 1761 (Brossier, B. Angers MSS. 727, p. 131).

[42] Port, *Dict.*, II, 289-90; dom Piolon, 'Un professeur à l'Université d'Angers, Joseph Mabaret', *Rev. hist. litt. arch. d'Anjou*, III (1869), p. 132.

[43] Uzureau, 'Le Jansénisme en Anjou 1713-1730', *Rev. des Facultés Catholiques de l'Ouest*, Dec. 1914, pp. 402-3, 386; and 'La Faculté d'Angers contre le Jansénisme', *ibid.*, Feb. 1914, pp. 518-23.

[44] See below, pp. 174ff.

[45] Uzureau, *Rev. des Facultés Catholiques de l'Ouest*, Dec. 1914, p. 386.

[46] 'Paul Gilly, doyen du Chapitre Saint-Laud-lès-Angers', *Anjou hist.*, XXVI, p. 14; 'Claire Omo, professeur à la Faculté de Théologie d'Angers, *ibid.*, XXII, pp. 16-19.

[47] Bachelier, *Le Jansénisme à Nantes* (1934), p. 257.

[48] See E. Préclin, *Les Jansénistes du xviiie siècle et la Constitution civile du Clergé* (1928).

[49] Lens, I, p. 270.

[50] J. Leflon, *Etienne-Alexandre Bernier, évêque d'Orléans, et l'application du Concordat*, 2 vols. (1938-9), I, p. 3.

[51] The syndic of the diocese asked the agents-general of the Clergy of France for copies of letters addressed to his bishop, as he was generally in the capital (A. Nat. G 8 620, plaq. 53, 1 Feb. 1774). M. de Grasse was not, however, entirely absent from his diocese in his latter years, as has been said (see 'Mgr de Grasse évêque d'Angers', *Anjou hist.*, I (1900-1), pp 626 ff.).

[52] See p. 38 following.

CHAPTER II

[1] For the various bells, see the notes by 'E. L.' (the abbé Emile Longin) in his edition of Thorode, *Notice de la Ville d'Angers, 1772* (1897), pp. 373, 367, 293, 345, 313, 205, 218, 92-7. For the Jacobins, A.M.L. 13 Q 11. There was one bell at the Prêtres de la Mission (A.M.L. 13 Q 14), two at the Écoles Chrétiennes ('Inventaire', 30 May 1792, A.M.L. 13 Q 9, p. 42). At La Fidelité there were two in the main tower and one over the sacristry (P.V. Municipality, 26 April 1790, A.M.L. 13 Q 10).

[2] M. L. de Farcy, *Clochers, Sonnerie, Horloge et Porche de la Cathédrale d'Angers* (1872), p. 32; Péan de la Tuillerie, *Description*, p. 58; Rangeard, 'État...' (B. Angers MS. 1020 (894), f. 23); A.M.L. G 271, p. 663 (Jan. 1775); A.M.L. G 1014, f. 25 (12 Dec. 1782); A.M.L. G 942 (May 1784); État Civil, Hôtel de Ville, Angers, GG 185, f. 51, p. 33, cap. 77.

[3] 'La Cathédrale d'Angers pendant la Révolution', *Anjou hist.*, XXV (1925), p. 135.

[4] Péan de la Tuillerie, p. 56.

[5] Besnard, I, p. 133.

[6] 'Réglémens pour une Communauté de Filles dans un pensionnat' (B. Angers MS. 412 (399) p. 9). Custumal of the Carmelite friars (1728), A.M.L. 86 H 4, p. 19.

[7] A.M.L. G 1116, p. 170 (9 Sept. 1762); Port, *Inventaire ... des Archives ... de la Mairie*, p. 144.

[8] Some idea of how rich and how numerous vestments were can be gleaned from the inventories of churches in the early years of the Revolution. For example (if such detail is not thought too frivolous) here are the figures for chasubles alone in some churches: Toussaint 7 (A.M.L. 13 Q 5), Carmelites 18 (A.M.L. 13 Q 8), La Croix 7 (13 Q 8), La Baumette 44, mostly old (13 Q 15), Pénitentes 13, Ursulines 20, parish of Saint-Evroul 11, Écoles Chrétiennes 14, etc.

[9] De Moleon, *Voyages Liturgiques de France*, pp. 84-8 (date of the edition is 1757, but the original travels date from the early years of the century).

[10] 'Journal des Usages du Séminaire d'Angers', Letourneau, App. III, p. 405.

[11] 'Les Cérémonies religieuses à Angers avant la Révolution', *Anjou hist.*, XIII, pp. 572-4.

[12] 'Détail des employés et des exercices du Séminaire d'Angers' (c. 1737), *Anjou hist.*, XXV (1925), p. 79.

[13] 'Le chapitre de la Cathédrale d'Angers avant la Révolution. Processions', *Andegaviana*, XXIV, pp. 64 ff.; A.M.L. G 271, pp. 661-2, 670; A.M.L. 86 H4, f. 30.

[14] For what follows, De Moleon, pp. 91, 100, 81, 93-7; Péan de la Tuillerie, p. 65; Piganiol de la Force, *Nouveau Voyage en France* (1780).

[15] Péan de la Tuillerie mentions this, but not De Moleon. It was Locke (*Travels in France, 1695-1679*, ed. J. Lough, 1953, p. 223), however, who noticed that the faces carved on the water pots would have been idolatrous to Jews.

[16] For very similar ceremonies of the 'Three Marys' on Easter day at Troyes, see A. Prévost, 'Histoire de la Maîtrise de la Cathédrale de Troyes', *Mems. Soc. Acad. d'Agriculture, des Sciences, Arts et Belles-Lettres du Département de l'Aube*, 3rd Ser., XLII (1905), p. 336.

[17] As in note 14 above; but for the procession of Saint-Julien, Mme Letondal 'Mémoires' *Anjou hist.*, V (1904-5), p. 13; for the procession of the Cordeliers on the Monday of the octave of Corpus Christi, which the Carmelites were bound to attend, A.M.L. 86 H 20, p. 16; for the Easter Monday procession of Saint-Pierre, E. L. in Thorode, p. 310, and for the dragon of Saint-Serge, A. de Soland in *Méms. Soc. Agric.*, I (1850), pp. 244-5.

[18] 'A.G.', 'La Procession de la Saint-Marc et les Rogations en Anjou avant la Révolution', *Anjou hist.*, 1953, p. 45.

[19] A.M.L. G 272, p. 699; G 942, f. 21; G 273, f. 463.

[20] A.M.L. G 272, p. 699; G 942, f. 60(b).

[21] 'Le Chapitre de la Cathédrale d'Angers avant la Révolution. Processions', *Andegaviana*, XXIV, pp. 65-8.

[22] Péan de la Tuillerie, *Description*, p. 226; A.M.L. G 942, ff. 21, 33(b), 29.

[23] Full details of the *neuvaine* of 23 April-1 May 1785 in A.M.L. G 1014, f. 121; cf. ff. 288, 312. Saint-Sérené was also popularly invoked for 'serene' weather, J. Levron, *Les Saints du pays angevin* (1946), p. 115.

[24] 'Mémoire pour M. du Chapitre de Saint-Laud d'Angers' (c. 1763), A. Nat. H 1633, no. 253.

[25] For lists of relics see E. L.'s notes in Thorode, pp. 56-7, 265-6, 309, 345-6; Port, *Dict.*, I, pp. 54-8, 33; Godard-Faultrier, 'Extrait d'un Inventaire des

Saintes Reliques conservées dans le Trésor de l'Église d'Angers', *Méms. Soc. Agric.*, 2nd Ser., III (1852), pp. 95 ff.

[26] Locke (1678), p. 223.

[27] Péan de La Tuillerie, *Description*, pp. 58–9.

[28] A.M.L. G 272, p. 305 (24 Sept. 1782); E. Chevrier, 'Notice sur les Églises de Sablé', *Rev. hist. et arch. du Maine*, I (1876), pp. 408–9.

[29] A.M.L. G 1013, p. 185. Notice the emphasis on authenticity. A doubtful relic would be inventoried with a note to this effect—'a little box of crystal, in which is enclosed, *"dit-on"*, a corporal stained with the Precious Blood' (Inventory at Saint-Martin, 1787, A.M.L. H 27, p. 140).

[30] Thorode, pp. 137–8.

[31] 'La paroisse de Saint-Samson-lès-Angers', *Andegaviana*, XXIV, p. 137.

[32] Port, *Dict.*, I, p. 189; 'La paroisse de Lesvière-lès-Angers' au xviiie siècle', *Anjou hist.*, XXI, p. 9.

[33] Péan de la Tuillerie, p. 17; Piganiol de la Force, p. 170.

[34] Thomas Marwood's Diary (1701) in the 'Beddingfeld Papers', *Catholic Record Soc. Misc.*, VI (1909), p. 103.

[35] Joseph Grandet, *Considerations et pratiques de piété pour honorer Jésus Christ au Saint-Sacrament* (1716) in *Anjou hist.*, XIV, pp. 5–19; Desjobert, 'Notes d'un voyage en Anjou' (1780) in *Andegaviana* XI, p. 120.

[36] A full list of the tableaux for the years 1770, 1780 and 1785 is given by dom Chamard in 'Le Sacre d'Angers', *Revue de l'Art Chrétien*, IV (1860), pp. 149–52.

[37] Municipal Registers (B. Angers MS. BB 130, ff. 77, 31).

[38] V. Dauphin, 'La Corporation des Ciriers d'Angers'. *Mems. Soc. Agric.*, 2nd ser., XXVI (1923), p. 24; Lehoreau, 'Cérémonial de l'Église d'Angers' (early eighteenth century) in *Anjou hist.*, XV, p. 565.

[39] Otherwise called the *Clocheteur des Trépassés*, who in some provincial towns still went round at night with his bell crying 'Réveillez-vous, gens qui dormez, priez Dieu pour les trépassés'—parodied by profane wits as 'Prenez vos femmes, embrassez-les' (see *Le Voyageur à Paris, tableau pittoresque et moral de cette Capitale* (1797), I, pp. 72–3; the work is by an Angevin).

[40] Lehoreau, *Anjou hist.*, XV, pp. 567–8.

[41] V. Dauphin, 'Les anciennes corporations d'Angers. Les juridictions consulaires', *Mems. Soc. Agric.*, 6th Ser., IV (1929), p. 163.

[42] 'A propos du Sacre d'Angers', *Anjou hist.*, XII, pp. 608–11; Grandet, *Anjou hist.*, XIV, p. 581.

[43] See 'Note sur des Fouilles pratiquées au Tertre Saint-Laurent', *Mems. Soc. Agric.*, VI (1849), pp. 222–5.

[44] Grandet, in *Anjou hist.*, XIV, p. 582.

[45] Municipal Reg., B. Angers MS. BB 130, ff. 50, 91. In 1777, dean Duchilleau of Saint-Laud records in his accounts—'à Mr. Mabeaud pour le jour du Sacre pour ma part d'un repas qu'il avoit commandé chez un traiteur 4*l. 7s. 6d.*' (A.M.L. G 946, p. 2).

[46] Hamelin, 'Un voyage en Anjou' (1782), *Anjou hist.*, IX (1908–9), p. 41.

[47] Mme Letondal, *Anjou hist.*, V (1904–5), p. 12.

[48] Hamelin, *op. cit.*, p. 42.

[49] A.M.L. G 273, f. 294 (23 May 1788); G 269, p. 652 (22 May 1780); Brossier, B. Angers MS. 730, p. 219; for the parish of Saint-Maurille A.M.L. G 1732, ff. 31, 35(b), 36 (year 1777).

[50] Le Moy, *Cahiers*, pp. 258, 250; E. Rondeau, 'Le Sacre d'Angers', *Méms. Soc. Agric.*, 5th Ser., V (1902), pp. 34–5; Municipal Reg. (Mairie), I, p. 58 (April 1790).

[51] B. Bois, *Les Fêtes révolutionnaires à Angers de l'an II à l'an VIII* (1793–99) (1929), pp. 26, 42.

[52] A.M.L. G 273, f. 183 (4 June 1787).

[53] 'A propos du *Sacre* d'Angers 1741', *Anjou hist.*, XII, p. 590.

[54] *Arrêt de la Cour de Parlement* (11 July 1786), Caps. 82, 83. A copy is found in the parish register of Saint-Pierre, État Civil, Hôtel de Ville, Angers, GG 185, p. 34. It was not until 26 April 1792 that the municipality of Angers prohibited churchwardens from demanding this tribute—on the ground that it was a tax and that taxes could only be levied by the national legislature! (Municipal Register (Mairie) II, p. 180(b)).

[55] *Nouvelles ecclésiastiques*, 25 Sept. 1750, p. 155.

[56] Besnard, I, p. 120.

[57] For a discussion of suitable tests, see G. Le Bras, *Introduction à l'histoire de la pratique religieuse en France* (1942), pp. 24, 36–9, 52.

[58] *Extrait des Registres du Parlement, concernant la Police générale de la ville d'Angers* (14 May 1777), B. Angers H 2090, nos. 6 and 7.

[59] E.g. the testaments of Charles Louet (1746) and of Mathurin Margariteau (1779) in Gontard de Launay, *Recherches généalogiques et historiques sur les familles des maires d'Angers* (1893), II, p. 268, and J. Levron 'L'intérieur d'un honnête homme au XVIIIe siècle', *Anjou hist.*, 1953, pp. 75–9. In 1778 the wife of a master-baker gave 200l. to the parish of Saint-Evroul to found a requiem and two low masses each year for her husband's soul (A.M.L. G 1694, f. 32(b)). The impression of decline is derived from the lists of foundations of religious houses; I have not had time to work through the archives of notaries to confirm this. The generous gifts to the Lazarists (p. 84, below) are exceptional.

[60] Blordier-Langlois, 'Autobiographie', *Rev. hist. litt. arch. d'Anjou*, I (1867), pp. 194–5.

[61] *Mémoires de l'abbé Baston, chanoine de Rouen*, ed. J. Loth and Ch. Verger (1897–99). Extracts are printed in *Anjou hist.*, X.

[62] 'Les Missions décennales à Angers avant la Révolution', *Anjou hist.*, XVI, pp. 585–7.

[63] 'La Béatification et la canonisation de Sainte-Chantal à Angers et à Saumur', *Andegaviana* IV (1906), pp. 286–9. Cf. 'prodigious' crowds at the Ursulines in 1775 (Rondeau, 'L'église des Ursulines', *Méms. Soc. Agric.*, VIII (1905), p. 327).

[64] *Nouvelles ecclésiastiques*, 4 Sept. 1751, p. 144.

[65] Port, *Inventaire-sommaire des Archives Départementales, Maine-et-Loire, Série G* (1880), pp. 32–3; cf. *Andegaviana*, XXIII, p. 127.

[66] 'Le chapitre de la Trinité à la fin du XVIIIe siècle', *Anjou hist.*, XVIII, p. 208.

[67] Besnard, I, pp. 196–7.

[68] A *monitoire* was an injunction by ecclesiastical authority, on the request of a lay judge, to reveal anything one might know of a certain crime, under pain of excommunication. It would normally be read out by curés at the *prône* of their parish mass on three successive Sundays (Guyot, XL, pp. 209–25). Angevin confessors ruled that a *monitoire* did not oblige a man to give evidence against his relatives down to the fourth degree ('Consultation de cas de conscience', MS. Univ. Rennes 221, p. 38). For two interesting examples of the use and abuse of the *monitoire*, see A. Coquerel, *Jean Calas et sa famille* (1869), pp. 91–2, and G. Walter, *Hébert et le Père Duchesne* (1946), p. 16.

[69] Lehoreau in *Andegaviana*, XVII, pp. 6–7. A theological handbook of the diocese of Angers published in 1712, gave an extensive discussion of *monitoires* on the ground that they were 'frequently used in France' (see the remarks of the *Journal de Trevoux*, Oct. 1713, p. 1834). For an interesting *monitoire* of 1701, see B. Angers MS. 767, no. 1.

x

[70] *Le Parfait Notaire apostolique* (1775), I, p. 692.

[71] Port, *Inventaire ... des Archives ... de la Mairie*, pp. 313, 134, 137, 139, 141.

[72] Besnard, I, pp. 87–90; *Nouvelles ecclésiastiques*, 10 July 1754, p. 111; 4 Sept. 1754, p. 143. (The bishop is heavily censured for granting a *monitoire* against the satirists but not against the pamphleteer, who was his own vicar-general.) One might observe here that compared with other legal documents or other ecclesiastical ceremonies, a *monitoire* was absurdly cheap—30 sous to the diocesan officials, 10 sous registration fee, 10 sous to a curé for publication (P. Alletz), *La Discipline de l'Église de France* (1780), p. 117.

[73] Cf. Champion, *Le France d'après les cahiers* (1921), pp. 194–5.

[74] Municipal Reg., B. Angers MS. BB 132, f. 114(b).

[75] Thorode, p. 307.

[76] Péan de la Tuillerie, p. 41; Letourneau, *Histoire du Séminaire*, app. III, p. 412; *Processionale Andegavense* (1788), B. Angers S.T. 269, p. 8.

[77] Pierre Le Loyer, *Discovres des Spectres ou Visions et Apparations d'Esprits* (1608), p. 607.

[78] Rangeard, 'État historique, ecclésiastique et civil de l'Anjou', B. Angers MS. 1020, f. 22.

[79] Cit. C. Bila, *La Croyance à la Magie au XVIIIe siècle en France dans les contes, romans et traités*, *Thèse*, Paris (1925), p. 135. Bila seems to be in error in ascribing this article to Diderot (see J. Assézat, *Œuvres complètes de Diderot*, XVI (1876), p. 35n.).

[80] Port, *Dict.*, II, p. 442.

[81] See Bila, *op. cit.*, pp. 38, 52–3, 62–3, 138. For clergy ridiculing superstition, p. 136.

[82] Port, *Dict.*, II, 376 (P. Hunault); III, 61 (F. Paulmier).

[83] Curé Robin, *Le Mont-Glonne, ou recherches historiques sur l'origine des Celtes...* (1784), *Œuvres de M. Robin*, I, p. 160.

[84] The cathedral paid its preachers 500*l.* for their course. (A.M.L. G 271, pp. 661–2, 13 Jan. 1775).

[85] Merlet de la Boulaye, letter of 21 July 1767, B. Angers MS. 634.

[86] E.g. at the parish of Saint-Maurice in 1772 and 1776 (A.M.L. G 271, pp. 389, 391; Brossier, B. Angers MS. 729, p. 73(b)). For details of a parish mission in 1738, see 'Une mission à Saint-Maurille d'Angers', *Anjou hist.*, XVII, pp. 363–5.

[87] 'Les missions décennales à Angers avant la Révolution', *Anjou hist.*, XVI, pp. 572–87; for interesting details on mission technique early in the century, see 'Recueil de Sermons pour la mission d'Angers' (1712), (B. Angers MS. 259 (250)).

[88] René-Jean Bailly's life of Vaugirault, in *Anjou hist.*, VII, 1906–7, pp. 497–8.

[89] Rangeard, 'État...' in *Andegaviana*, VI, pp. 144–5.

[90] Rondeau, 'Saint-Michel du Tertre d'Angers', *Méms. Soc. Agric.*, 4th Ser., IV (1890), p. 282.

[91] Péan de la Tuillerie, p. 308.

[92] A.M.L. G 1171, f. 78 (27 Jan. 1790); A.M.L. G 1781 (complaint by the lay warden and treasurer, 16 July 1783).

[93] See the new statutes of 1782 (A.M.L. G 1676).

[94] R.P.F. Marie Bernard Ducondray, 'La Confrérie du Rosaire en Anjou du XVe siècle à la Révolution', *Rev. Anjou*, N.S., XI (1885), pp. 75–8. For the place of this confraternity in the Dominican order generally, see R. P. Mortier, *Histoire des Maîtres Généraux de l'Ordre des Frères Prêcheurs*, VII (1914), pp. 188–203.

⁹⁵ Fr. Jean Donatien Levesque, 'Corporations, communautés seculaires, confréries ... du Tiers-Ordre dans l'ancien couvent des Frères-Prêcheurs d'Angers', *Anjou hist.*, 1953, pp. 121–46.

⁹⁶ Thorode, 'Notice sur la ville d'Angers' (1773) in *Anjou hist.*, XXVII (1927), p. 32.

⁹⁷ For this confraternity see *Très-Humbles et Très-Respectueuses Représentations ... de la noble Confrérie des Bourgeois ... à Monseigneur le Comte de Provence* (1774), B. Angers MS. 767, no. 7. Suchet, curé of Saint-Michel de la Palud & Huchelou, curé of Saint-Julien were members in 1790 ('Extrait du Registre des Conclusions de la Société des Nobles Bourgeois...' 19 Aug. 1790 (B. Angers MS. GG 363)). Printed forms of admission and invitation are found in A.M.L. J 3134.

⁹⁸ 'Un différand entre le Présidial et la Municipalité d'Angers, 1743', *Andegaviana*, 1937, pp. 22–4.

⁹⁹ Brossier, B. Angers MS. 730, p. 35, 727, p. 18(b).

¹⁰⁰ Brossier, B. Angers MS. 726, p. 617, 730, p. 166(b) (date 1764). It was on a 1st April!

¹⁰¹ Brossier, B. Angers MS. 730, p. 45(b).

¹⁰² A.M.L. G 1014, f. 25 (Dec. 1782).

¹⁰³ A.M.L. G 942, f. 13(b) (Saint-Laud); G 1171, f. 41 (Saint-Pierre) G. 1014, ff. 26, 121, 122, 268 (Saint-Martin).

¹⁰⁴ A.M.L. G 269, p. 640 (1 May 1780).

CHAPTER III

¹ Port, *Dict.*, I, p. 82.

² See, for example, F. J. Fétis, *Biographie universelle des musiciens*, 8 vols. (1860–5), II, p. 456; III, p. 31; IV, pp. 61, 91; V, p. 265; VI, pp. 55, 333; VII, pp. 341, 3, 92.

³ O. Marcault, *Le Diocèse de Tours*, II, p. 285.

⁴ 'Personne n'ignore que, depuis le moyen âge jusqu'à la Révolution, les maîtrises des églises cathédrales et collégiales de France ont été, avec la chapelle royale, des centres actifs de culture et d'enseignement musical' (M. Brenet, *Les Musiciens de la Sainte-Chapelle du Palais*, Soc. Internat. de Musique, Section de Paris, 1910). 'Tous les chanteurs qui ont eu quelque célébrité ont reçu leur éducation musicale dans les maîtrises...' (Portalis to Napoleon, 30 June 1805, cit. Marcault, p. 286). For examples—Marmontel, *Memoirs* (Eng. trans., 4 vols., 1850), I, p. 376; Fétis, I, pp. 5–6, 387; II, pp. 172, 403; III, p. 200; IV, pp. 438–9; V, pp. 256, 281, 438; VII, p. 109.

⁵ M. Brenet, 'Sebastien de Brossard, 165?–1730', *Méms. Soc. de l'Hist. de Paris et de l'Île de France*, XXIII (1896), pp. 75, 91. For examples, 'Les premiers Pianistes Parisiens', *Rev. Musicale*, April 1923, p. 196. It was customary to allow able choir-boys to have motets and masses of their own composition performed in church (see Brenet, *Les Musiciens de la Sainte-Chapelle*, pp. 286, 302, 306–9; Clerval, *L'ancienne Maîtrise de Notre-Dame de Chartres* (1899), pp. 92, 113, 307; 'La revue des Maîtres de Chapelle et musiciens de la Métropole de Rouen', *Précis analytique des travaux de l'Académie de Rouen*, 1850, p. 221.

⁶ A. Cellier, 'Les Motets de Michel-Richard de la Lande', *Rev. musicale*, Feb.–March 1946, p. 21; Fétis, IV, pp. 5, 102; P. Longlas des Clavières, 'Les Ancêtres de Grétry', *Rev. musicale*, Jan. 1923, p. 225. The ancedote concerning Rameau originates with Maret, *Éloge historique de M. Rameau* (Dijon, 1766)

who cites the authority of the secretary of the Academy of Clermont. A similar tale, with better evidence to support it, is told of Rameau's brother. C. Girdlestone, *Jean-Philippe Rameau* (1957), accepts both stories, suggesting that one brother imitated the whimsical device used by the other.

[7] Clerval, *L'ancien Maîtrise de ... Chartres*, pp. 50-1, 81-2, 92-8, 102-3; A. Prévost, 'Histoire de la Maîtrise de la Cathédrale de Troyes', *Mems. Soc. Acad. d'Agric. ... du Département de l'Aube*, 3rd Ser., XLII (1905), pp. 263-5.

[8] La Bruyère, *Les Caractères* (ed. Hachette, 1916), p. 426.

[9] For the royal chapel, de Luynes, *Mémoires sur la Cour de Louis XV* (ed. L. Dussieux and E. Soulié, 1860), II, p. 65; VI, pp. 436-7; VII, pp. 9, 280; IX, pp. 8, etc.

[10] R. Viollier, 'Jean-Joseph Mouret', *Rev. musicale*, July-Aug. 1938, pp. 19-21.

[11] *Journal et mémoires de Mathieu Marais, 1715-1737*, ed. M. De Lescure, 4 vols. (1863), IV p. 458; Marmontel, I, pp. 331, etc.; Luynes, IX, p. 9.

[12] G. Sceats, *The Liturgical use of the Organ* (1922), p. 7.

[13] Duforq, 'Les grandes Formes de la musique d'Orgue', *Rev. musicale*, 1937, p. 228; R. Aigrain, *Religious Music* (E.T.) (1931?), p. 228. See the reference to Daquin's imitation of the nightingale in Mercier's *Tableau de Paris*, II, p. 82, and to Balbastre in C. Burney, *The Present State of Music in France and Italy* (1773), p. 38.

[14] P. C. C. Bogaerts, *Études sur les Livres choraux qui ont servi de base dans la publication des livres de chant Grégorien édités à Malines* (1855), pp. 118-20.

[15] *Tableau de Paris*, II, p. 81. For the history of the 'secularization' of Church music—'part of the drift of European culture from the church to the stage', see W. Mellers, *François Couperin and the French Classical Tradition* (1950?), pp. 146-9, and C. Girdlestone, *Rameau*, pp. 73-6, 104-5. By its very nature, church music has always been open to such accusations. Dr. F. Sternfeld has drawn my attention to a passage in Erasmus (see Reese, *Music in the Renaissance* (1954), p. 448) which has the same ring as this quotation from Mercier.

[16] For 'Theophilanthropy' see below, pp. 291-4.

[17] A.M.L. G 273, pp. 30 (17 March 1786), 170 (28 March 1787); G 274 (14 March 1788), p. 418 (27 March 1789).

[18] A.M.L. G 272, p. 1 (5 Oct. 1780); Rondeau, 'L'église des Ursulines', *Méms. Soc. Agric.*, VIII (1905); 'Précis des discours dans l'église... de Saint-Martin' (17 Nov. 1773), B. Angers MS. 1045.

[19] De Moleon, *Voyages liturgiques*, p. 84.

[20] Besnard, I, p. 132.

[21] X. de la Perraudière, 'Voyage à Rome en 1750 par M. Robin, curé d'Anjou', *Rev. des Facultés Catholiques de l'Ouest*, V (1894-5), p. 281.

[22] A.M.L. G 269, p. 254 (Aug. 1777); G 271, p. 502 (Sept. 1773), p. 556 (April 1774). The expenses for the eve of Saint-Maurice were normally 300*l.*; for the chapter's attempt to reduce this, G 273, p. 85 (Aug. 1786); p. 212 (Sept. 1787). For instrumentalists from Saumur and Poitiers, G 269, p. 39 (April 1776); G 271, p. 502 (Sept. 1773).

[23] A.M.L. G 272, p. 110 (June 1781); G 273, p. 225 (9 Nov. 1787).

[24] *Affiches* in 'Variétés religieuses angevines, fin du xviiie siècle', *Andegaviana*, IV (1906), p. 23.

[25] C. Port, *Artistes Angevins* (1881), p. 138.

[26] Port, *op. cit.*, pp. 10-11; in 1761 there had been some question of his becoming *maître de musique* of Chartres (Clerval, *L'ancienne Maîtrise de Notre-Dame de Chartres*, pp. 101-2). 'Sa musique était exacte, mais son style n'était pas amusant' (*Affiches* 1782 in *Anjou hist.*, III (1902-3), pp. 481-2).

[27] Brossier, B. Angers MS. 730, p. 78.

[28] 'Variétés religieuses angevines, fin du xviiie siècle', *Andegaviana*, IV (1906), p. 5.

[29] *Affiches* in *Anjou hist.*, XVII, p. 159, and *Andegaviana*, IV, pp. 24–5.

[30] A.M.L. G 271, p. 702 (March 1775); G 269, p. 201 (May 1777).

[31] A.M.L. III Q 1 (Estimation *Biens Nat.*), no. 431.

[32] Port, *Dict.*, III, pp. 747–8; A.M.L. G 273, p. 277 (March 1788).

[33] Port, *Artistes Angevins*, p. 298; A.M.L. G 269, pp. 114, 109, 383; G 271, p. 749.

[34] A.M.L. G 269, p. 383; G 273, pp. 180, 132, 74; 'Département de Maine-et-Loire. Traitement des officiers des chapitres d'Angers' (5 Feb. 1791), A. Nat. D xix. 80, file 612, no. 10. The fund which furnished their revenues was called 'la Bourse des bacheliers'.

[35] A.M.L. III Q 1 (Estimation *Biens Nat.*), nos. 323, 339, 432 (houses of Rosé, Pochard, and Bardoul).

[36] Verses of Follet, in A.M.L. G 299.

[37] A.M.L. G 269, p. 13; G 273, p. 427; Brossier, B. Angers MS. 729, pp. 139, 385, 87.

[38] A.M.L. G 271, p. 495.

[39] A.M.L. G 271, pp. 400 (Nov. 1772), 672 (Feb. 1775).

[40] Cf. A.M.L. G 271, pp. 545 (Feb. 1774), 555, 636 (Feb. 1775). For the dress, De Moleon, p. 83; Brossier, B. Angers MS. 730, p. 89.

[41] See 'Inventaire des meubles de la psalette' (A.M.L. 13 Q 24) for details of arrangements.

[42] A.M.L. G 269, p. 82; G 271, pp. 7, 345, 544; G 273, pp. 2, 165 (April 1787), 245 (Jan. 1788). For the change of 1780, A.M.L. G 269, p. 646 (12 May 1780).

[43] A.M.L. G 269, pp. 92, 113, 252.

[44] A.M.L. G 271, pp. 520, 522.

[45] A.M.L. G 269, p. 452 (30*l.* given); G 271, p. 313 (96*l.* given to a boy sent away because of 'des infirmités qui pouvaient se communiquer aux autres enfants qu'en outre il étoit sans aucune espèce d'aptitude pour apprendre la musique').

[46] Brossier, B. Angers MS. 730, pp. 28, 19, 237.

[47] A.M.L. G 269, p. 631 (April 1780).

[48] Port, *Artistes*, p. 12; Clerval, *Chartres*, p. 125. One imagines, comparing this salary with that of choir-men, that there must have been many additional perquisites.

[49] A.M.L. G 942, p. 72 (June 1786)—increase of the salary of the organist of Saint-Laud from 250*l.* (G 942, f. 28(b)) to 400*l.* on condition that this practice ceases. For the salary of the cathedral organist rising from 500*l.* to 800*l.*, see A.M.L. G 273, p. 236 (Dec. 1787), p. 357 (Nov. 1788); special gratifications were also given, e.g. for publishing a piece of music. In June 1783 the organist of Saint-Martin's was given a rent-free house because his salary did not correspond with others (A.M.L. G 1014, f. 48). Saint-Aubin paid 400*l.*, Toussaint 175*l.*, Ronceray 150*l.* with board and lodging (A.M.L. H 1255, p. 41; Petition of 20 Nov. 1792 in A.M.L. 1 L 981), the Carmes 50*l.* (P.V. municipality, 28 April 1790, A.M.L. 13 Q 8). A comparison of organists' salaries with those in the town of Troyes shows the same rise throughout the century, but at Troyes the general level is lower (A. Prévost, 'Instruments de musique usités dans nos églises...', *Méms. Soc. acad. ... de l'Aube*, 3rd Ser., XLI (1904), pp. 93–4, 106, 122).

[50] Petition in A.M.L. G 948.

[51] Saint-Martin: 4 choir-men, wages 474*l.*, 350*l.*, 340*l.*, 400*l.*
Saint-Laud: a subcantor 360*l.*, 3 choir-men, wages 360*l.*, 360*l.*, 200*l.*

Saint-Maurille: a subcantor 300*l.*, 4 choir-men one at 360*l.*, the rest at 300*l.* (P.V. Dept. 2 Oct. 1790, A.M.L. 1 L 68).

Saint-Pierre: 4 choir-men at 342*l.* each. (A. Nat. D XIX 80, file 612, no. 10).

[52] A.M.L. G 1014, f. 194 (1786); G 1013, ff. 13, 345 (1780). The senior of the two choir-boys cost the chapter 100*l.* p.a. (P.V. Dept. 10 Nov. 1790, A.M.L. 1 L 68). For the 'serpent', see C. Burney, *The Present State of Music in France and Italy*, pp. 11-12—'In French churches there is an instrument on each side the choir called the *serpent*, from its shape, I suppose, for it undulates like one. This gives the tone in chanting, and plays the base when they sing in parts. . . The *serpent* keeps the voices up to their pitch, and is a kind of crutch for them to lean on.'

[53] A.M.L. G 1014, ff. 281-2.

[54] A.M.L. G 942, f. 24(b); 'Cantatille pour accompagner le bouquet que prestent a Monseigneur l'Eveque d'Angers au 1er jour de may les enfants de choeur de la cathedrale', by canon d'Estriché of Saint-Laud (c. 1734?) B. Angers MS. 554 (519), II, p. 101; *Processionale Andegavense* (1788), (B. Angers S.T. 269), p. 8. The old Angevin carols were collected and published in 1774 and in 1780 (Port cites Grimault, *Noëls Angevins*, 1876).

[55] Péan de la Tuillerie, *op. cit.*, p. 9.

[56] 'Journal de mon voyage de Rome l'an 1716' (by a Carmelite of Angers), B. Orléans MS. 474, pp. 70-1; J. A. Pocquet de Livonnière, 'Voyage d'Angers à Rome' (c. 1760), B. Angers MS. 1368, p. 24.

[57] Port, *Dict.*, I, p. 52; Lehoreau, in *Anjou hist.*, XV, pp. 235-6.

[58] E. L. in Thorode, pp. 216-17.

[59] The parish of Saint-Maurice adopted the Roman altar in 1718 (E. L. in Thorode, p. 167) and Saint-Laud in 1720 (J. L[evron], 'La paroisse Saint-Laud d'Angers', *Anjou hist.*, 1954, p. 116).

[60] See Port's inventory of Series G of the Departmental archives, pp. 163, 231; also A.M.L. G 1722, f. 81(b)-82 (parish Saint-Maurice 1784); G 1694, i. 23(b) (Saint-Evroul 1771); 'Le clergé du Ronceray et de la Trinité. . .', *Andegaviana*, XXVI, p. 10 (1760); A.M.L. 62 H 5 (Saint-Aignan 1758, 1788); Mme Letondal's Memoirs, *Anjou hist.*, V, p. 12; Levron, 'Saint-Laud', *Anjou hist.*, 1954, p. 116.

[61] E. Champion, 'J.-J. Rousseau et le vandalisme révolutionnaire', *Révolution Française*, LV (1908), p. 26.

[62] Port, *Cartulaire de l'Hôpital Saint-Jean*, p. 31; E. L. in Thorode, pp. 332, 219, 213, 327, 344, 363-4; Port, *Dict.*, I, p. 200.

[63] E. L. in Thorode, pp. 228, 169, 319, 247; see also pp. 176, 313-14, 384, 183, 158, 149, 300, 318, 149, 159. E. Lefèvre-Pontalis, 'L'Église abbatiale du Ronceray', *Congrès archéologique de France*, LXXVIIe session, 1911, II, p. 125.

[64] Thorode, pp. 64 ff.; Port, *Dict.*, I, p. 52; Péan de la Tuillerie, pp. 59-60.

[65] Dufourcq, *Esquisse d'une Histoire de l'Orgue en France du xiiie au xviiie siècle* (1935), p. 407; Port, *Artistes Angevins*, pp. 3-4.

[66] J. Denais, *Monographie de la Cathédrale d'Angers* (1899), p. 14.

[67] Denais, p. 14; Urseau, 'Angers', *Congrès archéologique de France*, LXXVIIe session, I (1911), p. 167.

[68] Péan de la Tuillerie, pp. 44-5, 87. For another Angevin's admiration of the obelisk at St. Peter's see 'Journal de mon voyage de Rome', B. Orléans MS. 474, pp. 71-2.

[69] Pinier, 'Ancienne Église Saint-Martin', *Congrès archéologique de France* as above, p. 204; G. H. Forsyth, *The Church of Saint-Martin of Angers* (Princeton, 1953), p. 196; Brossier, B. Angers MS. 730, p. 30(b); Urseau, *op. cit.*, p. 168; A.M.L. G 272, p. 142 (Aug. 1781).

[70] Urseau, 'La Peinture décorative en Anjou du xiie au xviiie siècle', *Rev. d'Anjou*, LXXIX (1919), p. 194.

[71] Port, *Dict.*, III, p. 646; Denais, p. 16.

[72] See A. Lejard, *French Tapestry* (1946), pp. 30–1. For the date of manufacture see L. de Farcy in *Bull. Soc. Nat. Antiquaires de France*, 1912, pp. 229 ff.

[73] Joubert, 'Rapport sur les Tapisseries de la Cathédrale de Saint-Maurice', *Méms. Soc. Agric.* 2nd Ser. I (1850), pp. 101–10.

[74] A.M.L. G 270, p. 288.

[75] A.M.L. G 272, p. 228 (27 March 1787), p. 230; L. de Farcy, 'Les Ateliers de Réparation des vielles tapissieries à Angers', *Méms. Soc. Agric.*, XII (1909), p. 133. For the chapter of Saint-Maurille selling tapestries to pay for woodwork, see A.M.L. G 1116, f. 69 (cited in Port's inventory, p. 164).

[76] A.M.L. G 272, p. 349 (Sept. 1782); De Beauregard, 'Recherches sur le Tombeau du Roi René, Duc d'Anjou', *Méms. Soc. Agric.* IV (1839), pp. 31–3. Contract for the woodwork, B. Angers MS. 747 (673), no. 10. On royal permission, Port's inventory of series G in the Dept. archives, p. 32.

[77] Farcy, *L'Ancien Trésor de la Cathédrale d'Angers*, p. 89; A.M.L. G 273, p. 318 (July 1788); Port, *Artistes*, pp. 209–10. A canon gave 3,000*l.* of his own money towards the choir (Brossier, B. Angers MS. 730, p. 89).

[78] Babeau, *La ville sous l'ancien régime* (1884) II, pp. 129–30; Lacombe, *Talleyrand, évêque d'Autun* (1903), pp. 65–6; Champion, *op. cit. Révolution Française* LV (1908), pp. 25 ff., 467. For other examples, as also for references to occasional manifestations of a reverse tendency, see R. Lanson. *Le Goût du Moyen Age en France au XVIIIe siècle* (1926).

[79] A. Blunt, *Art and Architecture in France, 1500–1700* (1953), pp. 240–1.

[80] Sir R. Blomfield, *A History of French Architecture, 1661–1774*, 2 vols. (1921), II, pp. 190, 192.

[81] J. Mondain-Monval, *Soufflot, sa vie—son œuvre—son esthétique* (1918), pp. 425–6, 431.

[82] Mondain-Monval, *op. cit.*, p. 458. See *Bull. de la Soc. nat. des Antiquaires de France*, 1943–4, pp. 70–1 for references to E. Gauthey, *Observations sur la physique, etc.* (1774), and Lalande, *Voyage ... en Italie* (1786). See also Thorode, p. 22.

[83] R. Lanson, *Le Goût du Moyen Age en France au XVIIIe siècle* (1926), pp. 36–8. For this and other examples, see especially J. Lestocquoy, 'La Persistance du style gothique au XVIIe et XVIIIe siècle', *Rev. du Nord*, XXIV (1938), pp. 103–8.

[84] Rangeard, 'Sur le progrès des sciences et des beaux arts sous le règne de Louis le Grand' (1783), B. Angers MS. 639, f. 3. For curé Robin's praise of the tower of Saint-Maurice, 'un morceau d'architecture quoique gothique, des plus delicats qu'on puisse voire en France', see 'Discours sur l'antiquité de l'église de Saint-Pierre' in parish register, État Civil Angers, GG 181, p. 24.

[85] P. Laugier, *Essai sur l'architecture* (1755), p. 173.

[86] See correspondence of 1760–1 in B. Angers MS. 634 also 'Mémoire ou Discours sur les principales circonstances de la vie de Michelange buonaroti par M. l'abbé Laugier pour sa réception à l'académie d'Angers', B. Angers MS. 638, ff. 41 ff.

[87] *Observations sur l'Architecture* (1765), pp. 117, 129–30, 137–8, 237, 150.

[88] *Le Voyageur à Paris, tableau pittoresque et moral de cette capitale*, 3 vols. (1797), p. 4; E. L. in Thorode, p. 205 (cf. pp. 216–18).

[89] *Essai sur l'Architecture*, p. xv; cf. *Observations*, pp. v, 84.

[90] Cf. L. Hautecœur, *Histoire de l'Architecture classique en France* III (1950), p. 388; M. Levi, *Inventaire des Papiers de Robert de Cotte, premier architecte du Roi, 1656–1735* (1906), pp. xxv ff.

[91] L. De Lens, *L'Université d'Angers*, I (Faculté des Droits) (1880), pp. 138, 84–7, 71, 90–92.

[92] B. Bois, *La Vie scolaire et les créations intellectuelles en Anjou 1789–99* (1929), p. 6.

[93] Port, *Dict.*, I, pp. 77–8; Lens, I, pp. 119–24; 'Les Collèges de l'Université d'Angers', *Anjou hist.*, 1928, p. 5.

[94] X. de la Perraudière, 'Voyage à Rome en 1750 par M. Robin, curé d'Angers', *Rev. Fac. Cath. de l'Ouest*, V (1894–5), p. 52.

[95] Pilastre in 1792 (Bois, p. 17).

[96] Besnard, I, pp. 122, 125 (cf. Bois, pp. 18–19). In addition to these abuses in practice, in the conferring of law degrees nobles had special official privileges, but 'La noblesse n'est comptée pour rien en Théologie et Médecine' ('Mémoires du clergé. Quelques instructions concernant les matières bénéficiales', B. Angers MS. 397, f. 17(b)).

[97] A. Dupuy, 'Les Épidémies en Bretagne au xviiie siècle', *Annales de Bretagne*, II (1886–7), pp. 190–1. If medical knowledge was irrelevant to obtaining the degree, some doctors were not ignorant (A. Boquel, *La Faculté de Médecine de l'Université d'Angers, 1433–1792* (1951), p. 88).

[98] J. Leflon, *Bernier*, I, p. 3 (12 June 1786).

[99] Besnard, I, pp. 161–2, 122, 202.

[100] Rangeard, 'Compliment burlesque au concierge de l'Académie des sciences et Belles lettres d'Angers', B. Angers MS. 557 (521), f. 100(b).

[101] 'La bassesse de la flatterie érigée en loi' (Rangeard, 'État', *Anjou hist.*, VI, pp. 17–27. *Andegaviana* V, p. 453). For an example, Canon Guillot's verses on the comte de Provence, 1773 (B. Angers MS. 1045, nos. 2 and 3).

[102] Discourse of 7 March 1770, MS. Univ. of Rennes, 213, f. 100.

[103] According to J. Jeanvrot, 'Volney', *Révolution Française*, XXXV (1898), p. 283. But more than one provincial Academy has been named in connexion with Voltaire's jest (Clogenson, 'Des Relations de Voltaire avec les Académies, et en particulier avec l'Académie de Rouen', *Précis analytique des travaux de l'Académie ... de Rouen*, 1849, p. 233).

[104] *Nouvelles ecclésiastiques*, 8 Oct. 1760, p. 180.

[105] F. Uzureau, 'Ancienne Académie d'Angers. Les dernières Rentrées publiques avant la Révolution', *Méms. Soc. Agric.* 5th Ser., II (1899), pp. 356–61.

[106] Uzureau, *loc. cit.*; 'Les Angevins et la Famille Royale à la fin de l'Ancien Régime', *Anjou hist.*, II (1901–2); B. Angers MS. 556, (520); Uzureau, 'Les Évêques d'Angers et l'Académie', *Méms. Soc. Agric.*, VIII (1905), p. 98.

[107] See Uzureau, 'La Société royale d'Agriculture d'Angers 1761–93', *Méms. Soc. Agric.*, XVII (1914), pp. 45–58; 'Registre de la Société d'agriculture, de commerce et des arts', B. Angers MS. 1263, f. 33.

[108] The letters of Cotelle to Bertin are in A. Nat. H¹ 1509, dossier I, pièces 3, 17; dossier 12, pièce 2; dossier 17; dossier 19, pièces 125, 130.

[109] *Travels*, 27 Sept. 1788.

[110] E. Stoye, *Vincent Bernard de Tscharner, 1728–1778* (1954), p. 127.

[111] Bois, p. 72; La Revellière-Lépeaux, *Mémoirs* (ed. R. David, 1895), I, p. 59. Sup. Gen. of Congregation of Saint-Maur to La Revellière, 24 April 1786, B. Angers MS. 633.

[112] 'La Franc-Maçonnerie en Anjou xviiie–xixe siècles', *Anjou hist.*, IX, pp. 234–5.

[113] Brossier, B. Angers MS. 727, p. 32(b).

[114] 'La Loge du *Tendre Accueil* à Saint-Maur et à Angers', *Anjou hist.*, XXIV (1924), pp. 140–4. This lodge belonged to the *Grande Loge de France* (A.M.L. III F 12 (8)). For the lodge *Père de Famille*, Bois, p. 78.

[115] 'Aux armes, à l'ordre maçons,
Chargez, alignez vos canons' (*Anjou hist.*, XXIV, p. 145).

[116] C. Port, *La Vendée Angevine* (1888), I, p. 3.

[117] 'Sur les mauvais livres', MS. Univ. of Rennes 213, ff. 130 ff. He is particularly referring to the works of d'Holbach published between 1766 and 1770.

[118] See especially his *Cahier* in A.M.L. J 3134 (papers of Pantin among the papers of the Soland family). See also in J 3135, 'Messaline, tragédie' and the 'Méditation sur le caresme de 1740 par M. De Voltaire'. (For this latter, too incompetent in versification to be by Voltaire, see R. Pomeau, *La Religion de Voltaire* (1956), p. 195.)

[119] Mercier du Rocher, *Mémoires* (in C.-L. Chassin, *La Préparation de la guerre de Vendée*, I, pp. 464–5, 470). Similarly, for J. A. Berthe's (born 1765) reaction against his parents' desire for an ecclesiastical career for their son, see B. Angers MS. 616 (autobiography).

[120] Letters from Rome (8 Dec. 1765), Florence (21 July 1767), London (17 June 1777), Rome (22 Dec. 1777, 4 March 1778), in B. Angers MS. 634.

[121] F.-J. Grille, *Lettres, mémoires et documents … sur la formation, le personnel, l'esprit du 1er bataillon des volontaires de Maine-et-Loire* (4 vols., 1850), I, pp. 123–5.

[122] Bois, *La Vie scolaire*, pp. 92–3.

[123] Meynier, *La Revellière-Lépeaux*, p. 92; *Almanach ou Calendrier d'Anjou pour l'an de grâce 1750* (B. Nat. Lc^{29} 11), p. 31.

[124] 4 March 1758 (A. Nat. H 1633, nos. 82, 86).

[125] 'Mémoire à Monsieur Frère du Roi', 4 Dec. 1786, and reply of *Présidial*, 23 Jan. 1787 (A. Nat. R5 123).

[126] The abbé Sigorne wrote to Emery the superior of the Seminary on 27 June 1779 urging the devising of a reply to Buffon (MSS. Emery, Saint-Sulpice, IX, 9583). The actual thesis as sustained on 10 Aug. of the same year is found in the Emery papers, IX, 9187.

[127] C. Robin, *Le Mont-Glonne… (1774) Œuvres de M. Robin*, I, p. 152.

[128] Bois, *La Vie scolaire*, pp. 41–3.

[129] For Barat's orations of 1773, 1779, and 1781 see 'Les *rentrées* publiques à Angers (1773)', *Anjou hist.*, VII, p. 240; and Uzureau, 'Ancienne Université d'Angers. Les dernières *Rentrées publiques* avant la Révolution', *Rev. des Facultés Cath. de l'Ouest*, VIII (1898), pp. 369, 371.

[130] *Affiches* 13 Dec. 1782 (see 'Ancienne Académie d'Angers. Les dernières *Rentrées publiques* avant la Révolution', *Méms. Soc. Agric.*, 5th Ser., II (1899), p. 359).

[131] B. Angers MS. 638, p. 38.

[132] 'Sur l'irréligion et sur la réligion', B. Angers MS. 513 (493), f. 127. On Prévost, see Bois, pp. 43–4; Blordier-Langlois, 'Sur quelques discours prononcés a l'Académie…', and 'Discours prononcés par François Prévost', *Méms. Soc. Agric.*, V (1839), pp. 249–50, 282.

[133] 'Éloge de M. Le Corvaisier, Secrétaire Perpétuel de l'Académie d'Angers, par M. l'abbé Rangeard, son successeur…' [Fréron] *L'Année littéraire*, III (1761), p. 252.

[134] To Préseau at Angers, Avignon, 28 Dec. 1764 (B. Angers MS. 634).

[135] 'Discours sur l'illusion et le danger des Sistems' (1762), B. Angers MS. 1671, pp. 8–9. For the way in which orthodox apologetics swung to using Newton and to this extent forsaking Malebranche and Cartesianism, see Aram Vartanian, *Diderot and Descartes. A Study of Scientific Naturalism in the Enlightenment* (1953).

[136] 'Éloge du Roi Louis XV', B. Angers MS. 639, p. 119.

[137] Poems of canon d'Estriché of Saint-Laud, B. Angers MS. 554 (518), pp.

22(b), 25, 27(b), 29. On d'Estriché (died 1740) see Rangeard, 'Académiciens d'Angers auteurs, leur vie et leurs ouvrages', B. Angers MS. 639, p. 134(b).

[138] Speeches of 1776 and 1780, Uzureau, *Rev. Facultés Cath. de l'Ouest*, VIII (1898), pp. 368, 370.

[139] A discourse to the Academy, 1781 (B. Angers MS. 556 (520), f. 105).

[140] 'Le philosophe chrétien', B. Angers MS. 426 (413), pp. 197, 90. 'Mortel, pourquoi refuserois-tu de croire? Diras-tu que c'est la raison que te fait douter? Je suis aussi partisan que toi de la raison sacrée: ... elle m'est aussi chère que la foi, puisqu'elle en est la base.'

[141] 'Poésies de M. l'abbé Rangeard', B. Angers MS. 556 (520), f. 68.

[142] '...deux Bustes, représentant Voltaire et Rousseau, en plâtre noirci, vendus et adjugés au Sr Rigaliour, pour cinquante sols—2*l.* 10*s.*' ('Vente des meubles et effets de la ci devt abbaye de Saint-Aubin d'Angers', 23 July 1792, A.M.L. 13 Q 1.)

[143] *Traduction en vers François, de l'Élégie Latine, ou Ovidianum de M. Claude Robin*... (*Œuvres de M. Robin*, I, p. 8); *Le Montglonne* (*ibid.*, p. 65).

[144] 'Lettres Inédites de ... Cotelle de la Blandinière ... membres de l'Academie d'Angers, à Titon du Tillet (1748–57)', *Méms. Soc. Agric.*, 4th Ser., II (1888), p. 86.

[145] Bougler, *Mouvement Provincial en 1789, et biographies des députés de l'Anjou* (1865), p. 34.

[146] *Droit exclusif des Curés aux Dixmes de leurs Paroisses*, pp. 22 ff. (For this pamphlet see below, p. 364.)

[147] E. L. in Thorode, pp. 20, 134–5, 212.

[148] Thorode, pp. 1, 188.

[149] J. Leflon, *M. Emery*, pp. 61, 27. *L'esprit de Sainte-Thérèse* was published in 1775.

[150] V. Dauphin, 'La Corporation des ciriers d'Angers', *Méms. Soc. Agric.*, XXVI (1921), p. 24.

[151] The most complete edition is that of 1785 in 24 vols. From 1703 onwards volumes were being published, being originally given as monthly lectures from April to November each year (*Journal de Trevoux*, Oct. 1713, p. 1809).

[152] A. Lombard, *L'abbé Du Bos, un initiateur de la pensée moderne, 1660–1742* (1913), p. 31.

[153] The phraseology is P. Hazard's. (*La Crise de la conscience Européenne 1680–1715* (1935), I, p. 66; *La Pensée Européenne au 18e siècle* (1941), I, pp. 326–7.)

[154] E. Carcassone, *Montesquieu et le problème de la constitution français au XVIIIe siècle* (1927), pp. 182–236.

[155] *Projet de l'Histoire d'Anjou* (A. Nat. K 1144, no. 39), p. 9.

[156] [Adrien Baillet] *Topographie des Saints* (Paris, 1703), pp. 52–6. Rangeard's lives of these saints have been printed in *Rev. de l'Anjou*, I (1854). For Saint-Lezin, see J. Arnauld d'Andilly, *Vies de plusieurs Saints illustres de divers siècles* (1664), pp. 287–95—the writer was a brother of the bishop of Angers of the same name.

[157] R. Pouhardin, *Cat. MSS. Coll. Duchesne et Bréquigny. B. Nat.* (1905), Coll. Duchesne 58, fo. 59; P. Paris, *Les MSS. Français de la B. du Roi* (1839), IV, p. 331, V, pp. 77, 196–7.

[158] V. Godard-Faultrier, 'Église d'Angers. Bibliothèque de l'Evêché', *Méms. Soc. Agric.*, VI (1849), pp. 214–21.

[159] C. Port, *Inventaire Sommaire des archives départementales, Maine-et-Loire*, Ser. G (1880), p. 164; Ser. H, pp. 4–5, 188.

[160] Ch. Urseau, *Cartulaire Noire de la Cathédrale d'Angers* (1908), p. xii.

[161] See Port's *Inventaire Sommaire des archives départementales*, Ser. G, p. 31.

[162] Register of the deliberations of the clergy of Anjou, B. Angers MS. 734 (660), ff. 91, 91(b).

[163] Rangeard, 'État...', *Anjou hist.*, VI, p. 579.

[164] A.M.L. G 1013, p. 174; G 268, p. 209 (in Port's inventory, pp. 151, 32).

[165] G. Dufour, 'J.-B. Leclerc. L'exil et la mort', *Méms. Soc. Agric.*, 6th Ser., VII (1932), p. 18; B. Nat. MSS. Clairambault, V (1309), p. 135 (Laure's *Catalogue*, II, p. 415).

[166] Rangeard, in *Anjou hist.*, XXVI, p. 146; Breval, II, p. 25. It is true that neglect of historical treasures was not a new phenomenon, and that in this respect the eighteenth century was an improvement upon its predecessors. For sixteenth- and seventeenth-century scandals, see P. Marchegay and E. Mabille, *Chroniques des Églises d'Anjou* (1869), pp. v–xv; E. L. in Thorode, pp. 312, 104, xii.

[167] 'Tableau des archives...' (1771), A.M.L. H 15.

[168] 15 March 1782, B. Angers MS. 1748 (VI).

[169] See page 119. For *lods et ventes*, see p. 66; for *deshérence*, p. 65.

[170] Canon Dutertre to D'Alichoux, 20 Feb. 1780 (A.M.L. G 279).

[171] Register of the clergy of Anjou, B. Angers MS. 734 (660), ff. 91, 107.

[172] Information concerning these and other individuals is taken from Port's *Dict.* and E. L.'s notes to Thorode, except where otherwise stated. Touraille's 'Histoire d'Anjou' is in B. Angers MS. 1003. Bruneau de Tartifume's description of Angers was published by Th. Civray in 1933 (2 vols., *Soc. des Amis du Livre angevin*).

[172a] J. Le Long, *Bibliothèque historique de la France* (1719); no. 4270. For Jean de Launoi, H. Busson, *La Religion des Classiques, 1660–1685* (1948), pp. 302, 307–9.

[173] Yvonne Mailtert, 'Fondation du Monastère Bénédictin de Saint-Nicolas d'Angers', *Bibl. de l'École des Chartres XCII* (1931), p. 44; H. Stein, *Bibliographie générale des Cartulaires français* (1907), p. 17; *Bibliothèque des écrivains de l'Ordre de Saint-Benoît* (1778), IV, p. 115.

[174] *Histoire de Sablé*, preliminary 'Epistre'.

[175] De Beauregard, 'Recherches sur le tombeau du Roi René, Duc d'Anjou', *Méms. Soc. Agric.*, IV (1839), p. 31.

[176] See the names Audoys, Deville, Prévost, Pierre Ayroult, Trottier in Port's *Dict*. For another lawyer, Vattier, see the letter of a Benedictine of Marmoutiers to a canon of Saint-Pierre, 31 July 1755, B. Angers MS. 633. The craze for ancestor hunting was neatly satirized by a canon of Appoigney-les-Regennes who published three learned brochures about the mayors, physicians and seigneurs of Angers of his own family and was thanked by the municipality, *Présidial*, University and Academy before his writings were found to be a hoax (Port, *Dict.*, III, pp. 576–8. A copy of Thomasseau de Cursay's *Guerrier sans reproche* (1775) is found in A.M.L. J 809).

[177] Published in 1897 by E. L. (the abbé E. Longin).

[178] Brossier, B. Angers MS. 726, entry 'Église'. On Brossier generally, see 'Les Chanoines de la cathédrale d'Angers pendant la Révolution', *Anjou hist.*, XXIII (1923), pp. 83–4.

[179] Cf. the comment of Le Gendre, 'A quoi ne réussissent point des gens adroits, fort appliqués et qui ont toujours en argent comptant quatre cent mille écus dans leurs coffres! Il y a longtemps qu'on le dit de la congrégation de Saint-Maur' (*Mémoires de l'abbé Le Gendre, chanoine de Notre-Dame*, ed. M. Roux (1863), p. 400).

[180] For this work generally, see M. Lecomte, 'Les Bénédictins et l'histoire des provinces au XVIIe et XVIIIe siècle', *Rev. Mabillon*, XVII (1927), pp. 237 ff.; XVIII (1928), pp. 39 ff.

[181] M. Lecomte, 'La publication des *Annales Ordines Sancti Benedicti*', *Mélanges et Documents publiés à l'occasion du 2ᵉ centenaire de la mort de Mabillon*, p. 257.

[182] M. Lecomte, *Rev. Mabillon*, XVIII (1928), p. 110.

[183] Le Long, *Bibliothèque*, no. 14946; *Bull. Soc. nat. antiqu. de France*, 1921, pp. 214-18; L. Webber-Jones, *Classical and Medieval Studies in honour of Edward Kennard Rand* (N. York, 1938), p. 144. See also 'Deux Lettres de dom Pierre Constant à dom Edmond Martène', *Rev. Mabillon*, XXXVI (1946), p. 62.

[184] Though there is the example of dom Ros of Saint-Nicolas (see the letter of 12 May 1746 in *Analecta Juris Pontificii*, no. 117 (1874), cols. 787-9). Dom Taillandier (see below) found the charter house of Saint-Aubin in disorder in 1752, and the documents of Lesvière were in confusion in 1790 (E. L. in Thorode, p. 284).

[185] *Analecta Juris Pontificii*, no 117 (1874), cols. 789-90. On dom Rivet, see *Bibliothèque ... des écrivains de l'Ordre de Saint-Benoît* (1777), II, pp. 476 ff., and 'L'Histoire littéraire de la France par dom Rivet et autres', *Rev. Mabillon*, II (1906-7), pp. 210 ff. and 254.

[186] L. Brière, 'Dom Jean Colomb, Bénédictin de l'abbaye Saint-Vincent du Mans. Correspondence inédite', *Rev. historique et archéologique du Maine*, I (1876), pp. 504-12.

[187] 'Relation du voyage de dom Taillandier en Bretagne' (ed. dom Plaine), *Rev. de Bretagne et Vendée*, 4th Ser., II (1872), pp. 97 ff.

[188] 'Lettres inédits des Bénédictins de Saint-Maur', *Revue Bénédictine*, XXV (1908), pp. 242-3.

[189] The correspondence of Housseau and Rangeard is published in *Rev. hist. arch. du Maine*, I (1876) as above; II (1877), pp. 262, 265, 515-517 and III (1878), pp. 415-17, 419. For Housseau's collaborators, see P. Lauer, *Coll. des MSS sur l'histoire des provinces de France. Inventaire*, 2 vols. (1905), II, p. xxix.

[190] Port, *Dict.*, I, p. 624. Cf. Mornet's edition (G.E.F.) of the *Nouvelle Héloïse*, I, pp. 355, 368.

[191] Rangeard, 'Sur la mort de Mlle de la Guénerie auteur de quelques romans moraux', B. Angers MS. 556 [520], f. 67.

[192] Bougler, *Mouvement Provincial*, p. 35. Cf. among Rangeard's papers, 'Mandemens fait pour M. de Grasse qui me les avoit demandés', B. Angers MS. 639, pp. 69 ff.

[193] *Rev. hist. et arch. du Maine*, I (1876), pp. 443-4, 445, 111-13; II, pp. 264, 265; 'Les Notaires en Anjou vers le milieu du XVIIIᵉ siècle', *Anjou hist.*, 1949, p. 27; *Cat. gén. MSS. Bibl. Publ. Fr.* (*Le Mans*) XX (1893), p. 124; M. Cotton, *Cat. gén. MSS. Bibl. Publ. Fr.* (Tours), XXXVII (1900), II, pp. 821-2.

[194] E. Mabille, *Cat. analytique des Diplômes ... relatifs à l'histoire de Touraine ... dans la Collection de Dom Housseau* (*Soc. arch. de Touraine*, XIV, 1863); Lauer, *op. cit.*, I, pp. xxix-xxx. Housseau had earlier contributed to vol. XI of the *Historiens de la France* (C. de Lam, *Bibliothèque des écrivains de la Congrégation de Saint-Maur* (1882), p. 183). In Nov. 1787 Dom Villevieille of St. Germain-des-Prés asked permission to see the charters of the cathedral of Angers (A.M.L. G 273, p. 220).

[195] P. Marchegay, 'Conseils sur la manière d'étudier et d'écrire l'histoire d'une province', *Rev. des Provinces de l'Ouest*, IV (1856-7), p. 433n.

[196] 'Lettres de Barthélemy Mercier abbé de Saint-Léger à Jean Tonnelet Chanoine régulier de l'abbaye de Toussaint, 1775-1777', *Méms. Soc. Agric.*, 4th Ser., III (1889), pp. 37-9.

[197] 'Essai sur l'Etablissement des Bretons dans l'Armorique...' (1767);

'Dissertation sur les ... Princes qui ont regné en Anjou jusqu'à la dernière réunion à la couronne en 1480' (1775), B. Angers MS. 1671.

[198] Gaudin, curé of Saint-Nicolas, 'Anecdotes Angevines' (1774), B. Angers MS. 1550(6), ff. 15, 18.

[199] *Traduction en vers François, de l'Élégie Latine, ou Ovidianum de M. Claude Robin* ... (B. Angers, 103–627) printed in *Anjou hist.*, XXXIX (1939), pp. 178–201.

[200] *ibid.*

[201] Port, *Inventaire* ... *des Archives* ... *de la Mairie*, p. 274.

[202] E. L. in Thorode, pp. 372, 10, 131, 11, 12; Péan de la Tuillerie, p. 131; Brossier, B. Angers MS. 726, p. 41.

[203] Thorode, p. 18.

[204] In 1748 (Port, *Dict.*, III, pp. 265–6).

[205] *Le Mont-Glonne* (1774), *Œuvres de M. Robin*, I, p. 206.

[206] For high praise of Robin's views two generations later, see Bizeul, 'Voie Romaine de Nantes à Angers', *Annales de la Soc. Royale acad. de Nantes et du département de la Loire-Inférieure*, VIII (1837), pp. 145–8.

[207] *Le Camp de Caesar au village d'Empyré* ... *ou dissertation sur l'antiquité de l'église de Saint-Pierre* (1764), (B. Angers 103, 627), pp. 22–3, 57 ff.

[208] 'Le pèlerin apostolique ou les pensées diverses à l'occasion d'un voyage de Rome', B. Angers MS. 1841 (147), f. 12.

[209] *Le Mont-Glonne*, I, p. 206.

CHAPTER IV

[1] *Mémoire pour les Doyen, Chanoines et Chapitre de l'Église d'Angers au sujet de l'obéissance féodale, qui leur est demandée* ... (1774), B. Angers MS. 747 (673), no. 23.

[2] A.M.L. G 271, p. 593 (8 July 1774). For the cathedral's fiefs in country districts, see J.-F. Bodin, *Recherches historiques sur l'Anjou et ses monumens* (2 vols., 1821–3), II, pp. 100–2.

[3] A.M.L. G 271, p. 550 (28 Feb 1754).

[4] 'Deshérence', i.e. escheat. A.M.L. G 273, p. 82 (11 Aug. 1782), pp. 328, 338, 508, etc.

[5] A.M.L. G 273, p. 144, gives an idea of the expenditure on children. In 1782 the chapter obtained 345*l*. 19*s*. from the escheat of the goods of Louis Allard, a servant. 150*l*. of this was given to a foundling girl who had been trained in tailoring and was now being subsidized to buy a bed and furniture (G 273, p. 82).

[6] A.M.L. G 273, p. 49 (May 1786).

[7] *Arrêt de la Cour de Parlement* (1786), État Civil, Hôtel de Ville, Angers. GG 185, p. 51.

[8] C. Loizeau de Grandmaison, *Inventaire-sommaire des archives départementales, Indre-et-Loire*. *Sér G*. (1882), p. 1. Bodin, *Recherches* II, p. 101; 'Le Chapitre de la cathédrale d'Angers avant la Révolution', *Anjou hist.*, XIX, p. 114. But the bishop of Angers had to pay for a quarter of the repairs to the cathedral (Piales, *Traité des Réparations* (1761) II, p. 378).

[9] Lehoreau, *Anjou hist.*, XV, pp. 227, 235.

[10] See the collection of notes on the privileges of the cathedral in B. Angers MS. 747 (673), f. 5, cf. A.M.L. G 272, p. 173; G 273, p. 233; G 273, pp. 22, 30; Brossier, B. Angers MS. 730, pp. 39, 57, 25. 'Spiritual affinity' is the relationship between god-child and god-parent. See (Alletz) *La Discipline de l'Église de France* ... (1780), p. 19. When an individual had no fixed residence, 'fixation

of domicile' by ecclesiastical decree was necessary before his banns could be called.

[11] A.M.L. G 273, pp. 20 (Feb. 1786) and 139 (March 1787).

[12] Brossier, B. Angers MS. 730, p. 62.

[13] A.M.L. G 271, p. 613 (Aug. 1774); G 269, pp. 440 (Jan. 1779), 447, 450–1.

[14] 'M. Le Noir de la Cochetière, vicaire général d'Angers', *Anjou hist.*, XXXIX, p. 153. From A.M.L. 1 L 980, 'Traitement de ceux qui composaient l'Église cathédrale', it appears that the basic income of a canon was about 3,800*l.*, the dean getting double. The Civil Constitution pension was calculated as 1,000*l.* plus half the remainder of previous income, and canons here are given 2,325*l.* basic pension. Piganiol de la Force (VIII, pp. 81–2), the official *Pouillé* of the diocese (1783, ed. Uzureau, 1904, p. 41) and Chatizel even (*Lettre*, 1785, p. 126—see below, p. 201), greatly under-estimated the value of a canonry.

[15] Port, *Dict.* I, 524.

[16] Register of deliberations of the clergy of Anjou. B. Angers MS. 734 (660), f. 132(b) (18 Aug. 1788).

[17] A. Nat. D XIX, 57, file 214, no. 17 (1 June 1790). When pensions under the Civil Constitution of the Clergy were settled, Boulnoy was allowed 1,430*l.* for his additional benefices; as this was half their value, he must have been drawing 2,860*l.* originally, though probably this does not take into account the expenses of which he complains. Louet appears to have enjoyed 1,770*l.* from additional benefices, and other canons of the cathedral are recorded as having had from this source—3,950*l.*, 1,738*l.*, 1,250*l.*, 738*l.*, 1,188*l.*, 922*l.*, 604*l.*, 392*l.* ('Traitement de ceux qui composaient l'Église cathédrale', A.M.L. 1 L 980).

[18] A.M.L. G 272, p. 569.

[19] A.M.L. G 348 (accounts in an old register of the chapter).

[20] For canonical houses, see estimations for the sale of *Biens Nationaux*, A.M.L. III Q 1, nos. 293, 295, 317, 348, 352, 353, 413, 294. De la Brosse rented out his residence in the rue du Vollier (*ibid.*, 415), and Louet leased out the house in the parish of Saint-Michel du Tertre which came to him as *maître école*, living himself in the archdeaconry, rue montée de l'évêché (*ibid.*, 178, 294). Canons Chalopin, Waillant, and La Haye-Montbault had country-houses; no doubt others had too.

[21] There were 29 prebends, all except three being in the collation of the bishop. The three exceptions were: a stall annexed to the abbey of Toussaint, which was under royal patronage, another conferred by the abbot of Saint-Serge, and one in the collation of the chapter on the nomination and presentation of the 'canon of the week'. The Dean was elected by the chapter, subject to confirmation by the archbishop of Tours.

There were in addition seven 'dignitaries' appointed by the diocesan bishop; these were—the three archdeacons (of 'Angers', of 'Outre Loire' and of 'Outre Maine', with areas of jurisdiction corresponding to these titles), the *Trésorier* (Treasurer), the *Chantre* (Precentor), the *Maître École* (Chancellor of the University) and the *Pénitencier* (the bishop's representative to absolve reserved cases). The two last-named always held a prebend. The others generally did so in practice, but this was not essential and a dignitary who was not a canon could not enter chapter.

As our subject does not include diocesan administration the dignitaries have not been considered except in their role as canons.

One should note that the *Théologal* (who preached on the first Sunday in the month except in March and December and had to be the holder of a degree in Theology) was not, as in many churches, a dignitary; his office was simply an obligation attached to the prebend of Saint-Jacques (*Pouillé* of 1783, ed. Uzureau (1904), pp. 41–2; E. L. in Thorode, pp. 109–14).

[22] Even so, he claimed to be of an old family (Brossier, B. Angers MS. 727, p. 108).

[23] For dates of birth and of appointment, see 'Les chanoines de la cathédrale d'Angers pendant la Révolution', *Anjou hist.*, XXIII (1923), pp. 81–94.

[24] De La Chenaye-Desbois and Badier, *Dictionnaire de la Noblesse* (3rd ed., 1843), XVI, p. 264. Gontard de Launay, *Recherches sur les familles des Maires d'Angers* (1893) I, p. 148.

[25] *ibid.*, XII, p. 492; Henri Jougla de Morenas, *Grand Armorial de France*, IV, p. 480, 'One of the oldest families of Anjou' (Brossier, B. Angers MS. 727, p. 97).

[26] De La Chenaye-Desbois and Badier, XIX, p. 805.

[27] M. de Saint-Allais, *Nobiliaire Universel de France* (1814), I, pp. 384–5.

[28] De La Chenaye-Desbois and Badier, VI, pp. 762–3.

[29] *ibid.*, XV, pp. 718–19.

[30] *ibid.*, X, pp. 856–60.

[31] F. Uzureau, *Un Prêtre Français pendant l'émigration : M. de la Corbière, chanoine d'Angers* (1909); for the family, see Lainé, *Archives généalogiques et historiques de la Noblesse de France*, VII (1841), p. 95; II (1829), p. 8. Concerning other canons, for Poulain de la Guerche, see Gontard de Launay, *op. cit.*, I, pp. 144–5 (son of a *conseiller* of the *Présidial* of Angers); for La Haye Montbault, P. de Farcy, 'Catalogue des gentilshommes d'Anjou lors de la recherche de la noblesse de 1666', *Rev. hist. de l'Ouest*, VI (1890), p. 6, also 'Armorial d'Hozier', copies by M. Sauvage, B. Angers MS. 1827, *cahier*, 26, p. 390.

[32] 'Les chanoines de la cathédrale d'Angers pendant la Révolution', *Anjou hist.*, XXIII, pp. 94, 88; Brossier, B. Angers MS. 730, pp. 63(b), 227. For the pages, see A. Babeau, *La Vie Militaire sous l'Ancien Régime* (1890), II, pp. 40–1.

[33] 'Les aumôniers du Calvaire d'Angers pendant Révolution', *Anjou hist.*, XIX (1918), pp. 135–6.

[34] *Relation Sommaire . . . de ce qui s'est passé dans l'Assemblée du Clergé de Paris Intra Muros* (printed by Aulard) *Révolution Française*, XXVI (1894), p. 65. For the professorial right by which D claimed the benefice, see Piales, *Traité . . . des Gradués* (1757), III, pp. 323, 334–5, 349–63, 393.

[35] A.M.L. G 273, pp. 189, 195, 319 (June 1787–July 1788).

[36] A.M.L. G 269, pp. 519, 572–3, 612 (1779–80).

[37] A.M.L. G 269, p. 482 (April 1779).

[38] A.M.L. G 273, pp. 151, 170–1 (March–April 1787).

[39] Brossier, B. Angers MS. 729, pp. 100–101, 104, 100; 727, p. 205; 730, p. 64(b).

[40] A.M.L. G 269, p. 706; G 272, pp. 5–6 (Nov. 1786); G 272, pp. 7, 11.

[41] A.M.L. G 272, pp. 208–10. Apart from Waillant the only case of sexual immorality which we have found among the clergy of the town at the end of the old régime is a reference to Cotelle dean of Saint-Martin 1756–77, who in his youth had committed escapades which obtained posthumous mention in the *Liste de tous les prêtres trouvés en flagrant délit chez les filles* (1790). Gossip about curé Robin's housekeeper was groundless and was soon silenced. It was in backward and isolated areas of France that drinking and wenching curés were still found (see, e.g., J. Faivre, 'Le Bas-clergé Franc-Comtois au milieu du XVIIIe siècle'; *Annales Révolutionnaires*, VII (1914), pp. 1 ff; G. Hardy, 'L'Anti-cléricalisme paysan dans une province française avant 1789', *ibid.*, V (1912), pp. 605 ff.; and for one area of rural Anjou, R. M. Andrews, *Les Paysans des Mauges au 18e siècle* (*Thèse*, Paris, 1935), p. 183).

[42] *Nouvelles ecclésiastiques*, 3 April 1753, p. 56. It is said that canon de Montriou died at Rome in 1777 at the very moment when a bishopric awaited

him (Port, *Dict.*, I, p. 731). For bishop de Vercel, see canon Guillot's adulatory writings, B. Angers MS. 1671.

[43] Le Noir de la Cochetière's *Journal* in 'M. Le Noir de la Cochetière, vicaire général d'Angers,' *Anjou hist.* XXXIX, pp. 146-7.

[44] 'Les vicaires généraux d'Angers pendant la Révolution', *Anjou hist.*, XXI, pp. 79-84.

[45] In March 1784.

[46] Waillant, Brossier and Le Noir de la Cochetière were masons.

[47] 'M. Louet vicaire général d'Angers 1725-1800'; *Anjou hist.*, XIX (1918-19), pp. 29-30; Port, *Dict.*, II 548; Brossier, B. Angers MS. 729, p. 26.

[48] See Uzureau, 'Un Mystique à la veille de la Révolution. Urbain-Élie Cassin', *Andegaviana*, XXVII (1927), pp. 212-45.

[49] 'Obsèques des Chanoines à Angers avant la Révolution', *Anjou hist.*, XVII, p. 261.

[50] Blordier-Langlois, *Angers et l'Anjou sous le régime municipal*, pp. 265-6.

[51] A.M.L. G 271, pp. 612, 616; G 269, p. 95.

[52] Lehoreau, *Anjou hist.*, XV, p. 238; 'Obsèques . . .' *Anjou hist.*, XVII, p. 266.

[53] Thorode, p. 49.

[54] B. Angers MS. 768, no. 36; A.M.L. G 942, pp. 35, 45, 59 (April 1785); G 1014, p. 121 (May 1785); G 942, pp. 131(b), 24(b), 128. The chapters of Saint-Laud and Saint-Martin were also united in confraternity with the chapter of Saint-Pierre-de-la-Cour of Mans. (The vicomte Menjot d'Elbenne and the abbé L.-J. Denis, *Le Chapitre Royal de l'église de Saint-Pierre-de la Cour* (1910), pp. 70, 229.) The cathedral of Angers had similar fraternal arrangements with the chapter of Compostella in Spain (J. Contrasty, *Le Clergé Français exilé en Espagne 1792-1802* (1910), pp. 258-9).

[55] A.M.L. G 1014, pp. 58, 121, 150, 192, 222.

[56] A.M.L. G 1013, p. 382 (Nov. 1781); G 1014, p. 38 (April 1782).

[57] A.M.L. G 942, p. 22 (Oct. 1782).

[58] A.M.L. G 1170, p. 244 (Nov. 1773).

[59] A.M.L. G 1170, pp. 241 (Nov. 1773), 244. For Jubeau, Port, *Dict.*, II, p. 420.

[60] A.M.L. G 1117, p. 99 (May 1776); G 1171, p. 47 (Aug. 1787).

[61] A.M.L. G 272, pp. 524 (April 1784), 566, 569.

[62] Lehoreau, *Anjou hist.*, XV, p. 238.

[63] Gautreau de Villeneuve's inventory, 1787 July, *Andegaviana* XXVI, p. 265.

[64] A.M.L. G 272, p. 566 (July 1784). Estimates by the cathedral. The figures given in *Tableau de la Province d'Anjou* (1762) in *Mém. Soc. Agric. . . .* 4th series, II (1897), pp. 419-20, are much too low.

[65] Péan de la Tuillerie, p. 330.

[66] A.M.L. G 272, p. 566 (July 1784)

[67] A.M.L. G 1117, p. 191(b).

[68] A.M.L. G 1117, p. 157(b) (Jan. 1785).

[69] A.M.L. G 272, p. 566.

[70] The total for 1784 was 2,745*l*. See A.M.L. G 1014, pp. 65, 66, 80, 89, 90, 99.

[71] A.M.L. G 1014, p. 246.

[72] A.M.L. G 1117, p. 157(b) (Jan. 1785).

[73] A.M.L. G 1014, p. 65 (Jan. 1783).

[74] A.M.L. G 272, pp. 567-8. That is, subtracting from the figures here given by the cathedral the estimated value of canonical houses (3,400*l*. and 3,670*l*.) and adding to the figure for Saint-Pierre the 600*l*. laid out on foundlings.

[75] 'Mémoire pour M. Du Chapitre de Saint-Laud d'Angers', A. Nat. H 1633, no. 253.

[76] A.M.L. G 272, p. 568. One tenant took over a house in 1779 with its door and window frames missing (Petition, 23 Feb. 1791, A.M.L. 19 Q 5). Another had to spend 7,000*l.* on repairs (Petition, 23 Dec. 1790, A.M.L. 19 Q 7).

[77] 100*l.* paid for a boy of 10 years to be brought up to the trade of a weaver; A.M.L. G 1117, 182(b) (Saint-Maurille).

[78] The figures can be collected from the register. A.M.L. G 1014.

[79] See 'Département de Maine-et-Loire. Traitement des officiers des chapitres d'Angers', A. Nat. D XIX 80, file 612, no. 10.

[80] 'M. Gautreau de la Grois, vicaire général d'Angers', *Anjou hist.*, XXVII, p. 84.

[81] Enclosure to Mgr Jarente, bishop of Orleans, in Cotelle to Bertin, A. Nat. H¹ 1509, dossier 12.

[82] The dean of Saint-Laud notes in his accounts for 1777 that 138*l.* 12*s.* are due to him for 231 masses (A.M.L. G 946). He is 6 sous out in his calculations.

[83] P.V. Directory Department, 18 July 1790, A.M.L. 1 L 68.

[84] The pensions allotted under the Civil Constitution of the Clergy, which include *half* the value of the house and of supplementary benefices are a good indication. Dean Duchilleau of Saint-Laud is to receive 2,509*l.*, other canons of that chapter 1,902*l.*, 1,299*l.*, 1,000*l.*, 1,363*l.*; canons of Saint-Martin, 1,831*l.*, 1,663*l.*, 2,676*l.*; of Saint-Maurille, 1,000*l.*, 2,073*l.*, 1,871*l.*, 1,894*l.*; of Saint-Pierre, 1,774*l.*, 1,930*l.*, 1,942*l.*, 1,490*l.*, 1,336*l.*, and the dean of Saint-Pierre, 2,636*l.* Canons of La Trinité run from 1,199*l.* to 1,323*l.* ('Régistre contenant les traitements des ci-devant chanoines', A.M.L. 2 L 132).

[85] See Estimations for the sale of *Biens Nationaux*, A.M.L. III Q 2, IV, no. 281; III Q 1, no. 10; III Q 1, nos. 7 and 42, 250, 287.

[86] 'Situation du Sieur Pierre Tremblé' in notaries' archives, A.M.L. II E, 2,643. Tremblay left 40,000*l.* for his heirs. Some of this no doubt came to him by inheritance, e.g., 2 houses and 5 gardens came to him from 'Mme Veuve du Tremblier' (Port, *Dict.*, III, p. 296).

[87] A.M.L. G 942, p. 103 (Feb. 1788).

[88] A.M.L. G 1014, pp. 272, 274. Cf. the arrangement of canon Boylesve with the chapter of Saint-Maurille to spend 4,000 to 5,000*l.* on repairs provided he can keep the house if he resigns after 25 years of exercise (Brossier, B. Angers MS. 727, p. 126).

[89] Brossier, B. Angers MS. 727, pp. 115, 120.

[90] Cotelle, the dean of Saint-Martin who died in 1777, was well known to have been pushed up by Court influence—Rangeard refers quite openly to this in his 'Eloge historique de M. Cotelle', B. Angers MS. 639, p. 88. Notice, however, the other type of canon of Saint-Martin. The abbé Barat, born at La Chapelle Saint-Florent, had one brother a grocer at Cholet and another a country curé. He had served as curé of Epié and had obtained a doctorate in theology before being appointed to a canonry (Port, *Dict.*, I, p. 198).

[91] De La Chenaye-Desbois and Badier, *Dictionnaire de la Noblesse*, XVIII, col. 337.

[92] *op. cit.*, III, cols. 944, 947.

[93] 'M. Gautreau de la Grois, vicaire général d'Angers', *Anjou hist.*, XXVII, pp. 81–5. The Gautreau brothers were joint owners of the handsome country-house of 'Douzillé' near Angers (Port, *Dict.*, II, p. 61).

[94] Uzureau, 'Les chanoines d'Angers pendant la Révolution', *Mém. Soc. Agric.*, 1925, p. 85.

[95] *Extraits du Livre de raison de M. le Chanoine Daburon de Mantelon*, Letourneau, *Histoire du Séminaire*, app. V, p. 422.

[96] Uzureau, *op. cit.*, *Mém. Soc. Agric.* ... 1925, gives the details.

[97] A.M.L. G 1170, pp. 403–4.

Y

[98] A.M.L. G 1014, p. 6 (June 1782).

[99] A.M.L. G 1117, pp. 104–104(b), (July 1777).

[100] A.M.L. G 942, p. 16(b), (1782).

[101] A.M.L. G 1117, p. 172(b), (Jan. 1787).

[102] A.M.L. G 1117, pp. 102(b)–103.

[103] A.M.L. G 946 (account book of Du Chilleau, 1777–8, pp. 13, 16, 17 and back).

[104] Mme Letondal, *Mémoires, Anjou hist.*, V (1905–6), p. 12.

[105] Port, *Dict.*, II, p. 692. For his ode on the marriage of the baron de Landreau and Mlle d'Escoubleau, see *Affiches*, 7 Jan. 1785, p. 7.

[106] See p. 77.

[107] Port, *Dict.*, II, p. 204.

[108] *ibid.*, I, 762–3, 727.

[109] 'Les vicaires généraux d'Angers pendant la Révolution', *Anjou hist.*, XXI, pp. 79–84.

[110] 'M. Gautreau de la Grois, vicaire général d'Angers', *Anjou hist.*, XXVII, p. 82 (date is 30 Aug. 1766).

[111] A.M.L. G 273, pp. 173, 206; 132, 356; 225, 226. At the cathedral there were two succentors, four *corbelliers*, four chaplains ('sous chantre' is here translated as 'succentor' and *maire-chapelain* as chaplain), two deacons, and two *épistoliers* (Rangeard, 'État ... de l'Anjou avant la Révolution de 1789', B. Angers MS. 1020 (894), f. 25). For curious details concerning these officials, see E. L. in Thorode, pp. 116–22.

[112] A.M.L. G 942, pp. 45, 118(b), Saint-Laud, 1784, 1788. The sacrist of Saint-Martin was also succentor, with 1,140*l*. (A. Nat. D XIX 80, file 612, no. 10).

[113] A.M.L. G 1117, pp. 42, 65(b), 71(b) (Saint-Maurille). At Saint-Martin, a total salary of 650*l*. was given (A.M.L. G 1014, p. 152).

[114] A.M.L. G 1117, p. 76(b); G 942, p. 40, give Saint-Maurille and Saint-Laud 300*l*. A. Nat. D XIX 80, file 612, no. 10, gives Saint-Martin 350*l*. For a tonsured clerk who was sub-sacrist and *épistolier* at Saint-Martin, see 'L'Église Saint-Martin d'Angers et son personnel pendant la Révolution', *Anjou hist.*, 1949, pp. 68–9. For salaries generally, see P.V. Directory Department, 2 Oct. 1790, A.M.L. 1 L 68, which gives chaplains of Saint-Pierre and Saint-Martin 729*l*. and 600*l*. Income from saying masses might be about 40*l*., then there might be gifts of corn or wine from the chapter (see a petition of 1790 in A.M.L. 1 L 980, and P.V. Directory Dept., 29 Oct. 1790).

[115] A.M.L. G 1013, pp. 25, 26 (Aug. 1769).

[116] A.M.L. G 1117, p. 143(b); G 1171, p. 28; G 942, p. 111(b); G 1014, p. 234; G 273, pp. 44, 47 (dates, 1783–1788).

[117] Lehoreau indeed denied them this title ('Cérémonial', III, p. 132); but see E. L.'s comments in Thorode, p. 278.

[118] See 'Les chanoines de la Trinité d'Angers et l'abbesse du Ronceray', *Anjou hist.*, XVIII, pp. 46–9; and 'Le clergé du Ronceray et de la Trinité avant la Révolution', *Anjou hist.*, XXVI, pp. 134–5.

[119] See *Mémoire Signifié pour les Chanoines, Curé, Maires-Chapelains & Chapelains & Communauté de l'Église Plebeaine et Paroissiale de la Trinité d'Angers* (B. Angers, S.J. 407, no. 11) and *Arrest du Parlement* (1750) B. Angers, MS. 1748 (VI).

[120] *Mémoire* as above, p. 23.

[121] *Anjou hist.* as above, XXVI, pp. 134–5.

[122] He was summoned to wall up three windows which overlooked the abbey cloisters. *Mémoire Signifié Pour Me Charles-François Boufteau, Prêtre ... Appellant de la Sentence de la Sénéchaussée d'Angers ...* (1768) B. Angers, S.J. 407, no. 18. The case of the abbess is in S.J. 407, no. 20.

[123] *Mémoire Signifié pour Dame Léontine Desparbez de Lussan-Bouchard d'Aubeterre, Abbesse de l'Abbaye Royale du Ronceray*... (Mame, Angers, 1782) B. Angers, S.J. 311 (7), no. 16, pp. 34–41.

[124] See MS. notes (date 1781) in the margins of *Mémoire Signifié* ... etc. of 1750, B. Angers, S.J. 407, no. 13.

[125] 'Les chanoines de la Trinité...', *Anjou hist.*, XVIII, p. 60.

[126] *Mémoire Signifié*... B. Angers, S.J. 311 (7), no. 16, p. 1.

[127] *Mémoire Signifié Pour M^{res} Nicolas Duval & Jean-Urbain le Roy Chanoines*... (1782) B. Angers, S.J. 311 (7), no. 15, p. 21. 'Leurs Aumoniers!'

CHAPTER V

[1] Charming sketch plans of the houses of Saint-Aubin, Saint-Serge, Saint-Nicolas, and Lesvière are found in Peigné-Delacourt (pref. by L. Delisle) *Monasticon Gallicanum* (1890), II, planches 141, 144, 142, 143.

[2] Lehoreau, *Anjou hist.*, XV, p. 225.

[3] See the return to the *Chambre ecclésiastique* of July 1786 in A.M.L. H 34, H 24; L. Bourgain, 'Contribution du clergé à l'impôt sous la monarchie française', *Rev. Quest. Hist.*, XLVIII (1890), pp. 117–18. Total receipts varied from year to year, and there is room for disagreement as to what deductions of charges should be allowed before stating a figure for available income. Total recepts in 1781 were 58,123*l.*, in 1784 68,891*l.* (A.M.L. H 193—Cellarer's accounts).

[4] In 1765, 19,000*l.* (dom Busson's visitation, in *Anjou hist.*, XV, pp. 12–13). The monks had 15,887*l.* then. In 1768 the *Commission des réguliers* noted the income of the monks alone as 17,758*l.* (*Anjou hist.*, IV, pp. 168–9).

[5] Seven in 1765 (*Anjou hist.*, XV, pp. 12–13). Besnard was a student in the seventies (I, pp. 168 ff.). A good deal of the detail which follows is from Besnard, I, pp. 170–3.

[6] 'Les derniers jours de l'abbaye de Saint-Aubin d'Angers', *Anjou hist.*, XVII (1916–17), pp. 67–81.

[6a] F. Uzureau, 'L'Abbaye de Saint-Aubin d'Angers, XVIIIe siècle', *Rev. Mabillon*, X (1919), pp. 113 ff., citing *Nouvelles ecclésiastiques*, 1769. For the furniture of comfortable bedrooms, see inventory of 22 April 1790 (A.M.L. Q·1).

[7] For this condition in the order of Saint-Maur see dom A. Du Bourg, 'Vie Monastique dans l'abbaye de Saint-Germain des Prés', *Rev. Quest. Hist.*, LXXVIII (1903), p. 456.

[8] Thorode, p. 286 (note); dom Busson's visitation, *Anjou hist.*, XV, p. 18; *Comm. des réguliers*, 1768, *Anjou hist.*, IV, p. 169.

[8a] There had been 12 monks here in 1704, and 6 in 1765 (Uzureau, 'Les derniers jours du prieuré de Lesvière-lez-Angers (1790)', *Rev. Mabillon*, XI (1921), pp. 313–14.

[9] P.V. Directory Dept. 20 Nov., 26 Dec., 9 Nov., 28 Oct. 1790. A.M.L. 1 L 68.

[10] Estimation *Biens Nat.*, A.M.L. III Q 2, III, no. 29. (28 April 1791); petition for annulment of the sale, 21 Feb. 1791, A.M.L. 19 Q 5.

[11] A.M.L. E 4337 (Petition of inhabitants concerning paving charges, 1774).

[12] Estimation *Biens Nat.*, III Q 1, no. 505.

[13] Report of March 1791 on A.M.L. 16 Q 2.

[14] Lainé, *Archives généalogiques*, VII, pp. 36–7.

[15] Dom Busson's visitation, 1765, *Anjou hist.*, XV, p. 15; *Commission des réguliers*, 1768, *Anjou hist.*, IV, p. 169. The *total* revenues in 1790, before any deductions were made, were 41,084*l.* (A.M.L. 13 Q 2). Since 1767 Saint-Nicolas had also been saddled with a pension of 1,200*l.* a year for another sinecurist,

Charles de Bouillé, who was only in minor orders (18 August 1790, A.M.L. 16 Q 2).

[16] Estimation *Biens Nat.*, A.M.L. III Q 1.

[17] Lehoreau, *Anjou hist.*, VIII, p. 257.

[18] Aimé de Soland, 'Église Abbatiale de Saint-Serge et Saint-Bach', *Mems. Soc. Agric.*, 2nd Ser., I (1850).

[19] *Anjou hist.*, XV, p. 17; IV, p. 169 (as above). Documents on the quarries (1750) in A.M.L. C 28 (carton). For a pension which proved a burden on the revenues of Saint-Serge, see A.M.L. 16 Q 4.

[20] P.V. of the ceremony by Sigogne, notary of Angers, A. Nat. file 'Succession de l'abbé de Hérouville', in T 222 (confiscated papers of emigrés, etc.).

[21] 46,000*l.* worth of repairs were here involved (A. Nat. T 222, file 21, nos. 16 (1 June 1787) and 4.

[22] 'Réponse à l'assignation...' A. Nat. T 222, file 'Succession... Hérouville'.

[23] *ibid.*, file headed 'Torrelly l'abbé'.

[24] Letter 14 Dec. 1784 from sequestrator of Hérouville's property, A. Nat. T 222, file 18, nos. 5 and 6.

[25] A. Nat. T 222, file 18, no. 12. In the end the bishop extracted only 5,000*l.* from the Hérouville family (statement of bishop, 9 Dec. 1790, A.M.L. 16 Q 4).

[26] *Anjou hist.*, IV, p. 169

[27] Port, *Inventaire.... Mairie*, pp. 268–9, 270; 'Les derniers jours de l'abbaye Saint-Nicolas-lès-Angers', *Anjou hist.*, XXI, pp. 19 ff.

[28] I.e. nine, Laubry, *Traité des Unions des Bénéfices* (1778), p. 145.

[29] For the decline in the numbers of religious from 1770–1790 see the statistics in Gérin, 'Les monastères Franciscains et la Commission des Réguliers, 1766–1789', *Rev. des Questions historiques*, XVIII (1875), pp. 88–9; and generally, see S. Lemaire, *La Commission des Réguliers, 1760–1780* (1926).

[30] Dom Martène, *Histoire de la Congrégation de Saint-Maur* (ed. Dom G. Charvin 1928), I, p. 263; IV, pp. 114–17.

[31] Brienne's words, Gérin, 'Les Bénédictins Français avant 1789', *Rev. des Questions historiques*, XIX, (1876), p. 482. For the Benedictine 'anarchy', see L. Deries, 'Dom Poirier', *Rev. Mabillon*, XX (1930), pp. 52–3.

[32] *Corresp. hist. des Bénédictins Bretons* (ed. A. de la Borderie 1880), pp. 160–3, 169–70.

[33] Given in Schmitz, *Histoire de l'Ordre de Saint Benoît* (7 vols., 1956).

[34] A. Rostand, 'L'oeuvre architecturale des Bénédictins de la congrégation de Saint-Maur en Normandie, 1616–1789', *Bull. Soc. Antiqu. Normandie*, XLVII (1939), pp. 182–222.

[35] For Saint-Nicolas, Port, *Inventaire... Mairie*, pp. 268–9, 270; E. L. in Thorode, pp. 216–18.

[36] E. L. in Thorode, p. 219.

[37] It was the abbé Prévost, E. Harisse, *L'abbé Prévost, histoire de sa vie et de ses oeuvres* (1896), pp. 250–1.

[38] F. Rousseau, *Moines Bénédictins martyrs et confesseurs de la foi pendant la Révolution* (1926), pp. 343–4; for Braux, Port, *Dict.*, I, pp. 478–9.

[39] Loaisel de Tréogate, J.-M., *Ainsi Finissent les grandes passions*, Paris, 1788.

[40] The house was joined to the Congregation of Sainte-Geneviève in 1629 (P. Feret, *L'abbaye de Sainte-Geneviève et la Congrégation de France* (1883), II, pp. 25–30). For its place in the congregation generally, see Dom Beaunier, *Recueil hist. des Archevêchés, Abbayes et Prieurés de France* (ed. 1906), pp. 245–9.

[41] *Anjou hist.*, IV, p. 170; Capitular Register, A.M.L. H 1260, pp. 130, 145 (4 April 1777, 9 March 1789).

[42] 30 April 1790, A.M.L. 13, Q 5.

[43] E. L. in Thorode, p. 25.

[44] Saint-Aubin ceded a garden to Toussaint in 1719 (A.M.L. H 20, map).

[45] Estimation *Biens Nat.*, A.M.L. III Q 1, no. 237.

[46] 'Tableau des Biens et Revenus ... de la maison de Toussaint...', Sept. 1780 (A.M.L. H 1248).

[47] 1182*l.* a year (A.M.L. 13 Q 5).

[48] If the butcher's bills are any indication: 1,449*l.* Easter to Easter 1771–2; 1,794*l.* March 1776–Dec. 1776 (A.M.L. H 1255, pp. 7–8); and in 1790 the butcher claimed 1,993*l.* owing (P.V. Dept., 12 Nov. 1790, A.M.L. I L 68). But one should take into account the fact that the chapter general of the province of Britanny met here. The abbot's share of the revenue was officially given out to be 3,500*l.* (Durand de Maillane, *Dict. de Droit Canon* (1776), I, p. 7).

[49] A.M.L. H 1260, p. 118.

[50] A.M.L. H 1255, pp. 43, 85, 80, 82, 59.

[51] De La Chenaye-Desbois & Badier, *Dictionnaire de la Noblesse*, XV, p. 719. Port, *Dict.*, III, p. 81.

[52] Strictly speaking eight, for the Recollets had two houses, one in the Saint-Laud area and one further out at La Baumette.

[53] 'Les Dominicains d'Angers et de Craon pendant la Révolution', *Anjou hist.*, XXI, pp. 213–14; Port, *Dict.*, I, pp. 70–1; [A. Launay], 'Monographie du Couvent des Capucins d'Angers', *Annales Franciscaines*, 1886, pp. 595–6; Armel, 'Les Franciscains de Maine-et-Loire pendant la Révolution', *Rev. d'Anjou*, 1907, pp. 53 ff; for the Augustins, A.M.L. 13 Q 6; for the Carmelites A.M.L. 13 Q 8.

[54] 'Registre concernant les affaires de la faculté de théologie d'Angers', B. Angers MS. 1244, pp. 47–51 (b). This is not an official register of the Faculty but a collection of precedents for the use of monastic houses against the secular doctors. For the lawsuit of dom Roualt 1718–19, see Cl. Pocquet de Livonnière, *Coustumes du Pays et Duché d'Anjou* (1725), II, col. 1050.

[55] P. Ubald, 'Les Frères Mineurs et l'Université d'Angers', *Études Franciscaines*, VI (1901), p. 71. (Note that at the Cordeliers, there were still two doctors of theology, out of 11 inmates, in 1789.)

[56] A. Léon, 'Couvents de Récollection de la Province Observante de Touraine-Pictavienne au XVIIe et XVIIIe siècles', *Études Franciscaines*, XXXVI (1924), pp. 624 ff.

[57] B. Angers MS. 555, pp. 42–6. This is a mid-century comic song ridiculing an Oratorian who had turned Capuchin; written in a seminary.

[58] A.M.L. 87 H 5, pp. 1–10, 2.

[59] A.M.L. 91 H 33, p. 32.

[60] Lehoreau, *Anjou hist.*, XV, p. 266.

[61] A.M.L. 86 H 20., pp. 4–31. (Including the income from masses said in the chapel of the *Présidial* from 1781 onwards, A.M.L. 86 H 5.)

[62] 10, 123 (A.M.L. 13 Q 8).

[63] Commission of 1786, *Anjou hist.*, IV, p. 171. *Rev. de l'Anjou*, XXX (1895), pp. 66–7, 69 (nn.); 24 April 1790, A.M.L. 13 Q 8. For questions about the ownership of this wine, 26 Jan. 1791, see A.M.L. II Q 55–6.

[64] In 1728 they had only 2,331*l.* income (A.M.L. 91 H 17). In 1783 their receipts were 4,931*l.*, though in the following year they appear to have been much higher (A.M.L. 91 H 32, pp. 11–15). Their expenditure in 1783 was rather more than 6,000*l.* (A.M.L. 91 H 33, pp. 32–50).

[65] E. L. in Thorode, p. 330.

[66] A.M.L. 91 H 33, pp. 33, 131. Their butcher's bill for 10 months was 300*l.*

[67] E. L. in Thorode, p. 331. But their furniture was simple enough, e.g., one

of them had two curtains, a carpet, a table, a dilapidated desk, an armchair with a moth-eaten cushion and an old cupboard containing eight books (13 Aug. 1790, A.M.L. 13 Q 11).

[68] A.M.L. 13 Q 6–27 April 1790, 24 Aug. 1790 and sale, 24 Nov. 1791.

[69] See above, p. 48.

[70] A.M.L. III Q 2, vol., III, no. 15. (Estimation of *Biens Nat.*) For the right of Recollets to own property, see M. Courtecuisse, *Tables Capitulaires des Frères Mineurs de l'Observance et des Récollets de Bretagne, 1476–1780* (1930), I, pp. lxiv–lxviii.

[71] 26 Aug. 1790, A.M.L. 13 Q 8.

[72] E. L. in Thorode, pp. 368, 370; Municipal Register, B. Angers MS. BB 130, f. 15 (b).

[73] See E. L. in Thorode; also dom L. Guilloreau, *L'Obituaire des Cordeliers d'Angers* (1902), pp. 48, 49; Fr. de Sessevalle in *Rev. d'histoire Franciscaine*, II (1925), pp. 545–9; and V. Chichmarec, *ibid.*, VII (1930), p. 356.

[74] E. L. in Thorode, pp. 309, 313–14, 340–45, 350.

[75] *ibid.*, pp. 309, 313–14; 'Les derniers jours du couvent de la Baumette', *Anjou hist.*, XLI, pp. 27–8.

[76] E. L. in Thorode, pp. 340–6.

[77] *ibid.*, pp. 326–7.

[78] See the liasse containing plans for building in A.M.L. 91 H 17; also Estimation *Biens Nat.*, A.M.L. III Q 1, no. 238.

[79] Lehoreau, *Anjou hist.*, XV, p. 266.

[80] Estimation *Biens Nat.*, A.M.L. III Q 1, no. 442.

[81] Uzureau, 'Le Couvent de la Baumette-lès-Angers', *Rev. d'histoire Franciscaine* VIII (1931), p. 357. For its historical importance in the history of the Recollets, see H. Lemaître, 'Géographie historique des établissements de l'ordre de Saint-François en Touraine', *ibid.*, VI (1929), p. 308.

[82] Uzureau, *loc cit.*, p. 9.

[83] 'Les derniers jours...', *Anjou hist.*, XLI, pp. 27–8.

[84] 'Le *cahier* de Saint-Samson-lès-Angers', *Anjou hist.*, XI, p. 500.

[85] Rangeard, 'Etat ... de l'Anjou...', B. Angers MS. 1020 (894), f. 46; description of house in A.M.L. III Q 2, vol. III, no. 187.

[86] Also a house in Angers; see lease to Jean René Pantin in 1780, A.M.L. J 3134.

[87] 'Maison de la Mission d'Angers' (MS. volume), B. Angers MS. 878, 'Obligations de la Maison de la Mission', ff. 1 ff.

[88] *ibid.*, ff. 18, 17(b). From 1768 to 1789, gifts for these purposes, missions and to found masses total just over 28,000*l*. Presumably most of this was invested with the Clergy of France.

[89] And one lay brother (Inventory of 16 May 1792, A.M.L. 13 Q 14). The inventory of their furniture in May 1792 shows that they had enough silver to lay three places at dinner, enough arm-chairs for all to sit in the parlour—but 21 chairs in their drawing-room were merely on loan to the house (A.M.L. 13 Q. 4).

[90] 'L'Oratoire d'Angers, 1619–1792', *Andegaviana*, XV (1914), p. 477. For one or two other foundations establishing offices and sermons, see E. L. in Thorode, p. 383.

[91] A. Crosnier, 'Le chevalier de Caqueray et ses souvenirs', *Rev. des Facultés Catholiques de l'Ouest*, IV (1894), pp. 881–2.

[92] F. Uzureau, 'Anciens collèges de la province d'Anjou. Les distributions des prix à la fin du XVIIIe siècle', *Anjou hist.*, I, pp. 11, 13.

[93] *Mémoires de Larevellière Lépeaux*, (Paris, 1895), I, pp. 15, 18–19.

[94] 'L'Oratoire d'Angers 1619–1792', *Andegaviana*, XV, p. 476.

[95] 80l., except for the *professeur* of mathematics, B. Bois, *La Vie Scolaire* ... *en Anjou*, p. 46.

[96] *Mémoires*, I, pp. 18–19.

[97] Bois, *La Vie scolaire* ... p. 48; the abbé Baston, *Mémoires* (ed. Loth & Verger, 3 vols.), I, p. 165.

[98] Bois, p. 48.

[99] See Port, *Dict.*, under names. For Héron, Blordier-Langlois, 'Autobiographie' *Rev. hist. arch. Anjou*, I (1867), pp. 192 ff. The squaring of the circle project is in B. Angers MS. 499 (473), date 1782.

[100] Speeches of 18 May 1790, in Uzureau, 'Anciens collèges de la province d'Anjou', *Anjou hist.*, I, p. 21n.

[101] G. Rigault, *Histoire général de l'Institut des Frères des Écoles Chrétiennes* (7 vols., 1938 ff.), II, p. 511 (cf. p. 613).

[102] *ibid.*, pp. 497–8, 507 ff.

[103] *ibid.*, pp. 498, 524, 320.

[104] The Frères had three *maisons de force* of this kind; payments of about 500l. a head were made (*ibid.*, pp. 278, 538). For a list of such institutions in France generally, see G. Vauthier, 'La maison de Charenton en 1790', *Annales hist. de la Révolution Française*, III (1926), p. 266.

[105] 'Les Frères des Écoles Chrétiennes à Angers, XVIII siècle', *Anjou hist.*, XV, pp. 571–81.

[106] Date 1763 (Rigault, II, p. 479).

[107] A.M.L. 90 H 3 ('Bien public', no. 4, 367).

[108] In 1778 (A.M.L. 90 H 1).

[109] Rigault, II, p. 554.

[110] *ibid.*, p. 557. In 1790 there were 30 (A.M.L. 90 H 3, 25 Feb. 1790).

[111] Was the rule observed? One pupil at the Rossignolerie stated that they were flogged with a five-corded whip on the fingers. This, he maintained, was an improvement on the Jesuits, who preferred another part of the anatomy (H. Pinguet, 'La vie bourgeoise de M. Boneau', *Anjou Hist.*, 1953, p. 204). For what follows, see Rigault, II, pp. 592, 609, 550, 558–62, 472, 533, 535.

[112] 'Au nom de Dieu et sous la protection de la glorieuse Vierge Marie, j'entreprends le commerce, cette année mil sept cent quatre-vingt-dix'.— inscription on the arithmetic books of Auget of Saumur (Rigault, II, pp. 531–2).

[113] Port, *Inventaire* ... *Mairie*, p. 129; A.M.L. E 4334 (date 1766).

[114] A.M.L. 95 H 25.

[115] Bois, 'L'Enseignement primaire en Anjou', *Rev. d'Anjou*, 1909, p. 225. See also 'Les Frères des Écoles Chrétiennes et la Municipalité d'Angers, XVIIIe siècle', *Anjou hist.*, XVI, pp. 142–7.

[116] Municipal Reg., B. Angers MS. BB 130, ff. 108(b), 109. The Oratory had proposed to found a School of Mathematics in 1783 (B. Angers MS. GG 359).

[117] Rigault, II, p. 556 n. 3.

[118] *ibid.*, pp. 478–80. The right of the Institute to hold property within the whole area of the jurisdiction of the Parlement of Paris was at stake in this case.

[119] For his career, Rigault *passim*.

[120] 'Les paroisses du diocèse d'Angers avant le Concordat. Nominations aux cures', *Anjou hist.*, IV, p. 458.

[121] (Bretaudeau), *Notre Dame du Ronceray* (Angers, 1895), pp. 103–9, 112. Regulations for reform were made in 1686 but were never carried out (Uzureau, 'Deux abbayes angevines au XVIIe siècle', *Rev. Mabillon*, 1914, pp. 335 ff.).

[122] A.M.L. E 693, cit. R. H. Andrews, *Les Paysans des Mauges au 18e siècle* (1935), pp. 62–6.

[123] Bretaudeau, p. 242; *Anjou hist.*, 1932, pp. 93 ff.; 'Tableau de la Province

d'Anjou 1762–6', *Mems. Soc. Agric.* 4th Ser., II (1897), p. 425; *Mémoire Signifié pour Me Charles-François Boufteau* (1768), B. Angers S.J. 407, no. 18, p. 3.

[124] Uzureau, 'Les Communautés de femmes du diocèse d'Angers en 1790', *Méms. Soc. Agric.*, IX, p. 113.

[125] 'État actuel de l'abbaye Royalle du Ronceray' (1773), B. Angers MS. 1748, VI.

[126] P. M. Masson, *Une Vie de femme au xviii*e *siècle. Madame de Tencin. 1682–1749* (1910), p. 7n.

[127] Statement of canons Duval and Leroy in 1785, *Anjou hist.*, XVIII, pp. 211–12.

[128] Grandet, 'Notre-Dame Angevine' in Uzureau. 'L'Abbaye du Ronceray au début du XVIIIe siècle', *Rev. Mabillon*, XXXIX (1920), pp. 38–9.

[129] Bretaudeau, pp. 217–18.

[130] De La Chenaye-Desbois and Badier, *Dict. de la Noblesse.*, III, cols. 385–6. The family expected to obtain good abbeys for its unmarried daughters, cf. 'L'Abbaye Cistercienne de Leyme au diocèse de Cahors', *Rev. Mabillon*, XVI (1925), pp. 205–6.

[131] *Recueil des Instructions données aux ambassadeurs de France (Rome)* (ed. Hanoteau, 1911), XVII, p. 429. Cf. Brossier, B. Angers MS. 730, p. 13. For his previous embassy to Spain, *Recueil*, XII, bis (1899), p. 326.

[132] B. Pocquet, *Histoire de Bretagne* (1914), VI, pp. 341–66.

[133] 'La maréchale d'Aubeterre', *Andegaviana*, 1927, p. 145.

[134] In 1773 there were 35 nuns ('État', *Anjou hist.*, 1932, p. 93); in 1790 there were 23 ('Les Religieuses du Ronceray d'Angers pendant la Révolution', *Anjou hist.*, XXXI, pp. 104 ff.). There were also five girls, ages 20 to 25, waiting to make their professions (A.M.L. 13 Q 3, 26 April 1790).

[135] 'Les Visitandines d'Angers pendant et après la Révolution', *Anjou hist.*, IX, pp. 56–61. For Darlus de Montclerc and his purchase of lands and fiefs for 62,000*l.* in 1769, see *Archives du Cogner* (pub. by L.-J. Denis, Le Mans), Ser. E (1909), pp. 43–4, and J.-X. Carré de Busserolle, *Catalogue analytique d'aveux de fiefs rendus par des familles ... de l'Anjou ... (XVII*e *et XVIII*e *siècles)*, (Tours, 1885), p. 146.

[136] Mme Letondal, *Mémoires, Anjou hist.*, V, p. 9.

[137] For Jeanne-Jacquine Moutardeau, see 'La déportation des Religieuses Angevines', *Anjou hist.*, XXIX, p. 161.

[138] A.M.L. 13 Q 10 (26 April, 1790).

[139] 'Les Calvariennes d'Angers', *Anjou hist.*, VI, p. 460; Uzureau, 'Les Carmélites d'Angers, XVIIe et XVIIIe siècles', *ibid.*, V, pp. 561 ff.; Chaulbert, 'Le Carmel d'Angers, 1626–1792', *La Province d'Anjou*, X (1935), pp. 86–7. Dowries were admitted to be an abuse ('Consultations de cas de conscience avec les résolutions', MS. University of Rennes 222, ff. 191–2.—This is an Angevin document).

[140] A.M.L. 13 Q 7.

[141] Crosnier, *Histoire de la Congrégation de Saint Charles d'Angers* (1930), p. 54. In the house of La Croix nuns were established with a dowry of 1,200 to 2,000*l.* Families who could not pay this capital sum were expected to try to find 150*l.* a year *pension*. All nuns, with or without a dowry, had to bring a 'trousseau' of 600*l.* (A.M.L. 13 Q 8, 30 Nov. 1792.)

[142] Discourse to the Academy of Angers, 7 March 1770, MS. University of Rennes 213, f. 125.

[142a] Dates of arrival in Angers in Rangeard, 'État ... ' B. Angers MS. 1020. For details of the foundation of the Visitation at Angers in 1636, see E. Catta, *La Visitation Sainte-Marie de Nantes, 1630–1792* (1954), pp. 153, 344.

[143] E. Rondeau, *Histoire du Monastère des Ursulines d'Angers* (*1618–1910*) (Angers, 1911), p. 177.

[143a] 'Le Bon Pasteur d'Angers 1688–1795', *Anjou hist.*, XXXV, pp. 8–9; for the Petite Pension, see below, p. 100.

[144] The curé of Saint-Maurille, etc., to the mayor, 27 Jan. 1786, B. Angers MS. DD 16.

[145] Port, *Dict.*, I, p. 75.

[146] A. Nat. H 1654, no. 32 (10 Feb. 1731).

[147] Lehoreau, in 'La Banque de Law et les Angevins', *Anjou hist.*, II, pp. 547–8. The standard method of investment (by disguised loans) left such institutions peculiarly vulnerable (cf. B. Pocquet du Haut-Jussé, 'La Vie temporelle des communautés de femmes à Rennes au XVIIIᵉ siècle', *Annales de Bretagne*, XXXI (1915–16), p. 101.

[148] A. Nat. H 1654, no. 60.

[149] Port, *Dict.*, I, p. 73.

[150] A. Nat. H 1654, no. 20 (15 Nov. 1727).

[151] A. Nat. H 1654, no. 61 (Jan. 1730).

[152] Uzureau, 'Tableau de la Province d'Anjou, 1762–66', *Méms. Soc. Agric* ... 4th Ser., II (1879), pp. 425–6.

[153] A. Nat. G 8 620, file 53 (Superior to agents-general, 8 Aug. 1772).

[154] 31 August 1790, A.M.L. 13 Q 8 (misfiled). Another 'État' gives 11,900*l.* as the figure.

[155] A.M.L. 13 Q 8.

[156] 6,748*l.* A.M.L. 13 Q 8.

[157] 6 Oct. 1790, A.M.L. 13 Q 8.

[158] 29 Nov. 1793, A.M.L. 13 Q 14. But in 1790 the revenues were noted as higher—5,787*l.* ('Tableau Général des Revenues des hospices ... 1790', drawn up in year VI, A.M.L. 1 L 989).

[159] 'Les Visitandines d'Angers ...', *Anjou hist.*, IX, p. 45.

[160] Letters of Marie Hyacinthe de Montecler, *économe*, 2, 17, and 29 Nov. 1776, A. Nat. H 1654, nos. 54, 55.

[161] There was a basic yearly income of 178*l.* from the leases of two houses and a shop. By Nov. 1792 debts totalled over 12,000*l.* (A.M.L. 13 Q 7).

[162] 220*l.* rents and the interest on 8,700*l.* capital (Crosnier, pp. 72–3).

[163] E. Rondeau, *Histoire du Monastère des Ursulines*, pp. 172–7.

[164] Mme Letondal, *Mémoires, Anjou hist.*, V, pp. 10–11. She was being a little unfair. La Croix had connexions with two hospitals in country towns (6 Oct. 1790, A.M.L. 13 Q 8).

[164a] Besnard, I, p. 134; M. G. Bayer, 'Le Guignolet d'Angers', *Rev. d'Anjou*, LVII (1908), pp. 25 ff.

[165] 20 rooms for boarders (26 April 1790, A.M.L. 13 Q 10).

[166] 30 Nov. 1792, A.M.L. 13 Q 8.

[167] 29 Nov. 1793, A.M.L. 13 Q 14.

[168] Crosnier, pp. 60 ff.; for La Croix, A.M.L. 13 Q 8. At the Bon Pasteur in 1792 there were 7 actual sisters, 24 endowed or fee-paying residents for life, and 14 received for life without dowry, though yearly payments were made on behalf of some (A.M.L. 13 Q 7).

[169] 'État de la Maison des dames religieuses de Sainte Catherine ordre de Cîteaux', A.M.L. 13 Q 8.

[170] 'Cérémonial des Religieuses de la Fidelité d'Angers pour les Vetures, et pour l'election d'une Prieure devant Monseigneur l'Evêque' (1744), B. Angers MS. 1815, p. 12—this is a nineteenth-century copy.

[171] Crosnier, pp. 370–2.

[172] Details from A.M.L. 13 Q 16 (20 April 1790).

[173] 28 Sept. 1792, A.M.L. 13 Q 8.

[174] 26 Aug. 1790, A.M.L. 13 Q 8; 16 Oct. 1792, A.M.L. 13 Q 8.

[175] Details from Penitents (30 May 1792, A.M.L. 13 Q 14); Calvaire (14 Sept. 1790, A.M.L. 13 Q 8); Crosnier, pp. 54–5; Bon Pasteur (31 May 1792, A.M.L. 13 Q 7); Ursulines (20 April 1790, A.M.L. 13 Q 16).

[176] Uzureau, 'Les communautés religieuses de femmes dans le diocèse d'Angers en 1790', *Mém. Soc. Agric. ...*, IX, pp. 115–16.

[177] A. Nat. H 1653, no. 43.

[177a] 7 March 1770, MS. University of Rennes 213, f. 125.

[178] Mme Letondal, *Mémoires, Anjou hist.*, V, p. 10.

[179] *ibid.*, p. 11; 'Projet d'Établissement d'un hôpital d'Enfants trouvés dans la ville d'Angers', B. Angers MS. GG 363; *Journal du Département de Maine-et-Loire*, 19 Jan. 1791, A.M.L. 148 L 1.

[180] Uzureau, *loc. cit.*; *Méms. Soc. Agric. ...*, IX, p. 118; Bois, *La Vie Scolaire*, p. 112; Péan de la Tuillerie, pp. 182–3.

[181] There were 32 beds for them at the Visitation (31 Aug. 1790, A.M.L. 13 Q 17) and 24 'with green curtains' at the Ursulines (16 Sept. 1790, A.M.L. 13 Q 16).

[182] 'Réglemens pour une Communauté de Filles', B. Angers MS. 412, pp. 18(b), 20(b), 21.

[183] *Nouvelles ecclésiastiques*, 16 Jan. 1789, in *Anjou hist.*, XIX, pp. 38–41.

[184] J. Neveu, 'Une fête chez les Ursulines avant la Révolution', *Méms. Soc. Agric.*, XII (1937), pp. 108–15.

[185] Rondeau, *Histoire du monastère des Ursulines*, pp. 200, 204–5

[186] *Nouvelles ecclésiastiques*, as above, p. 40.

[187] Cosnier, *La Charité à Angers* (1889), pp. 106, 296–7; Mme Letondal, *Mémoires, Anjou hist.*, V, p. 11. Their course lasted for three months. Some were trained gratuitously, others were charged a small fee (Crosnier, *Hist. Congrégation de Saint Charles*, p. 66).

[188] C. Port, *Cartulaire de l'Hôpital Saint-Jean d'Angers* (1870), pp. 92, 64.

[189] Port, *Dict.*, I, pp. 98–9; in April 1791 there were 189 old men, 102 boys, 100 girls, 11 pensioners ('État', A.M.L. 1 L 989).

[189a] 'Les Incurables d'Angers avant la Révolution', *Anjou hist.*, III, pp. 22–3. Port, *Dict.*, I, p. 100. *Tableau de situation de l'Hôpital des Pauvres Incurables*, 4 Sept. 1791, B. Angers MS. 1157.

[190] A further 27,000l. from invested monies brought total revenue in 1790 to 93,032l. ('Tableau Exact ... des biens que possédait en 1790 l'hospice civil...' A.M.L. 1 L 989).

[191] C. Port, *Inventaire des Archives anciennes de l'Hôpital Saint-Jean d'Angers* (1870), p. xxxi. The monopoly of the sale of meat in Lent was worth 2,400l. p.a. Municipal Reg. (*Mairie*), II, p. 27(b)—1 March 1791. It was farmed out of course—see correspondence of 1787 in A.M.L. E 13.

[192] Port, *Cartulaire*, pp. 90–2.

[193] Municipal Reg., B. Angers MS. BB 130, f. 126.

[194] Lehoreau, *Anjou hist.*, II, pp. 547–8; 'État des Biens fonds ... de l'hôpital de la ville d'Angers' (1791), A.M.L. 1 L 989. For funerals, see *Instruction à l'occasion des Jurés-Crieurs de la Ville ... d'Angers* (1761), B. Angers MS. 1154. Generally, see also 'État', 1 Jan. 1792, B. Angers MS. 1154.

[194a] 'Tableau Général des Revenues des hospices civils du Canton d'Angers en 1790', A.M.L. 1 L 989.

[195] Port, *Cartulaire*, p. 33. For the composition of the boards of management of the various hospitals see *Almanach de la Province d'Anjou*. (1790). B. Nat. Lc[29] 12, pp. 65–7.

[196] For its composition, *'Changements qu'on propose à l'Acte de Fondation de l'Hôpital des Incurables'*, B. Angers MS. 1157, p. 3.

[197] Report of the commission of investigation, 6 Sept. 1789, pr. on pp. 6–18 of *Lettre Ecrite à MM. les Curés d'Angers, par M. Delaunay l'aîné, Avocat*. B. Angers H 2094. Cf. 'Notes sur quelques abus', B. Angers MS. 1157.

[198] E.g. Saint-Aubin gave 1,810*l.* a year to the Hôpital Général (A.M.L. H 34). The bishop voluntarily gave 300*l.* too (A.M.L. G 33).

[199] Letter of the administrators, 13 Feb. 1791 (A.M.L. 1 L 988).

[200] 'Réglement pour l'Hôpital des Pauvres Incurables ... fait par M. De Vaugirault, Évêque d'Angers le 16 mars 1751' (1789), B. Angers H 2094, pp. 9–10.

[201] Uzureau, *Méms. Soc. Agric.*, IX, pp. 127–8.

[202] And 20 unpaid domestic helps ('État', A.M.L. 1 L 989).

[202a] *Tableau*, 4 Sept. 1791 (B. Angers MS. 1157).

[203] Cosnier, p. 116.

[203a] 'Réglement', pp. 7–8; 'Les Hôpitalières d'Angers pendant la Révolution', *Anjou hist.*, V, p. 378.

[204] See letter of the Superior Gen. in Paris, 4 March 1784 (A.M.L. F 6).

[205] 'État ... de l'Anjou...', B. Angers MS. 1020, f. 53.

[206] L. La Combe, 'Denise-Marie Boussinot, supérieure de la Communauté de Saint-Charles, 1759–1829', *Anjou hist.*, I, pp. 591–4, 726; and Crosnier's monograph.

[207] Port, *Dict.*, I, p. 74. For references to the wife of M. Charpentier, a wine merchant of the rue Saint-Denis, confined here, and to one Geneviève Gravelle, accused of libels against the great and sent to the Penitents of Angers by ministerial order—also to the *gouvernante* who aided them by smuggling letters out (date 1751), see F. Ravisson, *Archives de la Bastille*, XVI (1884), pp. 197–207.

[208] 'Le Bon Pasteur d'Angers 1688–1795', *Anjou hist.*, XXXV, pp. 8–18; Lehoreau, *Anjou hist.*, XV, p. 285.

[209] 'Bureau Général de Charité. Porro unum est necessarium' n.d. (1789). (B. Angers H 2933), p. 11.

[210] A bibliography of fact and fiction in those matters can be compiled from G. May, *Diderot et la Religieuse* (1954).

[211] Besnard, I, p. 291.

[212] A.M.L. 87 H 7, pp. 123–5 (26 Aug. 1757).

[213] The following is worth citing as a curiosity. It is written on the back of a volume of pious meditations. 'Meditation on the passion of Our Lord Jesus. 4th volume—I condemn in this manuscript, which was given to me by my superiors, anything blasphemous or unorthodox which may be contained there, as also the slightest appearance of error or what is contrary to the sentiments of the Church. Angers 10 September 1786. Fr. Lactance Joubert, *religieux récollet'* (MS. University of Rennes 208—see *Cat. gen. MSS. Bibl. Publ. France. Université de Paris et Univ. des Dépt.* (1918), pp. 597–8).

[214] C. Bloch, *L'Assistance et l'État en France à la veille de la Révolution* (1908), especially pp. 365–6, 372.

CHAPTER VI

[1] See C. Port, *Les Artistes Angevins*, under the names.

[2] Port, *Artistes*, pp. 303, 297; Bretaudeau, *Ronceray*, p. 212.

[3] Agreement of 1780, with petition of 23 Dec. 1790 (A.M.L. 19 Q 7).

[4] A.M.L. D 31 (1778); A.M.L. G 273, pp. 79, 33 (1786).

[5] 1786–9 (A.M.L. H 151, file 2).

[6] 'Mémoire des ouvrages que moy éperon à faites [sic] et fournis', 12 Sept. 1789 (A.M.L. H 12).

[7] A.M.L. H 1255, pp. 43, 67, 71, 74, 80, 82.

[8] A.M.L. H 1255, pp. 4, 49, 70, 80, 82, 39, 61, 63, 75, 92, 31, 43, 53.

[9] A.M.L. 78 H 14 (Augustins, April 1789).

[10] A.M.L. G 33 (Laundry list, 1773).

[11] Toussaint, A.M.L. H 1255.

[12] For lists of debts, see A.M.L. 13 Q 1 (Saint-Aubin—over 7,000l. owed to the butcher); 13 Q 6 (Augustins); 13 Q 12 (Lesvière); 13 Q 8 (Carmes), etc.

[13] See, for examples: A.M.L. G 1171, 1 May 1788. (Milscent, on becoming *lieutenant particulier* of the *sénéchaussée*, hands over the functions of *sénéchal* of the fiefs of Saint-Pierre to Victor Bodi); Brossier, B. Angers MS. 730, p. 35(b). (The *avocat* of the cathedral receives 100l. p.a. honorarium); A.M.L. G 942, f. 9 (20 sols a day extra to the feudist of the chapter of Saint-Laud for taking the assizes); A.M.L. 1 L 68, P.V. Directory Dept., 27 Oct. 1790 (Chopin, receiver of the abbey of Saint-Aubin was paid 1,200l. p.a.). A.M.L. H 4, p. 423 (Saint-Aubin transfers office of *sénéchal* of the jurisdiction of the priory of Château-gontier from an *avocat au présidial* of Angers to one of Châteaugontier). For the notary of the Jacobins and the *sénéchal, procureur, greffier* and *sergent* of the *Trésorier* of the cathedral, see E. L. Thorode, XI, in pp. 110–11. There were sixteen seigneurial courts in Angers, all dependent on ecclesiastical institutions (Métivier, *Des anciennes institutions judiciaires de l'Anjou* (1851), pp. 5–10).

[14] Estimation *Biens Nat.*, A.M.L. 111 Q 1, no. 417.

[15] A. Nat. D XIX 61, file 61, no. 2 (29 June 1790).

[16] See above, chap. 111.

[17] A. Nat. D XIX 61, file 61, no. 2 (29 June 1790).

[18] For 48l. p.a. (A.M.L. H 1255, p. 94).

[19] 'Le noble confrairie des Bourgeois', B. Angers MS. 767, no. 2.

[20] Péan de la Tuillerie, p. 85; A. Nat. D XIX 61, file 61, no. 2. The Seminary employed a verger for its church of Saint-Julien, at 20l. p.a. (Accounts, 1779, A.M.L. G 35).

[21] *Arrêt de la Cour de Parlement*, 11 July, 1786, p. 35, in the parish register of Saint-Pierre (État Civil Angers, GG 185, f. 51). The cathedral also had a very expensive real *Suisse* from Switzerland (A.M.L. G 271, p. 170).

[22] Saint-Maurice, Grille's accounts (B. Angers MS. 748, no. 8, f. 4(b); Lesvière, A.M.L. G 1663, f. 2 (1785).

[23] Parish accounts 1756–89, A.M.L. 62 H 5.

[24] A.M.L. G 1712, f. 56.

[25] *Arrêt de la Cour de Parlement*, as above, in État Civil, GG 185, f. 51, p. 34.

[26] A.M.L. G 942, f. 124 (Saint-Laud); P.V. Directory Dept., 12 Oct. 1790. A.M.L. 1 L 68 (Saint-Aubin); A.M.L. G 35 (Seminary accounts, 72l. p.a. to bell-ringers at Saint-Julien).

[27] A.M.L. H 1255, p. 45 (1781), p. 98 (1781–9), p. 96 (1779).

[28] A.M.L. D 31, file 3 (1779–80).

[29] The Carmelites employed two gardeners (A.M.L. 13 Q 8); the Penitents had a gardener, a sacristan, a porter, a baker and an infirmary help as well as four other servants (A.M.L. 13 Q 14); the nuns of Sainte-Catherine had 7 house servants, a sacristan, an errand boy and a gardener (A.M.L. 13 Q 8).

[30] P.V. Department, 23 July 1790 (A.M.L. 1 L 68); A.M.L. 1 L 9 and 9 bis, pp. 31–2; see also A.M.L. 16 Q 3.

[31] A.M.L. 16 Q 2 (9 April 1791).

[32] A.M.L. 16 Q 4 (17 Oct. 1792).

[33] Petitions to Directory of District, 20 Nov. 1792 (A.M.L. 1 L 981; see also A.M.L. 16 Q 3).

[34] P.V. Directory Dept., 29 Oct. 1790 (A.M.L. 1 L 68).

[35] Register of servants' wages and duties, A.M.L. H 1255, p. 20.

[36] A.M.L. H 1255, pp. 14–15, 10–13.

[37] Deliberations of parish of Lesvière, 1785. A.M.L. G 1663, f. 2.

[38] Deniau, *Histoire de la Vendée*, I, p. 194.

[39] The statistics I have collected are too incomplete to be worth recapitulation. This is the general impression however. The monks of Saint-Serge gave 1,440*l.* alms in the winter of 1789–90, and this was regarded as a usual sum (District to Department, 29 Nov. 1790, A.M.L. II Q 55–6). Cf. for Saint-Aubin, A.M.L. 13 Q 1).

[40] B. Angers MS. 638, p. 38.

[41] *Affiches*, in 'Les Angevins et la Famille Royale ...', *Anjou hist.*, II, pp. 505–6; Munic. Reg. BB 130; f. 124(b). A sojourn in jail awaited militia men who were moved by enthusiasm to fire extra salvoes. (A. Nat. H 1633, no. 40).

[42] A.M.L. G 1014, f. 58; 'Le chapitre de la Cathédrale d'Angers avant la Révolution', *Anjou hist.*, XXIII, p. 7, also *Andegaviana*, XXIV, p. 66.

[43] Munic. Reg. BB 131, f. 22(b).

[44] J. Levron, *La Bourse de Commerce d'Angers au 18e siècle* (1933), pp. 45–6.

[45] François Prévost, Nov. 1755, 'Présidial d'Angers. Discours de Rentrée', B. Angers MS. 513, f. 127.

[46] Munic. Reg. BB 130, f. 128(b) (Dec. 1783). The cathedral yielded in the following July (BB 131, f. 29).

[47] A.M.L. G 273, pp. 270–1 (March 1788, reply of cathedral to cathedral of Puy en Vellay); for others keeping records, A.M.L. G 1014, p. 58 and Registre des délibérations de la juridiction consulaire d'Angers', *Anjou hist.*, XVI, p. 133.

[48] *ibid.*, *Anjou hist.*, XVI, p. 133.

[49] 'On s'étonne que les hommes portent les désirs des distinctions jusques au pied des autels: c'est par cette reflexion que commencent presque tous les traités sur cette matière; mais il faut bien que ceux qui ont droit à des honneurs publics les obtiennent dans les églises, puisque dans notre constitution le peuple n'a plus d'occasions de s'assembler ailleurs.' (Guyot, *Répertoire universel et raisonné de Jurisprudence civile, criminelle, canonique et bénéficiale* (81 vols., 1776–1786), XXI, pp. 264–5.)

[50] Port, *Dict.*, II, p. 506. Disputes over precedence in churches were settled by Royal Courts. Ecclesiastics could make decisions 'on the spot, to avoid scandal, and provisionally only', (Alletz), *La Discipline de l'Église de France* (1780), p. 34.

[51] Mezeray (*syndic*) to Duchesne, 30 Dec. 1772, 31 Jan. 1773, 23 Sept. 1773; reply of 29 Aug. 1773 (A. Nat. G 8 620).

[52] Mezeray to the abbé Dulau, 28 Dec. 1773, 6 May 1772 (A. Nat. G 8 620).

[53] Letters of abbess, 11 Feb., 23 Feb., 22 April, 1774; 27 Jan. 1775 (A. Nat. G 8 620).

[54] A. Nat. G 8* 2610, no. 387; G 8* 2451, pp. 42, 43; G 8 620 Mezeray to the abbé de la Rochefoucauld, 20 March 1776, and copy of Turgot's letter of 23 Oct. 1775. (The first two references here are consultations of the council of lawyers.)

[55] A. Nat. G 8* 2607, no. 69 (27 Feb. 1772), no. 137 (21 April 1772); G 8* 2596, no. 106 (19 March 1766).

[56] Ecclesiastics were liable to capitation on the number of servants they employed, but this was the affair of the central government and appeals against

assessment were made directly to the intendant; see letters of a canon of Saint-Martin and of the dean of Saint-Pierre, in 1789 and 1786, in B. Angers MS. CC 172.

[57] *Arrest du Conseil d'Estat ... Portant defenses aux Maire & Eschevins de la ville d'Angers de contraindre les Ecclesiastiques ... au payment des droits d'entrée des vins de leur cru ...* (1653), A. Nat. G 8 614.

[58] Letters of Belot (10 Sept. 1719) and Mezeray (4 Aug. 1773) in A. Nat. G 8 620; A. Nat. G 8* 2609, no. 21.

[59] Mezeray to agents-general, 13 Feb. 1759, A. Nat. G 8 620.

[60] Correspondence of Sept. 1773–Sept. 1774, A.M.L. H 2.

[61] Mezeray to the abbé Dulau, 1 Feb. 1772, A. Nat. G 8 620; cf. A. Nat. G 8* 2607, nos. 69 and 137.

[62] A.M.L. E 4337 (date 1774); Munic. Reg. BB 132, f. 103(b) (1787); A.M.L. G 942, ff. 112, 116 (date 1788).

[63] Enclosed in de la Brosse to Duchesne, 16 Feb. 1787, A. Nat. G 8 620.

[64] Mezeray, 5 Sept. 1772, A. Nat. G 8 620.

[65] A. Nat. G 8* 2597, no. 259 (14 July 1767); Letters of Mezeray 4 Dec. 1771, 1 Sept. 1773, 5 Sept. 1772, 4 Aug. 1773, 20 Feb. 1779, and of de la Brosse 16 Feb. 1787 (all in A. Nat. G 8 620); Consultation of council of lawyers, 21 Feb. 1775, A. Nat. G 8* 2804.

[66] See the register of the agents-general, A. Nat. G 8* 2570, nos. 42, 49, 68, 173; Consulations of lawyers, A. Nat. G 8* 2451, ff. 42–3; and memoirs enclosed in Le Roux's letter of 14 March 1766 and 'Observations' on them, A. Nat. G 8 620.

[67] Letters of Le Roux, 4 March, 15 March 1766, A. Nat. G 8 620.

[68] Mezeray, 8 Nov. 1774, A. Nat. G 8 620.

[69] 'Mémoire pour demoiselle Renée Coudraye. ...' (31 March 1786). A. Nat. T 222, file 21, nos. 6 and 7. The bishop also had the repairs of Saint-Serge and of Saint-Martin-ès-Aire, Troyes, on his hands.

[70] Brossier, B. Angers MS. 729, f. 107(b), 108; MS. 727, f. 210.

[71] The *cens* (yearly feudal rent) was generally trivial—e.g. the Petits Pères paid 3s. 2d. to the fief of Saint-Maurille and 12s. 4d. to that of Saint-Aubin, while the Rossignolerie paid 60l. to the fief of Saint-Martin. It was feudal incidents which were a burden. For an unpopular minor due of a different kind (*à droit de bac* on ferrymen, exercised by Saint-Laud), see Municipal Register, (*Mairie*) 1, p. 93(b) (14 June 1790).

[72] See the case of the canons of Toussaint and a tobacconist's shop, *Proc. syndic* Dept. to District of Angers, 10 Nov. 1790, A.M.L. 1 L 124.

[73] *Mémoire, sur une question de Desherance. Pour Martin Pinson & Marie Jamin, sa Femme, Défendeurs: contre Messieurs les Doyen, Chanoines & Chapitre de Saint-Martin ...* (Angers, 1777), B. Angers S.J. 311 (7), no. 27. The *Mémoire* of Jacques Trottier against Saint-Nicolas is in S.J. 311 (7), no. 29.

[74] Munic. Reg. BB 130, ff. 66(b)–67. For what follows, see 'Jacques Boullay du Martay, maire d'Angers (1742–1803)', *Andegaviana*, XXIX, p. 134; 'La municipalité d'Angers avant la Révolution', *Andegaviana*, V, pp. 205–9; Blordier-Langlois, *Angers et l'Anjou sous le Régime Municipal*, (1843), pp. 325, 331–2, 334–6, 339, 340, 343.

[75] This can only be justified if the area covered by feudal superiorities as well as directly owned is being considered. Of the 2,811 houses in the main city area listed by Thorode, 513 were owned by ecclesiastical corporations—chapters owned 214 of them and abbeys 84 ('Récensement des maisons d'Angers vers 1780', B. Angers MS. 1172).

[76] Port, *Inventaire ... Marie*, p. 153. The bishop was willing to agree to the

demolition of the church, but the cemetery of Saint-Denis and two houses belonging to the Seminary stood in the way of the project (Munic. Reg. BB 120, f. 75(b)).

[77] Munic. Reg. BB 131, f. 7; BB 130, ff. 133–4, 142.

[78] Munic. Reg. BB 132, ff. 52, 76(b), 78, 126; BB 133, f. 20(b).

[79] Munic. Reg. BB 130, f. 44.

[80] They were allowed to enclose ground previously left open (Munic. Reg. BB 130, ff. 39(b), 44).

[81] Munic. Reg. BB 130, f. 138; BB 131, ff. 51(b), 52(b). (Cf. Port's note in Péan de la Tuillerie, pp. 181–2.)

[82] Munic. Reg. BB 132, f. 140.

[83] Munic. Reg. BB 132, ff. 145(b)–6. In 1786 there had been an investigation by the town into Saint-Serge's title to certain lands near the city walls (Letter of Bardoul, 19 April 1786, A. Nat. R 5, 123).

[84] P.V. *Commission intermédiaire*, A.M.L. C 166, ff. 78(b), 80(b).

[85] Letter of Pocquet de Livonnière, 26 Nov. 1766, A. Nat. H 1 1509.

[86] Ch. Urseau, *Étude sur l'Instruction primaire avant 1789 dans le diocèse d'Angers. Documents inédits.* (1893), p. 11.

[87] See Guyot, *Répertoire de Jurisprudence*, II, pp. 74–5.

[88] 2 Dec. 1749, A. Nat. G 8 620, file 50. For a later complaint, 'Le *cahier* du chapitre de Saint-Martin d'Angers', *Anjou hist.*, XXXI, pp. 216–17. For the edict of 1749, Isambert, *Recueil ... des anciennes Lois*, XXII, pp. 226–35, and an interpretative Declaration in 1762, pp. 323–8.

[89] See the registers of the correspondence of the agents-general, A. Nat. G 8* 2600, no. 234; G 8* 2569, no. 212; G 8* 2578, no. 50; no. 184, no. 234, no. 245, no. 328; G 8* 2579, no. 20; G 8* 2610, no. 387; G 8* 2614, no. 37, no. 81. See, also, consultation of council of lawyers, G 8* 2459, ff. 444–5, 448; and letters of *syndics* of the diocese, 14 Feb. 1776, 20 March 1776, 10 July 1771, 23 May 1771, 22 July 1771, 15 Aug. 1780, 3 June 1784, in A. Nat. G 8 620. For the legal position concerning the *droit d'amortissement*, see Durand de Maillane, *Dictionnaire de Droit canonique et de pratique bénéficial* (1776) I, p. 150; also the *Rapport de l'Agence, contenant les principales affaires du Clergé .... 1775–1780* (1785), pp. 94–5, clxiv–clxvi, concerning the leasing out of some uncultivated land by the canons-regular of Toussaint in 1773.

[90] Mezeray to de Beauvais, 19 Feb. 1774, A. Nat. G 8 620. Actually the first sommation was to the chapter of Saint-Martin, 27 Dec. 1773 (B. Angers MS. 768, no. 39).

[91] Letters of abbot of Saint-Serge, 22 Nov. 1774, and of chapter of Saint-Martin, 20 Sept. 1774 (A. Nat. G 8 620, files 49 and 53).

[92] 'Mémoire pour les Doyen, Chanoines et Chapitre de l'Église d'Angers', B. Angers MS. 747, no. 23.

[93] A. Nat. G 8* 2609, nos. 373, 403.

[94] Bishop of Angers to the agents-general, 21 July 1775 (A. Nat. G 8 168). Canon Roustille to agents-general, 22 July 1774 (A. Nat. G 8 620, file 53). For the renewal of trouble in 1776, see the dean of Saint-Laud, 31 Dec. 1776, and Mezeray, 5 Oct. 1776 (A. Nat. G 8 620).

[95] 'Observations' (on a letter of the chancellor of the duc d'Orléans, of April 1782), A. Nat. G 8 614.

[96] See 'Déclaration concernant les inhumations'; 10 March 1777, Isambert *Recueil*, XXIII, pp. 391–4; *Rapport de l'Agence ... 1775–80* (1785), pp. 4–5.

[97] See Guyot, *Répertoire ... de Jurisprudence*, II, p. 32; 'Eloge de Mʳ Dupaty, médecin', B. Angers MS. 1671; Dupuy, 'Les Epidémies en Bretagne au 18ᵉ siècle', *Annales de Bretagne*, I (1886), pp. 120–40. For the church of Saint-Evroul in Angers, Brossier, B. Angers MS. 726, f. 987; for the parish church of

Saint-Maurice, 'L'Église paroissiale de Saint-Maurice', *Anjou hist.*, 1949, p. 46.

[98] Letters of *échevins* of Tours, 5 Sept. 1776, B. Angers MS. DD 16.

[99] 'Les Cimetières d'Angers', *Anjou hist.*, IX, pp. 466–8; *Andegaviana*, 1927., pp. 4–6. The cost of buying land from the chapel of Guinefolle was 4,930*l.* (*Extrait du Procès-Verbal relatif à l'établissement des nouveaux Cimetières* (1783), B. Angers MS. DD 16). Saint-Nicolas and Saint-Samson being outside the town retained their old cemeteries. (*Tableau de Répartition de la Dépense pour l'établissement des Nouveaux Cimetières*, B. Angers MS. DD 16.

[100] Port's note in Péan de la Tuillerie, p. 191.

[101] Deliberations of parish, 3 Aug. 1777, A.M.L. G 1669, f. 23(b).

[102] Parish Saint-Maurille, A.M.L. G 1732, f. 55; Port, *Inventaire ... Mairie*, p. 221.

[103] A.M.L. G 1014, ff. 132–3; G 1732, f. 55.

[104] *Anjou hist.*, IX, pp. 476–8.

[105] A.M.L. G 1732, f. 55; G 1712, f. 69; (discussions of parishes of Saint-Maurille and Saint-Julien).

[106] 27 Jan. 1786, B. Angers MS. DD 16. Cemetery disputes of the kind we have described took place in many towns. For interesting examples, see J. Ricommard, *La Lieutenance générale de police à Troyes au XVIIIe siècle* (1934), pp. 165–8.

[107] Rangeard, 'État ... d'Anjou ...' (extracts concerning chapels in *Anjou hist.*, VII, p. 470).

[108] Lehoreau, *Anjou hist.*, XV, p. 294; Péan de la Tuillerie, p. 166.

[109] Thorode (extract in *Anjou hist.*, XXVII, p. 31).

[110] Munic. Reg., 12 June 1784, 24 Feb. 1785, BB 131, ff. 19(b), 55.

[111] Estimation *Biens Nat.* A.M.L. III Q 1, art. 129; Corresp. Dept, to the deputies of Maine-et-Loire in Paris, 4 June 1791. A.M.L. 1 L 155; 'Tableau des biens ... de la maison de Toussaint', 30 Sept. 1780. A.M.L. H 1248.

[112] E. L. in Thorode, pp. 323, 326, 327 (dates 1771, 1769).

[113] 'État ... Saint-Aubin', 1786. A.M.L. H 34; Estimation *Biens Nat.*, A.M.L. 11 Q 1, p. 9.

[114] Petition, an II, A.M.L. 16 Q 1.

[115] 'L'Université d'Angers 1787–1790', *Andegaviana*, XIX, p. 125; A. Boquel, *La Faculté de Médecine de l'Université d'Angers 1433–1792*, p. 16; Blordier-Langlois, *Angers et le Département de Maine et Loire 1787–1830* (1837), I, p. 229; Estimation *Biens Nat.*, A.M.L. 111 Q 1, no. 238; Le Moy, *Cahiers*, p. 65.

[116] Le Moy, *loc. cit.* V. Dauphin, 'La Corporation des Apothicaires d'Angers', *Méms. Soc. Agric.*, 6th Ser., VI (1931), p. 15; C.-L.-T. Portais, *L'abbé Gruget, curé de la Trinité d'Angers ... 1751–1840* (1896), pp. 138–9.

[117] Thorode, note by E. L., p. 286; *Affiches*, in 'Variétés religieuses angevines du XVIIIe siècle,' *Andegaviana*, IV.

[118] *Affiches* as above.

[119] A.M.L. G 269, pp. 286–7 (23 Dec. 1777).

[120] A.M.L. G 271, pp. 22–3, 40, 42, 43. For reactions in the parish of Saint-Evroul, see below, p. 166.

[121] A.M.L. G 271, p. 621 (Sept. 1774. Not to come into effect until 1784).

[122] A.M.L. G 942, f. 15 (Feb. 1782); G 1697 (Feb. 1789); B. Angers MS. 758, no. 36 (1782); A.M.L. G 1670, f. 16 (7 Aug. 1785). These are references to the chapter and parish of Saint-Laud and the parish of Saint-Denis.

[123] De Tocqueville, *L'Ancien Régime et la Révolution* (O.U.P. ed., 1916), pp. 195–6.

[124] E. Coyecque and H. Debraye, *Cat. gén. MSS. Bibl. publ. de France, Paris. Chambre des Députés* (1907), p. 342.

[125] L. Tuetey, *Cat. gen. MSS. Bibl. publ. de France. Archives de la Guerre* (1911), pp. 376, 378.

[126] A.M.L. 95 H 25.

[127] E. L. in Thorode, p. 377. (The Seminary of Saint-Charles cared for aged priests).

[128] E. L. in Thorode, pp. XXVI, 230, 238.

[129] Munic. Reg. BB 131, ff. 9(b), 10; BB 131, ff. 50, 60(b); BB 132, f. 38(b).

[130] 'Description de la ville d'Angers au début du xviii siècle', *Anjou hist.*, XV, p. 239n.

[131] Munic. Reg. BB 130, f. 134(b) (30 Jan. 1764).

[132] For the year 1787, see Munic. Reg. BB 132, f. 67; A.M.L. G 273, pp. 117, 119, 124. The Assembly of the Clergy of Anjou appointed a committee of two canons, the prior of Saint-Nicolas and curé Chatizel to help the municipality in Jan. 1787. For 1788, Munic. Reg. BB 132, f. 141; BB 133, f. 4(b). For 1789, see the *cahier* of the chapter of Saint-Martin, (*Anjou hist.*, XXXI, p. 217) and of Saint-Laud (A.M.L. G 942, f. 126, cap. 21). One should notice that the union of an abbey to an episcopal see normally took place *inside* a particular diocese— the proposed merger of an abbey of the diocese of Angers to the see of Séez was an unusual suggestion (see the list of abbeys of France in Durand de Maillane, *Dictionnaire de Droit Canonique* (1776), I, pp. 2–8).

[133] Munic. Reg. BB 130, f. 134(b), (30 Jan. 1784).

[134] Munic. Reg. BB 131, f. 20(b); BB 132, ff. 141, 142.

[135] Petitions of the town to *Monsieur*, 12 Jan. and 14 Feb. 1784, in B. Angers MS. GG 363.

[136] E.g. Tours and Le Mans.

[137] Munic. Reg. BB 130 ff. 70 (16 Nov. 1782), 77; BB 131, f. 3(b); BB 132, f. 127(b) (10 April 1788). See also the bishop's letter to his curés, 27 June, 1788 (B. Angers MS. 1156).

[138] Port, *Inventaire ... Marie*, p. 164.

[139] Port, *Dict.*, I, p. 99.

[140] 'Project d'Etablissement d'un hôpital d'Enfans trouvés ...' I Oct. 1769 (B. Angers MS. 1156). The canons of Saint-Pierre were estimated to be paying 600l. a year for the upkeep of foundlings (A.M.L. G 272, f. 566) and Saint-Maurille's expenses were supposed to be heavy (*loc. cit.*, f. 568). For the small expenses of the Seminary on the fiefs of Saint-Julien and Saint-Maimbeuf, see A.M.L. G 35.

[141] Munic. Reg. BB 131, f. 3(b) (March 1784); BB 132, f. 121(b), 125 (March 1788) and discussions of parish of Saint-John Baptist, A.M.L. 1712, f. 68 (24 Feb. 1788). For the government's views on the obligations of feudal overlords in Angers, Tours and Le Mans, there is a letter of Orry to the intendant in A.D. Indre-et-Loire, C 319. (cit. Catalogue, p. 47).

[142] Bardoul to the business agents of *Monsieur*, 1786. A. Nat. R 5 123.

[143] 'Pourquoi on voulait transférer à Lesvière l'Hôpital général d'Angers (1687)', *Andegaviana*, XXXIII, p. 277 ff.; B. Angers MS. 1156, f. 1. Suitably prompted by his Jesuit confessor, Louis XIV himself had vetoed the proposition of 1687, declaring that the citizens' arguments for confiscation, if valid, would entitle them to take the bishop's palace (Dom Martène, *Histoire de la Congrégation de Saint-Maur*, VII, p. 14–17).

[144] *Très-Humbles ... Représentations ... de la noble Confrérie des Bourgeois* ... (1774), B. Angers 767, no. 7.

[145] *Très-Humbles et Très-Respectueuses Représentations que prennent la liberté de faire à Monseigneur le Comte de Provence les Officiers Municipaux d'Angers* (12 Jan. 1774), B. Angers MS. GG 363.

Z

[146] 'Projet d'Etablissement d'un hôpital d'Enfans trouvés dans la ville d'Angers' n.d. B. Angers MS. GG 363.

[147] Boullay to the municipality, 26 July 1787. B. Angers MS. GG 363.

[148] The letters patent (Nov. 1787) and the survey of the house (21 March 1768) are in B. Angers MS. GG 363. The property of the *Confrèrie des Bourgeois* was united to the new foundation. In June 1788 the bishop wrote to his curés urging them to use their good offices with seigneurs of fiefs (B. Angers MS. 1156).

[149] Munic. Reg. 132, ff. 125 (25 March 1788).

[150] See *Discours sur Angers, relativement à l'industrie et au commerce* (1787) pp. 11, 27 (B. Angers H 2036); *Anjou hist.*, XV, pp. 26–9; Blordier-Langlois, *Angers et l'Anjou sous le régime municipal*, pp. 350–2.

[151] 'L'Oratoire d'Angers 1619–1792', *Andegaviana*, XV, pp. 437–6.

[152] *ibid.*, pp. 490, 478–82, 485; 'A l'Université d'Angers 1755–65', *Anjou hist.*, XXX, pp. 146–7.

[153] 27 Feb. 1765, A. Nat. H 1633, no. 206.

[154] Munic. Reg. BB 132, ff. 139, 141 (July 1788). In view of these projects it is interesting to note the great alarm caused in Angers in May of this year by a rumour that its university was to be transferred to Tours ('L'Université d'Angers, 1787–1790', *Andegaviana*, XIX, p. 116).

[155] F. Dumas, *La Généralité de Tours au XVIIIᵉ siècle. L'Intendant du Cluzel*, (1894), p. 100.

[156] 'Conseil de ville Au Roy et à Nos seigneurs de son conseil', A.M.L. C 44.

[157] See, e.g. Munic. Reg. BB 130, f. 86; BB 131, ff. 19(b), 33(b); BB 132, ff. 20, 21, 104(b).

[158] Munic. Reg. BB 132, ff. 107(b)–108, 8 Jan. 1788.

[159] *ibid.*; also, BB 132, f. 129; and Memoir of 1 April 1788, in *Anjou hist.*, IX, pp. 376–84.

[160] Munic. Reg. BB 133, ff. 50(b)–51; 63(b); BB 134, ff. 18(b)–19.

[161] Munic. Reg. BB 134, ff. 19–21(b).

CHAPTER VII

[1] Lehoreau, *Anjou hist.*, XV, pp. 245, 248, 246, 241. In all estimates of population, reference should be made to the figures of births, marriages and deaths in 'Le clergé paroissial d'Angers et la Constitution Civile', *Anjou hist.*, VI, pp. 168–70.

[2] See L. Rondeau in *Méms. Soc. Agric.*, II (1868), p. 377.

[3] By the curé, 16 Dec. 1768 (A.M.L. G 1722, f. 43).

[4] Lehoreau, *Anjou hist.*, XV, p. 236. This pre-eminence is confirmed by such statistics as we have concerning the number of households which maintained a servant. In 1730 the numbers of servants recorded in the parishes of Angers was as follows: Saint-Maurille 361; Saint-Michel du Tertre 202; Saint-Maurice 107; La Trinité 105 (remember its huge population); Saint-Denis 91; Saint-Pierre 83; Saint-Aignan 67; Saint-Michel de la Palud 62; Saint-Martin 48; and so on (V. Dauphin, *Angers il y a deux cents ans, 1730. Étude économique et social d'après le registre de la Capitation* (1931), p. 7).

[5] Parish deliberation, 13 April 1766 (A.M.L. G 1712, f. 26(b)).

[6] A.M.L. G 1762, f. 460; Rangeard, 'État d'Anjou', *Anjou hist.*, VII, pp. 470 ff.; Thorode, p. 153n. The town population of Saint-Michel de la Palud largely consisted of artisans (M. Boisseau du Rocher, 'Le Faubourg Bressigny', *Méms. Soc. Agric.*, 7th Ser., XVII (1943), p. 93).

[7] Thorode, p. 158n.; Lehoreau, *Anjou hist.*, XV, pp. 251–2.

[8] A.M.L. G 1694, f. 21(b) (13 April 1769).

[9] L. Rondeau, 'Saint-Michel du Tertre d'Angers', *Méms. Soc. Agric.*, 4th Ser., II (1888), p. 200; 4th Ser., IV (1890), p. 289; J. Grandet, 'Notre-Dame Angevine' (1704), in *Anjou hist.*, XX, p. 193.

[10] M. Boisseau du Rocher, *Méms. Soc. Agric.*, 7th Ser., XVII (1943), pp. 110–15. Thorode, 'Récensement des maisons d'Angers, Mars 1780', B. Angers MS. 1172, pp. 5 ff.

[11] Port, *Dict.*, II pp. 317–18; *Anjou hist.*, XXIV, p. 227; Portais, *Gruget*, p. 142; Gautreau (1784) in *Anjou hist.*, XVIII, p. 205; Thorode, pp. 174–6n.

[12] Péan de la Tuillerie, p. 44.

[13] 'La paroisse de Saint-Nicolas-lès-Angers', *Anjou hist.*, XXII, p. 1; Lehoreau, *Anjou hist.*, XV, p. 250.

[14] M. de Pignerolle was present at the parish deliberations of 27 May 1787, A.M.L. G 1663, f. 2.

[15] Lehoreau, *Anjou hist.*, XV, p. 284. Boatmen and ferrymen were a byword for irreligion. ('Consultations de cas de conscience', M.S. Univ. of Rennes 221, pp. 84, 131).

[16] 'La Paroisse de Lesvière-lès-Angers au xviiie siècle', *Anjou hist.*, XXI, p. 7.

[17] Statistics sent to the *Commission intermédiare* of the provincial Assembly, A.M.L. C 190; see also 'La paroisse de Saint-Laud d'Angers', *Anjou hist.*, XX, p. 66.

[18] For the area, see M. Boisseau du Rocher, 'Les Faubourgs Saint-Michel et Saint-Samson', *Méms. Soc. Agric.*, 7th Ser., XVII (1943), pp. 110 ff.

[19] 14 April, 1766, B. Angers MS. 734, f. 56.

[20] 'Le clergé paroissial d'Angers et la Constitution Civile', *Anjou hist.*, VI, pp. 168–70.

[21] Lehoreau, *Anjou hist.*, XV, p. 295.

[22] Robin, *L'Ami des Peuples*, pp. 39–44.

[23] 'Plan pour formation des cures, en la ville et les fauxbourgs d'Angers ... proposé par un inconnu', B. Angers MS. 793, no. 10.

[24] J. Leflon, *Bernier* (1938), p. 6.

[25] Deliberations of clergy of Anjou, B. Angers MS. 734, f. 56 (14 April 1766).

[26] A.M.L. G 1694, f. 21(b).

[27] See pp. 59, 65.

[28] 'Le chapitre de la Trinité d'Angers à la fin du xviiie siècle', *Anjou hist.*, XVIII, pp. 205 ff.

[29] Munic. Reg. B. Angers, BB 131, f. 50(b).

[30] A.M.L. G 942, f. 126.

[31] Bernier, curé of Saint-Laud, 10 Oct. 1790 (Leflon, *Bernier*, p. 6).

[32] Details concerning places of birth etc. are from 'Les 23 vicaires de la ville d'Angers pendant la Révolution' and 'Les 19 curés....', *Anjou hist.*, XII, pp. 272 ff., 134 ff. (The reference to 19 curés in this latter article is explained by the fact that Saint-Léonard and Saint-Augustin were included within the municipal boundaries by the law of 27 April 1791.)

[32] See his signature on the parish accounts of Saint-Aignan, 1777, A.M.L. 62 H 5.

[34] 'Les curés de Saint-Joseph d'Angers', *Anjou hist.*, XIII, p. 643.

[35] Thorode, 'Récensement des maisons d'Angers vers 1780', B. Angers MS. 1172, p. 64.

[36] *Lettre du Curé de Sainte-Croix à M. de la Brosse....* (B. Angers S.T. 403), p. 3.

[37] *Traduction ... de l'Élégie Latine, ou Ovidianum de M. Claude Robin* (B. Angers 103, 627), p. 5.

[38] 'Les 23 vicaires...' *Anjou hist.*, XII, pp. 275–7.

[39] 'Correspondence de M. Houdet', *Anjou hist.*, XII, p. 249.

[40] *ibid.*

[41] 'L'abbé Gruget', *Anjou hist.*, XXIV, p. 224.

[42] Leflon, *Bernier*, I, pp. 1, 2, 5.

[43] Besnard, I, pp. 149–50.

[44] *Le Parfait Notaire Apostolique* (1775), II, p. 332.

[45] Abbé Baston, *Mémoires*, extracts in *Anjou hist.*, X, p. 352.

[46] Letourneau, *Histoire du Séminaire d'Angers*, pp. 18–19; Besnard, I, p. 151; 'Détail des employés et des exercices du Séminaire d'Angers' (c. 1735), *Anjou hist.*, XXV, p. 77.

[47] Besnard, I, pp. 161–2.

[48] 'Journal des usages du Séminaire d'Angers', Letourneau, app. III, p. 404.

[49] The inventory of the Seminary library, 28 Feb. 1791 (A.M.L. 13 Q 26) shows that about one-eighth of the books concerned piety and the spiritual life, and one-eighth Roman, Civil and Canon Law. Theology, representing half the total, was well supplied with the Fathers, Councils, controversy, preaching, ecclesiastical history, but the doctrine section was thin. Books on the history of France (482), on foreign lands (219) and the arts generally (483) were comparatively few.

[50] Cit. H. Bremond, *A Literary History of Religious Thought in France*, trans. K. L. Montgomery (1936), III, p. 434.

[51] For the state of the clergy of Angers c. 1650 before the reforms of Henri Arnauld, see A. Debidour, *La Fronde angevine, tableau de la vie municipale au XVIIᵉ siècle* (1877), pp. 197–8.

[52] P. Pourrat, *Jean-Jacques Olier, fondateur de Saint-Sulpice* (1932), pp. 156–7.

[53] *ibid.*, pp. 176–84, 159, 160. For the doctrine of Papal infallibility in the Seminary of Angers in the early eighteenth century, see Dom P. Piolin, 'Un Professeur à l'Université d'Angers. Joseph du Mabaret', *Rev. hist. lit. arch.*, *Anjou*, III (1869), pp. 136–7.

[54] *Nouvelles ecclésiastiques*, 25 Dec. 1732, p. 245; 16 Jan. 1740, p. 11; 23 Oct. 1747, p. 170; 10 July 1754, p. 111; 21 May 1756, p. 85; 8 Oct. 1760, p. 180; 27 March 1775, p. 45; 22 May 1789, p. 83.

[55] Letourneau, pp. 406–9; 'Détail des employés', *Anjou hist.*, XXV, p. 78.

[56] J. Leflon, *Monsieur Emery*. I, p. 29.

[57] Putting aside as a manifest fable a tale of riotous practical joking which accompanied a visit of the abbé de Talleyrand to Angers (given in A. de Soland, *Bull. hist. et monumental de l'Anjou*, 1854, pp. 190–2). 'Un certain esprit de luxe' denounced in a circular of 1 March 1783 refers simply to the necessity for regular retreats and the fact that some tutors in seminaries had changed the furnishings of their rooms without the agreement of their local superior (the Angevin copy of this circular is in MSS Emery, Saint-Sulpice, X, ff. 391–3).

[58] Besnard, I, pp. 160–1.

[59] Lyonnet, *Histoire de Mgr d'Aviau du Bois-de-Sanzay, successivement archevêque de Vienne et de Bordeaux* (2 vols., 1847), I, pp. 52–3. At this time (1753) he was eighteen. He was ordained priest in 1760 and took his doctorate at Angers (pp. 65, 670–1).

[60] Besnard, I, pp. 152–3.

[61] The average of eleven of the vicaires of Angers in 1789 was 32·3 years. The average age of seven of the curés on the date of their appointment had been 34.75 years.

[62] See, for the rights of graduates in the diocese, 'Une nomination ecclésiastique à Angers au 18ᵉ siècle', *Andegaviana*, XX, pp. 137–40.

[63] See 'Les paroisses du diocèse d'Angers avant le Concordat. Nominations aux cures', *Anjou hist.*, IV, pp. 449 ff.

[64] *ibid*.

[65] See Canon Bailly's *Notice* on bishop Vaugirauld in *Anjou hist.*, VII, p. 491.

[66] 'La paroisse Saint-Laud d'Angers', *Anjou hist.*, xx, p. 65.

[67] Port, *Dict.*, III, pp. 223–4.

[68] Chesnau of Saint-Pierre du Lac (near Beaufort) to the ecclesiastical committee of the Constituent Assembly, 17 Nov. 1789, A. Nat. D XIX 51, file 85.

[69] Figures of income in 1730 are in 'E.L.'s' notes to Thorode; for 1783 see the *pouillé* of that year in *Anjou hist.*, I, pp. 342–4; for Saint-Samson, A.M.L. H 770; for Saint-Nicolas, *Anjou hist.*, XXII, p. 10; for Saint-Evroul, Port's note in Péan de la Tuillerie, p. 105; for the cathedral's 200*l.* to Saint-Maurice and Saint-Evroul, A.M.L. G 271, p. 619, G 1694, f. 22(b); for Lesvière accepting a *congrue* of 500*l.* in 1768, A. Nat. G8, 79.

[70] Portais, *Gruget*, pp. 122, 127; 'L'abbé Gruget', *Anjou hist.*, XXIV, pp. 226–7; 'Le chapitre de la Trinité d'Angers à la fin du 18ᵉ siècle', *Anjou hist.*, XVIII, p. 25.

[71] A.M.L. 1 L 981, nos. 38, 2, 40, 46.

[72] Clerical taxation on these chapels was two-thirds of that on the cure, see 'Mémoire a Consulter' and report of Dumesnil, 28 April 1789 in A. Nat. G 8 620.

[73] A.M.L. 2 L 132, pp. 203, 194. For curé Robin's presentation of his nephew, a country vicaire, to a chapel depending on the cure of Saint-Pierre, see his parish register, Etat Civil, Angers GG 181, 31 Jan. 1767.

[74] Curé Farrayres to Boumard, 2 Sept. 1785, A.M.L. G 1690.

[75] In 1779, Chotard received 44*l.* 16*s.*; Robin 47*l.* 2*s.*; Boumard 44*l.* 14*s.*; ('Distribution faitte à Mrs. les Docteurs Regents', A.M.L. D 31).

[76] B. Angers MS. 748, no. 8, f. 4(b); A.M.L. G 1722, ff. 50(b)–51.

[77] Besnard, I, pp. 244–5; B. Angers MS. 748, no. 8, f. 4.

[78] G. Lefebvre, *Les Paysans du Nord* (1924), p. 278. Diderot, *Jacques le Fataliste* (*Œuvres*, Pléide ed., 1935, p. 333); p. 59 above; Lefebvre, citing *Mémoires* of the abbé Fabry, in *Annales Historiques de la Révolution Française*, XII (1935), p. 70.

[79] A. Lefort, 'Le prix de la vie dans un presbytère angevin au milieu du xviii siècle', *La Province d'Anjou*, II (1927), pp. 250 ff.

[80] See below, p. 161.

[81] P.V. Estimation, *Biens Nat.*, A.M.L. III Q 2, vol. IV, no. 1 (Saint-Aignan), no. 2 (Saint-Evroul), no. 3 (saint-Michel de la Palud), no. 5 (Sainte-Croix); see also no. 8 (Saint-Denis), no. 10 (Saint-Pierre).

[82] *ibid.* no. 4 (Saint-Martin), no 7 (Lesvière); A.M.L. III Q 2, vol. III second series of numberings 30 (Saint-Samson).

[83] Documents of seizure, 28 April 1789, A. Nat. G 8 620.

[84] See A. Nat. D XIX file 224 (12), 2 May 1790.

[85] 'Les paroisses du diocèse d'Angers avant le Concordat. Nomination aux cures', *Anjou hist.*, IV, pp. 471, 456.

[86] 'Le clergé paroissial d'Angers et la Constitution Civile', *Anjou hist.*, VI, pp. 168–70.

[87] 'Le chapitre de la Trinité d'Angers à la fin du 18ᵉ siècle', *Anjou hist.*, XVIII, p. 208.

[88] A.M.L. G 1694, f. 22.

[89] Besnard, I, p. 234.

[90] Robin, *Le Montglonne*, p. 208.

[91] *Mémoire instructif pour les maitres de cérémonies ... au Sacre de Saint-Julien, suivant le nouveau plan de ce sacre exécuté pour la première fois en 1784*, pr.

by G. Hautreux, 'Une Procession angevine au xviiie siècle', *Rev. historique de l'Ouest*, II (1886), pp. 157–68.

⁹² On some great festivals the *curé primitif* might also monopolize the celebration of divine service in the parish church (see pp. 168 ff).

⁹³ See *La Semaine religieuse d'Angers*, 8 June 1919; 'La Paroisse de Saint-Jacques-lès-Angers', *Andegaviana*, XXIII, p. 128; 'L'abbé Gruget...' *Anjou hist.*, XXIV, p. 228; for the ritual see [Carré], *Recveil curieux et édifiant, sur les Cloches de l'Église avec les cérémonies de leur Bénédiction* (Cologne, 1757), pp. 41–6.

⁹⁴ See 'La paroisse Saint-Laud d'Angers', *Anjou hist.*, XX, p. 66; and *Cérémonial de la prestation de serment d'une sage-femme ... par un Curé du diocèse d'Angers* in Dr. O. Couffon, *Les Cours d'accouchement en Anjou à la fin du xviiie siècle* (Angers, 1913), App. II, pp. 87–91.

⁹⁵ Couffon, p. 86.

⁹⁶ *Affiches*, Aug. 1780, in 'Les marriages Angevins à la fin du xviiie siècle', *Anjou hist.*, III, p. 428.

⁹⁷ Bodin, *Recherches* II, pp. 396–7; Besnard, I, p. 235. Though he kept within his theological context, Canon Jubeau of Saint-Maurille seems to have been another preacher who was not afraid of informalities (*Nouvelles ecclésiastiques*, 27 March 1775, p. 49).

⁹⁸ Couffon, App. II, p. 89.

⁹⁹ A.M.L. G 1693. The other notes are in A.M.L. G 1692. It is not possible to give detailed references, as the notes are largely unpaged.

¹⁰⁰ A.M.L. G 1692, 'Jugement', p. 14 and a *cahier* containing a sermon on Exodus XX, 'Non moechaberis'.

¹⁰¹ Cf. A. Bernard, *Le Sermon au xviii siècle, 1715–89* (1901), pp. 382–3.

¹⁰² Sermon on Capernaum (A.M.L. G 1692); 'Spectacles ou comédies' (A.M.L. G 1693).

¹⁰³ 'Troisième Dialogue sur le jubilé' (A.M.L. G 1692).

¹⁰⁴ Eighteenth-century catechism from the library of the Seminary of Angers, inscribed 'j'apartiens à Marie Chauvigné', MS. University of Rennes 219, p. 4.

¹⁰⁵ 'Catechismes ou Instruction de la Doctrine Chrétienne', again from Angers, MS. University of Rennes, 220, pp. 2–3, 10–11, 27, 29.

¹⁰⁶ *ibid.*, pp. 34–85 (Prayer), pp. 96–168 (Sacraments).

¹⁰⁷ *ibid.*, p. 24. In 1772 in the parish of Saint-Pierre there were 55 boys and 61 girls for confirmation, ages varying from 7 to 11 (Parish Register, État Civile, Angers, GG 181, *ad fin*).

¹⁰⁸ Robin, *Montglonne*, p. 208.

¹⁰⁹ Port, *Dict.*, I, pp. 101, 162; 'Variétés religieuses angevines du xviiie siècle', *Andegaviana*, IV, p. 6; 'La Faculté de Médecine d'Angers en 1754', *Anjou hist.*, XXXIX, pp. 203–4.

¹¹⁰ C. Port, *Inventaire Mairie*, pp. 199, 200. The practice is referred to by Mme de Genlis, *Mémoires* (Paris, 1825), I, p. 50; also by the duc de Luynes, *Mémoires sur la Cour de Louis XV* (ed. L. Dussieux and E. Soulié, 1860), II, p. 207.

¹¹¹ The cathedral gave approximately 1,000l. a year to be shared among 15 or so curés in needy districts. In March 1789, 14 curés received a total of 980l. (A.M.L. G 273 pp. 406–8); in Feb. 1790, 17 curés received a total of 1,321l. (A.M.L. G 273, p. 519). Saint-Pierre only voted small amounts, 'taking into account the hardness of the season and the needs of the poor' (A.M.L. G 1171 f. 31 (1786), f. 53 (1788), f. 67 (1788).

¹¹² E.g. 'Fondation pour les pauvres dans la cy devant paroisse de Saint-Michel du Tertre' (1791), A.M.L. I.L. 989, file 2.

[113] 'Le chapitre de la Trinité d'Angers à la fin du xviii siècle', *Anjou hist.*, XVIII, p. 206.

[114] Robin's note in his parish register, État Civil, Hôtel de Ville, Angers, GG 183, f. 102. See C. Port, 'L'Hiver en Anjou', *Rev. hist. lit. arch. d'Anjou*, N.S., II (1880), pp. 203-4.

[115] Munic. Reg. B. Angers MS. BB 134, f. 23. Cf. 'Notes sur quelques abus reprochés à l'administration des Incurables', B. Angers MS. 1157.

[116] E. Queruau-Lamerie, 'L'Instruction secondaire à Angers pendant la Révolution', *Revue de la Révolution*, 1887, p. 140.

[117] Louis Grimaud, *Histoire de la Liberté d'enseignement en France*, I, *L'Ancien Régime* (1944), p. 31. A good deal of anti-clerical zeal has been expended in the past to show that France under the old régime was ill-provided with facilities for elementary education. M. Port showed how true this was of his own Angevin countryside and demolished arguments drawn from 'scattered evidence and wandering schoolmistresses' (*La Vendée Angevine*, I, pp. 71 ff). A similar gloomy picture can be painted by considering some other (though by no means all) rural districts (e.g. M. Schnerb, 'L'Enseignement primaire dans le Puy-de-Dôme pendant la Révolution', *Annales hist. de la Révolution Française*, 1935, pp. 97 ff; for the contrasting views of Dupuy and Bernard and Henri Sée on Brittany see *Annales de Bretagne*, IV (1888-9), pp. 365 ff., V (1890), p. 3, XXV (1909-10), pp. 101-2; XLII (1936-7), p. 170). In towns the situation varied greatly: good in Angers, deplorable in Reims (G. Laurent, 'Jean-Baptiste Armonville, conventionnel ouvrier', *Ann. hist. Rév. Franç.*, 1924, p. 224).

The conclusion seems to be:

(i) that education for the poor, where available, owed much to the efforts of ecclesiastics, but that they considered their work in this respect from a narrowly clerical viewpoint (cf. A. Babeau 'L'Intervention de l'État et l'instruction primaire en Provence sous la Régence', *Rev. Hist.*, XLVI (1891), pp. 300 ff).

(ii) that there was little enthusiasm among the laity for the education of children of the common people, and that the existence of schools very largely depended upon the incidence of pious benefactions and legacies (see Schnerb, *op. cit.*, p. 98).

[118] Port, *Inventaire ... Sér. G....*, p. 239, 232, 238, 231-2; Brossier, B. Angers MS. 727, p. 149(b).

[119] Port, *Inventaire ... Sér. G....*, p. 231.

[120] Port, *Inventaire Mairie*, p. 269; Capit. Reg. Saint-Aubin, 5 Dec. 1745, A.M.L. H 4, p. 392.

[121] E. L. in Thorode, pp. 147-8. Cf. above, p. 100. For the work of François Chollet (born 1659) in setting up parish schools in Angers see C. Urseau, *L'Instruction primaire avant 1789 dans les paroisses du diocèse actuel d'Angers (1890)*, pp. 185-7.

[122] 'Fondation pour les pauvres'.... A.M.L. 989, file 2; Rondeau, 'Saint-Michel du Tertre', *Méms. Soc. Agric.*, 4th Ser., IV (1890), p. 284.

[123] Munic. Reg. B. Angers MS. BB 120, f. 74, 2 April 1763; see 'Notice sur l'Instruction Primaire à Angers, 1789-1800', *Rev. de l'Anjou* XXIX (1894), p. 130; for the two schools of Saint-Michel de la Palud, A.M.L. G 1758; the curé of this parish gave a legacy to a school in the countryside in 1754 (B. Bois, 'L'Enseignement primaire en Anjou, Pièces justificatives', *Rev. d'Anjou*, N.S., LIX (1909), pp. 56-60).

[124] 'La paroisse Saint-Julien d'Angers', *Andegaviana*, XXIX, p. 55.

[125] See typical contracts in *La Révolution Française* XXXIV (1898), pp. 237-9 and L(1906), pp. 47-8.

[126] Péan de la Tuillerie, p. 474; for the building, A.M.L. G 1792.

[127] Munic. Reg. B. Angers MS. BB 120, f. 74.

[128] Urseau, *'L'Instruction primaire dans les paroisses du diocèse actuel d'Angers'*, pp. 31–2; A.M.L. 1712, f. 5.

[129] Port, *Dict.*, I, p. 84.

[130] Guyot, *Repertoire* ... *de jurisprudence*, I, p. 442, XLIX, p. 139.

[131] See above, page 21.

[132] Declaration of 9 April 1736, Isambert, *Recueil* XXI, pp. 405–6.

[133] *Le Parfait Notaire Apostolique*, I, p. 219.

[134] Cf. (Alletz), *La Discipline de l'Église de France* (1780), p. 3; Dupuy, 'L'Administration Municipale...', *Annales de Bretagne*, V (1889–90), p. 664. For the legal requirement, see the regulations of Parlement for the diocese of Angers, par. 9, État Civil, Hôtel de Ville, Angers, GG 185, f. 51. The tiny parish of Saint-Aignan paid 1l. 13s. a year for registers (A.M.L. 62 H5).

[135] He was paid only for copies of entries given to private individuals (Chassin, *Les Cahiers des curés*, p. 71), and well he might be in days when a baptismal extract might be more than 100 words in length (see the one in A.M.L. J 3134). For other details concerning the burden imposed on the clergy by the keeping of registers, see M.-L. Fracard, *La Fin de l'Ancien Régime à Niort* (n.d.), pp. 80–1.

[136] *Copie du Certificat du Sieur Curé de Saint-Pierre d'Angers; concernant l'altération faite sur un de ses Registres* (1770) (B. Angers S.J. 311(7), no. 21).

[137] E.g. In the registers at Saint-Nicolas, *Anjou hist.*, XXII, p. 5.

[138] Parish Registers of Saint-Pierre, État Civil, Hôtel de Ville, Angers, GG 181, ff. 256, 183, 102; extracts printed by Port, 'L'Hiver en Anjou' *Rev. hist. lit. d'Anjou*, N.S., II (1880), p. 203–4.

[139] Printed in Port, *La Vendée Angevine* (1888), 2 vols., I, pp. 373–5.

[140] P. Sage, *Le 'Bon Prêtre' dans la littérature française d'Amadis de Gaule au Génie du Christianisme* (1951), pp. 443, 357–8, 380, 205, etc.

[141] Sermon, 'Honneur aux prestres', A.M.L. G 1692.

[142] 'Sa vie doit être une censure publique', 'Curés' in sermon notes, A.M.L. G 1692.

[143] See F. Duine, 'Les Généraux des paroisses Bretonnes. Saint-Martin de Vitré', *Annales de Bretagne*, XXIII (1907–8), p. 4; G. Coolen, *Helfaut, Essai sur l'administration d'une paroisse sous l'ancien régime* (Saint-Omer, 1939, *Méms. de la Soc. des Antiquaires de la Morinie*, tome XXXVII); Babeau, *Le Village sous l'ancien régime* (1878), p. 133; L. Froger, 'De l'organization et de l'administration des fabriques avant 1789, au diocèse du Mans'; *Rev. des Questions hist.*, LXIII (1898), pp. 406–36.

[144] L. Rondeau, 'Saint-Michel du Tertre d'Angers', *Méms. Soc. Agric.*, 4th Ser., IV (1890), p. 287. Cf. at the parish church of Saint-Denis—'nous avons trouvés dans le jubé une petite armoire fermante a trois clefs servant d'archives de la fabrique, ouverture faittes nous avons trouvé ein liasse de lettre' (original spelling), A.M.L. 13 Q 20, 9 May 1791.

[145] For the same tendencies in the countryside of Anjou see R. H. Andrews, *Les Paysans des Mauges au 18e siècle* (These, Paris, 1935), p. 169.

[146] Guyot, *Répertoire de jurisprudence*, XLIV, p. 414.

[147] There is a copy attached to the parish register of Saint-Pierre, État Civil, Hôtel de Ville, Angers, GG 185, f. 51, *Arrêt de la Cour de Parlement, portant réglement pour l'administration des biens et revenus des fabriques des paroisses situées dans l'étendue du Diocèse d'Angers* (11 July 1786).

[148] Pocquet de Livonnière, *Coustumes du Pays et Duché d'Anjou* (1725), II, cols. 1092–3; cf. also *Anjou hist.*, XX, pp. 193–6.

[149] A.M.L. G 1712, f. 26(b).

[150] A.M.L. G 1694, f. 19(b).

[151] Portais, *Gruget*, pp. 160–1, 167–8.

[152] A.M.L. G 1732, ff. 1, 2, 14, 15, 16(b), 17.

[153] The sealing fee was 30s. (B. Angers MS. 748, no. 8).

[154] A.M.L. G 1694 (Saint-Evroul), f. 19(b), March 1765; G 1722 (Saint-Maurice), f. 95(b), Jan. 1789; G 1663 (Lesvière), f. 6, Jan. 1789.

[155] A.M.L. G 1694, f. 35(b), April 1783.

[156] A.M.L. G 1712 (Saint-Julien), f. 21, April 1764.

[157] *ibid.*, f. 68, Feb. 1788.

[158] A.M.L. G 1669, f. 15, Sept. 1774.

[159] A.M.L. G 1694, f. 27(b), Sept. 1774.

[160] A.M.L. G 1712 (Saint-Julien) (1765); G 1670 (Saint-Denis), f. 6(b); Portais, *Gruget*, pp. 160–1; A.M.L. G 1663 (Lesvière), f. 2 (1785, 1787).

[161] A.M.L. G 1669, f. 10(b) (1773).

[162] A.M.L. 62 H 5. He was followed by Jean le Favre, *bourgeois*, who held office for the 13 years following 1777.

[163] Final account, 30 Dec. 1790, in A.M.L. G 1696.

[164] No one of any consequence could pray without a chair to lean on, said the anti-clerical wits—
'Faites vous apporter à tous deux une chaise
Car pour entendre Dieu il faut être à son aise'
('Messaline, tragedie', A.M.L. J 3135).

[165] A.M.L. G 271, p. 611 (1774); the farm of the chairs brought in 1,000*l.* in 1770, and 1,200*l.* in 1785 (Brossier, B. Angers MS. 730, p. 61(b)). The abbey of Toussaint farmed its chairs for 30*l.* p.a. (A.M.L. H 1248, p. 16 (1776).

[166] Saint-Pierre, A.M.L. G 1777, f. 3 (1789).

[167] A.M.L. G 1670, f. 4(b); A.M.L. G 1694, f. 14; A.M.L. G 1732, ff. 2–3. The charge was 12s. at Saint-Aignan (A.M.L. 62 H 5).

[168] A.M.L. G 1696; B. Angers MS. 748, no. 8 (Grille's accounts, Saint-Maurice); A.M.L. G 1764 (accounts of René Desjardins, Saint-Michel de la Palud); Rondeau, 'Saint-Michel du Tertre', *Méms. Soc. Agric.*..., 4th Ser., IV (1890), p. 283. At Saint-Jacques, seats brought in 100*l.* p.a. (A.M.L. G 711, accounts of Pierre Bénion, 1770).

[169] A.M.L. G 1670, f. 5.

[170] A.M.L. G 1670, f. 6.

[171] A.M.L. G 1670, f. 13.

[172] A.M.L. G 1712, f. 56(b). The sacristan was given 10s. as gratuity.

[173] Rondeau, 'Saint-Michel du Tertre', *Méms. Soc. Agric.*, 4th Ser., IV (1890), p. 283.

[174] Saint-Michel de la Palud 67½*l.*, Saint-Pierre 60*l.*, Saint-Laud 11*l.*,—see accounts in A.M.L. G 1764; G 1777; G 1698; Saint-Jacques, 102*l.*, 90*l.* (A.M.L. 13 Q 22, Feb. 1792); Saint-Julien, 72*l.*, 40*l.*, 25*l.*, 30*l.* (A.M.L. 13 Q 22); Saint-Samson 8*l.* (A.M.L. 13 Q 26).

[175] A.M.L. H 4, p. 392 (reference to houses of Saint-Michel de la Palud in capitular register of Saint-Aubin); and accounts A.M.L. G 1763. For Lesvière, A.M.L. G 1663, f. 3(b). For some tiny cottages owned by Saint-Julien, A.M.L. 13 Q 22.

[176] A.M.L. G 1698, 'État des Revenus et charges de la fabrique de la Paroisse de Saint-Germain alias Saint-Laud', 1786; A.M.L. G 1696; A.M.L. G 1777; for an investment with a monastery, A.M.L. H 4, p. 387. For the parish of Saint-Jacques, A.M.L. 13 Q 22.

[177] Grille's accounts, B. Angers MS. 748, no. 8. Compare the scattered revenues of Saint-Julien ('Revenu des pauvres de Saint-Julien' 1791, A.M.L 1. L 989).

[178] G 1669 (Saint-Denis), 15 Aug. 1771.

[179] G 1694 (Saint-Evroul), Aug. 1772.

[180] P.V. District of Angers, 10 Aug. 1790, A.M.L. 2 L 2, p. 55.

[181] For what follows see the complete accounts from 1754–90 in A.M.L. 62 H 5. The church consisted of four walls with two windows and a door, a rood screen gallery, and some wainscotting, altogether estimated to be worth only 300*l*. (P. V. Estimation, *Biens Nat.*, A.M.L. III Q 2, III, no. 30).

[182] E.g. the hand of the minutes of the assembly of Saint-Laud changes when the curé is absent through illness, A.M.L. G 1697, f. 6(b).

[183] Portais, *Gruget*, p. 162.

[184] A.M.L. 62 H 5 (parish accounts), Years 1773, 1776, 1784.

[185] A.M.L. G 1712, ff. 23, 25(b), 24(b), (July 1765).

[186] A.M.L. G 1694, f. 21(b).

[187] A.M.L. G 1694, f. 23 (April 1769).

[188] A.M.L. G 1722, ff. 50(b)–51.

[189] A.M.L. G 1670, ff. 2(b)–3.

[190] A.M.L. G 1712, f. 32(b) (March 1769). For examples of curés buying (or being presented with) articles of ecclesiastical silver, etc. which they used for the benefit of their churches, see A.M.L. 13 Q 24 (Saint-Michel de la Palud); 13 Q 18 (Saint-Aignan); 13 Q 24 (Saint-Maurice).

[191] A.M.L. G 1712, f. 33 (Jan. 1770).

[192] A.M.L. G 1712, f. 35 (June 1771).

[193] A.M.L. G 1772, f. 43(b).

[194] Portais, *Gruget*, pp. 127, 162.

[195] For the legal position, see Pialès, *Traité des Réparations* (1761) II, pp. 283 ff., 307–19. For the kind of disputes which arose in the countryside and their connexion with peasant anti-clericalism see G. Hardy, 'L'administration des paroisses au XVIIIe siècle. Les réparations de bâtiments ecclésiastiques', *Rev. d'Hist. moderne et contemporaine*, XV (1911), pp. 6–23.

[196] A.M.L. C 24 (Parish to the intendant May, 1779).

[197] A.M.L. C 24 (Feb. 1781, 25 May 1781); A.M.L. G 1170, f. 353.

[198] Report of the cathedral representatives at the parish assembly, 6 March 1775 (A.M.L. G 271, p. 686).

[199] Besnard, I, pp. 147–8. Compare the cathedral sending deputies to the assemblies of Saint-Laud and Saint-Maurice (A.M.L. G 272, pp. 301–2; G 269, p. 486; G 271, p. 686).

[200] A.M.L. G 1669, f. 15(b).

[201] See Courtillé's letter of 8 July and other documents in A. Nat. G 8 620.

[202] A.M.L. G 1669, ff. 16–17.

[203] *ibid.*, f. 27.

[204] *ibid.*, f. 21.

[205] A.M.L. G 1669, f. 25 (22 Feb.).

[206] A.M.L. G 1669, ff. 28, 27.

CHAPTER VIII

[1] Cf. Rangeard's later comment—'Mais de tous les abus qui renversèrent l'ancien ordre, le plus scandaleux fut celui qui prodiguant à des mains oisives le salaire de l'ouvrier laborieux, laissa s'établir et subsister dans l'église, pour en dissiper ou en profaner les biens, ceux qu'on a si improprement appelés du nom de *curés primitifs*' (*Procès-Verbal historique des actes du clergé député à l'Assemblée des États-Généraux* (1791), *B.M.* F.R. 140 (15), p. 12).

[2] Lehoreau, *Anjou hist.*, XV, p. 249.

[3] A.M.L. H 444, f. 252.

[4] 'Transaction entre Monsieur l'abbé de Saint-Serge, Mr. le Trésorier de l'Eglise d'Angers et MM. des Eglises collegialles de Saint-Maurille et Saint-Jean Baptiste en Saint-Julien touchant les Portions Congrues de MM. les curé et vicaire de la Paroisse de Saint-Samson', A.M.L. H 770, cf. the Seminary accounts, A.M.L. G 35 (1779).

[5] 'La paroisse de Saint-Jacques-lès-Angers', Andegaviana, XXIII, p. 127.

[6] Saint-Aubin paid 206l. in lieu of grain rents (A.M.L. H 34 (1786)); for Saint-Michel du Tertre, see Rondeau, Méms. Soc. Agric., 4th Ser., IV, p. 285.

[7] 'Le chapitre de Saint-Laud d'Angers', Andegaviana, XXX, p. 9. For small properties belonging to various cures (capital value of land given in brackets), see A.M.L. P. V. Estimation, Biens Nat.: Saint-Maurille (1,900), III Q, vol. II, cahier 8, nos. 52–72; Saint-Evroul (?) III Q, vol. II, 14 Oct. 1790; Saint-Laud (3,500l.), III Q 2, vol. III, no. 22; Saint-Maurille (500l.), III Q 2, vol. III, no. 22.

[8] See p. 355, note 114.

[9] See Préclin, Les Jansénistes du XVIIIe siècle et la Constitution civile du clergé (1928), pp. 392 ff.

[10] 'La paroisse de Saint-Nicolas-lès-Angers' Anjou hist., XXII, p. 10. Lesvière, which had had 300l. congrue, 45l. in lands and 13l. in tithes also got the new congrue of 500l. (A. Nat. G 8 79).

[11] 'La paroisse de Saint-Nicolas', as above.

[12] 'La paroisse de Saint-Jacques-lès-Angers', Andegaviana, XXIII, p. 127.

[13] A.M.L. G 271, pp. 4–6 (7 Jan. 1769); Brossier, B. Angers MS. 730, f. 127(b), (30 Dec. 1768).

[14] The cathedral wanted to impute surplice fees against the congrue and insist that property abandoned must be in good repair (A. Nat. G 8 620, file 53, 14 Aug. 1768). The first request was turned down (A. Nat. G 8* 2598, no. 391). The cathedral abandoned its title of curé primitif on 31 Dec. 1768 (act of renunciation at end of parish register, État Civil, Angers, GG 33—Cf. f. 544 also.

[15] Brossier, B. Angers MS. 730, p. 208 (8 May 1769); in April 1769 the parish assembly of Saint-Aignan paid 6l. to the avocat Benoist for a consultation against the union (A.M.L. 62 H 5). For the general idea of uniting small parishes to relieve tithe owners of the burden of a higher congrue, see Reg. Clergé Anjou, B. Angers MS. 734, f. 56.

[16] A.M.L. G 1694, f. 21(b).

[17] ibid.

[18] A.M.L. G 271, pp. 22–3, 42.

[19] A.M.L. G 1765, f. 19.

[20] Reference mislaid. Probably 'Le chapitre de la Trinité', Anjou hist., xviii.

[21] Canon Mezeray to agents general of Clergy, 27 July 1768. A. Nat. G 8 620, file 53.

[22] For the cathedral's episcopal jurisdiction, see above p. 57.

[23] A.M.L. G 269, p. 31 (March 1776).

[24] Brossier, B. Angers MS. 727, pp. 139(b)–150(b); cf. 728, p. 83(b), 726, pp. 113, 64. For Saint-Evroul cf. the 'humble supplication' of its curé concerning the date of his patronal festival, 1786 (Parish register, Etat Civil, Angers, GG 33).

[25] See Thorode, under various parishes.

[26] Lehoreau, Anjou hist., XV, pp. 248–9.

[27] 'Les chanoines de La Trinité d'Angers et l'abbesse du Ronceray', Anjou hist., XVIII, pp. 46–7.

[28] Port, Dict., I, p. 55. 'Ainsi l'abbesse étoit propriétaire de l'autel', Rangeard later observed (Procès-verbal historique des actes du Clergé député à l'Assemblée des Etats-Généraux (Paris 1791), B.M. F.R. 140 (15), p. 28n.).

[29] *Anjou hist.*, XVIII, as above; Portais, *Gruget*, p. 159; *Mémoire Signifié pour les Chanoines, Curés ... de l'Eglise plebeiane & paroissiale de la Trinité...* (1750) B. Angers S.J., 407, 11.

[30] See Thorode and Lehoureau for these and the following details.

[31] 'La paroisse de Lesvière-lès-Angers au xviiie siècle', *Anjou hist.*, XXI, p. 7.

[32] Lehoreau, *Anjou hist.*, XV, pp. 241, 238.

[33] The chapter of Saint-Maurille offered the parishioners half property rights in the two bells if they would share in the repairs (A.M.L. G 1732, f. 46, Aug. 1782). An agreement of 1762 to put the parish bell in the tower of the canons was never implemented (G 116, f. 170).

[34] Saint-Laud, 1784 (A.M.L. G 942, f. 45).

[35] Portais, *Gruget*; For the share of the parish of Saint-Laud in repairs (half roof of nave, one side of cloister, half gallery), see A.M.L. C 190.

[36] Guyot, *Répertoire de Jurisprudence*, IX, p. 434; A. Nat. G 8 2812, p. 274; cf. Cl. Pocquet de Livonnière, *Coustumes du Pays et Duché d'Anjou* (1725), II, col. 1037.

[37] A. Nat. G 8* 2564, no. 221.

[38] Cf. De Moleon, *Voyages liturgiques*, p. 83.

[39] Extracts from the 'Coutumier du Grand Séminaire', *Anjou hist.*, XVIII, pp. 33 ff.

[40] 'La paroisse Saint-Julien d'Angers', *Anjou hist.*, XXXI, p. 67.

[41] A.M.L. G 1712, f. 13(b) (April 1759); G 1712, f. 52(b) (Jan. 1783).

[42] Thorode, note, p. 151.

[43] A.M.L. G 1722, ff. 43–43(b).

[44] A.M.L. G 116, f. 170 (Sept. 1762).

[45] A. Nat. G 8* 2813, p. 395 (Register of Consultations).

[46] A.M.L. G 116, ff. 185, 228, 240.

[47] A. Nat. H 1633, no. 253 (Memoir of chapter to Bishop of Orleans) no. 252 (letter to the comtesse de Brienne).

[48] A.M.L. G 1732, ff. 5(b), 10, 13.

[49] A.M.L. G 1732, ff. 2–3, 4.

[50] A.M.L. G 1732, f. 8 (26 Jan. 1766).

[51] *Nouvelles ecclésiastiques*, 12 Sept. 1763, p. 149. Bishop de Grasse's *Ordonnance et Instruction Pastorale ... portant condamnation de la Doctrine contenue dans les Extraits des Assertions* (1763), B.M. 4091 aa 31, is a great onslaught on Probabilism and a defence of the Parlement and of the Gallican Articles of 1682.

[52] See Port, *Dict.*, III, pp. 670–1, and above, p. 8.

[53] *Nouvelles ecclésiastiques*, 16 Jan. 1740, p. 9; 6 Nov. 1750, p. 179; 9 Oct. 1753, p. 164. For his exclusion of Jansenists from Jubilee indulgences *ibid.*, 23 Jan. 1752, p. 15.

[54] *ibid.*, 3 Oct. 1740, p. 160; 28 Aug. 1747, p. 138; 23 Oct. 1747, p. 169; 6 Nov. 1750, p. 180.

[55] *ibid.*, 25 Nov. 1731, p. 235; Aug. 1733, p. 121. The Augustins remained firm at this time however (*ibid.*, 20 April 1733, p. 59) and three years later a Recollet of Angers was discovered hearing the confessions of Jansenists by night in a church at Nantes (A. Bachelier, *Le Jansénisme à Nantes* (1934), p. 226). The collapse of Dominicans and Oratorians was of course largely a result of official pressure on their central organization (A. Gazier, *Histoire générale du mouvement Janséniste* (2 vols. 1922), II, pp. 328, 327).

[56] *Nouvelles ecclésiastiques*, 20 Nov. 1748, p. 185 (cf. 25 Dec. 1732, p. 246); 6 Jan. 1735, p. 24; 19 Nov. 1744, p. 185. Also Rangeard, 'Etat', B. Angers MS. 1020, f. 49. Some of the temporalities were united to the house of La

Fidelité at Angers (see P. V. Municipal Officers, La Fidelité, 26 April 1790,
A.M.L. 13 Q 10). I have not been able to find a copy of L. Delaunay's monograph (1917) on La Fidelité of Saumur.

   [57] *Nouvelles ecclésiastiques,* 25 Sept. 1750, p. 154; 6 Nov. 1750, pp. 178–9.
For an earlier Oratorian denial of the bishop's claim to have converted one of
their number, see *Lettre d'un Theologian à M. l'Évêque d'Angers* ... (1747),
A.M.L. III F³, no. 2.

   [58] *Nouvelles ecclésiastiques,* 16 Jan. 1740.

   [59] *ibid.,* 1742, p. 40; 23 Jan. 1752, p. 15.

   [60] *ibid.,* 9 Oct. 1753, pp. 162–3.

   [61] Brossier, B. Angers MS. 726, f. 135.

   [62] *Au Roy, et a Nosseigneurs les Commissaires Généraux du Conseil* (1754?)
and MS. 'Memoire concernant l'affaire des douze curés qu'on nom cardinaux'
(Jan. 1754) in Parish Register Saint-Pierre, Etat Civil Angers, GG 181; A. Nat.
G 8* 2581, no. 14 (12 Feb. 1753); G 8* 2582, nos. 27, 34; G 8* 2583, no. 9 (Jan.
1755); G 8* 2584, no. 23; G 8* 2585, no. 59 (1 March 1757). A letter of the abbé
de Beauvais, 22nd June (no year) in A. Nat. G 8 620 also refers.

   [63] *Nouvelles ecclésiastiques,* 16 Jan. 1752, pp. 15–16.

   [64] A.M.L. H 4, pp. 419–21 (28 Feb. 1753).

   [65] Evocations were particularly objected to (see the remonstrances of March-
April 1753 in J. Parguez, *La Bulle Unigenitus et le Jansénisme politique* (1936),
pp. 135–6).

   [66] *Nouvelles ecclésiastiques,* 10 July, 1754, pp. 111–12; 4 Sept. 1754, p. 143;
21 May 1756, p. 85.

   [67] *ibid.,* 24 July, 1758, pp. 123–4.

   [68] For Rangeard's later comments on this power see *P. V. historique* (1791),
pp. 18–19.

   [69] E. Appolis, 'Entre Jansénistes et Constitutionnaires: un tiers parti', *Annales économies, sociétés, civilisations,* 1951, pp. 154 ff.

   [70] *Mémoires pour l'Histoire des Sciences et des Beaux Arts (Journal de
Trevoux),* Sept. 1710, pp. 1520–1.

   [71] E. Préclin, *Les Jansénistes du XVIIIᵉ siècle et la Constitution civile du
clergé, 1713–91* (1928), p. 81.

   [72] Hardy, *Le Cardinal de Fleury et le mouvement Janséniste* (1925), p. 62.

   [73] Letter of 12 May 1746, *Analecta Juris Pontificii,* no. 117 (1874), col. 788.

   [74] See below, pp. 182–9.

   [75] *Au Roy et à Nosseigneurs les Commissaires Généraux du Conseil* (1754?) in
Parish Register Saint-Pierre, Etat Civil Angers, GG 181, p. 5.

   [76] *ibid.,* p. 24.

   [77] *ibid.,* p. 4.

   [78] *ibid.,* pp. 2–3, 26, 29, 36.

   [79] *ibid.,* p. 44.

   [80] *ibid.,* p. 36.

   [81] Port, *Dict.,* II, p. 296. Bishop de Grasse (born 1720) was his father's second
surviving son. François, the eldest, inherited the vast family estates in Picardy
and San Domingo—it was said that the alleys of his woods were swept when he
went hunting and that his linen was sent to the Antilles to be laundered. A
third son had a military career, the fourth was the notorious Admiral (documents concerning the controversy over his sea-battle of 12 April 1782 found
their way into the bishop's library at Angers—B. Angers MS. 487). Just as
naturally as the unmarried girls of this family went into exclusive convents,
Jacques de Grasse was sent to the Church to collect an income. He became
bishop of Vence at the age of 34 and did not appear in his diocese until two
years after being consecrated. He was 38 when he was transferred to Angers

(see the Marquis de Grasse and M. Emile Isnard, *Histoire de la Maison de Grasse*, 2 vols. 1933), I, pp. 228–36).

[82] Besnard, I, pp. 98–9; Uzureau, 'L'Abbaye de Saint-Aubin d'Angers (XVIIIe Siècle)', *Rev. Mabillon*, X (1919), pp. 113–15.

[83] Besnard, *loc. cit.*

[84] *Nouvelles ecclésiastiques*, 25 June 1764, p. 103; 16 Jan. 1767, p. 15.

[85] *Conférences ecclésiastiques du Diocése d'Angers sur la Grace* (1748), Bodl. 8 B Sa 414, vol. III pp. i–iv. For other 'Jansenist' allegations against the *Conférences*, see below, p. 199 and B. Hauréau, *Histoire littéraire du Maine* (4 vols., 1843), IV, p. 283.

[86] *Nouvelles ecclésiastiques*, 30 Jan. 1785, p. 17.

[87] C. A. Sainte-Beuve, *Port-Royal* (ed. Doyon & Marchesné, 9 vols., 1926–8), VI, p. 242.

[88] *Clemens Papa XIII ad Episcopos Andegavensem, Alesiensem, Nolanum et Sartatensem* (Rome, 1765), B.M. 4051 aaa 45.

[89] The municipality of Angers had prevented them from establishing a sugar refinery in Angers (C. Port, *Inventaire ... de la Mairie*, p. 147; *Nouvelles ecclésiastiques*, 14 Aug. 1754, p. 132). A striking example of the kind of hatred which the Jesuits could evoke is found in G. Boussinesq and G. Laurent, *Histoire de Reims* (3 vols., 1933), II, pp. 211–13.

[90] Leflond, *M. Emery*, I, pp. 37–8.

[91] *Nouvelles ecclésiastiques*, 8 Oct. 1760, p. 180; 9 Oct. 1753, p. 162.

[92] Brossier, B. Angers MS. 726, pp. 957–67; 730, pp. 180(b), 182, 186, 34(b).

[93] See below, p. 187, Cf. pp. 132–3.

[94] The *arrêté* of the Parlement of Paris (9 May 1760) was a preliminary move in the campaign against the Jesuit order (P. Dudon, 'De la suppression de la Compagnie de Jésus, 1758-1773', *Rev. des Question historiques*, CXXXII (1938), p. 86).

[95] *Nouvelles ecclésiastiques*, 30 Jan. 1761, p. 20.

[96] Isambert, *Recueil*, XXII, pp. 405–17, 441–2. For the bishop's Gallican activities in 1765 (in alliance with the University of Angers and the Parlement of Paris), see Bois, *La Vie Scolaire*, p. 42.

[97] For this see below, p. 190.

[98] Mezeray to the agents general of the Clergy of France, 16 July 1765; also 26 June, 3 July, 10 July (A. Nat. G 8 620).

[99] See Mezeray's letters as above; also A.M.L. G 940, f. 135(b); A.M.L. G 116, ff. 236, 237.

[100] Blordier-Langlois, *Angers et l'Anjou sous le régime municipal*, p. 315; A. Nat. H. 1633 (Carton of privileges of the town of Angers), no. 33—'nouvelle constitution de l'hôtel de ville d'Angers.'

[101] *Nouvelles ecclésiastiques*, 25 June 1764, p. 103.

[102] A. Nat. G 8* 2813, p. 553; A.M.L. G 270, p. 70.

[103] A.M.L. G 270, p. 69 (26 May 1767).

[104] A.M.L. G 1013, f. 117 (25 Feb. 1773).

[105] A.M.L. G 270, p. 144 (27 Aug. 1781).

[106] *Journal de Madame Craddock, Voyage en France, 1783–1786* (French trans. by Mme O. D. Balleygiver, 1896), p. 273.

[107] J.-F. Bodin, *Recherches*, II, p. 391.

[108] Robin, *Montglonne*, p. 208.

[109] Port, *Dict.*, III, p. 268; *Traduction en vers François, de l'Elégie Latine, ou Ovidianum de M. Claude Robin, Curé de Saint-Pierre d'Angers, Auteur du Montglonne* (B. Angers 103, 627), pp. 4–5.

[110] 400l. a year, before the *congrue* was raised to 500l. in 1768 (A. Nat. G 8 79 (Angers)).

[111] Port, *Inventaire Mairie*, pp. 273–4.

[112] 'Claude Robin, dernier curé de Saint-Pierre d'Angers, 1714–1793', *Anjou hist.*, XXXIX, p. 197; Besnard, I, p. 236.

[113] X. de la Perroudière, 'Voyage à Rome en 1750 par M. Robin, Curé d'Anjou,' *Revue des Facultés Catholiques de l'Ouest*, 1894, pp. 52–3, 63, 292. (This is an edition of the major part of Robin's MS. 'Le pèlerin apostolique ou les pensées diverses . . . à l'occasion d'un voyage de Rome', B. Angers MS. 1841.)

[114] See Lehoreau, *Anjou hist.*, XV, p. 245; L. Rondeau, 'L'Eglise Saint-Pierre d'Angers et le Curé Robin', *Méms. Soc. Agric.* . . ., II (1868), pp. 379–80; the *pouillé* of 1783 gives the income as 890*l.* (*Anjou Hist.*, I (1900), p. 344).

[115] Robin took possession on 13 January 1752 (Parish Register, Etat Civil, Angers, G.G. 180, f. 8).

[116] L. Rondeau as above, pp. 382–4. Rondeau's article is a summary, with full quotations, of Robin's own *Exposé signifié, suivi de la demande en complainte formée par Messire Claude Robin* . . .

[117] A. Nat. G 8* 2812, p. 274 (8 Oct. 1759). The other details of this affair are in Rondeau, pp. 382–4.

[118] Rondeau, pp. 386–9, 393.

[119] *Exposé*, in Rondeau, p. 393.

[120] A.M.L. G 1170, f. 256 (22 June 1774).

[121] *Exposé* in Rondeau, pp. 390–1.

[122] A.M.L. C 24 (Statement of the parishioners' case to the intendant—undated).

[123] Letter from Versailles to the intendant, 23 Feb. 1781, and order of Council of 8 May 1781 (A.M.L. C 24).

[124] Robin to intendant 25 May 1781, A.M.L. C 24.

[125] A.M.L. G 1170, f. 386 (24 May 1782); f. 353 (1788).

[126] P.V. parish assembly of Saint-Pierre, 8 Sept. 1783, 9 March 1784, 22 Feb. 1784, 23 Feb. 1784 (B. Angers MS. DD 16).

[127] *Exposé* in Rondeau, pp. 389, 380; A.M.L. G 1170, f. 256 (22 June 1774); A.M.L. G 1177, transaction of 20 Jan. 1787.

[128] Port's note in Besnard, I, p. 243; Port, *Dict.*, III, pp. 268–70.

[129] A.M.L. G 1177 (20 Jan. 1787).

[130] *L'Ami des Peuples, ou Mémoire intéressant pour l'Eglise et pour l'Etat . . . addressé à Monseigneur l'Evêque d'Angers, en l'Année 1760, par un curé du diocese* (Angers, 1764). *Ouvres de M. Robin*, B. Angers, 103, 627.

[131] *Exposé signifié*, see above, note 116.

[132] *L'Ami des Peuples*, p. 6; *Exposé*, in Rondeau, p. 378.

[133] *L'Ami des Peuples*, p. 32.

[134] *Exposé*, in Rondeau, p. 384.

[135] *L'Ami des Peuples*, pp. 30–1.

[136] *ibid.*, p. 31n. Though, naturally enough, canons were the particular objects of curé Robin's scorn, his works also make it clear that he was prepared to apply the same devices of antiquarian research to humble the pride of the great monasteries of Anjou. He praises the original penitence and abstinence of monks and their learning, but regrets their acquisition of property. Across the river the great abbess of Ronceray ruled, but Robin would have it set on record that 'in fact, by origin, the abbess was nothing more than a sister of charity, as it were, or schoolmistress set over the education of girls and receiving her institution to office from the church and dean of Saint-Pierre'! ('Dissertation sur l'antiquité de l'Eglise de Saint-Pierre', 20 April 1760), in Parish Register Saint-Pierre, Etat civil, Angers, GG 181, pp. 25, 35).

[137] *Traduction en vers François, de l'Elégie Latine, ou Ovidianum de M. Claude Robin* . . ., p. 8.

[138] *Le Camp de Caesar au Village d'Empyré ... ou Dissertation sur l'Antiquité de l'Eglise de Saint-Pierre* (1764) B. Angers 103, 62, p. 57.

[139] Besnard, I, pp. 238-40, 279.

[140] Pauvert had deputized for Robin in the confessional and taken the gift left behind (Besnard, I, pp. 244-5).

[141] *Le Mont-Glonne*, p. 212.

[142] *Affiches*, 23 Dec. 1785.

CHAPTER IX

[1] Guyot, *Répertoire ... de Jurisprudence*, VII, p. 45; XVII, pp. 169-70.

[2] For a comment on the 'electoral' procedure for the metropolitan area of Tours, see *Nouvelles ecclésiastiques*, 26 March 1760, p. 67.

[3] G. Lepointe, *L'Organisation et la politique financière du Clergé de France sous le règne de Louis XV* (1923), pp. 29 n. 2, 97.

[4] See '*La Chambre ecclésiastique du diocèse d'Angers*', *Anjou hist.*, XXIII, pp. 64ff. Also see Chatizel, *Lettre de MM. les Curés du Diocèse d'Anjou à Monseigneur l'Illustrissime et Révérendissime Évêque d'Angers* (1785), B. Angers 3324, p. 31.

[5] On 20 Aug. 1759 it was decided that there should be four meetings a year ('Regître pour servir à inserer les Conclusions et deliberations du Clergé d'Anjou' (B. Angers MS. 734), f. 20(b)).

[6] *Anjou hist.*, XXIII, p. 66; Chatizel, p. 30.

[7] A.M.L. G 272, p. 36 (7 Feb. 1781).

[8] Reg. Clerg. Anj., B. Angers MS. 734, ff. 32, 63(b), 75(b), 80, 84, 103(b), 104. It was said later that the bishop's will prevailed in the 'elections', (de la Brosse, 31 Aug. 1786, A. Nat. G 8 620). At that time, however, there was very good reason for creating an impression that there had been powerful episcopal control.

[9] See Rangeard's accusations in *Dialogue entre un curé, un chanoine de cathédrale, son curé primitif, et un philosophe* n.d. (B. Angers 100,041), p. 11; and Boumard's in 'Mémoire à consulter' A.M.L. G 1691; and P.V. of 12 May 1785, A. Nat. G 8 620 ('honoraires assés considerables').

[10] *Anjou hist.*, XXIII, p. 66. cf. Rangeard's later comment—'Le syndicat, espèce de magistrature financière, et presque souveraine dans la répartition de l'impôt devenu, dans certain diocèses, l'heritage des chapitres' (*P.V. historique des actes du clergé* (1791),p. 16).

[11] 'Le comité particulier des chanoines' (*Lettre à Messieurs les Curés du Diocese d'Angers*, 1789 (B. Mus. $\frac{910.C9}{9}$, p. 13).

[12] In 1773 these totalled 3,500*l.* (Reg. Clerg. Anj., B. Angers MS. 734, f. 102; cf. 84(b), 85(b)).

[13] Reg. Clerg. Anj., B. Angers MS. 734, ff. 44(b), 47(b), 51(b), 54, 61.

[14] Reg. Clerg. Anj., B. Angers MS. 734, ff. 4(b), 8, 12, 17, 25(b), 37(b), 44(b), 53, 59.

[15] Reg. Clerg. Anj., B. Angers MS. 734, ff. 115 (b)–116(b) (July 1784). The Seminary owed six years' arrears in 1779, totalling 2,457*l.* (see accounts in A.M.L. G 35).

[16] An ordinary member was paid 120*l.*, the secretary 220*l.*, the *syndic* 240*l.* (Reg. Clerg. Anjou, B. Angers MS. 734, f.20(b)). In 1786 these fees were raised to 200*l.*, 300*l.* and 500*l.* respectively (*ibid*, f. 123).

[17] In 1762 it was agreed that the son would succeed to office on his father's death—and he did in fact become Receiver two years later. On his death a

brother-in-law took over (Reg. Clerg. Anj., B. Angers MS. 734, 40(b), 48, 107(b)).

[18] *ibid.*, f. 85.

[19] 'Le prix exhorbitant des denrées et matières de première nécessité', 'Tout étoit extremmement cher' (*ibid.*, ff. 85, 112(b), 110(b)).

[20] Reg. Clerg. Anj., B. Angers MS. 734, ff. 30(b), 23(b), 111.

[21] *ibid.*, f. 111(b); Mezeray to the agents general, 10 Oct. 1772, 31 Jan. 1773, A. Nat. G 8 620. The offices were bought in 1693 for 11,000*l.* Louis XIV put up the offices of Apostolic Notaries for sale in 1691. In some towns the Royal Notaries bought them up (V. Nouel de Kéranqué, *Essai sur la communauté des notaires Royaux et Apostoliques de Rennes au XVIIIᵉ siècle* (1904), pp. 24, 30).

[22] A Nat. G 8 2461, f. 569. The Royal Notaries also pointed out that Apostolic Notaries were unknown in the primitive church (!), that they did not come under the ordinary authority of civil magistrates, that their registers were ill-kept and that they competed with Royal Notaries for the right to do legal business concerning sales, leases and inventories involving the property of benefice holders (*Mémoire pour les Conseillers du Roi et de Monsieur. Notaires à Angers, contre le Clerg*é *de la Province d'Anjou* (B. Angers H. 2090), pp. 8, 10, 11–12, 18).

[23] *Rapport de l'Agence, contenant les principales affaires du Clergé ... 1775–1780* (1785), p. CXLIV—cf. pp. 87–9. The report is by the abbé de la Roche-foucauld and the abbé de Jarente.

[24] Reg. Clerg. Anj., B. Angers MS. 734, ff. 90–1.

[25] A. Nat. G 8* 2461, f. 572.

[26] Reg. Clerg. Anj., B. Angers MS. 734, f. 92.

[27] A.M.L. G 269, ff. 386–7. The bishop's expenses had been 3,372*l.* (Reg. Clerg. Anj., f. 94(b)).

[28] Port, *Dict.*, II, p. 296. But it is not true that Mgr de Grasse lived 'continuously' in Paris, see *Affiches* in 'Mgr de Grasse, évêque d'Angers'. *Anjou hist.* I, p. 626.

[29] A.M.L. G 269, ff. 389–90.

[30] Reg. Clerg. Anj., B. Angers MS. 734, f. 96.

[31] A. Nat. G 8* 2462, f. 26 (Dec. 1778).

[32] *ibid.*, ff. 26, 28–9, 34.

[33] Reg. Clerg. Anj., B. Angers MS. 734, f. 96.

[34] *ibid.*, ff. 102(b), 104; Letter of Mezeray 20 Feb. 1779, A. Nat. G 8 620; [Chatizel] *Lettre de MM. les Curés du Diocèse d'Anjou à Monseigneur l'illustrissime et Révérendissime Evêque d'Angers* (1785), B. Angers 3324, p. 108; *Lettre à Messieurs les Curés du Diocèse d'Angers* (1789), British Museum $\frac{910\,a\,9}{9}$, p. 7.

[35] Letters of the Bureau (16 Sept. 1766), Mezeray (22 Oct. 1766), and replies, especially to the bishop (26 Sept. 1766) in A. Nat G 8 620. See also A. Nat. G 8* 2611, nos. 56, 59.

[36] Mezeray to the abbé Dulau 11 Aug. 1770, A. Nat. G 8 620; Dulau to Mezeray 12 Sept. 1770, A. Nat. G 8* 2611, no. 153.

[37] Mezeray to Dulau, 6 May 1772, 7 March 1775 (A. Nat. G 8 620), Dulau to Mezeray 14 May, 1772, (A. Nat. G 8* 2611, no. 206).

[38] A.M.L. G 271, pp. 431–2; *Affiches* 7 May 1774. The tax was from half a livre to 5*l.* a year (see accounts of 1789 in A.M.L. G 279).

[39] For this paragraph see E. Préclin, *Les Jansénistes du XVIIIᵉ siècle et la Constitution civile du clergé* (1928).

[40] Leflon, *M. Emery*, p. 32. 'Vous en aurez été touché plus qu'un autre, Emery tells Rangeard, 'parce que vous lui étiez attaché' (MSS, Emery, Saint-Sulpice, X, f. 387).

AA

[41] Payment in 'Evêché d'Angers, Devis de réparations 1782–7', A. Nat. T 222.

[42] *Lettres du Baron de Castelnau, officier de Carabiniers, 1728–93*, ed. Baron de Blay de Guex, pref. A. Chuquet (1911), p. 304.

[43] Henri Jougla de Morenas, *Grand Armorial de France* (*Soc. du Grand Armorial de France*) *Supplément* (1952), p. 193.

[44] See A. Sicard, *L'Ancien Clergé de France. Les Evêques avant la Révolution* (5th ed., 1912).

[45] *Mémoires et Notes de Choudieu* (ed. Barrucand, 1897), pp. 17, 14–15.

[46] Biographical notes in Port, *Dict.*, I, p. 771; Bougler, *Mouvement Provincial en 1789, et biographies des députés de l'Anjou* (1865), I, p. 508.

[47] 'Une Correspondance en 1791', *Andegaviana*, IV (1906), p. 233.

[48] F. H. Tresvaux, *Histoire de l'Eglise et du diocèse d'Angers* (2 vols., 1859), II, p. 344; 'Un imprimeur angevin: Charles-Pierre Mame (1746–1829)', *Anjou hist.*, XXVIII, pp. 203–4.

[49] Tresvaux, II, p. 343.

[50] Brossier, B. Angers MS. 726, p. 967.

[51] To the abbé de Barral, 22 March 1786 (A. Nat. G 8, 620); to Barentin, 11 Jan. 1789 (A. Nat. AA 62, Dossier 1550, plaq. 3ᴮ, no. 96).

[52] 'Un mystique à la veille de la Révolution', *Andegaviana* XXVII, p. 216; to the intendant of Tours, March 1786 (*Inventaire-Sommaire des Archives Départmentales. Indre-et-Loire* ed. C. L. de Grandmaison (1878), p. 29; Mme Letondal, 'Mémoires', *Anjou hist.*, V, p. 10).

[52a] No doubt Mgr de Lorry's years at Tarbes, a centre of clerical discontent, have a good deal to do with his attitude to the lower clergy of Anjou. But this is a subject which I have not had time to study. E. Lafforque, 'Histoire des Evêques du diocèse de Tarbes', *Revue des Hautes-Pyrénées*, XXIV (1929), p. 69, shows the sad economic state of the curés of Tarbes, but does not discuss the bishop's attitude.

[53] E. Queruau-Lamerie, *L'abbé Chatizel de la Néronière, curé de Soulaines* (Laval, 1899) B. Angers 103435, p. 6.

[54] *Traité du Pouvoir des évêques de France sur les empêchements de marriage* (Avignon, 1782) (B. Angers S.T. 814), pp. 114–15, 124–6, 131–5. Convenient comparisons for Chatizel's arguments are found in a standard collection of Richerist doctrines put out by the canonist Maultrot three years before— [Maultrot] *Les Droits du Second Ordre, défendus contre les apologistes de la domination épiscopale* (1779).

[55] *Traité*, p. 82.

[56] *ibid.*, pp. 117–22.

[57] According to a catechism in use in the diocese of Angers the Pope could give a simple priest power to confirm in an emergency (eighteenth-century Catechism from the library of the Seminary at Angers, MS. University of Rennes 219, p. 168).

[58] *Traité du Pouvoir des évêques...*, pp. 123, 128–30, 141–2.

[59] *ibid.*, pp. 127–30, 131n., 143–5n.

[60] Letourneau, *Séminaire*, pp. 121–2. One might cite Cotelle de la Blandinière's obituary notice—'On remarque dans tous les traités de morale qui sont sortis de sa plume, beaucoup d'ordre et de clarté ... et surtout, un profond respect pour l'autorité de l'église et des pasteurs du premier ordre. Longtemps curé, il fut bien éloigné de contracter cet esprit presbytérien, triste avant— coureur de cet esprit d'égalité mal entendu...' (*Annales Catholiques ou suite des Annales Religieuses, Politiques et Littéraires*, 1797, no. 26, pp. 92–3).

[61] *Traité des cas réservés au Pape; Traité des cas réservés aux évêques* (1785). For contemporary comment see *Nouvelles ecclésiastiques*, 22 Dec. 1785, pp. 20–8; 3 April 1786, pp. 53–6. Préclin's discussion is found on pp. 342 ff. of his work.

[62] *Conférences ecclésiastiques sur la Hiérarchie, pur servir de suite et d'appui aux Conférences d'Angers* (Paris, 1785) III, pp. 526-7, 377, 7, 20, 43, 291.

[63] 3 vols., 1787. For comment see *Nouvelles ecclésiastiques*, 6 Nov. 1787, p. 172; Préclin, pp. 358-9.

[64] *Conférences ecclésiastiques sur les synodes pour servir de suite et d'appui aux Conférences d'Angers en formant le quatrième volume de celles sur la hiérarchie* (Paris, n.d.), pp. 38-9, ii.

[65] *ibid.*, pp. 52-3, 60, 62, 113-14, 143, 156, 191-2, 195.

[66] *ibid.*, pp. xxiii-xxiv, 274-5.

[67] See *Nouvelles ecclésiastiques*, 30 Oct. 1789, pp. 173-8; 6 Nov. 1789, pp. 177-178.

[68] E. Queruau-Lamerie, *L'abbé Chatizel*, p. 17.

[69] De la Brosse, *Lettre du Syndic du Diocèse d'Angers à MM. les Curés* (1789) (B. Angers H 3325), p. 16.

[70] [Rangeard], *Dialogue entre un curé, un chanoine de cathedrale ... et un philosophe.* n.d. (B. Angers 100,041), p. 12.

[71] [Chatizel], *Lettre de MM. les Curés du Diocèse d'Anjou à Monseigneur l'Illustrissime et Révérendissime Evêque d'Angers* (1785) (B. Angers 3324), p. 9.

[72] pp. 30-1, 34-6.

[73] pp. 47, 19, 32, 39. Chatizel's claim concerning common law is well borne out in Guyot, VII, p. 43.

[74] pp. 28, 39, 40-3.

[75] p. 71. Chatizel's accusations against the bishop and the cathedral were never satisfactorily refuted. The great abbeys seem to have paid a more reasonable share of taxation; Saint-Aubin paid 6,825*l.* in 1786, Toussaint paid 1,562*l.* in 1780 (A.M.L. H 34; H 1248). In 1784 it seems that the chapter of Saint-Pierre paid rather less than one tenth of its income in taxation (A.M.L. G 272, p. 566—estimate by the cathedral).

[76] *Avertissement de l'Assemblée Générale du Clergé d'Anjou présidée par Monseigneur l'Illustrissime & Révérendissime Evêque, à tous les Bénéficiers du Diocèse* (Angers, 1786), B. Nat. LK³ 1097, p. 40.

[77] *ibid.*, pp. 50-1.

[78] *ibid.*, pp. 41-3, 49.

[79] *ibid.*, pp. 39, 58-9.

[80] *ibid.*, pp. 38, 59, 74.

[81] *ibid.*, pp. 9, 10, 27-8.

[82] *ibid.*, pp. 14-15.

[83] *ibid.*, loc. cit.

[84] *ibid.*, p. 28. Compare the 'standing orders' (as it were) of the diocese in this matter. 'Dans quelques diocèses, cette election se fait dans les Sinods, dans d'autres diocèses, elle se fait dans une assemblée générale, dans d'autres c'est le bureau luy même qui nomme aux places vacantes ... Comme il n'y a rien ladessus de prescript par aucun règlement du clergé, il parôit que chaq' diocèse peut suivre a cet égard son usage' ('Mémoires du clergé. Quelques instructions concernant les matières bénéficiales, avec le Pouillé d'Anjou', B. Angers MS. 397, ff. 132(b)-133).

[85] Reg. Clerg. Anjou (B. Angers MS. 734), ff. 120-120(b).

[86] *Extrait des Registres du Conseil d'Etat* (A. Nat. Ba 13, liasse 9). These new regulations are also in Reg. Clerg. Anjou, ff. 121(b)-3.

[87] G. Lepointe, *L'Organisation et la politique financière du clergé...*, pp. 99, 106.

[88] 22 March 1786 (A. Nat. G 8 620).

[89] As the canons of the cathedral minuted, A.M.L. G 273, f. 26. Cf. the view of the canons of Saint-Pierre, A.M.L. G 1171, 3 May 1786.

[90] Reg. Clerg. Anj. (B. Angers MS. 734) f. 121(b). See also A.M.L. G 942, f. 213. (Saint-Martin).

[91] 'Mémoire à consulter', A.M.L. G 1691. (Carton concerning the parish of Sainte-Croix.) Two country curés also signed their protest.

[92] *Extrait des Registres* ... (A. Nat. Ba 13, liasse 9), pp. 3–4 (arts. II, III, IV).

[93] The Assembly allowed 1,213*l.* for their expenses, Reg. Clerg. Anj. (B. Angers 734) f. 125(b)).

[94] *ibid.*, ff. 125, 125(b).

[95] *ibid.*, f. 125(b).

[96] Letter of Courtillé of 20 Sept. 1775 (A. Nat. G 8 620, file 'Angers, Paroisses de la Ville. Saint-Denis Saint-Laud').

[97] De la Brosse to agents-general, 13 June 1786 (A. Nat. G 8 620).

[98] A.M.L. G 942 (Saint-Laud), f. 76(b).

[99] De la Brosse, 13 June (A. Nat. G. 8 620).

[100] Reg. Clerg. Anj. (B. Angers MS. 734), f. 125.

[101] A.M.L. G. 273 (Cathedral) p. 313 (1 July 1788), p. 316 (4 July 1788). (Note that the curé of Saint-Nicolas now sat in place of Chotard.) For a complaint see [Rangeard], *Dialogue entre un curé, un chanoine*, etc., p. 11.

[102] 22 March 1786 (A. Nat. G 8 620).

[103] 9 July 1786 (A. Nat. G 8 620).

[104] De la Brosse to the agents-general, 29 June 1786 (A. Nat. G 8 620).

[105] See Courtillé's letter of 20 Sept. 1775 (A. Nat. G 8 620, file 'Angers Paroisses de la Ville'). For the cathedral Rogation procession incident, see above, p. 181.

[106] 'Remarques que j'ay fait en lisant l'histoire ecclésq. de M. Fleuri'—on a detached sheet numbered 32 and headed 'Curés' (in Boumard's hand), A.M.L. G 1692.

[107] See the 'Mémoire' attached to de la Brosse's letter of 21 Aug. 1786 (A. Nat. G 8 620).

[108] The history of this case is found in de la Brosse's letter of 29 June 1786 and in the P.V. signed 'Chollet huissier de l'hôtel de ville', 12 May 1785, and in the 'Mémoire a Consulter' enclosed in de la Brosse's letter of 21 Aug. 1786, all in A. Nat. G 8 620. The sum is variously mentioned as 14*l.* 5*s.*, 16*l.*, 5*s.*, and 18*l.* 5*s.*

[109] De la Brosse, 21 Aug. 1786 (A. Nat. G 8 620).

[110] De la Brosse, 29 June 1786 (A. Nat. G 8 620).

[111] De la Brosse, 29 June 1786 (A. Nat. G 8 620).

[112] A. Nat. G 8* 2465, f. 449.

[113] 21 Aug. 1786 (A. Nat. G 8 620).

[114] Bishop of Angers to the agents-general, 9 July 1786 (A. Nat. G 8 620).

[115] A Nat. G 8* 2465, f. 449.

[116] De la Brosse, 21 Aug. 1786 (A. Nat. G 8 620).

[117] Record of seizure by Pierre François Dumesnil, 'huissier audiencier au siège de la police royale d'Angers' (A. Nat. G 8 620).

CHAPTER X

[1] F. Uzureau, 'Une Révolution judiciaire à Angers, 1787–88', *La Révolution Française*, LXXXI (1928), pp. 225–7.

[2] 'L'Assemblée Provinciale d'Anjou, 1787–1790', *Anjou hist.*, IX, pp. 131–2.

[3] Louis-Charles duc de la Trémouille, *L'Assemblée Provinciale d'Anjou d'après les archives de Serrant*, 1787–9 (1901), p. 47.

[4] He claimed descent from a Robert Walsh who was governor of Carlisle for Henry II in 1174 (*Extrait d'histoires et de Titres concernant la maison de Walsh* (1768), A.M.L. II E 2750) and, or alternatively, from Philip Walsh who was doing great deeds in Ireland about this time. In 1753 the family was recognized in France as possessing *ancienne noblesse* and took out naturalization papers in 1755 (La Trémouille, *Une Famille royaliste Irlandaise et Française* (1901), pp. 83–91). For Walsh's bid for popularity while a member of the Provincial Assembly of Anjou see J. de Reau de la Gaigonnière, *La Commission intermédiaire de l'assemblée provinciale d'Anjou* (1911), pp. 20–1, 24.

[5] P. Renouvin, *Les Assemblées Provinciales de 1787* (1921), p. 182.

[6] C. Berlet, *Les Tendances unitaires et provincialistes en France à la fin du 18e siècle* (Univ. de Nancy, Fac. de Froit, 1913), p. 73. Uzureau, 'L'Assemblée Provinciale d'Anjou et l'élection de la Flèche', *Méms. Soc. Agric.*, XIII (1910).

[7] Blordier-Langlois, *Angers et le Département de Maine-et-Loire 1787–1830* (2 vols., 1837), I, pp. 25–8.

[8] *ibid.*, I, pp. 319–22. For the subordination of the provincial assemblies at Tours, Angers and Mans to a general assembly at Tours, see J. du Reau de la Gaigonniere, *op. cit.*, pp. 9, 15, 136–7, 40.

[9] A Meynier, 'Une grande période électorale en Anjou. Les élections aux Etats-Généraux de 1789', *Rev. de l'Anjou*, XLIII (1901), p. 209.

[10] Blordier-Langlois, I, pp. 322–6.

[11] As the curés complained later, *Projet d'un Mémoire des curés du Diocèse d'Angers relativement à la convocation des Etats-Généraux*, Proust, *Archives, de l'Ouest*, A iv, p. 28.

[12] A. Meynier, *Un représentant de la bourgeoisie angevine à l'Assemblée Nationale Constituante et à la Convention Nationale, L.M. La Revellière-Lépeaux, 1753–1795* (1905), p. 101.

[13] Blordier-Langlois, I, pp. 31–4.

[14] A.M.L. G 273, ff. 362, 375 (Dec. 5).

[15] Portais, *Gruget*, p. 185. For the meeting of 9 Dec. see Munic. Reg. B. Angers MS. BB 133, ff. 10–11(b). For parish discussions, A.M.L. G 1772 (Saint-Maurice), ff. 92(b)–93; G 1663 (Lesvière), f. 5; G 1712 (Saint-Julien), f. 69; G 1732 (Saint-Maurille), ff. 62(b)–63.

[16] *Extrait du Procès-Verbal de l'Assemblée Générale de la Ville d'Angers du 24 décembre 1788* (B. Angers H 2032). The discussions were approved by a further assembly on 24 Dec. See also 'Projet de rétablir les Etats de la Province d'Anjou', *La Révolution Française*, LXV (1913), p. 371. The petition included a further request that nobles be not allowed to stand as deputies for the commons, and that their financial and legal employees be not allowed to vote. The *Présidial* dissented from the first of these stipulations (Munic. Reg. B. Angers MS. BB 133, f. 10).

[17] H. Carré, *La Noblesse de France et l'opinion publique au xviiie siècle* (1920), p. 335.

[18] A Meynier, *Rev. de l'Anjou*, XLIII (1901), pp. 213, 217; *La Revellière-Lépeaux*, pp. 105–7.

[19] *De la noblesse du 2e ordre, par un gentilhomme angevin, noble d'extraction* (Nov. 1788), see Blordier-Langlois, I, pp. 24–6.

[20] *Dialogue sous le Ballet de la Paroisse de Saint-Michel-du-Tertre entre le Bedeau de la Paroisse, un Avocat, et un Etudiant en Droit* (B. Angers H 2034), p. 18. For Walsh comte de Serrant's personal campaign in the countryside—kissing babies, giving balls and hunting parties to the lesser gentry, banquets to curés and alms to the poor, see *Lettre à un Seigneur d'Anjou accusé de tromper le Peuple*, 28 Feb. 1789 (B. M. $\frac{911 \text{ c } 11}{1 \text{ & } 2}$, pp. 5–7.

[21] *Lettre d'un membre du Tiers-Etat de la Province d'Anjou à Monsieur le comte de W— S— T—* (B. Angers H 2034), Angers, 28 Dec. 1788.

[22] *Arrêté de Messieurs les Etudiants en Droit* 2 Feb. 1789 (B. Angers H 2031, nos. 10 & 11) ; *Arrêté des jeunes citoyens de la ville d'Angers*, 4 Feb. 1789 (B. Angers) H 2034). See also B. Pocquet, *Les origines de la Révolution en Bretagne* (1885), II, p. 280.

[23] Brette, *Recueil de documents relatifs à la convocation des Etats-Généraux de 1789*, IV, pp. 620–1.

[24] See A. Le Moy, *Cahiers de Doléances des Corporations de la Ville d'Angers pour les Etats-Généraux de 1789* (*Coll. Docs. Inéd. sur l'hist. écon. de la Révn. Franç.*, 1915), pp. lxvii–cxix.

[25] 'A. M. le Duc de Praslin, président de l'assemblée provinciale d'Anjou', 'Vers pour être mis en chant après le rappel du Parlement de Paris' (B. Angers MS. 556, ff. 97, 110, 85–6; and cf. f. 142). The letter to Héron picturing Louis as the dupe of a frivolous queen (early '89?) is in F. Grille, *Lettres ... et documents ... sur ... la formation du Ier Bataillon des volontaires de Maine-et-Loire* (4 vols., 1850), I, pp. 6–7.

[26] In Proust, *Archives*, A IV, pp. 31–4.

[27] They are found, together with strong support of the commons against the nobility in 'F. F. curé de H ...' *Instructions des Curés du diocèse d'Angers à leurs députés aux Etats-Généraux, rédigés par un curé du diocèse d'Angers* B. M. $\frac{910.c.9).}{11}$

[28] Saint-Laud (12 March 1789) in A.M.L. G 942, f. 125; Saint-Martin in *Anjou hist.*, XXXI, pp. 215–18.

[29] 'Protestation' B. Angers MS. 711, f. 10(b).

[30] *Mémoires et Notes de Choudieu* (ed. Barrucand, 1897), p. 8.

[31] *Cahier* in Proust A IV, pp. 31–4; cf. A.M.L. G 942, f. 125; *Anjou hist.*, XXXI, pp. 215–16. The bishop urged the deputies to the Estates-General to 'restore our Holy Religion to its ancient splendour, and protect it against the insults and outrages of unbelief' (*Mandement de Monseigneur l'Evêque d'Angers, qui ordonne des Prières pendant la tenue des Etats-Généraux*, 5 May 1789 (B. Angers H 2030), p. 4).

[32] 'F. F. curé de H...', *Instructions*, pp. 13–18.

[33] See p. 241. below.

[34] A Le Moy, *Cahiers ... des Corporations ... d'Angers*, pp. 34, 42, 45, 71, 76, 81, 116, 120.

[35] *ibid.*, pp. ccx, 59.

[36] *ibid.*, pp. 59, 227, 236, 111, ccx, 33, 37.

[37] *ibid.*, pp. 13–14, 33, 49, 80.

[38] See pp. 220–1 below.

[39] Le Moy, *op. cit.*, pp. clxxxvi–vii, ccix, 34, 58, 71, 80, 85, 110, 224.

[40] *ibid.*, pp. 45, 219.

[41] *ibid.*, p. 219.

[42] *ibid.*, pp. 11, 27, 35, 44, 50, 72, 111.

[43] *ibid.*, pp. ccix, 14, 26, 33, 59, 220; and cf. pp. 115–16. above.

[44] *ibid.*, p. 57.

[45] Cf. Meynier, *La Revellière-Lépeaux*, p. 147.

[46] *La Sentinelle du Peuple*, 25 Dec. 1788 (B. Angers H 2034), pp. 6, 10.

[47] See p. 220 below.

[48] *Addresse à la Noblesse et au clergé de la Province d'Anjou* (B. Angers H 2034), pp. 6–7.

[49] *Avis au Tiers-Etat de la Province d'Anjou* (B. Angers 100.016), pp. 3–21, Mongodin agrees that all the orders should pay equal taxation, however (p. 211).

⁵⁰ *La Confession d'un Pauvre Roturier Angevin à l'occasion d'un Avis au Tiers-Etat de la Province d'Anjou* (B. Angers H 2034), pp. 6, 14–15, 8.

⁵¹ *Eclaircissemens sur trois questions des Conférences d'Angers* (Paris 1789), B. Nat. Lb 1288, especially pp. 10–13, 18–19, 30–1, 36–7, 49, 76–77.

⁵² *Extrait des Registres du Conseil d'Etat* (1770 Jan.), A.M.L. II E 2750.

⁵³ *Arrest du Parlement de Paris qui maintient & garde Messire de Walsch, comte de Serrant dans la propriété & jouissance des Arbpes sur les chemins existans dans l'étendue de sa Haute-Justice* (22 Aug. 1786), A.M.L. II E 2750. This sentence cancelled that of the *sénéchaussée* of Angers of 10 Jan. 1785.

⁵⁴ *A Messieurs de la Commission Intermédiaire de l'Assemblée Provinciale d'Angers* (1788) A.M.L. C 20. For d'Autichamp, see P. V. Comm. Interméd. A.M.L. C 166, f. 66.

⁵⁵ A.M.L. G 273, ff. 117 (2 Jan. 1787), 119 (5 Jan.). On 6 Jan. de la Brosse was in touch with the municipality (Munic. Reg. BB 133, f. 35(b)).

⁵⁶ *Extrait des Registres ... de l'Assemblée Générale du Clergé d'Anjou* in *A Messieurs de la Commission Intermédiaire* (A.M.L. C 20), p. 20.

⁵⁷ *Lettres du Baron de Castelnau, officier de Carabiniers 1728–1793*, ed. Baron de Blay de Guex, pref. by A. Chuquet (1911), p. 316.

⁵⁸ *A Messieurs de la Commission Intermédiaire* (A.M.L. C 20), p. 4.

⁵⁹ The duc de la Trémouille, *L'Assemblée Provinciale de l'Anjou*, pp. 95–6.

⁶⁰ This letter is printed in *Anjou hist.*, XVIII, pp. 190–3.

⁶¹ P. V. Comm. Interméd. A.M.L. C 166, ff. 64(b), 66, 67, 69(b), 74.

⁶² *Lettre du Baron Suisse au Noble Breton* in *Analyse de la Brochure Des conditions nécessaires à la légalité des Etats-Généraux* (B. Angers H 2034), pp. 18–19.

⁶³ Meynier, *La Revellière-Lépeaux*, p. 104.

⁶⁴ Brette, IV, p. 624.

⁶⁵ Uzureau, 'Les Elections du Clergé d'Anjou aux Etats-Généraux de 1789', *Méms. Soc. Agric.*, 5th Ser., VI (1903), pp. 385–6. For suspicions of the clergy up to this time, see *Le Patriote Angevin* (B. M. $\frac{911 \text{ c. } 11)}{21}$, no. III, March 1789 (accusation that nobles and clergy want open voting for deputies to the Estates-General).

⁶⁶ Intendant to *Garde des Sceaux*, 25 March 1789 (A. Nat. Ba 13, liasse 9, plaque 3).

⁶⁷ *P. V. des Séances particulières de l'ordre de la Noblesse des Sénéchaussées d'Angers, Beaufort, Baugé, Château gontier et la Flèche*, in Proust, A IV, p. 47. The comte de Provence followed suit on 3 April (Brette, IV, p. 625).

⁶⁸ *Instructions et Pouvoirs donnés par Messieurs les Gentilshommes des cinq sénéchaussées d'Angers à leurs Députés*, Proust A IV, pp. 72–4.

⁶⁹ A.M.L. G 273, pp. 409–10 (June 1783).

⁷⁰ The rules are found in B. Angers MS. 1204. There are MS. Collections concerning the Order in the B. Nat. (*Collection Clairambault* and *Anc. Suppl. Franc.*, no. 24108) also in the municipal libraries of Nancy and Carpentras.

⁷¹ A.M.L. G 273, p. 414 (20 March, 1789), see also p. 416 (21 March).

⁷² *P. V. des Séances ... de la Noblesse*, Proust A IV, pp. 51–2.

⁷³ *ibid.*, pp. 52–3. The marquis did not obtain his chapter of noble canonesses. So in February 1790 he renounced his rights to the nation and obtained an honourable mention from the National Assembly (*Correspondence de M. M. les députés des Communes de la Province d'Anjou avec leurs commettans* (B. Angers H 2025), IV, pp. 149–50, 16 Feb. 1790). At last he had been successful in hawking his ancestors.

CHAPTER XI

[1] A. Le Moy, *Cahiers ... des Corporations ... d'Angers*, p. 49. In many places it was customary for a vicaire to make an annual tour of the parish collecting money towards his stipend.

[2] Le Moy, p. clxxvii, cf. p. ccix.

[3] *ibid.*, pp. 43, clxxvii, ccix.

[4] *ibid.*, pp. ccviii, 80, 93–4, 224.

[5] *La Confession d'un Pauvre Roturier* (see above, p. 215).

[6] *Bureau Général de Charité. Porro unum est necessarium* (B. Angers H 2033).

[7] A.M.L. G 942, f. 126 (cap. 27).

[8] *Lettre circulaire de quelques membres du Tiers-Etat d'Anjou à MM. les Curés du diocèse, convoqués pour l'Assemblée du 16 Mars* (B.M. $\frac{910.c.9}{10}$, pp. 3–4, 8.

[9] Le Moy, p. 58.

[10] *Projet d'un mémoire des curés du Diocèse d'Angers, relativement à la Convocation des Etats-Généraux* (B. Angers H 2032, no. 10). This brochure is also found in A. Nat. B. a 13 liasse 9, pl. 2; it is reprinted in Proust, A IV, pp. 21–8.

[11] *Anjou hist.*, XXXI, p. 217; A.M.L. G 942, f. 125(b).

[12] 'Mémoire de la Commission Intermédiaire de l'Assemblée Provinciale d'Anjou contenant ses voeux sur la forme et la Convocation des Etats-Généraux.' A. Nat. Ba 13, liasse 9, pl. 1.

[13] *Projet d'un mémoire*, Proust A, IV, p. 27.

[14] *ibid.*, pp. 21–4.

[15] A. Nat. Ba 13, liasse 9, pl. 5.

[16] P. de la Gorce, *Histoire religieuse de la Révolution Française*, I (1909), p. 92.

[17] *Droit Exclusif des Curés aux Dixmes de leurs Paroisses, ou lettre à M. de Gr ... pour être présentée à l'Assemblée générale des Etats de la Nation* (B. Angers, 100.042), pp. 5, 11, 15.

[18] *ibid.*, pp. 4, 7, 25–7, 30, 50, 53.

[19] *ibid.*, p. 68.

[20] Rangeard had been a friend of Bishop de Grasse (see above p. 53, also Guy de Chateaubriant, 'Deux Lettres du xviii siècle', *Méms. Soc. Agric.* 6th Ser. XIII (1938), pp. 64-6) and was accused of communicating to that prelate a document which would aid him in a lawsuit against the chapter (Bougler, *Biographie des députés de l'Anjou depuis l'Assemblée Constituante jusqu'en 1815* (2 vols. 1865), I, pp. 31–2). Rangeard subsequently lived in poverty for some time as *prieur-curé* of Saint-Aignan until the bishop found him a good living. Even so, considering his abilities, Rangeard might still have hoped for something better (see M. Emery's letter of 3 April 1784 in MSS. Emery, Saint-Sulpice, vol. X; ... 'j'ai toujours regretté que vous fussiez relégué dans une campagne, et je suis toujours étonné qu'avec aussi peu d'encouragement, vous avez eu le courage d'acquérir tant de connoissance').

[21] *Droit Exclusif des Curés ...*, p. 62.

[22] *Dialogue entre un curé, un chanoine de Cathédrale, son curé primitif, et un philosophe* (B. Angers 100.041), pp. 7, 13.

[23] *Lettre à Messieurs les curés du Diocèse d'Angers* (B. Mus. $\frac{910 c 9}{9}$, pp. 4–5, 13, 6–8. This pamphlet must have been published at the end of January 1789 (see p. 3).

[24] *ibid.*, pp. 9, 13–14.

[25] *Projet de Plaintes et Demandes pour être présenté pour des Curés du Diocèse*

d'Angers, à l'Assemblée Générale du 16 Mars 1789. (B. Mus. $\frac{910 \text{ c } 9)}{7}$, pp. 17–20, 5–6.

[26] *ibid.*, pp. 9–13.

[27] *ibid.*, pp. 15–16, 7–9.

[28] *ibid.*, p. 23.

[29] De la Brosse, 9 Jan. 1789 (A. Nat. Ba 13, liasse 9, p. 1).

[30] Letter of Chatizel, 23 Dec. 1788 (B. Angers MS. 618, printed in F. Grille, *Bric-à-brac*, 2 vols. (1853), I, pp. 82–4).

[31] Letter of 23 Dec. as above.

[32] De la Brosse, 9 Jan. 1789 (A. Nat. Ba 13, liasse 9, pl. 1; cf. Proust A, IV, p. 30); the bishop, 11 Jan. 1789 (A. Nat. AA 62, dossier 1550, pl. 3B, no. 96).

[33] *Lettre de M. le Curé de Soulaines, en réponse à celle de M. le Syndic du Clergé du Diocèse d'Angers*, 24 March, 1789 (B. Angers H 3326), p. 5.

[34] A.M.L. G 273, p. 405.

[35] *Lettre du Syndic du Diocèse d'Angers à M.M. les Curés* (B. Angers H 3325), p. 16 (see above p. 201 also).

[36] *ibid.*, p. 24. Cf. Chatizel's *Lettre* of March 24 as above, pp. 8–9.

[37] *Lettre du Syndic*, p. 4.

[38] *ibid.*, p. 1.

[39] In the *sénéchaussée particulière* of Angers (which was the largest sub-division of the total electoral area) there were 462 parishes of the diocese of Angers, and 182 parishes depending on other bishops.

[40] 9 Jan. 1789 (A. Nat. Ba 13, liasse 9, pl. 1).

[41] If they lived over two leagues from Angers. For the question of the legality of obtaining a substitute see Milscent's letter & draft reply in the affirmative (A. Nat. Ba 13, liasse 9, pl. 2).

[42] 22 Feb. 1789 (A. Nat. Ba 13, liasse 9, pl. 2).

[43] Boumard, Rangeard and the curés of Saint-Maurice, Saint-Julien, Saint-Michel de la Palud and Saint-Aignan, 10 March 1789. Reply to Boumard, 14 March (A. Nat. Ba 13, liasse 9, pl. 3). A reply to Boumard from Necker is also found in A.M.L. G 1691.

[44] A.M.L. G 1171, f. 70; G 942, f. 125. Cf. *Cahier* of Saint-Martin in *Anjou hist.*, XXXI, p. 215.

[45] See lists of attendance in Uzureau, 'Les Elections du Clergé d'Anjou aux Etats-Généraux de 1789', *Méms. Soc. Agric.*, 5th Ser., VI (1903), pp. 343–79.

[46] This meeting is described (angrily) in the 'protestation des bénéficiers simples, réguliers et chanoines de l'Eglise d'Angers contre les opérations de l'assemblée du clergé de 1789. 30 mars 1789' (B. Angers MS. 711). See also *Précis des Réclamations fait par le Chapitre de l'Eglise d'Angers* (B. Angers H 2028 (6) and A.M.L. G 273, f. 417; also the intendant's letter of 31 March 1789 (A. Nat. Ba 13, liasse 9, pl. 3).

[47] De la Galissonière, 17 March 1789 (A. Nat. Ba 13, liasse 9, pl. 3).

[48] The same, 18 March (*loc. cit.*).

[49] Uzureau, *Méms Soc. Agric.*, 5th Ser., VI, pp. 384–5, 388.

[50] *ibid.*, pp. 383, 384, 387.

[51] *ibid.*, p. 383. 'Protestation' (B. Angers MS. 711), f. 15(b). The Secretary elected was the abbé Coulonnier, curé of May, a stern and businesslike individual, as his yearly law-suit (over tithe) with his parishioners demonstrates (Deniau, *Histoire de la Vendée* (6 vols., 1878), I, p. 122). His age and failing eyesight, however, made his appointment an unsuitable one—see below.

[52] Uzureau as above, pp. 388, 390. Intendant's letter of 25 March (A. Nat. Ba 13, liasse 9, pl. 3).

[53] Uzureau, pp. 391–2.

[54] *ibid.*, p. 394.

[55] The *cahier* is printed in Proust, *Archives*, A, IV, pp. 35–6.

[56] Uzureau, p. 369. According to the minutes, Chatizel had a large majority, but these minutes were badly drawn up in the first place. The intendant reported on March 25th that Chatizel had 500 votes, and the bishop 300 (A. Nat. Ba 13, liasse 9, pl. 3). He also says that Rangeard received 700 votes against the bishop's 78.

[57] Uzureau, pp. 398–402.

[58] Chatizel, *Lettre* ... , 24 March; for Boumard, *Lettre du Curé de Sainte-Croix d'Angers à M. de la Brosse, soi-disant Syndic du Clergé d'Anjou* (March 26, 1789) (B. Angers S.T. 403), pp. 6–7.

[59] Uzureau, p. 402.

[60] A.M.L. G 273, ff. 417–18 (March 27), f. 419; G 942 (Saint-Laud), f. 121(b); G 1014 (Saint-Martin), f. 267; G 1171 (Saint-Pierre), f. 71.

[61] 'Protestation des bénéficiers simples, réguliers et chanoines de l'Eglise d'Angers contre les opérations de l'assemblée du clergé de 1789, 30 Mars 1789 après midy' (B. Angers MS. 711), ff. 20(b)–21, 19, 18(b).

[62] Report of intendant, 7 April 1789 (A. Nat. Ba 13, liasse 9, pl. 3).

[63] Uzureau, p. 403. The cathedral makes the interruption appear dignified, of course (A.M.L. G 273, f. 419, 3 April 1789).

[64] A.M.L. G 273, ff. 421–2.

[65] Uzureau, p. 405.

[66] 31 March 1789 (A. Nat. Ba 13, liasse 9, pl. 3).

[67] 5 April (A. Nat. Ba 13, liasse 9, pl. 4). Cf. A. Brette, 'La Collection Camus aux Archives Nationales', *La Révolution Française*, XXII (1891), p. 201.

[68] A.M.L. G 273, f. 444 (15 April 1789).

CHAPTER XII

[1] [Rangeard], *Procès-verbal historique des actes du clergé* (Paris, 1 May 1790) B.M. F.R. 140 (15), p. 37.

[2] *Moniteur*, no. 4, p. 23 (28 May 1789); no. 5, p. 26 (3 June).

[3] Rangeard, *op cit.*, pp. 80, 82. (For Rangeard's patriotic verse written in the capital in 1789 see *Prière à Dieu*, B.M. F. 925(15).)

[4] *Journal inédit de Jallet curé de Chérigné, député du clergé de Poitou aux Etats-Généraux de 1789, précédé d'une notice historique par J. J. Brethe.* (Fontenay-le-Comte, 1871), p. 71.

[5] A. Houtin, *Les Séances des députés du Clergé aux Etats-Généraux de 1789. Journaux du curé Thibault et du chanoine Coster* (Soc. de l'Hist. Révolution Française) 1911, p. 38 (Thibault).

[6] *Correspondence de MM. les députés des communes de la Province d'Anjou avec leurs commenttans* (printed Angers, 1789; B. Angers H. 2025), I, pp. 179, 180.

[7] *Corr. deps. Anjou*, I, p. 204. All three Angevin curés voted for the verification of powers in common on 19 June (Houtin, pp. 145–5).

[8] On 25 June he was a member of a deputation of the clerical minority sent to concert policy with the intransigeant nobles (Thibault, in Houtin, p. 31), and he was one of the 23 clergy who filed a declaration of protest before finally taking their seats in the National Assembly (Houtin, p. 150).

[9] J. M. Thompson, *The French Revolution* (1951 ed.), p. 62; citing the English ambassador.

[10] *Corr. deps. Anjou*, I, pp. 452, 453, (18 July, 21 July).

[11] *ibid.*, I, pp. 385–6.

[12] The account is given by Robin in his parish register (in C. Port, *La Vendée*

Angevine (1888), I, pp. 3, 373–5). The edge is taken off this thrilling narrative when we compare it with a more sober narration in *Extrait des Registres du Bureau de la Correspondence du 17 Juillet* in *Corr. déps. Anjou*, I, pp. 329–32.

[13] Meynier, *La Revellière-Lépeaux*, p. 196; Port, *Vendée*, p. 373; E. Gabory, *La Révolution dans la Vendée* (1925), I, p. 36.

[14] P. Caron, 'Un Témoignage sur les événements de juillet 1789', *Revue Historique* CXVI (1914), pp. 295–6.

[15] 23 July 'Correspondence de M. Houdet, vicaire a Angers, à son frère, chirurgien à Saint-Florent-le-Vieil (1789–91)', *Anjou hist.*, XII, pp. 250–1 (also in *La Révolution Française*, LXI (1911), pp. 456–7). Cf. the report of the deputies in Paris, 22 July (*Corr. Déps. Anjou*, I, pp. 424–8).

[16] *Lettre de Messieurs les députés du Clergé d'Anjou à Messieurs les curés du diocèse* (B. Angers H 2032) — printed in *Anjou hist.*, XL (1940), pp. 210–11.

[17] On 22 August the deputies of Anjou informed their constituents that it was the Assembly's will that such committees should act as municipalities until new legislation was devised (*Corr. Déps. Anjou*, II, pp. 193–5). For links between the committee and similar bodies in other towns see Bosvieux and Tholin, *Inventaire ... des archives communales entérieures à 1790. Ville d'Agen* (1884,) p. 67.

[18] Reg. Clerg. Anjou. B. Angers MS. 734, ff. 134(b) (17 April), 135(b) (28 July). The royal treasury was, however, responsible in the end (f. 138(b)).

[19] Marquis de Lostanges, 12 Aug. 1789, *Rev. Hist.*, CXVI, p. 296.

[20] *Corr. Déps. Anjou*, II, p. 80; Port *Vendée*, I, p. 64. Walsh, comte de Serrant, left France on 19 July with the first wave of emigrés (*Une Famille royaliste Irlandaise et Française*, pp. 79–80).

[21] *Corr. Déps. Anjou*, I, p. 339n.; 'Etablissement de la milice Angevine', *Anjou hist.*, V, p. 193. For a country curé blessing the flag of his parish militia in October (by permission of canon Louet, vicar-general) see Deniau, *Histoire de la Vendée*, I, p. 98.

[22] Uzureau, 'Anciens collèges de la province d'Anjou', *Anjou hist.*, I, pp. 18–19.

[23] Port, *Vendée*, I, p. 104.

[24] *Extrait du Registre des délibérations du Comité permanent d'Angers* (B. Angers H 2031, no. 22).

[25] Uzureau, 'Suppression de la gabelle en Anjou, 1789', *Méms. Soc. Agric.*, XVI (1918), p. 13.

[26] *L'Observateur Provincial* (A.M.L. 151 L 1), no. 2 (22 Oct.), no. 4, p. 23. Milscent, a deputy of the commons, had resigned earlier (letter of the deputies of 18 Oct. in A.M.L. 1 L 152).

[27] *Corr. Déps. Anjou*, III, pp. 100, 118. Rabin, however, resigned on 5 November (*ibid.*, III, p. 130). For the activities of Angevin deputies in the National Assembly in this affair of the *gabelle*, see Le Hodey de Saultchevreuil, *Journal des Etats-Généraux*, V, pp. 181–2, 497–9; VI, pp. 158–61.

[28] Parish Reg. Saint-Evroul (Etat Civil, Hôtel de Ville, Angers, GG 34, f. 493); see C. Port, 'L'Hiver en Anjou', *Rev. hist. lit. arch. d'Anjou*, N.S., II (1880), p. 201.

[29] Leclerc, *L'Ami des Indigents* (1789), in E. Queruau-Lamerie, 'Notice sur les Journaux d'Angers pendant la Révolution', *Rev. d'Anjou*, XXIV (1892), p. 144.

[30] *Compte Rendu à la Commune de la Ville d'Angers par le Comité Permanent le 10 Septembre 1789* (B. Angers H 2033); cf. A.M.L. G 273, f. 464 (cathedral's gift on 29 July).

[31] Reg. Clergé Anjou. B. Angers MS. 734, f. 136; cf. A.M.L. G 273, ff. 481, 482, 484.

[32] A.M.L. G 273, f. 485; cf. *Anjou hist.*, XXV, p. 134.

[33] *Administration de Charité pour la ville d'Angers* (1789) (B. Angers H 2094), pp. 20–1. For votes of parish assemblies in Jan. 1789 in favour of a *bureau de charité* see A.M.L. G 1732, f. 64; G 1663, f. 6; G 1712, f. 71(b); B 1722, f. 95(b).

[34] *Bureau Général de Charité. Porro unum est necessarium* (B. Angers H 2033), pp. 21–4.

[35] Munic. Reg. BB 134, f. 23. See also *En l'Assemblée générale de la ville d'Angers* (B. Angers H 2094), p. 5.

[36] *Lettre Ecrite à MM. les curés d'Angers, par M. Delaunay, l'aîné, Avocat* (B. Angers H 2094), p. 5.

[37] *Affiches* in *Anjou hist.*, IV, pp. 477–9; see also 'Les municipalités de Saint-Augustin, Saint-Laud, etc.', *Andegaviana*, 1927, p. 335.

[38] E. Charavay, 'Documents Inédits. Les Jeunes Bretons et Angevins en 1790', *La Révolution Française*, XVII (1889), pp. 281–3.

[39] F. A. Aulard, *La Société des Jacobins. Recueil de Documents* (1889), I, p. 58. For the deputation at the bar of the National Assembly see Le Hodey de Saultchevreuil, *Journal des Etats-Généraux*, IX, pp. 397–8.

[40] J. A. Berthe, 'Histoire et Faits d'Armes de la Garde Nationale d'Angers' (1839), B. Angers MS. 1059.

[41] Port, *Vendée*, I, p. 99. The best description of the scene is in the abbé Huard's letter of 4 Aug. cited below. Delaunay's *Discourse* to the King in the name of the National Guards of Maine-et-Loire (17 July 1790) is found in B. Nat. 8° LB³⁹ 3797.

[42] Port, *Dict.*, III, p. 81.

[43] 'Corr. de M. Houdet', *Anjou hist.*, XII, pp. 251–4.

[44] Bois, *La Vie Scolaire et les créations intellectuelles en Anjou, 1789–99*, p. 124.

[45] Blordier-Langlois, I, p. 96.

[46] P. V. Commission intermédiare, A.M.L. C 166, f. 241(b).

[47] *Procès-Verbal de l'Assemblée des Electeurs du Département de Maine-et-Loire* (B. Angers H 2033). At the end of June this assurance was formally renewed before the *conseil général* of the department (Port, *Vendée*, I, p. 106).

[48] 'Etablissement de la milice nationale Angevine', *Anjou hist.*, V, pp. 194–6.

[49] Given in full in Blordier-Langlois, I, pp. 342–3. As printed by the National Assembly by a decree of 15 June 1790, it is found in B. Angers H. 2038. cf. *Moniteur*, no. 168, pp. 685–6, and *L'Observateur Provincial* (A.M.L. 151 L 1) 3e Partie, no. 12, pp. 46–7.

[50] *Nouvelles ecclésiastiques*, 28 Aug. 1790, pp. 137–9.

[51] A.M.L. G 273, f. 569 (29 July 1790); P. V. Dept. A.M.L. 1 L. 68 (29 July); Cf. Bourgain in *Rev. d'Anjou*, XXXVII (1898), p. 17.

[52] Letter of the abbé Huard from Angers, 4 Aug. 1790 (B. Angers MS. 633). It is Huard who notes that three canons were present.

[53] Port, *Vendée*, I, pp. 106–7.

[54] For Bardou, see Port, *Dict.*, I, p. 205; for his singing of the *vide Thoma* in 1786 'avec un sentiment et une grace inexprimable' see *Affiches* (in *Andegaviana*, IV, pp. 24–5), for his discontent in 1789, see A.M.L. G 273, p. 427, (20 April 1789).

[55] 26 May 1790, A. Nat. D XIX 55, file 177 bis., no. 17.

[56] Delaunay, *Description fidèle de ... la cérémonie de la Confédération Nationale du 14 juillet 1790*, published by Gaetan in *La Révolution Française* XI (1886), pp. 15 ff.

[57] *L'Observateur Provincial*, printed at Pavie's Angers (A.M.L. 151 L 1), no. 1, pp. 4–5 (Oct. 1789); no. 6, pp. 34–5 (Nov. 1789); 2e Partie, no. 6 (Feb. 1790); 3e Partie, no. 17, p. 65 (June–early July 1790).

[58] 'Corr. de M. Houdet', *Anjou hist.*, XII, pp. 251–4.

[59] Meynier, *La Revellière-Lépeaux*, pp. 274–5.

[60] A. Michon, *Essai sur l'histoire du parti Feuillant, Adrien Duport* (1924), p. 80, citing Chénier, 24 Aug. 1790.

[61] Especially the eight who defended the porte Saint-Michel (J. A. Berthe's autobiography, B. Angers MS. 616). Soland was their leader. 'Je pense, mon cher Soland, que vous allez avoir la croix de Saint-Louis' wrote La Gallissonière from Paris, 2 Oct. 1790 (A.M.L. J 3135).

[62] Port's note in Besnard, I, p. 235.

[63] *Affiches*, 29 Nov. 1790 (see Gabory, *La Révolution et la Vendée*, I, pp. 94–95); *Récit exact d'une insurrection* ... in *L'Observateur Provincial* 4e Partie, nos. 12 and 13, p. 45. For the supposed connections of the plotters see C.–L. Chassin, *La Préparation de la Guerre de Vendée*, I, pp. 124–5. It seems clear that the high price of bread and corn was the essential cause of the rising. See Municipal Register (*Mairie*), I, pp. 135, 138(b), 140(b), etc., and, for the measures of the municipality to ensure supplies subsequently, *ibid.*, pp. 147–147(b).

[64] Blordier-Langlois, I, p. 144; Meynier, *La Revellière-Lépeaux*, p. 227; Choudieu, *Mémoires*, p. 57. For the importance attached to the tocsin and money found on rioters, cf., reports of Sept. 14 and 18 to the National Assembly, *Moniteur*, no. 259, p. 1070; no. 263, pp. 1089–90.

[65] 'Corr. de M. Houdet', *Anjou hist.*, XII, p. 262. For the accusation that a priest had exhorted people in the parish of La Trinité to join the rioters, see Merlet de Boulaye's letter in B. Angers MS. 634.

[66] See letter of De Houlières (Sept.) and of the deputies in Paris (3 Oct.) in A.M.L. 1. L. 152. 'Examine in your prudence,' wrote the deputies of Anjou from Paris, ' if it would not be more fitting to withdraw your request for artillery'.

CHAPTER XIII

[1] *La Confession d'un Pauvre Roturier Angevin* ... (B. Angers H 2034).

[2] Munic. Reg. BB 133, ff. 50(b)–51 (15 Feb. 1789).

[3] *Cahier* (Proust, *Archives* A IV, p. 32). According to the intendant, when the clergy declared its willingness to surrender immunity from taxation, it insisted that this did not mean that it would surrender its property (25 March, A. Nat. Ba 13, liasse 9, pl. 3).

[4] 'Le cahier du chapitre de Saint-Martin d'Angers', *Anjou hist.*, XXXI, pp. 216–17; A.M.L. G 942, f. 126 (cap. 20).

[5] *Droit Exclusif des curés aux Dixmes* ... (B. Angers 100.042) pp. 20–30.

[6] *Lettre à Messieurs les curés* ... (B.M. $\frac{910\,c\,9}{9}$, pp. 10–11. The date is Jan. 1789.

[7] A. Le Moy, *Cahiers*, p. ccviii.

[8] *ibid.*, pp. 58, 85.

[9] *ibid.*, p. 34 (the grocers propose to abolish tithe also, p. 227).

[10] *ibid.*, pp. 34, ccx, 38, 24, 13–14, 20.

[11] *ibid.*, p. 150; 'Le cahier de Saint-Samson-lès-Angers, 1789', *Anjou hist.*, XI, pp. 500–1.

[12] A. Le Moy, *Cahiers*, p. 22.

[13] *ibid.*, pp. 224, 261.

[14] And pamphleteers, cf. Boyd C. Schafer, 'Quelques jugements des pamphlétaires sur le clergé à la veielle de la Révolution', *Annales historiques de la Révolution Française* XVI (1939), pp. 110–22. See also N.-F.-M. Marion, *Histoire financière de la France depuis 1715* (6 vols., 1914–31), II, p. 39.

[15] Cf. Guyot, *Répertoire de jurisprudence*, II, pp. 74–5; D'Argenson, *Mémoires* (ed. E. J. B. Rathery, 9 vols., 1859–67), VII, p. 266.

[16] *Corr. Déps. Anjou*, II, p. 141.

[17] *Lettres de l'abbé Barbotin*, ed. A. Aulard, *Soc. Hist. Révn. Franç.* (1910), pp. xiv, 51–2.

[18] Marion, II, p. 25. The cathedral of Angers had handed in its silver 'pour le soulagement de l'état' in Dec. 1759 (Brossier, B. Angers MS. 726, pp. 67; 727, p. 50).

[19] 6 June 1789, *Moniteur*, p. 29.

[20] *Moniteur*, no. 64, pp. 263–4.

[21] *Moniteur*, no. 72, p. 296; no. 122, p. 492. For other proposals between Volney's and Talleyrand's, see S. Harris, *The Assignats* (1930), pp. 9 ff.

[22] J. Leflon, *La Crise révolutionnaire, 1789–1846* (*Hist. de l'Eglise*, ed. A. Fliche and V. Martin, XX, 1949), p. 49.

[23] *Corr. Déps. Anjou*, III, p. 80.

[24] Cf. Cernon's views, in Marion, II, p. 57, and Thomas Lindet's letter of 10 Jan. 1790 (A. Montier, *Correspondance de Thomas Lindet ... pendant la Constituante et la Législative* (*Soc. Hist. Rév. Franç*, 1899), pp. 47–8). In Oct. 1790 the District and Commune of Angers congratulated the National Assembly on the approaching sale of Church property as being 'le seul moyen de ramener la paix, en éteignant pour jamais les prétentions des opposants et en augmentant le nombre des amis de la révolution par la jouissance et l'amour de la propriété' (Municipal Register, *Mairie*, I, p. 161, 15 Oct. 1790).

[25] *Addresse de la Municipalité d'Angers à l'Assemblée Nationale*, in *Extrait des Registres de la Municipalité d'Angers contenant les Instructions relatives à la vente des Biens Domaniaux & Ecclésiastiques* (1790) (B. Angers, H 2028, no. 11), p. 4. For the discussion, Municipal Register (*Mairie*), I, pp. 19, 22, 32–3.

[26] De Houlières, mayor, to the president of the Ecclesiastical Committee of the Assembly, 14 (?) May, 1790 (A. Nat. DXIX 55, file 170, *pièce*, 1).

[27] Blordier-Langlois, I, p. 123.

[28] *Moyen très simple de vendre promptement, et sans dépréciation tous les biens, de main-morte, par M. de Volney, Moniteur*, no. 122, p. 492 (1 May 1790).

[29] Aulard, *La Société des Jacobins, recueil de documents*, I, pp. 58–9.

[30] By the decree of 17 April 1790 the administration of ecclesiastical property was vested in the civil authorities.

[31] P.V. District, A.M.L. 2 L 2, pp. 3, 26. For Feuillatreau, see above p. 106.

[32] P.V. District, A.M.L. 2 L 2, pp. 35, 37, 136.

[33] See letters of the *Proc. gen. syndic* of the Department, 29 Oct., 30 Oct. (A.M.L. 1 L 124).

[34] Deputies in Paris to Department, 28 Oct. (A.M.L. 1 L 152).

[35] P.V. Dept. 9 Nov. 1790 (A.M.L. 1 L 9 and 9 bis. p. 15), 30 Nov. 1790 (A.M.L. 1 L 68).

[36] A. Latreille, *L'Eglise Catholique et la Révolution Française* (1946), I, p. 81.

[37] The legislation is summarized in Aulard, *La Révolution Française et les Congrégations* (1903), pp. 13–20.

[38] See 'Les religieuses du Ronceray d'Angers pendant la Révolution', *Anjou hist.*, XXXI, p. 101; E. Rondeau, *Histoire du monastère des Ursulines d'Angers*, p. 229; 'Les Visitandines d'Angers pendant et après la Révolution', *Anjou hist.*, IX, p. 46; Uzureau, 'Les Carmélites d'Angers, XVII et XVIIIe siècles', *Anjou hist.*, V, pp. 561 ff.; 'Les Calvairiennes d'Angers 1619–1906', *Anjou hist.*, VI, p. 460. At the *Filles-Dieu* one sister asked to end her vows (Port, *Dict.*, I, p. 74). Two nuns of Sainte-Catherine chose to profit by the decrees, but one of these proposed to retire to the hospital of Saumur and the other to live as a *pensionnaire* in some other religious house (26 April, 27 Aug. 1790, A.M.L. 13 Q 8). The nuns of La Fidelité were firm on 26 April but by 27 Aug. when the

District administrators made their visitation, one chose freedom and seven others, though they stayed on, reserved a right to change their minds (A.M.L. 13 Q 10).

[39] Leflon, *La Crise Révolutionnaire*, pp. 55–6.

[40] These replies, from A. Nat. DXIX 1, are printed by Uzureau in 'Les Communautés religieuses de femmes dans le diocèse d'Angers en 1790', *Méms. Soc. Agric* ... IX (1906), pp. 113 ff.

[41] P.V. visit municipality, 26 April 1790 (A.M.L. 13 Q 3).

[42] 'Les Visitandines ...', *Anjou hist.*, IX, p. 44; Jeanne-Jacquine Moutardeau's 'Relation', *Anjou hist.*, XXIX, p. 162 (Pr. under the title 'La déportation des Religieuses Angevines').

[43] 22 July, 5 Aug. 1790 (A.M.L. 13 Q 4); P.V. Department 29 Oct. (A.M.L. 1 L 68).

[44] 27 July 1790 (A.M.L. 13 Q 12).

[45] 30 April 1790 (A.M.L. 13 Q 5).

[46] 28 April, 23 August 1790 (A.M.L. 13 Q 8).

[47] 27 April 1790 (A.M.L. 13 Q 8). See also (A. Launay), 'Monographie du couvent des Capucins d'Angers', *Annales Franciscaines*, 1886, p. 595.

[48] 'Les Dominicains d'Angers et de Craon pendant la Révolution', *Anjou hist.*, XXI, p. 213; 'Les derniers jours du couvent de la Baumette', *Anjou hist.*, XLI, pp. 26 ff.

[49] 24 April 1790 (A.M.L. 13 Q 8); P.V. Department 27 Oct. (A.M.L. 1 L 68) and later P.V. Department 17 Nov. (A.M.L. 1 L 9 and 9 bis.). P.V. District, 15 July (A.M.L. 2 L 2, p. 32); Municipal Register (*Mairie*), I, p. 75(b). See also Armel, 'Les Franciscains de Maine-et-Loire pendant la Révolution', *Revue d'Anjou*, 1907, pp. 15 ff.

[50] 'P.V. de visite au décès d'un religeux', 21 June 1790 (A.M.L. 13 Q 8).

[51] A.M.L. II Q 55–6.

[52] M. Chartier, 'A travers les papiers Caprara. Bénédictin d'Angers et bibliothécaire de Cambrai. René Marchant', *Revue du Nord*, XXIV, (1938), p. 188.

[53] Decree of 20 Feb. 1790.

[54] Municipal Register (*Mairie*), I, p. 106; II, p. 4; P.V. District, 2, 3, 5 July (A.M.L. 2 L 2, pp. 16, 19, 21); P.V. Department 2 July (A.M.L. 9 and 9 bis, Carton 9–10, p. 14).

[55] 28 April 1790, (A.M.L. 13 Q 8).

[56] 'Les derniers jours ... de la Baumette', *Anjou hist.*, XLI, pp. 26 ff.

[57] 28 April 1790 (A.M.L. 13 Q 12); P.V. Department, 21 July, 24 July (A.M.L. 1 L 68).—See also A.M.L. 1 L 9 and 9 bis, pp. 22(b)–23; Uzureau, 'Les derniers jours du prieuré de Lesvière-lez-Angers (1790)', *Rev. Mabillon*, XI (1921), pp. 313 ff.

[58] 27 April 1790 (A.M.L. 13 Q 6).

[59] 'Les derniers jours de l'abbaye de Saint-Nicolas-lès-Angers', *Anjou hist.*, XXI, pp. 20–2.

[60] 20 Aug. 1790, 'Corr. M. Houdet', *Anjou hist.*, XII, p. 258.

[61] The Lazarists and the 'Seminary of Saint-Charles' (an almost defunct institution which cared for old priests)—see P.V. Dept. 3 July, 20 Nov. 1790 (A.M.L. 1 L 9 and 9 bis.).

[62] Bois, *La Vie scolaire* ... p. 112; E. Rondeau, *Ursulines*, p. 213. The Dept. had originally accepted their claim to be an educational establishment, cf. P.V. Dept. 9 July (A.M.L. 1 L 9 and 9 bis, ff. 36(b), 42(b)–43).

[63] See for what follows, 'Les derniers jours de l'abbaye de Saint-Aubin d'Angers', *Anjou hist.*, XVII, pp. 67–81, and Uzureau, 'La Formation du Département de Maine-et-Loire et les derniers jours de l'abbaye de Saint-Aubin d'Angers, *Rev. Mabillon*, XXXIII (1913), pp. 33–49.

⁶⁴ For monks beginning to move their effects to lodgings in town see A.M.L. 13 Q 1 (27 April 1790).

⁶⁵ Departmental assemblies were to indicate 'aussitôt après leur formation' which houses were to be suppressed (*Lettres Patentes du Roi*, 12 Feb. 1790, cap. iv, in A.M.L. 121 L 1).

⁶⁶ A. Nat. D XIX 61, file 301, no. 6 (30 June 1790).

⁶⁷ Bertrand de Broussillon, *Cartulaire de l'abbaye de Saint-Aubin d'Angers* (3 vols., 1903), I, p. viii. For an accusation that some monks had taken away valuable books and sold others, see the letter to Rangeard of 13 Oct. 1790 (B. Angers MS. 634).

⁶⁸ I have assumed that the details of these arrangements were from the first those laid down in Estimation of *biens nationaux* in A.M.L. III Q 1, no. 197. For officials being given accommodation see P. V. Dept. 12 July 1790 (A.M.L. 1 L 9 and 9 bis. ff. 41–41(b)).

⁶⁹ May 1790, A. Nat. D XIX 55, file 170, *pièce* 1.

⁷⁰ 'Les derniers jours de ... Saint-Aubin', *Anjou hist.*, XVII, p. 81.

⁷¹ P.V. Dept. 28 June 1790 (A.M.L. 1 L 12 (ter), p. 9); cf. P.V. District, 7 June (A.M.L. 2 L 2, pp. 2, 14, 31); and P.V. Dept. 21 July (A.M.L. 1 L 68), and Jan. 1791 (A.M.L. 1 L 125). See also *L'Observateur Provincial*, 3ᵉ Partie, no. 24, p. 93).

⁷² See Estimation of *biens nationaux*, A.M.L. III Q 1, 30 Sept.–27 Nov. 1790.

⁷³ Cf. 'Loyers des maisons qui appartient à la communauté', A.M.L. 86 H 20, pp. 35–6.

⁷⁴ 'Tableau des Biens et Revenus ... de la maison de Toussaint', 30 Sept. 1780 (A.M.L. H 1248); Estimation *biens nat.*, A.M.L. III Q 1, pp. 13–29 (also arts, 199 and 200). For Saint-Aubin, see Estimation *biens nat.*, III Q 1, pp. 7–13.

⁷⁵ Estimation *biens nat.*, A.M.L. III Q 2, vol. IV, 2nd Series, no. 1 (2 July 1791); III Q 2, vol. III, 2nd Ser. of numberings, no. 23.

⁷⁶ 'Achats de biens nationaux par la ville d'Angers', *Anjou hist.*, III, pp. 632–4.

⁷⁷ Estimation *biens nat.*, A.M.L. III Q 2, vol. II (8th *cahier*—1 Dec. 1790), nos. 51 to 72. To complete the total add, A.M.L. III Q 2, vol. IV, no. 11; III Q 2, vol. III, 2nd Ser. numberings nos. 7 and 29; and land worth 560*l.* held by the Seminary in A.M.L. III Q 2, vol. IV.

⁷⁸ The main inventory for Saint-Laud is A.M.L. III Q 2, vol. II (Oct. 1790–Jan. 1791). Additions are recorded in III Q 2, vol. III, no. 2, which is land belonging to the chapter of Saint-Martin; also under date 21 April 1791 a further 23,300*l.* worth of land is recorded. Seventy-four of the items in the parish of Saint-Laud, worth 275,000*l.* had belonged to ecclesiastical institutions of the town of Angers itself, e.g. the cathedral had 96,000*l.* worth, the chapter of Saint-Laud 37,000*l.* worth, the Visitation 32.000*l.*, and the chapter of Saint-Martin 28,000*l.*

⁷⁹ *L'Observateur Provincial* 5ᵉ *Partie*, no. 16, p. 59 (end Dec. 1790). 'The sale of ecclesiastical property comes a year too soon,' wrote a substantial citizen who divided his time between his house in the rue Saint-Evroul and his country mansion at Chalonnes. 'Seeing that my finances are disarranged at the moment, I won't do so well out of it as I would if I had my funds available; on the other hand, I wouldn't be able to round off my property as I can do today if I let the occasion pass.' He took the opportunity. (G. Dufour, 'Jean-Antoine Vial', *Rev. de l'Anjou*, N.S., XIII (1921), p. 47). The date is 28 Dec. 1790. For La Revellière's purchases see *Annales hist. de la Rév. Franc.*, 1928, pp. 67–8.

⁸⁰ Marion, II, pp. 300–1, 126–7.

⁸¹ *Affiches*, in *Anjou hist.*, III, pp. 438–9.

[82] *Adjudication de Biens Nationaux*, n.d., n.p. (B. Angers H 2033).

[83] Bournisien, 'La Vente des Biens Nationaux', *Rev. historique*, C (1909), p. 38.

[84] Noailles to the Dept., 12 Sept. 1790 (A.M.L. 1 L 909). Cf. other letters in this carton and a letter of the comte de Dieusie, 12 Oct. 1790 in A.M.L. 1 L 152.

[85] Municipal Register (*Mairie*), I, pp. 131 (20 Aug.), 164(b), 180(b). In Jan. 1791 commissioners arrived from the Ministry of War to look at Saint-Nicolas (*ibid.*, II, p. 10(b)) and on 12 Feb. they reported that the location was an excellent one (p. 20).

[86] *ibid.*, I, pp. 168, 131(b), 164.

[87] *ibid.*, p. 164 (23 Oct. 1790).

[88] Municipal Reg. (*Mairie*), pp. 192(b), 196(b), 12 and 15 Dec. 1790; municipal deliberation, 15 Dec. 1790, pr. *Anjou hist.*, XX, pp. 331–5, under the title of 'La Voirie d'Angers 1790–1'. For the purchases, see L. Bourgain, *L'Église d'Angers pendant la Révolution et jusqu'en 1870* (1898), p. 43. For the Botanical garden, G. Robison, *La Revellière-Lépeaux* (New York, 1938), p. 38; Blordier-Langlois, I, p. 166, Municipality to district, 31 Aug. 1792, A.M.L. 19 Q 7 (ref. difficulties in getting hold of the vicarage of Saint-Samson).

[89] Bourgain, *Rev. d'Anjou*, XXXIII (1898), p. 189.

[90] See especially A. Boutillier du Retail, 'Les Privilégiés et les achats de Biens Nationaux dans le département de l'Aube', *La Révolution Française* LVI (1909), pp. 210–11, and Lecarpentier, *La vente des biens ecclésiastiques pendant la Révolution Française* (1908), p. 116.

[91] A. Nat. F 7 6774, plaq. 11 and 12.

[92] Municipal Register (*Mairie*), I, p. 8 (27 Feb. 1790); Lens, *L'Université d'Angers* I (Faculté des Droits), p. 254.

[93] Municipal Register (*Mairie*), I, p. 25(b) (13 March); (20 Aug.).

[94] 'Les municipalités de Saint-Augustin, Saint-Laud, Saint-Léonard et Saint-Samson à Angers, 1787–1795', *Andegaviana*, XXVII (1927), p. 335. For the petition of the monks of Saint-Serge backed by the municipality of Saint-Samson, see Municipal Register (*Mairie*), II, p. 8 (3 Jan. 1791).

[95] There are masses of petitions for the settlement of debts in A.M.L., Ser. Q. Noteworthy is prior Tonnelet's plea in favour of Madeleine Piron, laundress of Toussaint—very eloquent, with a Latin epigram (5 Oct. 1790, A.M.L. 16 Q 5).

[96] See especially the petition of Jean Luck, organ builder, who had spent a great deal on repairing a house belonging to the chapter of Saint-Maurille. The nation, he said, should give him the same terms as the chapter, 'à moins que les idées de justice ayent changé avec la Révolution' (23 Dec. 1790, A.M.L. 19 Q 7).

[97] 24 Sept. 1790, *Moniteur*, no. 269, p. 1113. On 8 Oct., Viger of Angers published a defence of the *assignat* pointing out that it was backed by Church lands and was thus immune from the weaknesses of Law's Scheme. (B. Angers H 2030, no. 38.)

[98] 'Corr. de M. Houdet', *Anjou hist.*, XII, p. 258.

[99] 'Les derniers jours de ... Saint-Aubin', *Anjou hist.*, XVII, p. 80.

[100] 'Un adversaire de la Révolution. Henri Bodard ...', *Anjou hist.*, XLVIII, pp. 10–16.

[101] As happened at Ecouffant and Sainte-Gemme (near Segré)—see *Proc. gen. syndic* of Dept. to National Assembly, 2 Nov. 1790 (A.M.L. 1 L 124); P.V. Dept., 20 Nov. (A.M.L. 1 L 9 and 9 bis) and proclamation in A.M.L. 141 L 4.

[102] Cf. *Corr. secrète de l'abbé de Salamon*, ed. de Richemont, pp. 469–70, cit. C. Ledré, *L'Église de France sous la Révolution* (1949), p. 62.

[103] *L'Observateur Provincial, 3e Partie*, no. 7, pp. 26–7 (May 1790).

[104] *L'Observateur Provincial*, 5ᵉ *Partie*, no. 6, p. 22 (Nov.); no. 15, pp. 4–5 (Dec.); no. 16, pp. 57–9 (intervention by Choudieu).

[105] See above, p. 239.

[106] P.V. District, 1 Dec. 1790 (A.M.L. 2 L 2, p. 163). Cf. dom Gaudon, looking after Saint-Aubin's wine harvest and asking for a reward of two barrels 'à un prix modique' (Viger to Department, 20 Oct. 1790, A.M.L. II Q 55–6).

[107] Blordier-Langlois, I, pp. 342–3.

CHAPTER XIV

[1] A. de Lameth, *L'Histoire de l'Assemblée Constituante*, extracts publ. by G. Michon in *Annales Hist. de la Révolution Française*, IV (1927), pp. 227–8; Talleyrand, *Mémoires* (ed. C. J. V. A. de Broglie, 5 vols., 1891–2), II, p. 123. Choudieu the Angevin anti-clerical said afterwards, 'we ought not to have imposed any oaths on them (the clergy) other than those exacted from citizens generally' (*Mémoires et Notes*, p. 14).

[2] For the foregoing, see in particular E. Préclin, *Les Jansénistes du XVIIIᵉ siècle et la Constitution civile du Clergé*; A. Mathiez, *Rome et le clergé française sous la Constituante* (1911), p. 81; B. Groethuysen, *Jean-Jacques Rousseau* (1949), pp. 313, 318–19, 333; A. Latreille, *L'Église Catholique et la Révolution Française*, I, p. 83. One might add that Voltaire himself wished to retain a subordinate Gallican Church.

[3] Mathiez, *op. cit.*, pp. 114–15, 121, 186, 318–19.

[4] *ibid.*, pp. 193, 259, 263, 335–7; dom Leclercq, *L'Église constitutionnelle* (1934), p. 43. For the interest of the clergy of Angers in the debates in Paris, see the letter of the abbé Huard to Merlet (who was in the capital), 4 Aug. 1790 (B. Angers MS. 633).

[5] The bishop of Angers was one of them (Barruel, *Collection ecclésiastique ou recueil ... des ouvrages faits ... relativement au clergé, à sa Constitution civile*, 14 vols., I (1791), p. 249).

[6] 29 March 1790, A. Nat. D XIX 57, file 214, no. 17.

[7] 22 May, 26 May, 29 June, A. Nat. D XIX 55, file 177 bis, no. 16; 56, file 201, no. 17; 61, file 61, no. 2. For further applications, see P.V. Dept., 20 Nov. 1790 (A.M.L. 1 L 68).

[8] A.M.L. G 273, f. 569 (9 July 1790); Municipal Register (*Mairie*), I, p. 110.

[9] Blordier-Langlois, I, p. 127.

[10] Cf. P.V. District, 5 July 1790 (A.M.L. 2 L 2, p. 21).

[11] Dom Leclercq, *L'Église constitutionnelle*, pp. 180–247.

[12] *Proc. gen. syndic* Dept. to District of Saumur, 11 Nov. (A.M.L. 1 L 124).

[13] A.M.L. G 273, f. 593 (18 Sept.); G 942, f. 145(b); 'La cathédrale d'Angers pendant la Révolution', *Anjou hist.*, XXV, p. 134.

[14] Uzureau, 'Les chanoines d'Angers pendant la Révolution', *Méms. Soc. Agric. ...* XXVIII (1925), p. 83.

[15] 15 Nov. 1790, Saint-Maurille (A.M.L. 13 Q 24); 20 Nov. Saint-Martin (A.M.L. 13 Q 24). Cf. Saint-Pierre, 15 Oct. 1790 (A.M.L. 13 Q 25).

[16] *Adresse à nosseigneurs de l'Assemblée Nationale*, 27 Feb. 1790. (There is a copy of this petition among papers relating to Tours in A. Nat. D XIX.)

[17] 'La cathédrale d'Angers pendant la Révolution', *Anjou hist.*, XXV, p. 135.

[18] Leflon, *Bernier*, pp. 6–7; *Anjou hist.*, XLVII, pp. 168–9.

[19] 'Plan pour formation de cures...', B. Angers MS. 793, no. 10.

[20] A.M.L. 1 L 966. See also 'La Chapelle Saint-Sébastien à Angers', *Anjou hist.*, XLI, pp. 129–30; for the views of the inhabitants of the *faubourg Bressigny* later on, Municipal Register (*Mairie*), II, p. 61 (31 May 1791).

[21] P.V. Dept., 20 Nov. 1790 (A.M.L. 1 L 68).

[22] 'Corr. de M. Houdet', *Anjou hist.*, XII, p. 267.

[23] 26 Dec. 1790, 'Les derniers jours de la paroisse Saint-Martin d'Angers', *Anjou hist.*, XLVII, pp. 112–13 (the original petition is in A.M.L. 1 L 966).

[24] The P.V. with full details of parish boundaries is in A. Nat. D XIX 80, file 611. The *proc. gen. syndic* of the District and the mayor of Angers handed in their plan to the Dept. on 6 Nov. (P.V. Dept., A.M.L. 1 L 9 and 9 bis.).

[25] 'Le clergé constitutionnel d'Angers 1791–1802', *Anjou hist.*, XVI, pp. 156–7. On the actual implementation of the reorganization, see E. L.'s notes in Thorode, pp. 149, 182–3.

[26] Leflon, *Bernier*, p. 6; S. Gruget, *Histoire de la Constitution civile du Clergé en Anjou* (as printed in *Anjou hist.*, II, p. 618). Gruget's history was also published as a separate volume by Uzureau (Angers, 1905).

[27] A. Mathiez, 'Les Philosophes et la Séparation', in *La Révolution et l'Église* (1910), p. 23.

[28] C. Ledré, *L'Église de France sous la Révolution*, p. 71.

[29] P.V. Dept., 16 Nov. 1790 (A.M.L. 1 L 9 and 9 bis.). For a list of territorial gains and losses caused by the Civil Constitution see *Études de Géographie ecclésiastique : le diocèse d'Angers* (Rodez, 1898) B. Nat. LK^3 1398, pp. 14–15.

[30] *Proc. gen. syndic* to the 'Bishop of the Department of Maine-et-Loire', 3 Dec. 1790 (A.M.L. 1 L 194*).

[31] See the next letter, 5 Dec. (A.M.L. 1 L 194*).

[32] Jurists of the old régime held that the normal method of translating the seat of a bishopric or of setting up a new see was by agreement of Pope and King with consultation of neighbouring bishops (Guyot, LXII, pp. 87–91; XIX, pp. 241–3). On the legal arguments concerning boundaries, see especially L. Sciout, *Histoire de la Constitution civile du Clergé* (4 vols., 1872–81), I, pp. 210–11, 217, 220–1, 223–4.

[33] A. Le Moy, *Cahiers ... d'Angers*, pp. clxxvi–vii.

[34] See B. F. Hyslop, *French Nationalism in 1780 according to the General Cahiers* (1934), p. 104.

[35] See R. Reuss, *La Constitution civile du Clergé et la crise religieuse en Alsace 1790–1795* (2 vols., 1922), I, pp. 26, 136, 152.

[36] Brette, *Recueil*, II, p. 175.

[37] *Moniteur* no. 161, p. 657; no. 167, p. 683; cf. *Corr. Deps. Anjou*, pp. 334–5. The discourse was printed and distributed by order of the National Assembly. I wish to express my great gratitude to the librarian of Carpentras (Vaucluse) who in answer to my enquiry concerning a copy in his care (MS. 1739, ff. 27–31) generously sent me a complete typescript.

[38] Mathiez, *Rome et le Clergé ...*, pp. 27–8.

[39] For a list of these matters compiled by a vicar-general of Rouen, see C. Ledré, *Une Controverse sur la Constitution civile du Clergé, Charrier de la Roche et le chanoine Baston* (1941).

[40] E. Lavaquery, *Le Cardinal de Boisgelin, 1732–1804* (2 vols., 1920), II, pp. 81, 82, 105.

[41] As the chapter of Saint-Brieuc said (see its deliberations ed. L. Dubreuil in *La Révolution Française*, LXX (1917), p. 355).

[42] Mathiez, *op. cit.*, p. 240. Braesch, *1789, l'année cruciale* (1940), p. 265, shows the mistakes of the Assembly very clearly.

[43] For an exaggerated account of the Gallican motives of the episcopate, see Lévy-Schneider, 'L'Autonomie administrative de l'épiscopat française à la fin de l'ancien régime', *Revue Historique*, CLI (1926), pp. 17–19.

[44] 'Whatever our kings could do, the representatives of the nation, in whom resides all primary sovereignty, can also do, and by a more eminent title,' said

the municipality of Morlaix (July 1790); see H. Zivy, 'L'Évêque de Saint-Pol-de-Léon et la Constitution civile du Clergé', *La Révolution Française*, LIV (1908), p. 38.

[45] Cf. Boisgelin's opinion, Lavaquery, II, pp. 115, 119.

[46] Gruget, *Histoire de la Constitution civile du Clergé en Anjou (Anjou hist.*, II, pp. 615–16). Gruget will be quoted often in this chapter. Mathiez's warning (*Annales Révolutionnaires*,. III (1910), pp. 133–4) concerning the reliability of works of this kind must be borne in mind; even so, Gruget, biased as he was, appears to have been an extremely honest man, whose word may be taken on matters of fact, though not of interpretation.

[47] Port, *Vendée*, I, p. 118.

[48] Gruget, *Anjou hist.*, II, p. 623.

[49] The P.V. of proceedings on 16 January is in A.M.L. 1 L 962. On this first day curés Gaudin and Follenfant took the oath, vicaires Taillebuis, Fautras and Viger, eight Oratorians, two Cordeliers and one Carmelite, and the two Mongazons, minor chaplains of the cathedral.

[50] One should add Voillement, *maître de musique* of the cathedral, to this list.

[51] Cf. E. Bouchez, 'Nicolas Servant, curé de Nanteuil-la-Fosse, vicaire épiscopal de la Marne', *Travaux de l'Académie Nationale de Reims*, CXXI (1910), p. 112.

[52] Gruget, *Anjou hist.*, II, p. 617.

[53] *L'Observateur Provincial, 5e Partie*, no. 23 (11 Jan.), pp. 85–7; no. 24, pp. 89–91. *Journal du Département de Maine-et-Loire*, no. 1 (c. 12 Jan.); no. 2 (19 Jan.), p. 28.

[54] Port, *Dict.*, I, p. 323.

[55] Gruget, *Anjou hist.*, II, pp. 618, 620, 624.

[56] Besnard, I, p. 237.

[57] Gruget, *Anjou hist.*, II, p. 618.

[58] *ibid.*, III, p. 47.

[59] Printed in *Anjou hist.*, XIV, pp. 40–1.

[60] Gruget, *Anjou hist.*, II, p. 620; III, p. 49.

[61] The brother at Mazé retracted later (*Anjou hist.*, VI, pp. 327–9).

[62] The examples paraphrased above are from G. Aubert, 'La Révolution à Douai', *Ann. hist. Rev. Franc.*, XII (1935), p. 535; H. Hausser, 'Le Serment à la Constitution civile dans deux paroisses Bourguignonnes', *La Révolution Française*, LV (1908), p. 40; and 'Registre de l'état civil de Mouy, Oise, 1791', *ibid.*, I (1881), p, 341.

[63] *Discours patriotique, sur les avantages de la Constitution, considérés par rapport à la Religion, et par rapport à l'Humanité*, Angers, 3rd ed., 1790 (B. Angers H 2036), pp. 7, 9, 5. The *proc. gen. syndic* of the Department acknowledged receipt of a copy of this pamphlet on 21 Nov. 1790 (A.M.L. 1 L 124).

[64] *Journal du Département de Maine-et-Loire*, no. 2 (19 Jan.), p. 12.

[65] Gruget, *Anjou hist.*, II, pp. 620, 623.

[66] Meynier, *La Revellière-Lépeaux*, p. 238.

[67] *Discours prononcé par M. Bénaben de l'Oratoire . . . le jour de sa réception au Club des Amis de la Constitution . . .*, (B. Angers H 2036), p. 2.

[68] He took the oath on 27 Dec. (*Moniteur*, no. 362, p. 1493). For an argument to follow his example, see *proc. gen. syndic* District to a country curé 14 Jan. (A.M.L. 1 L 194*).

[69] Gruget, *Anjou hist.*, III, p. 48. Du Chesnay took the oath himself, but on 21 March 1793 he retracted (Port, *Dict.*, III, p. 490).

[70] Port, *Dict.*, I, p. 786.

[71] According to Gruget. Local rumour ascribed a cynical boutade of the same

kind to Bassereau, curé of Lion d'Angers (Deniau, *Histoire de la Vendée*, I, p. 137).

[72] Besnard, II, pp. 35–6.

[73] 'Le clergé du Ronceray et de la Trinité avant la Révolution', *Anjou hist.*, XXVI, p. 139; Gruget, *Anjou hist.*, III, pp. 233, 49, 54.

[74] Gruget, *Anjou hist.*, III, pp. 240, 225–6. A contemporary in another part of France thought that satisfaction with a régime which had released them from their vows and awarded good pensions was an important motive inclining monks to become jurors (A. Cournot, *Souvenirs*, ed. E. P. Bottinelli, 1913, p. 28).

[75] 'Les derniers jours de ... Saint-Aubin', *Anjou hist.*, XVII, pp. 67 ff.; 'Les derniers jours ... de la Baumette', *Anjou hist.*, XLI, p. 28; Gruget, *Anjou hist.*, III, pp. 225–6; Armel, *Rev. d'Anjou*, 1907, pp. 16–21. For Soulet's text-book for use in seminaries of the Constitutional Church, see Barruel, *Journal ecclésiastique*, June 1792, pp. 757–814.

[76] Gruget, *Anjou hist.*, III, pp. 53–4.

[77] Gruget, *Anjou hist.*, IV, p. 49. According to the *Journal du Département de Maine-et-Loire*, no. 2 (Jan. 19), pp. 14–15, Ferré delayed because he was not sure whether to swear before the municipality of Angers or that of Saint-Samson, which was due to be reunited to Angers shortly.

[78] 'Corr. de M. Houdet', *Anjou hist.*, XII, p. 269.

[79] Port, *Dict.*, II, p. 144.

[80] E.g. at Revel in the diocese of Toulouse, and at Nancy; see A. Thoroude, *De la vente des Biens Nationaux particulièrement dans le District de Revel* (1912), pp. 63–5, and G. Constantin, 'Le Serment constitutionnel dans la Meurthe', *Revue des Questions historiques*, XC (1911), p. 460.

[81] See for a fine example 'Documents: La Commune de Baubigny (Côte d'Or) pendant la Révolution', *La Révolution Française*, LXIV (1913).

[82] For the importance of the difference between these two formulae, see Reusse, *La Constitution Civile ... en Alsace*, I, p. 83.

[83] Mathiez, *Rome et le Clergé ...*, pp. 473–4.

[84] Municipal Register (*Mairie*), II, p. 12(b). cf. P.V. Dept., 24 Jan. 1791 (A.M.L. 1 L, 69)—'il serait dangereux de laisser des ecclésiastiques fonctionnaires publics éluder la loi'.

[85] 17 June 1790, *Moniteur*, no. 169, p. 690.

[86] '*Observations sur la nouvelle circonscription des paroisses, par M. l'abbé Grégoire, député*, Barruel, *Collection ecclésiastiastique*, VII, pp. 3–22.

[87] Gruget, *Anjou hist.*, II, p. 622.

[88] Gruget, *Anjou hist.*, II, p. 617.

[89] Leflon, *La Crise révolutionnaire ...*, p. 73.

[90] Gruget, *Anjou hist.*, III, p. 159. Bardoul took the oath on 23 Jan.

[91] Lavaquery, *Boisgelin*, II, p. 137.

[92] 'Corr. de M. Houdet', *Anjou hist.*, XII, pp. 268–9. (cf. *La Révolution Française*, LXI (1911), pp. 457–9).

[93] 'Le Serment si impolitiquement ordonné,' said an Angevin curé who took the oath (curé Rousseau of Mazé to Rangeard, 8 Nov. 1791, B. Angers MS. 634).

[94] Port, *Dict.*, I, p. 645. Chatizel and Martinet both signed the minority protest regretting the Assembly's refusal to declare the Catholic, Apostolic and Roman religion the exclusive religion of the state (Barruel, *Collection*, XIV, pp. 10, 11).

[95] Gruget, *Anjou hist.*, II, p. 618.

[96] Gruget, *Anjou hist.*, III, p. 227.

[97] Beurrier, 30 Sept. (B. Angers MS. 616).

[98] *L'Observateur Provincial, 5ᵉ Partie*, nos. 17 and 18, pp. 61–3. It was Delaunay who ten months later brought up the case of a married benefice holder of Maine-et-Loire and by so doing obtained tacit (secular) agreement to clerical marriage (P. Sagnac. *La Législation civile de la Révolution Française* (1898), pp. 281–2). In 1789 La Revellière had campaigned against the obligation of clerical celibacy (A. Mathiez, *Les origines de cultes révolutionnaires* (1904), p. 66).

[99] *Journal du Département de Maine-et-Loire*, no. 1, p. 27. The first 'civic baptism' in France apparently took place at Strasbourg on 13 June 1790 (Mathiez, *op. cit.*, p. 43). So far, of course, these patriotic ceremonies were additions to, not substitutes for, religious ceremonies (see M. Dommanget, 'La Dechristianisation à Beauvais', *Annales Révolutionnaires*, VII (1916), pp. 235–6, and 'Les Sacrements civiques', *ibid.*, XI (1919), p. 170.

[100] Bougler, *Mouvement Provincial* I, p. 495.

[101] 'La Faculté de Théologie d'Angers à la fin du 18ᵉ siècle', *Anjou hist.*, XXIII, pp. 20–2. In addition to canons and parish priests, the following were doctors of the Faculty—Montalant of the little Seminary, Turmeau of the Seminary, dom Mansel of Saint-Aubin, and Maumousseau, an honorary canon of Saint-Pierre (for the first of these, see *Anjou hist.*, XIX, pp. 117–18).

[102] Gruget, *Anjou hist.*, II, pp. 48–9.

[103] See his appeal to the Dept., 22 March 1791 (Port's note in Besnard, I, p. 237).

[104] Besnard, I, p. 237.

[105] Letourneau, *Séminaire*, p. 222; 'Le Séminaire d'Angers', *Anjou hist.*, XI, pp. 492–3.

[106] Letter of a director to the curé of Alonnes, 18 Feb. 1791 ('Les Sulpiciens d'Angers pendant la Révolution', *Anjou hist.*, XXVI, pp. 83–4).

[107] 'M. Elias, directeur au Séminaire d'Angers, 1739–1793', *Anjou hist.*, XXI, pp. 74–5.

[108] 'Le Séminaire . . .', *Anjou hist.*, XI, pp. 492–3.

[109] *Nouvelles ecclésiastiques*, 25 June 1764, p. 103.

[110] 'L'Aumonier du Calvaire d'Angers contre la Constitution civile du Clergé', *Anjou hist.*, XLIII, pp. 46–8.

[111] Cotelle de la Blandinière to Rangeard, Aug. 1791 (Letourneau, *Séminaire*, p. 223).

[112] In the debates on Avignon, 17 Nov. 1790 (*Moniteur*, no. 324, p. 1339).

[113] *Traité du pouvoir des évêques de France sur les empêchements de marriage* (1782), B. Angers S.T. 814, pp. vii–viii. It was standard doctrine that the Pope was subject to a General Council (*Conférences ecclésiastiques sur les synodes pour servir de suite d'appui aux Conférences d'Angers en formant le quatrième volume de celles sur la hiérarchie* (B.M. 862 a 1 20), p. 195).

[114] Chatizel, *Traité*, pp. 82, 121–2.

[115] *ibid.*, pp. 38, 123.

[116] *ibid.*, pp. 163–4.

[117] *ibid.*, pp. viii–ix, 6–7, iii. Cf. the insistence of an Angevin curé—very critical of the exactions of Papal officials —that nothing must break French unity with the Papacy. ('F. F. curé de H . . .', *Instructions* (1789), p. 14).

[118] Gruget, *Anjou hist.*, III, pp. 228–9.

[119] P.V. Dept., 20 Jan. 1791 (A.M.L. 1 L 69).

[120] A. Nat. D XIX 80, file 611, nos. 20 and 23.

[121] For La Providence, see *Anjou hist.*, XIV, p. 41; for the Ursulines, Bois, *La Vie Scolaire*, p. 113; for La Croix, *Proc. syndic* District, 7 May 1791 (A.M.L. 1 L 194); for the Carmelites, the same, 17 April 1791 (A.M.L. 1 L 194). When one of the Mongazon brothers, chaplain of La Providence, announced his

intention of taking the oath there was a sensation among the nuns. 'They run thither and hither, crying out scandal, impiety and heresy. A runner is despatched to fetch the ecclesiastical superior (i.e. the former dean of Saint-Martin) who responds at once to the invitation of the despairing convent.' (*Journal du Département de Maine-et-Loire*, no. 2 (19 Jan.), p. 9). The nuns explained the dismissal of Mongazon by saying they preferred to have the dean saying their masses as he asked no fee (17 Jan. 1791, A.M.L. 13 Q 14). The Frères des Écoles Chrétiennes had decided to leave town if the oath was asked of them (*Anjou hist.*, XXXI, pp. 32–6).

[122] According to the *Nouvelles ecclésiastiques* he acted 'par déférence pour la pluralité' (4 June 1792, p. 90).

[123] Gruget, *Anjou hist.*, IV, pp. 361–2. He announces his intention of leaving soon in a letter to a friend on 1 March (A.M.L. 1 L 959 microfilm).

[124] 'L'application de la Constitution civile du Clergé en Maine-et-Loire', *Anjou hist.*, XVI, p. 62. For the municipality's purchase of 3,755*l.* worth of furniture, Register (*Mairie*), II, p. 67(b).

[125] Port, *Vendée*, I, pp. 145–8.

[126] *L'Observateur Provincial, 6ᵉ Partie*, no. 15, p. 57.

[127] Gruget, *Anjou hist.*, IV, pp. 361–2, 366–7.

[128] J. Denais, 'Hugues Pelletier, évêque constitutionnel de Maine-et-Loire', *Rev. hist. lit. arch. Anjou*, XII (1874), p. 159.

[129] *A Frère Hugues Pelletier, invaseur du siège épiscopal d'Angers* (see Bourgain, *Rev. d'Anjou*, XXXIII (1890), p. 71).

[130] Port, *Dict.*, III, p, 69.

[131] P.V. in A.M.L. 1 L 960. There had been a 'false start' with the elections on 7 March (*Journal du Département de Maine-et-Loire*, no. 5, p. 110). The parish of Saint-Laud was taken over on 27 March ('La Constitution civile du Clergé et la municipalité d'Angers', *Anjou hist.*, XIII, pp. 368–9).

[132] Besnard, I, p. 46. On 18 Feb. the parish of Saint-Laud had petitioned to be allowed to retain its pastor (A.M.L. 1 L 960).

[133] Gruget, *Anjou hist.*, IV, pp. 494–7. People now went to the masses of non-jurors in the chapels of nunneries, etc. (P.V. District, 27 April 1791, A.M.L. 2 L 2; Dept. to President of the National Assembly, 23 April, A.M.L. 1 L 125).

CHAPTER XV

[1] Letourneau, *Séminaire*, p. 179.

[2] Parish Register, État Civil, Hôtel de Ville, Angers, GG 183, f. 329.

[3] 'M. Le Noir de la Cochetière, vicaire général d'Angers', *Anjou hist.*, XXXIX, pp. 148–9.

[4] Leflon, *Bernier*, p. 10; 'L'application de la Constitution civile du clergé en Maine-et-Loire', *Anjou hist.*, XVI, p. 61.

[5] Meynier, *La Revellière-Lépeaux*, pp. 279–80; Port, *Vendée*, I, p. 208; for similar orders to Saint-Serge, 25 July 1791, A.M.L. 13 Q 4. For the departure of the directors of the Seminary, see J. Meilloc, *Les Serments pendant la Révolution* (ed. Uzureau, 1904), pp. 10–11.

[6] 'Les Frères des Écoles Chrétiennes à Angers (1791)', *Anjou hist.*, XXXI, pp. 32–6; Rigault, III, pp. 54, 131, 167–8.

[7] A.M.L. 1 L 959 (20 May 1791 and late July).

[8] Port, *Vendée*, I, p. 208.

[9] Blordier-Langlois, I, pp. 197–200; *Discours prononcé par M. Bénaben de l'Oratoire ... le jour de sa réception au Club des Amis de la Constitution ...* (B. Angers H 2036), p. 2.

[10] Port, *Vendée*, I, pp. 128, 135–7; *Dict.*, I, p. xxxiii. For clerical propaganda against the Constitutional Church in the countryside, see Deniau, I, pp. 133–5.

[11] Port, *Vendée*, I, pp. 196, 206–7, 389–90.

[12] Port, *Vendée*, I, pp. 214–25. A draft of this order is found in the Soland papers, A.M.L. J 3135.

[13] F. Grille, *Lettres ... et documents sur ... la formation ... du 1ᵉʳ battalion des volontaires de Maine-et-Loire*, I, pp. 93–4.

[14] Meynier, *op. cit.*, p. 240. For Proust's masquerade, see above, p. 42.

[15] Port, *Vendée*, I, p. 230.

[16] Municipal Register (*Mairie*), II, pp. 68(b), 88–9, 91.

[17] Gruget, *Anjou hist.*, V, pp. 35–6, 39, 42, 41; *Nouvelles Affiches du Département de Maine-et-Loire*, I (19 Nov. 1791), p. 8; Blordier-Langlois, II, p. 115.

[18] Municipal Register (*Mairie*), II, p. 83(b); A.M.L. 19 Q 5 (17 Aug. 1791).

[19] See the description of the abbey in April 1792 in Municipal Register (*Mairie*), II, p. 177.

[20] Blordier-Langlois, I, pp. 203 ff.

[21] Copy of a letter to the Committee of Alienation in 1791 (A.M.L. I L 125). For examples of the sort of difficulties, see A.M.L. 19 Q 5 (Guillaume Janneau and A.M.L. II Q 55–6 (Pierre G...(?)...amier).

[22] 'Quelle doit être l'influence de la Révolution sur notre langue et sur notre littérature?' B. Angers MS. 1641 (92).

[23] Blordier-Langlois, I, pp. 353–55.

[24] Meynier, *op. cit.*, p. 243. Note that on 29 June a hundred armed men had raided the rectory of Soulaines, broken the furniture and expelled Chatizel from his parish. (Letter of Chatizel, 26 August 1791 in *Journal Ecclésiastique*, p. 85).

[25] On 1 Nov. religious communities re-opened their chapels to the public—but they were compelled to close them again on the 4th (A.M.L. 2 L 130, no. 75).

[26] Rangeard to the Department, 28 Nov. (?) 1791 (A.M.L. 1 L 966). The particular trouble here was that parishioners of Brain objected to the union of their parish with that of Andard.

[27] J. Leflon, *La crise révolutionnaire*, p. 90.

[28] Meynier, pp. 250, 251, 252.

[29] Port, *Vendée*, I, pp. 304–5; 'La persécution religieuse en Maine-et-Loire', *Andegaviana*, XXVI, p. 348.

[30] Chassin, *La Préparation de la Guerre de Vendée*, II, pp. 369–77.

[31] List in *Anjou hist.*, 1905, pp. 474 ff.

[32] Municipal Register (*Mairie*), III, p. 1.

[33] Port, *Vendée*, I, pp. 349–55; Godard-Faultrier, *Le Champ des Martyrs* (2nd ed.), p. 72. According to Deniau (I, p. 194) canon Gilly of the cathedral, infirm and almost blind, was carried to prison on a chair. Barruel (*Histoire du Clergé pendant la Révolution* (1793), p. 231) tells this story of canon de la Forestière, who died soon after being imprisoned. For the unpopularity of refractory priests at this time, see Bois, *La Vie scolaire*, p. 179, and the letter of 28 June in B. Angers MS. 627. For subsequent Angevin support for a 'dictatorship of public safety', see J. Belin, *La logique d'une idée-force. L'idée d'utilité sociale pendant la Révolution, 1789–92* (1939), pp. 541–2.

[34] Canon Bizotin of Saint-Maurille and Martin a sub-cantor of the cathedral, broken by illness, offered to subscribe to the Civil Constitution of the Clergy to avoid arrest. The mayor, Pilastre, a friend of La Revellière-Lépeaux, went to their lodgings to receive their subscriptions and humanely offered to them the new oath of Liberty and Equality, which was easier to tender consciences than the old oath to the Civil Constitution (F. Uzureau, 'A propos du Serment de

Liberté et d'Egalité', *Révolution Française*, LXX (1917), pp. 445–8). Canon Bardoul took the civic oath on 20 June (Municipal Register (*Mairie*), III, p. 2).

[35] As there were no students the servants were paid off on 26 June (Dept. to District, A.M.L. 2 L 132).

[36] Blordier-Langlois, I, pp. 244–5; Meilloc, *Les Serments pendant la Révolution*, pp. 15–16, cf. p. 138, above.

[37] According to Deniau (I, p. 202) they received sordid treatment by their guards here.

[38] Port, *Vendée*, II, pp. 15–16, 26–30. Apart from discomfort, they were not victimized en route, except by being targets for obscenities (Barruel, *Histoire du clergé pendant la Révolution* (1793), pp. 552–3).

[39] A. Lallié, *Les Noyades de Nantes* (2nd ed., 1879), p. 126.

[40] For conditions, see letter in Godard-Faultrier, *Le Champ des Martyrs* (3rd ed., 1869), p. 277.

[41] See below, p. 292. For their good reception on landing, see A.-C. Sabatié, *La déportation révolutionnaire du clergé Français* (2 vols., 1910), I, p. 162.

[42] A.M.L. 1 L 963 (under 4 Dec.).

[43] A.M.L. L 375, see 'Les 19 curés de la ville d'Angers pendant la Révolution', *Anjou hist.*, XII, pp. 136–8.

[44] Blordier-Langlois, I, pp. 259–60.

[45] 'Situation du Sieur pierre tremblé chanoine à Saint-Martin à Angers', A.M.L. II E 2643.

[46] Bois, *La Vie scolaire*, pp. 117–18, 506–7; Queruau-Lamerie, 'Les religieuses d'Angers et de Beaufort pendant la Révolution', *Rev. d'Anjou*, LXXXI (1920). For the orders to leave (Sept. 1792) and subsequent inventories and sales, see A.M.L. 13 Q 3 (Ronceray), 13 Q 8 (Sainte-Catherine, Carmelites, La Croix), etc.... Ronceray became a military hospital (A.M.L. 2 L 134—16 pluviôse an II).

[47] Bois, *La Vie scolaire*, pp. 106–7. Sometime in 1792 Mame the printer purchased the buildings of the collège (F. Grille, *Bric-à-brac*, I, p. 175).

[48] Blordier-Langlois, I, pp. 245–6, 207–9. For damage to the church of the Augustins, see A.M.L. 13 Q 6. The tomb of Bertrand de Beauvau (see above, p. 219) was destroyed.

[49] Municipal Register (*Mairie*), III, pp. 44(b), 48(b) (19 Sept. 1792); F. Grille, *La Vendée en 1793* (1851), II, pp. 30–1.

[50] See Uzureau in *Rev. Mabillon*, XI (1921), p. 317.

[51] Municipal Register (*Mairie*), III, p. 76(b) (15 Nov. 1792).

[52] Blordier-Langlois, I, pp. 266, 269 (Dec., 1792).

[53] Besnard, II, p. 387 (Port's note).

[54] For another example of his complacency towards patriots (19 June 1792), see M. Saché, 'Le Citoyen Morainville, 1759–1807', *Rev. d'Anjou*, 1921, p. 136.

[55] Bois, *La Vie scolaire*, p. 131.

[56] 28 Dec. 1791 and 27 July 1792 (Uzureau, 'Le premier mariage civil à Angers', *Annales révolutionnaires*, VII (1914), pp. 56–3); *Anjou hist.*, VII, p. 620.

[57] Bois, *Les Fêtes révolutionnaires à Angers de l'an II à l'an VIII* (1793–99) (1929), pp. 8–9.

[58] Port, *Dict.*, III, p. 748.

[59] On 8 March 1793 the municipality authorized dom Renaudin, prior of Saint-Serge, to depart for Spain. He probably stayed in Nantes (F. Rousseau, *Moines Bénédictins martyrs et confesseurs de la foi pendant la Révolution* (1926), p. 204). But in view of the charges against him, Bernier would have been in danger if he had come forward.

[60] Leflon, *Bernier*, p. 14n. One of the Sulpicien directors of the Seminary of Angers perished in the September massacres (Meilloc, p. 11).

[61] Port, *Vendée*, II, pp. 58–9.

[62] Chassin, *La Vendée patriote, 1793-1800* (1894), II, p. 79.

[63] *ibid.*, II, pp. 95–98.

[64] *ibid.*, II, pp. 102, 331. The municipality had given permission for the cap of liberty to be hoisted there on 24 July 1792 (Register (*Mairie*), III, p. 16(b)).

[65] Though he preached a two-hour sermon there on the wickedness of the sale of church property (Deniau, II, p. 194).

[66] Blordier-Langlois, I, pp. 312, 315, 318, 276, 365. For Rosé, Port, *Dict.*, III, p. 305; for Boniface, see below, p. 289. The committee requisitioned a confessional from the church of Saint-Laud for a sentry box (A.M.L. 13 Q 23).

[67] Port, *Dict.*, p. 81.

[68] Blordier-Langlois, I, p. 336.

[69] Bois, *La Vie scolaire*, pp. 231–3.

[70] Queruau-Lamerie, *Rev. d'Anjou*, 1920, p. 9.

[71] Blordier-Langlois, I, p. 324.

[72] Bois, pp. 108, 239–40. In Aug. 1793 Mévolhan petitioned the Convention to colonize Australia—'this isle of the Southern Sea will one day be peopled with free men who will owe to the French in Europe their happiness and their liberty' (Port, *Dict.*, II, p. 669).

[73] Blordier-Langlois, II, p. 374.

[74] Besnard, II, p. 54 (Port's note). Taillebuis, constitutional curé of Saint-Nicolas, followed their example (*Anjou hist.*, VI, p. 284).

[75] Port, *Dict.*, III, p. 224.

[76] Bois, *Fêtes*, pp. 19, 20, 22. For Coquille, see above, p. 266. He had had a rough passage as constitutional curé of Beaupreau (Port, *Vendée*, II, p. 33n.).

[77] P. Marchegay and E. Mabille, *Chroniques des Églises d'Anjou* (Soc. de l'hist. de France, 1869), p. iv; C. Urseau, *Cartulaire noir de la Cathédrale d'Angers* (1908), p. vi.

[78] For the siege, see Blordier-Langlois, I, pp. 369 ff.; Chassin, *La Vendée patriote*, III, p. 351; F. Grille, *Bric-à-brac*, I, p. 378.

[79] The *Club de l'Est* was finally ended on 23 March 1794; the *Club de l'Ouest* was installed in La Trinité on 24 May.

[80] There were 1,123 death sentences passed in Angers. In addition 1,020 people died in the prisons as a result of bad conditions (Greer, *The Incidence of the Terror* (1935), pp. 32, 141–2).

[81] Blordier-Langlois, I, p. 430. Cf. Boniface's crazy 'Vive la Guillotine' letter of 16 ventôse, an II in B. Angers MS. 616.

[82] Chassin, *op. cit.*, III, p. 348.

[83] Bois, *Fêtes*, pp. 26–7. Bardou, formerly of the cathedral choir, sang republican canticles (Port, *Dict.*, I, p. 205).

[84] *Anjou hist.*, XII, pp. 146, 275; Besnard II, p. 63 (Port's note); Deniau III, pp. 572, 563, 573–4; Uzureau, *Un martyr de la foi en 1794* (1913).

[85] F. Rousseau, *Moines Bénédictins martyrs et confesseurs de la foi pendant la Révolution*, p. 167; Uzureau, 'Dom Chabanel prieur de l'Evière', *Méms. Soc. Agric.*, 1905, p. 418, *Andegaviana*, 1907, pp. 192–201.

[86] Port, *Dict.*, II, p. 120 (citing Grille). Queruau-Lamerie says she died in prison.

[87] Port, *Dict.*, II, pp. 317–18; L. La Combe, 'Denise-Marie Boussinot, supérieure de la communauté de Saint-Charles', *Anjou hist.*, I (1900–1), pp. 594, 726–7; Meilloc, p. 21. She did not formally become a sister until

March 1796 (A. Crosnier, *Histoire de la Congrégation de Saint-Charles d'Angers*, p. 78).

[88] Uzureau, *Les filles de la charité d'Angers pendant la Révolution: martyre des sœurs Mairie-Anne et Odile* (1902), p. 48.

[89] Uzureau, *La déportation des religieuses angevines* (1909); *Anjou hist.*, 1903, pp. 34 ff.; 1906, pp. 459 ff.

[90] Blordier-Langlois, I, pp. 414-15. According to Lallié, they were deported, according to Godard-Faultier (*Le Champ des Martyrs* (2nd ed., 1855), p. 115) 14 of them were suffocated by the stifling conditions on the boat taking them to Nantes.

[91] List in Queruau-Lamerie, 'Les Prêtres d'Angers noyés à Nantes...' *Rev. d'Anjou*, LXIX (1914), pp. 261-4. See also *Corresp. et papiers de Bénaben* (ed. A. Launay 1886), pp. 144-162. Some priests were also marched out of Angers; curé Gouppil of Saint-Evroul died at Doué after a death-march conducted by his nephew the apothecary (6 Dec.), see *Anjou hist.*, XII, p. 141, and 'Le terroriste Gouppil', *ibid.*, XII, pp. 192 ff. A minor ecclesiastic of La Trinité, the abbé Cochet also died at Doué (Deniau, III, pp. 306-7, 604).

[92] Blordier-Langlois, I, pp. 260-1; dom F. Chamard, *Les Vies des saints personnages de l'Anjou* (3 vols., 1863), III, p. 501. There is a pathetic note of the sale of Robin's effects, 10 Sept. 1794, in A.M.L. II E 2390. They brought 244*l.*—a coat and vest of black cloth went for 20*l.* to an old clothes dealer, 'la femme Perisseau'.

[93] 6 Dec. 1793, *Correspondence of Jean-Baptiste Carrier ... during his mission in Brittany, 1793-4*, ed. E. H. Carrier (1920), p. 141.

[94] C. Mellinet, *La Commune et la milice de Nantes* (n.d. 12 vols.), VIII, p. 146.

[95] G. Martin, *Carrier et sa mission à Nantes* (*Thèse*, Paris, 1924), p. 267.

[96] A. Lallié, *Les Noyades de Nantes* (2nd ed., 1879), pp. 153, 114, 126 (dom Champeaux had been scheduled for deportation to Spain in 1792 but had petitioned successfully against this).

[97] The full story is given by Lallié in *Rev. de Bretagne et Vendée*, 5th Ser., III (1878), pp. 286-7.

[98] Carrier, *Correspondence*, p. 150.

[99] Port, *Dict.*, I, p. 303. He was referring to the *noyades* in general. For another example of Bénaben's gloating over the defeated, see Chassin, *La Vendée patriote*, III, p. 420. For the phrase 'Château d'Eau', cf. G. Lenôtre, *Les Noyades de Nantes* (1912), p. 231.

[100] Bois, *La Vie scolaire*, pp. 431-2.

[101] See L. Jacob, *Fabre d'Églantine chef des 'Fripons'* (1946), pp. 187-8, 190-5, 312; A. Mathiez, *La Conspiration de l'Étranger* (1918), pp. 33, 43 ff.; D. L. Dowd, 'Jacques-Louis David, artist member of the Committee of General Security', *American Hist. Rev.*, LVII (1951-2), p. 885.

[102] It was then that Volney was released from prison. 'I find that the very word *ambition* oppresses me,' he wrote, and was preparing to retire to America for a while (see the correspondence of Volney and La Revellière-Lépeaux ed. A. Mathiez in *Annales Révolutionnaires*, III (1910), pp. 169-70, and H. Fleischmann, *ibid.*, p. 582, and Mathiez, 'Volney *commissaire observateur* en 1793'; *ibid.*, IV (1911), p. 532.

[103] Port, *Dict.*, I, p. 22.

[104] J.-B. Leclerc, *Essai sur la propagation de la musique en France, sa conservation et ses rapports avec le gouvernement*, Prairial, an IV (B.M. 557—d. 35(1)), p. 51.

[105] Bois, *Fêtes*, p. 75.

[106] Port, *Dict.*, III, p. 224. In the *Annales de Religion*, May 1795, he published

an appeal for religious liberty—the original is in B. Angers MS. 557, ff. 23(b)–24, 'Contre l'intolérance en matière de religion et de culte'.

> Le droit du culte qu'on est maître
> De rendre à l'auteur de son être,
> Ne peut nous être contesté,
> Et si l'on peut lier notre âme,
> C'est quand le pouvoir qu'on réclame
> Gêne d'autrui la liberté.

Two of the Frères des Écoles Chrétiennes were keeping a school at this period. They closed in September 1797 rather than take the oath of Fructidor (Rigault, III, pp. 418 ff.). In July 1797 the abbé Boussinot, brother of Denise-Marie, was baptizing and marrying in the chapel of the Petite-Pension (Crosnier, p. 82).

[107] During the period of repression from Nov. 1797 onwards, 141 clergy of Maine-et-Loire were arrested. On July 1798 domiciliary visits in search for priests, emigrés, Chouans and English spies were made in Angers (Blordier-Langlois, II, p. 106). But of our old clergy of Angers only one seems to have been deported (see below, p. 293).

[108] Noel certainly died before 1802; Gaudin died an emigré. Except where otherwise stated, in the following pages information concerning the fate of curés is taken from 'Les 19 curés de la ville d'Angers pendant la Révolution', *Anjou hist.*, XII, pp. 134 ff., and information concerning vicaires, from 'Les 23 vicaires de la ville d'Angers pendant la Révolution, *ibid.*, XII, pp. 272 ff. For Follenfant, *Anjou hist.*, VI, pp. 168–70.

[109] Port, *Vendée*, I, p. 208.

[110] 'M. Elias, directeur du Séminaire d'Angers (1737–93)', *Anjou hist.*, XXI, p. 75.

[111] 'Les derniers jours de l'abbaye de Saint-Aubin d'Angers', *Anjou hist.*, XVII (1916–17), pp. 167 ff.

[112] *Anjou hist.*, VI, p. 291.

[113] Deniau, II, pp. 310–11; cf. pp. 42, 86, 89. For a remarkable escape when like Balzac's Colonel Chabert he lay hidden for hours under dead bodies, see III, p. 404.

[114] J. Contrasty, *Le Clergé Français exilé en Espagne 1792–1802* (Toulouse 1910), pp. 259–9. Information about the Angevins on pp. 52–3, 103, 109, 114, 116, 118–19, 303.

[115] 'Nous étions plus de deux cents à sa table', said Breton afterwards (V. Pierre, 'Le clergé Français en Espagne', *Rev. des Questions Hist.*, LXXV (1904), pp. 491–2), Breton became tutor to a noble family (Port, *Dict.*, I, p. 489). For his brother, a captain in the Republican armies, see *Souvenirs du Comte de Contades* (1885), pp. 196–7.

[116] E.g. Breton, and Forest (Port, *Dict.*, II, pp. 173–4). Coulonnier curé of May (see above, p. 228) died in Spain in 1796 (Port, *Dict.*, II, p. 730).

[117] 'L'on comptait les morceaux destinés pour mon ventre' ('Aventures comico-tragiques du curé de Saint-Georges, François de nation, Espagnol de Force'—see Port, *Dict.*, II, p. 745).

[118] Chassin, *La Préparation de la guerre de Vendée*, III, p. 100. There were, however, many hardships (E. Sol, *La Prison, l'exil, les pontons* (1926), pp. 377–89).

[119] F.-X. Plasse, *Le Clergé français réfugié en Angleterre* (1886), II, p. 416.

[120] See his letter of 8 May 1815 in *Anjou hist.*, VI, pp. 327–9.

[121] But a French ship intercepted the vessel in which he was bound for London (from whence he was to leave for China), Port, *Dict.*, II, p. 696.

[122] Port, *Dict.*, I, p. 645.

[123] Régis de l'Estourbeillon, *Les Familles françaises à Jersey pendant la Révolution* (Nantes 1886), p. 317. Bancelin and de la Corbière escaped via Jersey (*ibid.*, pp. 276, 314). It is possible that the abbé Le Blanc of the diocese of Angers referred to as dying at Reading in 1797 was the minor ecclesiastic of that name at the cathedral of Angers (J. C. Weale, *Register of Burials in the old French Cemetery at Reading—Catholic Record Soc. Misc.*, XXXII (1932), p. 188). Dom Blisson of Saint-Serge is last heard of at Rouen in 1792 taking out a passport for Ostend (F. Rousseau, *op. cit.*, pp. 315, 179).

[124] 'Corresp. de M. Houdet', *Anjou hist.*, XII, p. 270; Godard-Faultrier, *Le Champ des Martyrs* (2nd ed., 1855), pp. 155-7.

[125] Régis de l'Estourbeillon, p. 408; Port, *Dict.*, II, p. 548; 'M. Louet, vicaire-général d'Angers, 1725-1800', *Anjou hist.*, XIX, p. 30; cf. *Anjou hist.*, IX, p. 48.

[126] F. Uzureau, *Un Prêtre français pendant l'émigration. M. de la Corbière, chanoine d'Angers* (1909), pp. 4, 32, 33. (Also printed in the *Revue de Lille*, 1909.)

[127] For Chaloigne, 'Les curés de Saint-Joseph d'Angers', *Anjou hist.*, XIII, pp. 649-50n.; for Follenfant, nephew of the curé of that name, *Anjou hist.*, VI, pp. 168-70 (he hid at Laval for part of the time, see Deniau, III, p. 616); for Mauxion, vicaire de La Trinité, *Anjou hist.*, VI, pp. 168-70. Pineau, an ex-Cordelier, also remained concealed in Angers ('Le clergé de Saint-Barthélemy-lès-Angers pendant la Révolution', *Anjou hist.*, XXVI, p. 25). One of the pious ladies who concealed Gruget was the sister of La Revellière-Lépeaux (Deniau, III, p. 59).

[128] V. Pierre, *La Terreur sous le Directoire* (1887), II, p. 443. Dom Boislinard of Saint-Nicolas and dom Dagorgne cellarer of Saint-Serge are also found in the prisons of the Île de Ré and Oléron (F. Rousseau, *op. cit.*, pp. 343-4, 315).

[129] 'Le Séminaire d'Angers', *Anjou hist.*, XI, p. 494.

[130] Where he enjoyed the company of Marmontel, see *Memoirs of the life of Marmontel written by himself* (4 vols., 1805), IV, pp. 271-2.

[131] A. Nat. AA 62, Carton 1550. Plaq. 3^A, no. 4. For his interrogation by the police in 1796, see A. Nat. F⁷ 3682, cit. Uzureau in Meilloc, p. 27; for his refusal to ally with the Constitutional Church, see P. Pisani, *L'Église de Paris et la Révolution* (4 vols., 1909), II, p. 231.

[132] Copy of letter of Lecoz bishop of Rennes, 13 Nov. 1797 (A.M.L. I L 959).

[133] 27 Jan. 1798, A.M.L. I L 959.

[134] Port, *Dict.*, I, p. 771.

[135] *Enquête administrative, 1796* (A.M.L. 378), printed in *Anjou hist.*, XIV, p. 504.

[136] *ibid.*, p. 504.

[137] Queruau-Lamerie, 'Les Fêtes décadaires d'Angers et l'Institut de musique du citoyen Voillemont', *Rev. d'Anjou*, 1922, p. 35.

[138] See above, p. 287, also 'Discours lus à l'autel de la cathédrale sur la Religion' (1797), B. Angers MS. 639, ff. 121-37.

[139] 'Les Brittaniques, Ode', B. Angers MS. 557, ff. 11(b)-16(b). This ode was read publicly after his death at the *Fête de la Paix* (10 nivôse an VI), Bois, *Fêtes*, pp. 138-9.

[140] Gazier, 'Henri Grégoire', *Rev. hist.*, IX (1879), pp. 116-17n.

[141] Port, *Dict.*, III, p. 81.

[142] M. Chartier, 'A travers les papiers Caprara...', *Rev. du Nord*, XXIV (1938), pp. 189, 193, 190-1.

[143] 'Les derniers jours de l'abbaye de Saint-Aubin', *Anjou hist.*, XVII, pp. 67 ff.; Besnard, II, pp. 125, 105.

[144] *Enquête*, 1796, *Anjou hist.*, XIV, p. 503.

[145] *ibid.*, pp. 506, 503. Loyau died in 1799 or thereabouts (Armel, *Rev. d'Anjou*, 1907, p. 16).

[146] Its buildings were a ruin pervaded by the stench of rotting cows' feet left there by the managers of a short-lived tallow factory (A.M.L. 16 Q 2, report of 25 prairial, an III).

[147] Port, *Dict.*, I, pp. 478-9.

[148] Bois, *Fêtes*, pp. 84, 108, 115, 131; Bois, *La Vie scolaire*, p. 339.

[149] *Etienne Bernier ... Lettres*, ed. J. Leflon (Reims, 1938), p. 7.

[150] Blordier-Langlois, II, p. 393.

[151] Bois, *La Vie scolaire*, pp. 488, 475; Rigault, III, p. 455.

[152] On 19 Feb. 1800 it was reported that 'la reprise du culte catholique est générale' (Uzureau, 'La Séparation de l'Église et de l'État dans un grand diocèse (1800-2)', *Rev. des Sciences ecclésiastiques et de la science catholique*, VIII (1907), pp. 701-12). In 1800 M. Meilloc began sending young Angevins up to Paris to be clandestinely ordained by the bishop of Saint-Papoul (see Mgr F. Trochu, *L'abbé Charles Foyer ... 1771-1842* (1948) for one of them). For Meilloc's activities concerning the question of oaths of fidelity to the state, see the letter of 10 Aug. 1801 in MS. Emery Saint-Sulpice), VIII, 8024. For other activities, Meilloc, pp. 30 ff.

[153] Blordier-Langlois, II, pp. 129-30.

[154] Uzureau, *loc. cit.*

[155] 'Quel bonheur pour vous et pour moi, mes Frères...' (*Etienne-Alexandre-Jean-Baptiste-Marie Bernier, Curé de l'Église de Saint-Laud, vicaire-général de la Rochelle ...* A.M.L. II E, 241).

[156] For bishop de Lorry's willingness to authorize fidelity to the constitution in 1800, see *Annales philosophiques, morales et littéraires ou suite des Annales catholiques* (1800), I, p. 272; II, p. 128; III (1801), pp. 151, 153. His pastoral letter of July 1801 ordering subjection to duly constituted secular authority is in MS. Emery (Saint-Sulpice), VIII, 8028. On 11 Aug. 1801 the prefect of Maine-et-Loire referred to him as 'a feeble character, never having at any time won public confidence' (Uzureau, '*Les premières applications du Concordat dans le diocèse d'Angers*' (1901), p. 3).

[157] Besnard, II, p. 20.

[158] Bernier, *Lettres*, p. 9.

[159] Cf. p. 62, above.

[160] Bernier, *Lettres*, p. 24 (he exaggerates).

[161] Leflon, *Bernier*, pp. 300-9 and for the incidents at Saint-Serge described below.

[162] Bernier, *Lettres*, p. 8. 'Voilà donc M^r notre Évêque installé. *Les Affiches d'Angers* assurent qu'il a fait le miracle de rétablir la concorde dans le clergé d'Angers ... quant à une réconciliation réelle, je n'y croirai jamais' (Letter of the abbé Minier, 18 prairial, an X, B Angers MS. 627).

[163] For Ferré's allies in this propaganda, see Port, *Dict.*, II, pp. 74-5; I, pp. 337-8. For the suggestion, early in 1801, that Ferré should become the new constitutional bishop, see Uzureau, 'Les Prêtres constitutionnels de Maine-et-Loire, 1795-1802' in Meilloc, p. 352.

[164] Port, *Dict.*, II, p. 144.

[165] 'Les curés de Saint-Joseph d'Angers', *Anjou hist.*, XIII, pp. 643, 649-50n.; L. Cosnier and E. Pavie, *Saint-Joseph d'Angers, L'église—la paroisse* (1896), pp. 24-6. One ought to mention that Chatizel returned to his parish at Soulaines.

[166] Leflon, *Bernier*, pp. 297-9.

[167] See his *Précis des dévotions à la Vraie Croix qui ont lieu dans l'église*

paroissiale de Saint-Laud (1804) reprinted in *La Semaine religieuse d'Angers*, 25 March 1928, pp. 250–1.

[168] Follenfant returned to Saint-Maurice as a vicaire before going to a parish. For these vicaires, see 'Le Clergé paroissial d'Angers et la Constitution Civile', *Anjou hist.*, VI, pp. 168 ff. and 'Les 23 vicaires. . . .'. *ibid.*, XII, pp. 272 ff. For Forest, formerly of Saint-Michel du Tertre, see Maupoint's biography (1864).

[169] Bernier, *Lettres*, p. 24.

[170] For the re-opening see the reminiscences of the abbé Quinton, *Au clergé angevin* (1841) in MS. Emery (Saint-Sulpice), III, 3153, pp. 7, 14.

[171] Blordier-Langlois, II, p. 143; Port, *Dict.*, II, p. 204; III, p. 604; II, p. 696; Blordier-Langlois, II, pp. 256–7; Port, *Dict.*, II, p. 640; Maupoint, *Vie de Mgr Montault-des-Isles* (1844), p. 396.

[172] *La Semaine religieuse d'Angers*, 8 June 1919.

[173] Armel, *Rev. d'Anjou*, 1907, pp. 53 ff.

[174] L. Cosnier, *Les Sœurs hospitalières* (2nd ed., 1882), pp. 59–62. See the comment in Gruget's unpublished memoirs in Godard-Faultrier, *Le Champ des Martyrs* (2nd ed., 1855), p. 192.

[175] One had joined during the Terror, one had taken the oath of Liberty and Equality to be able to carry on, one had been imprisoned (Crosnier, *Hist. de la Congrégation de Saint-Charles d'Angers*, p. 96).

[176] D. Gérard van Calven, 'Les Bénédictines de Notre-Dame du Calvaire', *Rev. Bénédictine*, X (1893); Uzureau, *Les premières applications du Concordat dans le diocèse d'Angers* (1901), p. 3.

[177] Bois, *La Vie scolaire*, pp. 397–8 (date 1799).

[178] *ibid.*, pp. 474, 480.

[179] *L'Education publique doit-elle être confiée au Clergé?* (November 1817), B. Nat. Ld⁴ 4362, p. 35.

[180] Port, *Dict.*, II, pp. 147, 30–1. Voillemont died in 1814. A requiem of his own composition was sung at the cathedral (*ibid.*, III, p. 748).

[181] For Brossier, *Anjou hist.*, XXIII, p. 84; for Marchand, *Rev. du Nord*, XXIV, pp. 190–3; for Jagault, Deniau, III, p. 591; for the monks of Lesvière, *Rev. Mabillon*, XI, p. 318; for Janin, *Anjou hist.*, VI, pp. 327–9; for Cordeliers and Capuchins, Armel, *Rev. d'Anjou*, 1907, pp. 19 ff.; for the Sulpiciens, Meilloc, *Les Serments pendant la Révolution*, pp. 11–12, and MS. Emery (Saint-Sulpice), I, 286 (date 1810); for the others, Port, *Dict.* under the names. Locatelli came back and lived near Angers from 1830 to his death in 1851.

[182] Besnard, II, pp. 258, 285, 140; I, p. 289.

[183] It would take us too far afield to give authorities for what follows. But Prosper Mérimée's description of the historic buildings of Angers in 1836 must be mentioned—*Notes d'un Voyage dans l'ouest de la France*, pp. 313–41. There had been a disastrous fire at the cathedral in 1831, but the façade had been rebuilt exactly as before.

[184] E. Renan, *Souvenirs d'Enfance et de Jeunesse* (1883), *Préface*.

[185] Joachim Du Bellay, *Les Regrets* (c. 1552), XXV.

SOURCES AND AUTHORITIES

(A) MANUSCRIPT MATERIALS

(I) *Departmental Archives, Maine-et-Loire*

Series C (Civil archives)

C 20 documents concerning the affair of the 'Trees' before the *Commission intermédiaire* of Provincial Assembly of Anjou.
C 24 concerning vicarage repairs, Saint-Pierre.
C 44 municipal petitions to royal Council.
C 166 P.V. *Commission intermédiaire* Prov. Ass.
C 190 Statistics sent in to the above.

Series D   D 31 archives Faculty of Theology

Series E   E 4337 street lighting, 1774

Notaries archives (see Catalogue by J. Levron, *Répertoire numérique des Séries IE et IIE, titres féodaux et titres de familles* (1947).
II E 2390 Curé Robin of Saint-Pierre.
II E 2643 Canon Tremblay of Saint-Martin.
II E 2750 Walsh, comte de Serrant.
I have not worked through the notaries archives listed in J. Levron's *Répertoire numérique de la sous-série 5 E Notaires* (1940).

Series F   III F³ pamphlets

III F 12 masonic documents

Series G (Secular Clergy)

See C. Port, *Inventaire Sommaire des archives départementales: Maine-et-Loire, Série G* (1880).

(i) *Archives of the Évêché*
G 4   Episcopal mandements, 1592–1789.
G 5   Brochures on ecclesiastical matters.
G 33 Accounts, etc., of temporalities.
G 35 Accounts of seminary (rendered to the bishop).

(ii) *Chapters*
(i) Cathedral of Saint-Maurice
(*a*) Capitular registers:
G 269 (1776–1780); G 270 (1767–1768); G 271 (1769–1775); G 272 (8 Oct. 1780–1785); G 273 (1786–1790).
(*b*) other documents:
G 275 reg. of collations to benefices
G 279 the *Grand archidiaconé*
G 348 Canon Brossier's personal accounts, 1766–1771, in an old register
(ii) Chapter of Saint-Laud:
G 940 register, 1755–1771; G 942 register, 1780–1790; G 946 personal accounts of dean Du Chilleau, 1777–1791.

(iii) Chapter of Saint-Martin:
    registers—G 1013 (1768–1782); G 1014 (1782–1790).
(iv) Chapter of Saint-Maurille:
    registers—G 1116 (1754–1778); G 1117 (1766–1790).
(v) Chapter of Saint-Pierre:
    registers—G 1170 (1750–1784); G 1171 (1783–1790).

(iii) *Parishes*

Lesvière
    G 1663 parish assembly deliberations, 1685–1791.
Saint-Denis
    G 1669 and G 1670 parish assembly deliberations, 1765–1780 and 1781–1785.
Sainte-Croix
    G 1676 docs. ref. Confraternity Holy Sacrament.
    G 1690 letters to curé Boumard, 1786–1789.
    G 1691 Boumard's papers.
    G 1692 Sermon notes, chiefly Boumard's.
    G 1693 extracts from the Fathers, etc., by Boumard.
Saint-Evroul
    G 1694 assembly deliberations.
    G 1696 parish accounts, 1729–1785.
Saint-Laud
    G 1697 assembly deliberations and wardens' accounts, 1782–1792.
    G 1698 legacies and foundations, 1530–1786.
Saint-Jacques
    G 1711 accounts, 1741–1791.
Saint-Julien
    G 1712 assembly deliberations, 1750–1790.
Saint-Maurice
    G 1722 assembly deliberations, 1751–1789.
Saint-Maurille
    G 1732 assembly deliberations, 1765–1789.
Saint-Michel de la Palud
    G 1764 parish accounts, 1598–1790.
    G 1762, 1763, 1765 registers of revenues and charges and inventory of documents (1740, 1733).
Saint-Pierre
    G 1777 parish accounts, to 1789.
    G 1781 Confraternity of the Purification.
La Trinité
    G 1785, 1786, 1787, 1792, documents concerning property and business affairs.

Note: Some documents of the type listed in this section are found elsewhere.
    (i) The magnificently kept parish accounts of Saint-Aignan are in A.M.L. 62 H 5, owing to its status as a *prieuré-cure* under the abbey de la Roe (Mayenne).

390   FRENCH ECCLESIASTICAL SOCIETY

(ii) Extracts of the parish proceedings of Saint-Pierre, not otherwise available, are in B. Angers DD 16 (years 1783–1784).

(iii) The accounts of warden Grille (Saint-Maurice) are in B. Angers 748, no. 8.

Series H (Regular Clergy)

See C. Port, *Inventaire sommaire des archives départementales antérieurs à 1790: Maine-et-Loire. Archives ecclésiastiques. Série H* (1898); and J. Levron, *Répertoire numérique des archives départementales de Maine-et-Loire antérieurs à 1790. Série H (fin)* (1954).

(a) *Benedictine Abbeys*
Saint-Aubin
H 2 privileges; H 4 capitular register, 1660–1758; H 12 repairs, 1480–1789; H 15 archives; H 34 revenues, 1786; H 151, file 2, repairs to ornaments.
Saint-Nicolas
H 444 register of receipts.
Saint-Serge
H 770 abbatial manse.

(b) *Toussaint*
H 1248 property, Sept. 1780; H 1255 register of payments to servants and tradesmen.

(c) *Mendicant Orders*
Augustinians
78 H 14 accounts.
Carmelite Friars
86 H 4 (Custumal); 86 H 20 (general eighteenth-century documents).
Cordeliers
87 H 32 receipts.
Dominicans
91 H 17 revenue, repairs, reconstruction; 91 H 32 receipts, 1781–1790; 91 H 33 expenditure, 1781–1790.
Minims
93 H 2 professions, deaths, 1752–1755, 1774–1778.

(d) *Écoles Chrétiennes*
90 H 1 acquisition of Rossignolerie, 1770–1778.
90 H 3 business, 1773–1796.

(e) *Oratory*
95 H 25 corresp., 1762–1773.

(f) *Missionaires*
94 H 1 professions, deaths.
(Note 62 H 5 is parish accounts Saint-Aignan, see above under G.)

Series J
J 809 dossier of Thomasseau de Cursay.

J 3134, 3135 and 3136. Papers of the Soland family, chiefly valuable for the papers of René-Jean Pantin.

Series L (Departmental and District administrative documents during the Revolution)

See J. Levron, *Répertoire numérique de la Série L. Administration départementale de 1789 à l'an VIII* (1951).

(a) *Minutes of Sessions of Department*
   1 L 68 (July–Dec. 1790); 1 L 69 (Jan.–March 1791); 1 L 9 (28 June 1790–14, July 1790); 1 L 9 (bis) (3 Nov. 1790–14, Dec. 1790); 1 L 12 (ter) (Printed minutes of Sessions).

(b) *Administrative Correspondence of Department*
   to District, National Assembly and its committees, etc. (1 L 124; 1 L 125; 1 L 155; 1 L 194*).
   to deputies of Maine-et-Loire at Paris (1.L. 152).
   to the constitutional bishop (1 L 959).
   1 L 909 is letters received ref. creation of a military academy.

(c) *Other documents in the Department files*
   1 L 962 P.V. of oaths to Civil Constitution, January 1791.
   1 L 963 refusal of oaths, lists of priests arrested or deported.
   1 L 966 organization of parishes.
   1 L 980 pensions of clergy.
   1 L 989 poor, etc.
   121 L.I. letters patent.
   141 L 4 proclamations.
   2 L 130 refractory clergy.
   2 L 132 clergy salaries.
   2 L 134 Ronceray.

(d) *Minutes of Sessions of District*
   2 L 2; 2. L. 3.
   1 L 981 ecclesiastical pensions.

Series Q (Sale, inventory and management of Church property)

(a) *Series of registers enumerating and estimating value of the property*
   II Q 1; III Q vols. I and II; III Q 2 vols. III and IV.

(b) *Inventories* of the religious houses, visitations by municipal and district authorities, replies of monks and nuns, sales of furniture.
   13 Q 1 to 13 Q 17:
      13 Q 1 (Saint-Aubin); 2 (Saint-Nicolas); 3 (Ronceray); 4 (Saint-Serge); 5 (Toussaint); 6 (Augustinians); 7 (Bon Pasteur); 8 (Calvaire, Capuchins, Carmelites, Carmel, Sainte-Catherine, Cordeliers, La Croix); 9 (Écoles Chrétiennes); 10 (La Fidelité); 11 (Jacobins); 12 (Lesvière); 13 (Oratoire); 14 (La Providence, Pénitentes, Lazaristes, Petit Pension); 15 (La Baumette); 16 (Ursulines); 17 (Visitation).

(c) *Inventories* by municipality and District of parish and capitular churches, sales, etc.
   13 Q 18–13 Q 27:
      13 Q 18 (Saint-Aignan); 20 (Saint-Denis); 21 (Saint-

Evroul); 22 (Saint-Jacques, Saint-Julien); 23 (Saint-Laud);
24 (Saint-Martin, Saint-Maurille, La Madeleine, Cathedral);
25 (Saint-Michel du Tertre, Saint-Michel de la Palud, Saint-
Pierre); 26 (Seminary, Saint-Samson); 27 (La Trinité).

(d) II Q 55–56. Corresp. District and Department concerning the
sequestration.

(e) 12 Q 126, 127, etc., to 177. The actual sales.

(f) 16 Q 1–26 petitions of creditors of religious institutions.

(g) 19 Q 1–4. Corresp. District with *Comité d'aliénation* of National
Assembly.

(h) 19 Q 5. Corresp. Department and District.

(i) 19 Q 7. Corresp. Municipality to District.

Archives of the Hôtel-Dieu in A.M.L. F 6, E 13 (correspondence).

(II) *Archives Nationales, Paris*

AA 62, dossier 1550, pls. 3^A, 3^B, 3^C.

B a 13 (pl. 1, liasse 9).

The key documents, including reports of the intendant, concerning the elections and *cahiers* for the Estates-General.

D XIX, Documents of the Ecclesiastical Committee of the National
Assembly.

A vast mass of cartons, indexed only by Departments. Indispensable to the local ecclesiastical historian in view of the large
numbers of petitions, statistical summaries, etc., which were forwarded to Paris from the provinces.

F^7 6774[26] Corresp. of marquis de Lostanges (markings by the Comité
de Sûreté Générale).

G 8 and G 8* the papers of the Clergy of France.

G 8 79 is the file of the Clergy of France concerning the augmentation
of *congrues*—arranged by dioceses.

G 8 168—feudal claims of *Monsieur*.

G 8 614.

G 8 620 pl. 49, pl. 50 and mass of following documents.

This is the chief dossier of the Clergy of France for Angevin
business—contains the original letters of the *syndic* of the diocese
to one of the agents-general or to M. Duchesne, the *avocat* of the
Clergy of France, and drafts of replies, chiefly by M. Duchesne.

G 8* 2557–2619; 2451–2466; 2781–2833.

A series of registers—of the business affairs of the Clergy of
France and of the meetings and opinions of its council of lawyers.
Affairs concerning individual dioceses can be located by reference
to the contemporary indices, G 8* 2622–2626; 2467; 2834.

H 1654 documents on the nunneries of the diocese of Angers.

H 1633 carton concerning the privileges of the town of Angers.

H 1509 Society of Agriculture—corresp. of dean Cotelle.

K 1144 (liasse 'Angers').

R^5 documents concerning the apanage of *Monsieur*.

T 222 personal papers of bishop de Lorry.

(III) *Municipal Library, Angers*—referred to as 'B. Angers'

  (*a*) *The archives of the old municipality of Angers*
      See C. Port, ~~*Inventaire analytique des archives anciennes de la*~~
    Mairie d'Angers (1861).

    (i) Municipal registers.
        BB 120 (July 1765–May 1769)
        BB 129 (Oct. 1779–July 1781)
        BB 130 July 1781–March 1784)
        BB 131 (March 1784–July 1785)
        BB 132 (July 1785–Sept. 1788)
        BB 133 (Nov. 1788–June 1789)
        BB 134 (June 1789–Feb. 1790)
        (The registers after this are kept at the Town Hall of Angers—see below).

    (ii) Other documents—
        CC 44; CC 172; DD 16 (Cemeteries, 1776–1786); FF 16–32 (abandoned children, 1764–1789); FF 33 (police measures concerning Lent butchers); GG 359 (Oratory, 1783); GG 363 (*Enfants trouvés*, 1774–1790).

  (*b*) *Documents in the Municipal Library proper*
    See *Catalogue général des manuscrits des bibliothèques publiques de France. Départements.* XXXI (1898).

This collection includes poems, sermons, works of erudition, discourses to the Academy, etc., private correspondence, journals of travels as well as collections of documents of institutions.

The numbers of the items quoted in the text are given below, but a note of the contents is given only in the case of the more important materials; in general, the references to the text describe the nature of the evidence that is being used.

B. Angers 259; 397; 412; 426; 489; 513; 553–4; 555; 556–7; 611; 616; 627; 638; 639; 711; 726–730 (Canon Brossier's 'L'ami du secrétaire', an alphabetical index and analysis of the capitular decisions of the Cathedral chapter up to 1761—in five volumes.)

733–734 (Register of the Clergy of Anjou, 1699–1713 and 1756–1790—'Regître pour servir à inserer les conclusions et délibérations du clergé d'Angers'—an essential source for the history of the diocese); 747; 748; 758; 767; 793; 878 (MS. volume, 'Maison de la Mission à Angers'); 1019; 1020 (Rangeard, 'État historique, ecclésiastique et civil de l'Anjou avant la Révolution de 1789'); 1045; 1059; 1154; 1157; 1172 (Thorode, 'Récensement des maisons d'Angers vers 1780'); 1204; 1244 (misleadingly mentioned in the printed catalogue of 1898—is not an official register of the Faculty of Theology, but a collection of precedents to aid monastic doctors against the secular ones); 1368; 1550; 1641; 1671; 1748; 1815 (a 19th-century copy); 1841 (Robin, 'Le pèlerin apostolique', 1750).

(IV) *Archives of the Mairie, Angers*

Here, the registers of the deliberations of the municipality from February 1790 are stored.

Vol. I   21 Feb. 1790–15 Dec. 1790
Vol. II   17 Dec. 1790–14 June 1792
Vol. III 14 June 1792–September 1792
Vol. IV   Sept. 1792–October 1793

(V) *État Civil, Angers*

The parish registers, both for the period before 1790 and the period after that date, are stored here.

I have used principally the register for the parish of Saint-Evroul GG 33 and those for Saint-Pierre GG 180, 181, 182, 183. A good deal of the information which one would normally have wished to abstract from parish registers has been fully used by Canon Uzureau in his many articles in *Anjou historique*.

(VI) *Library of the Seminary of Saint-Sulpice, Paris*

The papers of M. Emery; vols. I, IV, VIII, IX, X.

(VII) *The University Library, Rennes*

(This library is contained with the municipal library, but their MS. collections are still kept separate).

The following eighteenth-century items have an Angevin provenance. MSS. 208; 213 (Discourses to Academy of Angers); 220 (Catechism); 219 (Catechism, from library of *Grand Séminaire*, Angers); 221 ('Consultations de cas de conscience avec les resolutions').

(VIII) *Municipal Library, Orléans*

MS. 474 'Journal de mon voyage de Rome en 1716' by a Carmelite friar of Angers. (Misdated in *Catalogue ... bibliothèques publiques de France*.)

B. PRINTED WORKS

This bibliography is limited to items relevant to Angevin local history. Excluded from it are materials which have been used for the purpose of comparing Angers with other parts of France, or for tracing the careers of Angevins outside their own province. Also excluded are the monographs on music, architecture, etc., which are the obviously indispensable guides in writing a book of this kind, and the general histories of eighteenth-century France and of the French Church (Mathiez, Lefebvre, Préclin, Lavaquery, Leflon, Latreille, etc.) which are too well-known, and to which my debt is too obvious to need recapitulation here. Bibliographical economies of this kind, omissions of the obvious, are, perhaps, the most conclusive evidence I could supply of my indebtedness. In the note on Angevin historians and antiquaries, most secondary works used are mentioned, though articles in journals, except in a few cases, have not been listed individually.

I. CONTEMPORARY PRINTED WORKS

(i) BOOKS AND PAMPHLETS

ANON. *Lettre d'un Théologien à M. l'Évêque d'Angers*, 1747 (A.M.L. III F³, no. 2).

ANON. *Avertissement de l'Assemblée Générale du Clergé d'Anjou présidée par Monseigneur l'illustrissime & révérendissime Évêque, à tous les bénéficiers du Diocèse*, Angers, 1786 (B. Nat. Lk³ 1097).

ANON. *Discours sur Angers, relativement à l'industrie et au commerce*, 1787 (B. Angers H 2036).

ANON. *Lettre d'un membre du Tiers-État de al Province d'Anjou à Monsieur le comte de W——— S———T.* Angers, 28 Dec. 1788 (B. Angers H 2034).

ANON. *Processionale Andegavense*, 1788 (B. Angers S.T. 269).

ANON. *A messieurs de la Commission Intermédiare de l'Assemblée Provinciale d'Angers*, 1788 (A.M.L. C 20).

ANON. *Dialogue sous le Ballet de la Paroisse de Saint-Michel-du-Tertre entre le Bedeau de la Paroisse, un Avocat, et un Etudiant en Droit* (B. Angers H 2034).

ANON. *Relation Sommaire . . . de ce qui s'est passé dans l'Assemblée du Clergé de Paris Intra Muros*, publ. by Aulard, *Révolution Française*, XXVI (1894).

ANON. *Lettre de Messieurs les députés du Clergé d'Anjou à Messieurs les curés du diocèse*, 29 July 1789 (B. Angers H 2032; pr. *Anjou hist.*, XL (1940)).

ANON. *Précis des réclamations fait par le chapitre de l'Église d'Angers*, 30 March 1789 (B. Angers H 2028 (6)).

ANON. *Arrêté de Messieurs les Étudiants en Droit*, 2 Feb. 1789 (B. Angers H 2031, nos. 10 and 11).

ANON. *Arrêté des jeunes citoyens de la ville d'Angers*, 4 Feb. 1789 (B. Angers H 2034).

ANON. *Lettre circulaire de quelques membres du Tiers-État d'Anjou, à M.m. les Curés du diocèse, convoqués pour l'Assemblée du 16 Mars*, B.M. $\frac{910\ C\ 9}{10}$.

ANON. *Bureau Général de Charité. Porro unum est necessarium.* n.d. [1789] (B. Angers H 2033).

ANON. *Lettre du Baron Suisse au Noble Breton*, in *Analyse de la Brochure . . . Des Conditions nécessaires à la légalité des États-Généraux* (B. Angers H 2034).

ANON. *Projet d'un Mémoire des curés du Diocèse d'Angers, relativement à la convocation des États-Généraux* (B. Angers H 2032; A. Nat. Ba 13, liasse 9, pl. 2; prin. Proust, *Archives de l'Ouest*, A IV, pp. 21–8)

ANON. *Lettre à un Seigneur d'Anjou accusé de tromper le Peuple*, Angers, 28 Feb., B.M. $\frac{911\ C\ 11}{1-21}$.

ANON. *Éclaircissemens sur trois questions des Conférences d'Angers*, Paris, 1789 (B. Nat. Lb³⁹ 1288).

ANON. *Le voyageur à Paris, Tableau pittoresque et moral de cette Capitale*, 3 vols., 1797 (Bodl. Douce M. 463).

ARNAULD D'ANDILLY, J. *Vies de plusieurs Saints illustres de divers siècles*, 1664.

[BAILLET, ADRIEN] *Topographie des Saints*, Paris, 1703.

BARRUEL, A. *Collection ecclésiastique ou recueil complet des ouvrages faits depuis l'ouverture des États-Généraux, relativement au clergé, à sa constitution civile*, 14 vols., Paris, 1791–3.

—— *Histoire du Clergé pendant la Révolution* (1794).

BÉNABEN, L. *Discours prononcé par M. Bénaben de l'Oratoire ... le jour de sa réception au Club des Amis de la Constitution* (B. Angers H 2036).

BOUMARD. *Lettre du curé de Sainte-Croix d'Angers à M. de la Brosse, soi-disant syndic du Clergé d'Anjou*, 26 March 1789 (B. Angers S.T. 403).

[CARRÉ, DOM RÉMI] *Recueil curieux et édifiant, sur les cloches de l'Église, avec les cérémonies de leur bénédiction*, Cologne, 1757.

CHATIZEL, P.-J. *Traité du pouvoir des évêques de France sur les empêchements de marriage*, Avignon, 1782 (B. Angers S.T. 814).

[CHATIZEL] *Lettre de Mm. les Curés du diocèse d'Anjou à Monseigneur l'illustrissime et révérendissime Évêque d'Angers*, 1785 (B. Angers 3324).

CHATIZEL. *Lettre à Messieurs les curés du diocèse d'Angers*, 1789, B.M. $\frac{910\,c\,9}{9}$.

—— *Lettre de M. curé de Soulaines, en répose à celle de M. le Syndic du Clergé du diocèse d'Angers*, 24 March 1789 (B. Angers H 3326).

[CHATIZEL?] *Projet de Plaintes et demandes pour être présenté pour des Curés du diocèse d'Angers à l'Assemblée Générale du 16 Mars 1789*, B.M. $\frac{910\,c\,9}{7}$.

COQUILLE, J.-B. *Discours patriotique, sur les avantages de la Constitution, considérés par rapport à la religion, et par rapport à l'humanité*. Angers, 3rd ed. 1790 (B. Angers H 2036).

DE LA BLANDINIÈRE, C. *Conférences ecclésiastiques sur les synodes pour servir de suite et d'appui aux Conférences d'Angers en formant le quatrième volume de celles sur la hiérarchie*, Paris, n.d. (B.M. 862, a. 1. 20).

—— *Conférences ecclésiastiques sur la Hiérarchie, pour servir de suite et d'appui aux Conférences d'Angers*, Vol. III, Paris, 1785, B.M. 862 a $\frac{1}{19}$.

DE LA BROSSE. *Lettre du Syndic du diocèse d'Angers à Mm. les curés*, 1789 (B. Angers H 3325).

DELAUNAY, J. *Lettre écrite à Mm. les curés d'Angers, par M. Delaunay l'aîné, avocat*, 1789 (B. Angers H 2094).

—— *Description fidèle de ... la cérémonie de la Confédération Nationale du 14 juillet 1790* (publ. by Gaetan in *La Révolution Française*, XI (1886), pp. 15–88).

—— *Discours au roi, prononcé le 17 juillet 1790 par Joseph Delaunay d'Angers, parlant au nom des gardes nationales du département de Maine-et-Loire*, Paris, 1790 (B. Nat. 8° Lb³⁹ 3797).

'F. F. CURÉ DE H.' *Instructions des curés du diocèse d'Angers à leurs députés aux États-Généraux, rédigées par un curé du diocèse d'Angers, 1789*, B.M. $\frac{910 \text{ c } 9}{11}$.

LAUGIER, M.-A. (Jesuit). *Essai sur l'Architecture, nouvelle edition, revue, corrigée & augmentée ...*, Paris, 1755 (Bodl. Douce L 348).

—— *Observations sur l'Architecture*, Paris, 1765 (Bodl. 8°Σ 188).

LE LOYER, PIERRE. *Discours des spectres ou visions et apparations d'esprits*, Paris, 1608.

LE LONG, J. *Bibliothèque historique de la France*, Paris, 1719.

[MAULTROT, G.-N.] *Les Droits du Second Ordre, défendus contre les apologistes de la domination épiscopale*, 1779 (B.M. 5707 a 10).

DE MOLEON. *Voyages liturgiques de France ou recherches faites en diverses villes*, Paris, 1757.

MONGODIN (CANON). *Avis au Tiers-État de la Province d'Anjou* (B. Angers 100-016).

POCQUET DE LA LIVONNIÈRE, CL. *Coustumes du Pays et Duché d'Anjou avec le commentaire de Mʳ Gabriel Dupineau*, 2 vols., Paris, 1725 (B.M. 1891 f 8).

PRÉVOST, A.-F. *Histoire de Marguerite d'Anjou Reine d'Angleterre*, 4 vols., Amsterdam, 1740 (Bodl. 55 c 90).

RANGEARD, J. 'Éloge de M. le Corvaisier, secrétaire perpétuel de l'Académie d'Angers, par M. l'Abbé Rangeard ...' *L'Année Littéraire* (Fréron) vol. III, 1761 (Bodl. Meerm. Subt. 8° 58).

—— *Dialogue entre un curé, un chanoine de cathédrale, son curé primitif, et un philosophe* (B. Angers 100.041).

—— *Droit exclusif des curés aux dixmes de leurs paroisses, ou lettre à M. de Gr—— pour être présentée à l'Assemblée générale des États de la Nation* (B. Angers 100.042).

—— *Prière à Dieu pour être présentée au Roi et a l'Assemblée Nationale; par M. Rangeard, député du Clergé d'Anjou*, 1789 (B.M. F. 925 (15)).

—— *Procès-verbal historique des actes du clergé*, Paris, 1 May 1790 (B.M. F.R. 140 (15)).

LA REVELLIÈRE-LÉPEAUX, L.-M. *Adresse à la noblesse et au clergé de la Province d'Anjou* (B. Angers H 2034).

ROBIN, CL. *L'Ami des Peuples, ou mémoire interessant pour l'Église et pour l'État ... adressé à Monseigneur l'Évêque d'Angers, en l'Année 1760, par un curé du diocèse*, 1764, Oeuvres de M. Robin (B. Angers 103. 627).

—— *Traduction en vers François, de l'Élégie Latine, ou Ovidianum de M. Claude Robin, curé de Saint-Pierre d'Angers, auteur du Montglonne*, Oeuvres de M. Robin (B. Angers 103. 627) pr. in *Anjou hist.* (1939).

—— *Le Camp de Caesar au village d'Empyré ... ou Dissertation sur l'Antiquité de l'Église de Saint-Pierre*, 1764 (B. Angers, 103. 627).

—— *Le Mont-Glonne ou recherches historiques sur l'Origine des Celtes*, 1784 (B. Angers 103. 627).

ROBIN, CL. *Exposé signifié, suivi de la demand en complainte formée par Messire Claude Robin*, extracts pp. L. Rondeau in 'L'Église Saint-Pierre d'Angers et le curé Robin', *Méms. Soc. Agric.* II (1868).

[VOLNEY, J.] *La Confession d'un pauvre roturier Angevin à l'occasion d'un Avis au Tiers-État de la Province d'Anjou* (B. Angers H 2034).

(ii) NEWSPAPERS

The *Affiches d'Angers* (B. Angers H 5423) was the town's one newspaper at the end of the old régime. During the revolutionary years, Angers had some ephemeral news-sheets (*L'Observateur provincial*, A.M.L. 151 L 1; *Journal du Département de Maine-et-Loire*, A.M.L. 148 L 1; *Le Patriote angevin*, B.M. $\frac{911\ C\ 11}{21}$.

For many areas of France, the Jansenist *Nouvelles ecclésiastiques* is a mine of information, sardonically presented, on religious affairs. Anjou is no exception.

(iii) ORDINANCES, PROCLAMATIONS AND OFFICIAL PUBLICATIONS

Ordonnance de Monseigneur l'Évêque d'Angers portant condamnation de deux imprimez, 1704 (Bodl. G Pamph. 2240, no. 4).

Arrest du Parlement de Paris du 25 juin 1750 pour l'Église de la Trinité d'Angers ... 1750 (B. Angers MS. 1748 (VI)).

Extrait des registres du Conseil d'État, Jan. 1770 (A.M.L. II E 2750).

Extrait des registres du Parlement, concernant la police générale de la ville d'Angers, 14 May 1777 (B. Angers H 2090, no. 687).

Extrait du procès-verbal relatif à l'établissement des nouveaux Cimetières, 1783 (B. Angers MS. DD 16).

Arrêt de la Cour de Parlement, portant réglement pour l'administration des biens et revenues des fabriques des paroisses situées dans l'étendue du diocèse d'Angers, 11 July 1786 (in parish register of Saint-Pierre, État Civil, Angers, GG 185, p. 34).

Arrest du Parlement de Paris qui maintient & garde messire de Walsch, comte de Servant dans la propriété & jouissance des Arbres sur les chemins existans dans l'étendue de sa Haute-Justice, 22 Aug. 1786 (A.M.L. II E 2750).

Arrêt de la Cour de Parlement, 11 July 1786 (Copy in parish register Saint-Pierre, État Civil, Angers, GG 185, p. 34.)

Extrait des registres ... de l'Assemblée Générale du Clergé d'Anjou, in *A messieurs de la Commission Intermédiaire* (A.M.L. C 20).

Extrait du procès-verbal de l'Assemblée Générale de la Ville d'Angers du 24 décembre 1788 (B. Angers H 2032).

Administration de Charité pour la ville d'Angers, 1789 (B. Angers H 2094).

Mandement de Monseigneur l'Évêque d'Angers qui ordonne des prières pe dant la tenue des États Généraux, 5 May 1789 (B. Angers H 2032).

Extrait du registre des déliberations du Comité permanent d'Angers, 17 Sept. 1789 (B. Angers H 2031).

Comte Rendu à la Commune de la ville d'Angers par le Comité permanent le 10 Septembre 1789 (B. Angers H 2033).

Procès-verbal de l'Assemblée des Électeurs du Département de Maine-et-Loire (B. Angers H 2033).

Adresse de la Municipalité d'Angers à l'Assemblée Nationale in *Extrait des registres de la Municipalité d'Angers contenant les instructions relatives à la vente des Biens Domaniaux & Ecclésiastiques*, 1790 (B. Angers H 2028, no. 11).

Adjudication de Biens Nationaux (B. Angers H 2033).

(iv) LEGAL MEMOIRS (ex parte statements of a case by plaintiffs or defendants)

Mémoire signifié pour les chanoines, curé, maires-chapelains & chapelains & communauté de l'Église plebeiane & paroissiale de la Trinité d'Angers, 1750 (B. Angers S.J. 407, no. 11).

Au Roy, et a Nosseigneurs les Commissaires Généraux du Conseil, [1754?], in parish register of Saint-Pierre, État Civil, Angers GG 181.

Mémoire signifié pour m^e Charles-François Boufteau, prêtre ... appellant de la sentence de la Sénéchaussée d'Angers, 1768 (B. Angers S.J. 407, no. 18). Also see reply of abbess, S.J. 407, no. 30.

Copie du certificat du Sieur Curé de Saint-Pierre d'Angers: concernant l'altération faite sur un de ses Registres ..., 1770 (B. Angers S.J. 311 (7), no. 21).

Très-humbles et très-respectueuses représentations ... de la noble Confrérie des Bourgeois ... à Monseigneur le Comte de Provence, 1774 (B. Angers MS. 767, no. 7).

Très-humbles et très-respectueuses représentations que prennent la liberté de faire à Monseigneur le Comte de Provence les Officiers Municipaux d'Angers, 12 Jan. 1774 (B. Angers MS. GG 363).

Mémoire pour les Doyen, Chanoines et Chapitre de l'Église d'Angers au sujet de l'obeissance féodale, qui leur est demandée ..., 1774 (B. Angers MS. 1747, no. 23).

Mémoire, sur une question de Desherance. Pour Martin Pinson & Marie Jamin, sa Femme, défendeurs: contre messieurs les Doyen, Chanoines & Chapitre de Saint-Martin ..., 1777 (B. Angers S.J. 311 (7), no. 27).

Mémoire pour les Conseillers du Roi et de Monsieur, Notaires à Angers: contre le Clergé de la Province d'Anjou, 1779 (B. Angers H 2090, notaires d'Angers, no. 4).

Mémoire signifié pour M^{res} Nicolas Duval & Jean-Urbain Le Roy Chanoines ..., 1782 (B. Angers S.J. 311 (17), no. 15).

Mémoire signifié pour Dame Léontine Desparbez de Lussan-Bouchard d'Aubeterre, Abbesse de l'Abbaye Royale du Ronceray ... 1782 (B. Angers S.J. 311 (7), no. 16).

(v) LAW BOOKS

ANON. *Le Parfait Notaire apostolique*, 2 vols., Paris, 1775.

[ALLETZ, P. A.] *La Discipline de l'Église de France d'après ses maximes et ses décisions répandus dans la collection des Mémoires du Clergé,* Paris, 1780.

DURAND DE MAILLANE, P.-T. *Dictionnaire de Droit canonique et de pratique bénéficial,* 2 vols., 1776.

GUYOT, P.-J. *Répertoire universel et raisonné de jurisprudence civile, criminelle, canonique et bénéficiale,* 64 vols., 1775–83 + 14 vols. suppl., 1786.

LA ROCHEFOUCAULD-BAYERS (P.-L. DE) AND JARENTE. *Rapport de l'Agence, contenant les principales affaires de Clergé* ... *1775* ... *1780,* Paris, 1785.

LAUBRY, M. *Traité des Unions des Bénéfices,* Paris, 1778

PIALES, *Traité* ... *des Gradués,* 6 vols., Paris, 1757.

——*Traité des Réparations,* 4 vols., Paris, 1762.

(vi) ALMANACS, GUIDE BOOKS AND REPORTS OF TRAVELLERS

ANON. *Almanach ou Calendrier d'Anjou pour l'an de Grace 1750* (B. Nat. Lc^{29} 11).

ANON. *Almanach de la Province d'Anjou, Apanage de Monsieur, ou étrennes angevines* ... *pour l'Année 1790* (B. Nat. Lc^{29} 12).

BREVAL, JOHN. *Remarks on Several Parts of Europe,* 2 vols., 1738.

CRADDOCK, MME. *Journal, Voyage en France* (French trans. by Mme O. D. Balley-giver), 1896.

EXPILLY. *Dictionnaire géographique, historique et politique des Gaulles et de la France,* 6 vols., 1762.

LOCKE, J. *Locke's Travels in France, 1675–1679 as related in his journals, correspondence and other papers.* Ed. John Lough, C.U.P., 1953.

MARWOOD, THOS. *Diary,* in the 'Bedingfeld Papers', ed. J. H. Pollen, S.J., *Catholic Record Soc. Miscellanea,* VI (1909).

PÉAN DE LA TUILLERIE. *Description de la ville d'Angers et de tout ce qu'elle contient de plus remarquable,* 1778, ed. C. Port, Angers, 1869.

PIGANIOL DE LA FORCE, J.-A. *Nouveau Voyage en France,* 2 vols., Paris, 1780.

RUTLAND, DUKE OF. MS. *H.M.C.,* XIV (1), 1894.

STANHOPE, PHILIP HENRY, fifth Earl. *Notes of Conversations with the Duke of Wellington* (1888).

DOM TAILLANDIER. *'Relation du voyage de dom Taillandier en Bretagne'* (ed. dom Plaine), *Rev. de Bretagne et Vendée,* 4th Ser., II (1872).

THORODE. *Notice de la Ville d'Angers,* 1772., ed. E. L. (i.e. the abbé Emile Longin), Angers, 1897.

WATERFORD, LADY. MS. *H.M.C.,* XI (VII), 1888.

WRAXALL, N. *A Tour through the Western, Southern and Interior Provinces of France,* 3 vols., 1777.

YOUNG, ARTHUR. *Travels in France and Italy,* 1792.

II. A NOTE ON SECONDARY AUTHORITES:
THE HISTORIANS AND ANTIQUARIES OF ANJOU

I. JOURNALS

The student of French provincial history has an obvious starting point for his researches: the local historical journals. Anjou is particularly rich in this respect. The essential publications are:

(i) *Société d'agriculture, sciences et arts d'Angers, Mémoires:* 1st Series, 6 vols., 1831–47; 2nd Series, 8 vols., 1850–7; New (3rd) Series, 1858–86; 4th Series, 11 vols., 1887–97; 5th Series, 28 vols., 1898–1925; 6th Series, continuing, 1926– . The title of the society underwent the following amendments—'Société nationale ...' 1850–2; 'Société impériale ...' 1853–69; 'Société nationale ...' 1870–1925.

(ii) *Revue de l'Anjou et de Maine-et-Loire:* Series 1, 5 vols., 1852–6; Series 2, 6 vols., 1857–60; Series 3, 4 vols., 1860–2. The Second Series was entitled *Revue de l'Anjou et du Maine.*

(iii) *Revue historique, littéraire et archéologique de l'Anjou,* 24 vols., 1867–80. Superseded (ii) above.

(iv) *Revue de l'Anjou,* 85 vols., 1880–1922. Superseded (iii) above.

(v) *La Province d'Anjou* (1926–).

(vi) *Anjou historique* (1900–).

(vii) *Andegaviana* (1904–).

Materials may be gleaned in:

Revue historique et archéologique du Maine (1876–); *Revue des Facultés catholiques de l'Ouest* (1891–1919); *Revue historique de l'Ouest* (1885–1901); *Revue de Bretagne et de Vendée* (1857–88), which became *Revue de Bretagne, de Vendée et d'Anjou* (1889–1901) and then *Revue de Bretagne* (1901–); *Revue des provinces de l'Ouest* (1853–9); *Répertoire archéologique de l'Anjou* (1858–67); *Annales de Bretagne* (1885–); *La Semaine religieuse d'Angers* (newspaper).

Isolated articles or notes directly referring to our theme have also been found in the following national journals:

Revue de l'Art chrétien; Revue Mabillon; Revue Bénédictine; Annales franciscaines; Études franciscaines; Revue de l'histoire de l'Église de France; Bulletin de la Société de l'histoire du Protestantisme français; Revue des Questions historiques; proceedings of the *Congrès archéologique de France; Revue de la Révolution; Revue historique; Révolution française; Revue du Nord.*

II. WORKS PUBLISHED BEFORE 1870

Blordier-Langlois, *Angers et le Département de Maine-et-Loire, 1787–1830* (2 vols., Angers, 1837) and *Angers et l'Anjou sous le régime municipal* (Angers, 1843) remain indispensable for a framework of events. For the writer, see his 'Autobiographie', *Rev. hist. lit. arch. d'Anjou,* I (1867). Otherwise, few secondary works of value for the purpose of this study appeared before M. Célestin Port turned to Angevin history. The journals also are fairly barren. Tresvaux, *Histoire de l'Église et du diocèse d'Angers*, (Paris, 1858) is disappointing. A few personal details may be gleaned from Bougler, *Mouvement provincial en 1789. Biographie des députés de l'Anjou depuis l'Assembée constituante jusqu'en 1815* (2 vols., Paris, 1865), J.-F. Bodin, *Recherches historiques sur l'Anjou et ses monuments* (2 vols., Saumur, 1821–3), and (for the revolutionary period), V. Godard-Faultrier, *Le Champ des Martyrs* (Angers, 1852—later editions 1855, 1869, 1881). Some interesting collections of documents were published in this period, but the eighteenth-century religious history of Anjou is only indirectly illustrated in them (P. Marchegay, *Archives d'Anjou*, 3 vols., Angers, 1843–54; F.-J. Grille, *Lettres, mémoires et documents … sur la formation du Ier bataillon des volontaires de Maine-et-Loire* (4 vols., Paris, 1850) and *Le Bric-à-Brac* (2 vols., Paris, 1853). Proust's *Archives de l'Ouest, 1789–1800* (2 vols., Paris, 1868), however, contains crucial documents relative to the elections to the Estates-General.

III. CÉLESTIN PORT

The techniques of modern research came into the local historiography of Anjou with M. Port, departmental archivist of Maine-et-Loire, whose two magnificent dictionaries have been basic for this study—*Dictionnaire historique, géographique et biographique de Maine-et-Loire* (3 vols., Paris, 1878) and *Artistes angevins* (Paris, 1881). A primary source of great value for the study of ecclesiastical life in Angers on the eve of the Revolution is F.-Y. Besnard, *Souvenirs d'un Nonagénaire*, which Port edited in 1880 (Paris) with very full scholarly notes. He performed a similar task for Péan de la Tuillerie's guide book to Angers, originally published in 1778 (Angers, 1869). In addition to these works of reference and scholarship, M. Port also published *La Vendée angevine* (2 vols., Paris, 1888), an anti-clerical chronicle, chiefly of value for the primary material it embodies. Port's inventories are models of their kind and occasionally give interesting extracts from the documents (*Inventaire analytique des archives anciennes de la Mairie d'Angers*, Paris, 1861; *Cartulaire de l'hôpital Saint-Jean d'Angers*, Paris, 1870; *Inventaire des archives anciennes de l'hôpital Saint-Jean d'Angers*, Paris, 1870; *Inventaire-sommaire des archives départementales, Maine-et-Loire, Série G*, Angers, 1880).

IV. FROM M. PORT TO CANON UZUREAU

With the advent of the Third Republic, the growing importance of the issue of Church v. State seemed to draw Angevin historians towards the eighteenth-century Church and its clash with the Revolution; M. Port showed this interest on the anti-clerical side, historians like M. Queruau-Lamerie illustrate this influence on the Catholic side. The most useful secondary work published in this period is G. Letourneau, *Histoire du Séminaire d'Angers* (Angers, 1895); special mention must also be made of 'E. L.' (the abbé Emile Longin), who edited Thorode's *Notice de la ville d'Angers* in 1897 with a wealth of curious detail in the footnotes, freely presented to historians of the future in the same generous spirit which canon Uzureau's later career was to show.

Some information may also be gathered from L. de Farcy, *Clochers, sonnerie, horloge et porche de la Cathédrale d'Angers* (Angers, 1872); L. Cosnier, *La Charité à Angers* (2 vols., Angers, 1889–90)—and other works and articles by these two authors—from L. de Lens, *L'Université d'Angers I* (*Faculté des Droits*), (Angers, 1880); C.-L.-T. Portais, *L'abbé Gruget* (Angers, 1896); E. Queruau-Lamerie, *Le Clergé du département de Maine-et-Loire pendant la Révolution* (Angers, 1899), and *L'abbé Chatizel de la Néronière, curé de Soulaines* (Laval, 1899); L. Bourgain, *L'Église d'Angers pendant la Révolution et jusqu'en 1870* (Angers, 1898); C.-L. Chassin, *La Préparation de la guerre de Vendée, 1789–1793* (Paris, 3 vols., 1892); and *La Vendée patriote, 1793–1800* (4 vols., Paris, 1894); Ch. Urseau, *L'Instruction primaire avant 1789 dans les paroisses du diocèse actuel d'Angers* (Paris, 1890). The local historical journals are much richer in relevant articles in this period, notably from the pens of E. Rondeau (see especially 'Saint-Michel du Tertre d'Angers', *Méms. Soc. Agric.*, 4th Ser., IV, 1890), Queruau-Lamerie and J. Denais.

A good deal of valuable original material was published between 1870 and 1901. Of memoirs, those of La Revellière-Lépeaux (ed. R. David, 3 vols., Paris, 1895), Choudieu (ed. Barracand, Paris, 1897), and Mercier du Rocher (ed. C.-L. Chassin in *La Préparation de la guerre de Vendée*, vol. I, Paris, 1900) provide good examples of varied hues of anti-clerical opinion, and X. de la Perraudière published a substantial portion of curé Robin's racy account of his pilgramage to Rome (*Rev. des Facultés catholiques de l'Ouest*, V, 1894–5). A fascinating correspondence between Rangeard and dom Housseau was made available by L. Brière (*Rev. historique et archéologique du Maine* I, 1876; II, 1877; III, 1878) and the duc de la Trémouille published correspondence from the archives of the Serrant family which is indispensable to a knowledge of Angevin events from 1787–9 (*L'Assemblée provinciale d'Anjou d'après les archives de Serrant, 1787–9*, Paris, 1901). The correspondence of Bénaben (ed. A. Launay, Paris, 1886) is of value only for the revolutionary years. The various journals also contain more documents—the fashion was beginning which was to lead to the amazing documentary collections of the abbé Uzureau.

V. CANON UZUREAU

Without canon Uzureau's vast publication of Angevin documents, this book could not have been begun. Most of this writer's work was put out in the form of brief 'articles' which are, in essence, transcripts of original sources, though the correlation and editing of the materials is such that it would be unjust to refer to them simply as a source. The lists of ecclesiastical personnel, the details concerning parishes and monasteries and the biographical notes which Uzureau provides are, like the dictionaries of Port, his anti-clerical predecessor, essential bases for reference. In his journals, *Anjou historique* (1900–   ) and *Andegaviana* (1904–   ), canon Uzureau published, year by year, a mass of material, much of it belonging to the eighteenth century. A full list of my indebtedness would include 69 items from the first periodical and 15 from the second. In *Anjou historique* one finds reports of travellers (IX, XLI), extracts from liturgical memorialists like Grandet and Lehoreau (II, XV, XVI, XVII and XIV), from the *Affiches*, the local newspaper, and from parish registers (in almost every number), *cahiers* (XXXI, see also *Andegaviana* XI, XII), invaluable personal memoirs like those of Mme Letondal (V), Jeanne-Jacquine Moutardeau (XXX) and Gruget (II), the correspondence of the abbé Houdet (XII, also in *Révolution française* LXI, 1911), documents from the old seminary (XVIII, XXV), reports on the monasteries by a Benedictine visitor (XV), or the *Commission des réguliers* (IV), the administrative enquiry of 1796 (XIV) which is indispensable for a knowledge of the fate of individual clergy during the Revolution.

I have taken liberties in giving references to *Anjou historique* and *Andegaviana*. In cases where canon Uzureau's contribution was an 'article' rather than a document, or in which his source is not stated or its actual words quoted (often it is a parish register) I have retained his own title; otherwise I have cited the title or the nature of the document rather than the heading, descriptive of its general interest, which its learned editor devised. Thus from *Andegaviana*, IV (1906), I cite *Affiches* instead of 'Variétés religieuses angevines, fin du XVIIIe siècle', and from *Anjou historique*, XXIX (1929), I cite Jeanne-Jacquine Moutardeau's 'Relation' rather than 'La déportation des religieuses angevines'.

Canon Uzureau also published materials in journals other than his own. Ten contributions relative to our theme are in the *Méms. Soc. Agric.*, from the years 1897, 1899, 1903 (particularly important, concerning the clergy and their elections to the Estates-General), 1905, 1906, (bis), 1910, 1914, 1915, 1918; two are in the *Revue des Facultés catholiques de l'Ouest* (1898, 1914), four in the *Revue Mabillon* (1914, 1919, 1920, 1921), three in the *Révolution française* (1914, 1917, 1928), one in the *Revue d'histoire franciscaine* (1931) and one in the *Revue des sciences ecclésiastiques et de la science catholique* (1907).

Separately printed are:

Les premières applications du Concordat dans le diocèse d'Angers, 1801–3, 1901.

Les Filles de la Charité d'Angers pendant la Révolution; martyre des soeurs Marie-Anne et Odile, 1902.

Les Serments pendant la Révolution (by M. J. Meilloc, edited by Uzureau, 1904).

Pouillé du diocèse d'Angers, 1783, 1904.

Un Prêtre français pendant l'émigration; M. de la Corbière, chanoine d'Angers, 1909. (Also in *Revue de Lille* for that year).

Les victimes de la Terreur en Anjou, listes des personnes décédés dans les prisons d'Angers, 1912.

Un Martyr de la foi en 1794: M. Laigneau de Langellerie, aumônier du Carmel d'Angers, 1913.

After the death of canon Uzureau in March 1947, *Anjou historique*

M. Lefevre-Pontailis, M. Pinier, M. O. Raguenet de Saint-Albin, M. Saché, M. A. Lefort, M. Chaulbert, M. C. Dufour, M. Chartier, M. J. Levron, Fr. Jean Donatien Levesque, 'A.G.', M. H. Pinguet, M. J. Neveu, M. Boisseau du Rocher and M. Guy de Chateaubriant, for many a piece of interesting information.

continued under the editorship of M. J. Levron, the [
archivist of Maine-et-Loire; it is still in being and sti[
original materials in the tradition established by its found[

VI. MORE RECENT WORKS

Both for the documents it contains and for its introdu[
Moy's edition of the *cahiers* of the town of Angers is indispe[
inédits hist. Révolution française, 2 vols., Angers, 1915–16).][
background of Angevin life is described in the monog[
Dauphin—a study of the social structure of the town of A[
from the capitation register (*La Province d'Anjou*, 1931, al[
printed) and articles on the town's industries and corpor[
Méms. Soc. Agric., XXVI (1923), N.S., IV (1929), IV (19[
Rev. de l'Anjou, N.S., LXVI (1913). See also J. Levron, [
Commerce d'Angers au 18ᵉ siècle (Angers, 1933). A. Meynie[
of La Revellière-Lépeaux (Angers, 1905), has, in some r[
replaced by that of G. Robison (New York, 1938), but it rem[
for a knowledge of Anjou in 1789. My interpretation of th[
Angevin bourgeoisie is substantially that given by Meynier[
important article, 'Une grande période électorale en Anjou.[
aux États-généraux de 1789', *Rev. de l'Anjou*, XLIII (19[
*La Vie scolaire et les créations intellectuelles en Anjou, 17[
1929), is a definitive monograph which has been my cons[
reference; the same author's *Les Fêtes révolutionnaires à A[
II à l'an VIII* (Paris, 1929), is important for the revolut[
One of our curés rose to great position and his career is the[
masterly biography: J. Leflon, *Etienne-Alexandre Be[
d'Orléans, 1762–1806* (2 vols., Paris, 1938); see also M. Le[
of Bernier's correspondence (Reims, 1938) and, for the s[
M. Emery (2 vols., Paris, 1943). The superb *Histoire général[
des Frères des Écoles chrétiennes* by G. Rigault (8 vols., Pa[
gives an exhaustive account of one of the ecclesiastical in[
Angers. E. Rondeau's *Histoire du Monastère des Ursulin[
1618–1910* (Angers, 1911), gives a full account of the Ursu[
Crosnier's *Histoire de la congrégation de Saint-Charles d'Ange[
(Angers, 1930), is useful. For a definitive work of a differ[
G. H. Forsyth Jnr., *The Church of Saint-Martin at Anger[
1953), a magnificently produced and scholarly architectural[
logical survey.

Materials may be gleaned in books not directly concer[
theme of this essay; the most important were O. Marcault's l[
diocese of Tours (3 vols., Tours, 1918); Dr. O. Couffon's acc[
century midwifery courses (Angers, 1913); R. M. Andrews on[
of the *Mauges* (*Thèse*, Paris, 1935), and A. Boquet's mono[
Angevin Faculty of Medicine (Angers, 1951). The loc[
journals also yield a richer harvest in the modern period. I[
the amazing production of canon Uzureau, I am indebted t[
P. P. Ubald and Armel, M. L. La Combe, M. G. Bayer[

INDEX